Western Ethics

For Karen and Lisa

WESTERN ETHICS

An Historical Introduction

Robert L. Arrington
Georgia State University

Copyright © Robert L. Arrington, 1998

First published 1998

Transferred to digital print 2004

2 4 6 8 10 9 7 5 3 1

Blackwell Publishers Inc.
350 Main Street
Malden Massachusetts 02148
USA

Blackwell Publishers Ltd
108 Cowley Road
Oxford OX4 1JF
UK

Library of Congress Cataloging in Publication Data

Arrington Robert, L., 1938–
   Western ethics : an historical introduction / Robert L. Arrington.
       p.   cm.
   Includes bibliographical references and index.
   ISBN 0-631-19415-0 (hardback : alk. paper). — ISBN 0-631-19416-9 (pbk. : alk. paper)
       1. Ethics—History.   I. Title.
   BJ71.A77   1998
   170'.9—dc21   97-8618
                                                                   CIP

British Library Cataloguing in Publication Data

A CIP catalogue record for this book is available from the British Library.

Commissioning Editor: Steve Smith
Development Editor: Mary Riso
Desk Editor: Alison Truefitt
Production Manager: Lisa Eaton

Typeset in 10½ on 12½ pt Ehrhardt
by Ace Filmsetting Ltd, Frome, Somerset
Printed and bound in Great Britain by Marston Book Services Limited, Oxford

This book is printed on acid-free paper.

170
R44453

Contents

Preface

As its title indicates, this book is an introduction to the field of Western ethics through a study of its history. The chapters that follow contain descriptions of the major ethical theories found in the history of Western philosophy.

Ethics, like most philosophical subject matter, can be introduced either historically or systematically (thematically). The latter approach directs attention to the recurrent problems and issues that ethical philosophers discuss, usually by way of indicating the different positions that various historical and contemporary thinkers have taken on one or more of the issues. The historical approach proceeds by probing the manner in which a single ethical theorist, or a group of them holding many of the same opinions, addresses a variety of ethical issues. Most of the problems of concern to current ethical thinkers can be found in the works of the major historical figures over the course of the centuries, and so a study of the history of ethics can provide considerable information about the perennial issues. It is hoped that the present work will achieve this result.

The historical approach has some advantages over the systematic one. One of its virtues is that it can convey the manner in which ethical problems are related to one another and demonstrate how the answers to these problems need to be coherently organized within an overall philosophical perspective. Another advantage is that for many readers the historical approach is more accessible than the systematic one. Philosophical problems in the abstract are sometimes difficult to grasp, and it is often easier to represent these issues in one's mind by means of the overall philosophies of actual thinkers living in specific periods of time. The greatness of the individual philosophers ensures that their thought is timely and relevant. The ethical problems that an Aristotle or Kant grappled with are in many respects the same problems we are thinking about today, as can be seen in the last chapter where parallels are drawn between historical positions and current trends in Anglo–American ethics.

The studies in this book survey the history of Western ethical philosophy from the time of Socrates and the Sophists in the fifth century BCE to the philosophy of Nietzsche at the end of the nineteenth century CE. Special attention is given to theories that have exerted considerable influence on contemporary ethics, namely those of Aristotle, Hobbes, Hume, Kant, and Mill. The recent interpretive or critical literature on these figures is enormous, and an attempt has been made to identify different interpretations and to pinpoint important contributions to the understanding of their ethical theories.

Any person writing a history of ethics, even one of an introductory nature such as the present effort, is faced with a problem. One wants to try and place the philosophers studied in the context of their own times and cultures. These cultures have changed over the centuries, making cross-cultural comparisons risky. The Aristotle of the fourth century BCE is not grappling with exactly the same issues as is a twentieth-century CE philosopher, not even a contemporary "virtue ethicist." At the same time, most philosophical histories of ethics are not written solely to explain the ethical thought of a particular period (or periods) of time – certainly this one is not. Their goal, and the goal here, is to illuminate the study of ethics by looking at past accomplishments. Consequently, one will inevitably single out elements that are of concern to us today, and this agenda may result in, if not a distorted picture of times past, at least a slanted one. One can only face up to this risk, and try to meet it by attempting to be as accurate as possible and, within the limits of one's purpose and space, providing as much detail of the original theories as possible.

A word about the term "ethics" or "ethical philosophy." As used herein, this term refers to the philosophical study of morality. What, one may ask, is morality? Philosophers disagree over the concept of morality, and many of them would deny that what a Plato or Aristotle is talking about is morality at all. In the minds of many of the latter philosophers (often called deontologists), morality is given its most accurate and profound representation in the philosophy of Immanuel Kant, and, as we shall see, the perspectives of Kant and the ancient Greek thinkers are different in many respects. And both are different from the utilitarian point of view found among many British ethical thinkers. Moreover, Kant's successor, Hegel, explicitly distinguishes between the moral life and the ethical life. In spite of this widespread opinion about the distinctiveness of the concept of morality, the operating assumption in the present work is that the Greeks, the Kantian deontologists, and the British utilitarians are all studying morality. As ethical philosophers, they offer different theories as to what morality consists in or ideally should consist in. The present study will take morality to be any practice in which the ideas of good and bad, good and evil, right and wrong, or obligation and duty play a *central* role. Still more generously, morality will be conceived to be any endeavor in which one seeks to answer Socrates' question about how one should live one's life. With this broad and ecumenical concept of morality in mind, ethics can be equated with moral philosophy.

Throughout the book, the author's aim is to offer detailed and sympathetic accounts of the moral philosophies examined. Detailed, because it is believed that more superficial descriptions would be of little value. Sympathetic, because it is hoped that readers will come to appreciate the genius and greatness of all these moral philosophers, even though they may disagree, as they must, with one or more of their particular theories. Frequently an effort will be made to indicate the problems and shortcomings of the individual theories. In doing this, however, the goal is not to denigrate or refute the theories but rather to encourage the reader to seek solutions to the problems, often from within the perspectives of the theories themselves. Such constructive criticism serves the practice of philosophy better, in the author's opinion, than carping demolition efforts.

In most of the chapters, a single major work of the moral philosopher studied is singled out for examination. These works are widely available and might profitably be read alongside this history. Moreover, at the end of the book there is a list of recommended readings keyed to the various chapters. These readings are more advanced than the studies contained in this book, but they are nevertheless accessible and interesting.

As the last chapter makes clear, the history of Western ethics does not end at the beginning of the twentieth century. But one must stop somewhere, especially after having written such a long book. Exhaustion and some modicum of sympathy for the reader are effective motives for doing what is always difficult – ending a project for which one has deep affection.

Acknowledgments

I have many people to thank for assistance in preparing this book. My colleagues David Blumenfeld, Jim Humber, Grant Luckhardt, Tim Renick, and Iakovos Vasiliou read and commented on selected chapters, and John Beversluis and Richard Parry gave me valuable advice on two of the chapters. Several of the anonymous readers for Blackwell Publishers made very helpful suggestions. An early draft of one of the chapters was read before the Philosophy Club at the University of Reading. For secretarial assistance, I greatly appreciate the support of members of the staff in the Department of Philosophy at Georgia State University: Ellen Logan, Nikki Heiser, and Kelly Nardell. Georgia State University, through the good offices of Dean Ahmed Abdelal, provided a leave of absence during which work on the book was begun. Most of all, I thank my wife Margarita for her constant encouragement, patience, and good humor throughout the long period of research and writing.

We are grateful for permission to reproduce the following copyright material:

Cambridge University Press: *Moral Philosophy from Montaigne to Kant: An Anthology*, vol. II, ed. J. B. Schneewind, 1990. William B. Eerdmans Publishing Co.: St. Augustine, *The Writings Against the Manichaeans and Against the Donatists*, Select Library of the Nicene and Post-Nice Fathers of the Christian Church, vol. IV, ed. Philip Schaff, 1979. The Free Press, a division of Simon and Schuster: *Greek and Roman Philosphy after Aristotle*, ed. Jason Saunders, © 1996 by Jason L. Saunders. Hackett Publishing Company: Aristotle, *Nicomachean Ethics*, trans. T. Irwin, 1985; Thomas Hobbes, *Leviathan*, ed. Edwin Curley, 1994; Plato, *Meno*, trans. G. M. A. Grube, 1981; Plato, *Republic*, trans. G. M. A. Grube, rev. C. D. C. Reeve, 1992. Harvard University Press, Loeb Classical Library: Diogenes Laertius, *Lives of Eminent Philosophers*, vols I and II, trans. by R. D. Hicks, 1925. Macmillan Publishing Co.: Jeremy Bentham, *The Works of Jeremy Bentham*, vol. I, ed. John Bowring, 1962 (originally reprinted by Russell and Russell, New York, NY, 1962). New Directions Publishing Corporation: Henry Miller, *The Colossus of Maroussi*, © 1941 by Henry Miller. Oxford University Press: David Hume, *A Treatise of Human Nature*, ed. L. A. Selby-Bigge, 2nd edn, rev. by P. H. Nidditch, 1978; Peter Abelard, *Peter Abelard's Ethics*, trans. D. E. Luscombe, 1971; G. W. F. Hegel, *Hegel's Philosophy of Right*, trans. T. M. Knox, Clarendon Press, 1942. Prentice-Hall, Inc./Macmillan: David Hume, *An Inquiry Concerning the Principles of Morals*, ed. Charles Hendel, © 1957. Princeton University Press: Spinoza, *Ethics*, in *A Spinoza Reader*, trans. and ed. E. Curley, 1994. Random Century Publishing Group, Ltd./Routledge: I. Kant, *Groundwork of the Metaphysics of Morals*, trans. H. J. Paton, in his *The Moral Law*, 1950. Random House Inc.: F. Nietzsche, *On the Genealogy of Morals*, trans. Walter Kaufmann, © 1967. Simon and Schuster/Macmillan: I. Kant, *Critique of Practical Reason*, 3rd edn, trans. Lewis White Beck, © 1993. University of Toronto Press/ Routledge: John Stuart Mill, *Collected Works of John Stuart Mill*, vols X and XVIII, ed. J. Robson, 1969.

Despite every effort to trace and contact copyright owners prior to publication this has not always been possible. We apologize for any apparent infringement of copyright and, if notified, we will be pleased to rectify any errors or omissions at the earliest opportunity.

1

Socrates and the Sophists: An Invitation to Ethics

The founder of ethical philosophy in Western civilization was a short, ugly, snub-nosed, poor and unemployed, modestly dressed and barefooted man named Socrates. He lived in ancient Greece as a citizen of the city-state of Athens during the fifth century BCE. He was, ironically, executed by his fellow Athenians on grounds of immorality. Socrates was not the first Western thinker to engage in ethical reflection about morality, but his ideas have been responsible for some of the main directions of thought about right and wrong and good and bad throughout the subsequent 2,500 years of Western philosophy. Furthermore, Socrates the man stands even today as a revered example of a person who truly lived the moral life. Although sometimes criticized for not doing enough to fight the injustices perpetrated by others, he was committed to never engaging in an unjust act himself. He always listened to his conscience and did what he thought was right – even when doing so put him in grave danger. In fact, his insistence on never committing an unjust act provoked his own execution at the hands of the Athenians. Astonishingly, Socrates acceded to his execution *on moral grounds*.

Socrates died in the year 399 BCE after being tried by the citizens of Athens for corrupting the youth and not believing in the gods of the Athenian city-state. He was seventy years of age at the time of his execution. He had been born an Athenian citizen – the son of a stonemason – and he spent almost all of his life within the city of Athens, a city he loved and to which he was always loyal. Although he served (honorably and courageously) as a soldier on several occasions and, in rare instances, as an official in the governance of the city, to our knowledge he never held a regular job or regular political office. Most of his time was spent talking to the people of Athens, young and old, citizens and visitors, about the meaning and course of their lives – usually urging them to change their ways! His message to them was: the unexamined life is not worth living for a human being. His counsel: pay attention to the most important thing in life, your soul or character; seek goodness and justice, for these alone benefit the soul. And he offered his fellow citizens the following assurance: nothing can harm the good and just person, while the wrongdoer courts unhappiness and misery. "For I go around doing nothing but persuading both young and old among you not to care for your body or your wealth in preference to or as strongly as for the best possible state of your soul ..." (*Apology*, 30a–b).[1]

Such a message was not well-received by all Athenians, many of whom came to resent his criticisms and to feel that his self-described role as a "gadfly" was detrimental to the city. But a handful of Athenians came to believe, as the Oracle at Delphi had in fact asserted, that no one was wiser than Socrates. When he was arraigned on the charges of impiety and corruption of youth, his friends came to his assistance, first pointing out how he could win acquittal and subsequently arranging for his escape. In response, in a moving and morally elevating series of actions that have inspired readers throughout the ages, Socrates argued that it would be contrary to justice to engage in normal "courtroom" tactics or to escape from a state and a set of laws which he loved, to which he owed much, and to which he had sworn allegiance. He demanded and drank the cup of poisonous hemlock. And so he died – according to Plato one of the wisest, one of the most just, and one of the happiest of men.

Socrates wrote nothing; he only talked (endlessly, it seems). We know of his actions and ideas primarily through the writings of Plato, who had been his student and who went on to become one of the greatest philosophers of all time. Plato wrote dialogues, in almost all of which a character named "Socrates" is the main speaker. Determining which ideas in the dialogues came from the historical Socrates and which came from Plato himself is referred to as "the Socratic problem." It is not a problem that has been resolved even today to the satisfaction of all scholars. Experts are generally agreed, however, that in the early dialogues, such as *Euthyphro*, *Apology*, *Protagoras* and *Crito*, and perhaps in the transitional *Meno*, Plato lets the character "Socrates" speak for the historical Socrates, expressing and defending beliefs that Socrates actually held. The so-called "middle dialogues," including the *Phaedo*, *Symposium*, and *Republic*, present Plato's own ideas (even though the character "Socrates" continues to be their spokesperson), but these ideas are not always clearly demarcated from those of Socrates. However in Plato's masterpiece, the *Republic*, the ideas are clearly his own, at least after the first book of this lengthy work.

The dialogues are artistic masterpieces, highly dramatic, beautifully written, engaging and enduring. Plato was not only a great philosopher, he was also a great artist and one of the greatest Greek prose writers. While we can and should appreciate his artistry, it does cause us difficulties in establishing the connection between the philosophical content of the dialogues and Plato's and Socrates' own views. Difficulties of interpretation often arise in the case of works having the form of dialogues, more so than with treatises. These difficulties are especially evident with regard to the actual thought of Socrates, as can be seen from the fact that subsequent philosophical schools equally claiming to follow Socrates – such as the Cyrenaics and Stoics – developed philosophies quite antithetical to one another.

Socrates' Antecedents: Three Strands of Greek Thought

In his ethical thinking, Socrates was reacting in large measure to ideas about morality that were prevalent in fifth-century Greece. Among these ideas were, in the first place, the concepts informing the popular culture, most of which came from the still-influential Homeric myths. These myths, derived from Homer's eighth-century poems *The Iliad* and *The Odyssey*, perpetuated the cult of the hero, for whom personal honor and self-aggrandizement were the highest values. Also present in Socrates' fifth-century Athens were ideas about morality that resulted from political developments in Greece, ideas, for example, about the rule of law and justice. These political/ moral notions became particularly influential with the development of an early form of democratic government in Athens. Indirectly such ideas had their source in the work of the pre-Socratic philosophers of nature such as Anaximander and Empedocles, who, rejecting the idea that human destiny was controlled by the whimsical and capricious decisions of the Olympian gods, interpreted events in terms of an all-encompassing rational and intelligible order of nature. This philosophical development led to the notion that there might be a rational order of values as well. Finally, one found in fifth-century Athens a distinctive set of ideas about conduct enunciated by a group of thinkers called the Sophists, itinerant teachers who, for recompense, taught techniques for political success within the Greek city-states. Practicality, success, and adaptability were central values for most of the Sophists, although the claim of some of them that virtue can be taught led to the idea that there can be rational ethical discussions. Other Sophists preached a more radical doctrine praising immorality and self-indulgence. For thinkers of the latter stripe, conventional morality is to be rejected – it is no more than a false story designed, in the interest of those holding power, to mislead the masses about the facts of human nature and conduct. In Socrates' eyes, both the conservative sophistic emphasis on success and conformity and the radical sophistic call to individual wilfulness were dangerous. They constituted alternatives to true morality and threatened to undermine it.

Socrates' thought must be grasped in relation to all three of the above developments. First, he set out to repudiate some of the essential ingredients of Homeric morality. Second, he sought to describe the nature of true morality as a rational enterprise. And third, he mounted a defense of morality – morality as it ought to be understood – against the influence and arguments of the Sophists.

Before we consider the general philosophical propositions that constitute Socratic ethics, let us look at two specific ways in which Socrates challenged the ordinary moral views of mid- to late fifth-century Athenians. These challenges will give us a glimpse of Socrates' style and his famous devotion to reason. The first concerns the relationship between the gods and morality; the second, the issue of vengeance.

The Gods and Morality

In the early dialogue *Euthyphro*, Socrates is engaged in a discussion with Euthyphro, a religious "seer," about the nature of piety or godliness. Euthyphro is in the process of prosecuting his father for murder – on the grounds that his father tied up a hired laborer (who had killed one of the house slaves) and left him out in the cold, with the result that the man soon died. In prosecuting his father, Euthyphro considers himself to be doing what is pious, and Socrates wants to know why he thinks this – especially in light of the fact that the bond between father and son was particularly important in the morality of the time, so much so that Euthyphro's act would be seen as highly questionable by most people. What, after all, is piety or godliness? Does Euthyphro know?

> So tell me now, by Zeus, what you just now maintained you clearly knew:
> what kind of thing do you say that godliness and ungodliness are, both
> as regards murder and other things; or is the pious not the same and alike
> in every action, and the impious the opposite of all that is pious and like
> itself, and everything that is to be impious presents us with one form or
> appearance in so far as it is impious?   (*Euthyphro*, 5c–d)[2]

What, in other words, are the characteristics found in all pious actions by virtue of which they are pious and as a result of which they differ from all things that are impious? This is an example of Socrates' famous "What is it?" question: a demand for a definition of the subject matter under discussion and a question he thinks we must be able to answer if we are to know what we are talking about.

One of Euthyphro's attempts to comply with Socrates' request is as follows: "Well, then," he replies, "what is dear to the gods is pious, and what is not is impious" (7a). Socrates immediately points out that the gods often differ and disagree with one another. Given this fact, it follows that what is dear to or pleases one god often displeases another. Thus Euthyphro's definition would lead to the absurd conclusion that some things are *both* pious *and* impious – pious by virtue of being dear to some of the gods, and impious by virtue of being displeasing to others. But it cannot be the case that one and the same thing is both pious and impious. Such a state of affairs would be self-contradictory and therefore irrational.

When Euthyphro corrects his definition of the pious and states that it is what *all* the gods love, Socrates pursues the discussion by raising another famous question: "Is the pious loved by the gods because it is pious, or is it pious because it is loved by the gods?" (*Euthyphro*, 10a) In order to answer this question, he inquires whether something's "being loved the gods" results from the fact that the gods love it, or whether, on the contrary, they love it because it is loved. The latter option is an odd one, since "being loved" isn't something independent of the fact that someone loves it. Thus Euthyphro can only agree that the former is the case (that something is loved because the gods love it). Likewise, Socrates points out that a thing is seen because someone sees it (it being senseless to say they see it because it is seen). Being loved and being seen are properties a thing has as a result of the fact that someone experiences it a certain way. But the feature of "being pious" is quite different. It is not the *product* of someone experiencing something in a certain way (e.g., loving or taking pleasure in it) but rather is the *reason* they experience it this way. Therefore Euthyphro and Socrates agree that the gods love certain actions *because* those actions are pious; they are not pious because the gods love them. Piety has an objective nature independent of how it may be perceived or experienced. The gods' love of a pious act is simply their response to the fact that this act has the essential properties that make an act pious. That the gods love the virtue of piety may be a fact about piety, but it is not the fact about piety that *makes it* piety. The latter must be an objective property or set of properties that the virtue of piety has independently of how it is perceived by someone, even by the gods.

Socrates continues to press for a definition of piety, understood now as the essential characteristic of pious actions by virtue of which the gods love them. Unfortunately, Euthyphro is unable to provide such an definition, and the dialogue ends with the religious spokesman in a state of confusion. Socrates then draws the telling moral: if Euthyphro doesn't know what pious acts are, how can he be so confident that he is doing the pious thing in prosecuting his father? Surely in venturing such an extreme action he must *know* that his act is a pious one? "If you had no clear knowledge of piety and impiety, you would never have ventured to prosecute your old father for murder on behalf of a servant" (*Euthyphro*, 15d). Faced with such a predicament, Euthyphro takes quick leave of Socrates, saying that he will inform him of the nature of piety on another occasion. At this point the dialogue ends.

If we change the terminology slightly and talk, not about gods but about God, Socrates has raised a question in the *Euthyphro* that many of us might profitably consider even today. Is an action right because God commands it, or does he command it because it is right? Many believers in the Christian, Jewish, and Muslim traditions think God is the source of right and wrong, and one way of expressing this view is to see it as a version of the position rejected by Socrates: an act becomes right as a result of God's commanding it. Such a "divine-command" theory of ethics entails that an act is wrong *because* or as a result of the fact that God tells us not to do it. Someone adopting this position should consider the question whether or not *any* act would become right just because God commanded it? Would an act of murder become right if God commanded us to undertake it? But how could he command such a thing, we might protest; surely he would not! But what is to prevent him, if an act is right simply because he commands it? Anything he commands thereby becomes right, even if it is murder, rape, or theft! If such a notion of God and rightness gives us pause, as perhaps it should, this must be because we hold God and his commandments to a higher standard: God will (can?) command only what a *good* person or being would command, or what *morality* requires. This line of thought might drive us to conclude that there are moral truths independent of God, and that if an all-good God commands an act, it is because the act is itself right or obligatory. From which it would follow that God commands an act because it is right; it is not right because God commands it.

There is another aspect to this problem that raises the issue of rationality. If God's command *alone* made an act pious or right, would not this command be capricious and whimsical? There would be no reason for God's command, no reason grounded in the independent rightness of what he commands. If an act is right simply because God commands it, both God's command and the rightness of the act appear arbitrary – God could *equally well* have commanded otherwise. God should have a reason for what he commands, and the very best reason is that he knows the act he commands is, in accordance with morality, objectively right.

A person who raises questions like the above may easily be regarded with suspicion – and perhaps seen as undermining the belief in the gods or God. In fact, Socrates was a religious believer ("I do believe in them as none of my accusers do" (*Apology*, 35d)), although not necessarily a believer in the traditional Greek gods; he was not the atheist he was accused of being during his trial.[3] He worshiped the gods and lived a life of piety. At the same time, he considered it his duty to provide the most rational interpretation possible of the gods. It is inconsistent, he maintained, to think of the gods as the most perfect beings and also to view them – as most Greeks did – as acting capriciously or immorally. To be truly divine, the gods must be perfect. If they are perfect, they must act for good reasons. Thus when they command an act, they do so because the act *is* pious or in some other way virtuous; their reason for commanding it is that they see or know it has this moral property.

Vengeance: Is It Just?

Another disagreement Socrates had with the longstanding popular morality of the Greek people relates to the issue of vengeance. Most Greeks simply took it for granted that if a person harms you, you should harm that person in return. Indeed, a favorite conception of *justice*, one which Socrates wished to rebut, was that it consists in helping your friends and harming your enemies. Socrates disagreed vigorously and is the first major figure in Western philosophy to do so.

His argument against vengeance is found in the dialogue *Crito*. Early in this dialogue he obtains agreement from Crito that, just as some things harm the body and make it "corrupted," so injustice harms the "higher part of man" – the soul – while justice "improves" or benefits it.

> And is life worth living for us with that part of us corrupted that unjust action harms and just action benefits? Or do we think that part of us,

whatever it is, that is concerned with justice and injustice, is inferior to
the body?   (*Crito*, 47e–48a)[4]

Crito agrees that the "health" of the part of us in which right and wrong operate (the part "that is concerned with justice") is just as important as the health of the body. Socrates and Crito then agree that "the most important thing is not life, but the good life" (*Crito*, 48b), and Socrates is also able to gain Crito's assent to the proposition that the good life is the same as the just life. It follows from these agreements that "wrongdoing is in every way harmful and shameful to the wrongdoer" (*Crito*, 49b). Having established this conclusion, another immediately follows: "So one must never do wrong" (ibid.). And that proposition in turn implies "Nor must one, when wronged, inflict wrong in return, as the majority believe, since one must never do wrong" (ibid.). By a series of logical deductions, therefore, Crito is led to accept Socrates' conclusion that "One should never do wrong in return, nor injure any man, whatever injury one has suffered at his hands" (*Crito*, 49c). Vengeance, in other words, is always wrong: the age-old doctrine of an eye for an eye must be rejected. Crito has been given a lesson in rational thinking, in reasoning, as well as one in moral philosophy. One must be consistent in one's thoughts, and if one agrees, as Crito did, that wrongdoing harms the soul, one must be willing to repudiate the popular view in support of vengeance. Here we have Socrates' rejection of "what most people think" – the opinion of the many. We also find in this argument one of his fundamental moral convictions: acting immorally harms the soul of the person who engages in this wrongdoing.

The repudiation of vengeance gives us a good example of Socrates' moral methodology. He starts from an assumption that many of his fellow Athenians would accept – the goodness of justice. He then interprets this goodness as a benefit to the soul, with the corollary that injustice (and any wrongdoing) is harmful to the soul. Insofar as an act of vengeance involves harming others, it is a case of wrongdoing. Such an act is harmful even to the soul of the perpetrator of vengeance. Thus, contrary to popular opinion, vengeance is wrong. Common morality is inconsistent in approving vengeance and at the same time applauding the goodness of justice. A more rational morality would repudiate vengeance.

General Themes of Socrates' Ethics

These reflections lead us to some of the general themes of Socrates' ethical philosophy found in the Platonic dialogues. The following are the basic components of this philosophy:

1. The thesis that the unexamined life is not worth living for a human being.

2. The thesis that the proper, most important activity of a person is the care of her soul.
3. Socrates' disavowal of knowledge ("Socratic ignorance").
4. The Socratic paradoxes:
   (a) virtue is knowledge;
   (b) all of the virtues are one (the unity of the virtues);
   (c) a person does not voluntarily do wrong; therefore wrongdoing is the result of ignorance;
   (d) nothing can harm a virtuous person.

As we proceed, these themes will be expounded and developed more or less in the order indicated, although, as we shall see, most of them are intertwined and cannot be understood independently of one another.

"The unexamined life is not worth living for a human being." Nowhere else in Western literature has the call to ethical inquiry and philosophical reflection been expressed more forcefully. According to Socrates, not to reflect on the question of how to live one's life amounts to living a worthless life, and, as he also argues, an unhappy one. Unfortunately, most people spend little if any time examining their lives. It will behoove us to take a closer look at this unexamined life.

All of us enter a world populated by other people and dominated by society. Our parents, our relatives and neighbors, and our fellow citizens constantly tell us what to do, what to seek, how to run our lives. Early on it is hard to argue with them; indeed, more often than not we have no wish to argue. And so, in spite of the usual teenage rebellion, we normally grow up accepting the ideas of the society we inherit. The social atmosphere in which we live our early lives contains ideas about right and wrong and good and bad, i.e., about morality. It also contains ideas about religion and religious activities and beliefs, and the religious and moral notions are often interwoven. Furthermore, the social atmosphere incorporates ideas about appropriate personal goals and ambitions: what kinds of occupation are acceptable, what kind of person is an appropriate spouse, and so on. Almost without exception, we emerge from our early period of conditioning or socialization unhesitatingly and unreflectively subscribing to these ideals. Most of us choose an occupation and a set of personal goals from the set of options socially approved and sanctioned by our society. We choose a religion from the few sects available within our community. And we define the good life, as well as the moral life, as they are defined by our elders and our peers. In short, most of us live our lives in conformity to our society and culture. This is the kind of unexamined life that Socrates deems unworthy of a human being. Why?

Because few of us in such a condition pay any attention to our character or our spiritual life – what Socrates calls our *soul*. We simply don't have the time for, or sufficient interest in, such old-fashioned pursuits as the proper tendance of the soul, i.e., character development. For the most part, we seek pleasure, wealth, or fame, but we are seldom aware of precisely what motivates us and we seldom question the direction of our lives or make deeply informed choices about our goals. Perhaps most important, the overall structure of our values is unclear to us, and little attention is given to the ways our values fit together, or fail to do so. We are simply pushed and pulled by social pressures and by our own inchoate and impetuous desires. Although we may think otherwise, we are hardly in control of ourselves. Such an unexamined life, according to Socrates, is a sure recipe for disaster; it leads – inevitably, he thinks – to unhappiness.

Although, as we have noted, Socrates was a religious person, he did not mean anything by the notion of a soul that we today would think of as religious. The idea of a soul is often associated with the religious conception of an afterlife, but it is uncertain whether or not Socrates believed in immortality. Death, he claimed in the *Apology*, is one of two possibilities: (a) a transition to life in another world, or (b) eternal sleep – and he appears to accept the second option as being just as likely as the first. The soul for Socrates, and for most Greeks and Greek philosophers, is the animated "part" of ourselves – the difference between a corpse and a living body. It is also the "part" of a person that feels, desires, suffers emotions, thinks, and acts. It is more than one's body, to be sure, but not something that is necessarily *independent* of one's body. Immortal or not, it is immensely important – the most important part of ourselves, for it is on the basis of what we do, what we think, what we feel, and what we desire that we are happy or not. Our soul is the locus of happiness or, as is so often the case, unhappiness, and because our happiness is supremely valuable to us, we must tend to this soul. Tending to it requires *knowing* it. The motto inscribed over the entrance to the Temple of Apollo admonished each of those who entered to "Know thyself," and while this probably was a religious commandment to realize that one is a human being and not a god, it becomes a perfect motto for Socrates' quite different thought. The person who lives the examined life is the one who knows herself.

At the center of Socrates' concern is the notion of happiness. Happiness, he reasonably claims, is what everyone desires above all other things, but although we desire it, we are not always successful in attaining it. We frequently make mistakes about what happiness consists in, and we often mistakenly think that what makes others happy (or seems to) will also make us happy. Not knowing our true selves and their needs, we miss the mark. Our ignorance is therefore to blame for our failure. By promoting knowledge and self-knowledge, we promote happiness – our ultimate, true goal.

The Craft of Living Happily

In discussing knowledge and happiness, Socrates frequently appeals to what scholars call his "craft analogy." Individuals who have mastered a craft (*technē*) possess a knowledge (*epistēmē*) both of the ends of their activity and the means to achieving them. A shoemaker knows what a good shoe is, and how to make one. A horsebreeder knows what kind of equestrian offspring is desirable, and how to breed horses in order to obtain this result. The captain of a ship knows the ends and means of sailing, and so on. In the case of a craft, there is an end product that is determinate (definite) and clearly defined; and there are agreed-upon procedures for obtaining this end product. To learn a craft is to learn these things, and this knowledge is objective. No one disputes what being a good shoemaker or horsebreeder is.

For Socrates, living well or successfully requires that we see the activity of living as a craft, the end product of which is happiness. The procedures for attaining it are what he calls *virtues*, these being the modes of excellence, or excellent functioning, of the various states and activities that make up a human person, both in body and soul. Just as a certain kind of chisel functions well in doing its job, and a certain way of making violins succeeds in creating superb musical instruments, so certain activities of the soul function well in leading a person to happiness. What is required, then, if we are to be successful in attaining our goal of happiness, is that we be craftsmen of our own lives. And this requires knowledge: of what human beings are, of who we as individuals are, and of how we are to act in order to achieve happiness.

Scholars disagree about the precise way we are to understand Socrates' account of the relationship between the virtues and happiness. Are the virtues *means* to the attainment of happiness when happiness itself is something distinguishable from the virtues? Or are virtuous activities *components* of happiness such that happiness is constituted by, or embodied in, virtuous activity? The craft analogy suggests an instrumentalist interpretation, since the end or goal of a craft is usually something distinct from the activities involved in the craft – a shoe, for example, is something distinct from, although produced by, the skilled activity of the shoemaker. However, Socrates often seems to take it as self-evident that the virtues bring happiness; he never provides *evidence* or reasons to think that the virtues produce happiness, as he would have to do if they are alleged to be means to an independent end. Thus it can be argued that he equates virtuous activity and happiness. But scholars continue to debate whether Socratic virtues are to be engaged in because they are valuable *in themselves*, because they are components of happiness, or because they are *means to* something else, namely happiness, that is distinct from them and valuable in itself.

At this point we should take note of one way in which Socrates' thought parallels the popular Greek morality of his time. Ordinary Greek citizens frequently talked of virtue (*aretē*) and identified five basic virtues: temperance, piety, courage, justice, and wisdom. Socrates agreed that these are virtues; much of his philosophical activity was aimed at trying to understand exactly what they are – what they *essentially* are. In our discussion of the *Euthyphro*, we found Socrates and his friend discussing the question "What is piety?", and other dialogues deal with the virtues of courage and temperance in the same fashion. Most of the early dialogues consist of attempts to arrive at a definition of the virtue under discussion, at an account or identification of what all instances of it have in common and hence what can serve as a criterion or standard for saying that something is, or that someone has, this virtue. In these dialogues, Socrates wants to show several things about the virtues, one of which is that most people do not have a clear grasp of their nature. That their failure is worrisome results from the fact that, as the person in the street also vaguely realizes, each of the virtues is no more than a form of excellence, something of which everyone approves. Courage, for instance, is an excellence of behavior with respect to feelings of fear; temperance an excellence of behavior with respect to our appetites. What Socrates' friends do not fully realize is that these virtues are required for the attainment of happiness, and hence that practicing them is part of the craft of living a successful life. Most people, on the contrary, have picked up only superficial conceptions of the virtues that make up the common-sense morality of the society. Socrates' task is, first, to show them that these conceptions are inadequate and, second, to convince them that the virtuous life is the life that is required for happiness. His task is to demonstrate that the virtues, properly understood, are the tools or procedures of the craftsman's trade when the craft itself is life.

The Gadfly's Demonstration of Ignorance

But to succeed at this task of educating his fellow citizens, Socrates must first disabuse them of their conviction that they already know all there is to know about these matters. It is in this context that we find him making his famous claim in the *Apology* that he himself is unaware of having any wisdom – great or small. At his trial, as reported in the *Apology*, he tells the story of how his friend Chaerephon visited the Oracle of Delphi and asked the Oracle if it were true that Socrates is the wisest of men. The priestess of the Oracle answered affirmatively. Socrates was astonished at this announcement, and he claims to have searched far and wide to see if he could refute the Oracle by finding a person wiser than himself. But his search, he tells the trial judges, was unsuccessful. After approaching one reputedly wise person after another, conversations with them proved that they were not really wise at all but only thought they knew much. "I am wiser than this man; it is likely that neither of us knows anything worthwhile, but he thinks he knows something when he does not, whereas when I do not know, neither do I think I know; so I am likely to be wiser than he to this small extent, that I do not think I know what I do not know" (*Apology*, 21d). Thus Socrates concludes that insofar as he is conscious of his own ignorance, while the "wise men" think wrongly that they know a great deal, perhaps he, Socrates, is in fact the wisest of the lot. As he says regarding any knowledge of the afterlife, "It is perhaps on this point and in this respect, gentlemen, that I differ from the majority of men, and if I were to claim that I am wiser than anyone in anything, it would be in this, that, as I have no adequate knowledge of things in the underworld, so I do not think I have" (*Apology*, 29b).

Here we have the thesis of "Socratic ignorance" – Socrates' disavowal of knowledge. This disavowal is so apparently at odds with his evident brilliance that many readers and commentators consider it no less a paradox than the Socratic paradoxes we identify and discuss below.

Euthyphro, as we have seen, claims to know what piety is. He is so confident of his knowledge that he thinks of himself as acting from piety in legally prosecuting his own father for murdering a man: surely, he thinks, the gods will be pleased that he has not looked the other way just because it is his father who is the guilty party. Socrates demonstrates that Euthyphro knows far less about the nature of piety than he thinks (although the self-described religious seer never really gets the point). A person like Euthyphro is not the exception but the rule, both in ancient Athens and in the contemporary world. Most people have fervent views about right and wrong, good and evil, views they take to be true beyond any doubt – and they are often prepared to go to great lengths to get other people to agree with them or, at least, to do what they think ought to be done (witness the current debate over abortion). But Socrates was able to show the people to whom he talked that their moral convictions, strong as they were, did not amount to true knowledge – they were unable, as Socrates demonstrated, to give a definition of the subject matter of these convictions. The first step towards genuine moral knowledge would be for them to recognize their current lack of such knowledge. Only then could they begin the serious and difficult task of mastering the craft of living. Socratic ignorance, therefore, is the first step toward the attainment of wisdom.

Socrates himself never claims to have mastered the craft of living. After reducing his interlocutors to inconsistency and a state of confusion about particular virtues, he stops short of demonstrating the nature of these virtues. His primary aim is to show, through the practice of the *elenchus* (cross-examination, the art of refutation), that others, in spite of their pretensions, fail to understand this craft of living. Such a philosophical demonstration is the service he as "gadfly" provides his fellow Athenians: he shows them their ignorance and thereby sets them on the path to self-knowledge. But in doing so he remains faithful to his own claim to ignorance – although, some commentators think, without perfect consistency.

Virtue is Knowledge

Although Socrates seldom (if ever) provides a positive account of any of the virtues, he does affirm and argue for several general propositions about virtue and human nature. Included among these propositions are those commonly referred to as the "Socratic paradoxes." The label results from the fact that these claims seem to go dramatically against common sense and hence appear to be obviously false. (Unlike formal logical paradoxes, however, the Socratic ones do not amount to self-contradictions or inconsistencies.) The paradoxes certainly challenge us to think more deeply about human nature and action, so that, whatever the final judgment as to their truth or falsity, they perform the Socratic "gadfly" function of pulling us up short and forcing us to reexamine some of our common-sense beliefs about morality.

We shall first examine the Socratic paradox that flows from our discussion above: virtue is knowledge. Socrates' views are clearly expressed in the following passage from the *Meno*:

Socrates: The next point to consider seems to be whether virtue is knowledge or something else.

Meno: That does seem to be the next point to consider.

Socrates: Well now, do we say that virtue is itself something good, and will this hypothesis stand firm for us, that it is something good?

Meno: Of course.

Socrates: If then there is anything else good that is different and separate from knowledge, virtue might well not be a kind of knowledge; but if there is nothing good that knowledge does not encompass, we would be right to suspect that it is a kind of knowledge.

Meno: That is so.

Socrates: Surely virtue makes us good.

Meno: Yes.

Socrates: And if we are good, we are beneficent, for all that is good is beneficial. Is that not so?

Meno: Yes.

Socrates: So virtue is something beneficial?

Meno: That necessarily follows from what has been agreed.

Socrates: Let us then examine what kinds of things benefit us, taking them up one by one: health, we say, and strength, and beauty, and also wealth. We say that these things, and others of the same kind, benefit us, do we not?

Meno: We do.

Socrates: Yet we say that these same things also sometimes harm one. Do you agree or not?

Meno: I do.

Socrates: Look then, what directing factor determines in each case whether these things benefit or harm us? Is it not the right use of them that benefits us, and the wrong use that harms us?

Meno: Certainly.

Socrates: Let us now look at the qualities of the soul. There is something you call moderation, and justice, courage, intelligence, memory, munificence, and all such things.

Meno: There is.

Socrates: Consider whichever of these you believe not to be knowledge but different from it; do they not at times harm us, at other times benefit us? Courage, for example, when it is not wisdom but like a kind of recklessness: when a man is reckless without

	understanding, he is harmed, when with understanding, he is benefitted.
Meno:	Yes.
Socrates:	The same is true of moderation and mental quickness; when they are learned and disciplined with understanding they are beneficial, but without understanding they are harmful?
Meno:	Very much so.
Socrates:	Therefore, in a word, all that the soul undertakes and endures, if directed by wisdom, ends in happiness, but if directed by ignorance, it ends in the opposite.
Meno:	That is likely.
Socrates:	If then virtue is something in the soul and it must be beneficial, it must be knowledge, since all the qualities of the soul are in themselves neither beneficial nor harmful, but accompanied by wisdom or folly they become harmful or beneficial. This argument shows that virtue, being beneficial, must be a kind of wisdom.
Meno:	I agree. (*Meno*, 87c–88d)[5]

Knowledge or wisdom, then, is a *necessary condition* of any activity being beneficial, since without knowledge an activity or state of character may turn out to be harmful. Virtue, it is agreed, is good, that is to say, beneficial. Since knowledge alone is always beneficial, virtue is knowledge.

Following up this line of thinking, consider further the virtue of courage. We might think that courage is a matter of control over the emotion of fear. But is control over fear always a virtue? Not in the case of a hardened criminal who succeeds in robbing others in part because of her ability to control her fear. Control over fear becomes a virtue only when it is combined with a knowledge of good and bad, only when we control our fear in order to achieve what we know to be good ends and to avoid what we know to be bad ones. Knowing when to control one's fear to achieve the good and avoid the bad is *always* beneficial and thus always a virtue. Likewise for temperance. Control over our appetites, which many might think to be the proper understanding of temperance, is hardly a virtue if it reduces one's food intake to the point of illness or death. True temperance requires control over appetites in the interest of promoting the good and avoiding what is bad. And this in turn requires a knowledge of good and bad. Once again knowledge is central: temperance turns out to be the knowledge of when to control one's appetites in order to achieve health and other beneficial ends. Virtue, then, always involves knowledge, since it is this knowledge that points a person toward the good and ensures that her behavior is beneficial.

In claiming that virtue is knowledge, Socrates appears to be saying not only that knowledge is a necessary condition of virtue, something one must have in order to be virtuous, but also that knowledge is the very *essence* of virtue, that is, a necessary and *sufficient* condition of it. If one has knowledge, one will be virtuous; knowledge is all that is required. Such a strong thesis appears very dubious, as we shall see in more detail later. For the moment, we shall simply note that the strong thesis seems to fly in the face of our common-sense conviction that many knowledgeable individuals (who know the difference between good and bad) are not virtuous at all but on the contrary are scoundrels and criminals. Socrates' claim that virtue is knowledge, when knowledge is understood as a necessary and sufficient condition of virtue, is therefore a paradox.

Socrates' position becomes more plausible when we recognize another assumption he makes in the course of the argument, namely that all human beings desire the good – what benefits them – or that no one desires the bad. A long passage from the *Meno* brings out this point:

Meno: I think, Socrates, that virtue is, as the poet says, "to find joy
            in beautiful things and have power." So I say that virtue is to
            desire beautiful things and have the power to acquire them.
Socrates: Do you mean that the man who desires beautiful things desires
            good things?
Meno: Most certainly.
Socrates: Do you assume that there are people who desire bad things,
            and others who desire good things? Do you not think, my good
            man, that all men desire good things?
Meno: I do not.
Socrates: But some desire bad things?
Meno: Yes.
Socrates: Do you mean that they believe the bad things to be good, or
            that they know they are bad and nevertheless desire them?
Meno: I think there are both kinds.
Socrates: Do you think, Meno, that anyone, knowing that bad things are
            bad, nevertheless desire them?
Meno: I certainly do.
Socrates: What do you mean by desiring? Is it to secure for oneself?
Meno: What else?
Socrates: Does he think that the bad things benefit him who possesses
            them, or does he know they harm him?
Meno: There are some who believe that the bad things benefit them,
            others who know that the bad things harm them.
Socrates: And do you think that those who believe that bad things
            benefit them know that they are bad.
Meno: No, that I cannot altogether believe.
Socrates: It is clear then that those who do not know things to be bad
            do not desire what is bad, but they desire those things that they
            believe to be good but that are in fact bad. It follows that those
            who have no knowledge of these things and believe them to
            be good clearly desire good things. Is that not so?

15

Meno: It is likely.

Socrates: Well then, those who you say desire bad things, believing that bad things harm their possessor, know that they will be harmed by them?

Meno: Necessarily.

Socrates: And do they not think that those who are harmed are miserable to the extent that they are harmed?

Meno: That too is inevitable.

Socrates: And that those who are miserable are unhappy?

Meno: I think so.

Socrates: Does anyone wish to be miserable and unhappy?

Meno: I do not think so, Socrates.

Socrates: No one then wants what is bad, Meno, unless he wants to be such. For what else is being miserable but to desire bad things and secure them?

Meno: You are probably right, Socrates, and no one wants what is bad. (*Meno*, 77b–78b)

Socrates' argument here is a powerful one. If no one desires anything that she knows will bring harm to her, then she always *thinks* that the object of her desire is good. She may be in error about the matter, since what she desires may turn out to be disadvantageous to her. But no one desires something *knowing* that it is bad, and hence harmful to her. A person always desires what she believes to be good. In this sense, she always wants the good.

If nobody desires what is bad, if, on the contrary, everybody desires what is good and desires this more than anything else, then *knowing* what is good will lead to action in pursuit of this good. It follows, as Socrates claims, that knowledge is sufficient for virtuous activity. Given the universal desire to pursue what is good, i.e., what is beneficial to oneself, once one has a knowledge of what is good, one will pursue it. Such a claim has less of a ring of paradox about it than it originally appeared to have (although later we shall observe some other possible problems with it).

The Unity of the Virtues

The equation of virtue and knowledge suggests that there really is only one virtue, or that all of the virtues normally distinguished (temperance, courage, etc.) are in fact one, namely knowledge or wisdom. Thus we are led to the second Socratic paradox, the thesis of the unity of the virtues.

How can all the virtues be one? Can they be identical – courage, for instance, being the same virtue as temperance? Socrates himself, in seeking definitions of the various virtues, certainly suggests that these definitions, and hence these virtues, are quite different: he would not, for example, accept a plausible definition of courage – "knowledge of the fearful and the hopeful in war and in every other situation" (*Laches*, 194e–195a)[6] – as the definition of justice, say, or as the definition of any of the other traditional virtues. In what sense, then, are the virtues *one*?

Many commentators have found Socrates' thesis of the unity of the virtues so bizarre that they have in fact dismissed it. More recently, however, as a result of the work of the great Socratic and Platonic scholar, Gregory Vlastos, an interpretation has been given to this thesis which makes it consistent with other aspects of Socrates' thought and shows it to be an intelligible and plausible idea.[7] What Socrates wants to claim, according to this interpretation, is that any person who has one of the virtues has them all. As Socrates puts the question in the dialogue *Protagoras*: "Which of these two things is the case: That some men partake of one of these parts of virtue, others of some other part? Or is it the case that if a man has one he will of necessity have them all?" (329e2–4).[8]

Socrates, according to Vlastos, accepts the second alternative: to have one of the virtues is to have them all. One cannot be courageous and not also be temperate; one cannot be pious without also being just – and so on.

Once again the key to understanding such a claim is the emphasis Socrates places on the virtue of wisdom. All of the virtues, he maintains, are "parts" or species of wisdom. We have seen how knowledge is a necessary condition of any particular virtue: one cannot be temperate without being wise, i.e., without curbing one's desires by the use of reason; one cannot be courageous without being wise, since knowing what to fear and what not is clearly a form of wisdom. It follows that a courageous person cannot be foolish (i.e., lacking in wisdom), a just person cannot be foolish, and likewise for all of the virtues. As Socrates puts it, folly (foolishness) is the opposite of both courage and temperance (and, by implication, of all the other virtues). He then argues that two different things cannot have the same opposite, and he concludes from this claim that all of the virtues (courage, temperance, piety, justice, and wisdom) are the same, having as they do the same opposite, folly. Socrates' logic may be a bit shaky in this argument, but his line of thought clearly shows that he wishes to place all virtuous persons in one class, the class of individuals who are not foolish (lacking in wisdom). Thus if an individual person does not fall into the class of foolish persons, she will therefore be in the class of individuals who are courageous, temperate, pious, just, and – of course – wise. Thus, having one of the virtues, she will have them all.

A simpler way of grasping Socrates' thesis of the unity of the virtues is to reflect on what it means to be a wise person. Could a wise person also be cowardly? If so, given what courage and cowardice mean, this person would not know what to fear and what not to fear. But such a person would *not* be wise, lacking as she is in some essential knowledge. Similarly, a wise person could not be intemperate, for that too would mean a lack of knowledge (of when to curb one's appetites). Thus anyone who is wise will also have all the other virtues. The various virtues are coextensive, as Vlastos puts it: if one of them is found in a person, all will be. In this sense the virtues are one.

Wrongdoing Is Always Involuntary?

We are now in a position to consider the most famous of the Socratic paradoxes, the claim that if we know the good we shall pursue it and that if we do what is wrong we do so involuntarily and out of ignorance. Socrates expresses this paradox in a passage in the *Protagoras*:

> "Well, gentlemen," I said, "what about this? Aren't all actions praise-worthy which lead to a painless and pleasant life? And isn't praiseworthy activity good and beneficial?"
>
> They agreed.
>
> "So if what is pleasant is good," I said, "no one who either knows or believes that something else is better than what he is doing, and is in his power to do, subsequently does the other, when he can do what is better. Nor is giving in to oneself anything other than error, nor controlling oneself anything other than wisdom."
>
> They all agreed.
>
> "Well now. Is this what you mean by error, having false opinions and being mistaken about matters of importance?"
>
> They all agreed to that as well.
>
> "Now surely," I said, "no one freely goes for bad things or things he believes to be bad; it's not, it seems to me, in human nature to be prepared to go for what you think to be bad in preference to what is good. And when you are forced to choose one of two evils, nobody will choose the greater when he can have the lesser. Isn't that so?"
>
> All of us agreed to all of that.   (*Protagoras*, 358b4–d4)[9]

In the *Protagoras*, the question is raised whether or not we can know something is bad for us but nevertheless be "led on and distracted by pleasure" to pursue it. Most people ("the world") believe this is possible; both Socrates and Protagoras deny it, but it is up to Socrates to show why this widely held belief in the weakness of the will is in fact false. Weakness of will is said (by most people) to occur when an individual knows that an action is wrong but is overwhelmed by her desire for the pleasure she thinks the act will bring her – her will is not strong enough to resist the temptation. Socrates proceeds to demonstrate that in cases of this sort the individual who allegedly is led astray by pleasure actually does not have complete knowledge of the case. She does not realize that the act she chooses to perform – the one she believes is bad but thinks will bring her pleasure – will in fact turn out to be painful. She only mistakenly thinks the action she pursues will bring an overall balance of pleasure. Thus it is ignorance that leads her to choose the bad course of action; she falsely believes that her act will lead to overall pleasure for herself; she believes, that is, that her act will produce the good, but her belief is in error.

It is debatable whether or not Socrates actually agreed to the equation (suggested in the *Protagoras*) of the pleasant and painless life with the good life. In any event, his general message is clear. Whatever the nature of good and bad, we never pursue the bad voluntarily. Given our desire for the good (what benefits the agent), any action that results in something bad is the result of our not knowing that what we aimed at was bad (harmful) rather than, as we falsely believed, good. So wrongdoing is always involuntary and the result of ignorance. Once Socrates has brought Protagoras to see this, the two agree that "nothing is more powerful than knowledge" (357c) and that "no matter where it is it always conquers pleasure and everything else" (357c).

Now we can let our reservations about some of the earlier paradoxes come fully to the fore, for these reservations can be expressed in their most powerful form in relationship to the claim that wrongdoing is always involuntary. Surely, we earlier wanted to protest, knowledge of what is good and bad cannot guarantee that the person who has this knowledge will be virtuous and act for good and worthy ends! Can't we know what is good for us – beneficial – and still not pursue it? Can't our wills be weak? Don't we *voluntarily* do things we know to be harmful to us – we continue to smoke, for example, knowing full well that doing so can and often does cause cancer. Can't we, to take the case of the "other-directed" virtue called justice, know what justice requires toward others and still deliberately not promote it, out of indifference or hatred toward other people? Don't criminals deliberately harm others? How can Socrates get away with saying that no one ever deliberately and intentionally, i.e., voluntarily, does what is wrong? How can he say that when we do what is wrong we always act out of ignorance?

Some commentators see two distinct but related paradoxes in this area of Socrates' thought: a prudential paradox and a moral one. The prudential paradox lies in the claim that we never willingly pursue what is *bad* (what will harm us); the moral paradox consists in the assertion that we never willing pursue what is *wrong* (what will harm others). One well-known and highly regarded recent interpretation takes the explanation of the moral paradox to rest on the prudential one.[10]

Socrates' reasoning behind the prudential paradox is simple and powerful: we are often mistaken about our own true interests. A person may, for instance, pursue a degree in law, thinking that success in this effort will bring great benefit to her. In fact, working as a lawyer turns out to make her miserable. In choosing to pursue a degree in law, she was simply insufficiently knowledgeable of what is involved in being a lawyer, or insufficiently knowledgeable of her own likes and dislikes. She brought considerable harm on herself (loss of money and time in seeking the degree and subsequent misery in using it), but only out of ignorance. If she had known what it is to be a lawyer, and what it would be like for *her* to be one, she would not have chosen to do what she did; she did not *voluntarily* seek the resultant harm. In this case, as Socrates claimed, wrongdoing (acts that bring about harm and misery) clearly turns out to be involuntary and the result of ignorance.

But there are other cases. What about the cigarette smoker who continues to smoke in spite of having read all the dire statistics about the carcinogenic effects of doing so? Socrates could answer that in cases of incontinence like this the smoker really hasn't taken the statistics to heart – she hasn't faced up to the facts and thus can't really be said to believe the facts about the consequences of smoking. Or perhaps she thinks herself likely to be the exception – smoking after all doesn't always cause lung cancer or heart disease, and, not being very risk-averse, a person may be willing to take her chances. Interpreted in ways like these, the case of the cigarette smoker may offer no disproof of Socrates' paradox.

What about the moral paradox, the denial that we ever deliberately harm others? Wasn't Hitler an evil man who knew he was bringing misery to millions but nevertheless did so – in a highly deliberate and ruthless fashion? Likewise, didn't Stalin "voluntarily" exterminate millions of his own fellow citizens? Don't all of these examples show that one can voluntarily and knowingly do wrong or bring harm to others? Perhaps, but Socrates is probably not without a comeback. Hitler, given his paranoid ideological convictions, probably saw himself as producing a "higher good," for which "noble" goal taking the lives of what he considered to be a few million "subhuman and dangerous" beings was a necessary means. He didn't aim at what he took to be wrong; he aimed at what he took to be good. And so he didn't voluntarily do what he believed to be wrong. Of course, we are convinced that his paranoia and ideology were irrational, false in the extreme. But that simply shows that he acted out of ignorance. So the paradoxical statement that wrongdoing is involuntary and the result of ignorance may stand the test of a Hitler – or Stalin.

Another line of defense of the moral paradox – and one central to Socrates' position – goes like this: if we know what justice and injustice are (if we know what acts are just or unjust) *and* if we know that acting virtuously is always in our own interest, then we will never knowingly and willingly do what is unjust. To do so would involve us in deliberately pursuing what will harm us and make us miserable, which the prudential paradox rules out. It is clear that Socrates adopts this way of thinking in the dialogue *Gorgias*. His argument, however, relies on the premise that unjust acts (and vicious, non-virtuous ones in general) bring harm to the agent who performs them. In the minds of most readers, Socrates does not adequately defend this premise. One can say either that Socrates takes it for granted, or that, by the time Plato wrote the *Gorgias*, he (Plato) was developing his own line of thought, the full defense of which was only to be given in a later dialogue, the *Republic*.

No Harm Comes to the Just Person?

Finally, let us turn to the last of the Socratic paradoxes, the claim that no harm can come to a good and just person. Unfortunately, this too seems to fly in the face of experience. How many decent, in many cases noble, individuals have been brought down by the powers of corruption? Take the case of Socrates himself: he was condemned by the Athenians on charges that contained little truth, having initially been brought to trial as the likely result of, among other things, the resentment felt toward him by individuals who had been "shown up" by his elenctic investigations. Here is a man who is good, decent, and just, but one who is being harmed in the extreme by unjust fellow citizens. Doesn't the case of Socrates refute his own theory?

Socrates certainly didn't think so. He maintained to the end that he was not being harmed by his accusers or by the verdict of the jury. Not only was he already old and likely to die soon anyway, death would only provide him with an occasion to answer some questions which, as a philosopher, it was his business to answer. Furthermore, death was either a transition to an eternal life with the gods, which couldn't be very unpleasant, or an eternal "dreamless" sleep, which, if his previous experience held up, was one of the most desirable states of all. What harm, then, is being imposed on him? Most important, however, Socrates claims to be happy because, throughout his life and then at his trial, he has always done his best to be a good and just person. He has obeyed his divine "sign" (what, with some interpretive license, we might call his conscience) when it told him *not* to do certain things. He has honored the gods and served his city. He has led a life of virtue and *for this reason* he is a happy man. Nothing is more important than this. The virtuous person is the happy person, simply because he is virtuous, and no enemy arrows or fateful catastrophes can destroy such happiness. No harm can come to the virtuous individual.

Socrates clearly implies that the reverse of this proposition is also true: no happiness can come to an unjust man, to one who is not virtuous. Those who pursue a life of injustice may pile up riches and honors and enjoy abundant pleasures, but these do not a happy life make. The Greeks believed that virtue and excellence were the same thing, (the two English words are both translations of *aretē*), and that to live an excellent life is therefore to live a virtuous one. The excellent life is the one best suited to the attainment of the end of life, and it is agreed by all that this end is happiness. Hence it follows that the virtuous and just man, but not the unjust, is happy; the temperate, but not the profligate; the wise, but not the foolish. All of these virtues, as we have seen, are simply specific manifestations of the knowledge of what is good and what is bad. The virtuous person is the one who knows what is good, and, knowing this, pursues the good and avoids the bad. In doing so, the virtuous person attains the end of his craft, the life of happiness. The person lacking virtue, on the contrary, acts from ignorance of good and bad. Not knowing the good, mistaking something else for it, she fails to pursue the good. And this amounts to her failure to obtain happiness, since the good is nothing more than happiness. The wrongdoer is therefore the miserable person.

Seen in this fashion, Socrates' thought turns out to be remarkably consistent. Once we understand the nature of human action, as reflected in the so–called paradoxes, we shall see that the moral life is rationally justified. Any rational person, therefore, will lead a life of virtue and avoid a life of vice – and thereby achieve happiness.

Two Problems with Socrates' Views

Yes, but ... Is Socrates' argument really convincing? Two problems suggest themselves to most scholars. First, there is what they refer to as his intellectualism. Socrates' conviction that to know the good is to seek it implies that knowledge by itself is capable of motivating a person to act. If we know what is good, this knowledge alone will prompt us to act. Is this, we might ask, an acceptable conception of *motivation?* Many philosophers, past and present, are convinced that we act because of a combination of belief (knowledge) and desire, and that without desire, belief or knowledge will not be sufficient to motivate us to undertake any action. Knowledge or belief may inform us of what the facts are, or of what the consequences of our action will be, but unless we have a desire for those consequences, or unless we have some affective/conative response (some feeling or desire) to the facts, we shall take no action. Cognitive states such as belief or knowledge merely *inform* us, they do not *move* us. Given this conception of action, Socrates' belief that knowledge of good and bad is sufficient to cause us to act in a virtuous manner will be seen as rather unconvincing.

Such a criticism of Socrates ignores his claim – argued for, as we have seen, in the *Meno* – that all human beings desire what is good, what is advantageous and beneficial to them. In light of this doctrine, one can see his intellectualism in a different fashion. Even though knowledge for him is both a necessary and sufficient condition for acting virtuously, virtue is not strictly equated with knowledge. Also at the basis of virtue is the desire for the good. *Given* this desire, the only impediment to our acting virtuously is our false state of belief. If we straighten out our beliefs and arrive at true ones, then virtuous actions will follow; if we do not do so, vice will result. Against the background of the universal desire for happiness, knowledge is both the necessary and sufficient condition of virtue.

Even if this interpretation is correct, however, Socrates' position is still open to criticism. Do all persons have a desire for the good? And even if they do, is the desire for the good always the dominant desire? Don't we also have desires that are not grounded in a conception of the goodness of their objects, for instance, desires that simply erupt in us? And don't these latter desires sometimes get the better of our desire for the good? It can be argued that a more anarchic, impulsive conception of desire has more to recommend it than Socrates' conception. In fact, one can see Plato as coming to this latter view of desire, and as a result developing a very different response to the problem of ensuring virtuous action. He will look for a way of *controlling* the erupting, particular desires that sometimes overwhelm us, and thus he will not rely on our desire for the good to take over once knowledge has been attained.

Another concern that scholars have with Socrates' thinking relates to the notion of justice. To act justly is to act in a way that benefits others. Given the Socratic claim that knowledge (of good and bad) is sufficient for virtuous action, it seems to follow that if we know that a certain action will harm others we will not engage in this action. But is this in fact true? It certainly appears not to be. Socrates himself relies frequently on the more convincing argument that once we know what truly benefits *us* we will act on this knowledge. But knowing that an action will benefit others is not to know that it will benefit us. In fact, it will often be the case, from the standpoint of what is almost universal experience, that what benefits us harms others, and that what benefits others harms us. Thus it is highly questionable whether knowing that a mode of behavior will benefit others is sufficient to motivate us to act justly. From this line of thought it follows that Socrates has failed to show that we are adequately motivated to be just persons.

We noted above that Socrates can be interpreted either as *equating* virtue and happiness – as claiming that acting virtuously constitutes happiness – or as maintaining that acting virtuously is an instrumental *means* to the attainment of happiness, not happiness itself. The latter view seems to follow from his use of the craft analogy. If the craft analogy explains Socrates' conception of virtue, then he cannot simply assume that in being virtuous a person *thereby* is happy and that in lacking virtue a person *thereby* is unhappy or miserable. He has to prove that living a life of virtue in point of fact leads, instrumentally, to happiness. He needs to show that an unjust person turns out, as a *result* of his unjust actions, to be miserable. Socrates never proves these things, and to that extent he fails to prove his case that nothing bad can befall a just person. He never proves it *unless* he is after all committed to the proposition that happiness *consists* in virtuous behavior. Some scholars maintain that this in fact is his position; others disagree. It is for further research to determine which of these interpretations is correct.

But is it reasonable to say *either* that happiness consists in virtuous activity *or* that virtue leads to an independently identifiable happiness? Whatever the details, is Socrates' overall account of human nature a realistic one or just an overly optimistic, rather pious dream? It is certainly a controversial account, and it is time for us to turn our attention to some of Socrates' contemporaries who thought that, on the topic of virtue and happiness, and on other topics as well, Socrates was not facing the facts but was "up in the clouds" (as one comic Athenian poet, Aristophanes, actually pictured him in his famous satirical play, *The Clouds*).

The Sophists: Protagoras

One can read very little about ancient Greek society without hearing about the Sophists. These individuals were teachers who, wandering from one city-state to another, offered their services for money, promising to teach skills that would be useful in the affairs of life within the city-state, particularly political affairs. With the rise of democracy in the fifth century, such skills could be very valuable to citizens who needed to give speeches in the assembly and argue their favorite cause before their fellow citizens. The techniques of rhetoric were in demand, and many of the Sophists billed themselves as rhetoricians. Rhetoric, as they practiced it, was the art of being persuasive in speech and writing; its goal was success, not truth. Other Sophists taught techniques for getting the better of one's competitors or enemies, and their goal in this instance was, again, success – not justice.

It is not difficult to understand how the Sophists themselves became, in many instances, highly successful. They offered what the market demanded. But neither is it difficult to understand why in some quarters they came to have a bad reputation. It was said of them that they saw no shame in making the better cause appear the worse, if in doing so they and their clients came off winners. They seemed willing in many instances to use any trick available to them to advance their cause. Thus it is easy enough to see why the term "sophistical" has the derogatory meaning it has today: it suggests the practices of the ancient Sophists. And it is not too difficult to understand why Socrates' accusers often pictured *him* (erroneously) as a Sophist.

But this popular picture of the Sophists is not the whole story. Many of them had philosophical views and in fact used these convictions to justify their activities. Indeed, some of these sophistic philosophies consist of doctrines that many people today, especially those who see themselves as being "realistic" about such matters, consider nothing less than common sense. We shall briefly examine several of these sophistic philosophies.

The earliest and most famous Sophist was Protagoras of Abdera (490–420 BCE). He was widely known throughout Greece as well as in other parts of the ancient world, and he became highly esteemed and wealthy as a result of his teachings. He was a confidant of Pericles, the great leader of the Athenian democracy during its apex, and he was admired by Socrates (who nevertheless strongly disagreed with him on some points). Protagoras was one of the more moderate Sophists when it came to his philosophical views and his teachings. He was well-known for his claim that he could teach virtue, and hence for the more general thesis that virtue was something teachable. This was a somewhat radical message among the Greeks, since it was widely assumed by them that virtue was the prerogative of birth and rank. Protagoras's claim that virtue can be taught had a democratic ring to it. It also was congenial to Socrates' belief that virtue is knowledge. But other aspects of Protagoras's message were strikingly different from the philosophical teachings of Socrates.

Protagoras is what we call a *relativist*. In point of fact we know very little first-hand about his thought, for only one fragment (the first sentence of one of his books) has been preserved. For the most part, we have to flesh out his views from the writings of others who mention him and describe his thought. Plato went so far as to name a dialogue after him in which Protagoras and Socrates engage in debate, and he is prominently mentioned in another Platonic dialogue, the *Theaetetus*. But the one fragment we have of his writings conveys the fundamental principle of Protagorean relativism, and it is not difficult for us to expand this proposition into a more developed doctrine.

The first sentence of Protagoras's *On Truth* reads as follows: "Of all things the measure is man: of things that are, that they are; of things that are not, that they are not." *Man is the measure of all things* – this is the standard expression of Protagorean relativism. What does it mean? First of all, as we know from early commentators on Protagoras, it is a way of saying that the *individual person* is the judge of reality, the one who determines that some things exist and others do not. Second, this individual provides the measure, the standard or criterion, for existence and nonexistence. A measure of this sort is what shows that a thing exists (or not) and indicates how a thing is, i.e., what qualities it has. According to Protagoras, what an individual *experiences* and thus *believes* determines what exists and what does not, how things are and how they are not. Individual experience and belief, then, are the measure. No one has a way of determining existence and nonexistence that is independent of her own experiences and beliefs. No one can know of any reality other than what is "measured" by this standard.

We might agree with Protagoras that this individual perspective – a person's experiences and beliefs – determines the way things *appear* or *seem* to her. But Protagoras takes the argument a step farther. Plato, in his dialogue *Cratylus*,[11] expresses Protagoras's idea as follows: "so that as things *appear* to me, so they *are* for me, and as they *appear* to you, so they *are* for you." Protagoras is in effect denying that we can make a distinction between the way things appear and the way they are. Things *are* as they *appear* to be. No one can distinguish between how things are and how they appear because the only access one has to them is through their appearances. Let us consider some examples. How can we know whether the wind is warm or cold other than how it feels to us, or the taste of a peach except the way it tastes to us, or the color of a bowl except the way it looks to us? There is no more to the reality of these features for each of us than their appearances to each of us.

The quotation from Plato also shows us that Protagoras placed emphasis on the fact that different people see, taste, and feel things differently: appearances may vary from person to person. If you have a cold and your friend does not, a peach will likely taste one way to you and another way to her. Is it possible to say that the taste of one of you is correct and that of the other incorrect? How could you find out? Your tasting it again is likely to reveal the same taste to you, but if your friend tastes it again she too is likely to confirm *her* first taste. Nothing is proved either way about the real taste of the peach. Shall we bring in a third taster? What would this prove? The peach may produce in him a *third* taste, but this taste has no more authority – no greater ability to reveal the "real" taste of the peach – than your taste or your friend's. But what if the third person's taste agrees with your friend's? Doesn't this prove that your friend's taste was correct after all? It shows nothing of the sort, since both your friend's taste and that of the third observer may be, for all anyone knows, deceptive, while yours is accurate (or veridical, as philosophers say). "But I have a cold," you say, "so surely my taste buds are not working correctly." But to this one might respond: for all we know, the taste buds of a person with a cold are the ones that reveal the real taste of a peach. "For all we know" – but of course we really don't, and can't, know any such thing *or* its contrary. We have no way of knowing what is real independently of our individual experiences (tastes), and so we can never conclude that our own experience (taste) is in error. Thus the real taste of the peach for you is the way you taste it; the real taste for your friend is the way she tastes it, and the real taste for the third party is the way that individual tastes it. Each person is the measure of the taste of the peach.

There is an even more radical conclusion that seems to follow from Protagoras's claim that man is the measure. Common sense may tell us that, although the peach we eat may taste different to each of us, nevertheless it is the same peach we eat. But how can this be so? What is the peach for us other than its taste and its other sensory appearances. The only peach each of us encounters and "knows" is the peach that consists of the sensory appearances it provides us – and so, if there are different appearances, there are different peaches. As paradoxical as it may sound, we do not taste the same peach when it yields a different taste to each of us. Each person's world is to some extent different from the world of others.

Put another way: all beliefs are true. To quote from Plato one more time:

> Socrates: He [Protagoras] says, does he not, that things are for every
>   man what they seem to him to be?
> Theodorus: Yes, that is what he says (*Theaetetus*, 170a).[12]

A person's beliefs reflect the ways things seem to her. Just as we cannot distinguish between a true appearance and a false one, we cannot distinguish between a true belief and a false belief. This consequence in turn destroys the distinction between knowledge and belief, since belief is commonly thought to be susceptible of both truth and falsity while knowledge must always be true. If the true/false distinction cannot be drawn, however, and if an object *is* how it *appears* to an individual, then a person's belief, which reflects this appearance, is always true. Consequently it is *knowledge* a person always has, not mere belief. I *know* the taste of the peach, the warmth of the wind, the color of the bowl, and the nature of all the things I experience.

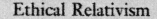

Ethical Relativism

So far we have presented Protagoras's relativism as a form of cognitive relativism about knowledge and the nature of reality. But it is easy enough, and justifiable enough in terms of other references by ancient philosophers to Protagoras's thought, to extend his relativism to the moral sphere. As Aristotle put it:

> Protagoras said that man is the measure of all things, meaning simply and
> solely that what appears to each man assuredly also *is*. If this is so, it
> follows that the same thing both is and is not, and is both bad and good,

and whatever else is asserted in contrary statements, since often a particular thing appears good (or beautiful) to some and the opposite to others; and the criterion is what appears to each individual (*Metaphysics*, 1062b13).

As a Sophist, Protagoras traveled considerably, and in his travels he observed the varied customs of the people he visited. He was in a position to note that different societies or cultures held different beliefs about almost all aspects of life: the relations of parent to child, sexual activities, marital expectations, the value of pleasure in life, the value of discipline, the role of art and music, business activities, politics, religion. These beliefs constitute a culture's values and morality. Is it possible to distinguish between cultural values or moralities that are true and those that are false, those that are rationally acceptable and those that are not? On what basis would we do so? To what could we appeal? In defense of itself, each culture will appeal to its own values, but such an appeal begs the question if one is trying to ascertain whether this culture's values, or those of a competing culture, are true or rationally acceptable. But if we appeal to a set of values of some *other* culture, we seem to beg the question *against* the values of the first culture. In light of the difficulty (impossibility?) of identifying a neutral and independent standard of comparison, it is easy to be drawn to the thesis of relativism: any set of values is acceptable for those who believe in them and unacceptable for those who do not. For *me*, the true values are *my* values – those of my society; for *you*, those of your society. For me, true morality is the set of moral convictions I and my fellow citizens adhere to; for you, true morality is the moral beliefs you and your fellows accept. Ethical relativism is the thesis that there are no moral values that are true independently of whether they are adhered to or not (later relativistic thinkers like to talk of a relativity of moral *principles*). This is the thesis that there are no moral values that are valid for (binding on) a person who does not accept these values (principles).

If relativism is popular in some quarters, it is heatedly denounced in others. Many see its widespread acceptance in the late twentieth century as representing the decline

Ethical relativism has been an influential theory throughout the history of Western philosophy. It appeals to philosophers and laypersons alike who are impressed by the fact that people argue incessantly over moral values and seldom if ever come to any agreement. Conflicts over morality occur at all places and all times, and there seem to be no procedures or techniques for resolving these disputes in a rational manner. Frequently societies go to war in order to uphold and extend their moralities – *by force*. In contemporary American and European society, the social homogeneity that previously existed has been seriously eroded if not destroyed, and it is very seldom that the entire society agrees on moral values. In today's world, Protagoras would likely have us believe that the true morality is that of the subculture, the gang, or even the individual. If an individual believes in a certain moral code, then it is true for her even if others vociferously disagree. These other individuals simply have a different moral code that is true – true for them. Pushed to its logical conclusion, relativism would justify each person in accepting her own morality.

If relativism is popular in some quarters, it is heatedly denounced in others. Many see its widespread acceptance in the late twentieth century as representing the decline of Western civilization and the cause of many of the problems faced by today's society. The dire warnings about the pernicious effects of relativism do not, of course, prove that it is not a true theory of morality. But aside from the sermons and the handwringing, there are some philosophical objections to relativism which should be noted. These objections were in fact registered by some contemporaries of Protagoras. The great Sophist failed to convince Socrates and Plato, and indeed many of their successors in the history of moral philosophy.

In Plato's dialogue *Theaetetus*, we find Socrates taking Protagoras to task by arguing that his practice as a Sophist is inconsistent with his philosophy.

> If whatever the individual judges by means of perception is true for him; if no man can assess another's experience better than he, or can claim authority to examine another man's judgment and see if it be right or wrong; if, as we have repeatedly said, only the individual himself can judge of his own world, and what he judges is always true and correct: how could it ever be, my friend, that Protagoras was a wise man, so wise as to think himself fit to be the teacher of other men and worth large fees; while we, in comparison with him the ignorant ones, needed to go and sit at his feet – we who are ourselves each the measure of his own wisdom? (*Theaetetus*, 161d–e)

Protagoras, the professional Sophist, bills himself as a teacher, and one thing he teaches is that to be successful a person should submit to the laws and customs of her own society. Socrates wants to know how, being a relativist, Protagoras can justify calling himself a teacher. A teacher is someone who is supposed to impart the *truth* to his students, often replacing their naive, immature beliefs with true ones. But this presupposes that the ideas Protagoras imparts to them have a greater degree of truth than the ones they have developed on their own. The notion of superior truth, however, is inconsistent with relativism. If one of the immature Athenian youths believed that he should flout the rules of Athenian society, then, according to relativism, it would be true (for him) that he should, and if Protagoras urges that, on the contrary, it is right to follow these rules, this conviction may be true for Protagoras but, by Protagoras's own admission, not true for the person who disagrees with it. How can Protagoras justify correcting these young people and teaching them how they really should behave?

Protagoras's response to this charge is weak. He admits that he cannot be engaged in the process of replacing false beliefs with true ones. But that, he says, is not his task. His role is to replace a set of beliefs that is likely to get a person into trouble with a set that will promote this person's success. Just as a physician cannot object to a sick man's claim that his food tastes (and thus is) bitter but can treat the patient so that he no longer tastes it as bitter, so the Sophist can replace a set of beliefs, which he must admit are true for the person holding them, with a *better* set of beliefs, better not in the sense of having more truth to them but in the sense of having more desirable consequences. And the student of the Sophist, just like the patient of the physician, will like the results and call them good. Abiding by the values and rules of one's society, Protagoras claims, is the best recipe for success in life, success being exactly what his students want. Thus Protagoras provides what today we would call a pragmatic justification of his activities as teacher: what he teaches is what works, what is useful – not what is true for everyone or true absolutely.

But *is* it true, we might ask, that following the values and rules of society is the best way to achieve success in life? Many young rebels think otherwise, and how can their beliefs be faulted from a relativist point of view? What success is to them, and what leads to this success, may be quite different from what they are for Father Protagoras. How can Protagoras claim to know what really is good for a person, or what really brings success? In the end, he can only know, by the principles of his own relativism, what is good for *him* or what conduces to success for *him*. His opinions on these matters are no better, however, that the value judgments of any other person. Therefore, he cannot legitimately claim to have superior ability to produce what the client wants, as he does claim in offering his services as a teacher.

There are still other problems with Protagorean relativism. To see these difficulties, we must distinguish two parts of this theory. On the one hand, Protagoras maintains that different people have different ideas about morality. This claim is what philosophers call the thesis of *cultural relativism*. It amounts to an empirical, factual assertion to the effect that there are fundamental moral disagreements among people. This hypothesis *may* be true, but then again it may not – the evidence we have, even today, is inconclusive. One reservation about its truth could be expressed in the following way. Although it is undeniable that people of different societies, as well as people in the same society, often disagree on moral issues, this does not necessarily show that they subscribe to different *fundamental* ethical principles. Their disagreement might be explained in terms of differences of belief with respect to *nonmoral* matters, religious convictions, say, or scientific ones. Or, in the case of people from different cultures, disagreement might be explained in terms of different material circumstances under which they live. Different circumstances of life in two cultures might call for different forms of behavior and do so in light of the very *same* moral principles the one culture shares with the other. For example, a society in which food is very scarce, or one in which there is a large differential between the number of males and females, might justifiably require quite different practices with respect to the distribution of food, or marriage relations, than would a society in which these material circumstances do not exist. And the two societies might appeal to the *same* fundamental moral principle – e.g., the demand that human need be satisfied – to justify their different social arrangements. The cultural differences in this case would reflect the divergent circumstances of life, not divergent moral convictions.

But assume that, after all is said and done, cultural relativism is true and there are different and conflicting sets of fundamental moral principles. Does it follow that one society's or one person's moral code is just as true as any other such code? Does it prove *ethical relativism*, the philosophical theory that denies there are any moral propositions true for all human beings, as an ethical *absolutist* would claim? Might not one or more of the different cultural principles be mistaken, and one of them true?

Of course, we would have to prove that some are false and the one true, but the simple fact of disagreement over principles does not in and of itself show that we cannot do this. It does not prove that the beliefs of each party are equally true – just because they are believed. Consider a case of disagreement outside the moral sphere – in the area of science. Chemists, nuclear physicists, and mathematicians sometimes disagree, but that hardly proves that the beliefs and theories of one party have no more merit that the those of the others. In science, disagreements can be overcome and truth, or at least probability, ascertained. Cultural disagreements with respect to morality do not, by themselves, prove that the same cannot be done in the moral sphere. But it does cause one to wonder how the truth of one set of moral views might be established over the claims of alternative moralities.

Still another objection to Protagorean relativism is found in the *Theaetetus*. If Protagoras is correct, Socrates observes, he must admit that his opponent who denies the relativity of values is also correct, there being no distinction between believing and knowing. Thus, if Protagoras is right, the moral absolutist who denies the relativity of values *knows* that values are absolute. But if he knows this, then Protagoras, who claims just the opposite, is wrong. So, if Protagoras is right, he is wrong. The theory, in a nutshell, refutes itself.

The Sophists: Thrasymachus and Others

Here we must leave Protagoras and look at the ethical views of another well-known Sophist. Perhaps the most famous sophistic theory of ethics is the one often attributed to Thrasymachus: "might makes right". Thrasymachus's actual statement, as reported in Plato's dialogue *Republic* is "I say that justice is nothing other than the advantage of the stronger" (*Republic*, 338c).[13] In this dialogue, Thrasymachus blasts Socrates for his pious messages, lambastes his character, and loudly affirms "the facts," viz., what rules the world is power; government is simply the control of the weak by the strong; rulers develop laws to further their own interests; and whatever the rulers demand is just and right. According to Thrasymachus, rulers govern, not in order to improve the condition of their people but to better their own lives. In fact, he argues, the greater the amount of control they exercise over people, the greater their own gain – hence tyranny, he thinks, is the best form of government. The tyrant, whose control over the people is absolute, is actually praised and applauded by the people far more than is the democratic ruler – out of fear, to be sure, but that fact does not render the applause less pleasant and rewarding.

Socrates has little difficulty identifying problems with the "might makes right" ethic. He asks Thrasymachus if the rulers can ever make mistakes about their advantage and their interests, and Thrasymachus has no choice but to agree that they can. Rulers are, after all, human and fallible. Thrasymachus had already claimed that the citizens of a society ought to obey the ruler or rulers (might makes *right*):

Socrates: Tell me, don't you also say that it is just to obey the rulers?

Thrasymachus: I do   (*Republic*, 339b).

But this claim, together with the admission that the rulers can make mistakes and formulate laws against their advantage or real interests, generates an inconsistency. What if the citizens determine that one of the laws of the state is, in fact, not to the advantage of the rulers? Should they obey it? If they do not do so, they violate the claim that obedience to the ruler is just; if they obey this law, then they do not act in the interest of the rulers, and hence they violate the claim that what is right is what is to the advantage of the stronger party. Insofar as the fundamental principle of Thrasymachus's theory generates this contradiction, the principle that might makes right must be rejected as false.

It is unclear whether or not Thrasymachus perceives the power of Socrates' argument, but for one reason or another he soon changes his tune. He begins to speak of the stronger party, not as the one who is just and right because of her power and might, but as the unjust person who happens to gain more out of life, precisely because of her *injustices*, than does the individual who always follows the precepts of justice. In the competition of life, he now claims, injustice pays better than justice. The unjust person, for example, will cheat on her taxes when she realizes there is little chance of being caught; the just person will never do this – consequently the unjust individual comes away from the tax season with more money in the bank. If elected to political office, the unjust person will have no scruples about taking bribes and will gain hugely therefrom; the just official will refuse to do so, but her very refusal will anger her constituents, who want a favor from her or a "piece of the action." Thrasymachus affirms that the greater the injustice, the greater the payoff: the more power, strength, and freedom it brings. But he is quick to say that even bag-snatching pays if you aren't caught at it.

If this second position of Thrasymachus is correct and the life of injustice is more rewarding than the life of justice, then Socrates, who affirmed exactly the opposite, is wrong. It is at this point in the *Republic* that Plato mounts his own distinctive defense of the Socratic position, a defense we shall consider in the next chapter.

Other Sophists, and non-Sophists as well, agreed with Thrasymachus (some with his "might makes right" formula and others with his "injustice pays" doctrine). Some of these Sophists developed ways of putting his points that soon became part of standard philosophical terminology in ancient Greek thought. The Sophist Antiphon proposed a distinction between *natural law* and *conventional law*. The latter consists of the laws established by human beings and governments; the former is the set of laws that govern our actions as a result of our human nature and our membership in the natural world. In Antiphon's opinion, it is better to follow the edicts of natural law than those of conventional law. Conventional laws attempt to suppress our natural instincts, and consequently they cause us to suffer frustration and disappointment

– and frequently pain. The fundamental natural law is the law of self-preservation, and conventional law is often opposed to self-preservation. Conventional law, for instance, requires that we not attack another individual until that person attacks us – but this entails giving the other person the advantage of the first strike, which often is fatal. Conventional law requires that we use the courts to settle our grievances, but success in the courts depends on our ability to give persuasive speeches (or to hire a good lawyer), which makes success uncertain. Better to take matters into our own hands outside the court of law. The individual who follows the law of nature, Antiphon concludes, is likely to live a better life than the one who follows man-made law.

An obstreperous thinker by the name of Callicles, although not himself a Sophist, takes the argument a step further. He too appeals to the law of nature and identifies this law as the real law of justice. According to nature, he maintains, one should give free rein to one's appetites and desires. Conventional conceptions of virtue constitute impediments to the natural life, a life in which happiness consists in the satisfaction of desire. Hence one should ignore these conventions and live a life of unbridled passion. Moreover, it is only natural that the strong control the weak, since this is precisely what natural law requires and ordains. Thus it is right for the strong to rule – this too is in accordance with nature. For Callicles and his friends, as Plato notes, "the height of justice is a conquest won by force" (*Laws*, 890a).[14] Conventional justice is simply the attempt of the weak to control the strong, and when this attempt fails, real justice is done and the natural order restored. Callicles believes, then, not only that defiance of conventional law will produce the happier, better life, but that such defiance is just and right because it is in accord with human nature and the law of the natural world. We have come full circle at this point, returning to the notion that might makes right.

A final step can be taken, one expressed as a conjecture (but not actually affirmed) by Glaucon and Adeimantus in the *Republic*. According to this theory, human beings following the law of nature often find themselves in conflict and frequently are threatened by others. Given the dangers and uncertainties of the "tooth and claw" form of existence entailed by the law of nature, they agree to establish a community under laws prohibiting the strong from preying on the weak. These laws define justice and other forms of proper social behavior. They are conventions, and their only justification is that they make life more tolerable for most people – in effect they constitute a compromise between the best and the worse conditions in which life can be lived. The laws thus have no intrinsic value; they are merely instruments to protect the average person from the voracious attacks of the strong. Hence if a citizen of society finds on occasion that she can break one of the conventional laws and get away with it, there is no good reason for her not to do so. Injustices and other acts that violate the conventions will be punished if their perpetrators are caught – but it is only the pain of punishment that is to be avoided, there being no stigma attached to being accused of injustice. The wise person will break the laws when she can do so with impunity. Only a fool will think that the laws should never be broken – such a fool will have failed to realize the conventional nature of the laws and the merely pragmatic justification of them. *Successful* injustice is better – more natural and rewarding – than justice as defined by the conventional rules of society.

Clearly there is a wide gulf between Socrates' ethics of virtue and the ethical theories of the Sophists, whether these theories stress relativism, power and might, or the value of injustice. The stage is set for a debate that will last many centuries. The Sophists throw out a bold challenge to anyone who would argue that such virtues as temperance and justice have supreme and objective value. They challenge us to prove that the moral life is the better one. They raise the urgent question whether or not it is possible to provide morality with a foundation that will allow it to resist, on grounds a rational person could accept, the onslaught of relativism and the claim that an unrestrained satisfaction of our appetites is the only legitimate goal in life. Plato, both coming to the defense of Socrates and passing beyond him, takes up this challenge.

2

Plato

Plato (428–348 BCE), descendent of an aristocratic Athenian family and student of Socrates, is one of the greatest philosophers in the history of Western civilization. Not only a major ethical thinker, he also made ground-breaking contributions in the areas of metaphysics (the theory of reality), epistemology (the theory of knowledge), and, closely related to his ethics, political philosophy. Alfred North Whitehead, the twentieth-century British-American philosopher, was paying tribute to the enormous influence Plato has had on subsequent thinking when he said that the rest of Western philosophy is but a series of footnotes to Plato. Plato's views had an incalculable impact during the ancient and medieval periods, and indirectly they have continued to exercise influence up to the present day. Even when these views are not fully embraced (and they seldom are today), they raise important questions and serve to identify recurrent general positions found in most philosophical debates – the *Platonist* points of view.

Our task in this chapter is to understand what Plato had to say about ethics or moral philosophy. We cannot do this in complete independence of his views on other subjects, particularly political philosophy, metaphysics, and epistemology, but an attempt will be made to keep references to these other views to a minimum. Our approach to Plato's ethics will be through the medium of his masterpiece, the *Republic*, a book that is required reading for any educated person (no less so today than in times past). Much of the political philosophy found in the *Republic* is unpalatable to most members of democratic societies. At the same time, they can recognize that the contents of this long dialogue are of the utmost importance, defining as they do a political and philosophical position that is perennial, immensely challenging, and, simply because we may disagree with it so fervently, demanding of a thoughtful and rigorous response. Moreover, although Plato's political philosophy and ethics are closely interwoven, we may find elements of his ethics that remain attractive today and are capable of being elaborated in independence of the political structure in which he placed them.

Plato needs to be seen as a "revisionist" in ethics. Although he articulates an ethical theory that preserves some of the notions about morality prevalent in his day, he rejects many of them, and he gives philosophically innovative interpretations of those he accepts. He agrees with most fourth-century Greeks in granting the importance of justice in the moral life – it is the central topic of the *Republic* – but he develops a highly novel theory of the *nature* of justice, a new way of understanding it which requires radical changes in our personal and political lives. Happiness is also central for both Plato and his fellow Greeks, but if we raise the question of what happiness *is*, Plato's answer is original and highly challenging. In general Plato wants to reorient our thinking about moral issues. He calls into question many common-sense answers to moral questions and seeks to convince us that philosophical reflection on these issues will lead to deeper insights and intellectually more responsible views about them.

The Allegory of the Cave

The conviction that philosophical reflection is needed in order to see through the frequent illusions of common sense is forcefully dramatized in the most famous part of the *Republic*, the Allegory of the Cave (*Republic*, 514aff).[1] Plato presents his thought here in the form of an allegory in order to characterize in a vivid and accessible way what he takes to be the moral, epistemological, and metaphysical plight of humanity. In everyday life, he asks us to believe, we are like prisoners who have been chained all their lives in a cave and forced to look constantly forward at the wall in front of them. On this wall are shadows cast by various statues of people and animals which are raised above a screen behind the prisoners, the source of light being a fire behind the screen. Never having seen anything else, or the mechanism whereby the shadows are cast, the prisoners believe the shadows are real people and animals. They identify and recognize recurring shadows and talk about them as if they were real. What would happen, Plato asks, if some of the prisoners were forced to turn around and confront the fire and the statues (a move, he suggests, they would resist, being accustomed as they are to their own limited world)? After momentarily being blinded by the fire, on regaining their vision they would at first take the statues displayed above the screen to be unreal. Only later would they see that these objects have more reality than their shadows on the wall. If the prisoners were then to emerge from the cave ("if someone dragged [them] away from there by force, up the rough, steep path"), they would once again be blinded, this time by the sun, and they would initially believe the objects – the people and animals – they encounter in the outside world were less than real. Finally, however, they would come to understand that these objects are in fact real and that the statues and the shadows of the statues were mere copies or reflections of things having greater reality. Thus they would learn that there are degrees of reality, degrees of knowledge or understanding, and degrees of truth. In the end they would have to be coerced into returning to the cave so as to enlighten the prisoners who remained in chains. The enlightened ones, the bearers of truth, would not, however, be graciously welcomed by the remaining prisoners, who would think them charlatans and denounce them for lying and inventing idle stories. The prisoners would be convinced only if they too were released and forced to undertake the ascent from the cave to the real world.

The Allegory of the Cave is richly symbolic and conveys a number of Platonic messages. For our purposes we shall take it as a means of conveying Plato's belief that everyday thought about morality is merely a set of vague images about so many shadows on a wall. Only if we free ourselves from this limited vision shall we be able to understand what justice really is. The real nature of justice will reveal itself only when we see it in the light of philosophical reason. The Allegory of the Cave also warns us that our enlightened views will be rejected by the many individuals who remain in darkness, and that they will want to vilify and punish us, just as the citizens of Athens denounced and executed Socrates.

Defining the Moral Life

Plato's *Republic* is an extended essay on justice and on the various metaphysical and epistemological dimensions of it. The dialogue is narrated by Socrates, who recalls and recounts an extended discussion that had earlier taken place in the house of Cephalus, an elderly and wealthy businessman. As usual, Socrates leads this discussion, whose participants also include his friends Glaucon and Adeimantus, as well as Thrasymachus, the belligerent moral skeptic we encountered in the last chapter. Cephalus himself appears early on to express his delight in seeing Socrates once again. He stays on for a while in order to answer Socrates' questions about old age and wealth. Old age, he says, is not such a bad thing: it frees one from the demons of sex and other bodily demands and allows one to enjoy the more refined pleasures of conversation.

> I was once present when someone asked the poet Sophocles:
> "How are you as far as sex goes, Sophocles? Can you still make love with a woman?"
> "Quiet, man," the poet replied, "I am very glad to have escaped from all that, like a slave who has escaped from a savage and tyrannical master" (*Republic*, 329b–c).

Old age, Cephalus points out, brings a great sense of calm and freedom. As for wealth, its greatest advantage is that it enables one to avoid those circumstances in which it becomes necessary to deceive and defraud others; it also permits one to pay one's debts and perform the offerings due to the gods. In these ways, wealth serves justice and brings peace of mind to the one who possesses it.

Cephalus's comments give Socrates his opening:

> A fine sentiment, Cephalus, but speaking of this very thing itself, namely
> justice, are we to say unconditionally that it is speaking the truth and
> paying whatever debts one has incurred? Or is doing these things
> sometimes just, sometimes unjust? (*Republic*, 331b–c)

In his ode to the peace of mind brought on by old age and wealth, Cephalus has
expressed the conventional understanding of the moral life: it is a matter of not doing
such things as deceiving and defrauding others, a matter of following simple rules
like "Tell the truth" and "Pay one's debts." Socrates wishes to look deeper. He points
out that paying one's debts or telling the truth is not *always* the just thing to do:

> I mean this sort of thing, for example: Everyone would surely agree that
> if a sane man lends weapons to a friend and then asks for them back when
> he is out of his mind, the friend shouldn't return them, and wouldn't be
> acting justly if he did. Nor should anyone be willing to tell the whole truth
> to someone who is out of his mind.
>   That's true.
>   Then the definition of justice isn't speaking the truth and repaying
> what one has borrowed (*Republic*, 331c–d).

Socrates then asks Polemarchus, Cephalus's son, for a better definition of justice. In
the discussion that follows, he leads Polemarchus to see that another traditional
conception of justice – doing good to one's friends and evil to one's enemies – is also
to be rejected. "Is it, then, the role of a just man to harm anyone?" Socrates asks
(*Republic*, 335b). As we saw in the last chapter, he goes on to argue that harming
anything – dog, horse, or human being – renders that thing worse off, less excellent,
by diminishing the virtue (*aretē*) which makes it a good or excellent thing of its kind.
Here Socrates is appealing to the Greek equation of virtue and excellence. To harm
a human being is to make that person "worse in human virtue." The specifically
human virtue, Socrates and his interlocutor agree, is justice – hence to harm a person
is to make that individual worse off with respect to justice, i.e., to make her *unjust*.
Now it becomes evident why harming one's enemies is something a just person cannot
do:

> Well, then, can those who are just make people unjust through justice?
> In a word, can those who are good make people bad through virtue?
>   They cannot.
>   It isn't the function of heat to cool things but of its opposite?
>   Yes.
>   Nor the function of dryness to make things wet but of its opposite?
>   Indeed.

Nor the function of goodness to harm but of its opposite?
Apparently.
And a just person is good?
Indeed.
Then, Polemarchus, it isn't the function of a just person to harm a friend or anyone else, rather it is the function of his opposite, an unjust person?
In my view that's completely true, Socrates.
If anyone tells us, then, that it is just to give to each what he's owed and understands by this that a just man should harm his enemies and benefit his friends, he isn't wise to say it, since what he says isn't true, for it has become clear to us that it is never just to harm anyone?
I agree   (*Republic*, 335c–d).

How, Plato (through Socrates) is asking, can a person be just who, in injuring her enemies, makes them unjust? How can such injustice be the result of justice? Thus the claim that justice is helping one's friends and harming one's enemies must be rejected.

As the action of the *Republic* proceeds, Socrates encounters the brash Thrasymachus. Thrasymachus has an altogether different conception of justice and morality from the one endorsed by either Cephalus or Socrates. "I say that justice is nothing other than the advantage of the stronger" (*Republic*, 338c). After some sharp responses from Socrates (see Chapter I, pp. 30–1), Thrasymachus expresses himself as follows:

> ... justice is really the good of another, the advantage of the stronger and the ruler, and harmful to the one who obeys and serves. Injustice is the opposite, it rules the truly simple and just, . . . and they make the one they serve happy, but themselves not at all. You must look at it as follows, my most simple Socrates: a just man always gets less than an unjust one   (*Republic*, 343c–d).

Thrasymachus's considered opinion, then, is that being moral is merely the unenlightened, misguided practice of doing what is good *for others*, for the strong, not for oneself. Being honest, keeping one's promises – all such moral actions benefit *someone else*. In Thrasymachus's eyes, such actions are foolish. The moral person fails to see that in the real world the unjust person comes out on top – the just individual is always a loser in comparison with the unjust. This moral person does not understand that the distinctions drawn between justice and injustice, and good and evil, are no more than conventional means by which the strong induce the weak to act in ways that benefit the strong themselves. Realistically, happiness is best achieved by behaving immorally on those occasions when one can get away with it. Far from Socrates' pious message (that the happy person is the virtuous one) being true, happiness, Thrasymachus affirms, is best attained by vice. And the bigger the vice, the better the chances of success and the greater the rewards – the perfectly vicious person *will not be caught*.

The *Republic* is in part an attack on the immoralism of Thrasymachus[2] and his claims to be realistic about human nature and human behavior – his claims, that is, to give a more honest and accurate account of them than Socrates. Plato's masterpiece is a passionate attempt to show that justice – true justice, that is – really does pay, that the life of the just person is better and happier than the life of the unjust person, and, indeed, that the life of the unjust person is in reality a miserable one. Socrates had attempted to demonstrate these very things, but, as we shall see, Plato's approach is different.

The *Republic* is also an attack on conventionalism, the view that moral distinctions are created by human beings and do not reflect any real distinctions in nature. At most, adherents to this view maintain, obedience to conventional moral rules works to one's advantage by earning one protection and public admiration and acclaim. There is no deeper justification for these rules. In Book II of the *Republic*, Plato has two of the participants in the discussion, Glaucon and Adeimantus, state as forcefully as possible the conventionalist case against Socrates and the moral life. Glaucon and Adeimantus are in fact friends of Socrates and are inclined to think him correct about morality, but so far they have not been convinced by what he has to say. Hence they pose objections in order to prompt him to come up with more convincing counter-arguments.

Gyges' Ring: A Skeptical View of Morality

One of their arguments consists of a recounting of the famous story of Gyges' Ring. As related by Glaucon, Gyges is a simple, modest, law-abiding shepherd who tends to his flock, gets along reasonably well with his fellow shepherds, and generally stays out of trouble. One day, while looking for a stray sheep, he stumbles across a skeleton which has a ring placed on one of its fingers. Thinking no harm will be done, he takes the ring and places it on his own finger. Later, while in the midst of other shepherds, Gyges notices that when he turns the setting of the ring inside his hand, his companions pay no more attention to him and in fact appear to think he is no longer there. Subsequent experimentation proves that turning the ring in this fashion actually renders him invisible, and he quickly sees the advantages he can reap from the possession of this marvelous instrument. So, quickly, he leaves the company and simple life of the shepherds and, with the help of his ring, goes to the court ... slays the king ... seduces the queen ... takes over the throne ... and lives ever after with great wealth, fame, and power.

And the moral of the story for us listeners and readers is ... wouldn't *we* do the same things if *we* came to possess this ring, if we could get away with them as Gyges did? Would any person continue to obey the principles of morality if she could break them without being caught and punished? Would she not, on the contrary, follow in the path of Gyges? More importantly, would any person have any *reason* to behave morally if she could get away with behaving immorally? The cynical suggestion behind this story is that people are just only because they are afraid of being caught and punished if they disobey society's moral rules. The normative lesson of the story is that if behaving justly is only a means to staying out of trouble, it has no intrinsic value, no value in itself – just behavior can reasonably be put aside if no longer needed. Justice, the suggestion goes, rather than being something desirable in itself – as Socrates had argued – is in fact something quite burdensome. We tolerate it only because it is the lesser of two evils – it frequently prevents others from harming *us*. Why should the just person continue to be just if she came to have the powers signified by Gyges' ring? Why should she do so, when she would be able to enjoy with impunity all the powers and pleasures she could wish for?

This view of morality, of course, is consistent with Thrasymachus's conviction: the strong person, the one who can get away with it, will always opt for injustice and the benefits it brings, and reasonably so. The happy person is the individual who is not intimidated by "morality" and has the will and strength to go after what everyone really wants: wealth, power, "the queen," and "the kingdom." Thrasymachian immoralism and conventionalism both express deep skepticism about the demands of morality.

The story of Gyges' Ring is a dramatic presentation of the skeptical point of view regarding morality and shows that Plato fully understands the appeal of such skepticism and the philosophical positions that sustain it. Plato sets for himself the demanding task of demonstrating that, in spite of the attractions of moral cynicism, the truly moral life is better than the immoral life. He seeks to prove that the life of a just person – even if devoid of the rewards often attaching to just behavior (e.g., esteem and honor) – is a happier life than that of an unjust person. He also wants to show that the unjust life is an unhappy one – that Gyges would be miserable as he sits on his throne with all the world bowing before him. Plato attempts to *justify* the moral life by proving that it is superior to its alternatives, including both the calculating life of self-interest and the life of conformity to the social conventions of the day. To prove these things is a tall order, but Plato sets out to do so (all the while, however, admitting the difficulty of his task, as is shown by the fact that Socrates constantly expresses uncertainty, gropes for answers, and offers the listener and reader, as the best he can come up with, mere images and analogies).

Three Kinds of "Good"

Plato defines his task more precisely by having Glaucon distinguish three kinds of good: (1) those things that are good simply in themselves; (2) those that are good both in themselves and as a result of their consequences; and (3) those that are onerous but good as a result of their consequences. Most people, Glaucon notes, think of justice as falling into the third class: in itself it is burdensome, but we pursue it in order to obtain the moral approval of our fellow human beings and the advantages that follow from this approval. The story of Gyges' Ring plays on option (3), for it demonstrates conditions under which it would be reasonable to set aside justice as a good precisely because under these conditions justice would no longer be a necessary means to other advantages. Thus the story interprets justice as falling exclusively into the third, instrumental category of goods. Glaucon pays little attention to category (1), illustrating this kind of good only by such things as the ephemeral pleasures of the moment which bring no harm in their wake. What Glaucon wants to know is whether Socrates can show that justice is a good that falls into category (2), the superior category. Can he show that justice (the Greek word for which, *dikaiosunē*, is virtually synonymous with "the moral life") is both good in itself and good by virtue of its consequences? And can he show that it is superior to any other good that may be found in any of the three categories? The remainder of the *Republic* is a long and convoluted positive answer to Glaucon's questions, an attempt to show that justice, while it does have beneficial consequences, is additionally something that has value in and of itself such that its very presence in us makes us better and happier persons.

It is important to keep in mind that Plato's ethical theory is an attempt to ground the validity of justice in facts – objective scientific facts, we moderns might say – about the deep underlying structure of human nature and society. His view is the antithesis of the theories of relativism and conventionalism. For Plato, the standards of morality are not created or fabricated by human beings; they are not the result of human decisions, preferences, or customs. They reflect *nature*, not arbitrary convention. And they are universal, which is to say they apply to all humankind because all human beings have essentially the same nature (although the variations among people, as we shall see, are important in defining the specific ideal roles of individuals). In Plato's view, the false theories of relativism and conventionalism (and immoralism) fail by virtue of having inadequate pictures of human nature. Once we understand what human beings are really like, we shall see that the moral life is the most rewarding one – for everyone. In the last analysis, then, Plato claims that he himself has the more "realistic" picture of morality – more accurate than that of Thrasymachus or Protagoras, whose theories of human nature are one-sided and incomplete.

Ideals and Essences

But Plato the "realist" is also an idealist. He is perhaps the greatest thinker in Western history to emphasize the reality of *the ideal*, claiming thereby that reality is not simply what we find in the actual world but contains as well the ideals toward which we strive and the ideal standards against which we measure the actual. The effective imprint of these ideals is everywhere. First, they are the goals that prompt the purposive actions of individuals and states. Second, they are the standards of measurement we use to measure and assess the actual things and facts in our everyday world. Norms and ultimate values – for these are what standards and goals are – exercise, therefore, an enormous influence on the course of human history.

For Plato, the ideal in fact has *more* reality than the actual. The ideal is unchanging and eternal, whereas the actual facts are forever changing, coming into being and then ceasing to exist. The ideal of justice, for example, is always the same, but the institutions striving to be just (and always falling short) are temporal entities which last for a while and then disappear. Ideals are what Plato in his theories of knowledge and metaphysics calls *forms*. They exist in an unchanging realm apart from the *particulars*, the individual objects, persons, and institutions which are found in the actual, ephemeral, spatio-temporal world. The forms are known, not through sense experience – which has only actual, ever-changing particulars as its objects – but through reason, pure intelligence of the sort exemplified in mathematical thought. It is reason that grasps the ideal objects in their unchanging reality: the ideal triangle, the ideal person, the ideal horse, the ideal state, etc. Forms are the *essences* of things, their essential natures in their full and perfect reality. The persons, states, and so on in the actual world reflect but do not fully embody their essences. There is no perfect triangle to be found in actual space, and there is no perfect person or state in history. Hence the reality of actual triangles, persons, states and all the other things we find in the world of the senses is incomplete and inferior to the reality of their essences. These essences thus become our ideals. As we pursue our efforts first to know and then to realize the ideals of human nature and the self, we seek to make ourselves more real, to become truly human, truly virtuous, truly just.

In one of his culminating visions, Plato maintains that goodness itself, the *form of the good*, is the ultimate cause both of our knowledge of the world and of the very reality of the world (*Republic*, 507bff). As he expresses this vision in the Allegory of the Sun, the form of the good is analogous to the sun, whose light makes things visible and whose power and nourishment are essential to their very existence. We can attain knowledge of what we find in the world only when we come to understand it in relationship to goodness and thereby comprehend its moral dimension. And, in a fashion that Plato admits we cannot fully understand, this goodness is "beyond being" and is the source of reality and all that is found in it. These mystical theses are not defended at length by Plato (he contends, after all, that we cannot fully grasp them), but they round out his picture of the world in which a true realist must also be an idealist. Spatio-temporal facts alone are not enough; the reality of the ideal is as stubborn and insistent as any fact. And at the very heart of reality is that ultimate ideal, true goodness.

The State and the Individual

The theory of human nature in which Plato seeks to ground morality has two parts, a theory of the state or society, and a theory of the psychology of the individual person (soul). Interestingly, he thinks that we should begin with the social/political theory: the state (or city, as he calls it, having in mind the Greek *polis* or city-state) is the individual *writ large*, and understanding its origin and structure will assist us in understanding the nature of the more elusive individual soul. As Socrates puts it:

> We say, don't we, that there is the justice of a single man and also the justice of a whole city?
> Certainly.
> And a city is larger than a single man.
> It is larger.
> Perhaps, then, there is more justice in the larger thing, and it will be easier to learn what it is. So, if you're willing, let's first find out what sort of thing justice is in a city and afterwards look for it in the individual, observing the ways in which the smaller is similar to the larger.
> That seems fine to me   (*Republic*, 368e–369a).

In Plato's mind there is an analogy between the state and the individual, with respect both to their parts and to the organization of these parts. Once we grasp these aspects of the state, we can then turn our attention to the individual, whose nature will as a result of the previous political studies be more readily and accurately understood.

How, Plato asks, did the state or organized society come into being? It originated, he claims, as a means of satisfying human need. "I think a city comes to be because none of us is self-sufficient, but we all need many things. Do you think that a city is founded on any other principle?" (*Republic*, 369b) On their own, individual human beings, possessing their distinctive abilities but also their personal weaknesses and limitations, would find it hard to satisfy their various needs, in particular their needs for food, clothing, shelter, and protection from enemies. Everyone would be better off if a division of labor were agreed upon by all so that some members of the group would provide certain services and other members would work to meet other common needs. Moreover, everyone would be well served if the division of labor were to occur in accordance with the natural talents of the various individuals concerned. Some people by natural ability are suited to be farmers and carpenters, others are better suited to serve as soldiers. Good farmers, those with a natural ability to farm, could provide ample food for the community and in fact more than most individuals on their own could provide for themselves. Good soldiers, those with the measure of spirit, strength, and courage needed for the job, could provide better protection for the entire community than most individuals could provide for themselves. Hence a state organized according to natural ability and talent would be more successful in satisfying basic human needs than a group of unorganized individuals.

Plato acknowledges that few people would remain content with a sufficiency of food, shelter, and clothing. His acknowledgement is a grudging one, however – indicative of an ascetic streak in him:

> Yet the true city, in my opinion, is the one we've described, the healthy one, as it were. But let's study a city with a fever, if that's what you want. There's nothing to stop us. The things I mentioned earlier and the way of life I described won't satisfy some people, it seems ... (*Republic*, 372e–373a).

Luxuries will be demanded, and additional territory desired. These cravings will lead to further specialization of effort. Soldiers will be needed, not just to protect the community from outside interference, but also to keep the peace within the community and to engage in territorial expansion through war. And leaders will have to be selected to arbitrate quarrels among citizens over the new luxuries and to make decisions about when to go to war and to seek more land. Gradually, then, there will develop three classes of citizens, what Plato calls the guardians, the auxiliaries, and the members of the productive or economic class. The guardians will be the leaders and rulers, those who establish laws and direct the state in times of war. The auxiliaries will implement the laws within the state and fight the battles required both for protection and for external expansion. The members of the economic or productive class (sometimes called the workers) will provide – through agriculture, industry, and commerce – the food, clothing, shelter, and luxuries required by the populace.

Such is the way a state would develop, Plato claims. At least, such is the way a *rational* state would develop, one that would be successful in attaining its goals and providing for the happiness of the society as a whole, i.e., for the collective body of its citizens. The rational state would take advantage of the natural differences to be found among human beings, allotting (indeed requiring) responsibilities or social functions in accordance with these differences.

> This was meant to make clear that each of the other citizens is to be directed to what he is naturally suited for, so that, doing the one work that is his own, he will become not many but one, and the whole city will itself be naturally one not many (*Republic*, 423d).

If other states did not use the natural division of talents as the basis for social differentiation, they would quickly lose out in competition with the rational state. Thus nature itself provides the standards upon which a successful (i.e., happy) social organization can be constructed.

So far it is only in the broadest strokes that we have sketched Plato's picture of a rational or ideal state. More needs to be said about the nature of the inhabitants and about their relationships to one another. The division into classes has been made on the basis of natural talents and proclivities, but specific qualities of mind (or soul) are required of members of each class if the entire organization is to function well. Clearly the leaders, the guardians, need to possess as much *intelligence* as possible, but this natural intelligence must be nurtured and developed in ways that will ensure that as mature leaders they develop policies supportive of the interests of the community as a whole. Plato believed the members of the productive class and to some degree the auxiliaries will always pursue their individual, private interests and hence will fail to grasp and pursue the good of the entire state. Understanding the good of the state as a whole, then, is the important function of the guardians. To fulfill it, their native intelligence must be perfected so that they can know what this good is, and their emotional life must be so formed that they wish for and pursue it. Thus leaders need the virtue of *wisdom*, this virtue being a power that enables them to do well what they are best suited to do. Their wisdom will enable them as statespersons, lawmakers, and arbitrators to act in the interest of what is truly good for the state and hence for all the citizens of it.

The auxiliaries also need to have certain natural talents which are shaped and nurtured into virtuous dispositions. They must, of course, be strong, but they also must be high-spirited, filled with civic pride, and prepared to fight for the cause of the city-state as a whole. And they must not be frightened of risks, threats, or attacks. They must have an abundance of what Plato calls *spirit*. Plato warns, however, that untutored and untrained spirit can be harsh and mean, and can lead quickly to war and repression. Thus the auxiliaries must learn to control their spirit and express it at the appropriate moments and in appropriate ways. Their spirit must be so molded that they follow willingly the edicts of the rulers, develop attachments and loyalties defined by the rulers' superior wisdom, and stick to these commitments in the face of temptation and conflict. Developing these dispositions of character is developing the virtue of *courage*. This courage is the distinctive virtue of the warriors, their disposition to perform well in *their* special role.

The members of the productive or economic class have their distinctive abilities too: abilities to engage in farming, industry, commerce, and the like. Physical skills of various sorts are needed for most of these activities, but wide-ranging and deep-thinking rational intelligence is not a requirement; neither is the high-spiritedness of the auxiliaries. Just as the "workers" are primarily involved in productive activities aimed at satisfying physical needs, the personalities of these individuals tend as well to be of a "physical" or materialistic nature, that is to say, personalities dominated by *appetite*, the desire for food, drink, and sex. But Plato warns that while such appetites may indeed motivate the workers to produce the articles needed to satisfy them, these very appetites can also stand in the way of successful performance. The drunk, the glutton, the sexual profligate is seldom the best farmer, shop worker, or businessperson. The virtue needed by the members of the productive class is that of temperance or *moderation*: control over the appetites and sensual pleasures so that they motivate but do not interfere with successful production. Hence the workers must be educated to cultivate moderation in their souls.

Moderation: The Key

As it turns out, moderation is not a virtue needed only by the workers. The leaders themselves also require it. Individuals who are born with great intelligence can sometime escape into the realm of pure intellect, forgetting the world and using their intelligence only to seek theoretical knowledge or, at worst, play intellectual games. In such cases, intelligence is out of control. To perform well, reason too needs to be reined in and directed toward the most important objectives.[3] Furthermore, the auxiliaries require moderation. The very pride that leads to the defense of one's country can become overweening or excessive, as all Greeks who knew their Homer were aware. It can degenerate into *hubris*, the fault of overweening pride. In becoming excessive, pride in country can be turned against one's own fellow citizens, generating a regime of terror and repression. This is a phenomenon very familiar to us in this last decade of the twentieth century, during which many military dictatorships have terrorized their own people in the interest of national pride. So the warriors of the ideal state need to be moderate as well as courageous: their spirit must be directed at wise objectives and not unleashed to pursue its irrational urges. All three classes, then, require the virtue of moderation.

There is a wider sense of moderation or temperance that Plato has in mind and applies to both the productive class and the other two classes. The chief elements of moderation, he thinks, are obedience to commanders and self-control over sensual pleasures. Moderation (*sōphrosunē*) was considered by the Greeks to be deferential behavior as well as avoidance of excess and vulgarity. Deferential behavior assumes that there is a hierarchy of places or positions in society and that a person recognizes her appropriate place and also recognizes the authority of those in positions above hers. Moderation in this sense is a matter of knowing one's place, knowing what behavior is appropriate for this place, and knowing what forms of recognition are due to those occupying other places. The Platonic application of such a notion is not difficult to surmise. The workers or members of the productive class must show deference to the rulers, acquiescing in the limits they place on the workers' pursuit of their material desires. Thus the limits required by temperance or moderation are the limits dictated by the intelligence of the guardians. Likewise the auxiliaries must recognize that it is their job to support and implement the policy decisions of the guardians. And the guardians themselves must accept that it is their job to rule (the more intelligent members of society are often reluctant, Plato thinks, to assume roles of leadership). There must be, then, general agreement as to who is in charge and a willing acceptance of this authority.

Plato also draws a close connection between moderation and self-control:

Yet isn't the expression "self-control" ridiculous? The stronger self that does the controlling is the same as the weaker self that gets controlled, so that only one person is referred to in all such expressions.

Of course.

Nonetheless, the expression is apparently trying to indicate that, in the soul of that very person, there is a better part and a worse one and that, whenever the naturally better part is in control of the worse, this is expressed by saying that the person is self-controlled or master of himself. At any rate, one praises someone by calling him self-controlled. But when, on the other hand, the smaller and better part is overpowered by the larger, because of bad upbringing or bad company, this is called being self-defeated or licentious and is a reproach.

Appropriately so.

Take a look at our new city, and you'll find one of these in it. You'll say that it is rightly called self-controlled, if indeed something in which the better rules the worse is properly called moderate and self-controlled   (*Republic*, 430e–431b).

Both a state and an individual have control over themselves, and thereby guide their own destiny, only when they manifest the virtue of moderation – in the case of the state, when "the desires of the inferior many are controlled by the wisdom and desires of the superior few" (*Republic*, 431c–d); in the case of the individual, when the baser desires of the concupiscent self are controlled by reason.

What would happen in the state whose development we are following if the workers were temperate, the police and soldiers courageous and temperate, and the leaders wise and temperate? We would have a state in which each one "does her own," that is to say, a state in which each does what she is best capable of doing and does it well, thereby contributing "her own" to the overall well-being of the state. In this way, the needs of all the citizens would be well served – each would receive her "due," her "own" – and the populace as a whole would be content and happy. Here we have a rational, ideal state. It is a state grounded in the nature of the human beings composing it, an organization of men and women erected on rational principles resulting from the recognition of the facts of human nature and the requirements for satisfying the needs and demands of this nature. Such a state would embody the virtue of *justice*. In this state, each citizen would obtain her due by giving her due, this being a concept of justice deeply, even though vaguely, embedded in the Greek mind. Plato's rendition gives it specificity and detail. Justice becomes for him a matter of balance and harmony among the citizens and the activities of these citizens. When everyone does her own, and does it well, we have balance and harmony; we have a state in which everyone then receives her own, her proper share; we have a just state. Justice is the virtue of the state as a whole, and it is realized when each of the parts of the state is manifesting the virtue appropriate to its specialized role.

But will things just naturally occur in this way? As an organized state emerges in response to the needs of human beings, will it necessarily take on the structure described above? Will its citizens naturally assume the virtues appropriate to them?

We surely know, as well as Plato knew, that the answers to these questions are negative. Plato spends considerable time in the *Republic* describing states that fall short of the ideal – some, like tyranny, considerably short of it. We cannot, then, just expect the ideal state to evolve on its own; we must take steps to bring it into being.

Education for an Ideal State

The secret to success in this endeavor, Plato firmly believes, is *education*. There must be an extensive and intensive education of the guardians and the auxiliaries. Plato is less than sanguine – indeed quite pessimistic – about the chances of educating the members of the productive class and bringing them to an appreciation of their role. Accordingly, for them he has some alternative methods in mind, which we shall examine shortly. Many pages of the *Republic*, however, are spent detailing the educational measures to be used in the case of the other two classes, and especially the class of the leaders.

The members of the guardian and auxiliary classes are selected on the basis of their natural talents and their ability to respond to education. They include talented women no less than men. They are separated off from the masses and appropriately educated from youth onward. Plato proposes a program to ensure the availability of the desired modes of intelligence and spirit – a program that some might denigrate as "genetic engineering." He also rejects what we would call a normal family life for the young guardians. They are not permitted to live with their parents, since doing so would lead them to form restrictive and unwise attachments to the members of their family. In fact, the family is to be abolished altogether so that the youthful guardians can emotionally attach themselves to the state as a whole and only to it.

Much of the early training of the guardians involves gymnastics and music and the fine arts, the former to train the body, the latter the soul. Plato is convinced that music and the other fine arts exert a powerful influence on people, one that, to his mind, is often deleterious. But if the future guardians are subjected to a proper aesthetic education they will learn to love the beautiful and loathe the ugly. Insofar as Plato also believes in a close connection between the good and the beautiful ("And gracelessness, bad rhythm, and disharmony are akin to bad words and bad character, while their opposites are akin to and are imitations of the opposite, a moderate and good character" (*Republic*, 401a)), he thinks this aesthetic education will in effect condition their minds to be attracted to the good and repelled by the bad. The city must take great care not to allow artists to create images of characters who are "vicious, unrestrained, slavish, and graceless." On the contrary, it must "seek out craftsmen who are by nature able to pursue what is fine and graceful in their work, so that our young people will live in a healthy place and be benefitted on all sides, and so that something of those fine works will strike their eyes and ears like a breeze that brings health from a good place, leading them unwittingly, from childhood on, to resemblance, friendship, and harmony with the beauty of reason"(*Republic*, 401c–d). This goal of inculcating an attraction to the good and repulsion from the bad will also be accomplished by the instruction in gymnastics and physical education, where the graceful motion and gesture – indeed the graceful body and beautiful comportment – are stressed. Training in these physical activities simultaneously involves inculcation of the virtues of moderation and courage: learning to control one's appetites is a part of good training; so is learning how to control one's emotions in order to keep one's concentration and a cool head; and learning when to take risks and when on the contrary it would be foolish to do so is an essential part of training.

From this early form of education the individuals selected for leadership roles as guardians pass on to instruction in more intellectual subjects. Mathematics, which represents for Plato one of the most advanced forms of intellectual activity, is at the center of the guardians' later education. Instruction at this level is designed to produce statespersons, individuals who can *reason* and thereby understand human nature and human society, and, perhaps more importantly, will be able to exercise rational control over their appetites and emotions. By the time they are ready for leadership, these gifted men and women will have become philosophers, and they can enter the world of "real life" as philosopher-kings. Thus would Plato adhere to his admonishment that "cities will have no rest from evils" (473d) until philosophers are kings and kings philosophers.

In the education of all the citizens, one of the main objectives is to instill in them an appreciation of the reasonableness of a society in which each class performs its special task: in which the guardians rule over all others, the auxiliaries provide protection for all, and the workers produce the goods needed by all. Successfully educated citizens will perceive this arrangement to be desirable, and they will willingly assume their proper roles. They will see the goodness and benefit of living in a just society in which each receives, as well as gives, his due. And, if all goes well and each in fact does his due, happiness and contentment is what each will receive.

Plato's Challenge to Democracy

Many contemporary readers react negatively to Plato's notion of an ideal state, largely because they perceive it to be rigidly authoritarian. To be sure, the leaders have great power. They develop the laws, they train the auxiliaries so that the latter will effectively enforce the laws, they direct all aspects of life in the state, and they are even authorized to lie to the people if the issue involved is important enough. Furthermore, Plato is explicit enough about his negative attitude toward democracy: it is for him an inferior form of government which seldom matches ability to task, especially when it comes to leadership, and which effectively reduces government to

Plato

mob rule. From the perspective of people accustomed to thinking of democracy as the best form of government ever devised, even if the best of the bad, the undeniable elitism and autocracy of Plato's ideal state are unacceptable.

Of course, Plato's views about these matters stand as a challenge to believers in democracy. Can they defend it against his indictment? To be fair to Plato, we must remember that he is attempting to construct the blueprint for a state which will ensure maximum happiness for the collective totality of its citizens. The demands placed on them are to be for their own good as this good is identified in light of what he proposes as an adequate theory of human nature and society. The rulers above all are to follow *reason* and not their own self-interest in developing the laws of the state. They are to promote the interest of the *whole*. In fact, Plato is careful to impose severe restrictions on the guardians to ensure that they will not use their positions of power to their own advantage and to the detriment of the other citizens. They are not permitted, for example, to own private property or to accumulate wealth. The guardians are to rule in the light of reason, for it is this activity, well performed, that will fulfill *them* and bring *them* the greatest happiness.

The Virtuous Soul: Appetites, Emotions, and Reason

Much more could be said about the ideal state in which philosophers are kings and kings philosophers – Plato's political philosophy is detailed and comprehensive. But our task is to use his picture of the state as an analog of the soul from which we are able to derive the natural features and virtues of the individual person. Ethics and political philosophy are not differentiated in Plato's mind – as a result of his insistence that human beings are essentially social and that there is no meaningful distinction between the private and the public spheres of life – and Plato uses his political analysis as a basis for determining the virtues of individual persons. His thesis is that the individual soul has a complexity that matches in composition and structure the complexity of the state. Furthermore, he believes that the virtues assigned to the different classes in the ideal state also apply to the different dimensions or "parts" of the individual soul. And, finally, he concludes that justice in the soul is analogous to justice in the state. Just as social justice is reached when all of the classes are doing well what they are best suited to do, with a resultant overall harmony and balance throughout the society, so too the individual soul attains the virtue of justice when all of its parts are performing their roles in an excellent fashion, with a resultant harmony and balance in the soul as a whole.

> Therefore, it necessarily follows that the individual is wise in the same way and in the same part of himself as the city.
> That's right.

And isn't the individual courageous in the same way and in the same part of himself as the city? And isn't everything else that has to do with virtue the same in both?

Necessarily.

Moreover, Glaucon, I suppose we'll say that a man is just in the same way as a city.

That too is entirely necessary.

And we surely haven't forgotten that the city was just because each of the three classes in it was doing its own work.

I don't think we could forget that.

Then we must also remember that each one of us in whom each part is doing its own work will himself be just and do his own.

Of course, we must.

Therefore, isn't it appropriate for the rational part to rule, since it is really wise and exercises foresight on behalf of the whole soul, and for the spirited part to obey it and be its ally?

It certainly is ...

And these two [the spirited and rational parts], having been nurtured this way, and having truly learned their own roles and been educated in them, will govern the appetitive part, which is the largest part in each person's soul and is by nature most insatiable for money. They'll watch over it to see that it isn't filled with the so-called pleasures of the body and that it doesn't become so big and strong that it no longer does its own work but attempts to enslave and rule over the classes it isn't fit to rule, thereby overturning everyone's whole life.

That's right   (*Republic*, 441c–442b).

And, to remind ourselves of Plato's ultimate objective, justice in the individual soul promotes the greatest possible individual happiness, just as justice in the state is tantamount to happiness for the state as a whole.

One of Plato's fundamental insights is that the human personality is a complex affair and that each of its various dimensions has its own needs and desires. Failure of the self to fulfill the needs and ends of any one or more of its parts will invariably lead to discontent and a lack of fulfillment of the total person. In Plato's view, the problem with the ethical theories of his opponents – those who advocate the self-interested pursuit of pleasure, or fame, or power – is that they fail to recognize human complexity and the diversity of needs and desires entailed by it. A hedonistic ethics – one which singles out physical pleasure as the only good – has an oversimplified view of human nature which is but a caricature of the human personality. To be sure, we desire pleasure – Plato never denies it – but we also desire, each of us in varying degrees, knowledge, personal accomplishment, honor, and the esteem of our fellows. Unless we acknowledge all of these desires and construct a recipe for life which allows for the fulfillment of them all, we shall not have proposed an ethical program that will issue in overall human happiness.

Clearly one of the main components of any person's personality is a set of physical *appetites*: bodily desires, cravings, urges, and drives. These are directed at physical things like food and drink, and sex and other bodily pleasures. As all of us know, these appetites can be overpowering. They need to be satisfied, but if no limit is placed on their satisfaction they can easily become the center of one's life, pushing everything else to the sidelines. Moreover, unchecked physical desires, e.g., erotic ones, lead to a state of affairs in which the level of pleasure required to satisfy these desires constantly increases, thereby producing inevitable frustration.[4] Appetites constitute what might figuratively be called the beast within us.

Of almost equal strength in most of us, perhaps even stronger in some, are our emotions: feelings of love, hatred, pride, shame, fear, bravado, jealousy, and, especially important for Plato, the love of honor and victory. These emotions are manifestations of what he appropriately calls *spirit*. We are all familiar with the high-spirited person from whom manifestations of strong emotion are frequent. We exhibit spirited pride when we cheer on our favorite sports team or display strong patriotism toward our country. More generally, spirit is that assertive element in us which pushes us towards the attainment of our goals. As appetites require satisfaction, emotions demand expression. Directly or vicariously, we seek occasions that will elicit from us sentiments of pride and joy, but also, on the darker side, anger and contempt. A rich life of the spirit can be immensely rewarding, whereas an impoverished one can be the cause of great dissatisfaction and emptiness.

Our spirited emotions, then, demand our attention. We have a deep desire for the rich emotional life and a fear of its diminishment. But our emotions also, as once again we all know, can get the better of us. A sports fan can become a fanatic who gives up most other aspects of life in order to be fully involved in the sport. A jealous husband can take drastic actions which bring great harm both to himself and others. A patriot is perhaps only a step away from being a villain. The military general can become so obsessed with victory that he commits numerous human rights violations. Just as appetites must be curbed, emotions must be controlled. It is easy to "lose control," and, as a result, commit actions and crimes for which we feel regret and remorse. Sometimes we can be in the grip of our spirited emotions to such a degree that we feel no pangs of conscience at the actions to which they drive us, at which point we enter into the pathological state of the psychopath or sociopath. Mental illness of various kinds can be attributed to emotional disturbances or an unbalanced emotional life.

Finally, in all of us there is what Plato calls *reason*. We are thinking beings, even if it often appears that many of us participate in this activity only on occasion and then at a fairly rudimentary level. But in reality, day-to-day life requires numerous mental skills and activities. The farmer has a degree of "know-how" just as does the nuclear physicist. Some intelligence is highly practical in nature, but even this demands a knowledge of a range of facts and an ability to perform mental operations in achieving a practical goal. Beyond that, open-minded observation of people will reveal that most of them have some curiosity about the world, about other people, and even about themselves. All of us, or almost all, want to understand what is happening around us; some, perhaps more than we are first inclined to believe, want to understand "the big picture," the veritable meaning of life. Reason thus exists in all of us, and reason too has its desires – to figure out a problem, to know the facts, to understand what is happening. Failure to satisfy these desires is to ensure their frustration and, accordingly, to lessen the quality of life. Many are the elderly who plead that they not lose control of their minds before the moment of death. We must acknowledge the presence and the importance of this intellectual dimension of our personalities.

All of us, then, have within us appetites, spirit, and reason. But each of us has a slightly different mixture of the three. There are people in whom appetites predominate, others in whom spirit is paramount, and some whose lives primarily revolve around intellectual activities. This differentiation is precisely the basis for Plato's identification of three political classes and for his assignment of a person to one of the three. Some people, indeed many, lead a life that primarily revolves around the satisfaction of appetite. For them, a life spent in pursuit of physical goods or the money needed to buy them is the most satisfying life. Others live for accomplishment and fame, or for a life of adventure that involves taking on the odds – spirit is at the center of their lives. And then there are the intellectuals, those creatures in whom reason predominates and who prefer to dedicate themselves to the life of the mind. As we have seen, making use of these differences among human beings is for Plato the best way to achieve a society whose various needs are met.

Plato believes not only that a person is born of a certain nature that fits her to play a specific role in society but also that this person is incapable of change and hence incapable of social mobility. He conveys this message in terms of what is often referred to as his Myth of the Metals – a "noble falsehood" he is prepared to convey to the members of society:

> "All of you in the city are brothers," we'll say to them in telling our story, "but the god who made you mixed some gold into those who are adequately equipped to rule, because they are most valuable. He put silver in those who are auxiliaries and iron and bronze in the farmers and other craftsmen. For the most part you will produce children like yourselves, but, because you are all related, a silver child will occasionally be born from a golden parent, and vice versa, and all the others from each other" (*Republic*, 415a).

Plato's last proviso in this tale leads him to allow that generational mobility is possible, and he warns the guardians to be on the lookout for children whose metal is not that of their parents. Mobility, of course, can be either upward or downward.

Justice in the Soul

But what about the individual herself? How should she organize her life? What do the demands and the dangers imposed by the three dimensions of her personality require if *her* needs are to be best met? Once again we need to speak in terms of virtues, in this case of those dispositions of character which enable one to realize in the fullest fashion the nature of one's own distinctive being.

In identifying these virtues, the analogy between state and individual comes to our assistance. Just as the guardians require the virtue of wisdom, so the rational part of the soul of the individual functions excellently when it manifests wisdom. Just as the auxiliaries of the ideal state must display the virtue of courage, so too the spirited, emotional dimension of the personality must manifest courage. And just as moderation is the primary virtue of the productive class, moderation is the virtue that ideally guides the activities of the appetitive soul. Moreover, moderation is a virtue suited to all three parts of the soul or personality, all three needing to avoid excess in the use of their powers and to acknowledge the place of reason and its right to direct the functioning of the other two parts. "And this unanimity, this agreement between the naturally worse and the naturally better as to which of the two is to rule both in the city and in each one, is rightly called moderation" (*Republic*, 432a). And finally, just as social justice is the hallmark of the ideal state as a whole, the virtue that is manifested when each class of citizens is doing what it is best suited to do, so too justice in the soul is the virtue of the fully realized individual person. The person whose soul manifests justice is one in which the various components of her soul are not in conflict: each component is performing its function well and thereby satisfying one set of the person's needs; no component is encroaching on the proper authority of the others and thereby overreaching its own authority; and each component recognizes and respects the proper activity of the others. Such an individual soul is, according to Plato, the *healthy* soul. "Virtue seems, then, to be a kind of health, fine condition, and well-being of the soul, while vice is disease, shameful condition, and weakness" (*Republic*, 444d–e). A healthy soul is one whose needs are met; it is not at war with itself; it achieves a state of balance. A healthy soul is a happy soul, its happiness consisting in the satisfaction of its various needs by means of the exercise of virtue in the three areas of need.

Plato set out in the *Republic* to show that the life of a virtuous person is a happy life and that it is good in itself as well as for its consequences. In identifying the happy person with one whose soul is healthy, Plato has made a strong case for his claim. Health, surely, is something we enjoy simply as health, simply for its own sake. None of us, if we are rational, would opt for a life of sickness and disease over a life of robust health. The healthy life bears its goodness or value up-front, "on its sleeve" – its value is unquestionable. But it is also instrumentally valuable; it is a necessary means to the attainment of most of the other specific values we pursue: the objects of our appetites, the causes to which our spirit rallies, the intellectual pursuits of our reason. So health falls into the second category identified by Glaucon: it is both good in itself and good as a result of its consequences. The just soul, being the healthy soul, therefore is good in itself and for its consequences.

Plato also set out to show that the life of an unjust person is in fact inferior in quality to that of a just person. He even made the bold claim that the unjust person is miserable, simply because he is unjust. Has Plato substantiated these radical claims? It appears that he has. If justice is harmony, balance, and health, then anything falling short of the just life will incorporate elements of disharmony, imbalance, and sickness.

> Surely [injustice] must be a kind of civil war between the three parts, a meddling and doing of one another's work, a rebellion by some part against the whole soul in order to rule it inappropriately. The rebellious part is by nature suited to be a slave, while the other part is not a slave but belongs to the ruling class. We'll say something like that, I suppose, and that the turmoil and straying of these parts are injustice, licentiousness, cowardice, ignorance, and, in a word, the whole of vice (*Republic*, 444b).

Such an unjust soul will be in conflict with itself, and consequently it will fail to satisfy the needs of one or more of its parts. Such a soul is unsatisfied, and, in cases of great conflict, in a state of anxiety and torment. Compared to the satisfied, healthy, just soul, the unjust soul is clearly the less happy, the more miserable of the two. A wise person, therefore, will always prefer the life of justice to the life of injustice.

At this point, we need to relate the ethical conclusion we have just reached to the political conclusion at which we arrived earlier. Each individual, we have said, needs to pursue the virtues appropriate to the three parts of her soul as well as the overall virtue of justice. But in the political setting, the lives of the auxiliaries and the workers are to be directed by, indeed controlled by, the policies and laws of the guardians. To a large extent the guardians will think for the soldiers and workers. In what way, then, are the soldiers and workers to exercise their own reason and thereby embody wisdom in their own individual lives? Is there not an inconsistency here between the ethical and the political thinking?

Not necessarily. The intelligence of the auxiliaries and workers will be aimed at the ends they pursue. They need to use intelligence in protecting the community and in producing the material goods required by the society. Hence there is ample room for wise soldiers and wise farmers and merchants. Nevertheless, the intelligence of the members of the auxiliary and working classes is less pronounced, and finally less rational, than that of the members of the guardian class. The latter display not only practical, instrumental, and strategic intelligence, they are also able to know the true nature of reality and to understand the laws that explain this reality by means of grasping the real objects of knowledge, the forms. They are able to know the ideal, essential nature of the human being and society and hence are able to ascertain what kind of soul and what kind of society are required if happiness is to be achieved. And they alone have this intellectual, philosophical grasp of the ultimate nature of happiness and the means to it. Putting this knowledge into practice, they must in many instances dictate to the auxiliaries and producers what form and course their social and individual lives will take. The guardians are playing *their* proper role, doing their own, precisely in making this contribution to the state. Hence, we can conclude, the operation of reason in the guardian class, while not eliminating the operation of reason – and the pursuit of wisdom – in the other classes, has a supervisory role with respect to the intelligence of the auxiliaries and producers. Within the limits set by this supervision, the latter are able to pursue wisdom in their respective and limited spheres.

Moreover, if the members of society – the members of all classes – have been given a proper education, they will have been trained to see the wisdom of the arrangement being proposed. Surely most citizens have the intelligence needed to understand that specialization of role and work is necessary in order for everyone to attain a satisfactory life. Most of them have the intelligence to observe that there are differences in level of intelligence among people and to conclude from this that it is in their *own* interests to have the guardians rule. The proper type of education would lead not only to the perception of these truths but also to their willing acceptance. This education would shape the emotional attitudes of people, developing in them an appreciation of balance and harmony, and thereby creating a positive emotional response to the order, balance and harmony of the ideal state. It must be remembered that in this state, the guardians and auxiliaries are not permitted to own private property or to accumulate wealth. Their job is to work to the advantage of all citizens, not to their personal or private advantage. This aspect of the arrangement of things in the ideal state will appeal to the emotional attitudes of the auxiliaries and workers and enable them to accept the rule of the guardians and to work for wisdom in their own proper spheres.

Where Plato and Socrates Differ

The points just made serve to illustrate a major difference between the thought of Plato and that of his teacher Socrates. It will be recalled that Socrates believed that virtue is knowledge, from which it follows that to know what is good will lead to the pursuit of that good. Moreover, there is no evidence that Socrates believed some citizens to be more capable of grasping truth, and hence goodness, than others. Hence for him knowledge alone (combined with the overriding desire for the good) will enable all citizens to be just and good – to avoid injustice and vice. We referred to Socrates' *intellectualism* in characterizing these views. It is clear that Plato is not an intellectualist of this sort. First of all, he does not believe that all citizens have the intelligence required to understand what is just and good; the intelligence of most is limited to more practical ambitions. They must be told by the guardians what to do in order to participate in the creation of a just state and a good life for all. Second, Plato insists on the importance of educating the emotions – the spirited element – of all citizens. Just as spirited auxiliaries are required in order to implement the dictates of the guardians, so the right emotional state of mind is required in order to put into practice the dictates of reason. Unless, as it were, one can appreciate the *beauty* of truth, one may not follow it where it leads. Through their education, the guardians themselves will have acquired a set of sensitivities and a mode of appreciation – in a word, a sensibility – that promotes the cause of truth. Pure reason and the grasp of truth are not enough for Plato: without the proper sensibility one can know the good and still *not* pursue it. Plato rejects the Socratic paradox that evil-doing is involuntary and the result of ignorance. For the good to be achieved, one must *abhor* evil, and one must *love* knowledge. It is the job of a proper education to instill these sentiments.

An Argument Against Plato

We shall conclude this discussion of Plato's ethics by considering one of the weightier objections recently brought against it.[5] This is the claim that, while Plato may have demonstrated something with his theory of justice, he has not proved what he set out to prove and his results leave us disappointingly short of what we expected of them. Plato wanted to show that such thinkers as Thrasymachus are wrong in their claim that the life of an unjust person is better than the life of someone who is just. Far better, according to Thrasymachus, to rob, steal, lie, break covenants, rape, murder – if you are strong and smart enough to get away with it. When Plato countered that a just person is actually happier, we were led to expect that he would demonstrate that a person who is just – *really* just, in Plato's view of things – will be happier in spite of *not* engaging in robbery, lying, rape and the rest. We expected him to prove that the person who is just according to our ordinary conception of justice will continue to be just in these same ways when he has attained justice according to the Platonic conception of it. But has Plato done this?

Let us grant that he has shown that a person whose soul exhibits the virtue of *Platonic* justice, namely a soul that is balanced and harmonious – one in which each part is contributing its proper share – will be a happy person, and perhaps even happier than the person who is unjust according to this model. Will such a healthy soul refrain from lying, cheating, or robbing others? It is unclear, for all Plato has demonstrated, that it will – at least so goes the criticism. According to this criticism, Platonic justice in the soul, while admirable enough, does not necessarily lead to ordinary justice. A healthy person may act unjustly toward others, and in fact may be all the more successful in her immoral endeavors as a result of being healthy. The difficulty can also be expressed by noting that health is a value for the person herself; ordinary justice is a value with regard to other people. Health is a self-regarding value; ordinary justice an other-regarding one. Consequently, has not Plato committed the fallacy of *ignoratio elenchi*, of drawing an irrelevant conclusion, or proving a proposition distinct from the one the argument was about in the first place? He may have proved that Platonic justice yields health but may not have proved that Platonic justice yields *justice*.

Another way of putting this argument is to say that if justice is defined – as is the case in the *Republic* – as a feature of character rather than of actions, then Plato would beg the question if he talks of or admits the reality of actions which are just independently of their being the actions that a just (i.e., well-balanced) soul would engage in.[6] Likewise, he would beg the question if he identifies unjust actions independently of their being performed by an unjust soul. But unless he can make these independent identifications, how can he know that a *just soul* (in the Platonic sense) will produce *just actions* (in the ordinary sense)? And an unjust soul, unjust ones?

Plato certainly thought he had answered Thrasymachus. He explicitly claims that the just soul will *not* engage in those actions toward others that we ordinarily label unjust, namely theft, treachery, breaking oaths and agreements, adultery:

> And would he have anything to do with temple robberies, thefts, betrayals of friends in private life or of cities in public life?
>
> No, nothing.
>
> And he'd be in no way untrustworthy in keeping an oath or other agreement?
>
> How could he be?
>
> And adultery, disrespect for parents, and neglect of the gods would be more in keeping with every other kind of character than his?
>
> With every one   (*Republic*, 443a).

And, contrary to the criticism we are examining, he seems *to argue* for this conclusion: a happy person, he claims, will not engage in theft and the like – "And isn't the cause of all this that every part within him does its own work, whether it's ruling or being ruled?" (ibid.) In other words, Plato thinks the cause of those actions ordinarily labelled unjust is an imbalanced state of the soul, a state in which one part – usually one or more of the appetites – is not "doing its own business," not obeying the dictates of reason. And in fact much of the injustice we encounter in life flows from greed or lust, which arguably are appetites out of control. Spirit too can be at fault, when the desire for glory and fame overwhelms reason and leaves numerous injustices in its wake. Spirit in this case will have abandoned its proper role. It must be noted that for Plato the opposite of justice is *pleonexia*, a matter of having and wanting more than one is entitled to. When appetite or spirit pursues more than it is entitled to, the result is precisely those actions denounced by all as unjust (except, of course, by Thrasymachus).

Plato himself does not have to argue that breaking promises, committing adultery, and so on are unjust in themselves. He simply needs to note that these action types are generally regarded as unjust and then to argue that an unbalanced soul, a soul that wants more than it is entitled to (in terms of the requirements of his own theory), often leads to precisely these kinds of action. We need to recall that the healthy balanced soul is one which follows the dictates of reason, and that reason is capable of knowing the *truth* about morality. Hence, if theft, treachery, adultery, etc. *are* unjust, reason will know this and will require appetite and spirit to refrain from these actions. In knowing these things, reason does not need to ascertain that the actions are unjust independently of their causation; it needs only to grasp that they are the consequences of the kind of soul that is unjust.

Finally, we must remember that Plato's healthy, just soul is pictured as a participant in a healthy, just state. The rulers of such a state clearly have an interest in the proper relationships among the parts of the state and therefore among all of its citizens. Most forms of injustice – ordinarily understood – involve taking what is not one's own, and it is precisely this type of infraction which would undermine the ideal state. Hence its rulers can be expected to prohibit and punish such injustices. To the extent, then, that the just individual is a member of a just state – and Plato thinks it unlikely that an individual can be fully just outside this context – this person will be *required* by the rational leadership of the state to act justly (in the ordinary sense) toward her fellow citizens.

In light of these considerations, it seems reasonable to think that Plato has achieved his goals. His analysis of justice in the soul shows us both how to avoid unjust actions toward others and at the same time how to achieve happiness for ourselves. What Plato has done is to take common conceptions of justice – which identify it in terms of specific types of actions (Cephalus, let us recall, took it to be a matter of telling the truth and paying one's debts) – and substitute for them a conception which understands justice in terms of a state of soul and the corresponding state of society. There is a definite advantage to Plato's procedure. Any particular type of action (say, returning what has been lent to one) can in certain circumstances be something that one ought *not* to do, even if more often than not it is the right or just thing to do (Socrates points out to Cephalus, for instance, that it is not right to return a weapon to its owner if that person is not in his right mind). Any definition of justice, then, which merely lists types of actions will always be open to the Socratic objection that there are counter-examples to it. Socrates and Plato demand that a search for justice (or any virtue) be a search for what all instances of justice have in common – the *essence* of justice which explains why particular acts or types of acts are just. In Plato's metaphysics, this common element becomes the Form of Justice, the ideal essence reflected more or less adequately in actual examples of the virtue. Justice cannot be defined in terms of action-types, because not all actions of any type will always be just. Thus the essence of justice must be defined differently, in terms of the characteristics of a just soul or state, which, having these characteristics, is always just. From a properly ordered, balanced and healthy soul or state, no injustice will ever flow because the order and balance amount to each part doing its own and receiving its own – but only its own. Plato sees himself, therefore, as giving us an analysis of justice that will support the moral observations of common sense in many instances, but one that will also correct them on occasion and explain *why* they are correct when in fact they are. Moreover, in showing us the essence of justice, the philosophical analysis of justice provides us with a *defense* of claims that particular acts are just, whereas common sense offers only alleged examples of justice without any grasp of why they are examples of it – and hence provides no defense against counter-claims.

Plato's ethical views are impressive, but there are problems with them which must be confronted. Internal difficulties within the theory – matters of inconsistency and invalid modes of argumentation – will likely suggest themselves to any close reader of the *Republic*. But these are not our concern. We want to know whether, when all is said and done, Plato's theory is *true* or at least reasonably correct. We want an overall assessment of the theory. What is to be said in this regard?

Difficulties with Plato's Ethics

Perhaps the major difficulty lies with the basic metaphor utilized by Plato in explaining his theory – the idea of justice as health. This metaphor is responsible for much of the theory's appeal. It would take a perverse mind – an irrational one? – to deny that health is a good, a value, something we ought to pursue. If justice is health, then justice too is truly a good. Moreover, if justice is health it may be possible to have a rational (scientific!) grasp of it, for health appears to be an objective state of affairs which can be analyzed and understood using objective methods of inquiry. We can look to experts (psychiatrists?) for ethical answers and ethical therapy.

But will the metaphor of health work? Is justice – or the good life – a matter of health in the soul? There are some reasons to think not. It is not obvious that all immoral individuals are mentally *ill*, not at least in our present understanding of this term. In fact, those who today are deemed mentally ill are thereby relieved of responsibility and blame for their wrongdoings, which is certainly not the attitude we take toward most immoral people. Furthermore, it is not obvious that all who fail to attain happiness do so because of an imbalance in their souls, and it is not obvious that happiness, when attained, consists in a lack of conflict within the soul. Couldn't the very lack of conflict result in a blandness and dullness of life – a mere homeostasis – which should not be equated with happiness? Perhaps more is needed for happiness than health; health may be a necessary condition of true contentment but not that state itself. Indeed, is it even a necessary condition of it?

Furthermore, there are questions about the epistemological status of the concepts of health and goodness (justice). *Physical* health is something we generally agree about, even if physicians and scientists occasionally debate the requirements for it.

The condition itself, we might say, is not *contestable* to any significant degree. But justice and goodness are highly contestable: we disagree and argue endlessly over what actions and social arrangements are just. Is it just, for instance, to take away the private property of a person and reallocate it to a poor person who has no property? Socialists who think in terms of a redistribution of wealth see this as simple social justice. Conservatives who think in terms of property rights and the rights of contracts believe such reallocation an abominable immorality. Such disagreements – which can be found in almost all areas of social interaction – are seldom if ever resolved to the satisfaction of all parties, and this fact suggests – but does not prove, as we saw in the last chapter – that moral issues are subjective, not objective. If they are subjective, rational people can disagree over them without disputants being correct and others incorrect. Thus, it might be argued, the concept of health, being objective, cannot be equated with the concept of justice, which is, at a minimum, contestable, and possibly subjective. And the same considerations might be brought against equating health and happiness. Is happiness objective, or is it subjective and relative, one person's happiness being another's misery?

But can't we all agree with Plato about the requirements for a just and happy self? In fact we do not agree. Artists might argue that reason stifles creativity and that a life of spirit unfettered by reason is the best way to fulfill oneself. Hedonists might respond to Plato by maintaining that pleasure is the only good and that the only value of reason is to help determine the means needed to achieve the maximum of pleasure and the minimum of pain. More generally, critics may urge that the rational life – orderly, moderate, controlled – may not be all that Plato makes it out to be. Isn't such a rational life simply the creation and ideal of *Western* civilization, reflecting the values, some would say, of white, Western males and their "ice" culture? Are there not other cultural ideals which are at least as valuable?

This line of questioning might lead one to inquire whether Plato came up with the right prescription for mental health. Is it, in fact, desirable for reason to control and suppress appetites and emotions? A thinker like Freud believed that while such repression is necessary for the survival of civilization, it also inevitably produces frustration and a lack of fulfillment in the individual.[7] From this perspective, individual unhappiness becomes the necessary condition for the continuation of society – not exactly what Plato envisaged.

And what about the relationship between happiness and individual liberty? Plato's political philosophy, intertwined as it is with his ethical one, suggests that liberty is not very important. Plato really has nothing to say about the liberty of individuals, except indirectly by denying that certain persons (most of us) should have it. But would we exchange our liberty – limited though it may be – for the type of allegedly complete happiness Plato aspires to? For most of us, isn't at least a modicum of liberty in fact an essential ingredient in happiness? Perhaps in thinking about Plato's philosophy we are inclined to imagine ourselves as members of the guardian class – and things sound fine. But most members of his society would not be guardians – the leaders are limited to a very small number of individuals. Would you like to be a businessman in Plato's state, or even a soldier? The problem is not so much a political one: that you would be told what to do; it is an ethical one: you would be restricted to a certain role, and your so-called fulfillment would be the result of performing well in that role. Even the guardians have no choice in their fate. Doesn't such a proposal rob one of one's humanity – the ability to choose a role (within limits, to be sure), to change roles if one wishes, and to determine the values one wants to achieve in life?

Plato, of course, would simply reject most of our values – or reinterpret them: he does, after all, stress the value of self-mastery, and this is a capacity closely related to personal and social freedom. Moreover, he thinks we really have no choice in the matter if we wish to be rational and realize our essential nature. But do we have an essential nature that restricts what goals we should aspire to and what occupations we should pursue? Many thinkers believe that nurture more than nature is responsible for who we are, and that consequently our nature is largely the product of the society we live in – hence not so essential after all. Or perhaps, as some contemporary thinkers called existentialists suggest, we are radically free to choose who we are – to choose our essence.[8] Furthermore, it is highly doubtful whether human beings are so markedly different with respect to reason, spirit, and appetite as to require separation into Plato's three classes. Isn't each individual's mixture of the three more balanced, and in the final analysis more standard and uniform, than he would have us believe? And can't we improve our reasoning skills, or our warrior skills, and thereby rise to a different category – something disallowed by Plato, who in his essentialist way believed that the nature of each of us is given once and for all?

It is not to be inferred that these questions cannot be answered by a confirmed Platonist. But they surely need to be answered. Plato's philosophy contains the first major ethical theory in a long line of distinguished theories, but that his theory was first proves neither that it was right nor that it was wrong. What we can conclude is that Plato offers us an interesting and significant proposal which must be taken very seriously, even today, if we are trying to get at the truth about morality and answer Socrates' question about how we are to live our lives. Plato's ethical theory is an option we must confront if we are to make an informed choice.

3

Aristotle

To have studied with Plato must be counted among life's most fortunate experiences. To have a pupil the caliber of Aristotle must be any great teacher's ultimate ambition. Plato and Aristotle, teacher and student, were both blessed, then, "by the gods," each equally rewarded by the other. History records few if any other examples of instructor and pupil who were both philosophical geniuses of the highest order and who both left behind philosophical accomplishments of the greatest significance.

Aristotle (384–322 BCE) was born in Stagira in the northern Greek province of Macedonia. He came to Athens at the age of seventeen to study with Plato, and he remained for twenty years in the Academy until Plato's death. Subsequently he served as tutor to the son of King Philip of Macedonia, the young man who was later to become Alexander the Great. Aristotle returned to Athens, at that time under Macedonian control, soon after Alexander was made regent for his father. Although he remained friends with Alexander until the latter's death, there is little evidence that he exercised much influence over the great warrior's thinking. Aristotle founded his own school in Athens, the Lyceum, and taught in it until anti-Macedonian feeling in the city forced him to flee. Having the example of Socrates before his mind, he refused, as he put it, to let Athens "sin twice against philosophy." The Lyceum, like Plato's Academy, continued to exist for eight hundred years; both were finally closed by a Christian emperor in Constantinople.

There are many similarities between the philosophies of Plato and Aristotle, especially in the area of ethics. But there are also sharp differences. Aristotle admired Plato greatly, but, as he put it, truth comes before Plato: "for though we love both the truth and our friends, piety requires us to honor the truth first" (*Nicomachean Ethics*, 1096a15).[1] It is sometimes said, with considerable appropriateness, that Aristotle brought Plato down to earth. He rejected Plato's Theory of Forms – which identified the essences of things with ideal, eternal forms existing in a non-spatial realm apart from the world of ordinary objects – and put in its place a notion of essence as the form of a material object, the form being what gives structure and intelligibility to a particular thing. This shift led Aristotle to place much more emphasis than Plato did on perceptual, empirical knowledge. In the area of ethics, Aristotle abandoned

Plato's mystical form of the Good ("it is not the sort of good a human being can pursue in action or possess") and restricted himself to a consideration of how the good life is to be achieved on earth and in this life. The difference between Plato's idealism and Aristotle's naturalism is marked and everywhere noticeable. It has led some commentators to exaggerate the difference by claiming that everyone is born either a Platonist or an Aristotelian. In our study of Aristotle's ethics, we shall take note of its differences from the ethics of Plato, but we shall also confront the fact that there are many similarities as well, especially with regard to the *issues* that focus the discussion.

Aristotle wrote two books on ethics, the *Nicomachean Ethics* and the *Eudemian Ethics*. There is a third work, the *Magna Moralia*, which scholars think was not written by Aristotle himself in spite of its largely accurate representation of Aristotelian ethics. For many years the *Eudemian Ethics* was not attributed to Aristotle, but scholars now think it was in fact written by him, although the time of its composition is still in doubt. For centuries, however, and still today, the *Nicomachean Ethics* is the central text for the study of Aristotle's ethical theory. Written in a straightforward, dry (and occasionally dull) style, it apparently consists of lecture notes, possibly dictated to his son Nicomachus. In spite of raising numerous interpretive difficulties, it is a book that is accessible to the contemporary reader – and a book filled with great wisdom.

Before we begin our study of the *Nicomachean Ethics*, a point needs to be made about Aristotle's method. Although Aristotle argues against ethical views held by specific individuals, he does not reject the fundamental ethical convictions of the members of his society. In particular, he thinks, the wise and virtuous members of this society hold beliefs that can be trusted. Rather than replace the accepted ethical convictions (of the wisest and best), he attempts to provide a philosophical clarification and defense of them, to develop their implications, and to set forth a systematic account of the moral world they define. This ethical activity does not amount to a simple vindication of a person's conventional moral beliefs. Some of these beliefs are rejected and even those retained are organized into a more coherent set of convictions (the common ends or goals of life are ordered in a more hierarchical manner which rearranges priorities and promotes more success in one's life as a whole).[2] It sets forth the ideal of an individual who, using reason, brings a level of depth and subtlety to moral thinking and the moral life which exceeds that of the average citizen. But Aristotle's thinking is not revisionist in the way Plato's is. It is a *refinement* of ordinary moral thought.

The Teleological Approach to Behavior

Aristotle begins the *Nicomachean Ethics* with a generalization that provides the key to his ethics and indeed to his philosophical thinking in general: "Every craft and every investigation, and likewise every action and decision, seems to aim at some good" (*NE*, 1094a1). This "good" is to be understood as a goal or, as Aristotle puts it, an end. All of deliberate human behavior, Aristotle is claiming, is goal-directed or purposive in character. As it turns out, nature in general for Aristotle is purposive: even the physical, non-animate domain consists of objects pursuing their natural ends. Aristotle is primarily responsible for the world-view that interprets all things in terms of their *telos*, the goal toward which they aim and move. This teleological approach to nature dominated Western thinking for two thousand years until it was rejected during the early modern period by the advocates of the newly emerged natural science. Many philosophers even today continue to think, however, that much of *human* behavior must be understood as goal-directed, as "aimed at some good." In taking this stand, they side with Aristotle and against the mechanistic stance of natural science when it comes to an understanding of human action. Whereas the mechanist would explain all action as being no more than bodily motions that are the inevitable result of prior physical causes, Aristotle and his followers maintain that identifying a person's intentions and reasons – her future goals and purposes – is the best way to understand why she acts as she does.

Aristotle notes that some of the goods or ends we aim at in action are things we need, or need to do, in order to attain other goods. They are *instrumental* goods or actions which are valued for the sake of what they produce or what they allow us to attain beyond themselves. The good of surgery, for example, is instrumental: we desire it, we aim at it, only because it leads to good health. In addition to instrumental goods, however, there are what we might call *intrinsic* values: actions, objects, or states of affairs that are valuable for their own sake. Health itself, Plato had claimed, is valuable in this way, although it is also instrumentally valuable because it allows us to attain still other ends, for example, mountain climbing or a long life. Another example of an intrinsic value might be love, or pleasure, or power, or anything one desires because of its own qualities.

Is There an "Ultimate End"?

In light of the distinction between instrumental and intrinsic ends, Aristotle poses an interesting question: is there an end we pursue for its own sake and do *not* pursue for the sake of anything else, an end which, furthermore, is the one for the sake of which we pursue *all other ends*? Is there, in other words, an "ultimate" end?[3] Is there a goal toward which we strive which leads nowhere beyond itself, a goal which is the ultimate goal of everything else we desire and do?

Aristotle gives an argument designed to prove that there must be an ultimate end. "Suppose, then, that ... we do not choose everything because of something else, since ... if we do, it will go on without limit, making desire empty and futile" (*NE*, 1094a20).

Unless there were an ultimate end, he claims, all our other desires would be empty and futile. Aristotle's argument here needs to be unpacked. He is noting, in the first place, that, if there were no ultimate end, we would always desire one thing for the sake of another, and that thing for the sake of still another, and so on. This dependency of one desired end on another would generate what philosophers call an infinite regress. Whatever we seek, we would seek in order to obtain something else, but we would seek this second thing in order to obtain a third thing, and the third in order to obtain a fourth, and so on ... without stopping. This chain of desires would never come to a halt, any end or object of desire found in it being something valued only because obtaining it would lead to the satisfaction of some other desire. In the second place, Aristotle is claiming that, given such an unending chain of desires and ends, any particular desire would be empty and futile because we would never be able to attain the *final* goal at which it aims; we would never be able to attain final satisfaction. This final goal would have to be an end desired for its own sake alone, but given the hypothesis of an infinite regress of goals, there would be no such final goal or end. No desire, then, could ever be completely fulfilled and satisfied. Consequently, every desire would be empty and futile. One commentator has described in the following picturesque terms what it would be like to live without an ultimate end: "Like children who quickly tire of their toys, they live on an endless treadmill of desire that never reaches a final goal, and they remain ever 'empty'."[4]

Another way to look at Aristotle's argument is as follows. If there were an infinite regress of desires and ends, we would never have a final or definite answer to the question *why* we should desire any particular thing, and thus we would never have a complete justification for any action aimed at satisfying a particular desire. Part of the justification for pursuing the object of the first desire is that attaining it is a means to attaining the object of another desire, and that a means to attaining still another. But we would never get a complete justification of the first desire because the series of desires would never come to an end. Without a complete justification of the initial and succeeding desires, these particular desires would be "empty and futile," that is to say, ungrounded,[5] unjustified.

Aristotle denies that there is such a infinite regress with respect to our desires and ends, and in his mind this entails that there is some *one* thing we desire for its own sake, do not desire for the sake of anything else, and for the sake of which we desire all other things. It is this end which brings the series of desires to a conclusion and stops the regress. (Aristotelian scholars debate whether or not his argument justifies the conclusion that there must be *one* ultimate end. Couldn't there be several different ultimate ends, each of which equally stops the regress?) This one ultimate end Aristotle calls "the best good," "the highest of all the goods pursued in action," which amounts to saying it is the supreme good.[6]

Clearly, if there is a supreme good, it is of utmost importance that we have a clear idea of what it is, for if we do "we are more likely to hit the right mark" in our efforts to achieve it. Fortunately, he thinks, most human beings ("both the many and the cultivated") are in at least verbal agreement regarding the supreme good: it is *happiness*. Moreover, he reports, they all consider happiness to be the same thing as "living well and doing well" (*NE*, 1095a15–20). The Greek term for happiness is *eudaimonia*. In fact, scholars have long debated whether "happiness" is the best way to translate this term into English. Most of them think it is the closest approximation available in spite of the fact, as we shall see, that our notion of happiness has connotations that do not accord with what Aristotle and the Greeks meant by "*eudaimonia*." An alternative translation is that of *success* – thus a person possessing *eudaimonia* is one who succeeds in life.[7] This translation, if taken to mean success in life as a human being and not just material success, works very well in certain contexts to reveal the significance of what Aristotle is saying.

Aristotle never takes issue with the identification of the supreme good with happiness or with the equation of happiness with living and doing well – here we find the nonrevisionist ethical thinker accepting, at least as a starting point for ethical reflection, the consensus view of his day. He immediately proceeds, however, to see whether happiness can meet the criteria he himself recognizes for the highest good (these criteria being reformulations of the conditions required for a single ultimate end). It must be, first, the *end* for which human beings pursue all other things. Second, it must be *unconditionally complete*, which means that it must be valued only for itself and not as a means to anything else. Third, it must be *self-sufficient* – "we regard something as self-sufficient when all by itself it makes a life choiceworthy and lacking nothing" (*NE*, 1097b10–15). A self-sufficient end is one to which nothing else can be added that would make life more choiceworthy. The self-sufficiency criterion may be thought to explain why there can be only *one* ultimate end: if there were two (or more) such ends, there would be something that could be added to each one of them that would make life more choiceworthy, namely the other end(s).[8] Only a single ultimate end can be self-sufficient. Happiness, Aristotle maintains, meets all three of the above conditions: it is an end at which we aim, it is not desired as a means to anything else, and nothing added to it makes it more valuable. Hence Aristotle agrees with the common opinion and accepts happiness as the highest or supreme good for human beings. What we need to do is to understand happiness in greater depth and detail and to avoid mistaken conceptions of it.[9]

Happiness: The Supreme Good?

It should be remarked right at the beginning of our study of Aristotle's ethics that his adoption of happiness as the supreme good is more controversial than it might first appear to be. The goal of happiness as living and doing well amounts to what one recent commentator described as "what all good parents want for their children."[10] But is it the end or goal of human life itself – the most valuable thing afforded by life? And should its pursuit be central to the moral life? History affords us examples of opinions to the contrary. Someone deeply influenced by the

Judeo-Christian tradition might think Aristotle's view ignores the truly supreme good: salvation or reunion with God. While it is true that the great Christian thinkers of the Middle Ages interpret the final goal of human life as happiness, they give it a deeply religious interpretation, identifying its highest realization with the vision of God available only in the afterlife. Many Christians regard happiness in this life as at best a secular value, not the supreme, religious one. In fact, in extreme cases they view the effort to attain happiness as a way of ensuring that one will *not* attain the supreme good of salvation – such would be the view of the puritan who sees the pursuit of happiness as self-centered and expressive of human pride. Aristotle's conception of the supreme good as happiness (a conception shared by Socrates and Plato) might be called a pagan or humanistic conception to distinguish it from ethical views often springing from the Judeo-Christian tradition.

One need not be a religious puritan to believe that Aristotle has gone awry in placing happiness at the center of the moral life. A later strain in moral philosophy, identified primarily with the eighteenth-century philosopher Immanuel Kant, takes the moral life to be the life of duty.[11] For Kant, it is strict adherence to duty for duty's sake which should constitute the motive for all human action. Doing one's duty, fulfilling one's obligations, being obedient to the moral law that imposes these obligations on one – these are to be the focus of moral effort, *not* the promotion of the ends of desire. In Aristotle, there is no suggestion that we have any *obligation* or *duty* to pursue our happiness or the means to it. We would be unfortunate, and perhaps lacking in intelligence, if we did not do so, but we would not for all that have violated an obligation. The concept of morality identified by Kant, one which remains very influential today, is a conception that differs in important ways from the ethics of Aristotle and most Greeks. Indeed, it is said by some scholars that the Greeks lacked any notion of duty in the Kantian sense. It is clear, then, that when we identify Aristotle, and Plato before him, as an important moral philosopher, we are not equating morality with the highly distinctive Kantian notion of morality. Aristotle represents the culmination of the classical Greek view that morality is a matter of individual human flourishing, a pursuit of the *natural* good for a human being. On this view, morality consists of strategies for bringing about happiness, by which the Greeks meant the fullest expression of our distinctively human nature – the achievement of the best, the most complete life possible in the world in which we live. Self-realization with respect to our full set of human potentialities is the aim – obtaining the natural human good is the ultimate object of morality.

If happiness is the supreme good, what exactly *is* it? On this issue, Aristotle notes, people disagree. "The many, the most vulgar, would seem to conceive the good and happiness as pleasure, and hence they also like the life of gratification" (*NE*, 1095b 16–17). People who identify happiness with pleasure pursue the enjoyment of bodily sensations and a life of sensual gratification. Aristotle rejects this view on the grounds that it equates human happiness with the life of the beasts: "a life for grazing animals" and hence a slavish life. While there is a "beastly" dimension to human nature, there is much more, and in Aristotle's view the ultimate good for human beings must reflect the distinctive aspects of human nature. Furthermore, people often disagree on what things are pleasant, which shows that these things are not objectively pleasant (pleasant by nature or pleasant in themselves) (*NE*, 1099a10–15) but merely subjectively so. Only that which is objectively good (or objectively pleasant)[12] can be equated with happiness. He goes on to report that more cultivated people identify happiness not with pleasure but with honor in the arena of political activity. Here again he disagrees: "This, however, appears to be too superficial to be what we are seeking, since it seems to depend more on those who honor than on the one honored, whereas we intuitively believe that the good is something of our own and hard to take from us" (*NE*, 1095b20–5). He also maintains that most human beings seek honor "to convince themselves that they are good," which shows, he thinks, that they really value virtue more than honor. Still others identify happiness with wealth. But while money is desirable, Aristotle points out that it is desired for what it can purchase, which indicates that there is, for those who pursue it, a goal higher than money itself. Moreover, he notes in passing, the life of money-making is in a way forced on a person (as a necessary means to other ends) and not a life chosen for itself.

Anatomy of the Soul: Reason and Appetite

None of these ordinary conceptions of happiness being satisfactory, Aristotle turns to the task of developing his own, constructive account. In doing so, he appeals to one of the fundamental principles of his teleological, goal-oriented conception of nature (and human nature): the notion of purpose and function. Everything in the world, according to this conception, has a distinctive function (*ergon*), and this function serves to identify its "good" – that at which it aims. "Well, perhaps we shall find the best good if we first find the function of a human being. For just as the good, i.e., doing well for a flautist, a sculptor, and every craftsman, and in general, for whatever has a function and characteristic action, seems to depend on its function, the same seems to be true for a human being, if a human being has some function" (*NE*, 1097b25). The good for artists and craftsmen depends on the function of their art or craft: the function of a musician is to produce pleasurable or beautiful music, the making of such music being the good at which the musician aims. When the musician achieves this good, she has fulfilled her function. Aristotle asks if a human being likewise has a function *just by being a human being*. Does a human being have a distinctive role to play? The organs and bodily parts of a human being obviously have their functions – the eye has the function of seeing, the ear hearing, the stomach digestion, and so on. Each of these plays a distinctive role in maintaining the life and well-being of a person, and they fulfill their functions if they perform well. What, then, is distinctive about the person herself, about the human being as a whole? After rejecting mere life, nutrition, growth, and sense-perception as distinctive features of human beings – because they are shared with other creatures – Aristotle locates the distinctive aspect of human nature in reason: "the remaining possibility ... is some sort of life of action of the part of the soul that has reason" (*NE*, 1098a1). Grasping the function of a human being, and thereby determining what the good of this creature is, requires an analysis of human rationality.

What, then, is this reason which sets human beings apart from the rest of nature and is thus their distinctive and essential function and form? Aristotle claims that the human soul has two parts to it. First, there is the rational part which actually engages in thinking and reasoning. Second, there is the irrational part, consisting of both the nutritive and appetitive dimensions of life. Although nonrational because it is not itself engaged in reasoning, the appetitive soul (consisting of appetites, feelings, desires, and emotions) can partake of reason to the extent of being influenced by it, following it, obeying it. For Aristotle, the other part of the nonrational soul, the nutritive aspect, is beyond the reach of reason and plays no significant role in the moral life. These distinctions allow us to see that there are two senses in which a human being "has" reason: (1) as a capacity for reasoning and (2) as a capacity for obeying reason. (1) resides in the rational soul; (2) resides in the appetitive part of the nonrational soul. The distinctiveness of human beings consists, then, in their possession of these two rational capacities.

If the supreme end and good for human beings is to be identified with the fulfillment of the distinctive human function, it must involve the *exercise* of the distinctive human capacities. Hence, a human being's function – and consequently her good, happiness – is identified with the actual exercise of reason in the two ways indicated: the activity of reasoning and the activity of obeying and following reason. After all, Aristotle argues, happiness being the highest good, it must consist in activity, since life as activity is fuller than life as a mere capacity. "We have found, then, that the human function is the soul's activity that expresses reason as itself having reason or requires reason as obeying reason" (*NE*, 1098a5).

Aristotle's claim, then, is that the function of anything is to be understood as the activity or manifestation of the feature that makes it distinctive. The function of any kind of thing or person is the same as the function of an excellent example of that thing or person. The excellent thing (person) is one who performs its (her) function "finely and well." Reason being the feature that sets human beings apart, excellence in reasoning (in the two senses identified) constitutes the excellent performance of the human function. Excellence in an activity is a notion we have encountered before: it is what the Greeks called *aretē*, virtue – "Each function is completed well when its completion expresses the proper virtue" (*NE*, 1098a15). Thus Aristotle can conclude, "the human good [happiness] turns out to be the soul's activity that expresses virtue" (ibid.).

Here we find Aristotle agreeing with both Socrates and Plato that happiness and virtue are inextricably linked. Furthermore, all three of them link virtue and reason. The pursuit of virtue via the exercise of reason and the consequent attainment of happiness is the essential theme of classical Greek ethics. But whereas Socrates' equation of virtue and the life of reason amounts to the vague suggestion that virtue is knowledge of the good and the bad, and Plato's similar equation is based upon a debatable devaluation of appetite and desire, Aristotle gives us a clear, attractive, and highly developed account of how reason and desire work together. The good life is the life *with or not without reason* (since there is more to it than mere thinking). The Aristotelian good for man does not commit one to the intellectualism of Socrates or the autocratic life of reason of Plato. Aristotle pictures the supreme good as the flourishing of the entire human personality in all its dimensions – in its appetitive and affective dimensions as well as its intellectual ones. For this reason, many philosophers judge Aristotle's ethics to be superior to that of his close predecessors.

The down-to-earth Aristotle always has his mind attuned to the messy motley of facts about human behavior which defies systematization, and this attitude leads him to a healthy skepticism regarding most generalizations and most moral principles. In his eyes, principles, at least in the area of ethics, are true "only for the most part," as rules of thumb or loose guidelines. In theorizing about the moral life, he maintains, the goal of precision is inappropriate, given the complexity and concrete nature of this life. Hence after giving us a generalization about the supreme good for humankind (happiness is the activity of the soul that expresses virtue), Aristotle immediately qualifies it. First, virtuous activity is something that must be achieved over a period of a complete life: "For one swallow does not make a spring; nor, similarly, does one day or a short time make us blessed and happy" (*NE*, 1098a15–20). Furthermore, happiness requires, in addition to virtuous activity, a modicum of "external goods" like good birth, good children, and beauty – "since we cannot, or cannot easily, do fine actions if we lack the resources" (*NE*, 1099b30).[13] It also appears to Aristotle, although he rightly puzzles over this matter, that what happens after one's death – what disgrace or honors come one's way, how one's children and other descendants behave – can affect the reality of one's happiness.[14] Hence happiness cannot just neatly be identified with a life according to rational virtue – external goods need to be added in order to achieve it. Nevertheless, it is "the activities expressing virtue that control happiness, and the contrary activities that control its contrary" (*NE*, 1100b5–10). The life of rational virtue, we might say, is the *essence* of happiness. It follows that Aristotelian happiness (*eudaimonia*) cannot be equated with momentary or periodic feelings of contentment (perhaps our contemporary conception of happiness) but is an objective matter extending across one's entire mature life and perhaps beyond.

The Virtues of Character

After highlighting the central importance of virtue for the study of the good for human beings, Aristotle goes on in the *Ethics* to give us an elaborate theory of *the virtues*. Virtue in general has been identified as the excellent functioning of the distinctive feature of human beings, their reason. We have also seen that there are two senses in which we have reason, the sense in which we engage in reasoning and the sense in which we have appetites and desires which, although themselves part of the nonrational soul, can listen to reason and obey (or *disobey*) it. When the first rational aspect of the soul is functioning well, we have, Aristotle tells us, *virtues of thought*, and when the second aspect listens to reason and follows its injunctions, we have *virtues of character*. The former are sometimes referred to by commentators as intellectual virtues, the latter moral virtues. As examples of intellectual virtues, Aristotle lists wisdom, comprehension, and intelligence, and as examples of virtues of character, generosity, temperance, courage, magnanimity, justice and numerous others.

It is often claimed that it is misleading in English to refer to the intellectual excellences (and to some degree the ones of character) as *virtues*, the English term "virtue" being inappropriate given its current standard meaning: the prim and priggish, the old-fashioned concern with chastity, etc. But surely no harm can come of this common translation if it is always kept in mind that the notion of virtue (*aretē*) has a special, clearly defined meaning for Aristotle – a meaning which applies no less in the intellectual than in the moral sphere. We should think of "virtue" as a technical term in Aristotle's ethics and thereby resist the tendency to assign it the connotations of *our* use of "virtue." Certainly nothing "slightly priggish," nothing "old-fashioned," is meant by *aretē*. It is, on the contrary, a robust and, for us, somewhat radical idea, and it is one which many contemporary ethical theorists are rediscovering as an invaluable tool in the study of morality. It should be noted that "virtue ethics," relying heavily on Aristotle's pioneering efforts, is a major branch of ethical theory today.[15]

Virtues of character occupy Aristotle for a large part of the *Nicomachean Ethics*, although in the end they are assigned a status secondary to the intellectual virtues. We are told, first of all, that they are virtues that pertain to appetites and desires, feelings and emotions – all these together making up the appetitive soul which achieves virtue by following the voice of reason. Desires, feelings and the other appetitive drives are among the major causes of our actions, and thus the moral virtues have a close connection to action. In fact, there are many virtues that apply directly to actions, to ways of behaving. Feelings and actions, then, are what are controlled by virtue. Virtue itself is not, according to Aristotle, a feeling or a mere capacity to have certain feelings or to engage in certain actions. Aristotle describes virtues as *states*; they are what we today would think of as states of character. Being morally virtuous is a matter of having a certain kind of character, of being a certain kind of person. A state of character in turn is what we might call a disposition or habit, a settled tendency to behave in certain ways and to have certain feelings, emotions, and desires. The moral life, then, involves developing and manifesting virtuous dispositions of character. And we need to remember that each of the states of character identified as a virtue is a state "that makes a human being good and makes him perform his function well" (*NE*, 1106a20). Virtuous states of character issue in feelings, emotions, and actions that represent the excellent performance of reason (in its second aspect, that of following or obeying reason).

Virtues are not natural states – we do not come into the world complete with a moral character and a set of moral dispositions. These settled tendencies of mind and body must be acquired through education and by habituation, by a person being trained in and by practicing the virtuous activities. We develop a state of character or disposition by repeating similar activities, and so "we become just by doing just actions, temperate by doing temperate actions, brave by doing brave actions" (*NE*, 1103a30–1103b1). The best advice Aristotle can give us here is to emulate the example of the good person, the individual who has already mastered the moral virtues and lives a life in accordance with them. Acknowledging that it is easier for a young person to develop moral virtues than an older one, Aristotle points to the importance of developing the right habits "right from our youth." Moral education, then, is absolutely central to the moral life. Unless we morally educate our children and thereby mold their characters in the right way, we cannot expect them to lead flourishing, happy lives later on.

The distinctive nature of Aristotle's conception of the moral life cannot be stressed too much. Being moral is a matter, not of following a set of rules imposed by some authority, but of being a certain kind of person and expressing one's moral character in words, feelings, and deeds. The emphasis we find in the *Ethics* is never on defining what is *right* or identifying what our *duty* is; the emphasis is always on what a *good person* would do.[16] The *motivation* for emulating the good person lies in the fact that being good means being the kind of individual who feels and acts in the ways that constitute the distinctively human life, and thus the *happy* life: happiness being what all human beings aim at as the ultimate good. Thus the right thing to do is defined via virtue rather than virtue via right conduct.

But in what does the manifestation of the virtuous states of character consist? What actions must we take and what feelings must we have if we are to be virtuous? What responses are called for if the appetites and feelings included in our nonrational soul are to obey the commands of the rational part? Many readers of the *Nicomachean Ethics* believe that Aristotle's answer to these questions is the key to his ethics and his major innovation in Greek ethical thought. Here we encounter his famous Doctrine of the Mean.

The Doctrine of the Mean

Aristotle develops this doctrine by noting that many states of the body "tend to be ruined by excess and deficiency" (*NE*, 1104a10). Both strength and health are examples. The strong person and the healthy one need food, but not too much or too little. Likewise, too much or too little exercise will ruin a person's strength and health. It is the mean between excess and deficiency, what he refers to as "the proportionate amount," which yields strength and health. Likewise, he claims, for those states of soul that we call virtues:

The same is true, then, of temperance, bravery and the other virtues. For if, e.g., someone avoids and is afraid of everything, standing firm against nothing, he becomes cowardly, but if he is afraid of nothing at all and goes to face everything, he becomes rash. Similarly, if he gratifies himself with every pleasure and refrains from none, he becomes intemperate, but if he avoids them all, as boors do, he becomes some sort of insensible person. Temperance and bravery, then, are ruined by excess and deficiency but preserved by the mean   (*NE*, 1104a15–25).

The brave person is afraid of what it is reasonable to fear and unafraid of things unreasonable to fear. She doesn't take foolish risks, but she is not afraid of threats that one can reasonably expect to turn aside if one stands firm against them – and she is certainly not afraid of insignificant threats ("of her own shadow"). If the cause is just and great, she will stand firm even while realizing that success is unlikely. One can say of the brave person that she feels fear on the right occasions and for the right things, and in those instances feels the right amount of fear. She also feels the right amount of confidence, and feels confidence on the right occasions, etc. Thus she achieves the mean with respect to the feelings of fear and confidence. Likewise, the temperate person lets her appetites prevail on the right occasions, with regard to the right objects, and in the appropriate amount. She seeks pleasure, but from the right things, at the right time, and to the appropriate extent. Thus, she achieves the mean with respect to the feelings of pleasure and the demands of appetite. And what about the feeling of anger? Here is how one commentator has described the possibilities: "Bad temper comes in a variety of forms: hot-tempered men get angry too quickly; choleric men get angry too often; 'bad-tempered' men get too angry when they get angry; violent men express their anger physically; and sulky or bitter men stay angry too long."[17] The mean rules out all of these manifestations of anger as excessive. But there can be too little anger as well, as is found in the slavish or stupid person.

Aristotle did not invent the notion of the mean – it had long been a part of popular Greek culture. What this culture referred to as *sōphrosunē* was basically the idea of "nothing in excess, nothing in deficiency"; *sōphrosunē* was sometimes thought of as the virtue of moderation (but, as we shall see, there are problems with the idea that the mean connotes moderation). Aristotle took over this common notion of the mean and gave it clearer articulation and greater substance. His originality lies in the way in which he philosophically interprets the common notion and the manner in which he expands the idea so that it becomes the *sine qua non* of all the virtues.

One of the major features of virtue as the mean, Aristotle tells us, is that it is not an absolute, arithmetic mean (as six is the arithmetic mean between two and ten) which would be the same for everyone; rather, it is the mean *relative to us*. The mean relative to us may vary from person to person, given the varying needs and circumstances of these individuals. For example, the amount of food that is appropriate for me, given my sedentary profession, is hardly the amount needed by an athlete. Likewise, what counts as courage for a trained soldier may be quite different from what counts as courage in the case of a philosophy professor, the intermediary between excess and deficiency varying according to the particulars of the individual case. In a sense, Aristotle is a *relativist*.[18] He repudiates the position of the *absolutist* who thinks there are "rules of virtue" which apply in every case and which can be appealed to in every instance to determine the correct or virtuous feeling or action. One and the same action will manifest virtue on the part of one person and not do so on the part of another. Nevertheless, Aristotle's position remains an *objectivist* one: if an action manifests virtue in the case of one individual, that it does so is an objective fact; moreover, any other person who was in the same situation, had the same needs, and was similar in other relevant respects would be required by reason to act in the same way. The fact of the matter is that people in many instances do differ with respect to the factors giving rise to the demands of virtue, although in other instances they find themselves similarly situated and therefore find reason imposing the same requirements of virtuous behavior on them.

The Doctrine of the Mean has frequently been misinterpreted to suggest that Aristotle is putting forth a doctrine of moderation. According to this view, he is recommending that we always strive to feel neither too much nor too little but rather the moderate amount: hence a little fear but not too much, a little pleasure but not too much, a little anger but not too much. This view of the matter is mistaken.[19] For one thing, according to Aristotle, there are situations, for example situations embodying injustice, which should provoke extreme anger in us, just as there are situations which rightly prompt us to feel extreme fear. While the *amount* of a feeling will on occasion be a factor in determining the mean, much more than quantity is involved in doing so. The mean, the intermediate, is a matter of having feelings of anger, pity, confidence (and so on) "at the right times, about the right things, towards the right people, for the right end, and in the right way" (*NE*, 1106b20). Assessed in these various dimensions, reason might well determine that on specific occasions the mean relative to the agent requires extreme confidence, great pity, or great anger. This, then, is no doctrine of moderation.

The truly virtuous person, however, is not just one who achieves the relative mean in her feelings and actions. She must also receive pleasure from doing so. Aristotle goes so far as to say that someone who is "grieved" by (unhappy about) abstaining from bodily pleasures (on the right occasions, in the right amount, etc.) is actually intemperate even if she does abstain (*NE*, 1104b5). A person who finds it painful to stand firm in terrifying situations, even if she succeeds in doing so, is nevertheless cowardly. Thus acting virtuously is something that must be done, as it were, in the right spirit.

This latter point explains a claim Aristotle makes which would otherwise be puzzling. As we have seen, Aristotle maintains that one becomes temperate by doing temperate things, just by engaging in just actions, and so on. But is it not true that "if we do what is just or temperate, we must already be just or temperate" (*NE*, 1105a20)? Aristotle avoids paradox here by distinguishing between, on the one hand, doing what is virtuous and, on the other, doing it "from the right state" or doing it as the fully virtuous person does it. We can act temperately without knowing and appreciating that our action is the temperate one, without deciding to do it *because* it is temperate, without our temperate action expressing a firm and settled temperate state of character, and without our receiving pleasure from our temperate action. The truly temperate person not only does the temperate act – achieves the mean between the extremes – but does this deliberately, choosing the mean because it *is* the mean. Such a person acts as she does in consequence of having an unchanging character which leads to such choices – precisely because they satisfy the mean – and she does so with pleasure. Aristotle's claim is that one becomes a temperate person of this sort, and, *mutatis mutandis*, virtuous in other ways, by engaging in acts that in fact are temperate, even if in those actions one is simply following a rule mechanically or following the example of someone else. But one exercises the *virtue* of temperance only when one acts from the right state, this being indicated by the fact that the act brings pleasure to the agent.

Aristotle's constant attempt to be faithful to the facts of experience – at the expense of neat generalizations – leads him to grant that "not every action or feeling admits of the mean" (*NE*, 1107a5). Envy and adultery he lists as a feeling and an act that are always base and never correct. They themselves, not their deficiencies or excesses, are base. "We cannot do them well or not well – e.g., by committing adultery with the right woman at the right time in the right way; on the contrary, it is true unconditionally that to do any of them is to be in error" (*NE*, 1107a15). That such feelings and actions are base and to be avoided is, presumably, the pronouncement of reason, even if reason's verdict in this case does not consist in identifying a mean.

Furthermore, Aristotle grants that in those instances in which there is a mean between excess and deficiency, it is not always the case that these positions on the ethical scale have agreed-upon names. The excessively confident person – or one who is deficient in fear – has no ordinary name, he tells us, but he goes on, sensibly, to characterize her as rash. Likewise, there is no name given to people who feel a deficiency of pleasure, but granting that there are such people, we can always come up with an appropriate description – Aristotle calls them "insensible." Taking case after case, Aristotle tries to show that the principle of the mean works to identify the state of character we think of as virtuous, whether we have a conventional name for it or not. Rather than follow him in this endeavor, we shall simply consider a brief table of selected virtues and vices that illustrates his results:

Habits of Feeling or Action	Deficiency	Mean	Excess
fear/confidence	rashness	bravery	cowardice
pleasures & pains	insensibility	temperance	intemperance
giving & taking money	ungenerosity	generosity	wastefulness
giving large amounts of money	niggardliness	magnificence	vulgarity
honor and dishonor	pusillanimity	magnanimity	vanity
anger	inirascibility	mildness	irascibility
pleasures in amusements	boorishness	wit	buffoonery

In all of the above cases and in other similar ones, the mean is to be interpreted as relative to the individual, not as absolute and hence fixed for everyone. Individuals displaying the mean in their character will decide (choose) what to do or feel as a result of reason's judgment as to what would be the mean in a given situation. The mild person, for example, will feel anger when reason indicates it is appropriate, will direct that anger at the appropriate persons, again indicated by reason, and will feel the amount of anger that reason deems appropriate. Thus Aristotle concludes: "Virtue ... is (a) a state that decides, (b) consisting in a mean, (c) . . . relative to us, (d) which is defined by reference to reason, (e), i.e., to the reason by reference to which the intelligent person would define it" (*NE*, 1106b35–1107a1). The person who has virtue in this complex sense is one whose appetites, feelings, and actions are guided by reason and who thereby is able to function well as the distinctive rational creature a human being is.

Motives and Pleasure

The complexities and subtleties involved in the definitions of many of the virtues emerge clearly in Aristotle's detailed examination of the case of bravery. This virtue, as we have seen, is a disposition to seek the mean regarding feelings of fear and confidence. Ever attentive to the particular case and always open to exceptions to the rule, Aristotle notes that fear of some things is actually "right and fine" and that a lack of fear is sometimes not a sign of courage but is actually "disgraceful." He has in mind things like a bad reputation – "for if someone fears bad reputation, he is decent and properly prone to shame, and if he has no fear of it, he has no feeling of disgrace" (*NE*, 1115a10). Likewise, the great fear we feel at committing "wanton aggression on children and women" is hardly a manifestation of cowardice but rather something right and fine. But other "bad things," Aristotle warns us, should not be feared at all, for instance, poverty or sickness, the reason being that they are not the result of vice and are not caused by ourselves. Not fearing poverty, however, does not amount to being brave, at least not in the primary or fullest sense of the term. Bravery, Aristotle maintains, is primarily manifested by fearlessness and confidence in times and acts of war, where the most frightening and terrifying condition is encountered: death. "Hence someone is called brave to the fullest extent if he is intrepid in facing a fine death and the immediate dangers that bring death – and this is above all true of the dangers of war" (*NE*, 1115a30–35). This person will feel fear but will nevertheless stand firm, being confident and hopeful. She will recognize that standing firm in these circumstances, at this time, and for this goal, is in accord with reason – "for the brave person's actions and feelings reflect what something is worth and what reason prescribes" (*NE*, 1115b15). Aristotle's account of bravery, as of many of the virtues, is highly nuanced and particularized, reflecting, he thinks, the complexity of life itself. Bravery is not a simple or straightforward matter, a fact clearly revealed in Aristotle's definition of bravery: "Hence whoever stands firm against the right things and fears the right things, for the right end, in the right way, at the right time, and is correspondingly confident, is the brave person ... " (*NE*, 1115b15).

Still another important detail, one already touched on in another context, emerges from Aristotle's discussion of bravery. It is easy, he thinks, to *simulate* bravery, to act as the brave person does without actually being brave. We can steel ourselves to stand firm even though we are excessively filled with fear; we sometimes stand firm because we are forced to do so by our superiors; or we impulsively rush into danger because of the emotion surging through us. In all these cases, we fail to act bravely because we do not act from the proper motive (in the right spirit, as we put it above). The brave person chooses to stand firm or to fight "because that is fine or because anything else is shameful" (*NE*, 1116a10). Virtue, we have been told, is a state that *decides*, that makes a choice, and the virtuous state makes a choice or decision for the right reason. The brave person must "aim at what is fine" in choosing to stand firm; such a person must not acquiesce to her superiors from a motive of fear, or be overrun by excitement. The brave person must decide to act as she does because reason counsels it and she thereby knows that it is fine; accordingly she acts to avoid doing something shameful and disgraceful.

Not only must the virtuous person act from the right motive, this person must, as we have seen, actually get pleasure from doing so. She must enjoy acting virtuously. This will happen when her character has been shaped in the right way through habituation. This fact about the virtuous person serves to distinguish her from still another individual who resembles her but in fact fails to be virtuous. This is the individual who is able to control herself and do what is fine and decent even though her feelings and emotions prompt her to go in the other direction. Such self-control is possible, Aristotle thinks, and it too is admirable. But it does not amount to acting virtuously, acting as a result of a disposition to seek the mean as determined by reason and to enjoy doing so.

The distinction we are considering here between the person of virtue and the person who exercises self-control in doing what is right is interesting because it throws more light on the difference between the ethics of Aristotle and the later "Kantian" notion of morality referred to above, a notion with which many of us operate today. If given a preference, Kant would have opted for the person of self-control over Aristotle's person of virtue: the former does her duty in spite of her desires to the contrary, thereby manifesting her ability to overcome her sensuous nature and to act as an autonomous moral agent. Aristotle's virtuous person, even though she does the right thing, gets pleasure from so doing, thereby making it difficult to know if she really did it for what Kant would consider the right reason (because it was her duty) or whether instead she did it because her physical person had been habituated to enjoy this kind of behavior. Aristotle's position clearly reflects his conviction that virtuous activity is a means to or, better, a constituent of the supreme good – happiness. Certainly if one behaves excellently and enjoys it, one is more likely to be happy than the person of great self-control who doesn't enjoy acting in the way required by excellence (virtue) but steels herself to do so anyway. The life of the latter person is one of constant struggle with the competing motives within her. The virtuous person faces no such struggle; her soul is unified and harmonious; she enjoys doing what she knows she must do in order to be virtuous. Such a person is truly *eudaimōn*, happy.

This concludes our discussion of the Aristotelian virtues of character. Before leaving the topic, however, it is good to reflect on the great originality of Aristotle's conception. What he is proposing in recommending a life of moral virtue is nothing less than the project of making an art of one's life, of using reason to shape one's inner being and outward behavior, polishing and perfecting them so as to obtain the proper proportions. Few of us today think that feelings, desires, and emotions need to be developed and cultivated; we simply accept most of them as they occur – as part of who we are. But this is to ignore that we are also rational creatures, or, if we do remember this, it is to keep our reason segregated from the rest of our personality. Aristotle's exciting suggestion is that reason works with the passions – to perfect them. Its role is not simply, as with Plato, to rule over them and keep them under control. Although Aristotle would admit that we can act wilfully and irrationally, there is no essential opposition between the passions and reason in his thought. He suggests a joint, cooperative venture between the two, with the passions serving as the raw material and reason operating as the hand of the artist, imposing form on the ingredients at hand, the result being a work of art, a life that manifests the best the raw material had in it and shows forth the genius of the artist. This is a bold and innovative conception of the moral life.

Voluntary, Involuntary, and Non-Voluntary Actions

In discussing the virtues of character, Aristotle highlights the notions of choice and action – selecting the behavior (and feelings as well, to the extent that we can be said to choose feelings and emotions) recommended by reason as the mean, and putting the prescription of reason into action. He rightly observes that such an account of the virtues presupposes that human beings can act voluntarily and thereby be responsible for their actions. As Aristotle notes, praise and blame are reserved for voluntary actions. Thus he enters into a pioneering investigation of voluntary behavior, a topic that is central to our understanding and evaluation of human action. The topic is also central from the point of view of jurisprudence and the philosophy of law. Our legal and judicial institutions apply punishments when people break the law, but these punishments, for the most part, are imposed only when lawbreakers voluntarily transgress a law. Given the unpleasantness of any punishment, and the severity of many, it is extremely important to know *when* a person breaks the law voluntarily. Aristotle's discussion of the topic introduces us to an issue that remains with us today – agonizingly so, given its practical importance and the fact that it is not easy to resolve. But Aristotle certainly took great strides toward resolving it.[20]

He singles out two conditions that render an action involuntary: force and ignorance. Force is the application of causes outside the personality of the person who acts: "what is forced has an external origin, the sort of origin in which the agent or victim contributes nothing – if, e.g., a wind or human beings who control him were to carry him off" (*NE*, 1110a1). Clearly, if we are carried off by a wind, we don't go voluntarily. If a wind blows our car into another, thereby causing us to have an accident, we do not voluntarily bring harm to the people in the other car. In a case like this, the driver of the car that bumps the other one "contributes nothing" to the accident. Likewise, a group of criminals may forcefully place an innocent person at the scene of a crime; this person for all that does not voluntarily participate in the crime. Hence when someone is caused to do something by powers outside herself, she can be said to act involuntarily.

Aristotle notes that there are cases in which we act under the influence of external causes (under duress, we would say) but still seem to act voluntarily. If a bank cashier hands over money after being told "Your money or your life" by an armed robber, external force is certainly being applied. But the cashier's action reflects the decision or the feelings of the cashier herself, and so she does contribute something to the action: "for in these sorts of actions he has within him the origin of the movement of the limbs that are the instruments of the action" (*NE*, 1110a15) – this origin, in many instances, being fear. In this respect, then, the cashier's action is voluntary. Aristotle calls such actions *mixed*; they are both voluntary and involuntary. But on the whole he considers them voluntary, and he argues for this conclusion by noting that we often praise or blame people who commit mixed actions (praise and blame being properly assigned, let us recall, only to voluntary actions). To take another example of a mixed action, imagine that we are on a sinking ship and throw all our possessions into the sea in order to lighten the load. Our action, although mixed, is on the whole voluntary. Although none of us would voluntarily throw away our possessions just to be doing so, the benefits attending to the act on *this* occasion – an occasion forced upon us – are enough to render it voluntary. Such acts, Aristotle tells us, are, after all, "choiceworthy."

While it seems reasonable to agree with Aristotle that an act whose origin is outside the agent is one which the person does involuntarily, it is frequently more difficult than it might seem to determine when this condition is satisfied. Mixed actions – in which there are both external and internal causes operating – give us an example of this difficulty. Moreover, could there not be actions whose origin was totally within an agent but which were nevertheless involuntary? Think of cases in which the internal cause is an obsession, a desire or wish that the agent cannot control or rid herself of. Isn't an obsession a sort of internal coercive force, and doesn't its presence lead us to deny that the agent who acts as a result of it does so voluntarily? Think of a person who compulsively washes her hands, or someone obsessed with the idea that she is Mary the mother of God – do they act voluntarily? Although Aristotle does not consider such cases, it might be possible to expand his notion of involuntary *forced* acts to include them.

Another condition that renders an act involuntary, according to Aristotle, is ignorance. If I do not know what I am doing, or do not know that doing such a thing has a certain effect, I do not engage in the act voluntarily. But the ignorance must be of a special kind. As Aristotle points out, "every vicious person is ignorant of the actions he must do or avoid" (*NE*, 1110b25) – namely the right or good ones – but this lack of moral knowledge does not render an act involuntary. It is ignorance "of particulars" regarding the action, its context, and its results which make an action involuntary (*NE*, 1111a1). If, in giving my aging aunt a cup of tea which unbeknownst to me contains arsenic, I bring about her death, I do not do so voluntarily. If someone shoots his son, mistakenly thinking him a burglar, his act is involuntary. Aristotle lists the following kinds of particulars relevant to any action: "They are: (1) who is doing it; (2) what he is doing; (3) about what or to what he is doing it; (4) sometimes also what he is doing it with, e.g., the instrument; (5) for what result, e.g., safety; (6) in what way, e.g., gently or hard" (*NE*, 1111a1-5). Although in acting one would presumably not be ignorant that it was oneself engaging in the act, and one would not be ignorant of *all* of the other relevant particulars unless one "were mad," ignorance of some subset of (2)–(6) is always possible, and "someone who was ignorant of one of these seems to have done an act unwillingly" (*NE*, 1111a15).

Aristotle distinguishes between an act being done in ignorance and one done because of ignorance. A drunken person may be ignorant of what she is doing, but the cause of her actions is her inebriated state, not her ignorance. But when a father shoots his son, thinking him a burglar, it is his false belief about the intruder (the false belief that he is a burglar) that causes him to act. In this case, the cause of his action is his ignorance. Only in the latter kind of case should we say that the person acted involuntarily.

Aristotle adds an important rider to the claim that an act is involuntary if it is done out of ignorance of the particulars. Under these conditions it is involuntary only if the agent, on learning of what she has done (on learning the facts), comes to regret the act or is pained at having done it. If there is no such regret or pain, the action done out of ignorance becomes, as Aristotle calls it, a non-voluntary act. He uses this additional regret/pain criterion for voluntariness to respond to a possible objection to his account. There are those who would claim that when we act, we always seek what is pleasant, or we seek to satisfy our desires or appetites. The desire for pleasure or the need to satisfy our appetites, although internal, *controls* our behavior and renders it involuntary – so goes the objection. We cannot prevent ourselves from acting as these motives prompt us to act, and therefore we act involuntarily. Aristotle responds by saying that actions of this type actually please us – as a result of the pleasure obtained or the satisfaction of the desire or appetite involved. Accordingly, they cannot be involuntary, insofar as an involuntary action must be one that leads to regret or pain. One does not act *unwillingly* if the cause of the action is internal (such as an emotion or appetite) and one is pleased to have acted in such a manner. This latter criterion might allow us to deal more decisively with the notion of inner compulsions considered above. If we are pained by the result of a compulsion, our act could be called involuntary; if we are not pained, our act could be classified as voluntary or non–voluntary.

The Virtues of Practical Reason

We should recall at this point that Aristotle divides the soul into irrational and rational parts. So far we have considered the virtues of the irrational soul, or at least that segment of it capable of listening to and following reason. Now we need to consider the rational soul itself and to identify its virtues, its ways of performing excellently so as to fulfill its function (*ergon*). These virtues are, we shall see, wisdom, intelligence, understanding, and comprehension.

In general, the function of the rational soul is the intellectual one of reasoning. But reasoning, according to Aristotle, comes in two forms. First, there is pure *theoretical reasoning* whose aim is to ascertain the essential, unchanging laws of the universe, i.e., to understand "beings whose origins do not admit of being otherwise than they are" (*NE*, 1139a5). This is the activity of the "scientific part" of reason. Its task is to grasp truths about those eternal things that could not be otherwise. Second, there is what Aristotle calls the "rationally calculating part," the part often referred to today as *practical reason*. Its job is to assist the soul in attaining *eudaimonia*. Practical reason investigates what is "up to us," what is temporal and variable, namely the actions we may or may not perform, and it advises us of the rational course of action. What we need to do is to ascertain the virtues of the two parts of reason – "we should find the best state of the scientific and the best state of the rationally calculating part; for this state is the virtue of each of them" (*NE*, 1139a15). The virtues of reason in general will be those modes of thought or states of mind which permit it to perform its scientific and practical tasks in the most excellent fashion. Theoretical reasoning will achieve virtue (excellence) when it grasps the truth about the way things in the world are and cannot fail to be. It will then manifest *sophia*, theoretical wisdom. The goal of practical reason being to assist the individual in attaining *eudaimonia*, it will manifest its virtues when it assists the character of a person in making correct decisions and engaging in correct actions. In doing so, it will reveal practical wisdom or intelligence (*phronēsis*).

Let us consider first some of the details of Aristotle's theory of practical reason.[21] As we shall see, there are two ways in which practical reason operates in the pursuit of *eudaimonia*. But first, some general characteristics of this form of reasoning can be noted. Practical reason manifests itself in *deliberation*, and it functions well when its activity expresses the virtue of *intelligence*. "It seems proper ... to an intelligent person to be able to deliberate finely about what is good and beneficial for himself, not [merely] about some restricted area – e.g., about what promotes health or strength

– but about what promotes living well in general" (*NE*, 1140a25). Thus the intelligent person does not have a narrow focus but rather is able to take her whole life into consideration. The end is the attainment of happiness. Unlike craft-knowledge, which aims at producing some object, intelligence aims only at producing the correct *action*. Actions are those things that are up to us and may or may not occur. Intelligence, then, is neither science nor craft-knowledge. Deliberation yields *decision*, and this decision is the origin of action. Aristotle defines decision as "a deliberative desire" (*NE*, 1139a20), since action, he maintains, is always motivated by *desire*, never by thought or belief alone – "Thought by itself ... moves nothing" (*NE*, 1139a35). As Aristotle claims at the very beginning of the book, we always act to attain an end, and desire or wish is "for the end" (*NE*, 1113a15), or as he tells us later, "desire is for the goal" (*NE*, 1139b1). But thought or reason must enter the picture as we deliberate over what to desire.

The first job of practical reason is to give guidance to the appetites, feelings, and emotions of the irrational soul, to direct this soul to those feelings and actions that constitute the mean in particular situations. There is, Aristotle believes, a sort of natural virtue in us that inclines us toward virtuous actions, but natural virtue is not virtue in the fullest and most precise sense. To attain the latter, deliberation is required. Deliberation involves an interplay of reason and desire. For one thing, reason can prioritize ends and thereby realign desires. Deliberation thus leads to desire molded or directed by reason, and when a decision is reached, the resultant deliberative desire is what moves one to act. When the decision is excellent "the reason must be true and the desire correct, so that what reason asserts is what desire pursues" (*NE*, 1139a20–25).

When well done, deliberation will include the virtues of *comprehension* and *understanding*. One role of deliberation, as we have just seen, is to determine the mean with regard to feelings or actions in specific contexts. To do this, it must be able to grasp or take into account all relevant aspects of the situation the agent finds herself in, thereby ascertaining the nature of the circumstances which bear upon proper or virtuous action. Doing this well amounts to comprehension, putting together the components of a complex situation in their proper relationships. Comprehension provides us with correct judgments about the nature and context of actions and feelings. Once a situation is comprehended in this fashion, the agent must be able to see what the moral demands of the situation are, i.e., what the proportionate action or feeling would be. Here, Aristotle thinks, we manifest intelligence if we come up with the correct decision or, as he sometimes expresses it, the correct prescription to action. General rules or principles of action may be appealed to in arriving at this decision, but since practical reason is concerned with particulars – particular situations and particular acts – we cannot simply rely on general rules to tell us what to do. There are three reasons for this. First, rules, being general, do not by themselves identify what specific actions we are to take. Second, no rules can encompass all the specific and changing detail of the circumstances of action. Third, rules must be applied to particular situations, and because of the first two factors, their application is never "mechanical" but demands an "eye" for what is required in the particular situation, i.e., for seeing this situation "aright." In order to arrive at a correct decision we must rely on a form of direct insight which, in light of the picture of the complex particulars already achieved through comprehension, yields an indication of what act or feeling would be the mean. We *see*, that is to say, what the overall situation demands of us with respect to the mean. Aristotle refers to this direct insight as a form of perception. He also suggests that it is the manifestation of the virtue of understanding in the practical sphere (*NE*, 1143b5). So, comprehension and understanding (of the perceptual variety) cooperate to determine the virtuous act or feeling. Together they constitute *phronēsis*.

Aristotle is notorious for his claim that deliberation is always focused on *means*, never on ends: "We deliberate not about ends, but about what promotes ends" (*NE*, 1112b10). His thinking here is not easy to understand, but it does suggest that in all deliberation there is some end that is presupposed and not itself debated. In our discussion above regarding deliberations aimed at identifying the mean of feeling and action, the end presupposed is that of happiness, since pursuing the mean is the way to promote happiness. Happiness itself is not in dispute: we do not deliberate over whether to be happy; we don't decide to be happy.

Deliberation and the Practical Syllogism

Deliberation about means is most obviously at work in the second activity of practical reason. Sometimes what we decide to do or feel will require that we take intermediary steps in order to accomplish a particular action or display a particular emotion. In cases such as these, deliberation is clearly about means and not ends. The exhibition of courage, for example, will require steps to be taken in preparation for battle; a life of temperance will necessitate that we take those actions needed to obtain the right amount of exercise, and so on. In ascertaining what these intermediary steps are, our deliberations will sometimes take the form of a *practical syllogism*.[22] A practical syllogism typically has a major premise which stipulates that certain kinds of things are good or desired, a minor premise which identifies a way of achieving one of these goods, and a conclusion which requires one to engage in an action of this kind.[23] Such deliberation is a matter of calculating the means (not *the mean*, which is the intermediate between excess and deficiency) to achieving a goal – in this case, the goal of virtuous action and happiness.

Correctness in practical reasoning consists, then, of two accomplishments. First, it must lead an agent to aim at what truly is good; it must, that is, identify a mean in action or feeling which is a component of happiness. Second, if this good that is aimed at cannot be accomplished directly, deliberation must identify the intermediary steps to be taken in order to accomplish it. Additionally, for the process of reasoning involved in these two undertakings to be correct, it must follow principles of valid argumentation and avoid false or invalid inferences. Thus, Aristotle concludes, "if having deliberated well is proper to an intelligent person, good deliberation will be the type of correctness that expresses what is expedient for promoting the end about which intelligence is true supposition" (*NE*, 1142b30). In other words, we deliberate well if we come up with a true (intelligent) thought about what end – what action or feeling (as a component of happiness) – we should pursue and if we identify the best, most expedient means for achieving this end.

Let us consider an example of deliberation. I may come to believe my physician's argument when he tells me that high cholesterol levels are dangerous and can be reduced by exercise. Thus I may accept the following "universal" statements or propositions: (1) "High cholesterol levels are dangerous and should be avoided" and "High cholesterol levels can be reduced by exercise." I also may come to accept my physician's claim that I have a high cholesterol level. Thus I assert the "particular" proposition: (2) "My high cholesterol level can be reduced by exercise" or "My exercising will reduce my high cholesterol level". If I deliberate intelligently about the matter, I shall draw the conclusion (3) "I ought to exercise" (or, as Aristotle suggests, I shall simply engage in the act of exercising – *if* I am a virtuous, i.e., intelligent, person). Propositions (1), (2), and (3) constitute a practical syllogism, and it is a syllogism like this which expresses intelligent deliberation over the means to virtuous activity. It has a universal premise (or premises) – what Aristotle calls the major premise – and a particular premise – what he calls the minor premise – and its conclusion is particular. The universal premise gives one a general truth or supposition about an end or a means to an end; the particular premise points to a specific act which is a means to this end, or an instance of the means identified in the major premise; and the conclusion indicates the particular act that is called for in light of the premises. It should be noted that if the minor premise were also universal, e.g., "low cholesterol levels prevent heart disease", no particular conclusion about a specific individual taking a concrete action could be derived from the major and minor premises. Thus a practical syllogism that ends with a recommendation to action must include general statements *and* particular statements. A practical syllogism is valid if the conclusion follows from the premises. In the example at hand, the conclusion that I should exercise follows from (1) and (2).

Of course, the practical syllogism we have been examining is only part of what arises from the exercise of intelligence. A person who becomes involved in this reasoning must also identify good health as a constituent of happiness *and* determine the amount of exercise that is appropriate. The latter task involves determining *the mean* with regard to exercise. Too much exercise is not an intelligent response to the knowledge that I have a high cholesterol level and must exercise to avoid this dangerous condition; neither is the deficient amount of exercise I now engage in. If I am intelligent, I will determine what amount is right for me, given my problem, my physical constitution, my current circumstances, and so on – and the right amount will be the mean between excess and deficiency.

Weakness of Will

As we all know from personal experience, determining what one ought to do with regard to activities like exercise does not always, in spite of one's best intentions, lead one to do these things. I may know that I ought to exercise thirty minutes a day and still not do so – my will may be weak. The problem of weakness of the will is one which concerned Socrates, Plato, and Aristotle: it is the problem of *akrasia* or incontinence, not doing what we know is good for us or doing what we know is not good for us. Socrates, we should recall, denied that *akrasia* ever occurs, since it would involve acting contrary to the knowledge of what is required to obtain a good or benefit. Plato, in separating the faculties of reason and appetite and setting them against one another, generated a psychological theory that explained how, contrary to Socrates and, for once, in accordance with accepted opinion, *akrasia* can and does occur. Aristotle agrees with Plato that Socrates' position is contrary to the facts, and he sets out to show how, given his own psychological theory, *akrasia* or incontinence can occur. One must ask oneself, however, if Aristotle really doesn't end up agreeing with Socrates. In fact, some scholars have argued that Aristotle tries to show how *both* Socrates and accepted opinion are correct on this score.[24]

Aristotle's approach to the problem involves making a distinction between two ways in which we can "have knowledge" (*NE*, 1146b30). A scientist who is verifying a certain physical theory in her laboratory knows her subject matter in a way different from the way she knows it when she is asleep. In the laboratory, she is actually aware of certain truths and facts; while asleep she is not aware of these things, although she has the capacity to call them to mind (to know them in the first sense) later on. Furthermore, a person knows the traffic laws in one way when she is awake, sober, alert, and driving with the full intention of obeying them; she knows these laws in a different sense when she driving while drunk. In the latter case, she still has a knowledge of these laws, but being drunk her knowledge is veiled by her state of inebriation. It is Aristotle's claim that when we suffer from weakness of the will we know what we ought to do but we know it in the second sense and not the first; we know it in a manner particularly like that in which the drunk driver knows how she ought to drive.

For Aristotle, weakness of the will is a matter of appetite clouding our knowledge of the minor premise of the practical syllogism whose conclusion indicates what we ought to do in our present situation. Returning to our example of exercise and high cholesterol levels, let us give an Aristotelian explanation of why, knowing what I do about high cholesterol levels in general and my own physical condition, I nevertheless do not engage in moderate exercise. Part of the appetitive aspect of my soul is a preference for the sedentary life and a strong distaste for energetic physical activity. This appetitive state leads me to "ignore" the particular fact that *I* have a high cholesterol level. I may do so by various forms of rationalization, e.g., saying to myself that the tests for cholesterol may have been in error, or that even if they were accurate I will be an exception to the rule, or that exercise is unnecessary in my case since I fully intend to go on a strict diet next week, and so on. In these ways, the full impact of the minor premise, "I have a high cholesterol level", is blunted to the extent that I am no longer fully aware of it. Not that I have forgotten it – it is simply clouded over by the presence of my aversion for exercise and my taste for physical inactivity. If these desires were not present, or if they were under control, I would fully realize that I am in a dangerous condition and consequently I would do something about it. My will is weak, I fail to do what my practical reasoning tells me to do, because the full impact of this practical reasoning is veiled from me by desire. This is a fault of my character – my feelings and actions are not being shaped by *phronēsis*, the excellent operation of practical reasoning. "The incontinent person knows that his actions are base, but does them because of his feelings, while the continent person knows that his appetites are base, but because of reason does not follow them" (*NE*, 1145b10).

The Virtues of Theoretical Reason

It remains for us to examine the virtues of the other aspect of reason, the part that is theoretical rather than practical: reason aimed at ascertaining the truth about the nature of things. In order to understand the virtues of theoretical reason, we must briefly describe the way in which Aristotle pictures the operation of this form of reason. Science, the knowledge of reality, he views as a deductive system of propositions similar in structure to the deductive system of geometry. In the case of geometry, we have a system of propositions – theorems, they are called – which follow logically or deductively from a set of propositions referred to as axioms. To say that the theorems follow deductively from the axioms is to claim that if the axioms are true, the theorems also must be true. If, for instance, parallel lines, which by definition are always an equal distance apart, never intersect, then a line intersecting one of them at a right angle will intersect the other at a right angle as well. In a deductive system, the truth of the axioms is transferred to the theorems that follow from them. What about the axioms themselves? These propositions are usually characterized as self-evident, so that their denial is necessarily false. "Parallel lines never intersect" is such a self-evident, necessarily true axiom. If such an axiom is and must be true, and if the theorems following from it must be true if the axiom is true, we can conclude with certainty that the theorems also are and must be true.

According to Aristotle, the science of nature has the same structure. It consists of a set of axiomatic laws about the very general nature of things, together with more specific laws that follow deductively from the axioms. Given this understanding of natural science, theoretical knowledge will be achieved through the exercise of two epistemic capacities. First there is the ability to think logically and derive theorems from axioms and then to derive still more specific theorems from the more general ones. Aristotle calls this "scientific knowledge." Additionally, there must be the capacity to see that the axioms are self-evidently true. This is done through a kind of intellectual intuition or mental perception (similar to what we saw at work in determining the proper course of action in a complex situation). Aristotle refers to the exercise of this capacity as *understanding*. Theoretical knowledge, then, consists of understanding plus scientific knowledge. When reason in its theoretical capacity is functioning well, achieving both understanding and scientific knowledge, it is manifesting the virtue of *wisdom* (*sophia*).

Aristotle makes it clear that *sophia* is concerned only with knowing the nature of things, not with productive knowledge (what we might call technology) or with action. It consists of a knowledge of universals – propositions about general types of things holding true universally – rather than, as is the case with practical reason, particulars (specific actions occurring at particular times and places). Scientific, theoretical knowledge aims at truth, at demonstrating what the general nature of things is. Practical reason, concerned as it is with action, aims at the good, the object of intelligent desire and feeling. As we have already noted, thought or scientific knowledge alone *moves nothing* – it simply lays out the eternal nature of things and does not by itself motivate a person to action. Only practical knowledge motivates and moves us to action, since it is driven by desire for an end.

It may appear to us today that the employment of reason in its practical and productive (technological) modes is at least as important, if not more so, than the operation of theoretical reason. Just the opposite was the case for Aristotle. He suggests that the life devoted to scientific knowledge, which he calls the life of study (sometimes translators refer to it as the life of contemplation), is the highest form of life, and, when it achieves the virtue of wisdom, the highest form of happiness. Indeed, in Book X of the *Ethics* he implies that the perfect life would be one devoted to study alone, with only minimal attention given to the nutritive and appetitive dimensions of the soul – just enough to allow a person to concentrate on the important matter of study.[25] Clearly he himself, being the great philosopher he was, preferred the life of study, the life of philosophizing and the pursuit of theoretical knowledge. He also notes that theoretical reason is godlike in nature, and hence it is what places us closest to the gods (whose activity, according to Aristotle, consists solely in contemplation). He concludes in Book X of the *Ethics* that the excellence of contemplation is the best of the various excellences and thus should be the dominant end we seek. But in other passages (and especially in the *Eudemian Ethics* when he is attending more to the average person than to the philosopher), he explicitly recognizes that happiness pertains to the human being as a whole. From this perspective, while theoretical wisdom may still be thought of as the highest virtue, it is not the equivalent of happiness since it is not self-sufficient. We are agents as well as thinkers, and from the perspective of the whole person, the virtues of character and the intellectual virtues constituting *phronēsis* are as essential as the virtue of theoretical wisdom.

It is clear why Aristotle ranks theoretical reason and knowledge so high. Early on in the *Nicomachean Ethics*, in seeking to define human happiness by identifying the human *ergon* (function), he does so by ascertaining what is distinctive about human beings, what sets them apart from all other creatures. We share the nutritive soul – procreation, nourishment, and growth – with all other forms of life, and we share appetite and some feelings with members of the animal kingdom. It is reason which sets us apart. One aspect of this reason is still tied to our animal nature – reason in its practical activity as a guide to feeling and action. Only theoretical reason and scientific knowledge truly distinguish us from the rest of nature. Hence this form of activity must be the human *ergon*, since nothing else in the natural world possesses the capacity for understanding and deductive scientific knowledge. If happiness is the well-functioning of the activities constituting the human *ergon*, then human happiness *is* study or contemplation. In achieving it, Aristotle tells us, we come as close as possible to the gods. It would be absurd, after all, to attribute virtues of character to the gods – they have no appetites that require temperance, no feelings of fear that require courage, and so on. The life of the gods can only be spent in contemplation, for they lack all material substance and are identical with pure reason itself. Human beings are not gods, but in pursuing a life dedicated to study and contemplation, they come as close to them as possible. In reading Aristotle, one wonders whether his aim is first and foremost to emulate the gods, or whether it is to seek the perfection appropriate for human beings with their dual nature. He can be read both ways.

Aristotle's Metaphysics

We shall conclude this discussion of Aristotle's ethics by briefly relating his ethical theory to his metaphysical picture of the nature of things in general, his picture of being *qua* being, as he put it in his definition of metaphysics. For Aristotle, nature consists of many individual substances, finite spatio–temporal entities which can be divided, at least in thought or by abstraction, into a material base and sensible and intelligible forms. The *forms* of an individual substance are what make it the kind of thing it is. These forms are the successors to Plato's eternal, non-spatial, separate Forms – Aristotle has brought them down to earth and turned them into the perceptible and intelligible characteristics of an individual, the properties which give an individual its identity as a being of a certain sort. The *matter* of a substance is the "stuff" out of which it is composed, the raw material which is shaped into a particular, distinctive thing by the thing's form.

In rounding out his picture of the universe, Aristotle postulates that, in addition to individual substances, there must be something out of which all of them arise. This something he refers to as *prime matter*, matter devoid of any form. At the other end of the spectrum, there is pure form, form that is not embodied in matter. This pure form is said to be identical with God. Aristotle's primary interest, and certainly ours in this study of ethics, is with the natural world of individual substances – those combinations of matter and form existing between prime matter and God. (We have seen, however, how the gods can complicate the picture for him in his search for an understanding of happiness.)

Aristotle the careful observer of nature could not help but be aware of the ever-present fact of change. All individual substances undergo change, losing one form or set of forms and taking on another. Consider, for example, the life of an individual human being. As it grows from baby to child, to adult, and then into a geriatric case, this individual substance changes its form: its size, its shape, its behavioral patterns, its thoughts, its feelings and emotions, and so on. Aristotle was interested in how we can explain this puzzling process of change. The puzzle, the problem of change, is the difficulty of understanding how something can become something other than what it already is and still remain the same individual throughout the process. How can I as a dour old man be the same as the smiling, bouncing babe of years past? Aristotle's answer is that a person *becomes* what she already *is*, that is to say, what she already is *potentially*. All the properties of the adult human being are already present in the babe and child, but in a state of potentiality, not actuality. Change is a matter of actualizing one's potentialities, a matter of actually becoming, becoming in fact, what one potentially is. Change can be understood, then, as a matter of realizing in actuality some of the forms one already has within oneself as potentialities. We may have multiple potentialities within us, but we actualize them only one at a time.

This brief sketch of Aristotle's metaphysics allows us to see why he is often said to offer us an ethical theory of self-realization. The moral life is devoted to achieving a certain character and a certain life of feeling, emotion, and action, together with an excellent intellectual life. These features of character, action, and thought are distinctive forms which turn us into specific kinds of persons (individual substances). We have these forms in us from the beginning as potentialities, and they come to realization as they become our actual features. The moral life aims to bring to realization, to actuality, the forms that make us essentially who we are, these being the forms of practical and theoretical rationality. We are essentially rational animals, even if in the early, immature stages of our lives we are only potentially rational.

Given that adult human life involves choice, we must choose correctly if we are to realize our essential potentialities and become what we essentially are. And we may, of course, choose incorrectly, thereby failing to actualize those potentialities and instead actualizing others. The study of ethics is to assist us in making the right choices and thereby in actualizing the potentialities that will make us the distinctive creatures we are. For Aristotle, this means that ethics will assist us in making choices that bring about our self-realization as rational animals. The mark of self-realization is happiness: the person who has actualized her essential potentialities is the happy person.

Aristotle himself did not draw the systematic connections between his metaphysics and his ethics. But when these lines of thought are made explicit, they reveal a philosophy that is profound and impressive in scope and coherence, and in its overall intelligibility and explanatory power. To the extent that Aristotle's ethical theory can be seen to fit together with his metaphysical picture of the general nature of things, his ethics gains in power. But this fit also, alas, makes the ethics vulnerable to the problems that attend the metaphysics. We shall conclude our discussion of Aristotle with a brief mention of some of the problems, metaphysical and otherwise, that scholars find in his ethics.

Criticism of Aristotle

One of Aristotle's more sympathetic critics, Alasdair MacIntyre, notes that the ethical theory rests on a metaphysical base, and he judges this base to be unacceptable in the contemporary world. "Aristotle's ethics," he writes, "presupposes his metaphysical biology."[26] MacIntyre describes this metaphysical biology as follows: "Human beings, like the members of all other species, have a specific nature; and that nature is such that they have certain aims and goals, such that they move by nature toward a specific *telos*. The good is defined in terms of their specific characteristics."[27] Presumably the metaphysical biology involves assumptions about the natural *telos* of reason as well as the *telos* of the various emotions. MacIntyre himself thinks it possible to provide an alternative account of the *telos* of a human being that does not take it to be universal (but accepts the facts of historical change) and grounds it in something other than biology (namely the social practices that make up the bulk of human activity). Whether he succeeds in this is another matter, but in rejecting Aristotle's teleological biology he has identified one of the main problems with Aristotle's ethics. We can develop this criticism in the following ways.

Do human beings really have a essence, or is it not in fact the case that they really have only a range of merely similar properties? Consider that Aristotelian *sine qua non* of the human species: rationality. Are all human beings rational – in anything like the same way? Isn't it in fact the case that different human beings possess this feature in very different ways, ranging from a very rudimentary level of mentality to genius? Aristotle is committed to a view called essentialism, which maintains that there are sets of necessary and sufficient conditions that must be satisfied for any individual substance to fall into a specific genus and species, a specific natural kind of thing. Individual persons, he thinks, must possess rationality as their essence in order to fall into the natural kind: human being. This theory has been widely criticized in recent years by philosophers who point out that only vague resemblances tend to link human beings to one another. There is no specific property of rationality found in all of us. Moreover, what individuals we decide to place in the class of human beings is not determined, as Aristotle thinks, by the presence of a natural kind in the world. Our classification scheme is arbitrary in as much as it is we ourselves, not nature, who draw the line between what falls into the class of rational beings and what falls outside it. In fact, different people, with different interests and needs, may well draw the line in different places. Is a fetus, for example, a human being? People today tend to disagree over the answer to this question, and it is unclear whether there is a "fact of the matter" in nature – a natural kind – to which we can appeal in order to resolve the issue.

But even if we have an Aristotelian essence, why must one identify it, as Aristotle did, with the distinctive feature of human beings – which is, according to him, reason?

Perhaps reason is just a feature we have that enables us to attain some other characteristic which is our essential nature – a follower of Darwin's theory of evolution might see this essential feature as survival and might interpret reason as one of many features in the animal kingdom promoting survival.[28]

Or why say, as Aristotle does, that the achievement of happiness is the hallmark of our having realized our essence? Perhaps the most brilliant intellects – the most rational creatures among us – are those who, capable of understanding life, become profoundly pessimistic and miserable. In their cases, they realize their Aristotelian essence, but they by no means become happy as a result of doing so. Their very rationality may reveal to them that life is meaningless and worthless – and this insight may justify to their minds the attitudes of withdrawal, indifference, and passivity (hardly the kind of responses required by Aristotle's concept of happiness).

And this happiness Aristotle talks about – has he described what it really is for all human beings? Or has he produced a conception of happiness that merely reflects the values of his own society, and perhaps those of other Western societies later influenced by the Greek model? Does the Aristotelian conception of happiness have universal validity?

Finally, has Aristotle really given us any help in determining concretely what happiness consists in? He tells us that it is a life of activity in accordance with virtue and that the virtues of character are to lead us to select the mean with respect to feeling and action. We are to feel the right amount of emotion or feeling in the context in which we find ourselves – but how do we know what the right amount is? All that Aristotle tells us is that it is relative to us and to the circumstances. The actual mean is to be ascertained by reason, but how do we know when this reason is working correctly? Have we no independent standard of the mean by appeal to which we can determine whether or not reason has judged correctly or incorrectly on a particular occasion. If Aristotle's response is that reason can be considered correct when it is that of a good or virtuous person, or when it accords with the good person's judgment, this assumes we know how to determine who is a good and virtuous person. But do we? Don't we need an independent standard for someone being this kind of individual? Does Aristotle give us this standard?

These are some of the questions a thoughtful student of Aristotle ought to raise. Aristotle may have given answers to these questions, but if so they are not obvious answers. Still and all, the profundity and reasonableness of Aristotle's ethics are so impressive that they surely require us to study the *Nicomachean Ethics* closely and carefully to see if we can find those answers.

4

Hellenistic Ethics: Epicurus and the Stoics

The period in the history of Greek and Graeco-Roman philosophy from the death of Alexander the Great (323 BCE) to the beginning of the Christian era is conventionally referred to as the Hellenistic period, whereas Greek philosophy prior to this time is categorized as falling into the Hellenic period. Most philosophers are inclined to view the Hellenistic period as inferior to the earlier, Hellenic one: the philosophies developed during it are thought to be largely derivative and less profound. If popular appeal is taken into account, however, Hellenistic philosophy must rank high, especially in the area of ethics. Two ethical theories, Epicureanism and Stoicism, emerged at this time and made a profound impact on the thought of the period, exerting influence far beyond the academic circles of the philosophers themselves. Although less influential in the subsequent history of thought than Platonism and Aristotelianism, they nevertheless remained live options in ethics throughout the centuries, and today they continue to find an appreciative audience.

Hedonism

It is difficult for contemporary readers, especially those who have observed Plato and Aristotle struggling with the complexity of human life in an effort to provide a recipe for happiness, to comprehend how the philosophy of hedonism came to exert such influence in the period after Aristotle's death. Hedonism appears to be a relatively simple, if not outright simplistic, view of the good life: it equates happiness with the attainment of pleasure and the avoidance of pain. Both Plato and Aristotle had stressed the inadequacy of such a philosophy of life; both of them thought that, while some pleasures are good, others are bad. Nevertheless, hedonism attracted many followers, and the most important hedonist of this time, Epicurus, opened a school in Athens, the Garden of Epicurus, which rivaled Plato's Academy and Aristotle's Lyceum in influence and remained vital for 500 years.

There is a standard historical explanation of the success of hedonism (and Stoicism as well), although it is one that can be challenged.[1] Alexander the Great, the Macedonian emperor whose empire extended from the northern part of Africa to the borders of India, completely changed the nature of life in Greece. Before Alexander, the *polis* or city-state had been the model of political organization throughout Greece. After Alexander, the city-states lost their authority, which passed to the centralized power of the empire. This dramatic political change entailed an equally drastic change for the Greeks in their modes of personal existence. Their basic ideas of human life, success, and happiness had been bound up with the political order of the city-state. It was within this unit that life was lived and had its meaning. Individuals, unless they happened to be slaves or barbarians (non-Greek speakers), lived their lives as citizens of a *polis*, and the role of citizen could not be clearly distinguished from the more personal aspects of life. One's identity and success were defined by one's participation in the life of the city-state with which one was affiliated. After Alexander, the city-state effectively disappeared: it lost its political authority and, as a result, its influence over the lives of its citizens. Without this source of identity, many Greeks experienced a sense of alienation, rootlessness, and meaninglessness. All of the ancient certainties were gone, and the individual was thrown back on her own resources of mind and body. Moreover, the political chaos that followed the death of Alexander subjected the Greeks to constant threats of subjugation, poverty, and death. These were harrowing times, and they called for radical, dramatic philosophies of life, not the patient, painstaking, and subtly reasoned accounts developed by Plato and Aristotle.

One response to such a threatening environment was to forget about the appeal of the contemplative life, which required peace and prosperity, to forget about the virtues, which only suited one for a successful life in the city-state, and to get down to basics. Life was short, the future uncertain – thus the only reasonable thing to do in such circumstances was to grab for oneself as much of life as possible. And for many Greeks "as much of life" meant "as much of pleasure." Maximize personal pleasure, make it as intense as possible, enjoy the moment to the fullest: such a recommendation had the ring of realism about it. After all, what else was there to live for?

Aristippus and the Cyrenaics

There were philosophers who spread this very message even before the Hellenistic period. They were called Cyrenaics; their leader was Aristippus (c. 435–355 BCE) of Cyrene, a city located in northern Africa. The Cyrenaics' philosophy was one of maximizing pleasure – attaining as much of it as possible in as intense a form as possible. Ironically, they saw themselves as followers of Socrates, whom they interpreted as stressing the life of individual happiness. Aristippus was a student and disciple of Socrates; he was also known as a Sophist by virtue of traveling from city to city offering instruction for fees (for which, we are told, Socrates rebuked him). When he returned to his native Cyrene – a city widely known for its pleasant quality of life – he too established a school in which he taught the principle doctrines of Cyrenaicism (whose name came from the name of Aristippus's home town).

None of Aristippus's writings are extant, and so we have only a sketchy idea of his philosophy. It appears that he preached that pleasure is the natural goal of life – the one thing that all human beings innately and always pursue. They seek pleasure instinctively and without reflection, although frequently, as a result of religious and philosophical influences, they can be perverted and led to deny (hypocritically) that pleasure is their one and only true goal. But in point of fact it is their natural pursuit, and the rational person will admit as much and turn her attention to the deliberate and vigorous cultivation of pleasure. "Seize the moment" – do not delay gratification – seems to have been the counsel of Aristippus. In an uncertain universe, take one's pleasures now – tomorrow may be too late. When asked about the painful consequences his life-style might entail, Aristippus shrugged them off, saying that he was unwilling to give up the *certainties* of present pleasure simply because of the *possible* pains to be incurred thereafter. The pleasures of reflection and contemplation – so often praised by philosophers – are in fact pale and slight: better to pursue the more robust and intense pleasures afforded by the human body – those of food, drink, and sex. Reason is important, yes, but its importance lies in the fact that, using all the knowledge at its command, it can increase the number of pleasures available to us. Aristippus is said to have maintained that we should not become slaves to pleasure: "it is not abstinence from pleasures that is best, but mastery over them without ever being worsted"[2] This statement may seem to imply an admiration for self-control – but it really suggests only that if we are "worsted by pleasure" we lose the ability to *increase* the amount of pleasure we can experience. By mastering pleasure, by using reason to seek out the most pleasure and most intense pleasures, we assure ourselves of getting the most out of life.

Aristippus's thinking should not be ignored or quickly dismissed. It represents a way of thought that has always been appealing and influential, especially in times when the "eternal verities" – those traditional values which give a broader meaning to life – are under threat or in a state of deterioration. Moreover, it appeals at any time to the self-proclaimed "realist" who thinks that morality is for the most part a "con-job" designed to ensure that most people will behave in ways beneficial to those in power. Such straightforward hedonism is the direct descendent of the ethics of Thrasymachus. It can be viewed either as a challenge to morality or as a conception of morality that puts itself forward as more in accord with the facts of experience than the convoluted thinking of a Plato or Aristotle.

The Problem with Hedonism

But while neither ignoring nor dismissing it, one can and should criticize it. Very little reflection is required to see that Cyrenaicism is not in accord with our common experience of life. For most of us (most of the time), tomorrow does roll around, and so does next year, and the next, and ... Because of the fact that most of us have a future, we quickly learn that we pay for the type of profligate life recommended by Aristippus. There are the hangovers to endure, the illnesses that follow, the enmity of our fellow creatures incurred by our self-centered attitude toward life, the resultant loss of opportunities, the diminishment of talent, the unfulfilled potentialities. Moreover, such a life of sensuality, as the Danish philosopher Søren Kierkegaard was to point out many centuries later, is not so easy to bring off as may appear.[3] One must constantly be attentive to opportunities for pleasure, vigilant against all obstacles to it, and cunning in order to avoid its unpleasant consequences. In the end, such severe vigilance is inconsistent with the happy-go-lucky style of life that is recommended. Furthermore, the philosophy of the Cyrenaics appears to succumb to what is sometimes called "the paradox of hedonism": the more one seeks pleasure, the less one's chances of obtaining it. Those whose lives are filled with pleasure more often than not are those who give no thought to pleasure in their busy pursuit of other goals and values – in fact, the pleasure they end up experiencing is the result of the fact that they pursued these other values with dedication and success.

But hedonism as a philosophy does not rise or fall with the Cyrenaics. It can be given a number of other expressions that turn it into a much more important and formidable philosophy of life. It receives one of these formulations in the hands of the Epicureans, Hellenistic philosophers who follow in the footsteps of Epicurus (341–271 BCE). This is the form of hedonism that flowered in the age after the death of Aristotle.

Epicureanism

It is an irony of history that "the Epicurean" and "Epicureanism" have come to be identified with the vulgar life of "wine, women, and song," the sensuous life of abandon led by the voluptuary and libertine, the pursuit of intense bodily pleasures. While this picture fits the case of the Cyrenaics, by no means is it consistent with the type of life recommended by Epicurus. The profligate life is in fact denounced by Epicurus, who thinks it a sure way to a miserable existence and an early death.

Epicurus developed a view that has come to be called *negative hedonism*. We shall allow him to put it in his own words. First, there is the explicit acknowledgement that "pleasure is the alpha and omega of a blessed life" and that "pleasure is our first and kindred good ... the starting point of every choice and of every aversion" (*Letter to Menoeceus*).⁴ As reported by Diogenes Laertius, Epicurus taught that "living things, so soon as they are born, are well content with pleasure and are at enmity with pain, by the prompting of nature and apart from reason."⁵ But, as he goes on to write in his *Letter to Menoeceus*, "By pleasure we mean the absence of pain in the body and of trouble in the soul" (*M*). The emphasis is always on avoiding certain kinds of experiences, viz., those which are painful. In fact, Epicurus firmly believes that the goal of "absence of pain" can only be achieved by avoiding the type of sensuous life recommended by the Cyrenaics. "When we say, then, that pleasure is the end and aim, we do not mean the pleasures of the prodigal or the pleasures of sensuality ... " (*M*). The only reason for pursuing positive pleasures, he argues, is that "when pleasure is present, so long as it is uninterrupted, there is no pain either of body or of mind or of both together" (*Principal Doctrines*).⁶ He also comments that "The magnitude of pleasure reaches its limit in the removal of all pain" (*PD*). His ultimate justification for these claims is that "the end of all our actions is to be free from pain and fear" (*M*). Thus by following the path charted by negative hedonism, we achieve the end, the goal, of all our actions.

Here, in explicit terms, we have a recipe for life in dangerous times, a recommendation for how to get through the mess of things without incurring that most undesirable experience, pain: seek health of the body and tranquillity of mind. But, of course, Epicurus's advice has validity in calm historical moments no less than in tumultuous ones. The secret of success is simplification: simplify your life and thereby avoid the many overt and covert threats to it. Thus Epicurus recommends that one develop a very modest diet (beans, bread, and water would suffice, he thinks, adding that cheese would turn it into a banquet). "To habituate one's self, therefore, to simple and inexpensive diet supplies all that is needful for health, and enables a man to meet the necessary requirements of life without shrinking, and it places us in a better condition when we approach at intervals a costly fare and renders us fearless of fortune" (*M*). The last point requires emphasis. If we are content with a simple diet that removes the pains of hunger and conduces to health, then we have little to fear from the future, for the ingredients of such a diet will seldom if ever be difficult to obtain. Moreover, this contentment with simple fare will not leave us disappointed when we cannot come up with the funds for an expensive meal – who needs it, after all? Thus Epicurus recommends a way of life that removes both *bodily* and *mental* pains – the bodily pangs of hunger, and the mental fears of what the future might bring together with the mental envy and resentment one might otherwise feel for what is beyond one's reach.

In determining what one should pursue and what one should avoid, Epicurus operates with a threefold distinction among our desires. "We must also reflect that of desires some are natural, others are groundless, and that of the natural some are necessary as well as natural, and some natural only" (*M*). Desires, then, fall into the following groups: (1) natural and necessary, (2) natural and unnecessary, and (3) groundless or non-natural. If the natural and necessary desires are not fulfilled, pain will result. The desire for food is natural and necessary, and if we do not attain food, we indeed find ourselves in pain. The desire for sexual activity is also natural, but, at least in Epicurus's eyes, it is not necessary. This desire arises out of the body, but pain does not result when it goes unfulfilled: "All such desires as lead to no pain when they remain ungratified are unnecessary, and the longing is easily got rid of, when the thing desired is difficult to procure or when the desires seem likely to produce harm" (*PD*). Finally, the desires that are groundless are those which are artificial, those that arise from convention or social customs rather than bodily need. The desire for fancy clothes is groundless – we need clothes, to be sure, but we do not need fancy ones, and no pains occur when our clothes are of simple cloth and we can easily overcome the longing for fancy dress. Other artificial desires include those for the honors and fame that result from political activities, which activities Epicurus thought a wise person would avoid insofar as in the end they usually lead to frustration and disappointment.

If we use as our criterion the satisfaction of natural and necessary desires, what kind of life would we live? In addition to the simple diet and the plain clothing, it would be "a quiet private life withdrawn from the multitude." *Be unknown*, Epicurus enjoins. He believes that many of our pains result from the frustrations, the haste, the conflicts, and the sheer nervousness of civic or public life. Best to withdraw from all that and live with a few close friends, enjoying their quiet company, discoursing and interacting with them alone. In fact, it was just this kind of life that Epicurus achieved, for himself and his pupils, in his Garden. The Garden was not only a school, it was also a home for those who chose to follow the wisdom of the master. There they ate their simple diet, wore their simple robes, and talked only of those things that brought comfort and contentment.

In addition to relating pain and pleasure to the different kinds of desires, Epicurus also develops a more technical categorization of these feelings. On the one hand, there is what he calls *kinetic pleasure*; on the other, *static pleasure*. Kinetic (or moving) pleasure results from the process of removing pains – hence eating is kinetically pleasant because it removes the pangs of hunger, and the satisfaction of other natural and necessary desires would likewise be kinetically pleasant. Kinetic pleasures are primarily bodily sensations (but there are also, as we shall see, kinetic mental pleasures); they occur when the body undergoes the process of returning to its natural state of painlessness – hence their description as *moving* pleasures. Static (or unmoving) pleasure is the state of complete and stable absence of pain and the enjoyment of this lasting condition. It is not a sensation, but it occurs as a result of having satisfied the natural and necessary desires and hence seems to presuppose the prior occurrence of pleasant sensations. This state is called "untroubledness" by the Epicureans, and is considered superior to kinetic pleasure and indeed projected as the ultimate goal of life. Such a state of the body, they argue, is its *natural* state, and pain and unfulfilled desires are disruptions of this natural state. In their doctrine of kinetic pleasure, the Epicureans were influenced by Plato's discussion of pleasure in the *Philebus*, where he defined pain and pleasure as processes of upsetting and restoring the natural state of equilibrium. But whereas Plato denied that this natural state is itself pleasurable, the Epicureans identify it as the maximally pleasant condition in life.

The goal of life includes not only static bodily pleasures but also static mental pleasures. The tranquil mind is, perhaps more than anything else, the key to a successful life. The mind is also, the Epicureans think, capable of various kinetic pleasures, for example the joy one experiences on meeting a friend. Moreover, the mind is able through memory to recall pleasant and painless events of the past, and it is able to anticipate pleasures to come. Epicurus himself in his dying days was said to reflect on the pleasures of previous philosophical conversations and to anticipate with delight the approaching release from the coils of pain in which all human life is wrapped. Thus in the midst of extreme pain (which, he mused, would, like all pains, be short lived), his mental pleasures predominated and led him to inform his companions that he was, on the very day of his agonizing death, a happy man. Whatever the positive value of these kinetic mental pleasures, however, they were greatly surpassed in value by the static pleasure of Epicurus's untroubled mind at peace with itself.

Philosophy and the Fear of Death

What the friends inhabiting the Garden of Epicurus talked about mostly was philosophy: they discoursed on the nature of the universe. Epicurus was convinced that the primary causes of human misery are false beliefs perpetuated by society, and hence that a proper understanding of the nature of things is essential for happiness. False convictions – about the universe, the gods, and human nature – lead to fear and anxiety, mental states that are extremely painful to human beings. Epicurus believed that he was able to see into the essential nature of things, and that the picture he drew of them would remove these sources of mental anguish. In fact, Epicurus's metaphysical beliefs – which we can label atomistic materialism – were largely unoriginal, having been developed over a century earlier by the Greek philosopher Democritus. Epicurus added some original twists to this metaphysics, but he largely took over – without proper acknowledgement, it should be noted – what had earlier been a leading rival of the metaphysical views of Plato and Aristotle. He is appropriately to be credited, however, with the full-fledged development of the hedonism that arises out of atomistic materialism.

One of the greatest causes of human unhappiness is the fear of death. But such fear, Epicurus argues, is groundless, being inconsistent with the nature of life and death.

Accustom thyself to believe that death is nothing to us, for good and evil imply sentience, and death is the privation of all sentience; therefore a right understanding that death is nothing to us makes the mortality of life enjoyable, not by adding to life an illimitable time, but by taking away the yearning for immortality. For life has no terrors for him who has thoroughly apprehended that there are no terrors for him in ceasing to live. Foolish, therefore, is the man who says that he fears death, not because it will pain when it comes, but because it pains in the prospect   (*M*).

He sums up this message with his memorable statement, "Death, therefore, the most awful of evils, is nothing to us, seeing that, when we are, death is not come, and, when death is come, we are not" (*M*). The only evils in life, the only things to be feared, are pains. If an event does not cause one to feel pain, there is no reason to fear its occurrence. But in order to feel pain, one must be alive: sentience requires life – a corpse feels nothing. The death of a human being, Epicurus maintains, is the end of sentience: nothing can be felt thereafter, neither pleasure nor pain. But if we cannot feel pain in death, we cannot be harmed by death, since only pain harms us. Thus there is no reason to fear death. Furthermore, the prospect of death should not produce pain, for while we are alive, we are not harmed by death unless we choose to fear it. And why should we fear it?

Atomistic Materialism

Epicurus is able to have great confidence in his argument because he generates it against the background of atomistic materialism – the thesis that everything that exists is material, consisting of collections of atoms moving about in empty space (the void). The atoms themselves are very small, although differing in size, shape, and texture. Each one is an indivisible unit incapable of being broken down into smaller parts. (Epicurus believes that the atoms do have parts, which account for their different sizes, but that these "minimal parts" can never exist on their own.) There are an infinite number of atoms in the universe, which means that space itself must be infinite in order to hold all of them. The atoms have weight (contrary to Democritus) and because of this feature their natural state is downward motion. Because they are in constant motion in the void, however, they initially meet no resistance and their original velocity is uniform.

For the atomistic materialist, human beings no less than physical objects are composed of atoms, a particular person being no more than a collection of atoms that maintains a stable identity for a period of time. Epicurus (following Democritus) develops an elaborate theory to explain how all aspects of human life – including feelings, emotions, perceptions, and thoughts – can be accounted for in terms of nothing more than the motions of atoms: the motions of atoms impinging on the body, and the internal motions that constitute mental activities and events. Thus perception is nothing more than the influence of very fine atoms (effluences) cast off from external objects which strike the sense organs and set up motions in them. We experience these motions as images of the external objects. Thought results when even finer atoms originating from an external object penetrate directly to the mind, without the intermediary of the sense organs, and set up the motions of thought. Feelings – most importantly the feelings of pleasure and pain – are the motions of atoms both in the mind and in the body, caused either by motions impinging from without on the body or by thoughts, which themselves, as we have just noted, are motions.

Epicurus believes in the soul, just as did Aristotle and Plato, and indeed most Greek thinkers. But for him the soul is purely material, consisting of very fine, smooth, round, and small atoms whose motions are quick and fast. According to Lucretius – a later Roman follower of Epicurus – the soul atoms are distributed throughout the body, with the rational activities (the *animus*) occurring in the chest and the other activities and motions (the *anima*) distributed throughout the rest of the body. The atoms of the soul act on, and are acted on by, the atoms of the body. The soul is said by the Epicureans to be the primary cause of sensation: on being "stirred" and stimulated by the bodily motions impinging on them, the soul atoms in turn produce in the body those sensations called pleasure and pain. When the body dies, the soul merely dissipates, and with it goes life, motion, and sensation. Thus when death occurs, a human being can no longer feel pain.

The metaphysics of atomism also provides Epicurus with arguments designed to alleviate other forms of mental anguish that stand in the way of human happiness. In his day, most Greeks retained the view of the gods that came down from the Olympian traditions. These gods, much wiser and stronger than human beings, frequently interact with their human subordinates, and their interventions in the lives of people are unpredictable and often have horrifying consequences. The importance of the gods for human affairs is captured in the very language itself, for, as A. A. Long has noted,[7] the Greek term for a happy person, "*eudaimon*," literally means having a favorable deity, whereas the word for unhappiness, "*kakodaimon*," connotes having a harmful deity. Hence most people lived in fear of the gods, and this fear was an obstacle to the state of "untroubledness" recommended by Epicurus. But rather than deny that the gods exist, as he might have done from the perspective of his materialism, Epicurus argues that they, being perfect beings, are not interested in the pitiful affairs of human beings. The gods are themselves immortal, and they are sublimely happy. Any intervention in human affairs would require passions and partiality, and these features are inconsistent with the undisturbed tranquillity of the gods: "A blessed and eternal being has no trouble himself and brings no trouble upon any other being; hence he is exempt from movements of anger and partiality, for every such movement implies weakness" (*PD*). In other words, "occupation and supervision, anger and favor, are not consistent with sublime happiness." Moreover,

Epicurus argues, the natural world is governed by strict laws that regulate the motions of the atoms. Given this regularity and lawfulness, it is clear that the gods do not manipulate the physical world so as to punish or reward human beings. The world of nature is left to operate according to its own devices. Hence human beings have nothing to fear from the gods, who live in splendid isolation from nature and the human sphere.

Fate and Human Freedom: The "Swerve"

Although a source of consolation with regard to the fear of the gods and the fear of death, atomistic materialism can *itself* be a cause of concern or anxiety. Most Greeks believed in something called fate, a mysterious chain of events that cannot be evaded or abrogated even by the gods. The fear of fate consequently was a debilitating psychological reality for them. A materialist like Epicurus had no choice but to denounce fate as an idle superstition – the only laws of cause and effect being those natural ones that operate to control the motion of the atoms. To this extent, the metaphysics of atomism can be seen as alleviating any mental pain resulting from fear of fate. But what about the laws governing the motions of the atoms themselves? Isn't this natural lawfulness the equivalent of fate? If human beings are nothing more than collections of atoms in motion, and if these atoms move in accordance with inexorable natural laws, human beings find themselves in the grip of an even stronger, all-pervasive necessity. Epicurus himself refers to the "merciless necessity" attributed to the laws by the previous nature philosophers. This natural necessity threatens human freedom no less than does mysterious fate. Such a troubling consequence of atomism is *not* congenial to Epicurus, and so he sets about to introduce an important variation into this metaphysical theory.

This variation is the infamous doctrine of the swerve. There is nothing in the extant writings of Epicurus himself about this doctrine, but Epicurus's Roman disciple Lucretius, in his famous and beautiful work, *On the Nature of Things*, gives us a detailed account which he attributes to the Master. The doctrine of the swerve is developed in the first place, not for the purpose of providing human beings with freedom from necessity, but for the purpose of explaining how the atoms could initially collide with one another so as to form the collections of atoms constituting particular physical objects and human bodies. According to Epicurus (Lucretius), the atoms were from time immemorial in a state of downward free fall in empty space. Insofar as space was empty, nothing would impede (by slowing down or speeding up) the motions of the atoms through it – all of them, therefore, would fall at the same speed in the same direction. How then could they initially collide and set up the chain reaction leading to the formation of physical objects? The Epicurean solution to this problem is the "announcement" that the atoms are able to swerve ever so slightly from their straight and downward paths, thereby coming into contact with, bumping into, the atoms adjacent to them and setting off the reaction needed. Clearly no such swerve has ever been observed. All that can be said in defense of the doctrine is that it explains what otherwise could not be explained: how the universe goes from a state of free fall to one of moving combinations of atoms. Ever so fortunately, the doctrine can also explain how human beings escape the fate of the causal nexus formed by the lawful motions of the atoms – human freedom consists in the ability of the atoms composing the human person to swerve from their regular, lawful path. "But a tiny swerve of the atoms at no fixed time or place brings it about that the mind itself has no internal necessity in doing all things and is not forced like a captive to accept and be acted upon" (Lucretius, *On the Nature of Things*, Book II). When necessity "raises its ugly head on the highway of life," we avoid it by swerving a bit to the left or a bit to the right. This is, to be sure, a picturesque and unconvincing doctrine, but it is one of the first attempts in Western history to explain how human beings can be free and at the same time part of the natural world – and, consequently, governed by its physical laws.

Happiness in Practice

Now that we have seen how, according to Epicurus, *theoretical* reason shows us how to avoid the mental pains resulting from a fear of death, the intervention of the gods, and fate, we can observe the manner in which he thinks *practical* reason contributes to the simple and happy life. Far from the preferred way of life being one of Cyrenaic abandon, it will be one guided by prudence (*phronēsis*, practical wisdom). The successful human being will be the one who exercises her reason in order to control her life, using it to determine how best to avoid pain. Such a person will not be greatly different from Aristotle's person of practical wisdom. Prudence or practical wisdom emphasizes the importance of temperance, of justice, and of true friendship, thus stressing the value of many of the virtues of character identified by Aristotle. But whereas Aristotle viewed the virtues as constituents of happiness, Epicurus has a much more instrumental conception of them. There is nothing intrinsically good about justice, he maintains. Justice simply consists of an agreement among human beings not to act harmfully toward one another in order to avoid the pains that would result if they acted without mutual consideration. Justice is thus a matter of convention, and its value lies only in the beneficial consequences which spring from it. Much the same can be said of a virtue like temperance. The only reason for acting temperately is that if one does not do so, one will usually be far worse off as a result.

   This, then, is one of the more influential "survival ethics" developed during the Hellenistic period as a means of coping with the changing and difficult times. If it simplifies the ethical landscape, perhaps this is merely the result of its effort to simplify life, thereby reducing the chances of damage and disaster. We should not underestimate its appeal – straightforward and elegant, it offers an unambiguous picture of the good life. And it seemed to work for the many citizens who looked upon Epicurus as Master and who acknowledged his insights and followed his precepts. Perhaps a lesson we should draw from the example of Epicureanism is that ethical truth needs to be sensitive to (shall we say relative to?) the circumstances in which it is articulated. The world of Aristotle and Plato was different from the world of Epicurus – is it reasonable in the face of such difference to expect the same recipes for happiness?

Problems of Epicureanism

In spite of its perennial appeal, there are philosophical problems with Epicureanism. We shall focus on the central difficulty inherent in its hedonism. What, we must ask, is meant by *pleasure* and *pain*? Epicurus speaks of them as opposites – contradictories: if we are in a state of pleasure, at least in a certain bodily location, we cannot at the same time be in a state of pain in that place, and vice versa. As Cicero puts it, "all those who are without pain are in a state of pleasure."[8] This follows from Epicurus's thesis that the absence of pain is pleasure. But if pleasure and pain are contradictories, it is equally the case that the absence of pleasure is pain. And this appears not to be the case: more often than not, given the absence of pleasure we simply feel nothing.

At least, we often feel nothing if pain and pleasure are taken to be sensations. Pain clearly can be a sensation, and pleasure too may on occasion be a felt sensation. But are all pleasures sensations? Are all pains? What is the sensation of pleasure one receives from reading Shakespeare or listening to Mozart? There is certainly no sensation one has as a result of doing so. And are all pains sensations? What about the mental anguish that Epicurus himself stresses? This clearly is not a sensation. In fact, the *summum bonum* recommended by Epicurus, the serene and untroubled life, the static *absence* of pain, is precisely a state in which we feel no sensations.

If we cannot equate pain and pleasure with sensations of fairly specific sorts, then what do these terms designate? It very much appears that Epicurus simply equates pleasure with whatever we enjoy or like, and pain with whatever we dislike – we enjoy an untroubled mind, therefore it is said to be pleasurable. But if this is true, what information is he giving us when he tells us that all human beings seek, desire, and enjoy pleasure – and avoid pain? Such a message amounts to the truism that everyone enjoys what she enjoys, likes what she likes, and avoids what she avoids. And the Epicurean enjoinder to pursue a life of pleasure and absence of pain is no more than the useless admonition that we pursue what we pursue and avoid what we avoid. Without a clearer, more specific definition of pain and pleasure, Epicureanism turns out to convey a fairly empty message.

Stoicism

To some minds, the ethics of Stoicism represents the intellectual apex of ancient Greek thought on the subject. As one esteemed historian of philosophy put it, "To the Stoic ethics belongs the glory that in it the ripest and highest which the ethical life of antiquity produced ... attained its best formulation."[9] The overall system of philosophy developed by the Stoics is a synthesis of many of the ideas originating from previous thinkers: we find in it echoes of the pre-Socratic philosophers Heraclitus and Parmenides; the influence of Socrates is apparent everywhere; and elements of Platonism and Aristotelianism play major roles in the system. But Stoicism is not just an eclectic attempt to pull together the strands of previous philosophical reflection. It stands as an original philosophy which, while undoubtedly incorporating elements from the past, puts them together in a fashion that required the special inspiration of the Stoic thinkers themselves.

From the historical perspective, and considering its impact on both academic and non-academic figures, Stoicism has been an immensely influential philosophy. During the Hellenistic period it competed on equal terms with Platonism, Aristotelianism, Epicureanism, and Skepticism (the other major movement of the time). Then it gained a foothold in Rome, where it exerted a major influence, first on Roman thought – Seneca, the famous senator and adviser to Nero, was a Stoic, and the Emperor Marcus Aurelius was an important Stoic philosopher and writer – and then on the thinkers of the early Christian period. The latter influence continued through the Middle Ages when Christianity dominated the Western intellectual world. In the modern period, thinkers such as Spinoza and Kant utilize Stoic thoughts and sentiments in developing their ethical theories, and eighteenth-century deism bears the marks of Stoicism. The influence of Kant being a major one in ethics even today, Stoicism has through him entered the contemporary world as well. In fact, when people today speak of "being philosophical" about some issue or series of events, the attitude or frame of mind they refer to is precisely the one recommended by the Stoics.[10] In the first part of this discussion we shall attempt to gain a general idea of what this "philosophical," Stoic attitude is. Then we shall turn to some of the details of the theory.

Stoicism is often classified along with Epicureanism as one of the survival philosophies developed when Hellenic culture began to unravel during and after the conquests of Alexander the Great. Like Epicureanism, it offers a prescription for dealing with life in troubled times. It is, however, a prescription that many highly civilized Greeks and Romans found more noble and sublime than the Epicureans' call to pleasure, even the negative pleasure recommended by Epicurus. The Stoics too recommend a life of peace and calm, but the meaning of their message, and the reasons they give for it, are strikingly different from those of Epicureanism. This becomes obvious as we take a look at their theory of the universe and of human nature.

What Must Be, Must Be

The universe, they claim, is a rational whole which can be identified either as Nature or as God. Within this whole, everything is related and interconnected. As Marcus Aurelius puts it in his famous *Meditations*, "Always think of the universe as one living organism, with a single substance and a single soul ... "[11] This one substance and soul is referred to as God, and this God *is* Nature. Thus we have what philosophers of religion call a *pantheistic* conception of the deity, one that does not set God apart from the world. Everything that happens in Nature occurs as a result of the divine laws governing it. These laws are the laws of reason – hence God or Nature is to be conceived of as a rational being, or as Reason itself. The laws of reason being the laws of God, the Stoics maintain that all things happen in accordance with divine providence, that is, because of God's will or purposes. These purposes are embodied in the rational laws actually controlling things, and the rational laws are the laws of *cause* and *effect* governing all of Nature. According to the Stoics, every event is the necessary result of prior causes, which themselves are necessitated by still earlier causes. In such a world, everything happens because it must happen; but what must happen is what God wills and is thus in accord with the rational and divine purpose. We human beings share in the divine reason – we have the "spark of the divine fire" in us (God being described by the Stoics as fire) – and therefore we can understand the rational principles that control Nature and ourselves. This rational capacity allows us to see that everything that happens to us does so necessarily, and that it happens because it is part of God's rational plan.

What if we believed in such a metaphysical theory of the universe? What in that case would be our attitude toward human life and human action? Given the metaphysics, it is not difficult to infer what the Stoic ethic amounts to in its essentials. Everything that happens has to happen, and, being the result of God's laws, it therefore happens for the best. The only appropriate attitude to take toward events, then, is to accept them, indeed to welcome them. It becomes foolish to wish that things might have turned out differently – they can't have and they shouldn't have! It is equally foolish to think that the future course of events can go in any of a number of different directions. What will be, must be, and there is no point whatsoever in trying to change the course of history. What will occur is eternally necessitated; there are no options, and there never have been. But because it is rational for things to unfold in this strictly determined fashion and because it is God's providential will that they do so, it is good that things happen exactly as they do. Insight into these matters thus brings immense consolation. Rather than living in fear of Nature, or the future, we come to feel at peace with ourselves and the world, knowing that only what is best ever occurs. And knowing that we are part of Nature and of God, we can feel our lives to be significant and fulfilled.

In the Stoic universe, it is senseless for us to think of planning our actions so as to obtain what we want or to improve our lives. *We* can't control the course of Nature; this course is predetermined from eternity. It is false to think we can bring about certain consequences and not others just by our willing them to happen, or by voluntarily deciding to act in certain ways. Here we have one of the earliest formulations of a non-consequentialist ethics, one which denies that what makes an act right or valuable is the value embodied in its consequences. For the Stoics, to think that being a good person, or a happy one, consists in bringing about beneficial consequences is to fail to understand the nature of things. Goodness and happiness do not consist in effective action. What, then, do they consist in?

Whether they are consistent in saying so or not, the Stoics maintain that the one thing we *can* control is our *attitude* toward what happens. Understanding that everything occurs in accordance with natural and divine law, we can mold our attitudes accordingly and accept whatever happens as necessary and beneficial. Or we can continue in our foolish attitudes and assume that we can, through our efforts, make a difference to what happens. On the one hand, we can be pained or frustrated by what occurs, or, on the other hand, we can accept the actual course of events without recoil (understanding its providential necessity). Wisdom resides in our learning to assent to whatever happens, thereby achieving freedom from the avoidance of pain and frustration as well as freedom from the pursuit of pleasure and ambition – both of which involve a rejection of the actual in light of what is foolishly thought to be a better outcome.

The Stoics are not unaware of the fact that there is considerable pain in the lives of many people; nor are they unaware of the fact that pleasure is a widely pursued goal. In their eyes, sensations of pain and pleasure in and of themselves are neither good nor bad. Pain becomes bad only through the attitude of aversion we take toward it; pleasure becomes good only through our passionate pursuit of it. But both the aversion and the pursuit are *contrary to nature*, revealing a failure to understand the necessity of all things. If we acknowledge this necessity, we can say with Marcus Aurelius that whatever is right for the universe is right for me. Then we can live our lives *in accordance with nature*, calmly accepting both the pain and pleasure because they form part of Nature's plan.

For the Stoics, the fact that our attitudes toward things are within our control is central to their understanding of the moral life. As indicated above, the moral life does not consist in any effort to bring about consequences of a certain sort. The moral character of what we do must be, they claim, the result of what we have control over, and we do not have control over the consequences of our actions. The Stoics keenly perceive the fact that, acting with the best intentions, things can and often do turn out far different from the way intended. What makes us men and women of good standing is not a matter of what we accomplish in life, but the attitude or motive with which we act. This motive we *do* have control over, and hence it alone has moral value (or disvalue) attaching to it. And the motive from which people of *good moral character* act is the wish to do whatever is in accord with nature. What accords with nature is what is rational. Consequently, the attempt to do what is rational is the one motive that bestows moral goodness and virtue on us – and rightness on our actions. To act in accord with nature or reason is our one duty, and if we do our duty, we shall as a matter of course be happy – come what may. The life of duty *is* the life of happiness.

This, then, is the general picture the Stoics sketch of Nature and human life. We now need to fill in some of the details, letting some of the Stoics speak for themselves and identifying more specifically some of the influences that helped shape their thoughts. We also need to acknowledge that the above picture reflects some five centuries of philosophical thought. Historians usually distinguish between Early Stoicism, Middle Stoicism, and Late Stoicism. We shall not pursue these finer distinctions but shall look primarily at the thought of the originator of Stoicism, Zeno of Citium, and at one of the late Stoics, Epictetus. And we must begin this more detailed account with a few words about one of the most picturesque characters in all of philosophy: Diogenes.

Diogenes and the Cynics

Diogenes (404–323 BCE) was not himself a Stoic but rather a follower of the philosophy known as Cynicism. Of all the influences on Stoicism, perhaps that of the Cynics was deepest. Diogenes was not so much a theorist as an itinerant moralist or preacher who traveled from city to city exhorting the citizens to put aside their foolish ambitions, false pleasures, and evil ways and to replace them with a simple life in accordance with nature and virtue. The story has it that he went from door to door with his lantern, looking for a real (or honest) man. His own life was an extreme example of the simple, natural kind of existence he recommended. Dressed only in a cloak, he slept in a tub (or jar) and ate only the simplest of foods. Once, after observing a child drink from its cupped hand, Diogenes threw away his cup, saying that it was clearly not essential to life. In aiming at a life in accordance with nature, he attempted to reduce his needs to the minimum. This effort, together with his indifference to all social and political distinctions, is admirably illustrated by the occasion on which he was approached by Alexander the Great. Alexander said to him that he had heard much about him and admired him greatly, so much so that he was willing to grant him anything he requested. Diogenes, who at the time was resting in his tub, responded by asking Alexander kindly to move out of his sunlight. Thinking that poverty was no mark of dishonor, Diogenes had no compunction against begging for the essentials of life. On one occasion he was observed begging from a statue, and when asked why, his response was, "to get practice in being refused."[12]

Diogenes and the other Cynics appear not to have any deep conception of what life in accordance with nature entails. Impressed by the simplicity and frugality of Socrates' life, they define what is natural primarily by opposing it to the artificial activities and desires associated with social life. Thus they denounce marriage, the construction of temples, and even the creation of coinage. Society itself is thought to be unnecessary, since the only *true* community would be an association of good and virtuous individuals. The virtuous person – a rare creature in Diogenes' eyes – is one who is indifferent to all externals: clothing, food, social positions, honors, power. These externals are renounced because reason shows them to be unnecessary for the good life and indeed an impediment to it – the person who seeks pleasure or fame more often than not becomes entangled in difficulties and led into unhappiness by the pursuit of them. The good life is the virtuous one, free from all external constraints and influences, free from duplicity, free from pomp. The founder of Cynicism, Antisthenes (ca. 446–366 BCE), expresses this doctrine in dramatic form by stating that he would rather go mad than feel pleasure.

By eliminating all artificial desires, the Cynics free themselves to a great extent from dependence on the external world. Knowing that they cannot control the world and hence cannot ensure that it will satisfy all of their artificial desires, they simply eliminate these desires. Knowing that they cannot control the attitudes and opinions other people have toward them, the Cynics become indifferent to public opinion. By mastering themselves – by controlling their desires and developing indifference to all things beyond their control – the Cynics free themselves from all frustration and disturbance. Independent in mind as well as in body, the Cynics' austere and ascetic lives represent their interpretation of Socrates' call to a virtuous life.

Zeno

Zeno of Citium (333–261 BCE), the father of Stoicism, studied not with Diogenes but with one of his successors, Crates. Legend has it that after reading about Socrates, Zeno came to Athens to study philosophy, and on the occasion when he asked the owner of a shop how to locate philosophers like Socrates, the shopkeeper pointed to a man passing in front of the shop and remarked: "follow that man." "That man" turned out to be Crates. Some years thereafter, around 300 BCE, Zeno began to lecture in the part of the central plaza known as the Painted Colonnade or Stoa, from whence comes the name Stoicism. By that time, he had developed his own philosophy and drew large crowds eager to hear about it. He became immensely popular, both for his message and for the upright life he lived. When he died in 261 BCE, the citizens of Athens produced a golden crown in his name and built a tomb for him at public expense, paying great honor to him in spite of the fact that he was not an Athenian citizen.

Although Zeno wrote several books, only fragments of these remain, and most of our knowledge of his philosophy comes to us second hand. A few quotations will give us a good picture of some of the main elements of his thought and that of his immediate followers, Cleanthes and Crysippus. Diogenes Laertius reports that Zeno was the first "to designate as the end 'life in agreement with nature,' which is the same as a virtuous life, virtue being the goal toward which nature guides us."[13] Cicero, the later Roman philosopher much influenced by Stoicism, but also a critic of it, tells us that Zeno "set forth that the end of goods is the morally honorable life, and that this is derived from the recommendation of nature"[14] and he claims that Zeno held there is "no life happy but the life of virtue" (*SVF*, I, 189; p. 111.)

The Socratic influence here is obvious: happiness consists in, is identical with, the life of virtue. What is more original, but bears the influence of the Cynics, is the idea that the virtuous life is the life lived in agreement with nature, and that nature has set up this type of life as the distinctive goal for a human being. Clearly we have here a teleological conception of human nature – its end or goal is happiness or virtue. This human nature is part of, and subject to the laws of, nature in general, so Nature, as it were, has posited virtue as the rational end of human life.

The life of virtue, Diogenes Laertius reports, is "a life in which we refrain from every action forbidden by the law common to all things, that is to say, the right reason which pervades all things, and is identical with this Zeus, lord and ruler of all that is."[15] Moreover, we live the virtuous life when all our actions "promote the harmony of the spirit dwelling in the individual man with the will of him who orders the universe."[16] Nature, of which our human nature forms a part, is thus identified both with Zeus and with reason – these two are in effect identical. We live in a world permeated by God and by reason, and this reason, this *logos*, sets for us a law we must follow in order to achieve virtue and be happy. To live a virtuous life is "to live consistently," to live a "smooth" life in accordance with rational principles rather than a rough, disorganized life according to impulse and passion: "for virtue is the state of mind which tends to make the whole of life harmonious."[17] A harmonious individual life is one which achieves consistency amid the constant changes that take place; and insofar as it is achieved by following the rational precepts of the divine *logos*, the individual life achieves harmony with Nature as a whole or with God.

What this harmony between the individual life and universal nature consists in has been admirably expressed by one commentator in the following way: "the goal of human existence is complete harmony between a man's own attitudes and actions and the actual course of events."[18] The actual course of events is, of course, the one ordained by the divine *logos*. Virtue, then, amounts to conformity, through the use of reason, to what must happen through the causative powers of the *logos*. Reason, showing us what will and must happen, indicates what we must accept and welcome if we are to be in harmony with Nature. Reason will enable us to detect the rigid chains of cause and effect which constitute the unfolding of all events in Nature. Accepting and welcoming these inevitabilities is the essence of virtue.

Zeno and the other early Stoics insist that, in the words of Cicero, "Good is absolute" and that "the value of virtue is ... singular and distinct; it depends on kind and not on degree."[19] Virtue, they maintain, is the *only* good, vice the only evil. Such an uncompromising stance is difficult to accept, and many philosophers of the times agreed with Aristotle that some "external goods" – for Aristotle these included health, beauty, and wealth – were also necessary conditions of happiness. But the Stoics stand their ground: everything other than virtue is at best *indifferent*. All externals, including pleasure, health, pain, and poverty, have no value in themselves. This is because all of them can be put to evil uses. As Seneca later puts it: "Good does not result from evil. But riches result from greed; therefore riches are not a good."[20] And again: "That which is evil does harm; that which does harm makes a man worse. But pain and poverty do not make a man worse; therefore, they are not evils."[21] Virtue alone, the Stoics argue, can never be put to evil uses or "make a man worse" – hence virtue alone has value and always has value.

But what about the things we ordinarily value – are we simply to dismiss them? Do the Stoics follow the Cynics in the latter's extreme asceticism? They do not. "All other things, Zeno said, were neither good nor bad, but nevertheless some of them were in accordance with nature and others contrary to nature ... He taught that things in accordance with nature were to be chosen and estimated as having a certain value, and their opposites the opposite."[22] These things which are neither good nor bad are called indifferent, and they include "all those things which neither benefit nor harm a man, such as life, health, pleasure, beauty, strength, wealth, fame, and noble birth."[23] Yet a distinction can be made among these things:

> Of things indifferent, as they express it, some are "preferred" others "rejected". Such as have value are "preferred'", while such as have negative, instead of positive, value are "rejected". Value they define as, first, any contribution to harmonious living ... ; secondly, some faculty or use which indirectly contributes to the life according to nature: which is as much as to say "any assistance brought by wealth or health towards living a natural life."[24]

Thus health can be selected (not "chosen" – only the good is chosen!) because it assists in promoting life. Health and other such *preferred* states or possessions are not, therefore, ignored, but they are assigned a position distinctly below that of virtue, which alone is truly good. Selecting and pursuing one of the indifferent values yields what were called *appropriate* actions. An act is considered appropriate, according to Cicero, if "a reasonable account can be rendered of its performance,"[25] if, that is, it can be demonstrated that it serves as a "means to the end of attaining the primary needs of nature."[26] But being appropriate does not give the act status as a moral act. Under certain circumstances, as we will see, it may even turn out to be immoral.

The Life of Reason

Appropriate acts are particularly recommended by the Stoics for the person who has not yet reached the age of maturity, the age when reason is fully developed. When we come into the world, we live first as creatures with natural impulses. Our natural impulses are directed toward "what belongs to one" or "what goes together with one" – what the Stoics describe as *oikeion*. Our first impulse, they argue, is to maintain our own life and constitution. Accordingly we avoid what we consider harmful and seek that which promotes our life and satisfies our natural impulses. In doing this, we select appropriate actions. Such a selection requires a rudimentary use of reason in the determination of the means needed to achieve the goals posited by natural impulse. The Stoics encourage appropriate actions because of the fact that they further the development of reason. A person reaches a point, however, when reason is capable of viewing life, not simply from the perspective of the goals of natural impulse, but from the vantage point of Nature in general. At this point, for instance, one is able to see that death is as natural as life – that it is part of life – and thus, instead of following our natural impulse to avoid death, we calmly accept it as being in accordance with nature. When reason is fully developed, a person attains the capability of acting morally, of doing what is right rather than what is naturally advantageous (appropriate) from her personal perspective.

The moral life requires the use of reason first in acquiring knowledge of nature as a whole and second in adopting principles of action consistent with this knowledge. "He who is to live in accordance with nature," Cicero tells us, "must base his principles upon the system and government of the entire world."[27] The knowledge required for virtue is the grasp of the laws of cause and effect governing all things; the principles of virtue those which propose actions in accord with the inevitabilities resulting from these laws. Some actions called for, e.g., those sustaining life, may be precisely those which were designated merely appropriate at the earlier stage. They acquire moral status and become morally obligatory because they are now seen to be the necessary effects of universal causation and hence in accord with nature. The person of moral virtue is the one who does what is right, the person who engages in right actions because she sees that they accord with nature, with reason. Frequently this will require a repudiation of natural impulse. We may observe on some occasions that pain is naturally inevitable, and hence instead of shunning it we accept it. Even the continuation of an individual life may on occasion be perceived by reason as inconsistent with natural law, in which case death is to be accepted – and in some instances furthered by one's own hand. (Legend has it that Zeno, after suffering a fall, took it to be a sign that his time had come and took his own life.)

The life of reason recommended by the Stoics is sometimes characterized as a life from which all passions and emotions have been extirpated – the life of Stoic apathy. This is an exaggeration, as we shall see, but to a large degree it is true and reflects one of the most distinctive aspects of Stoicism. Seneca, in contrasting Stoicism with Aristotelianism (the Peripatetics), writes: "The question has often been raised whether it is better to have moderate emotions, or none at all. Philosophers of our school reject the emotions; the Peripatetics keep them in check."[28] Diogenes Laertius describes Zeno's theory of the emotions as follows:

> Now from falsehood there results perversion, which extends to the mind;
> and from this perversion arise many passions or emotions, which are

causes of instability. Passion, or emotion, is defined by Zeno as an irrational and unnatural movement in the soul, or again as impulse in excess. The main, or most universal emotions, according to ... Zeno ... , constitute four great classes: grief, fear, desire or craving, pleasure.[29]

Being perversions, the passions are irrational; being causes of instability, they are mental disturbances. As impulses in excess, irrational and unnatural, they are feelings that are not guided by reason. In every case, a passion turns out to be a feeling that is inappropriate given the facts and the laws governing them. "Fear is an expectation of evil" (Diogenes Laertius reports),[30] but what we fear is some event in the natural world, which being necessitated by the divine and providential *logos*, is no cause for concern whatsoever and is certainly not evil. Only by letting feelings of fear outrun our reason, and hence our perception that everything happens for the best from the standpoint of Nature, do we fall into the perversion of fear. Fear amounts to an exaggeration and distortion of the significance of what is really only a morally indifferent event. Likewise, mental pains, those resulting from grief, envy, and even pity, are irrational interpretations of what happens in nature. To feel pity for a person who is viewed as unfortunate is to fail to grasp that nothing unfortunate has happened in the overall scheme of things.

Pleasure, too – not so much as a physical feeling but as enjoyment in the mind and the object of lust and craving – reflects still another irrational state of mind. In this case, the error consists in taking that which is morally indifferent and at best "preferred" as if it were *good*, when the latter, as we have seen, applies only to virtue. When physical feelings are misconceived as having the value of virtue, then we have the appearance of a passion. Passions, not the indifferent physical feelings themselves, are to be avoided.

The Stoics sometimes use strong language in their denunciation of the passions. To be a victim of passion is to be in the grasp of a "disease." The philosopher is the "physician of the soul" who assists one in recognizing the perversion of the passions and of attaining that state of apathy (*apatheia*) which constitutes liberation from them. At the same time, however, the Stoics themselves approve of certain emotions.[31] Joy or well-reasoned elation is appropriate, being based on reason, and so too are well-reasoned appetite and avoidance. And the love of parents for their children is approved, being based on the natural togetherness or belonging (*oikeiosis*) constituting the relationship between them. And as we shall see momentarily, the love of mankind is also considered rational – and indeed the foundation for the ideal Stoic society. Care must always be taken, then, to distinguish feelings and emotions that conflict with reason from those that accord with it. A life of apathy regarding indifferent things and of reasoned feeling regarding that which promotes natural ends makes up the emotional life of the wise person.

Stoicism contrasts sharply with Epicureanism when it comes to the role a person should play with respect to society and politics. Whereas Epicurus recommends withdrawal from society to life in a small congenial group and characterizes political life as a prison, the Stoics take a different view of the matter: "Nor yet will the Wise

Man live in solitude; for he is naturally made for society and action."[32] Not only is the Stoic sage a social creature, he is a member of the human race, and, Cicero reports, "The mere fact of their common humanity requires that one man should feel another man akin to him."[33] This sense of the brotherhood of humankind is the outgrowth of the togetherness and belongingness (*oikeiosis*) mentioned above; just as children naturally belong to their parents, all human beings naturally belong to one another. In this doctrine we find one of the grandest intellectual innovations in Western history – in the words of the historian Windelband, "one of the most powerful and pregnant creations in the history of the conceptions of human life."[34] Whereas previous philosophers, even Aristotle, had made a sharp distinction between Greeks and all other people, whom they termed Barbarians, the Stoics urge that this distinction is artificial. All human beings are brothers and sisters. The Stoics come to this belief because of their view that there is one rational law, one *logos*, for all of the world and hence all of humanity. "They hold that the universe is governed by divine will: it is a city or state of which both men and gods are members, and each one of us is a part of this universe; from which it is a natural consequence that we should prefer the common advantage to our own."[35] Whereas previous Greeks had distinguished people on the basis of their *polis* or their language (Greek or non-Greek), the Stoics claim that all human beings are part of one city, citizens of one state – the cosmopolis.

The divine rational law pervading all things is the source of the laws of this cosmopolis. "They say that justice, as well as law and right reason, exists by nature and not by convention ... "[36] As the non–Stoic commentator Philo puts it, "For this world is a great city, has one constitution and one law, and this is the reason of nature, commanding what should be done and forbidding what should not be done."[37] Here we have the beginning of the historically momentous doctrine of natural law. In the very nature of things we find the principles that should govern all human intercourse, and what these principles command is that we treat all human beings as equal. This is the basic principle of justice, which holds necessarily in the divine and rational constitution of things, even as it is so often broken and flouted in the actual irrational affairs of human beings and human states. Whatever else we think of the Stoics' philosophy, we must acknowledge that they are responsible for one of Western civilization's most distinctive and cherished political ideals.

Epictetus

Let us conclude our discussion of Stoicism by looking at the work of the late Stoic, Epictetus (50 BCE–30 CE). His is a voice that is distinctive and powerful (and always *practical*), even while the message is clearly grounded in the Stoic traditions we have identified. Epictetus was a Greek who had been enslaved in a Roman household. Although not well treated by his Roman owner, he was given his freedom when his remarkable philosophical talents came to light. Subsequently, he became a much loved teacher in Rome, and he left behind two works (transcribed by others) still widely read today, his *Manual* and the *Discourses*.

There is a story told about Epictetus that sums up much of his Stoic philosophy. It is said that one day his master became angry at him and as a result began to twist his arm. This continued for some time without any reaction from Epictetus, but finally he calmly said "Master, if you continue, you will break my arm." This, apparently, only raised the Roman's fury to greater heights, and he proceeded in fact to break Epictetus's arm – at which point Epictetus calmly observed "Master, I told you so." Here we have a picture of Stoic apathy toward that which is indifferent, physical feelings of pain and physical harm to the body. Here we have the calm, reasoned attitude of mind that turns an accident into an anticipated course of nature, and here too the resulting fortitude that raises a person above any conceivable harm.

The idea at the heart of Epictetus's thought is the distinction between things in our power and those that are not:

> Of all existing things some are in our power, and others are not in our power. In our power are thought, impulse, will to get and will to avoid, and, in a word, everything which is our own doing. Things not in our power include the body, property, reputation, office, and, in a word, everything which is not our own doing.[38]

Our attitudes, our thoughts, our responses to events, these are the things we can control, while what happens to our body or reputation is something over which we have no control. If something harsh happens to us, we are to ask, "Is it concerned with what is in our power or not?" "And if it is concerned with what is not in our power, be ready with the answer that it is nothing to you" (1). If one cannot avoid having one's arm broken, make no effort to avoid this happening. "Therefore let your will to avoid have no concern with what is not in man's power; direct it only to things in man's power that are contrary to nature" (2).

Not only are our thoughts and attitudes the only things we can control, they are the very things that make events dreadful or desirable: "What disturbs men's minds is not events but their judgment on events. For instance, death is nothing dreadful, or else Socrates would have thought it so. No, the only dreadful thing about it is men's judgment that it is dreadful" (4). And again, "Keep this thought by you: 'What distresses him is not the event, for that does not distress another, but his judgment on the event'" (16) and "For no one shall harm you, without your consent: you will only be harmed, when you think you are harmed" (30). Epictetus applies this way of thinking to matters both sublime and pedestrian – here is one of the latter: "Remember that foul words or blows in themselves are no outrage, but your judgment that they are so. So when any one makes you angry, know that it is your own thought that has angered you" (20). The foolish person is constantly blaming others for what is happening to her, but the only harm that comes her way is self-inflicted, through her own attitude to what happens. "The ignorant man's position and character is this:

he never looks to himself for benefit or harm, but to the world outside him. The philosopher's position and character is that he always looks to himself for benefit and harm" (48).

The secret to controlling one's thoughts and feelings lies in the recognition that the events toward which we direct them are totally beyond our control and that we only bring harm on ourselves if we dread, regret, or remonstrate over what happens to us. We will truly attain wisdom when we pattern our emotional reactions after events themselves, letting the latter guide the former. Thus, "Ask not that events should happen as you will, but let your will be that events should happen as they do, and you shall have peace" (8). Or, as he puts it later, "wish that only to happen which does happen" (32). When one's will is thus attuned to the actual and necessary course of events, one will live a life in accordance with nature – and attain perfect virtue, perfect peace, and perfect happiness. Such a life is invincible, since "You can be invincible, if you never enter on a contest where victory is not in your power." When you wish to happen what does happen, victory is always yours.

For Epictetus, following reason is a complex matter. It involves, first, "To understand Nature and follow her", but it also entails a life of principle, wherein one's actions are consistent over a lifetime: "Whatever principles you put before you, hold fast to them as laws which it will be impious to transgress" (50). Following this advice will produce that steadfastness of character so much admired by the Stoics, the character of a person who calmly knows how to deal with every contingency without nervously and erratically leaping this way and that, being pushed and pulled along by the fast-paced changes in the world. "Lay down for yourself from the first a definite stamp and style of conduct, which you will maintain when you are alone and also in the society of men" (32). The person of principle, as a later playwright put it, is the "man for all seasons."

Epictetus's advice is frequently quite concrete, applying his general message to the types of situations we so often confront in life. He advises, for example, the following: "In your conversation avoid frequent and disproportionate mention of your own doings or adventures; for other people do not take the same pleasure in hearing what has happened to you as you take in recounting your adventures" (33). Likewise, "If you try to act a part beyond your powers, you not only disgrace yourself in it, but you neglect the part which you could have filled with success" (37). Moreover, "And when someone says to you, 'You know nothing', and you do not let it provoke you, you are really on the right road" (46) And finally, "instead of displaying your principles to the multitude, show them the results of the principles you have digested" (46). That Epictetus and the other Stoics could combine such homespun wisdom with the most sophisticated philosophical musings on the nature of things undoubtedly contributed to their immense influence.

A Modern Stoic

As a parting example of Stoic doctrine, and as an indication of its abiding influence, I should like to quote from an author whom most people would *never* imagine to be a Stoic. The author in question was a recent American novelist and travel writer often thought to be nothing less than a hedonist and pornographer (and hence a follower of the Cyrenaics?). But consider the following passage:

> We awoke early and hired a car to take us to Epidaurus [an ancient healing center in Greece]. The day began in sublime peace ... The road to Epidaurus is like a road to creation. One stops searching. One grows silent, stilled by the hush of mysterious beginnings ... You are no longer riding through something – call it Nature, if you will – but participating in a rout, a rout of the forces of greed, malevolence, envy, selfishness, spite, intolerance, pride, arrogance, cunning, duplicity and so on ... It is the morning of the first day of the great peace, the peace of the heart, which comes from surrender. I never knew the meaning of peace until I arrived at Epidaurus ... The peace which most of us know is merely a cessation of hostilities, a truce, an interregnum, a lull, a respite, which is negative. The peace of the heart is positive and invincible, demanding no conditions, requiring no protection ... If it is a victory it is a peculiar one because it is based entirely on surrender, a voluntary surrender, to be sure ... What man wants is peace in order that he may live. Defeating our neighbor doesn't give peace any more than curing cancer brings health. Man doesn't begin to live through triumphing over his enemy nor does he begin to acquire health through endless cures. The joy of life comes through peace, which is not static but dynamic ... And without joy there is no life, even if you have a dozen cars, six butlers, a castle, a private chapel and a bomb-proof vault. Our diseases are our attachments, be they habits, ideologies, ideals, principles, possessions, phobias, gods, cults, religions, what you please ... Whatever we cling to, even if it be hope or faith, can be the disease which carries us off. Surrender is absolute: if you cling to even the tiniest crumb you nourish the germ which will devour you ... At Epidaurus, in the stillness, in the great peace that came over me, I heard the heart of the world beat. I know what the cure is: it is to give up, to relinquish, to surrender, so that our little hearts may beat in unison with the great heart of the world.

This remarkable passage, deeply Stoic in its inspiration, comes from a travel book, *The Colossus of Maroussi*, by Henry Miller.[39]

Stoicism is one of the most powerful, and many would say noble, ethical philosophies developed in the ancient Western world. We shall hear its reverberations later in this history of ethics. But it is an ethical theory that does have some significant problems, and we shall conclude by discussing several of them.

Problems of Stoicism

The Stoics were the first to assert the thesis of universal causation and determinism (although it was implicit in the earlier atomism of Democritus). According to this thesis, all events, including all human actions, have causes, and these causes necessitate the occurrence of the events that follow from them. If one accepts this doctrine, one believes that whatever happens is the one course required by the antecedent causes and that there is no alternative course of actions and events possible. What are we to say, in this case, about human freedom, the ability of human beings to make choices from real options so that whichever option they do select, they could equally well have acted otherwise? The Epicureans saw the threat of universal causation to human freedom and for this reason invented the notion of an unpredictable, uncaused swerve of atoms in order to avoid determinism. But the Stoics have nothing to do with the swerve; they are uncompromising determinists, the thesis of universal causation being essential to their philosophy. Nevertheless, they argue that some things, our attitudes and beliefs, are within our power, and they also present us with a complicated prescription for how we *ought* to act. Many philosophers see these latter elements of Stoicism as being inconsistent with the Stoics' own determinism.

Consider the case of our attitude toward sickness. According to the Stoics, it is up to us whether our illness is a misfortune or a matter of indifference – it depends on what attitude we take toward it. This seems to imply that it is possible for us to see the illness as a misfortune *and* possible for us to see it as a matter of indifference. But if universal causation is true, there will be a cause for our taking the one attitude or the other. And if the causes that exist prior to our forming the attitude lead us to perceive the illness as misfortune, *it is not possible for us to perceive it as a matter of indifference*. If, on the contrary, the causes lead us to assume the attitude of indifference, then it becomes impossible for us to see the illness as misfortune. Either one of the sets of causes or the other must exist, from which it follows that it is either impossible for us to feel misfortune or impossible for us to feel indifference. If one of these options is impossible, the attitude we actually take is necessary, in which case we really didn't have any *options* at all. And without options or choices, there is no such thing as freedom or voluntary behavior. And so, it seems, our attitudes and beliefs are not in our power.

The Stoics do not solve this problem; in fact, it is fair to say that they do not even attempt to solve it. Perhaps they did not see it as an issue. Aristotle, after all, had defined a voluntary action as an action whose cause lies within the agent, and if one thinks in terms of this definition those of our actions caused by our attitudes and beliefs (which lie within us) may be called voluntary. But is this really satisfactory? What should we say if it turns out, as it may well, that the causes of our attitudes and beliefs are a combination of genetic traits and educational influences. The latter lie outside us, and the former appear to be of such a "hardwired" nature that we have no control over them. If such are the causes of a person's attitudes and beliefs, no other attitudes and beliefs are possible for that person – from which it follows they are not really in this individual's power.

The problem of determinism makes questionable the consistency of the Stoics' theory of human nature with their theory of Nature. This possible inconsistency comes out in another way as well. Epictetus tells us "Do this" and "Don't do that" – he advises us, for example, not to talk too much about ourselves. But what if the causes that operate in the creation of one's personality, and subsequently within one's personality, make it inevitable that one endlessly talks about oneself. What sense does it make, then, to give such advice? "Don't talk too much about oneself" implies that one may or may not do this, and in effect says that the rational choice will be not to talk ... Giving advice, in other words, presupposes that the person advised has options and can make choices; determinism appears to deny this very assumption. Thus, we must ask, does it make sense for the Stoics to contrast the rational life with the life of ignorance and suggest that in the interest of pursuing happiness and virtue we should follow the one and not the other? Do we have a choice?

The problems we are considering here have become perennial philosophical issues. The debate rages today as to whether or not universal causation or determinism is inconsistent with freedom. Some philosophers think not – and hence offer hope to the Stoic. Others reject the Stoic claim to universal causation and argue that the fact of human freedom shows that not everything is caused. And still others throw in the towel, admit determinism, and sadly conclude that there is in fact no human freedom. If the Stoics do not solve this fascinating debate, at least they have the honor of being in on the early development of the problem.

The second major problem faced by Stoicism is the famous "problem of evil." This problem is shared by any religious doctrine that believes the world is under the control of divine providence and also postulates that God is perfect, good, or, as with the Stoics, rational. The problem is this: why, if God is rational, is there so much suffering and misery in the world? If God controls all things, why does this deity permit so much evil to occur? No one can deny that the world has always contained much suffering. Some of it is caused, no doubt, by human beings themselves; some of it is caused by natural "disasters" over which human beings have no control. But God has control over everything! Human beings are created according to God's providential plan, and they act out the role that divine providence has assigned them. So even the evil they cause can be traced directly back to God. Is not God responsible, then, for the evil that exists – for all of it!? If so, this makes God immoral; at least it does so if this God has the knowledge and power to prevent evil from occurring.

Very few religious believers, and they do not include the Stoics, wish to say that God is immoral or that he is limited either in knowledge or the ability to prevent evil. How, then, are they to explain the occurrence of evil? The most straightforward response, and the one given by the Stoics, is simply to deny the fact of evil. Thus Epictetus: "there is nothing intrinsically evil in the world" (27). Epictetus does not deny that many things *seem* to be evil, but in reality (intrinsically) they are not. The false appearances are the result of the fact that human beings interpret events from their own personal viewpoint and their impulse to survive and prosper – thus they may view a painful death as an evil. But from the perspective of the Whole, what happens to any person is required by the rational laws of Nature and God and hence is in accordance with natural and divine providence. Finite human beings simply cannot adequately comprehend the nature of the universe and fail to see that what happens always happens for the best. What is evil relative to a partial view of the matter is not evil relative to the correct, comprehensive vision of reality. Once we attain wisdom and can understand divine necessity, we will see that there is no evil in the world.

This type of answer to the problem of evil, although found in almost all religious doctrines, is a hard pill to swallow. The reality of suffering and pain are palpable and awful; the reality of a grand design in which this apparent evil is converted into something good and beneficial is at best the product of theory or faith. Many is the person who has lost the faith because of the concrete experience of evil. But for those whose acceptance of the theory is total, as was the case with many of the Stoics, it is possible to look suffering in the face without blinking.

Another problem encountered in Stoicism relates to their uncompromising claim that the life of virtue alone is good. Stressing as they do that virtue requires complete knowledge, and acknowledging that only the true sage possesses this knowledge, they face the question of what this means for the rest of us. We ordinary mortals, always ignorant to some degree, seem forever prohibited as a consequence of our normality from attaining virtue and happiness. This is a hard doctrine, and not one which serves well the goal of providing the type of security and peace of mind that Stoicism wished to offer. Compromises were in fact made, and some Middle Stoics urged that progress toward the ideal was possible and important; other Middle Stoics gave more significance to the "preferred" things in life and to the means of attaining the goals of impulse. Needless to say, critics of Stoicism, and they were many, jumped on these changes of heart and accused the Stoics of being inconsistent and of changing doctrine in order to obtain followers.

Finally, there is the problem of the Stoic concept of the world as a rational unity in which everything is connected and everything governed by providential, divine law. This is not a metaphysical theory that meets with great favor today. If we do not accept the metaphysics, can we still take the ethics seriously?

First of all, it is not clear that the metaphysics must be rejected. The scientific interpretation of the world, after all, is a *mathematical* one: the universe operates in accordance with laws, and these laws have mathematical expressions. Many philosophers see mathematics as the highest form of reason, and if one agrees, it follows that a mathematical universe *is* a rational universe. Moreover, recent ecological discoveries show how interrelated everything is on this planet. The life of one species depends on the lives of others, and the lives of all things are interrelated with environmental conditions on land and in the sea and water. Thus the interdependency of things stressed by the Stoics may be a fact. More speculatively, some cosmologists are beginning to talk about an ecological perspective on the universe itself, so that the many galaxies, black holes, and intergalactic dust(!) all form part of an interacting whole. If such speculations have substance, would this not vindicate Stoicism? To make a point not previously discussed, the Stoics were materialists – everything in the universe is matter. But they also thought of it as energy, the divine *logos* being described as a fiery breath that pervades all things. Some philosophers see a remarkable confluence between the early philosophical cosmology of the Stoics and contemporary scientific cosmology.

But even if such conjectures do not pan out, there is in Stoicism an ethical doctrine which may stand on its own. The emphasis on following principles, on being rational, on doing one's duty (in later Roman Stoicism), and on character do not necessarily depend on any particular metaphysical theory. When we arrive at the philosophies of Spinoza and Kant in the modern age, we shall hear echoes of Stoicism and encounter variations on Stoic ethics. It is an ethical theory that has perennial appeal.

5

Ethics During the Medieval Period

As we leave the ancient period, we enter the world of Christianity. We do not, however, entirely abandon the modes of thought developed and perfected in ancient Greece. The two greatest Christian thinkers of all times, St Augustine in the fourth and fifth centuries CE, and St Thomas Aquinas in the thirteenth, developed theologies and philosophies that attempted syntheses of the Christian message (or their interpretations of it) with Greek philosophy. Augustine was heavily influenced by Plato and the Platonist thinkers who followed him, especially the great Neoplatonist philosopher Plotinus. And Aquinas resurrected Aristotle and incorporated his thought into an explicit amalgam of Aristotelian and Christian beliefs. In one way or another, all of the medieval *philosophers* were concerned with issues whose origins were Greek. But, of course, the main and driving element in the philosophies of Augustine and Aquinas as well as of the other thinkers of this period is the Christian message itself, the doctrine of the one eternal God who is creator of the world and of humanity, the loving God who sent his son Jesus Christ to save human beings from sin, and the judgmental God who assigns his human creatures to heaven or hell in part as a result of the kinds of lives they live during their earthly sojourns (divine grace also enters the picture). The Platonic and Aristotelian concepts are used to articulate and interpret this message. They also provide it with universal scope or application: Augustine, Aquinas, and the other medieval thinkers see their philosophies as offering truths about humankind in general. In the studies that follow, what we want to look for is the highly distinctive form that the ideas and views originally coming from the Greeks assume when they are infused with basic Christian beliefs and values. The resulting ethical perspective is still very much with us today, although by no means universal even within Western culture.

Although they are surely the two most significant thinkers of the medieval period, Augustine and Aquinas are by no means the only important ones. The basic Christian message lent itself to a large number of different philosophical interpretations, and hence a variety of ethical outlooks. In this chapter we shall examine, in addition to the theories of Augustine and Aquinas, the ethics of Peter Abelard, a middle-period medieval thinker, and the ethical outlooks of John Duns Scotus and William Ockham, two late medieval philosophers. These three figures are particularly interesting because their ethical outlooks presage more recent developments in ethics.

St Augustine

Augustine (Aurelius Augustinas) was born in 354 CE in the north African town of Thagaste (located in what is now Algeria). His mother Monica was a Christian but his father Patricius remained a pagan. Given the forceful personality of Monica, Augustine and his brother and sister became believers early on, but Augustine, as he vividly describes in his masterful *Confessions*, soon strayed from the fold. First at the neighboring university of Madaura and then at the university at Carthage, he succumbed to the pleasures of the flesh, living to the hilt the bawdy and sensual life of a student. Later he began to cohabit with a concubine and fathered a son by her. But there was more to the young Augustine than the pleasure-seeker and libertine. Attracted to the intellectual life by the work of Cicero, he soon fell under the influence of a heretical Christian sect called the Manichaeans. The Manichaeans preached a dualistic doctrine in which the forces of good (God) are pitted against the forces of evil (the devil). It seemed to the young Augustine that this doctrine provided the best explanation available for the existence of evil in the world, including his own ever-apparent sin. How could a good God be responsible for so much evil? Is it not more reasonable to think that an independent force of evil exists in the world and competes with God?

After his student days, Augustine became a teacher of rhetoric at Carthage and then moved to Rome to continue his academic career. Never far away lurked the indomitable Monica, always hoping and attempting to dissuade him from his sinful and heretical life. It was in Rome that Augustine was introduced to the work of the Neoplatonists, the result being that he began to question and then to abandon the Manichaean and Ciceronian (skeptical) views he had previously held. More positively, under the influence of the Neoplatonists he began to appreciate the reality of the immaterial dimension of life and world. The writings of the Neoplatonists (Plotinus and Porphyry) directed his attention inward, to his soul, to his innermost, intangible being, and to the reality of the spiritual realm. Augustine was particularly attracted to Plotinus's resolution of the "problem of evil," the problem of reconciling the existence of evil in the world with the reality of a good and omnipotent deity. Plotinus's theory of "evil as privation" claims that evil is not something that exists as a positive factor in the world but signifies only a lack of being resulting from the inferior status of the created world. By denying that evil is some entity for whose existence God must be held responsible and blamed, Plotinus demonstrates that God is wholly good.

Later, when Augustine took a professorship at Milan, he was introduced to the

123

great Christian bishop Ambrose, with whom he was greatly impressed both intellectually and spiritually. It was in this context that he underwent his famous conversion to Christianity. The conversion occurred in a garden, where he overheard a child say "Pick it up and read it, pick it up and read it." He took this to mean the Bible, and on opening it to one of St Paul's epistles, he read: "No revelling or drunkenness, no debauchery or vice, no quarrels or jealousies! Let Christ Jesus himself be the armour that you wear; give no more thought to satisfying the bodily appetites."[1] He immediately came to see that no effort of will or intellect could save him from sin, and the realization dawned that his only hope lay through the power of God's grace. He came to understand that by God's grace he could turn his attention wholly to God and away from worldly desires and ambitions. Thus was he set on his life as a Christian. He soon returned to North Africa (in 388) where before long he was installed as the Christian Bishop of the town of Hippo. He remained in this post until his death many years later (430), serving both as a beloved pastor and as a highly esteemed Christian intellectual who was in the vanguard of many efforts to stem the tide of heretical doctrine. He was a prodigious and prolific writer, and he left us with an enormous body of books and pamphlets which have become seminal works of early Christian literature. In addition to his *Confessions*, his *The City of God* still ranks as one of the classics of Western civilization.

Our Chief Good

What does this Platonist and lately-converted Christian have to tell us about how we ought to live our lives? His ethics begins with a clearly recognizable Greek doctrine: "We all certainly desire to live happily; and there is no human being but assents to this statement almost before it is made"[2] Happiness is the aim (end) of life for all human beings, the goal toward which, as human beings, they naturally strive. But Augustine immediately asks, just as had Aristotle, what this happiness consists in. Some possibilities are clearly to be rejected: "But the title happy cannot, in my opinion, belong either to him who has not what he loves, whatever it may be, or to him who has what he loves if it is hurtful, or to him who does not love what he has, although it is good in perfection"[3] It is important to note the terms used by Augustine in describing these rejected possibilities. The central term is *love*, a term he employs very generally to include all forms of desire and striving – what we love is what we want and what we try to obtain through our actions. Consequently we are not happy if we do not obtain what we love; we are not happy if what we love turns out to be hurtful – either because it harms us or fails to satisfy us; and we are not happy if, while possessing what is "good in perfection," we fail to love it. Clearly the key to happiness is to discover what it is we already have which is good in perfection, and to come to love it. This will prevent us from failing to have what we love, and it will prevent us from loving what is hurtful. What is good in perfection is designated by Augustine as a human being's chief good, and thus happiness exists "when that which is man's chief good is both loved and possessed."[4]

What is this chief good? What is this perfection we possess and which we must love if we are to be happy? In answering this question, Augustine invokes the picture of the world embodied in the basic Christian conception of reality. This picture is a hierarchical one, incorporating, in Platonic fashion, the notion of levels of reality and perfection. All things have a place, a "rank and species," assigned to them "by the order of their nature." God is the being having perfect reality; the material world, being at furtherest remove from God, has least reality and is accordingly much inferior to God in its being. In between these two extremes we find human beings. Made up of body and soul, they share the materiality of the physical world but also the spirituality of the higher domain. *As a material being*, the human person has a large number of physical wants and desires (loves), the objects of which are themselves material. Clearly these objects of love are inferior to the spiritual things that are closer in reality to God. But *as soul*, the human person has the ability to love these higher things, and indeed to love God, the perfect being.

The Order of Love

The levels of reality are distinguished by Augustine, again in good Platonic fashion, in terms of their susceptibility to change. All things in the created world of space and time are in constant change, and all of them come to exist and subsequently perish. God, on the other hand, is immutable, unchanging and eternally existing. Change and perishing are signs of inferiority, while immutability is the mark of perfect being. Hence all beings can be ranked as inferior or superior in terms of their place on the mutable/ immutable scale. God is perfect being, and the material world imperfect being. Human beings have a perishable body but an immortal soul; thus they are intermediate on the scale of being. This metaphysical or theological conception gives substance to Augustine's distinction between kinds of love. To love that which is eternal is to love that which will always be present and will always satisfy one's desires, whereas to love that which is mutable and perishable will disappoint as a result of change, or cause grief as a result of perishing. Thus it is only rational to love the souls of other human beings more than their bodies, and more rational to love God than other human beings. It is *certainly* more rational to love God than to love perishing material objects and the perishing body. As the distinguished Augustinian scholar Etienne Gilson expressed it, "Men can be happy only in adhering with their whole heart to the immutable Truth and Wisdom, whose stability alone can redeem them from perpetual becoming in time."[5] Instead of restlessly moving from one profane love to another, never satisfied, we achieve stability through the eternal stability of the God we love.

The hierarchical structure of reality, together with the conception of the human being as possessing different degrees of reality within herself (soul being superior to body), sets the stage for defining "man's chief good."

> We must now inquire what is man's chief good, which of course cannot be anything inferior to man himself. For whoever follows what is inferior to himself, becomes himself inferior. But every man is bound to follow what is best. Wherefore man's chief good is not inferior to man. Is it then something similar to man himself? It must be so, if there is nothing above man which he is capable of enjoying. But if we find something which is both superior to man, and can be possessed by the man who loves it, who can doubt that in seeking for happiness man should endeavor to reach that which is more excellent than the being who makes the endeavor. For if happiness consists in the enjoyment of a good than which there is nothing better, which we call the chief good, how can a man be properly called happy who has not yet attained to his chief good?[6]

The notion that a thing's chief good is something superior to it, if there is something superior, leads Augustine to claim that the chief good of the body is not the (equally real) bodily states of pleasure, or beauty, or the like, but rather the higher reality, the soul. By this he means that the best condition of the body is to be ruled over by the soul. Hence the more virtuous the soul, the better off the body. What, then, is the chief good of the soul? What should it love and pursue?

> Let us see how the Lord Himself in the gospel has taught us to live; how, too, Paul the apostle – for the Manichaeans dare not reject these Scriptures. Let us hear, O Christ, what chief end Thou dost prescribe to us; and that is evidently the chief end after which we are told to strive with supreme affection. "Thou shalt love," He says, "the Lord thy God." Tell me also, I pray Thee, what must be the measure of love, for I fear lest the desire enkindled in my heart should either exceed or come short in fervor. "With all thy heart," He says. Nor is that enough. "With all thy soul." Nor is it enough yet. "With all thy mind." ... We have heard, then, what and how much we must love; this we must strive after, and to this we must refer all our plans. The perfection of all our good things and our perfect good is God.[7]

When we love God, we love that which is superior to us. God already dwells within us, but we may not in fact love this perfect good. If we turn our love away from inferior, material objects and redirect it toward this perfect being, we shall embrace the perfection of all good things. God, then, is our greatest good, and we attain it, and consequently happiness, by loving him. "To live well is nothing but to love God with all the heart, with all the soul, with all the mind."[8]

Augustine frequently expresses this doctrine in terms of the Biblical notion of beatitude: "the striving after God is, therefore, the desire of beatitude, the attainment of God is beatitude itself."[9] Beatitude is a state of happiness, more specifically the happiness of the virtuous person.[10] Such beatitude or happiness is not a theoretical contemplation of the sort Aristotle might approve of; rather it is a loving union with God, a fulfillment of one's entire intellectual and emotional needs and desires. This must be kept in mind, since Augustine the philosopher often uses intellectual terms in describing beatitude: "The happy life consists in rejoicing in the truth." Beatitude is the love of this absolute truth with all one's heart.

Peace

A central concept used by Augustine in describing the happiness of human beings is that of *peace*. Peace, he maintains, is desired by everyone: "Whoever gives even moderate attention to human affairs and to our common nature, will recognize that there is no man who does not wish to be joyful, neither is there any one who does not wish to have peace. For even they who make war desire nothing but victory – desire, that is to say, to attain to peace with glory. ... For even they who intentionally interrupt the peace in which they are living have no hatred of peace, but wish it changed into a peace that suits them better."[11] Even wicked individuals, he notes, "wage war to maintain the peace of their own circle, and wish that, if possible, all men belonged to them, that all men and things might serve but one head, and might, either through love or fear, yield themselves to peace with him!"[12] Thus the universal desire for happiness is revealed as a universal desire for peace. And peace is achieved through establishing order, an arrangement of human beings with harmony among them. "The peace of all things is the tranquillity of order."[13] And order, Augustine tells us, is "the distribution which allots things equal and unequal, each to its own place."[14]

Through war and aggression, wicked human beings may create a form of peace among themselves, but this peace is an unjust peace.[15] The order achieved and enforced in this fashion is a perversion of the natural order of the universe. Human beings, in their pride, their self-centeredness, are aping God. Abhorring equality with other human beings under God, evil individuals impose a rule of their own over their equals – they reject the just peace of God and love their own unjust peace. Clearly, then, to achieve the just peace, human beings must order themselves individually and collectively so as to achieve the natural order of things.

> The peace of the body then consists in the duly proportioned arrangements of the parts. The peace of the irrational soul is the harmonious repose of the appetites, and that of the rational soul the harmony of

knowledge and action. The peace of body and soul is the well-ordered and harmonious life and health of the living creature. Peace between man and God is the well-ordered obedience of faith to eternal law. Peace between man and man is well-ordered concord. ... The peace of the celestial city is the perfectly ordered and harmonious enjoyment of God, and of one another in God.[16]

The peace, then, that truly satisfies, that brings true happiness, is the peace which prevails when God's created order is preserved. It is a peace which exists when our loves are ordered according to the "place," the equality and inequality, of the objects of those loves. We must love God more than our fellow human beings; we must love all human beings equally as equal creatures of God; we must love material objects in the order and degree dictated by the rational soul, and we must love them less than we love the spiritual life of the soul and our fellow human beings. By ordering our loves in this fashion, we attain harmony within the individual soul, within the community of human beings, and within our relationship to God. Such harmony is perfect repose, such repose is perfect and just peace, such peace is true happiness.

Clearly, however, in reality it is the unjust peace we most often seek, not the just. Wicked human beings are wicked by virtue of the fact that the order of their loves is not the natural order established by God. They love material objects and pleasures more than the spiritual life; they love themselves more than they love their fellow creatures; and they even love themselves, and their vastly inferior bodily satisfactions, more than they love the perfect being, God. As Augustine sees it, this perverse order of their loves is the product of a failure or defect of will. Evil creatures have voluntarily turned their wills away from the objects of higher reality and perfection and toward lower and lesser ones. It is this perversion of the order of loves which is sin, and this sin is responsible for the evil that is manifest in the world.

The Two Cities

The failure of the will to acknowledge and honor the natural order of the objects of love is widespread, so much so as to generate a community of people whose loves are disarranged in the same manner. All of them can be said to love themselves more than they love God. This commonality crosses all ethnic and national boundaries and generates a "city" – not in a civic, political sense but in a psychological or moral/religious one. As one commentator has put it, "What constitutes one people is their union in pursuit of a common object of love."[17] The common object of love of all sinners is themselves and their material reality. In this way, sinners distinguish themselves from all those human beings who love God more than themselves. These latter individuals also, given their common object of love, create a "city." And so we find the basis for Augustine's celebrated distinction between the earthly city and the heavenly city, the City of Man and the City of God: "Accordingly, two cities have been formed by two loves: the earthly by the love of self, even to the contempt of God; the heavenly by the love of God, even to the contempt of self. The former, in a word, glories in itself, the latter in the Lord. For the one seeks glory from men; but the greatest glory of the other is God, the witness of conscience."[18] While the City of God has existed throughout all eternity, the City of Man came into existence with the Fall of human beings through Adam's disgrace. Throughout human history the two cities have been intertwined, some members of every nation being citizens of the one and others members of the other. Augustine also suggests that in this life we all at best possess dual citizenship. As fallen creatures, we are spiritual beings in conflict with our bodily vessels (a remnant of his Manichaeanism?). We are all sinners, and as such none of us in this life can ever be fully and exclusively members of the City of God. As history unfolds, each city tries to vanquish the other and recruit its citizens. But the division will continue until Judgment Day, when God will separate the cities and send their respective citizens either to heaven or hell, in accordance with their final choice of membership in the City of Man or the City of God.

The Moral Law

All human beings are capable of being citizens of the City of God, since all human beings, possessed of a rational soul, can know the laws of God and hence can love and rejoice in the Truth. These laws, which make up the Eternal Law (*lex aeterna*) – in distinction from the laws human beings create for the purpose of bringing order among themselves on earth (*lex temporalis*) – are known by human beings as the moral law. Recognition of the moral law by means of the rational soul is recognition of it through conscience. The moral law is simply an expression of the Nature of God – it is God's "sovereign reason." Hence, far from being arbitrary, it is totally objective and universal. It contains, among other injunctions, the laws of justice designed to order the relationships among human beings.

Through conscience we can know the moral law, but we cannot know it through our own efforts alone. It is only God's grace that permits finite mortals to comprehend the infinite truth. "The law was therefore given that grace might be sought; grace was given that the law might be fulfilled".[19] This grace is manifested through the "divine illumination" of our minds. It is God who illumines our minds and impresses upon conscience the contents of the moral law. Augustine uses such phrases as the law being "transcribed" on to the human mind and its "notion" being impressed on us, to describe this mysterious manner in which God as light allows our conscience, our reason, to be illumined and to grasp the truth. "The mind informs itself by the divine light through reason."[20]

What the moral law prescribes first and foremost is the love of God. Furthermore, it indicates the right order among the other objects of love. These dictates are in effect the principles of *virtue*, and thus virtue is "the order of love" or "rightly ordered love."[21] To be virtuous is to love things in the order and to the degree to which they should be loved given their place in the natural order of things. The virtuous person is therefore the wise individual who knows the moral law and follows it in her actions. And, as Socrates, Plato, and Aristotle had stressed, virtue leads to happiness: "And hence the chain of right choices of will is so to speak a path whereby they ascend to beatitude."[22]

Our minds, however, clouded as they often are by the love of inferior objects, frequently fail to perceive the moral law, and thus we fail to follow its precepts. We choose the inferior over the superior; we live a life of vice rather than virtue. As we noted above, the fault is a defect of will, since "The right will is ... well-directed love, and the wrong will is ill-directed love."[23] In this perversion of the will we find the origin of evil in the world – human beings are responsible for it because they turn their vision away from God and the eternal law, and they do so because they fail to arrange their loves in the right order. "For defection from that which supremely is, to that which has less of being – this is to begin to have an evil will."[24] Furthermore, "the defection of the will is evil, because it is contrary to the order of nature, and an abandonment of that which has supreme being for that which has less."[25] We bring evil into the world through the defection of our will, and we do so voluntarily – "the will could not become evil, were it unwilling to do so; and therefore its failings are justly punished, being not necessary, but voluntary."[26] Thus we are responsible for evil, and God's subsequent punishment of us for our evil actions is warranted.

The Problem of Evil

Placing responsibility for evil on the shoulders of human beings solves for Augustine a problem that had haunted him from the beginning of his intellectual career, indeed long before the time he was converted to Christianity. The basic puzzle for him is how there can be evil in a world created by God. The Christian God is supposed to create all things out of nothing, from which it seems to follow that this God is responsible for everything that exists in the world, including *evil*. But God is also supposed to be supremely good, supremely powerful, and supremely wise. Thus he would know how to create a world without evil; he would be able to do so; and given his goodness or beneficence, he would will to do so. How, then, can there be evil in the world?

The Manichaeans whose doctrines Augustine embraced as a young man had an answer to this puzzle. God, the principle of light and goodness, is *not* responsible for evil. God for them is not the only principle of creation – there is also the devil, the principle of darkness and evil, who operates in influencing the affairs of the world.

It is this negative creative source, therefore, which is responsible for evil. Such a theory, while highly plausible to some minds, including that of the young Augustine, achieves the goal of explaining evil only by limiting God. God is no longer thought of as infinite but rather as only one of two creative sources which produce and control the inhabitants and events in the material world. Thus God cannot be seen as the totally powerful being in whom orthodox Christians believe. Manichaeanism was therefore branded a heresy, and after his conversion Augustine was a leader in the fight against this heresy. But if not the Manichaean solution to the problem of evil, what other solution is there?

There is one thing that Augustine professes to know with certainty: "This I do know, that the nature of God can never, nowhere, nowise be defective, and that natures made of nothing can."[27] God cannot be responsible for evil, but created things ("natures made of nothing") can be. It is in his theological vision of created things as defective that Augustine finally comes to perceive the answer to the puzzle of evil. If there were some positive aspect of human nature that led individuals to act in ways that bring evil into the world, then we could ask why God created human beings with this characteristic. If, say, human nature is essentially aggressive, why does God create essentially aggressive human beings? God does create us, and he deliberately creates us with all the positive characteristics we have. Thus if evil is the product of one of these characteristics, the fault really lies with God – he should not have created us with this characteristic. But what if evil results, not from a positive feature of human nature, but from a negative one – from the lack of something? And what if the lack in question is the result simply of the fact that the human sinner is a *creature*, not the creator. If God the creator is perfect being, human beings, being created out of nothing, will be less than perfect being – they will lack perfect being. Their sin can then be understood to be the result of creaturehood, of the distance creatures are in their very being from the perfect reality of God. We cannot blame God for creating human beings with this lack, for they would not be creatures if they did not have this defect. Creatures could not have been created otherwise – thus we cannot consider God's creation of them, with all their defects, to have been the product of any lack of knowledge, power, or goodness on his part. Here we find Plotinus's "evil as privation" argument – and Plato's doctrine of degrees of reality – expressed in Christian terms.

Augustine's solution to the problem of evil, then, is his *negative* theory of sin and evil. Evil is not a positive reality, for which causal blame can be attributed to whomever or whatever brings it into existence. It is simply the lack of fully positive reality, the distance from God. Augustine frequently uses metaphors of light and darkness, and of sound and silence, to illustrate his theory. God is light, but creatures, being at such a far remove from God, are darkness. This darkness, however, is merely the absence of light. Likewise, silence is not a form of sound, a positive aural reality, but the lack of sound; it is not something we actually hear but rather the lack or absence of hearing. Human beings and their defective wills are not efficient causes of evil (actual realities that bring it into the world); they are defective causes – they act sinfully because they lack the reality of perfect goodness.

But why, we might ask, does God create human beings at all, if, being defective, they bring evil into the world? Augustine's answer is that human beings are given the power of choice by God. Because they are defective, they can choose evil, but they also have the ability to perceive the moral law and act on it. They have the ability to love inferior things and in doing so create evil, but they also have the ability to direct their love toward God and thus pursue the good. By virtue of the freedom of their wills, their ability to choose either "man or God," good or evil, human beings themselves are responsible for the existence of evil. They are created because God wants them to have the opportunity to love him, who is perfect goodness, and in granting them free will he gives them this opportunity. But if they do not avail themselves of it – voluntarily, as a result of their own choices – then, being creatures, they will not rise above their defective nature, and sin and evil will be the result.

Free Will

Does Augustine's answer to the problem of evil work? Few today find the negative theory of evil convincing, but there are those who appeal to human freedom in attempting to show how the fact of evil can be reconciled with the notion of an all-good creator.[28] In fact, the free-will defense, attributing evil to the free acts of human agents, is part of a very common "theodicy" found in recent philosophy of religion, a theodicy being this very attempt to understand evil in the light of creation by an all-perfect deity. But this theodicy has its critics. For one thing, much of the evil (the suffering and misery) in the world does not appear to be the result of human agency at all. Consider all the evil resulting from hurricanes, tidal waves, volcanic eruptions, and the like. Surely these events are not the result of the perverted human will. Can't God prevent these natural disasters from happening? If so, why doesn't he do so? If he cannot prevent them, doesn't this show him to be limited in ability or knowledge and hence imperfect? And why, the critic of the free-will defense continues, is there *so much* evil in the world? Couldn't God have created human beings with a greater disposition to do good, not, to be sure, a disposition so strong as to rule out choice and evil acts, but a greater inclination to love the good and hate evil? With respect to the negative theory of evil, we might agree that natural disasters are the inevitable (and negative) aspect of a created world, but we might still ask whether a created world, a created physical environment, must have all or so many of these dangers – just because it is created? Unless we share Augustine's extreme Platonism with its doctrine of levels of reality, an affirmative answer sounds very weak.

Augustine also struggles with the problem of how human beings can be thought to have free will if they are created by God and if God knows for all eternity what they will do. If they are created by God, isn't God responsible for their nature and therefore for the actions (including the sinful ones) that spring from it? And if God, being omniscient, knows everything that will happen, doesn't this knowledge entail that human beings will do exactly what God knows they will do and are incapable of doing anything else? If God knows that a person will sin at a certain time, this person has no choice, no options – she must sin at that time, in which case it is difficult to see how such a choice is free. Augustine answers these skeptical objections in ways that have become part of standard Christian apologetics. With regard to the claim that God's creation of human beings undermines their free will, he responds by saying that indeed God creates human beings, but he creates them *with freedom of the will*. It is this free will, not God, that leads to sin. With regard to the objection that God's omniscience is incompatible with human freedom, Augustine counters that one of the things God knows, in knowing everything, is that human beings *will* to sin and that they do so freely. Insofar as God knows this, it must be so (no one can *know* something that isn't so), and thus it follows that it is true that human beings freely will either to engage in sin or to be virtuous. Again, these "solutions" of Augustine's to the problems of divine omnipotence and omniscience are quite controversial.

Weak or strong, Augustine's answers to the problems inherent in the theistic world-view he adopts stand as major efforts of a Christian thinker to deal with these ethical and metaphysical questions. And his ethical theory as a whole, with its focus on love, stands as one of the major Christian attempts to answer Socrates' question about how we are to live our lives. Augustine shows how theists can be philosophical ethicists. One can, of course, reject the religious metaphysics, and one can reject the Platonic philosophical background. If one does so, one must wonder whether any use can still be made of Augustine's rich and fascinating idea of an order of love. It would be intriguing to speculate, but we must now move on and see what some other great Christian philosophers had to say about ethical issues.

Peter Abelard

Abelard (1079–1142 CE) is the most colorful figure in medieval thought and one of the most charismatic in Western intellectual history. Many of his students and colleagues thought of him as a contemporary Socrates, while others branded him a heretic and a rogue. Quarrelsome and combative, he crossed intellectual swords with many of the leading figures of his day, and he often lost out in the intellectual power struggles. He was condemned for heresy at the Council of Sens in 1141. Abelard also became notorious for his longstanding affair with Heloise – one of the great love stories of all times.[29] After being castrated as a result of a quarrel, he entered a monastery and Heloise joined a convent. Through correspondence, the two maintained an intellectual relationship for the rest of their lives.

While it has been necessary to piece together the elements of Augustine's ethics from a variety of sources, Abelard left us with several treatises in which his ethical thought receives more or less systematic treatment. We shall concentrate on the book he called his *Ethics*, its Latin name being *Scito te ipsum* or *Know Thyself*. The central topic of this work is *sin*, which for Abelard is the highest form of moral fault or guilt. His question is: what is sin, a matter of doing something wrong, a matter of having wrongful desires, or a matter of acting with a certain wrongful intention? His theory, which he argues for with great logical skill and numerous down-to-earth, often sexual examples, is that actions themselves are morally indifferent and that sin arises solely out of the intention with which one acts. His thoughts can be seen as a development of Augustine's "interiorism" with its emphasis on the soul's inward activities.

The *Ethics* begins with the statement "We consider morals to be the vices or virtues of the mind which make us prone to bad or good works."[30] He explicitly distinguishes these mental vices and virtues from bodily ones such as weakness and strength, implying that moral virtue and vice are not to be found in these bodily conditions. He also notes that there are good and bad things of the mind that do not pertain to morals and hence do not make human life worthy of praise or blame – things such as quickness of thinking or dullness of mind. His reason for excluding these from morals is that "since all these befall the wicked and the good alike, they do not in fact belong to the composition of morality nor do they make life base or honourable" (ibid.). A person whose mind is slow may still be honorable, and an individual with a quick mind may be exceedingly base. Mental vices are those traits of mind that "incline the will to something which is not at all fitting to be done or to be forsaken" (ibid.). A slow mind, ignorance, or a bad memory are not necessarily of this kind.

What is Sin?

But sin has yet to be identified. It is not to be equated with mental vices such as those just defined. One does not sin just because one has, for example, an irascible disposition, a tendency to become angry, any more than one sins simply because one has a bodily tendency to seek luxury. These mental and bodily vices (dispositions) are simply the conditions or "material" that can generate moral struggle. Whether or not we sin becomes a matter of the outcome of this struggle with vice. "And so vice is that by which we are made prone to sin, that is, are inclined to consent to what is not fitting so that we either do it or forsake it" (p. 5). It is this consent which is of the essence: "Now this consent we properly call sin, that is, the fault of the soul by which it earns damnation or is made guilty before God" (ibid.). Consent to vice is described by Abelard in theological terms – it is "contempt of God and an offense against him" (ibid.) – but as we proceed it will become clear that Abelard's concept of sin is something that can easily be seen as the highest form of moral fault in a non-theological sense. Abelard can be said to define a voluntaristic position in ethics which stresses the importance of volitions or motive. This is a position found, with a non-

Christian emphasis, in Stoicism, and much later, with a non-theological emphasis, in Kant. Abelard's arguments for his voluntarism show forth the perennial attraction of this ethical stance.

Abelard gives a precise characterization of the consent constituting sin. It is not to be identified with a "bad will" when this is understood as a desire to do something wrong. A person, Abelard argues, may consent to do something wrong without wanting to undertake this act. He gives the example of a person who kills his master because the latter is trying to kill him. The person, in acting out of self-defense, may have no desire whatsoever to kill his master. Nevertheless, he consents to kill him rather than to be killed himself, and "because he consented to a killing to which he ought not to have consented, this unjust consent of his which preceded the killing was a sin" (p. 9). We may wish to disagree with Abelard over the sinfulness of killing a person in self-defense, but we need to take with us his main point – that sinning, on the one hand, and wanting or desiring to do something wrong, on the other, are not the same thing. Sinning is a matter of assenting to something one knows to be wrong, or giving in to a desire to do something wrong, approving of this desire or deciding to follow its promptings. A bad will consists of desires to do what is unseemly or untoward; a sinful will is one that consents to these desires; and the highest form of moral rectitude is refusing to consent to the promptings of one's bad will.

Abelard considers an objection at this point. Granted that one sins without a bad will (without desiring to do wrong) when one sins under constraint (the conditions under which one kills another in self-defense might be thought of as a sort of constraint), what of those cases in which one sins willingly? Aren't the sin and the bad will the same in these cases (which probably form the majority of sinful acts)? "For example, someone sees a woman and falls into concupiscence and his mind is affected by the pleasure of the flesh, so that he is incited to the baseness of sexual intercourse. ... what else is this will and base desire than sin?" (pp. 13–14). Abelard's answer to this objection is instructive: "I answer that if that will is restrained by the virtue of temperance but is not extinguished, it remains for a fight and persists in struggling and does not give up even when overcome" (p. 13). The desires and lusts of the flesh (the bad will) constitute the material for a fight. Does a person give in to them or restrain them? The answer to this question determines whether or not the person sins. Sin exists only when one gives in, consents to, the concupiscence. "So sin is not lusting for a woman, but consenting to lust; the consent of the will is damnable, but not the will for intercourse" (p. 15). Lust is natural, Abelard thinks; it is always with us (it is part of "our weakness"), but it itself does not condemn us to sin. In fact, in prevailing over it we achieve our highest victory and glory.

Sin, as Abelard understands it, does not even require wrong actions on our part; it is enough that we consent to do what is unlawful. "The time when we consent to what is unlawful is in fact when we in no way draw back from its accomplishment and are inwardly ready, if given the chance, to do it" (p. 15). If, for example, we are prepared to give into our lust and engage in illicit intercourse whenever the opportunity presents itself, we are in a state of sin (in the "fullness of guilt") even without actually committing the act. In fact, to Abelard's radical way of thinking, doing the wrong deed does not make us more sinful than our simply being prepared to do it: "the performance of the deed adds nothing to increase the sin" (p. 15).

Sins need not be voluntary. One may not want to give in to lust: "There are people who are wholly ashamed to be drawn into consent to lust or into a bad will and are forced out of the weakness of the flesh to want what they by no means want to want." (p. 17). In embryonic form we have here a sophisticated theory of voluntary behavior which equates it with *wanting to want*.[31] Our "first-order desires," for instance the desires of the flesh, may not be consistent with our "higher- or second-order desires," for instance, the desire not to give in to the desires of the flesh. An act is voluntary, Abelard is saying, only if it is consistent with our second-order desires; and if it is inconsistent with them, it is involuntary. Hence the person who gives in to her lust but does not want to do so sins involuntarily. When one does not want to consent, but nevertheless does, one sins involuntarily.

The Moral Indifference of Actions

Perhaps the most controversial aspect of Abelard's ethics is his doctrine of the indifference of actions. In his words, "The doing of sin adds nothing to guilt or damnation before God" (p. 19). According to Abelard, one reason why others think that the act of sinning increases the guilt already incurred by the consent to sin is that the sinful act yields pleasure. But, Abelard responds, if the pleasure itself were sinful, then "spouses are not immune from sin when they unite in ... carnal pleasure" (ibid.). If it is said that marital intercourse should be engaged in without pleasure, Abelard objects that this is impossible, the resulting pleasure being unavoidable. And so, "It is clear from all this that no natural pleasure of the flesh should be imputed to sin nor should it be considered a fault for us to have pleasure in something in which it has happened the feeling of pleasure is unavoidable" (p. 21).

How, Abelard goes on to ask, could the actual commission of a sin increase the guilt already incurred by the consent to sin, given that the commission itself is a corporeal and external act and not one of the soul? "The doing of deeds has no bearing upon an increase of sin and nothing pollutes the soul except what is of the soul" (p. 23). Abelard further argues for this position by claiming that any given act, or kind of act, can occur without being sinful. First of all, any given kind of act can be done under coercion or through ignorance – "as for example if a woman is forced to lie with another woman's husband or if a man who has been tricked in some way or other sleeps with a woman whom he thought to be his wife ... " (p. 25). Abelard does not discuss these examples in any detail, but his point is clear enough. Almost any bodily action can be forced, in which case, as Aristotle has shown us, the person committing the act is not really responsible for it and ought not to be censured for it. Likewise, a person may undertake almost any act without understanding one or more of the important particulars regarding what she is doing, to whom she is doing it, with what, in what context, and so on – in which case, as Aristotle again pointed out, the person may be excused for the act. If any action can occur without incurring moral guilt (sin), then an act itself is morally indifferent. This does not mean that no act is wrong in itself, but only that the commission of an act is not what makes a person morally guilty (sinful). In Abelard's eyes, it is the consent to commit an act known by the agent to be morally wrong that brings sin upon this agent.

The claim that his contemporaries found most outrageous was Abelard's application of the above view to the case of the soldiers who killed Christ. It is clear, Abelard thinks, that these soldiers did not know what they were doing and did not know that what they were doing was wrong. In acting out of ignorance, they thereby committed no sin in executing Christ. This is one of Abelard's views that was condemned by the Council of Sens.

In a manner reminiscent of the Greek and Roman Stoics, Abelard notes that the only thing we always have control over are the acts of our soul or mind. "There are in fact many things by which we are restrained from action yet we always have dominion over our will and consent" (p. 27 – "will" is being used in this context as equivalent to consent or approval, not, as as in most contexts, as desire or natural will[32]). It is not just "up to us" whether we do what is right or what is wrong – external events may intervene to make it impossible to do good or to force us into doing something wrong. But whether or not we consent to acting in a certain fashion *is* "up to us," and our actual consent is what determines our guilt or our glory. Abelard deduces from these facts that moral commandments are in reality (even if they appear otherwise) directed at our consent, not at our bodily behavior. We can morally be commanded to do only what it is within our power to do, and consent alone is always within our power. Abelard has an interesting argument designed to show that moral prohibitions should not be understood to refer to a deed: "If a prohibition of this kind is understood, according to the sound of the words, to refer to the deed, he who wants to bear false witness or even consents to speaking it, as long as he does not speak it, whatever the reason for his silence, does not become guilty according to the Law" (p. 27). Abelard clearly thinks that consenting to bear false witness, even if one is deterred from doing so (perhaps by fear), is enough to make one morally guilty. And so the Law needs to be *interpreted*: "when it is said 'do not do this or that' the meaning is 'do not consent to do this or that' ... " (p. 27).

Abelard's arguments about the moral indifference of actions are suspect. He seems to have confused the fact that an act of a certain type can sometimes be caused or prevented by factors beyond our control with the quite different claim that actions are always out of our control. Actions we cannot avoid or engage in bring no merit or fault upon us, and, to be sure, there are many such actions. But not all of them fall into this category. When we bear false witness, we may do so knowingly and voluntarily. Are we not, in this case, to be censored for actually doing so? And is not actually doing so worse than having consented to do so, since we may always change our minds after having initially consented? So, when Abelard argues "Truly, it is not a sin to kill a man nor to lie with another's wife; these sometimes can be committed without sin" (p. 27), we want to reply that the fact that they can sometimes be committed without sin does not entail that they are always committed without sin. Abelard, however, seems to be of the opinion that what we do is never really within our control, from which it does follow that merit and blame should apply only to the voluntary act of consent. Be that as it may, he is surely right that moral praise and blame are often justified by the state of mind of the agent. Furthermore, in giving us a theory of moral culpability or blameworthiness, Abelard is undoubtedly correct in maintaining that consent and knowledge (matters of the soul) are of the essence. If a person does not intend to do what she in fact does, she is (at least usually) not considered blameworthy for her behavior. Hence Abelard's theory of the moral indifference of actions takes on credibility when it is seen as a theory of moral praiseworthiness and blameworthiness – which, after all, is what moral rectitude and sin are all about. "For God thinks not of what is done but in what mind it may be done, and the merit or glory of the doer lies in the intention, not in the deed" (p. 29).

A Subjectivist Theory?

Abelard is frequently criticized for having a *subjectivist* theory of ethics.[33] The charge is that by focusing exclusively on consent and intention, which are subjective matters, he provides no objective ground for the moral wrongness of acts. This accusation is problematic. After all, sin involves consent to a wrong or untoward act, which presupposes that the act itself *is* wrong. The sinful intention does not make the act wrong in Abelard's eyes; rather it is wrong because it is inconsistent with God's law. Moreover, seen as a theory of blameworthiness and praiseworthiness, not as a theory of right and wrong action, there is nothing objectionable about Abelard's focus on intention and consent. These matters – subjective if you will – *are* what make the difference between a wrong action for which we are to blame and the same action for which we are not to blame.

But Abelard sometimes talks in ways that can be construed as providing a criterion of good and bad actions. He suggests that an act is good if it flows from a good intention, and bad if from a bad one. Thus:

> Works in fact, which as we have previously said are common to the damned and the elect alike, are all indifferent in themselves and should be called good or bad only on account of the intention of the agent, not, that is, because it is good or bad for them to be done but because they are done well or badly, that is, by that intention by which it is or is not fitting that they should be done (p. 45).

And:

> ... so anyone's intention is called good in itself, although the work is not called good in itself but because it proceeds from a good intention (p. 47).

In these remarks, the subjective intention seems to give rise to the moral character of the act. This comes out clearly in Abelard's attempt to interpret in a positive fashion some Biblical examples that would otherwise be embarrassing. God commanded Abraham to sacrifice his son Isaac. How could a good God do such a thing ("Surely God did not command well a deed which it was not good to do?" (p. 31))? The answer lies in God's intention: he commanded this act in order to provide us with the example of Abraham's obedience, the constancy of his faith, and his love of God. Thus "This intention of God was right in an act which was not right" (ibid.). This shows that God is not to be blamed for commanding the killing of Isaac. Does it also show that God's action of demanding the sacrifice of Isaac was a good one, given his good intention? If God is to be acquitted of doing something wrong, and not merely absolved of blame for it, his right intention must make his act right. In suggesting as much, Abelard provides grounds for the claim that his theory is subjectivist.

In light of Abelard's focus on inner intention and consent, we might expect him to adopt what later is called a retributive theory of punishment, the theory that we ought to punish only those individuals who have an evil mind (*mens rea*) – which for Abelard would be a mind consenting to what is against the law. But this is not his position. Rather, he asks "why ought we sometimes to punish those whom we know to be innocent?" (p. 39), and his answer comes in the form of a consequentialist theory of punishment. Considering the example of a woman who accidentally suffocates her cold child by providing him the warmth of her own clothes, Abelard remarks, "However, when she comes before the bishop for satisfaction, a heavy punishment is imposed upon her, not for the fault which she committed but so that subsequently she or other women should be rendered more cautious in providing such things." (ibid.). It is clear that he sees nothing wrong with the judge's decision. Considerations of the good of society ("the common utility" (p.45)) are properly the basis for a judgment of punishment, not the fault of the agent. And when the good of society and the prevention of public injuries are taken into account, Abelard claims, a wrongful outward act is more likely to provide a bad example (or to cause more harm) than is a hidden, inner intention (p. 43). Thus we are justified in punishing a person for the act – even though the person may not have a "guilty mind." This is true, however, only of human judgments, not of divine punishments. God can grasp the inner intentions of an agent, whereas human beings are limited to a knowledge of the external behavior. Considering this behavior, they may punish (and are justified in doing so) solely on the basis of what was done, not on the basis of the inner state of mind. But this means that God alone judges us in a "true trial" (p. 41). "God considers only the mind in rewarding good or evil, not the results of deeds, and he thinks not of what comes forth from fault or from our good will but judges the mind itself in the design of its intentions, not in the outcome of an outward deed" (p. 45).

Today, many philosophers and jurists are inclined to accept a retributivist theory of punishment that justifies punishment only in the presence of *mens rea* (laws of strict liability constitute an exception to this, strict liability being assigned when an act has very serious social consequences even though the agent did not intend these consequences). For Abelard, this would mean that judges and jurors are "playing God." But it also means, on Abelard's own terms, that they take what is the higher moral ground. "God, however, distributes everyone's punishment according to the amount of fault, and all who offer equal contempt to him are later punished with an equal punishment whatever their condition or profession" (p. 45). Many today would find this to be a statement of ideal justice.

This, then, is Abelard's theory of consent and the moral indifference of actions. Intellectually speaking, this theory is not far from what we find, in the eighteenth century, in the Kantian idea of the good will. Here in twelfth-century France we have intimations of a theory that focuses on motive and duty (the kind of theory that later will be described as deontological in nature). But we also hear echoes of Aristotle and of the Stoics, for whom the idea of a good or virtuous agent is the central focus in moral deliberations, not the idea of a right or good action. But it is unlikely that Abelard was following Aristotle; the open and widespread discussion of the *Nicomachean Ethics* in medieval philosophy only came later. Most commentators credit Abelard's ethics with being entirely original, more so than most of his other philosophical views. And it is an ethics of enduring appeal.

There are problems with it, however. We have already noticed the ambiguity in Abelard's thought between a theory of moral responsibility and a theory of right or good action. Furthermore, concerns should be raised about the way he treats the relationship between intention and act. In claiming that actions are indifferent, Abelard seems to ignore the fact that some actions are identified (at least in part) by reference to intention. Murder, for instance, is an act of intentionally killing another person. Thus the act of murder cannot be said to be morally indifferent, as Abelard implies. To be sure, in focusing on the intention or consent, Abelard is identifying a major ingredient of the moral wrongness of murder. But murder does not become wrong solely because of the intention to kill – surely the fact that it is a matter of *killing* a human being enters into the determination of its moral status.

St Thomas Aquinas

Thomas Aquinas was born in 1225 CE in Roccasecca, Italy (near Naples). The son of a count and a member of a long-established feudal family, he outraged his family members when he entered the Dominican Order – at one point they went so far as to kidnap him and hold him prisoner in order to prevent his ordination. He studied and then taught theology in Paris, and his later career as a theologian included stays in Italy and then Paris again. Some of his writings were condemned by the Church soon after his death (1274), but shortly thereafter, given the shifting winds of religious politics, he was canonized. He is reputed to have been the first person raised to sainthood by virtue of his teachings and his thought rather than by virtue of the performance of miracles. His philosophy is considered one of the glories of the high Middle Ages, and he ranks even today as one of the most important philosophers in the history of Western civilization.

It is obvious in reading Aquinas that he was considerably under the influence of Aristotle. His admiration for Aristotle was so great that he referred to this Greek thinker simply as "The Philosopher." Aquinas's own philosophy, as we noted earlier, is a synthesis of Christian doctrine and Aristotelian thought. It has been claimed by some that his philosophy is merely eclectic and hence unoriginal, but this judgment ignores the genius involved in elaborating a systematic theory in which Aristotelian naturalism sits comfortably with the other-worldly attitudes of Christianity. As Aquinas saw it, Aristotle's work gives us deep insight into the secular dimension of human nature and the natural world. This secular view is not so much false as limited. Aristotle had no conception of the personal, providential God of Christianity (his deity being an entity who engages eternally in pure thought and pure thought alone). To attain an understanding of the Christian God, revelation is also required, and hence pure or natural philosophy is not enough. "Since, as we have shown, the natural power of understanding is not sufficient to see the essence of God, this power of understanding must come to it by divine grace."[34] But admitting this does not diminish the importance or truth of Aristotle's thought in understanding the natural order.

An Aristotelian Approach to Ethics

Aquinas's debt to Aristotle is perhaps even more apparent in his ethics than in other parts of his philosophy. As one commentator has put it, "Thomas was ... convinced that the teleological ethics of Aristotle was, in general, sound, and that the Greek philosopher's way of thinking provided a philosophical backbone, or, if preferred, a philosophical substratum for a Christian ethics."[35] Aquinas, like Aristotle, begins ethical inquiry with the question "What is the good for human beings?" Thus the notion of goodness is central to his ethics, as is the conviction that action is always aimed at an end or good, and ultimately aimed at the greatest, highest, most final good. But Aquinas's answer to the question of the good for human beings, while still very much Aristotelian in nature, has an obvious religious connotation, for the final good for a person turns out to be her *perfection*. Human perfection is what human fulfillment becomes when it is viewed as attaining a higher level of existence that puts human beings in touch with God and brings to completion God's plan for them. Life is seen by both Aristotle and Aquinas as a striving after the good, an attempt to achieve one's final end which alone brings fulfillment, the realization of one's potentialities, and happiness. But whereas for Aristotle one attains this end and lives the happy life in the natural world, among one's fellow citizens, for Aquinas the earthly life is but a preliminary step on the way to true happiness, achieved in the next life through union with God.

In his reading of human life and human nature, Aquinas reveals his religious perspective most clearly when he argues that nothing in the natural world totally satisfies our desires. A life of worldly goods, even a life of worldly virtue, leaves one dissatisfied and incomplete, with a sense that one has not made the most of one's life and not truly fulfilled one's inner nature and true purpose in life. Our desires remain unsatisfied by all temporal goods and accomplishments, and hence these desires reach beyond the temporal domain. Human beings are most strongly drawn to what fulfills and perfects them. As Aquinas puts it: "Because in all things whatsoever there is an appetite for completion, the final end to which each moves marks its own perfect and fulfilling good."[36] It turns out that this final end for human beings is God himself. "Our ultimate end is uncreated good, namely God, who alone can fill our will to the brim because of his infinite goodness."[37] We desire, most ultimately, to be united with God, to become one with him, to find our own joy and completion in him. Thus complete and self-sufficient happiness is possible for us only in the next life when, through the grace of God, we are united with him, behold him, and enjoy his infinite goodness. God alone, the infinite good, will "quiet the human heart."[38]

But in *this* life, as we live in preparation for the next, it is human reason which provides the tutelage and guidance required to attain earthly happiness. Although reason cannot grasp man's supernatural end or define the life in Christ by which it is to be attained, it can enable a human being to live the type of natural life ordained for him by God. And the picture Aquinas gives us of this life is essentially Aristotelian in nature. Human beings have a property or characteristic which sets them apart from all other things in the created universe: they are rational. The proper life for them to lead, then, is the life of reason. Reason is able to discern the ethical principles by means of which God intends us to live our lives. Furthermore, in living the life of reason, we are enabled to fulfill our potentialities, to actualize the modes of existence which move us closer to our final end, God. Reason permits us to grasp human nature and to live a life that accords with it. In doing so, reason puts us in touch with *natural law*, the law that reflects in human nature the eternal law of God.

Natural Law and Human Behavior

Let us see how some of these ideas work out in more detail. Human beings are purposive beings: they act in order to attain goals; their desires move them toward ends that will satisfy these desires. According to Aquinas, there are three kinds of desires, which he also refers to as appetites or inclinations. First, there are natural inclinations shared with all other creatures. Second, there are sense appetites, among which are both concupiscible appetites – love and desire for pleasure – and irascible appetites[39] – fear and the desire to shun the harmful. These are shared with animals. Then, third, there are rational appetites or will, whose object is the good as apprehended by reason. The latter appetites are conscious tendencies and ones over which we exercise control. In fact, in pursuing the objects of rational appetite, we manifest voluntary behavior or freedom of will which sets us apart from the rest of nature. *Free action* is of the essence of human nature. We express this nature when our sense appetites are molded and guided by reason.

How does reason or will direct our activities? Where or how does it obtain guidance concerning what things we ought to desire and pursue? These questions take us to the heart of the doctrine of natural law, a doctrine which, although it did not originate with Aquinas, is closely connected throughout subsequent history with his name and philosophy. The concept of natural law needs to be understood in terms of Aquinas's general definition of law and in relation to the concepts of eternal law and civil law. *Law* Aquinas defines as "an ordinance of reason for the common good, promulgated by him who has the care of the community."[40] This definition is most easily applied to the case of civil law, what Aquinas calls human law or positive law. A legislature is charged with the care of the community of citizens under its jurisdiction, and the legislators attempt, using their reason, to create laws that protect the public and provide it with the essentials of life. Such a law is backed up by *sanctions*, incentives to obey it – most fundamentally the punishments that attach to any infringements of it. The existence of civil law is a fact of life in any form of organized social existence, but it is not, according to Christian believers, the only law. There is also the law of God, the rules expressing the divine reason which manifest themselves in the divine providence ruling the world. Aquinas expresses this notion of a higher law in the following passage:

> Granted that the world is ruled by divine Providence ... it is evident that the whole community of the universe is governed by God's mind ... Since God's mind does not conceive in time, but has an eternal concept ... it follows that this law should be called eternal. Through his wisdom God is the founder of the universe of things and ... in relation to them he is like an artist with regard to the things he makes ... [Also] he is the governor of all acts and notions to be found in each and every creature. And so, as being the principle through which the universe is created, divine wisdom means act, or exemplar, or idea, and likewise it also means law, as moving all things to their due ends. Accordingly the Eternal Law is nothing other than the exemplar of divine wisdom as directing the motions and acts of everything.[41]

But can we grasp the rational order of God's mind and thus the order of Providence? Aquinas and other orthodox Christians deny that the corporeal human being, whose soul in this life is housed within the material body, can directly understand the mind of God. Fortunately, however, God's laws have been incorporated into human nature, which therefore reflects them. The goals that God would have us seek, the forms of behavior he would have us follow – all these are built into the behavior that is natural for us. Thus the precepts of eternal law correspond to the basic tendencies and inclinations (*inclinationes naturales*) of human beings. Natural inclinations direct us to goods, to those ends that God ordains as goods for human beings, as ways of perfecting human nature. By reflecting on these natural inclinations we become aware of what God has intended for us; we become aware of the human essence or ideal in accord with which God made us. And to this extent we come to appreciate God's Eternal Law. "Now this sharing in the Eternal Law by intelligent creatures is what we call 'natural law'."[42] Natural law is a dictate of reason, emanating from God's mind, reflected in natural inclinations, and apprehensible by human reason. Not all of God's laws, however, are reflected in human nature; those having to do with the religious obligations especially imposed on Christians are revealed by revelation.[43] This subset of God's laws is referred to by Aquinas as Divine Law. But human nature embodies the laws that govern the activities of all human beings *qua* natural creatures. Thus it embodies the laws that can be directly grasped by reason without the aid of revelation – laws dictating how all natural creatures should behave.

Natural Inclinations

What are these natural inclinations that reflect God's eternal laws? Given Aquinas's teleological conception of human nature, it follows that a basic inclination of all human beings is to seek the good – together with an equally basic inclination to avoid what is not good, i.e., what is evil. Thus the first, most general principle of natural law is "Desire the good and shun evil." This principle has an ontological foundation in the nature of human beings,[44] revealing as it does their most basic natural inclinations. Just as, Aquinas thinks, from the fundamental concept of "being" in the speculative or theoretical sphere we can derive the principle of non-contradiction ("a thing cannot simultaneously both be and not be"), so from the fundamental practical concept of "good" (as that which all things aim at) we can derive the principle commanding us to seek the good and avoid evil.[45] All other practical principles must be consistent with the basic demand that we seek good and avoid evil, just as all theoretical principles must be consistent with the principle of non–contradiction.

Other general natural inclinations or tendencies can be noted – reflecting the fact that human beings are simultaneously parts of physical nature, parts of the animal kingdom, and rational creatures. These inclinations yield additional general principles of natural law.[46] First, all human beings attempt to sustain their existence, from which natural fact we can derive the law "Conserve life and protect health." Some commentators have thought that the universal inclination to continue in existence yields the law that all life is to be respected and preserved. Second, being animals, humans naturally seek to propagate, from which inclination Aquinas derives the law commanding one to "Marry and multiply," or, more abstractly put, "Bring order into one's sexual activities and relations" (or, yet again, "promiscuity ought to be avoided").[47] Third, as rational creatures, human beings are subject to still other precepts: "There is in people an appetite for the good of their nature as rational, and thus it is proper to them, for instance, that they should know truths about God and about living in society. Correspondingly whatever this involves is a matter of natural law, for instance that people should shun ignorance, not offend others with whom they ought to live in civility, and other such related requirements."[48] As rational creatures we desire to know, and this inclination leads us to attempt to know the world and God. Moreover, human beings are social creatures who band together and live life as members of a group – hence the command of natural law to live peacefully in a civic community, as well as the commands (as Aquinas expresses them in his *Summa contra Gentiles*) not to injure others and not to hinder or obstruct their lawful activities. In general, "natural-law commands extend to all doing or avoiding of things recognized by the practical reason itself as being human goods."[49]

Primary and Secondary Precepts

In both his early writing on natural law – in the *Commentary on the Sentences* – and in his late, mature writing on the subject – in the *Summa Theologiae* – Aquinas makes a distinction between primary and secondary precepts of natural law. The basis for the distinction changes to some extent from the early statement to the later one. In the *Commentary on the Sentences*, Aquinas relates the distinction between primary and secondary precepts to another distinction between primary and secondary ends of human action. Any action that circumvents one of the primary ends of action will violate a primary precept of natural law, whereas any action preventing the realization of a secondary end, but not circumventing the primary end, will violate a secondary precept. For instance, the primary end of the matrimonial state is the propagation of the species, while the secondary end is domestic harmony or tranquillity ("peace in the family"). Monogamy serves both the primary and secondary ends. But, according to Aquinas, there may be circumstances in which polygamy is the best arrangement for ensuring the propagation of the species (presumably circumstances such as a large difference between the number of females and the number of males in a group). In such cases polygamy, even though it may violate the secondary end of matrimony, may still be approved as in accord with a primary precept of natural law. Accordingly, the moral demand for monogamous marriages is only a secondary precept. It appears that Aquinas made the distinction between primary and secondary ends of action in order to justify the fact that in the Old Testament the patriarchs are allowed to have more than one wife.[50]

The mature distinction between primary and secondary precepts of moral law, although already present to some degree in the earlier commentary, is fully developed in the *Summa Theologiae*. Here we are told that secondary precepts are those that are *derived from* primary precepts, either by a process of reasoning (demonstration) or a process of specification (determination) by which the general primary precepts are made concrete and determinate. Moreover, primary precepts are always true – they hold universally, which is to say, without exception, e.g., it is always wrong not to place some restrictions on one's sexual relations. Secondary precepts may not hold in some circumstances, so they are not strictly universal – the demand for monogamy is, therefore, a secondary, not a primary precept. Moreover, the primary precepts are *self-evident*. Any mind that understands the terms in which the primary precepts are expressed will grasp immediately that they are, and must be, true. Thus it is self-evident that human beings must live in society, and that they cannot do this if they harm one another and obstruct one another's lawful activities. Secondary precepts, on the contrary, are known in a manner subject to error. One may make a mistake in reasoning, for instance, one may make a mistake in deriving the secondary from the primary precepts. Although some experience of the world is necessary in order to understand any of the natural law precepts – none of them, therefore, is innate – rendering the vague primary principles specific and determinate requires considerable experience with human life and the world. It follows that the secondary precepts do not possess the self-evidence of the primary ones.

In making the distinction between primary and secondary precepts, Aquinas shows that he is attuned to the complexity of moral decision-making and understands the difficulty of arriving at moral judgments in the actual course of human life. While we do have the primary precepts as certain foundations and invariant guides, they do not address the detail of much actual moral experience. In concrete situations, reason is to be our guide, but self-evidence is unavailable and error always possible. Rational reflection on our actual experience is essential for determining what we ought to do in these concrete situations. Different situations may require different solutions, and we must always be on the lookout for mistakes, blindness, and bias in our experience and the judgments based on it. Furthermore, when one turns from the derivation of secondary precepts of natural law to the application of one of these precepts to a particular case, Aquinas follows Aristotle closely in emphasizing the need for what Aristotle called *perception*. It is the individual person who must judge whether or not the precept applies. Thus natural law doctrine, as least as taught by Aquinas, is not as rigid and formalistic as it is sometimes made out to be.

Reason, Human Goods, and the Will

It must be stressed that for Aquinas natural law is a dictate of reason, not a physical law.[51] For one thing, we are accustomed to think of physical laws as making it impossible for material things to act inconsistently with them. Stones and human bodies have no choice but to obey the physical laws of gravity. A dictate of reason, however, can be disobeyed. Hence in saying that humankind is governed by natural law, Aquinas is not claiming that we always in point of fact act in accordance with this law. Often, being the sinners we are, we fail to do so. Our failure is one of not living up to the dictates of reason as these dictates are embodied in what it is natural for us to desire and do.

Natural law prescribes the proper *goods* for human beings, the proper objects of desire, striving, and action. As the natural laws cited above indicate, these goods include some that we share with animals, e.g., propagation. Animals, however, act in this fashion without choice, which is to say, without reason. Rational human beings, on the contrary, are under an obligation to follow reason, their characteristic feature. Hence they should maintain themselves in existence and engage in sexual activities *because natural law demands it*. Physical goods thus become part of human good by virtue of being required by reason, by natural law. Thus, as one Thomistic philosopher has expressed it, "Sex is a human good, not just as such but insofar as it is engaged in consciously, purposively, and responsibly."[52]

Natural law is the set of propensities built into our nature which, if followed, will lead to the perfection of our being. Hence in seeking to fulfill or perfect ourselves, we must follow this law. The cardinal virtues, including temperance, courage, and justice, are in effect ways of following natural law and thus ways of perfecting our nature – as with Aristotle, they promote what we all seek: happiness. Aquinas follows Aristotle in thinking of a virtue as a habit (*habitus*) or disposition, not in the sense of an unreflective, unreasoning pattern of behavior but rather as an active tendency reflecting rational deliberation. Aquinas also follows Aristotle in believing that thought alone is not enough to produce actions and, *ipso facto*, good actions. The appetites or desires must be trained so as to follow reason and seek the good. The virtues include these trained, reflective desires, namely the concupiscible and irascible sense appetites transformed by the influence of reason into rational appetites or will. Once we have attained the virtues, they direct us in accordance with the precepts of natural law. Thus the guides to a proper, fulfilling and perfective human life are "the law without" and "the virtues within."

The notion of the will plays an important role in Aquinas's thought. Will is that faculty in us which tends toward or desires God, God being, as we have seen, our "best good", our ultimate, self-sufficient, and complete good. *Will* is an intellectual power that directs one to one's end. The use of reason in the determination of means to one's end is a matter of *choice*. In manifesting rational appetite, will expresses itself as love of the good, and hence love of God. Although in this life we cannot have complete or adequate knowledge of God, in knowing what we do about him through the use of reason (as well as from revelation), we can grasp him as our greatest good, and hence we can love him. It is in loving him that we come closest to him in this life, reaching out to him with our will in an effort to imitate him and ultimately to be united with him.

One of the essential aspects of the human will is that it is free. It has the capacity to seek and love God, but it also has the capacity to turn away from him and love the things of this world more than him – pleasure, say, or power. It has the capacity to follow virtue, but also the capacity to sin. It can follow natural law, or repudiate it. One exercises free will when one's actions proceed from the will in pursuit of ends apprehended by reason. Thus one's actions are voluntary when one knows what one is doing and when one desires the objects or ends of one's actions in light of one's knowledge of them. Again the influence of Aristotle is apparent. It is also noteworthy that Aquinas's concept of "free will" is not that of some interior and mysterious action of mind. It is, on the contrary, more like informed desire issuing in overt behavior.[53]

Moral Knowledge

Central to Aquinas's vision of human nature is his belief that human reason is capable of apprehending basic ethical principles and articulating an ethical system based on rational reflection. As we have seen, reason accomplishes this task by considering the nature of man in society and understanding the natural inclinations built into this nature by God. Part of the task involves grasping the first principles of natural law; another part consists in the deduction of more specific precepts from the first principles. According to Aquinas, rational human beings have the ability to recognize immediately that certain moral principles are true – this, for instance, is the case with the most general principle of natural law, "Seek good and avoid evil." This immediate grasp of truth is referred to by Aquinas as *synderesis*.[54] It is the result of a natural disposition or tendency built into human nature, and it is the practical equivalent of the disposition to grasp in an immediate and infallible manner the basic truths of logic and the first principles of theoretical reason. *Synderesis* is infallible; it provides a certain, indubitable insight into truth and therefore cannot be in error or lead us astray. It is the foundation of all moral knowledge, for if we could not apprehend with certainty morality's fundamental principles, there would be no moral knowledge at all.

Interestingly, Aquinas describes the deduction of specific moral precepts from the first principles as an exercise of *conscience*.[55] Today most people think of conscience as a sort of immediate vision of what is right or wrong, and they might be tempted to equate conscience with Aquinas's *synderesis*. But for Aquinas conscience is a matter of reasoning: the application of general principles to concrete situations. Conscience, for instance, will tell us how to conduct our sexual lives in the particular circumstances in which we find ourselves. The operation of conscience requires that we put together general principles and statements of fact that describe particular circumstances; with the principles and statements of fact as premises, we exercise conscience in deriving the conclusions that deductively follow from these premises. Mistakes are possible in such a process – mistakes not only about the matters of fact but about the logical relations between premises and conclusion. Conscience, then, is not infallible, but, according to Aquinas, it should nevertheless be our guide. It would be wrong for us not to follow it, even if it turns out to be in error.

A person who has perfected the power of practical reasoning has thereby developed a virtue, a *habitus*. This virtue is an intellectual one, designated by Aquinas as *prudence*. Prudence amounts to right reason about action, the tendency to think correctly about what ought to be done. But prudence is not simply an intellectual virtue; it is also a moral one. This reflects Aquinas's view that "For people to act well, it is requisite that not only their reason be well disposed through a *habitus* of intellectual virtue, but also that their appetite be well disposed through a *habitus* of moral virtue."[56] The prudent person is more, then, than one who possesses practical knowledge. Appetite, the will, must be shaped or molded by moral virtue, so that practical knowledge is put to use in action. Thus the prudent person is one who chooses well in accordance with practical reason.

Aquinas's system of philosophy permits the expansion of the above accounts of virtue and goodness in many directions and in great detail. Enough has been said, however, to give one a sense of how, borrowing from Aristotle, he developed a highly sophisticated Christian moral philosophy. Because of its elaborate and detailed metaphysical and epistemological dimensions, it appeals greatly to Christians who would not sacrifice reason as they pursue their faith and act as natural creatures in a providential world. Thomistic ethics in large part remains with us today in the form of the ethics of Roman Catholicism. And its doctrine of natural law has been of immense significance in Western culture since the time of Aquinas. Given this significance, it is appropriate that we conclude with a brief critical discussion of the notion of natural law.

Criticisms of Natural Law Theory

Many philosophers believe that the concept of "natural law" illegitimately combines a normative (evaluative) and a descriptive (factual) account of human behavior. Natural law is supposed to reflect our natural inclinations, the ways in which we tend to behave. In this sense, statements of natural law are descriptive accounts, and they are true to the extent that they describe our natural inclinations correctly. In doing so they give us an account of our essential human nature. But these natural inclinations also amount to ways in which we *ought* to behave if we are to behave as God commands or as divine reason demands. Hence to postulate natural inclinations is to put forward *norms* for behavior. These norms may or may not be met by actual behavior, insofar as, being creatures of free will, we may choose not to follow God's demands and thus may behave in ways inconsistent with natural law. Thus statements of natural law are normative, telling us how we ought to behave. In this way the theory of natural law combines both descriptive and normative accounts of human behavior. The question is whether this combination of factual and evaluative statements is a coherent one.

The concept of natural law offers the promise of providing a factual, objective basis for moral precepts. The argument of natural law theory goes like this: human nature being of a certain kind, it follows that deviations from the natural course of behavior are perverse and hence evil. As one commentator has put it "The idea here is that human beings are fulfilled or made happy in ways which can be seen by noting what they are (including how they act and what they are drawn to) ... "[57] But if human beings often do not act as natural law prescribes, then actual human nature is not reflected in natural law. Understood descriptively, statements of natural law are often *false*. In that case, natural law theory does not succeed in grounding moral precepts in human nature. Natural law theory may give us a normative set of moral principles, but it does not show how these principles are justified in light of human nature – for the good reason that natural law does not tell us the way human nature always in fact *is*. Thus the attempt of natural law theory to depict natural law as both normative and descriptive – to provide moral norms and their grounding in human nature – is perceived by many ethical thinkers to be incoherent and hence to fail.

A proponent of natural law theory might respond by claiming that the above argument fails to acknowledge the place of reason in natural law theory. Human beings are *rational* animals, which does not mean that they always follow reason but that they have a capacity, and, indeed, a natural inclination to do so. When human beings act in ways inconsistent with natural law, they are acting contrary to their rational inclinations. We all have a natural inclination to band together into social groups, but we do not always act in ways consistent with the rational insight that being social animals requires that we not harm others or infringe their lawful rights. We all have a natural sexual drive, but we do not always act in ways consistent with the rational insight that the goods aimed at by the sexual drive are not best achieved by a life of sexual promiscuity. Thus our rational inclinations, which are part of our nature as rational beings, can and do ground the normative imperatives of natural law.

But who, the critic might respond, is to say what ends and goods of human life are rational and thereby natural? How does "reason" determine, for instance, that the propagation of the species is the end of sexual activity, or of marriage? In calling such an end rational, isn't the natural law theorist simply assuming her own value judgments? Implicit, undefended value judgments may slip in at other junctures as well. It has been argued, for instance, that one cannot simply derive by reason the secondary precept "one must not kill" from the primary precept "one must not harm another person."[58] The inference from the one precept to the other requires the additional value judgment that killing a person is harming her. While many people may accept this judgment, many would not do so in an unqualified manner. What about euthanasia, for instance? This is an instance of killing a person, but is it also an instance of harming a person? Defenders of euthanasia would say no. Hence one might agree that one ought not harm an individual without agreeing that one ought not to kill that individual. Which is to say that not everyone agrees with the implicit judgment that killing a person is a matter of harming her. "Reason" and "nature" do not speak with an unequivocal voice with respect to the moral relation between harming and killing.

While such an argument is a strong one against a rigid doctrine of natural law, we have seen that Aquinas admits considerable flexibility into his account of natural law, specifically where it comes to the derivation of secondary natural law precepts and the application of these precepts to individual cases. Hence we should leave it an open question whether the criticism under discussion hits the mark when we limit ourselves to what Aquinas himself has to say about natural law.

But Aquinas is a good essentialist. He follows Plato and Aristotle in believing that human beings have an essence. Hence the ends at which human natural inclinations aim are essential ends, those that comprise the human essence. Reason is a faculty that allows us to comprehend essences, including our own, and hence to see that some ends are fulfilling of the human essence and for this reason are perfecting ends. If one rejects essentialism, as many philosopher today do, especially those who subscribe to the later philosophy of Wittgenstein,[59] then the notion that some ends are natural and essential will be uninviting. A critic of essentialism would maintain that human nature does not have neatly identifiable boundaries – there is no set of necessary and sufficient conditions for someone being a human being, or for some activity being distinctively human. Human beings and their activities come in a variety of "shapes and forms," and it is *we*, not human nature itself, who decide what is and what is not "human" or "natural." And different people may decide differently, so that there is no objective answer to the question of what a human being essentially is. But essentialism is by no means philosophically moribund, which means that natural law theory will still be with us for a while.

Voluntaristic Ethics

We shall conclude our study of ethics during the medieval period by considering very briefly the thought of two late medieval thinkers, John Duns Scotus and William Ockham. These two British philosophers provide us with additional evidence of the diversity of ethical outlooks found in the medieval period, all of which are nonetheless based on the basic premises of the Christian faith. Scotus and Ockham are particularly interesting because they begin to undermine the view, inherited by the earlier medieval ethicists from the Greeks, that ethical precepts are founded on the metaphysical ground of human nature. In different degrees, Scotus and Ockham give us *voluntaristic* conceptions of ethics which make the will and authority of God the foundation of moral rules. According to this view of the matter, it is because God commands, for example, that human beings not kill one another that it is wrong to do so. God's will imposes *obligations* on human subjects, and so the concept of obligation comes to play a more central role in ethical theory. Although for Scotus and Ockham these ethical ideas are still very much part of a spiritual view of the world, they may be seen as predecessors of the ethical theories of later materialistic thinkers like Hobbes in which *will* and *obligation* also play a pivotal role.

Duns Scotus

John Duns Scotus was born in 1265 or 1266 and died in 1308, at the tragically early age of forty-two. His family name was Duns, and he was dubbed Scotus or "the Scot" by the members of the Franciscan order which he joined. He was and still is considered one of the greatest, certainly one of the most subtle, of the medieval thinkers. Fortunately we have no need to look at the subtle, often mind-twisting distinctions he introduces into the discussion of metaphysics and epistemology. We shall concentrate on his claim that "the divine will is the cause of good, and so by the fact that he wills something it is good."[60]

This bold statement shows that Scotus is concerned with the question that vexed Socrates and others in pre-Christian days: is something good because God loves it, or does he love it because it is good? Scotus's answer, contrary to that of Socrates, is that God's willing something makes it good. This is why we refer to Scotus as giving us a voluntaristic account of ethics. In point of fact, however, Scotus proposes only a partial voluntarism. As we shall see, for him some but not all moral precepts are dependent on the divine will.

The question that must be posed is whether there is anything independent of the divine will which can serve as an objective origin of things good and right. Natural law theory of the sort found in Aquinas identifies human nature as such a ground. More precisely, this ground is the ideas in the mind of God which are exemplars of human nature and constitute the eternal law. God, for Aquinas, cannot will anything contrary to this eternal law, hence it becomes a source of morality independent of the divine will. Scotus is unhappy with this view because, to his mind, it places limits on God and destroys God's freedom of will. For Scotus, the will, human and divine, is absolutely free. To say that God *must* will in accordance with the eternal law – even if this law is identical with God's own exemplary ideas – is to repudiate his free will, and this is unacceptable. Thus Scotus wants to allow that God could will otherwise than he does. It seems to follow that there are no external restraints on what God's commandments can be. Cannot God will that *any* action is right?

Not completely, Scotus argues. God cannot will that idolatry is morally permissible, or that taking his name in vain is unobjectionable, since these actions are inconsistent with the human being's purpose in life, which is to love God. Moreover, insofar as God is the perfect and most desirable being of all, love of him is the only logically consistent response to him. "Love God," therefore, is the primary moral precept, and it cannot be set aside by God's willing otherwise. According to Scotus, it would be self-contradictory for God to will that his creatures not love him, and God cannot will a contradiction. Scotus and most other medieval thinkers see no problem in saying that God cannot will a contradiction. A contradiction is something logically impossible, and it follows from this that insofar as a self-contradiction does not describe a possible act, no limits on the possible acts God might undertake are created by granting that he cannot will what is self-contradictory.

With regard to other commandments that God gave to human beings, he *could* have willed otherwise. It is not logically impossible for God to will that human beings share all things in common; therefore any injunction to honor private property does not have the type of independent ground that the injunction to love God has. Furthermore, there would be no self-contradiction in willing the permissibility of murder or denying that monogamy is required. Clearly, as Biblical examples show, under some conditions God is willing to order the killing of a human being (Isaac) and to permit polygamy (the patriarchs). So, aside from the first three of the Ten commandments (and Scotus had doubts about the third one, concerning worshiping God on the Sabbath), moral precepts do not have the objective and independent underpinning of logic. These precepts are not themselves logically necessary, and they cannot be deduced from the first set of precepts which are logically necessary. In these cases, our obligation is to obey God's commandments *because* God has willed them.

But this is still not the complete picture of Scotus's ethical theory. He retains elements of natural law theory in his thinking, and he views the second set of God's ten commandments, those dealing with one's obligations to society and one's neighbor rather than to him himself, as having the underpinning of natural law. God created human beings in such a way that certain actions are harmful, given the human nature he placed in them. This nature consists of a subset of the essences or exemplars in his mind from which he freely selected during the act of creation. All such actions as adultery and lying are harmful, given human nature, and hence, according to Scotus, they are evil. It would be contrary to *right reason* to violate the precepts forbidding them. So even with regard to precepts whose denial would not be self-contradictory, there is an independent ground for many of them. Rational reflection on human nature can reveal the *content* of the natural law governing the relationships among human beings.

But even though the content of this set of commandments is determined by human nature, we have an *obligation* to obey them only because God commands them. His will, expressed in these commandments, is what places us under moral obligation. Right reason can discern what actions lead to our happiness or interfere with it, but reason cannot grasp that we have a duty to undertake or avoid these actions. The revelation of God's commandments is necessary in order for obligation to be incurred. Without God's acts of will, right reason would at best provide us with an ethics of self-fulfillment in which obligation plays no role.

Moreover, God *could* have created human beings with a different kind of nature. No limit can be placed on the creative activities flowing from God's free will. If God had created human beings differently, as he could have done, then he might have willed, for instance, that they bear false witness against one another. Moreover, many injunctions, such as not eating meat on Fridays, have nothing to do with human nature and happiness and are to be obeyed simply because God commands them. Divine law having to do with purely religious duties is a direct expression of God's commandments. In many ways, then, the moral order is contingent on God's will.

But clearly Scotus's voluntarism is limited. Most of God's commandments have either an absolute foundation in logic or a contingent foundation in natural law. God is limited in what he can command by the very nature he has freely given to human beings. Natural law is the foundation of the commandments concerning one's neighbor, and right reason can ascertain the content of these moral obligations. Nevertheless, in the end we are driven back to God's will, his will to create us as creatures of a certain kind, and his will as source of the commandments that place us under moral obligations.[61]

Ockham

William Ockham (or William of Ockham, as he is often called) – ca. 1285–1349 – denies the reality of independent and eternal divine ideas in God and hence the notion of divine exemplars that determine the nature of God's creatures. Just as God creates human beings, he also creates their essences, and could have created them otherwise. Nothing, then, constrains or limits God's creative activity. As an extreme nominalist, Ockham denies the reality of the common natures that constitute universal essences. For him there is no such thing as human nature in general. God creates, not common natures, but individuals. This theory allows Ockham to repudiate the idea that the Fall corrupts human nature, which we all allegedly share with Adam and Eve, and thereby brings guilt on all of us. There is no common human nature to corrupt. And thus Ockham severs all connection between a prior, or eternal, ontological background and God's moral laws. In Ockham, voluntarism in medieval philosophy receives its extreme expression.

Ockham, one commentator writes, "severs the bond between metaphysics and ethics and bases morality not upon the perfection of human nature (whose reality he denies), nor upon the teleological relation between man and God, but upon man's obligation to follow the laws freely laid down for him by God."[62] God's will takes the place of eternal exemplars or eternal law in the mind of God. The goodness of anything is dependent upon the will of that which creates it.[63] Human beings create hammers and saws, and thus good hammers and saws are those that are *as they should be* given the will of the human beings who bring them into existence. Human beings in turn are good insofar as they are as they ought to be, given the will of their creator, God. God himself cannot be said to be good, since he is uncreated and hence subject to no other will. Thus his will is free, and his free will is the sole source of goodness – and of how things ought to be.

God's omnipotence and freedom entail that God can impose on human beings whatever laws he wishes. His commandments are not constrained by any independent factors. It follows that God himself is under no obligations whatsoever. "Obligation does not fall on God, since he is not under any obligation to do anything."[64] Contrary to what Scotus had claimed, God could, if he wished, require that we hate him instead of love him.[65] Clearly, then, he could require of us that we bear false witness against one another, that we covet what others possess, and so on. Our obligations have no necessary content, as Scotus thought, but derive solely from God's commandments. Thus, "By the very fact that God wills something, it is right for it to be done ... "[66] Hence we can understand the Christian obsession with doing the will of God. As Copleston puts it, "The divine will is thus the ultimate norm for the Christian."[67]

But, as Copleston warns us, the above account is not a complete picture of Ockham's moral philosophy. Ockham, like Scotus, brings *right reason* into the picture and holds out the possibility of the human mind ascertaining through reason, rather than revelation, what is morally required of us. In order to see this we must make a distinction with respect to God's power. God in his *absolute power* can create human beings as he wishes and hence is free to command and forbid quite different acts from those he does command and forbid. But God in his *potentia ordinata*, in his power considered in the context of the world which he has created, commands those actions that are not harmful to human beings. These actions can be ascertained by human reason. Consequently, God commands that we follow reason, and it is *this* command that creates our obligation to do what reason advises. When reason ascertains that a certain act will harm us, it does not thereby place us under an obligation to avoid this act. Only God's will, as expressed in his commandment that we follow reason, does that.

In Ockham we have perhaps the purest example of a divine command theory of morality. An act is right because God requires it of us. There is no independent standard to which we can appeal to ascertain that God's commandments are themselves right and obliging. Even when we can discover through reason what is right and wrong, still this is so because of God's will to create human beings with the characteristics they have and because God commands them to follow reason. God is our creator, and thus the being on whom we depend for all that we are. As our creator, he has rightful authority over us.

Problems with Voluntarism

As even sympathetic commentators point out, it is not easy to render consistent all the things that Ockham and Scotus have to say about the ground of morality, and hence it is difficult to find their voluntaristic ethics acceptable.[68] Allowing that right reason can determine that many actions are right or wrong seems to place constraints on God's will, on what he can command or forbid. As we have seen, however, Scotus and Ockham still find ways to stress the centrality and ultimacy of God's will. But the more an unfounded or ungrounded will is identified as the source of morality, the more its edicts appear arbitrary and convey an impression of pure power without legitimation. If God's goodness is appealed to as a means of assuring us of the morality of his commands, new questions arise. It seems question-begging to claim that the commands of God require respect because of his infinite goodness. We can't know that he is good until and unless we have some independent reason for thinking that his commands are meritorious. Problems of this sort with voluntaristic theories of ethics will not disappear once we abandon a theological perspective. Thomas Hobbes, from a very different voluntaristic point of view, will grapple with the relationship between the rational laws of nature and the commands of an earthly sovereign.

6

Hobbes

In turning to the moral philosophy of Thomas Hobbes (1588–1679 CE), we enter for the first time into the period of modern philosophy. Hobbes, an Englishman, and his French contemporary René Descartes are the founders of modern philosophical thought. Their differences, however, are more noticeable than their similarities. Both stress the ability of unfettered reason – reason unaided by faith – to ascertain the nature of reality, but the pictures of reality they draw are dramatically different. Descartes is immortalized in the annals of thought for his mind/body dualism, according to which there are two fundamentally distinct kinds of things in reality, bodily or physical substances, on the one hand, and mental entities – minds or souls – on the other. In a living human being, these two metaphysically distinct things are joined together and even interact with one another. Death, however, involves the separation of a person's soul from her body. While it inhabits and interacts with the body, the Cartesian mind engages in acts of thinking, feeling, and willing; it is, in short, a thinking thing, without which the body is incapable of cognitive, affective, or voluntary activities. It is this Cartesian mind that Hobbes rejects. He is a monistic materialist instead of a dualist. For Hobbes, all reality is physical. The activities of thinking, feeling, and willing are no more than motions of the physical body, movements that occur as a result of the body's interaction with objects in the surrounding physical world. Hobbes's materialism – or more developed, sophisticated forms of it – is highly popular today, although Descartes' dualism had more impact on the thought of the seventeenth and eighteenth centuries.

Contractarianism

In the area of ethics, Descartes had little to contribute, whereas Hobbes developed a theory that is still considered one of the live options among ethical theories today.

He is the father of the form of ethical theory known as "contractarianism," the view that our moral (and political) obligations arise out of a contract we human beings make with one another as a means of fostering our survival and achieving a contented life.[1] Reason, according to Hobbes, counsels us to enter into a contract whereby we give up our unlimited liberties and place ourselves under the authority of a central power. Having made this contract, we subsequently find ourselves under an obligation to abide by it. Herein lies the origin of morality: obligation is a bond we create through voluntary contract.

For Hobbes, moral obligation and moral rules are necessary means for avoiding the horrifying consequences that would result from the absence of them. They are *not* desirable in and of themselves. "Obligation is thraldom," Hobbes tells us (*L*, xi, 7),[2] and much of his moral philosophy consists in showing us why we should voluntarily accept such an undesirable thing as thraldom. His answer, in essence, is that the constraint of obligation is the lesser of two evils. The alternative, a life free from the bonds of contract and morality, turns out to be a life that is "solitary, poor, nasty, brutish, and short" (*L*, xiii, 9). The moral life, restrictive though it may be because of the obligations it imposes on us, permits us not only to survive but also offers us our best chance for living a contented life. Morality is simply the better bargain.

Hobbes's conception of morality is clearly different from that of many of the thinkers we have considered hitherto. Plato and Aristotle, and many of their medieval followers, thought that the dictates of morality were intrinsic to human nature: to be fully human, or to achieve the human *telos*, requires that one follow the laws of morality. The moral life, in other words, is *constitutive* of human nature. Not so for Hobbes. Human nature can be understood without any appeal to morality (we shall see shortly what it looks like). The problem, as Hobbes sees it, is that, given human nature, we won't survive and certainly won't prosper unless we enter into a contract and thereby bind ourselves to fulfill the obligations we ourselves create. Morality is a means to a highly desirable end: survival and contentment. If in some sense virtue is its own reward for Plato and Aristotle, it is decidedly not its own reward for Hobbes.[3] It is simply the only way we can attain those other things we most fundamentally desire.

The State of Nature

The basic distinction we must grasp in order to understand Hobbes's moral and political theory is that between life in *the state of nature* and life in a *commonwealth* or political society. This distinction is not an historical or chronological one; Hobbes is not claiming that we (or our ancestors) first found ourselves in a state of nature and then created a commonwealth. As far as Hobbes knew, for that matter as far as we know today, all human beings have been born into and have grown up in something like a commonwealth. The state of nature is the condition of existence we would be in were we *not* members of a social group. It is a hypothetical condition, not an actual one (although Hobbes will point to some areas within our experience in which there exists something comparable to a state of nature). Hobbes's state of nature is the result of a "thought experiment": we ask ourselves what life would be like if we were not members of a commonwealth and hence were without the moral and political laws, and the means of enforcing them, entailed by membership in it. Can such a question be answered? Hobbes thinks it can by appealing to basic truths about human nature, specifically about the passions, and to facts about the environmental conditions under which we live. His general philosophy of materialism suggests to him a picture of raw human nature uncontrolled by civic rules and powers. It is to this picture that he turns in describing the state of nature.

Life in the state of nature is, according to Hobbes, a "war of every man against every man" (*L*, xiii, 13). There are several reasons for this being the case. First of all, life outside civil society would be an arena in which our natural passions, together with the scarcity of what we desire, drive us to incessant competition. "And therefore, if any two men desire the same thing, which nevertheless they cannot both enjoy, they become enemies; and in the way to their end, which is principally their own conservation, and sometimes their delectation only, endeavour to destroy or subdue one another" (*L*, xiii, 3). When there are not enough commodities and other goods to go around (and there never are), competition for these scarce resources leads to enmity and war.

Second, in such a tense situation, knowing that my neighbor will make every effort to obtain what she wants and consequently in all likelihood will try to deprive me of what I want, I quickly come to distrust this neighbor. My relationships to most of my fellow mortals is dominated by this mistrust, which Hobbes calls diffidence. This diffidence we have toward one another leads us to develop certain strategies for securing our safety. "And from this diffidence of one another, there is no way for any man to secure himself so reasonable as anticipation, that is, by force or wiles to master the persons of all men he can, so long till he see no other power great enough to endanger him" (*L*, xiii, 4). Hobbes warns that defensive strategies are not enough to protect ourselves: properly mistrusting others, we must anticipate attack and seek to subdue our enemies before they subdue us.

And there is another reason why anticipation is a wise strategy. "Also, because there be some that taking pleasure in contemplating their own power in the acts of conquest, which they pursue farther than their security requires, if others (that otherwise would be glad to be at ease within modest bounds) should not by invasion increase their power, they would not be able, long time, by standing only on their defense, to subsist" (*L*, ibid.). We must be realistic and acknowledge that some human beings are not moderate persons (like ourselves) who are interested only in protecting themselves; some human beings are dominators who take pleasure in imposing their wills on others and enjoy their power as an end in itself.[4] Against such as these, anticipation, a quick offensive attack, is better than a later defensive counterattack.

Third, although not all persons are dominators, all have a healthy interest in their own reputation, and this fact too causes problems in the state of nature: "For every man looketh that his companion should value him at the same rate he sets upon himself, and upon all signs of contempt, or undervaluing, naturally endeavours, as far as he dares (which amongst them that have no common power to keep them in quiet, is far enough to make them destroy each another), to extort a greater value from his contemners, by damage, and from others, by the example" (*L*, xiii, 5). In other words, our vanity and our desire for glory drive us into a war of every person against every other.

Hobbes sums up his description of life in the state of nature as follows: "So that in the nature of man we find three principal causes of quarrel: first, competition; secondly, diffidence; thirdly, glory. The first maketh men invade for gain; the second, for safety, and the third, for reputation" (*L*, xiii, 6,7). Given the facts of human nature and the realities of the world in which we live, quarrel, invasion, and war are inevitable.

We should add that in the state of nature human beings act on the basis of their appetites and passions, and these differ from one person to another. Calling different things good or evil as a result of their different appetites and passions, human beings come into conflict. Thus they are in a state of war "as by reason of the diversity of the present appetites, they mete good and evil by diverse measures" (*DC* 3, xxxi).[5] In the state of nature there is no common standard of good and evil, and therefore no way of resolving disputes short of conflict and war.

Hobbes makes it clear that war need not involve actual fighting. An abiding disposition to fight – in order to compete for the objects of one's desires, for fear of the competition, in pursuit of glory and reputation, or in defense of one's private values – is enough for him to declare a state of war. Given the conditions in the state of nature, a disposition to fight is ever-present among all its inhabitants, and hence the condition of war (of all against all) is satisfied.

There are certain assumptions built into this description of life in the state of nature, assumptions that Hobbes makes explicit. First of all, he is assuming that human beings are more or less equal with respect to their powers. This equality, he thinks, is evident in experience:

> Nature hath made men so equal in the faculties of body and mind as that, though there be found one man sometimes manifestly stronger in body or of quicker mind than another, yet when all is reckoned together the difference between man and man is not so considerable as that one man can thereupon claim to himself any benefit to which another may not pretend as well as he. For as to the strength of body, the weakest has strength enough to kill the strongest, either by secret machination, or by confederacy with others that are in the same danger with himself. And as to the faculties of the mind ... I find yet a greater equality amongst men than that of strength   (*L*, xiii, 1,2).

The latter claim, he argues, is substantiated by the fact that all human beings seem to think they are wiser than their fellow creatures – "But this proveth rather that men are in that point equal, than unequal. For there is not ordinarily a greater sign of the equal distribution of anything than that every man is contented with his share" (*L*, xiii, 2). (Hobbes's humor needs to be relished on those few occasions when he gives us a glimpse of it.) And his main point is that the strengths of either body or mind are so equally distributed among human beings that no one person or group will be able as a result of their natural powers to gain permanent control over the others.

Another assumption driving his argument is that there is no common power – no governmental authority – in place that is capable of forcing human beings to refrain from their warlike actions. This follows from the fact that we are discussing the state of nature, for by definition no governmental power exists in such a state. And if no person or group of persons is sufficiently superior in natural powers to overwhelm the others, then there will be no way to curb the warlike activities of the inhabitants.

Sometimes Hobbes paints the situation prevailing in the state of nature in the bleakest possible terms. He says, for instance:

> In such condition there is no place for industry, because the fruit thereof is uncertain, and consequently, no culture of the earth, no navigation, nor use of the commodities that may be imported by sea, no commodious building, no instruments of moving and removing such things as require much force, no knowledge of the face of the earth, no account of time, no arts, no letters, no society, and which is worst of all, continual fear and danger of violent death, and the life of man, solitary, poor, nasty, brutish, and short   (*L*, xiii, 9).

Hobbes does not think such a description an exaggeration, nor does he think that it reports a mere theoretical possibility. In his view, we actually have experience of a state of nature. He cites the case of the primitive people found in America during his time who live, in his estimation, without government and in the brutish manner depicted. Furthermore, in times of civil war – such as Hobbes's own time, in which the English Civil War occurred – there is a breakdown of government and a deterioration into a state of nature. Moreover, between sovereign states there is no effective government, and thus there is a state of nature on the international level. Finally, the passions and attitudes that prevail in a state of nature are apparent even *within* civil society, and they result in actions analogous to those we would find in the primitive state. Consider, for example, that, "when taking a journey [a man] arms himself, and seeks to go well accompanied; when going to sleep, he locks his doors; when even in his house, he locks his chests; and this when he knows there be laws, and public officers, armed, to revenge all injuries shall be done him." Furthermore, ask yourself "what opinion he has of his fellow subjects, when he rides armed; of his fellow citizens, when he locks his doors; and of his children and servants, when he locks his chests. Does he not there as much accuse mankind by his actions, as I do by my words?"(*L*, viii, 10). Human nature being what it is, we are always wise to be on guard, even in society, even with a policeman on the corner. The threat of violence and hostility, and of anarchy, are always with us.

It is clear that human life in the state of nature would quickly become miserable. In such a drastic, anarchic state, with death always lurking around the corner, life itself would be tenuous: "there can be no security to any man (how strong or wise soever he be) of living out the time which nature ordinarily alloweth men to live" (*L*, xiv, 4). Given that our fear of death is one of our strongest passions, this fear would impel us to seek to escape the state of nature. But how could we do so?

The Way Out: The Laws of Nature

Fortunately, even in the state of nature we would retain our reason, and it is reason that would show us what to do in order to leave behind our desperate and pitiable condition. Reason, according to Hobbes, is able to grasp general precepts or rules that instruct a person in what must be done in order to preserve her life. Such rules he calls *laws of nature*: "A Law of Nature (*lex naturalis*) is a precept or general rule, found out by reason, by which a man is forbidden to do that which is destructive of his life or taketh away the means of preserving the same, and to omit that by which he thinketh it may be best preserved" (*L*, xiv, 3). The laws of nature are the laws of prudence. They indicate what actions must be taken to serve the individual's self-interest, the most important aspect of which is her very survival. These laws, being discovered by reason, are objective reflections of the causal relationships between certain classes of actions and individual survival and well-being. Reason shows us the way out of our predicament in the state of nature.

Hobbes introduces the notion of a law of nature by way of contrast with the notion of a *right*. A right, he tells us, "consisteth in liberty to do or to forbear" (ibid.), liberty in turn being "the absence of external impediments, which impediments may oft take away part of a man's power to do what he would" (*L*, xiv, 2). I have a right, in other words, if there are no external impediments to my doing what I want to do. Hobbes clearly has in mind the kind of impediments found within society: laws, rules, regulations, and the enforcement thereof. These normative requirements limit a person's power to do what she would. In the state of nature, there are, by definition, no social constraints on action and the expression of power. Thus in the state of nature, a person has what Hobbes calls the "Right of Nature": "the liberty each man hath to use his own power, as he will himself, for the preservation of his own nature, that is to say, of his own life, and consequently of doing anything which, in his own judgment and reason, he shall conceive to be the aptest means thereunto" (*L*, xiv, 1). This Right of Nature, this liberty of every person, is unlimited in scope. In the state of nature "every man has a right to everything, even to one another's body" (*L*, xiv, 4). There are no impediments – no civic rules and regulations – to one person taking the life of another or enslaving another. The Right of Nature gives each one of us unlimited liberty to do as we please, so long as we see our actions as being necessary to protect and enhance our lives. The problems of life in the state of nature can be traced to the fact that in it each inhabitant possesses the Right of Nature.

This right, this unlimited liberty, disappears as soon as reason grasps and subscribes to the laws of nature, for laws, according to Hobbes, "determinith and bindeth" (*L*, xiv, 3). A law places one under an obligation, thereby imposing limits on one's liberty. A law of nature places one under an obligation to do certain things and not to do other things. Law involves the "thraldom" we spoke of earlier.

The First Law: Seek Peace

It is by limiting our liberty through the acknowledgement of the laws of nature and by replacing our unlimited liberty with obedience to these laws that we raise ourselves out of the state of nature. Reason sees what must be done:

> And consequently it is a precept, or general rule, of reason *that every man ought to endeavour peace, as far as he has hope of attaining it, and when he cannot obtain it, that he may seek and use all helps and advantages of war.* The first branch of which rule containeth the first and fundamental law of nature, which is *to seek peace, and follow it.* The second, the sum of the right of nature, which is *by all means we can, to defend ourselves* (*L*, xiv, 4).

We are instructed by reason to seek and to pursue peace, to give up our warlike condition in the state of nature, but we are also advised that if we have no reason to think that peace is possible we should revert to the strategies of war. If peace is not possible, the Right of Nature once again takes priority, and we have the right to defend ourselves by any action whatsoever. The first law of nature – "Seek peace" – is our best hope for survival, but the ever-realistic Hobbes recognizes that such a strategy may not work.

The Second Law: Lay Down the Right of Nature

Hobbes immediately proceeds to describe the second law of nature, the second general rule laid down by reason for defending ourselves:

From this fundamental law of nature, by which men are commanded to endeavour peace, is derived this second law: *that a man be willing, when others are so too, as far-forth as for peace and defense of himself he shall think it necessary, to lay down this right to all things, and be contented with so much liberty against other men, as he would allow other men against himself* (*L*, xiv, 5).

In seeking peace we are seeking to escape from the state of nature, "the condition of war of everyone against everyone" (*L*, xiv, 4). This war results from our unlimited liberty in the state of nature combined with our more or less equal power. Thus the only way to escape the condition of war is to give up, to renounce, our unlimited liberty, our right to all things. This is what the second law of nature commands of us. It does so, again, with certain conditions attached. We are to lay down our right to all things *if others are willing to do so too*. It would be foolish to do so unilaterally, for that would simply be to open ourselves to attack. Each of us is to renounce the Right of Nature if everyone else is willing to do so. Moreover, we are to renounce this right only to the extent necessary to attain peace and thereby protect ourselves. In ascertaining the amount of liberty we are to give up, Hobbes appeals to the law of the Gospel commonly known as the Golden Rule ("whatsoever you require that others should do to you, that do ye to them"). In Hobbes's appropriation of this rule, it requires each of us to be satisfied with as much liberty toward other human beings as we are willing to allow them with respect to ourselves.

In laying down or giving up our right to things, we may either renounce this right or transfer it to someone else. In engaging in either of these acts, we are removing an impediment to someone else's use of those same things or someone else's exercise of their right to them. In this way we are bestowing benefits on these other people. If we care not who receives the benefit, we are said to renounce our right; if we wish the benefit to accrue to some one or more particular persons, we are to speak of transferring our right to them, which amounts to a gift. We may, then, either abandon our right or give it away to other people.

Hobbes finds the source of both obligation and justice in the laying down of the Right of Nature:

> And when a man hath in either manner abandoned or granted away his right, then is he said to be OBLIGED or BOUND not to hinder those to whom such right is granted or abandoned from the benefit of it; and [it is said] that he *ought*, and it is his DUTY, not to make void that voluntary act of his own, and that such hindrance is INJUSTICE, and INJURY, as being *sine jure* [without right], the right being before renounced or transferred (*L*, xiv, 7).

The basic idea here is that in renouncing or transferring our right to all things, we thereby make a *commitment*, a promise, and in this way we create and impose upon ourselves an obligation to live up to the commitment or fulfill the promise. Herein lies the source of morality. There is no morality in the state of nature, since in that condition everyone has a right to everything whatsoever. As we have seen, having this right is a way of saying that there are no impediments, no restrictions, no laws, and no obligations standing in the way of a person appropriating and doing what she wants. But if I give up my right, I commit myself not to exercise it, and thus I am restricted in what I can do by the impediment I myself create, namely my promise not to exercise my right. Thus my duties and obligations arise from my laying down of the Right of Nature.

Likewise, justice and injustice arise out of the laying down of the Right of Nature. In the state of nature there is neither justice nor injustice: everyone has a right to whatever she can acquire. Hobbes interprets injustice as a kind of absurdity or contradiction – the inconsistency between voluntarily giving up the Right of Nature and then voluntarily assuming that very right again. Only after the renunciation or transference of rights can we speak of injustice – of violating our commitment to lay down our rights – and only then can we speak of justice – of honoring our commitment. Justice does not reside in the natural world; it is the creation of the voluntary actions of human beings.

Contracts and Covenants

The laws of nature recommend themselves to all rational human beings in the state of nature, and so all of them can be expected to lay down the unlimited rights they have in this state. Hence there will be mutual renunciation or transference of rights. This mutual interaction Hobbes calls a *contract*. When two or more individuals engage in a contract that commits them to future actions, they have formed a *covenant*, or a *covenant of mutual trust*. He notes that the contract or covenant need not be *express*, that is to say, it need not be explicitly conveyed and acknowledged by words. The sign or indication of a contract may be "by inference," and thus implicit or covert. Hobbes does not indicate exactly what such a covert contract might consist in, other than to say that "generally a sign by inference of any contract is whatsoever sufficiently argues the will of the contractor" (*L*, xiv, 14). Thus we can assume that a contract has been entered into if we have reason to think that such is the will of the parties involved. Insofar as human beings in the state of nature are rational, we do in fact have reason to believe that they have contracted with one other in the way needed to emerge from this untenable situation. We have reason to believe that they have agreed, even if not explicitly, to live within the moral limits they themselves, as rational agents, impose on themselves.

In engaging in a contract or covenant with one another, there are limits to the rights the parties can renounce or transfer, so that the contract itself is a limited one. A person cannot give up the right to resist any who "assault him by force, to take away his life." The very purpose of the contract is to protect one's life, hence giving up the right to defend this life would be inconsistent with the purpose of the mutual transference of right. Likewise, a person cannot give up the right to resist and avoid wounds, or to resist imprisonment (or avoid self-incrimination). Hobbes emphasizes that "Whensoever a man transferreth his right or renounceth it, it is either in consideration of some right reciprocally transferred to himself or for some other good he hopeth for thereby" (*L*, xiv, 8). A person enters into the social contract as a means of attaining "the security of a man's person, in his life and in the means of so preserving life as not to be weary of it" (ibid.). No person, therefore, can be expected to contract away her right to security of person or to the means needed to preserve life in a manner minimally acceptable to her. Even in the commonwealth created by the contract, a human being maintains the basic rights to these things.

The Third Law: Perform Covenants

Hobbes turns next to the third law of nature:

> From that law of nature by which we are obliged to transfer to another such rights as, being retained, hinder the peace of mankind, there followeth a third, which is this *that men perform their covenants made*, without which covenants are in vain, and but empty words, and the right of all men to all things remaining, we are still in the condition of war (*L*, xv, 1).

The second law of nature required us to make covenants, to agree to give up our unlimited liberty on the condition that other individuals would do so as well. And having made this covenant, each of us thereby incurs the obligation to do what we have contracted to do. But while reason may require us to enter into a contract, does it also require that we *live up* to this contract? In setting forth the third law of nature, Hobbes answers this question in the affirmative. Peace will not be attained and the war of all against all avoided unless people *perform* their obligations. Hobbes reminds us that "the definition of INJUSTICE is no other than *the not performance of covenant*" (*L*, xv, 2). Thus justice requires that we live up to our covenants.

The Case of the Fool

Hobbes is clearly concerned that the reasoning supporting the establishment of justice – the keeping of covenants – may not be as compelling as he would like. He is worried about the case of the skeptic – whom he calls "the fool" – who argues that reason does not always counsel just acts but, on some occasions at least, proposes unjust ones. The fool's argument, according to Hobbes, goes as follows: "'everyman's conservation and contentment being committed to his own care, there could be no reason why every man might not do what he thought conduced thereunto, and therefore also to make or not make, keep or not keep, covenants was not against reason, when it conduced to one's benefit'" (*L*, xv, 4). The fool's words are reminiscent of those of some of the ancient Sophists. According to the fool, reason would never counsel us to follow justice on those occasions when it would be in our individual interest not to do so. Reason tells us how to survive (to conserve ourselves) and how to obtain the satisfaction of our desires (our contentment), and it is easy enough to imagine occasions on which our survival or contentment would best be served by breaking our covenants and thereby committing an injustice. Surely on those occasions reason would advise us to commit those injustices! Thus the fool "questioneth whether injustice ... may not sometimes stand with that reason which dictateth to every man his own good" (*L*, xv, 4).

Although the fool's line of reasoning seems compatible with that of Hobbes, Hobbes nevertheless rejects it as spurious:

> ... in a condition of war wherein every man to every man (for want of a common power to keep them all in awe) is an enemy, there is no man can hope by his own strength or wit to defend himself from destruction without the help of confederates (where everyone expects the same defense by the confederation that anyone else does); and therefore, he which declares he thinks it reason to deceive those that help him can in reason expect no other means of safety than what can be had from his single power. He, therefore, that breaketh his covenant, and consequently declareth that he thinks he may with reason do so, cannot be received into any society that unite themselves for peace and defense but by the error of them that receive him, nor when he is received, be retained in it without seeing the danger of their error; which errors a man cannot reasonably reckon upon as the means of his security; and therefore, if he be left or cast out of society, he perisheth; and if he live in society it is by the errors of other men, which he could not foresee nor reckon upon; and consequently [he has acted] against the reason of his preservation, and so as all men that contribute not to his destruction forbear him only out of ignorance of what is good for themselves   (*L*, xv, 5).

This rebuttal to the fool's skepticism goes like this: (a) we cannot expect to survive by our own wit and strength alone; (b) confederates are needed in order for us to survive; (c) we can count on these confederates to help us only if they think we will live up to our covenants; (d) if we do not live up to these covenants, our confederates will help us only if they erroneously think we will live up to them; (e) it is irrational for us to think that we won't be discovered if we break our covenants; therefore we ought to keep our covenants and thereby act justly.

Is this a good argument? It relies heavily on the premise that unjust acts will be discovered and that we cannot count on our confederates' good will if they find out we have broken our covenants. We might think that there are occasions on which we could get away with a broken promise without someone else learning of it. But can we, in advance, have any certainty of succeeding in this fashion? And if we break our agreements often, then the chances of discovery become greater and greater. So, Hobbes concludes, the rational course of action – the one best designed to retain the help of our confederates – is to keep the covenants we have mutually made with them. Justice is the rational course of action.

Words Are Not Enough

The social contract together with the third law of nature creates obligations to deliver on one's commitment not to pursue all things as if one had a right to them. Hobbes refers in this context to the BONDS of obligation. How strong are they? How well will our promises work in limiting the exercise of our rights? Hobbes is not very optimistic about such covenants. Words alone, he claims, are of little avail, and people will be restrained in their actions only to the extent that they fear the consequences of continuing in a state of nature. But even this fear is not enough, Hobbes thinks. On their own, human beings cannot be trusted to live up to their agreements; given an opportunity, they will cheat. This tendency to cheat is acknowledged by everyone and hence is a source of fear that by entering into a contract they will make themselves vulnerable to the selfish machinations of others. Given this concern, unless some additional step is taken to ensure the performance of their covenants, people can be expected to act, often or often enough, in such a way as to ensure a reversal back to the state of nature. Thus the creation of bonds of obligation is not enough to bring about peace and hence survival. How is one to proceed?

Put otherwise, the contract into which a group of people enter is void, invalid, if there is a justified suspicion that the parties to the contract will not live up to it, and we have just seen that Hobbes thinks they will not do so if the matter is left up to them. Under what conditions would the contract be valid?

> If a covenant be made wherein neither of the parties perform presently,
> but trust one another, in the conditions of mere nature (which is a

condition of war of every man against every man) upon any reasonable suspicion it is void; but if there be a common power set over them both, with right and force sufficient to compel performance, it is not void (*L*, xiv, 18).

Hobbes tells us that "the bonds of words are too weak to bridle men's ambition, avarice, anger, and other passions, without the fear of some coercive power ... " (ibid.). Therefore, to seek peace through contract is not enough; there must also be a civil society possessing the coercive power to compel its citizens to abide by the contract into which they have entered. "But in a civil estate, where there is a power set up to constrain those that would otherwise violate their faith, that fear is no more reasonable; and for that cause, he which by the covenant is to perform first is obliged so to do" (*L*, xiv, 19). The fear that others will break the contract (that she who is "to perform first" will not do so) is sufficient to void the contract if additional measures are not taken to ensure that the promises made in the contract are kept. But the fear of the common power inherent in civil society, fear of the punishments this power will mete out for non-compliance, will be a motive sufficient for keeping these promises. With the assurance this brings that compliance will occur, the contract and the obligations incurred by means of it are valid and binding. Thus, to attain peace and escape the war of all against all, we must institute a "commonwealth."

Hobbes relates the need for a commonwealth to the conditions required for the establishment of justice. The bonds of obligation are not enough to bring justice into the world. Justice will come to exist only when people are forced by a central power to abide by their covenants. Thus Hobbes writes:

> Therefore, before the names of just and unjust can have place, there must be some coercive power to compel men equally to the performance of their covenants, by the terror of some punishment greater than the benefit they expect by the breach of their covenant, and to make good that propriety which by mutual contract men acquire, in recompense of the universal right they abandon; and such power there is none before the erection of a commonwealth. ... And therefore where there is no *own*, that is, no propriety, there is no injustice; and where there is no coercive power erected, that is, where there is no commonwealth, there is no propriety, all men having right to all things; therefore where there is no commonwealth, there nothing is unjust. So that the nature of justice consisteth in keeping of valid covenants, but the validity of covenants begins not but with the constitution of a civil power sufficient to compel men to keep them; and then it is also that propriety begins   (*L*, xv, 3).

The existence of the commonwealth alone ensures the conditions under which justice can exist, that is to say, under which promises will be kept.

Other Laws of Nature

Having articulated the first three laws of nature (to seek peace, to enter into a contract with others to give up the universal Right of Nature, and to keep one's covenants) Hobbes proceeds to identify and justify sixteen other such laws. It is unnecessary for us to consider all of these, but a few examples will indicate how Hobbes views reason, operating in the interest of security and contentment, to be the source of our moral obligations. Take, for instance, the fourth law of nature, which Hobbes calls Gratitude:

> As justice dependeth on antecedent covenant, so does GRATITUDE depend on antecedent grace, that is to say, antecedent free-gift; and is the fourth law of nature, which may be conceived in this form *that a man which receiveth benefit from another of mere grace endeavour that he which giveth it have no reasonable cause to repent him of his good will*. For no man giveth but with intention of good to himself, because gift is voluntary, and of all voluntary acts the object is to every man his own good; of which, if men see they shall be frustrated, there will be no beginning of benevolence or trust; nor, consequently, of mutual help, nor of reconciliation of one man to another; and therefore they are to remain still in the condition of war ...   (*L*, xv, 16).

Thus we see that our obligation to show gratitude to those who have befriended us is based on the fact that such an action or attitude is required if we are to remain at peace with one another and avoid the unacceptable conditions of the state of nature. Sociability is also required of us, and contumely – the declaration of hatred or contempt of another – is prohibited. And then there is the law requiring that we treat one another as equals – even if in point of fact human beings are *not* equal by nature:

> If nature therefore have made men equal, that equality is to be acknowledged; or if nature have made men unequal, yet because men that think themselves equal will not enter into conditions of peace but upon equal terms, such equality must be admitted. And therefore for the ninth law of nature, I put this *that every man acknowledge other for his equal by nature*. The breach of this precept is *pride*   (*L*, xv, 21).

Hobbes also formulates as a law of nature the rights that each of us retains as we conclude the social contract and enter into the commonwealth. The criterion governing the identification of these rights is that we should not insist on a right for ourselves that we are unwilling to allow others to retain for themselves as well. He lists as some of these rights the "right to govern their own bodies, [right to] enjoy air, water, motion, ways to go from place to place, and all things else without which a man cannot live, or not live well" (*L*, xv, 22). We can add to this list the ones already noted: the right not to incriminate oneself and the right to self-defense.

In describing these various obligations and rights, Hobbes sees himself as engaged in moral philosophy: "And the science of them [the laws of nature] is the true and only moral philosophy" (*L*, xv, 40). Morality is conceived to be a *science*, the rational study of what is required for survival and contentment. The basis of the moral science is the set of human desires and aversions – what we want, covet, and hate. We are led to engage in moral philosophy because of the simple and inescapable fact that we disagree with one another regarding the objects of our appetites and aversions and that this disagreement leads to conflict and, without much ado, the conditions of the state of nature. Hobbes's well-known expression of this conception of morality is as follows:

> *Good* and *evil* arc names that signify our appetites and aversions, which in different tempers, customs, and doctrines of men are different; and divers men differ not only in their judgment on the senses (of what is pleasant and unpleasant to the taste, smell, hearing, touch, and sight), but also of what is conformable or disagreeable to reason in the actions of common life ... And therefore so long a man is in the condition of mere nature (which is a condition of war) as private appetite is the measure of good and evil; and consequently, all men agree on this, that peace is good; and therefore also the way or means of peace (which, as I have shewed before, are *justice*, *gratitude*, *modesty*, *equity*, *mercy*, and the rest of the laws of nature) are good (that is to say, *moral virtues*), and their contrary vices, evil (*L*, xv, 40).

Although our appetites and desires differ and conflict with one another, and even though human reason issues conflicting judgments regarding "the actions of common life," as rational agents we can all agree on certain basic truths, the laws of nature. These laws set forth the requirements of morality. Thus out of our natural misery emerges the moral life.

The Commonwealth and the Sovereign

It is time now to turn our attention, although briefly, to the idea of the commonwealth and to Hobbes's account of the creation, powers, and functions of the sovereign. We begin by recalling the situation that leads to the necessity for a commonwealth:

For the laws of nature ... of themselves, without the terror of some power to cause them to be observed, are contrary to our natural passions, that carry us to partiality, pride, revenge, and the like. And covenants without the sword are but words, and of no strength to secure a man at all. Therefore ... if there be no power erected, or not great enough for our security, every man will, and may lawfully rely on his own strength and art, for caution against all other men (*L*, xvii, 2).

Therefore we must create such a power as will force us to keep our covenants. How are we to do so?

It will not be enough, Hobbes claims, simply to join together with family and friends in a defensive association. Others might do the same and the war of all against all would continue – now with the various associations at odds with one another. Nor is it enough simply to band together as a great multitude, for the conflicting voices within the multitude would cause any such coalition to collapse and the members to turn on one another. There is, Hobbes maintains, only one option:

The only way to erect such a common power as may be able to defend them from the invasion of foreigners and the injuries of one another, and thereby to secure them in such sort as that by their own industry, and by the fruits of the earth, they may nourish themselves and live contentedly, is to confer all their power and strength upon one man, or upon one assembly of men, that may reduce all their wills, by plurality of voices, unto one will, which is as much as to say, to appoint one man or assembly of men to bear their person, and every one to own and acknowledge himself to be author of whatsoever he that so beareth their person shall act, or cause to be acted, in those things which concern the common peace and safety, and therein to submit their wills, every one to his will, and their judgments, to his judgment (*L*, xvii, 13).

We agree among ourselves, that is to say, that we must give to one person (such as a king), or a group of individuals (such as Parliament), the power to control our lives and enforce the conditions of peace. We contract with one another, each saying in effect to all the others "*I authorise and give up my right of governing myself to this man, or to this assembly of men, on this condition, that thou give up thy right to him, and authorize all his actions in like manner*" (*L*, xvii, 13). This done, we have created a commonwealth: "This is the generation of that great LEVIATHAN, or rather (to speak more reverently) of that *Mortal God* to which we owe, under the *Immortal God*, our peace and defense" (ibid.).

The civil society we have created has the unity that we as separate individuals with conflicting goals do not possess in the state of nature. The unity resides in the singleness of power, whether that power be placed in the hands of one person or an assembly. We have created an artificial person as opposed to a natural one, and this artificial person is the Sovereign. We have also bestowed authority on this person (or the assembly). This authority is our own authority willingly transferred to the sovereign. The sovereign's actions henceforward are *our* actions; she is our agent who represents us. When the sovereign restrains us, it is in reality we who restrain ourselves. In obeying the sovereign we are simply following our own collective will. And it is by obedience to the sovereign that we are able to live in a condition of peace and prosperity.

Powers of the Sovereign

When Hobbes delineates the rights and powers of the sovereign, it is important to remember that he views the sovereign as an artificial person who is the representative of the people who, by contracting among themselves, create the commonwealth. Otherwise, one has the impression that Hobbes is recommending a highly repressive form of dictatorship or tyranny. Moreover, Hobbes's arguments for specific rights and powers often depend upon his conception of the sovereign as artificial person (which does not necessarily lessen the artificiality of some of these arguments).

Once constituted, Hobbes tells us, a sovereign cannot be deposed, for the following reason: "And they have also every man given the sovereignty to him that beareth their person; and therefore if they depose him, they take from him that which is his own, and so ... it is injustice" (*L*, xviii, 3). In deposing the sovereign the members of the commonwealth would be taking from the sovereign what they themselves have given – the sovereign's authority – and Hobbes sees this as the kind of inconsistency he has labelled injustice. Moreover, the citizens, having instituted one form of government – a democracy or aristocracy, say – cannot then force the sovereign to change this form to some other.

Second, the sovereign herself, or the sovereign assembly, cannot be in breach of the contract that created sovereignty, this for the reason that the sovereign was not party to the contract. The people contracted among themselves to lay down their universal right to all things and to institute a sovereign in order to ensure that their covenants are kept. The sovereign did not exist until called into being by the contract and hence could not have been party to the contract. Therefore the sovereign has not made a promise to the people or a covenant with them; there is no commitment on her part, then, that she might break.

Hobbes argues that a person, having agreed voluntarily to contract with others in giving up the Right of Nature, in seeking peace, and in agreeing to generate a sovereign, may not then reject the sovereign selected by the majority, even if this person had supported someone else to be sovereign or had advocated a different form of sovereignty: "For if he voluntarily entered into the congregation of them that were assembled, he sufficiently declared thereby his will (and therefore tacitly covenanted) to stand to what the major part should ordain" (*L*, xviii, 5). Here one of the basic principles of majoritarian democracy seems to find expression.

Once the sovereign is instituted in the manner described, this sovereign, being the kind of artificial person she is, can do no harm to her citizens.

> For he that doth anything by authority from another doth therein no injury to him by whose authority he acteth; but by this institution of a commonwealth every particular man is author of all the sovereign doth; and consequently he that complaineth of injury from his sovereign complaineth of that whereof he himself is author, and therefore ought not to accuse any man but himself; no nor himself of injury, because to do injury to one's self is impossible" (*L*, xviii, 6).

One cannot wilfully do injury to oneself, because, according to Hobbes, one always wills one's own good. And just as the sovereign cannot harm her citizens, the citizens cannot harm her. They cannot punish her and they cannot put her to death.

Duties of the Sovereign

The sovereign's duties are derived from her function, which is to further peace, survival, and contentment. Thus she is the person who judges what must be done in order to attain peace and avoid war. Moreover, given the great importance of public opinion concerning matters of war and peace – given the fact that these opinions can incite the populace to unreasonable stances, both warlike and peaceful – the sovereign is the judge of what opinions the populace shall have concerning these matters. The sovereign establishes a censor who "shall examine the doctrines of all books before they be published" (*L*, xviii, 9). Hobbes seems aware of the dangers of such censorship, and he engages in some sophistical reasoning in order to blunt the impact of his doctrine: "And though in matter of doctrine nothing ought to be regarded but the truth, yet this is not repugnant to regulating of the same by peace. For doctrine repugnant to peace can no more be true than peace and concord can be against the law of nature" (*L*, xviii, 9). (One looks in vain for a demonstration that a "doctrine repugnant to peace" cannot be true.) Moreover, if people are willing to take up arms to ensure the acceptance of an unorthodox opinion, this only shows that they are not members of the commonwealth in the first place, and therefore are not governed by a legitimate sovereign who can establish orthodoxy for them. In reality they are still in the state of nature and war.

It is important to note that the sovereign establishes the rules of what Hobbes calls propriety, what we might think of as private property and the realm of privacy. These rules dictate "what goods [a person] may enjoy, and what actions he may do, without being molested by any of his fellow subjects" (*L*, xviii, 10). That which is mine and that which is yours, that which is good and that which is evil – these are all established by the laws set forth by the sovereign. Moreover, the sovereign exercises judicial power, applying the laws she has created and deciding controversies in light of them. And the sovereign can both reward the lawkeepers and punish the lawbreakers.

In an executive capacity, the sovereign has the right to declare and conduct war, to call up a military for this purpose, and to levy taxes on the people in order to pay for the effort. In times of peace as well as war, she appoints all "counsellors, ministers, and officers" (*L*, xviii, 13), and she establishes the "titles of honour" that are awarded to those who deserve well of the commonwealth.

According to Hobbes, the rights of the sovereign are "incommunicable and inseparable" (*L*, xviii, 16): they cannot be given away by the sovereign to someone else and they cannot be divided up. The sovereign cannot, for instance, retain her judicial powers and give up her control over the military, for without the military she could not ensure that the laws would be executed. Her undivided power is close to absolute. She cannot do anything that infringes on the rights citizens retain in the commonwealth – the right to defend themselves, not to incriminate themselves, and so on – but these are but meager limits considering what the sovereign can and must do in order to achieve the very goal for which she was established: the overcoming of division among people and the attainment of peace. We can expect citizens to complain, whether the government be a monarchy or a democracy: "But a man may here object that the condition of subjects is very miserable, as being obnoxious to the lusts and other irregular passions of him or them that have so unlimited a power in their hands" (*L*, xviii, 20). But such complaints have no merit – those who complain exaggerate their small payments by the magnifying glasses of self-love and passion. They lack the telescopes (of moral and civil science) that would allow them to see what miseries would hang over their heads if they did not to make these small payments. Enlightened self-interest can look beyond the inconveniences of the moment and acknowledge that life in the commonwealth, even with its rules, laws, and limits, is the very best bargain a person can strike.

It remains for us to consider several general issues that arise in Hobbes's theory, issues that have taken on a perennial status in subsequent moral philosophy. These are the issues of egoism, determinism and human freedom, and relativism. The first concerns a thesis about the nature of human motivation. The second a claim about universal causality with implications for human freedom. And the third a question about the nature and validity of morality.

Psychological Egoism

Hobbes is often said to be a *psychological egoist* who claims that all human beings always act in their own self-interest, that is to say, for the purpose of obtaining what they consider a good for themselves. Egoism in this sense contrasts with *psychological altruism*, which insists that, at least on some occasions, human beings aim to promote the good of others. As psychological theories, egoism and altruism are conflicting empirical claims about the nature of human motivation. These psychological theories contrast with ethical or normative claims about how human beings *ought to act*. *Ethical egoism* is the claim that every person ought to act so as to promote her own self-interest, and *ethical altruism* the claim that everyone ought to promote the good of others.

Hobbes's psychological egoism is less apparent in *Leviathan* than in some of his earlier works, but the overall tone of the book is egoistic and there are occasional passages that seem straightforwardly so. Take for instance his statement that "of all voluntary acts the object is to every man his own good" (*L*, xv, 16). We act voluntarily when we do not act against our will, and our will, Hobbes is claiming, is always for something we perceive to be our own good. Even gift-giving follows this rule, "For no man giveth but with intention of good to himself" (ibid.). Furthermore, the argument of *Leviathan* conveys the impression that Hobbes is grounding morality and civil law in the self-interest of the individual contractor: a rational person sees that it is in her interest to give up the Right of Nature and abide by the laws of the sovereign. It is not surprising, then, that the traditional interpretation of Hobbes takes him to be an out-an-out psychological egoist.

The picture is more complicated, however, than initial impressions convey. Several recent scholars have challenged the traditional view and argued that *Leviathan* does not convey an egoist message.[6] These scholars point to definitions found in the book which clearly are not egoistic, for instance the claim that "*Desire* of good to another" is called Good Will, Benevolence, or Charity, there being no implication that such things as benevolence and charity do not exist (*L*, vi, 22). Moreover, some of the clearly egoistic definitions of earlier works are replaced in *Leviathan* by definitions that appear non-egoistic in nature – for instance, the notorious definition of *pity* in the earlier *Human Nature*, namely the "*imagination* or *fiction* of *future* calamity to *ourselves*, proceeding from the sense of *another* man's calamity"[7] gives way to "*Grief* for the calamity of another, is PITY, and ariseth from the imagination that the like calamity may befall himself" (*L*, vi, 46). If on observing the misfortune of others my only response is to fear that the same will happen to me, this "pity" is indeed self-regarding. But if I grieve for the misfortunes of others, even if I do so after imagining that the same may happen to me, at least I am grieving for *them*, not for myself. Such an emotion is other-regarding, and, as Hobbes himself says, it is associated with Compassion and Fellow Feeling. Such feelings do not sit comfortably with psychological egoism. Finally, the general argument of the book can be cast in terms that are not egoistic. We could allow a person a desire for the good of her loved ones, family, and friends and still generate the argument that this person ought to enter a commonwealth and take on the bounds of moral and legal obligation.

In deciding whether Hobbes is a psychological egoist we need a precise definition of the term "egoism" as a psychological term descriptive of human motiovation and behavior. There are at least three different definitions that have been offered for this term. First, there is the idea that psychological egoism stands for the claim that every person acts in order to satisfy her own desire. According to this interpretation, *what* a person desires is not the issue; rather the truth about human motivation turns on the question of whether one could ever act without having as one's primary goal or reason for acting the satisfaction of one's own desire, whatever the object of that desire might be. According to this way of thinking, a person might desire the good of many other individuals and still act egoistically, because what she really aims at is the satisfaction of *her* desire. Because the mere attribution of a desire to a person implies that the person wants to satisfy this desire, because saying of a person that she wants to satisfy her desire for *x* is a mere redundancy or tautology, this view has been called "tautological egoism."[8]

A second interpretation of psychological egoism maintains that a person acts egoistically because she always acts as she does because of past benefits or harms she has received from this kind of behavior. A person's "history of reinforcement" determines how she behaves subsequently. According to this theory, Mother Teresa helps the poor because early in her life she received rewards for doing so. This interpretation might be dubbed "causal egoism."[9] It defines egoism in terms of a causal thesis about behavior, a thesis which, in recent times, many psychologists have favored.

Finally, there is the definition of psychological egoism that relates it to our ordinary understanding of selfishness: we act egoistically (selfishly) if *what* we desire is our own good. Accordingly, we would act non-egoistically (unselfishly) if what we desire is the good of others. Seen in this way, the critical factor in deciding if a person acts egoistically is the content of her desire (hence we might call this "content egoism"). If the content is the good of oneself, then one acts egoistically; if the content is the good of someone else, one acts altruistically. According to this conception of egoism, in desiring the good of others a person would act altruistically even though it was her desire she sought to satisfy (tautological egoism) and even though she was motivated to act by previous benefits she had received for helping others (causal egoism).

In light of the quotation from Hobbes given above – " ... of all voluntary acts the object is to every man his own good" – it appears that at least in this passage Hobbes is a content egoist. But other passages in which he cites the good of others as the occasional object of our desire might lead us to conclude that, overall, he is only what Gregory Kavka has called a "predominant egoist."[10] According to this latter way of looking at the matter, a person's own well-being is the primary object of desire for that person, that is to say, the one that usually, but not always, takes precedence over altruistic values. Commentators have also found evidence of tautological egoism and causal egoism in Hobbes's work.

Ethical Egoism

Is Hobbes an ethical egoist?[11] Is self-interest the ultimate ethical goal for him – what we "ought" to seek? Again, some distinctions are required. Rational egoism asserts that promoting one's own interests is the rational thing to do; individual ethical egoism claims that everyone (morally) ought to promote *my* self-interest; and universal ethical egoism maintains that every person (morally) ought to pursue her own self-interest. Hobbes certainly is a rational egoist. To his mind, reason clearly requires working toward the satisfaction of one's self-interest; such satisfaction is a rational goal. It is also clear that Hobbes is not an individual egoist. But his conception of the laws of nature, which after all are normative guidelines, strongly suggests that he is a universal ethical egoist. These laws could be interpreted simply as the laws of rational egoism, but Hobbes does speak of them as moral laws (*L*, xv, 40; and *De Cive*, 3, xxxi). As moral, the laws of nature prescribe moral obligations: that everyone take the steps needed to ensure their existence and a minimally acceptable mode of existence. Thus these laws require morally that all human beings pursue their self-interest. Such is universal ethical egoism. It is important to note that the goal affirmed by the laws of nature is not gratification of one's immediate self-interest but rather satisfaction of one's overall, long-term self-interest. Thus Hobbes defends a form of *enlightened* ethical egoism.

There are philosophers who claim that the normative doctrine of egoism is not a *moral* doctrine. Morality, they assert, is an other-regarding practice requiring a concern for the well-being of other people. On these grounds they have questioned whether Hobbes has a moral theory at all.[12] We shall not take a stand on this issue. It may well be true that the ordinary concept of morality is other-regarding in nature. But ethical theorists do not always feel constrained by linguistic practices, and throughout Western history there have been philosophers who have put forward doctrines of egoism or prudence and have viewed them as describing the (true) nature of morality. Hence for our purposes it is appropriate to say that Hobbes should be seen as an ethical egoist.

Voluntary Behavior

Both psychological egoism and ethical egoism are highly controversial doctrines. This is particularly so in the case of the psychological theory, since it makes it appear that we are in the grip of a compulsion to do good for ourselves. We seem to have no choice about how we shall behave but are required always to do what we think best serves our interests. This implication raises the larger issue of whether as human beings we possess any such thing as *free agency*. Can we freely choose what we do, or do we necessarily act in order to satisfy some built-in pattern of motivation, e.g., to maximize our self-interest?

Hobbes's overall theory of human behavior seems to run counter to the notion that we possess free agency. He views behavior as simply another form of motion, and for him motions occur mechanically. Thus actions are the results of causal interactions among things in motion or at rest. As objects and states of affairs in the external world impinge on us, they set up motions in our minds (ideas) and motions in our "hearts" (desires and appetites). When we act "voluntarily" (when our action is not an involuntary tick or knee jerk response) what we do is the result of the mechanical interaction of the motions constituting our ideas and desires. As Hobbes explains it, our *going* and *speaking* depend on our thoughts of *whither, which way, and what* (*L*, vi, 1). Moreover, our going in a certain direction or speaking in a certain manner depends on what we desire to accomplish by doing so. Thus our going and speaking are but motions resulting from antecedent motions of thinking and desiring. These motions and their interactions, we are asked to believe, obey the mechanical laws that govern all motions in the universe. Given one set of motions, the consequent motions follow necessarily in accordance with these laws. In all of this law-governed activity, where is there any possibility of free or voluntary action?

It all depends, Hobbes says in effect, on what one means by "voluntary." If one uses this term to describe an act as having no prior cause (as a way of saying that no antecedent motions bring it about), then there is no free and voluntary behavior. But this is not necessarily what we mean by "voluntary." In giving his own definition of this term, Hobbes emphasizes, as most of us would want to do, the notion of the *will*. "For a *voluntary act* is that which proceedeth from the *will*, and no other" (*L*, vi, 53), he first tells us, and then he goes on to say of the will that it is "the last appetite in deliberating" (ibid.). In deliberation a variety of ideas pass through our minds, ideas of our doing this or that, together with the desires or aversions (appetites) that attach to these ideas. The thought that brings with it the greatest (idea of) pleasure generates the strongest desire, and this becomes the last appetite in the string of appetites involved in deliberation. This appetite or desire – this will – then causes us to act with a view to attaining or doing what we desire.

Isn't this entire process a mechanical one? Aren't we just doing what we have to do, without any possibility of free agency? Perhaps. But it is important to see that Hobbes's mechanical picture of human behavior is not inconsistent with "liberty," which he defines as the lack of external impediments (*L*, xiv, 2). If I act on the basis of my will, I thereby do what I most want to do on that occasion. Only if I am prevented by external impediments from doing what I want to do can I be said to be constrained or coerced, i.e., lacking in liberty. Thus on those occasions when the cause of my action is my will, it is proper to say that I act voluntarily. Voluntary action is consistent with the mechanical causation of action, as Hobbes sees it, because voluntary action is no more than a matter of doing what one wants to do. Hobbes, at least implicitly, is committed to a view of voluntary action that has come to be called "compatibilism." Free agency, liberty, voluntary action are compatible with the mechanistic, deterministic picture of the world because will is simply the last appetite in the process of deliberation.

Relativism?

Finally, let us look briefly at Hobbes's alleged *relativism*.[13] As we have seen, Hobbes views *good* and *evil* as being dependent on a person's desires and aversions:

> But whatsoever is the object of any man's appetite or desire that is it which he for his part calleth *good*; and the object of his hate and aversion, *evil*; and of his contempt, *vile* and *inconsiderable*. For these words of good, evil, and contemptible are ever used with relation to the person that useth them, there being nothing simply and absolutely so, nor any common rule of good and evil to be taken from the nature of the objects themselves, but from the person of the man (where there is no commonwealth), or (in a commonwealth) from the person that representeth it, or from an arbitrator or judge whom men disagreeing shall by consent set up, and make his sentence the rule thereof   (*L*, vi, 7).

This dense quotation contains a number of important points. First, it tells us that there is nothing good or evil *absolutely*, that is to say, in itself, in the nature of things themselves. Things, actions, people, and so on become good or evil only by being the objects of a person's desires or hatreds. But what one person may love, another may hate, what one will desire and pursue, another will avoid – and thus there is no common rule of good and evil. On the contrary, good and evil vary from person to person, society to society.

Hobbes does allow a common rule of good and evil within the commonwealth. This is because the sovereign is the artificial person created by consent of the governed, the person whose desires and aversions represent those of the citizens. Under these conditions of contract, one and only one set of things is good, namely those desired by the sovereign, and similarly for what is evil. But we must recall that the international situation is in effect a state of war pitting nation against nation, society against society, and thus the rule of good and evil for one society (what its sovereign determines to be good and evil) will be different from the rule of good and evil for another society (whose sovereign desires and hates different things). So we are back to the multiplicity of values we find in the state of nature. Never do we encounter things universally and absolutely good; they are only variably good or evil, relative to the individual person, or the artificial sovereign person, who makes them so by desiring or hating them.

It seems clear from these considerations that Hobbes offers us a *subjectivist* form of ethics which grounds moral values in the desires and aversions of individuals and not in the objective properties of states of affairs and actions. Insofar as these desires and aversions may vary from one person to another, and from one culture to another, the theory appears to be one of cultural relativism (see chapter 1). Is it also a theory of *ethical* relativism? Does Hobbes deny that there are universal moral truths binding on all human beings? Here the record is not so clear.

In the first place, as we have noted before, Hobbes not infrequently speaks of the laws of nature as moral laws. In *Leviathan* he writes that "the science of them [the laws of nature] is the true and only moral philosophy" (*L*, xv, 40), and in *De Cive* and other works the equation of the laws of nature and the moral law is explicit (e.g., *DC*, 3, xxxi). The laws of nature are universal truths known by reason, and they hold prior to the establishment of a commonwealth. It follows that there are universal moral maxims applying to all human beings at all times. The existence of such maxims is consistent with Hobbes's subjectivism: the maxims describe what must be done in order to realize what all human beings desire and to avoid what they all fear. But because they are true of all human beings, and true independently of whether they are believed to be true, these maxims constitute the principles of a doctrine of ethical absolutism, *not* ethical relativism.[14]

Some interpreters of Hobbes take the laws of nature to be the commands of the deity, and hence they interpret Hobbes as putting forward a divine–command theory of morality.[15] They point out that Hobbes equates laws with commands (*DC*, 14, i), and he as much as says that the person commanding the laws of nature is none other than God. This, too, is a non-relativist theory, whether it be a good interpretation of Hobbes or not.

Moreover, Hobbes stresses the fact that when human beings make promises or covenants with one another, they *bind* themselves to future actions. A person who has made a promise to give up the unlimited Right of Nature thereby has incurred an obligation to act in a certain way in the future. To be sure, these covenants or promises will be voided if there is reason to believe other people will not live up to their promises to do likewise. But the fact that obligations can be voided does not show that there were no obligations in the first place. And if our promises impose obligations on us, there are moral constraints in the world that are independent of human beliefs, desires, or civil law. In emphasizing them, Hobbes offers us a non-relativistic perspective on moral values.

Some contractarians view moral values as arising only after the creation of a commonwealth. These values are interpreted as what the parties to the contract agree to, or what the sovereign requires of citizens. We have seen that Hobbes does sometimes speak in this fashion, equating moral requirements with legal ones – and such a view is relativistic. But if the very act of making a covenant or contract is itself a moral act inasmuch as it imposes requirements on the parties to the contract which they are not at liberty to break at will, then contractarianism rests on a non-relativistic base.

As noted above, it is easy to see Hobbes as putting forth a theory of ethical egoism, which might be described as a theory of prudence or enlightened self-interest. According to this normative point of view, the ultimate value is the well-being of the individual, and the laws of nature prescribe the means for each individual to promote her long-range, overall (and hence enlightened) self-interest. In spite of the fact that it is the individual's self-interest that is primary, the theory of prudence is absolutistic in nature because it requires that everyone seek her enlightened self-interest as the rational thing to do, whether or not she believes she ought to do so or wishes to do so.

The debates over whether Hobbes is an ethical egoist and an ethical relativist are sure to continue. Surveying the various interpretations of Hobbes's moral theory, it is difficult to resist the conclusion that Hobbes is simply inconsistent and fails to articulate a single, coherent set of ideas. Hobbes scholars usually operate with a principle of charity and assume that there is a single interpretation that puts the pieces together in a plausible fashion. Be that as it may, the apparent inconsistencies cause interpretive difficulties at almost every step. Consider Hobbes's doctrine of contractarianism, which, as we noted at the beginning of this chapter, has had an enormous impact on moral and political thinking in modern times. This theory runs up against problems relating to the ground of moral values. Hobbes tells us, on the one hand, that good and evil are relative to our desires and aversions, but he also claims that by entering into a contract we promise to perform certain actions and that our entering into this contract therefore creates for us an obligation to deliver on our commitment. This obligation seems to arise from the act of contract, not from any desire that may attend it. Given Hobbes's apparent relativism, no contract I enter into is binding on me unless I desire it to be so. Given his contractarianism, my covenants are binding whether or not I wish to fulfill them. It is difficult to know which way to go on this issue.

Problems of Social Contract Theory

We shall conclude this discussion of Hobbes by considering two other problems that arise for his doctrine of a social contract. The first problem concerns what happens in the state of nature. Hobbes argues that all members of the state of nature would engage in a strategy of anticipation, attacking or making war on others before they could do the same. Insofar as everyone, being rational, would adopt the same strategy, a war of all against all would result. But wouldn't these rational agents be able to see that this sad state of war would be the result of their strategy? If so, they would have reason *not* to engage in anticipation. An alternative strategy of *lying low* or attacking only when attacked might suggest itself as the more rational approach.[16] But this alternative strategy would seemingly lead to a very different kind of life in the state of nature. So different, in fact, that the drive to create a commonwealth might not be necessary.

A second problem arises when we note that Hobbes is not committed to the belief that a contract actually took place at a point in history when human beings passed from the state of nature into civil society. In fact, he seems to say that the contract need not ever have occurred as an explicit act; it is, rather, a contract that is implicit, one we show through our behavior that we have made. We act in ways that indicate our willingness to comply with the will of the sovereign, for we reveal in innumerable ways our willingness to accept the authority of the sovereign as a means of protecting our survival and attaining a satisfactory life. But can we read such an implicit contract into our behavior? Can we demonstrate to a criminal, or a person engaged in civil disobedience, that she is violating a contract she previously made with the other citizens of the community? We certainly need a more detailed and convincing account of the criteria of implicit consent than Hobbes gives us if we are to be successful in claiming implicit consent.

The problem may be put another way. If the obligation we have to obey the sovereign is the consequence of promises we have made to one another to give up our Right of Nature, then these promises must be real. But if the contract we have entered into is merely implicit or hypothetical, our mutual promises are merely implicit or hypothetical as well. But hypothetical promises – promises one would have made, if ... – are not promises at all.[17] I must *actually* promise something in order to be obligated to do what I promise. Hobbes does not wish to assert that we actually promise anything. What is left, then, of our obligation to obey the sovereign and civil laws?

In spite of the above problems, Hobbes's basic idea of a contract holds great attraction for many people: morality is seen by them as a strategy we devise in our effort to defend and protect ourselves. Morality is not inherent in human nature – we could, after all, continue to kill one another in the state of nature; morality is simply the rational way to deal with our predicament. We impose moral obligations on ourselves and accept the authority of the sovereign and civil law because these are simply the most rational means we have to avoid death and distress.

7

Spinoza

Benedict Spinoza (1632–77 CE) is one of the most difficult philosophers in Western history to read and understand, but, as he tells us in the concluding sentence of his masterpiece, the *Ethics*, "all things excellent are as difficult as they are rare."[1] The main problem one encounters with the *Ethics* is that it is written in a deductive and semi-geometrical style. Spinoza is one of the so-called continental rationalist philosophers (the other two primary ones being Descartes and Leibniz), and his rationalism consists of taking logical or mathematical proof as the paradigm of knowledge. Beginning with axioms he considers to be self-evident, Spinoza proceeds to deduce theorems or propositions from these axioms. Once he shows his claims to be either self-evident or to have been deductively demonstrated, Spinoza makes ample use of them in subsequent demonstrations. If a statement is self-evident or deducible from axioms that are self-evident, it is known, with certainty, to be true; hence it can be used with assurance to prove other propositions that follow from it. Following the order of proof, then, is the first difficulty in understanding Spinoza.

A second difficulty derives from the fact that Spinoza begins each part of the *Ethics* by introducing the definitions of the terms or ideas he subsequently uses. The definitions are highly philosophical and expressed in language that often reaches back to the medieval period. Many of the concepts are hard to grasp, but everything depends on grasping them clearly and firmly. For the axioms are self-evident in light of the definitions of the terms involved.

With his definitions, axioms, and propositions (theorems), Spinoza systematically describes the world in its most general features. In fact, his philosophy – his metaphysics or theory of God, human beings, and nature – is one of the most systematic metaphysical theories ever generated. Once understood, this highly organized, deductive presentation is also one of the most impressive ever produced. If Spinoza is correct, he is able to *prove*, step by step, the most basic or fundamental propositions describing the cosmos. In proving them, he renders them certainly true; in organizing them into a system, he shows how all things "hang together" in the world. The result is intellectually gratifying: a vision of reality in which we can have total confidence and which gives us a systematic account of the totality of things. If ... he is correct!

We shall not follow Spinoza's detailed development of the initial parts of his system – his theories of God and the human mind. We shall have to content ourselves with a brief sketch of these doctrines. Once this sketch is concluded, we shall turn our attention to his applications of his metaphysical theories to human action and the quest for the human good. At that point, we shall follow Spinoza through the development of his argument in the last three parts of the *Ethics*.

Metaphysics

Spinoza is what we call a *pantheist*. Unlike the theology of theism (the theology accepted by most Christians, Jews, and Muslims), Spinoza's pantheism denies that God, on the one hand, and the world of nature and human beings, on the other, are separate and distinct entities. For the theist, God is eternal, and he creates, out of nothing, the world and time, which exist apart from him. God is, for the theist, a purely spiritual being. The physical world he creates is material, and human beings are mixtures of matter and spirit. As a pantheist, Spinoza denies that God is purely spiritual. God has a physical body, namely the world. God *is* the world. God and world, however, are not purely material. While we can understand God as physical, we can also understand the deity as spiritual, or as Spinoza prefers to put it, as mental. God is both extended matter and mental idea – extension and thought are two ways of grasping the nature of God. Extension and thought are, in Spinoza's terminology, two of God's essential features or *attributes*. The divine being is to be understood as the totality of extended matter *and* the totality of mental ideas. The equation of God and Nature has led some to call Spinoza a God-intoxicated man; it has led others to think of him as an atheist.

In Spinoza's philosophy, God is absolutely infinite, that is to say, unlimited, unbounded, unconditioned. God possesses an infinity of attributes, extension and thought being the only two of these attributes we can know. No finite thing can have an impact on God, since doing so would be a way of limiting him. And there can be only one infinite being since, if there were more than one, each of them would be limited by the other.

It follows from Spinoza's pantheism that we human beings are part of God. We are, in Spinoza's terminology, finite *modes* of the infinite substance God. This view contradicts common sense, insofar as the latter sees individual human beings as individual *substances* that possess considerable independence, self-determination, and individuality. For Spinoza, on the contrary, there is only one substance, equally called God or Nature. Only God/Nature is an independent, self-determining individual thing; we human beings are but parts of the whole, and our nature is determined in every way by other parts of the whole and by the laws (of Nature/God) that express the essential characteristics of this whole.

As modes of the absolutely infinite substance God, human beings are determinate features of the attributes thought and extension, both of which are themselves infinite. That is to say, we human beings are bodies – specific modifications of extension – and also minds – specific modifications of thought, i.e., specific ideas. Thought and extension being two ways of understanding any thing, it follows that human beings can be comprehended as a set of ideas *and* as a set of physical features. Our ideas are specific modifications of God's mind, and our bodies are specific modifications of God's body.

Mind and Body

Spinoza's theory of the nature and relationship of mind and body is one of the most obscure aspects of his philosophy, but it is also one of the most critical. First of all, mind and body must be understood as two ways of seeing or understanding *the same thing*. Thus a human being can be seen as a mind or as a body. Moreover, there can be no mind – no set of ideas – without a body, since an idea is always an idea of a body. i.e. is an idea "about" a body. It follows from this doctrine that there can be no survival of the human mind (or spirit or soul) after the death and destruction of the body. Spinoza denies the doctrine of personal immortality that claims the individual soul will survive death and continue to live everafter.[2]

Spinoza's theory of the nature of body and mind also has strange consequences for the understanding of the physical world. Just as there can be no idea without a body (of which it is the mental parallel), there can be no body without a corresponding idea. Thus the objects in physical nature have a mental correlate. Such a view can be seen as a form of animism which characterizes physical things as having (something like) souls. We must remember, however, that physical nature is the body of *God*, and to each modification of God's body there corresponds a divine *idea*. God is the total set of physical things (including human bodies) and the total set of ideas.[3]

Spinoza maintains that, contrary to the view of his predecessor, René Descartes, and perhaps to the common-sense view of things as well, mind and body never interact. The body does not produce ideas, and ideas (in the form of volitions or acts of will) never produce changes in the physical body. For Spinoza, mind and body are completely parallel, a body having its corresponding idea and an idea having its corresponding body, but without any impact of the one correlate on the other. Spinoza finds it impossible to conceive how thoughts and bodies, so essentially different in nature, could ever have causal relationships between them. How can an immaterial idea, which is not even in space, cause a physical thing like the body to move? Physical motion occurs only when one extended body comes into contact with another and conveys the force of motion to it. And how could the body, which always interacts with other bodies by means of physical impact in space, exert influence over a non-extended, non-spatial idea? Descartes, in desperation, appealed to the totally mysterious activity of the pineal gland to explain the alleged interaction. Spinoza, more consistently, denies that such interaction can occur.

Theory of Knowledge

If there is no mind/body interaction, then any and all explanations of what happens in the physical, extended world must be given solely in terms of the laws of extension and motion, i.e., in terms of physical bodies having causal impact on other physical bodies. Likewise, all explanations of what happens in the mental world must be in mental terms: we must explain one idea by appeal to other ideas. If physical explanations are always causal, what form do mental explanations take? They cannot be causal, since ideas are not spatial things which could come into contact with one another. According to Spinoza, the relationship between mental ideas is a *logical* one: some ideas *imply* other ideas, some of them *follow from* others. If, for example, we have the idea of a triangle, it follows that we have the idea of a three-sided figure inscribed upon a plane. The second idea is a deductive consequence of the first. Or again, if we entertain the thought that all human beings are mortal together with the thought that Socrates was a human being, we can infer, deductively, that Socrates was mortal. We can explain why a figure inscribed on a plane has three sides by noting that it is a triangle: its three-sidedness follows from its being a triangle. And we can explain why Socrates is mortal by seeing that Socrates is a human being and all human beings are mortal. Thus explanation in the realm of ideas takes the form of tracing the deductive relationships among these ideas.

Let us remember, however, that thought and extension are simply two ways of describing or thinking about the same thing. It follows that the causal order in physical nature corresponds to the deductive order in the realm of ideas. As we trace the deductive relationships among our ideas, we are in effect tracing the causal order among the physical objects that are the correlates of these ideas. Thus we understand the world, or Nature, by developing a deductive system of ideas which explains one idea as being the necessary consequence of other ideas – and we say, accordingly, that the one physical object (the correlate of the first idea) is the causal consequence of the others (the correlates of the other ideas). Hence the need for Spinoza to cast his own metaphysical theory of the world in deductive form.

It must be emphasized that deductive relationships involve relationships that are *necessary*. If something is a triangle, it *must* have three sides. If all human beings are mortal and Socrates is a human being, then Socrates *must* be mortal. There can be no exceptions to these relations; they always, necessarily, obtain. If we think of a deductive inference as having a set of premises and a conclusion, we can say that the proposition expressing the idea in the conclusion necessarily follows from the propositions expressing the ideas in the premises. This is the case, that is, if the deductive argument is a valid one; but to say that a deduction is valid is simply to say that if its premises are true, so too must be its conclusion.

Necessity and Freedom

Returning once again to the correlation between the deductive relationships in the realm of ideas and the causal relationships in the extended world of matter, we can see that the necessity found in the deductive relationships is mirrored by a similar necessity in the causal relationships. If one event causes another, then the second *must* occur if the first has occurred. If a lead ball is dropped from a position in the earth's atmosphere, it must fall to the ground. If a person has her head cut off, she must die. Causal necessity is the material equivalent of the logical necessity in the world of ideas. Therefore Spinoza is a strict determinist. Everything that happens in nature must happen; everything that happens in nature happens in accordance with the laws of physical nature, which laws express the necessary connections between causes and their effects.

Human beings, we should recall, are parts of nature. They have physical bodies which are under the control of the laws of nature. These bodies are in constant contact with other objects in their environments; some of the latter cause the human body to move in certain ways, just as the motion of the body itself causes things in the environment to move. All of this activity is governed by strict causality – nothing happens accidentally; everything that occurs must occur. When we add to this view of the human body the thesis that the mind cannot interact with the body, we come up with the result that the human body is totally under the control of Nature and its laws. There is no such thing as the body having the freedom to move one way or the other; given the causes in the rest of Nature, the body must move about in the ways it is caused to move. The human body is just one part of the total physical machine, Nature, and its behavior can be completely explained in terms of the laws governing this machine and the prior conditions of matter in motion.

Where, then, is human freedom? Spinoza denies that there is any such thing if it is thought to involve a violation of the causal order. Our bodies and their activities are the inevitable result of the physical forces at work in Nature. We are often bandied about by these forces, and the desires and appetites we form as a result of such forces move us hither and yon. As Spinoza puts it, "it is clear that we are driven about in many ways by external causes, and that, like waves on the sea, driven by contrary winds, we toss about, not knowing our outcome and fate" (IIIP59S).[4] We cannot control our bodies through the operation of the mind, and we cannot change the laws of nature. If human freedom requires such control or intervention, there is no such thing as human freedom. Once again Spinoza's thought comes into conflict with common sense (and with Descartes). We ordinarily think that we can make decisions, that we have at least limited dominion over our bodies, and that in exercising this control we engage in free, voluntary behavior. Not so, says Spinoza.

Is freedom, then, a total illusion? Much of the *Ethics* is an attempt to show that freedom is possible, but only if we understand what it really is. The popular conception of freedom as the exercise of free will is an illusion, but there is, according to Spinoza, a deeper sense of freedom, a freedom which is attainable. In fact, freedom ranks as one of Spinoza's highest values. The *Ethics* is designed to illuminate its nature and to show us how to obtain it. The goal of the book is to indicate the path by means of which we can escape from the slavery of the passions and become a self-determining, free human being.

The Practical Realm

The first step in finding this path is to understand the nature of human passions and actions. Part III of the *Ethics* gives us Spinoza's thoughts on these matters. Part IV describes the effects of the passions, or what Spinoza calls human bondage; and part V consists of his theory of human freedom. We shall now begin to follow the argument of these concluding sections of the *Ethics*.

In the closing pages of part II, Spinoza indicates the advantages that can come from applying his doctrine of God/Nature and his theory of the human mind to more practical matters. He writes:

> It remains now to indicate how much knowledge of this doctrine is to our advantage in life. We shall see this easily from the following considerations:
>
> A. Insofar as it teaches that we act only from God's command, that we share in the divine nature, and that we do this the more, the more perfect our actions are, and the more and more we understand God. This doctrine, then, in addition to giving us complete peace of mind, also teaches us wherein our greatest happiness, *or* blessedness, consists: namely in the knowledge of God alone, by which we are led to do only those things which love and morality advise ...
>
> B. Insofar as it teaches us how we must bear ourselves concerning matters of fortune, *or* things which are not in our power, that is, things which do not follow from our nature – that we must expect and bear calmly both good fortune and bad. For all things follow from God's eternal decree with the same necessity as from the essence of a triangle it follows that its three sides are equal to two right angles.
>
> C. This doctrine contributes to social life, insofar as it teaches us to

hate no one, to disesteem no one, to mock no one, to be angry at no one, to envy no one; and also insofar as it teaches that each of us should be content with his own things, and should be helpful to his neighbor, not from unmanly compassion, partiality, or superstition, but from the guidance of reason, as the time and occasion demand ...

D. Finally, this doctrine also contributes, to no small extent, to the common society insofar as it teaches us how citizens are to be governed and led, not so that they may be slaves, but that they may do freely the things which are best   (IIP49SIV).

In reading through this passage, which provides a good summary of Spinoza's ethical theory, one should remember that the divine decree of God may also be described as the Law of Nature. This law is equally the law of reason, and its edicts follow from one another with necessity. It is through knowing God or Nature – through reason – that we achieve true happiness and true freedom, our ultimate ethical goals.

Affects

Part III of the *Ethics* deals with the origin and nature of the *affects*, under which term Spinoza includes the feelings and emotions and other components of human nature that lead human beings to act in certain ways. He begins by saying that he will "consider human actions and appetites just as if it were a question of lines, planes, and bodies" (IIIPr). He contrasts this approach, which he views as the scientific one, with the normal way of explaining human feeling and action: "Most of those who have written about the affects, and men's way of living, seem to treat, not of natural things, which follow the common laws of Nature, but of things which are outside Nature. Indeed they seem to conceive man in Nature as a dominion within a dominion. For they believe that man disturbs, rather than follows, the order of Nature, that he has absolute power over his actions, and that he is determined only by himself" (IIIP). Such was the view of Spinoza's predecessor, Descartes, who thought that free acts of will could have an impact on the motions of the body – and hence disturb the order of Nature. Spinoza disagrees with this belief, claiming that the affects must be understood in the same way everything else in Nature is understood, namely "through the universal laws and rules of Nature" (ibid.), which laws are "always and everywhere the same" (ibid.). It follows that "the affects ... of hate, anger, envy, and the like, considered in themselves, follow with the same necessity and force of Nature as the other singular things" (ibid.). For this reason he can treat them like lines, planes, and bodies.

The class of affects, as we know from what has just been said, will include emotions like hate, anger, and envy. What exactly is an affect? Spinoza defines the term as follows: "By affect I understand affections of the body, by which the body's power of acting is increased or diminished, aided or restrained, and at the same time, the ideas of these affections" (IIID3). An affection for Spinoza is any modification (concrete determination) of the body or the mind. An affect is not merely an action-related bodily condition, since Spinoza explicitly says that it is also the idea of the bodily condition. One may say that there are bodily affects and mental affects, but one must always remember that there is a mental correlate of every bodily thing and characteristic, and vice versa. So to each bodily affect there corresponds the idea of that affect, which can be understood as a mental affect. An affect, then, is a state or disposition of the body or a state or disposition of the mind (a particular idea) which either increases or decreases the body's power to act. One commentator[5] equates this power to act with an organism's energy or vitality. Some affects inhibit action by reducing this vitality, others further it by increasing it. Clearly the freedom Spinoza seeks will turn out to be a matter of a person having affects of body and mind that enhance her power of acting; slavery, on the contrary, will be a matter of having affects that decrease this vital energy.

Active and Passive Emotions

Spinoza goes on, in an obscure passage, to say of the affects: "Therefore, if we can be the adequate cause of any of these affections, I understand by the affect an action; otherwise, a passion" (ibid.). Affects are therefore to be divided into two general classes: actions and passions. Some emotions are actions – or, more clearly expressed, active emotions – while others are passions – or passive emotions. Whether a particular affect falls into the one category or the other depends on the nature of the causality of the person who has the affect, i.e., whether this person is an *adequate* or *inadequate* cause of the affect. What could be meant by an adequate cause? Spinoza's definition is as follows: "I call that cause adequate whose effect can be clearly and distinctly perceived through it" (IIID1). An inadequate cause is one whose effect cannot be understood through it alone. Putting these definitions together, we can see that an affect is an action or active affect if the person who has it is its adequate cause, that is to say, if the affect can be understood (clearly and distinctly perceived) in terms of this person's own nature. If we can only understand an affect by explaining it in terms of external causes, that is, causes external to the agent herself, then the person who has the affect is not its adequate cause, and the affect is a passion, not an action. It is something that *happens to* the person, not something this individual *does* or something that manifests *her* nature. Active emotions are those that can be explained by, and hence manifest, the nature of the person who has them; passive emotions must be explained in terms of external causes.

As abstract and strange as these definitions may sound, they do seem to have some relationship to the way we normally talk about human beings and human behavior. If someone bumps me into the path of an oncoming train, this event is not something I do, not an action of mine; rather, it is something that happens to me. On the other hand, if I throw myself in front of the train, this is something I do – it is "by my own hand" that I take my life. Actions, then, as opposed to things that happen to us, do seem to result from our own nature, as opposed to the nature of other things. To Spinoza's way of thinking, these ordinary ways of talking embody many confusions, but they do show us how we can begin to think in his terms.

Spinoza's talk of passions is also not so very far from everyday speech. Emotions often overwhelm us. As a result of external events, they simply come upon us (through no decision of our own, as we might say), and we passively receive or undergo them. Insofar as we are passive with respect to these emotions, it is appropriate to think of them as passions. As noted above, one of the aims of the *Ethics* is to free us from the bondage of the passions. In our everyday understanding of passions, they certainly have the ability to put us in thrall. We can be so consumed by the passion of hatred or love, for example, that we lose control over ourselves.

If we try to relate what Spinoza tells us about active and passive emotions (actions and passions) to what he has said about affects that enhance or cripple the body's power of acting, we can see where his argument is going. Active emotions will enhance this power whereas passive ones will detract from it. Thus in seeking freedom, we shall be aiming at a life containing active emotions; and we shall strive to avoid a life of passions.

Adequate and Inadequate Ideas

In a highly original fashion, Spinoza proceeds to connect the above notions to the concept of an *adequate idea*. The first proposition deduced in part III is the following: "Our mind does certain things [acts] and undergoes other things, namely, insofar as it has adequate ideas, it necessarily does certain things, and insofar as it has inadequate ideas, it necessarily undergoes other things" (IIIP1). The mind, we must recall, has affects – namely the ideas that are the mental correlates of its bodily affects. If one of its ideas is adequate, proposition 1 tells us that the mind in this instance acts (has active emotions); if another of its ideas is confused or inadequate, this mental affect is therefore a passion. In this way actions and passions are linked up with adequate and inadequate ideas. And the connection carries through to the bodily dimension as well. If I have an adequate idea, not only does my mind act, my body also acts by virtue of the fact that the bodily affect is the correlate of the adequate idea. Clearly, if our goal is to be active rather than passive, both in mind and body, the secret is to attain adequate ideas.

What, we might ask, are adequate ideas? For our purposes, suffice it to say that they are to be construed as ideas that are clear and distinct and hence ideas that are true. They are also ideas that point toward an explanation of the bodily affects with which they are correlated. If I have an adequate idea, this idea can be deductively derived from other ideas that I have. By grasping these other ideas and the manner in which they entail the idea in question, I come to understand the bodily condition that is the bodily side of the idea, and this means that I understand how this bodily condition derives from other bodily conditions in accordance with the laws of Nature/God. By understanding how the idea is entailed by other ideas, I understand how the bodily condition of which it is the idea is causally derived from other material conditions reflected in the entailing ideas.

It follows from these considerations that my emotions are active if I understand them; and such emotions enhance my power to act, my energy or vitality. If I do not understand how the idea side of the affect follows deductively from other ideas I have, and hence how the bodily affect is caused by other objects in accordance with the laws of Nature, my affect is passive (a passion). As a result of this ignorance, my power of acting is inhibited. As Spinoza concludes in a corollary of proposition 1, "From this it follows that the mind is more liable to passions the more it has inadequate ideas, and conversely, is more active the more it has adequate ideas" (IIIP1C).

After defining actions and passions in terms of adequate and inadequate causes, and then adequate and inadequate ideas, Spinoza proceeds to point out that if a person has adequate ideas, these ideas are also adequate "in God." This means the idea and its logical consequences follow necessarily from God's essential nature. If a person has an inadequate idea, this idea does not follow from God's essential nature. We act, then, insofar as our affects follow necessarily from God's nature; otherwise, we are acted upon. And when we act, both God and ourselves can be said to be the adequate cause of the bodily correlate of this adequate idea. We act when we do what we perceive to follow necessarily from our own nature and from the very essence of God (or Nature).[6] Likewise, we act when our idea, being adequate, reflects the true nature of our own bodily condition; our bodily/mental action follows from, and can be explained solely in terms of, our own bodily/mental nature. We are passive victims when these things are not the case, when, that is, we do not understand the causes of our action. When we fail to comprehend the causes that lead us necessarily to act, we are the passive victims of these causes; when we understand these causes, we act and we are free.

The *Conatus*

One of the basic principles of Spinoza's theory of Nature (and human nature) is given by proposition 6 of Part III: "Each thing, as far as it can by its own power, strives to persevere in its own being" (IIIP6). There is in every natural being a *conatus*, a drive for self-preservation and self-maintenance, a striving to remain alive and to persevere in what it essentially is. Nature is dynamic in this sense, and to understand any thing in nature we must grasp its effort to realize and maintain its distinctive form of being. Indeed, Spinoza tells us, this *conatus*, or striving, constitutes a thing's actual essence (IIIP7).

As one commentator[7] puts it, the *conatus* provides us with the standard in terms of which we can judge whether an affect enhances an individual's power of acting or detracts from it. If an emotion aids a person in persevering in her distinctive being, then it increases this person's power to act; if an emotion intrudes upon, blocks, or inhibits the drive toward self-preservation, it reduces the power to act. Looking at matters from the other direction, if a person's ideas (mental affects) are true, and if therefore the person who has them is their adequate cause, then this person's drive to self-preservation has been enhanced.

Inasmuch as human beings can be seen as bodies and as minds, there is a mental *conatus* and a bodily one: "When this striving is related only to the mind, it is called will; but when it is related to the mind and body together, it is called appetite" (IIIP9S). Appetite, Spinoza concludes, is "the very essence of man, from whose nature there necessarily follow those things that promote his preservation" (ibid.). Appetite is the drive or *conatus* to achieve and maintain our distinctive being. When we are conscious of this appetite, we call it desire. In making appetite or desire so central to human nature, Spinoza is *in a sense* recognizing the centrality of the irrational (or nonrational) element in us. But insofar as we promote appetite and desire (the *conatus*) by having adequate ideas, the central importance of reason is also acknowledged.

It should be noted that Spinoza introduces an important qualification into proposition 6: "as far as it can by its own power" a person will strive to maintain her being. A human being is a finite mode, always subject to what is happening in the world around her. Often, and decisively so in the end, these surrounding forces are able to prevent us from persevering in our distinctive being. It is our nature to try to stay alive and be who we essentially are, but life is a constant battle to achieve these goals, and a battle we lose at the end.

The Source of Values

According to Spinoza, appetites and desires are the sources of our evaluations of things: "we neither strive for, nor will, neither want, nor desire anything because we judge it to be good; on the contrary, we judge something to be good because we strive for it, will it, want it, and desire it" (ibid.). Values, he is telling us, are not things in the universe independent of our desires and volitions; rather these values arise out of our strivings. Hence Spinoza's theory of value is a subjectivist one, similar to that of Hobbes. Our emotional reactions to things and events also are determined by the relation of these things to our strivings. We feel joy on those occasions when we see our *conatus* as being supported and furthered, and we feel sadness when, on the contrary, we think this *conatus* meets resistance or suffers a setback. Pleasure and pain can be explained in the same terms. "The *affect of joy which is related to the mind and body at once* I call *pleasure* or *cheerfulness*, and that of *sadness, pain* or *melancholy*" (IIIP11S). Spinoza also tells us that we feel joy when the mind passes to a higher perfection, and sadness when it passes to a lesser perfection. By passing to a higher perfection Spinoza means that a person is able to persevere in her distinctive being or increase her vital energy, thereby manifesting her being in action. A lesser perfection is a state wherein the *conatus* is frustrated and one's distinctive being is prevented from being manifested. When the body and mind rise to a higher perfection, we experience this as pleasure; when they fall to a lower level of activity, we experience pain.

The Primary Affects

Desire, joy, and sadness, Spinoza tells us, are the three primary affects, and all others can be explained as variations of these three. Love, for instance, is joy with an accompanying idea of an external cause, and hate is sadness together with the idea of an external cause. Desire is the conscious striving to maintain our being, and joy and sadness are the emotional reactions we have to the furtherance or diminishment of this drive. Thus we love what we perceive as enhancing our self-preservation and we hate what we perceive as threatening it. Such are the fundamental principles of Spinoza's psychology. Much of the remainder of Book III is a working out of the consequences of this theory and an application of it to the range of human emotions, feelings, and actions. One of these consequences, rather obvious in itself, is this: "We strive to further the occurrence of whatever we imagine will lead to joy, and to avert or destroy what we imagine is contrary to it, or will lead to sadness" (IIIP28), which is to say that we promote what we love and attempt to thwart what we hate, or, expressed another way, we promote what we think will lead to pleasure and avoid what will lead to pain.

Spinoza notes that love and hate, joy and sadness, and the various values that arise out of them, are relative. First of all, the effect an event will have on people varies: "Different men can be affected differently by one and the same object; and one and the same man can be affected differently at different times by one and the same object" (IIIP51). The effect an object will have on us is a function of whether or not it supports and furthers our drive to persevere in our distinctive being, and as the nature of different people varies, so will their reactions to the objects and events that affect these people. "Therefore, the desire of each individual differs from the desire of another as much as the nature, *or* essence, of the one differs from the essence of the other" (IIIP57D). And, insofar as our needs vary from time to time, our response to events will vary in time as well. It follows that our values often conflict:

> We see, then, that it can happen that what the one loves, the other hates, what the one fears, the other does not, and that one and the same man may now love what before he hated, and now dare what before he was too timid for.
>
> Next, because each one judges from his own affect what is good and what is bad, what is better and what worse ... it follows that men can vary as much in judgement as in affect   (IIIP51S).

Thus Spinoza is in a position to understand the great variation we find among people and cultures when it comes to moral values.

Spinoza can also explain the quarrelsomeness and competitiveness we so often encounter among human beings. We take joy in our power of acting – our power of furthering our *conatus* – and we are saddened by our lack of power (IIIP53 and 55). The joy we feel when we reflect upon ourselves and our power is, for Spinoza, self-love or self-esteem (IIIP55S).

> And since this is renewed as often as a man considers his virtues, *or* his power of acting, it also happens that everyone is anxious to tell his own deeds, and show off his powers, both of body and of mind and that men, for this reason, are troublesome to one another.
>
> From this it follows, again, that men are by nature envious ... *or* are glad of their equals' weakness and saddened by their equals' virtue.
>
> ... It is clear, therefore, that men are naturally inclined to hate and envy   (ibid.).

Here, perhaps, we find echoes of Thomas Hobbes, whose views were known to Spinoza and exerted an influence on him.

Affects and Inadequate Ideas

Spinoza next relates what he has had to say about the affects of joy and sadness to his doctrine of adequate and inadequate ideas. "When the mind conceives itself and its power of acting, it rejoices ... But the mind necessarily considers itself when it conceives a true, *or* adequate idea ... [Moreover] the mind conceives some adequate ideas ... Therefore, it also rejoices insofar as it conceives adequate ideas, that is ... , insofar as it acts" (IIIP58D). Clearly, then, joy or contentment, the satisfaction of our *conatus*, will be achieved to the degree that we entertain adequate ideas of ourselves. And to the extent that we have confused or inadequate ideas of ourselves, we shall be saddened. Thus is demonstrated once again the necessity of our obtaining a clear and accurate understanding of ourselves.

Spinoza gives us two concrete and central examples of how inadequate ideas can inhibit action, which is to say, how they can inhibit our persevering in our distinctive being. Take the case of self-esteem. This is "a joy born of the fact that we consider our own power of acting" (IIIP59, Def. XXV). On some occasions, we may experience this joy "accompanied by the idea of some deed which we believe we have done from a free decision of the mind" (IIIP59, Def. XXVIExpo). But there are, Spinoza has claimed (IIIDVI), no free decisions. Therefore this particular emotion of joy, this particular form of self-esteem, involves a false or confused idea. Rather than being an active expression of our nature, then, such self-esteem is just the opposite; it is a passion that inhibits our *conatus*. Likewise, repentance, being the effect of our viewing ourselves as having freely done something wrong, is also misplaced. To the extent that we feel such repentance, we operate with a confused idea of ourselves and fail to act in such a way as to express our true nature.

Let us sum up what we have learned in Part III of the *Ethics*. Spinoza gives us a set of terms – affects, active and passive emotions, adequate and inadequate causes, adequate and inadequate ideas, *conatus*, desire, joy, and sadness – and links them together. The result is a set of contrasting pictures: (1) a picture of a person who experiences passions or passive emotions, who is not the adequate cause of her emotions because she lacks adequate ideas of them, and who experiences sadness as a result of perceiving her drive to self-preservation being thwarted; (2) a picture of a person whose emotions are active and whose ideas are true and reflect the real nature of her body and its relation to Nature, a person who is herself the adequate cause of her emotions and thereby acts from her own true nature, and a person who feels joy because her drive to maintain her distinctive being is supported and enhanced. If we are seeking to identify the nature of freedom and true human happiness, clearly the second picture is the one we select. The first picture is a picture of slavery to the passions.

Human Bondage

Part IV of the *Ethics* is entitled "Of Human Bondage" and begins, appropriately, with a definition of "bondage": "Man's lack of power to moderate and restrain the affects I call bondage" (IVPr). Such bondage seems inevitable, since "the man who is subject to affects [passions] is under the control, not of himself, but of fortune" (ibid). As Spinoza demonstrates in proposition 2, "We are acted on, insofar as we are a part of Nature, which cannot be conceived through itself, without the others" (IVP2), the others being the other finite modes of Nature, which always impact on us, causing us to feel and do various things. These external causes have considerable power over us, and will lead, at some point, to our destruction: "The force by which a man perseveres in existing is limited, and infinitely surpassed by the power of external causes" (IVP3). The human condition is inevitable and inescapable; we are acted upon by external causes, and hence we cannot understand all of our behavior as following from our own nature alone. We do not have the self-sufficiency, the status of a substance, that we often mistakenly attribute to ourselves. The conclusion Spinoza draws from this is the inevitability of the passions: "Therefore, it is impossible that a man should undergo no other changes except those of which he himself is the adequate cause ... From this it follows that man is necessarily always subject to passions, that he follows and obeys the common order of Nature, and accommodates himself to it as much as the nature of things requires" (IVP4Dii and C).

The question we must raise, however, is whether we creatures of passion are necessarily in bondage to them. Do we have no power to moderate the passions? Are we always moved about, willy nilly, by them?

Before we can answer these questions, we must understand what Spinoza means by the knowledge of good and evil. He first notes that we call a thing good which is useful to our being, that is to say, which promotes our ability to act, to persevere in our being, to express our true nature. We call something evil if it has the opposite effects. Recalling that we feel sadness at whatever diminishes our ability to act, and joy at the opposite, he can then conclude that "The knowledge of good and evil is nothing but an affect of joy or sadness, insofar as we are conscious of it" (IVP8).

The knowledge of good and evil gives rise to desires – the desire to pursue what is useful to us and to avoid what threatens to diminish our ability to act. The desires that arise out of such knowledge can be opposed and overwhelmed by other, more violent desires. This is particularly true, Spinoza warns us, when the desires arising from a knowledge of good and evil pertain to the future and the desires conflicting with them are for the pleasures of the moment. Likewise, violent desires easily overwhelm us when our knowledge-based desires relate to things that *may* happen but then again *may not*, while the violent desire is for something already in existence. It is necessary for us to be aware of the ways in which we are inconstant and incontinent if we are to ascertain what knowledge and reason can do to moderate the passions.

Reason and Self-Interest

What does reason prescribe? What affects agree with the rules of reason? Spinoza's answer is this:

> Since reason demands nothing contrary to Nature, it demands that everyone love himself, seek his own advantage, what is really useful to him, want what will really lead a man to greater perfection, and absolutely, that everyone should strive to preserve his own being as far as he can. This, indeed, is as necessarily true as that the whole is greater than its part (IVP18S).

Many moral philosophers and moralists have claimed that morality requires us to eschew our self-interest; they have even equated self-interest with immorality. Spinoza rejects this line of thought. True morality promotes action that is to one's advantage and hence that is useful to the agent. Reason in effect demands that we be virtuous, since virtue "is nothing but acting from the laws of one's own nature" (ibid.). Such virtue should be desired for its own sake, since, as a result of the definitions built into the concept of virtue, "there is not anything preferable to it, or more useful to us, for the sake of which we ought to want it" (ibid.).

In advocating that we seek what is useful to us, that we strive to express our own distinctive nature, Spinoza may seem to adopt a theory of egoism. He does not, however, view it quite this way. First of all, he has claimed that reason commands that *everyone* seek his own advantage, which is quite different from the claim that everyone should seek *my* advantage. If this be egoism, it is *universal egoism*, not self-centered *individual egoism*. Moreover, Spinoza builds into the precepts of reason a demand for cooperation and complementarity among human beings:

> Man, I say, can wish for nothing more helpful to the preservation of his being than that all should so agree in all things that the minds and bodies of all would compose, as it were, one mind and one body; that all should strive together, as far as they can, to preserve their being; and that all, together, should seek for themselves the common advantage of all.
>
> From this it follows that men who are governed by reason – that is, men who, from the guidance of reason, seek their own advantage – want nothing for themselves which they do not desire for other men. Hence they are just, honest, and honorable (IVP18S).

Rational self-interest promotes the equal advantage of all persons and the coordinated actions designed to achieve this common advantage. All of us are, after all, interacting parts of a larger whole, God or Nature. The well-being of one depends intimately on the well-being of others. So it turns out that the person who rationally pursues her own interest is one who is just, honest, and honorable.

Virtue

Virtue, Spinoza has told us, is "nothing but acting from the laws of one's own nature." Thus virtue is equivalent to power, the power to seek one's own advantage and realize one's own being. It follows that "The more each one strives, and is able, to seek his own advantage, that is, to preserve his being, the more he is endowed with virtue; conversely, insofar as each one neglects his own advantage, that is, neglects to preserve his being, he lacks power" (IVP20). The drive to preserve one's own being, the drive to be virtuous, is itself a powerful one, although it can be defeated by external causes. Thus the foundation of virtue is the basic human *conatus*, the striving to preserve oneself. We fail as moral agents seeking our own advantage when we allow external causes to interfere with our drive to be ourselves and hence be virtuous. When this happens, we are controlled by other things, not by our own nature.

If one thinks through the matter, one can see why Spinoza claims that "A man cannot be said absolutely to act from virtue insofar as he is determined to do something because he has inadequate ideas, but only insofar as he is determined because he understands" (IVP23), that is, because he has adequate ideas. In having adequate ideas, a person *acts* rather than being impelled by passions and external causes. In acting, she seeks her advantage and exercises the power to preserve her being. Given the universal striving to preserve one's being, it follows that one strives as well to have adequate ideas, that is to say, to attain understanding. "What we strive for from reason is nothing but understanding; nor does the mind, insofar as it uses reason, judge anything else useful to itself except what leads to understanding" (IVP 26). In this way, the basic *conatus* is connected to the drive for understanding, and the striving to persevere in one's being becomes the striving to understand the world and our place in it.

The paradox that may seem to develop here is that the understanding we seek will in fact show that we are but parts of the whole and that our every action is the result of external causes acting on us. Would this not reveal that we never act from our nature alone but always from external causes as well? Would such an informed vision not demonstrate that the basic *conatus* is always frustrated? Would not understanding result in unrelieved sadness and acknowledgement of failure in our life goal? As we proceed, we shall attempt to see how this paradox is avoided.

The Knowledge of God

Spinoza's emphasis on understanding as our ultimate goal leads him to another of the central tenets of his moral theory: "Knowledge of God is the mind's greatest good;

its greatest virtue is to know God" (IVP28). God is a being "absolutely infinite, without which nothing can either be or be conceived" (IVP28D). God is, therefore, the greatest thing we can understand, and insofar as we strive for understanding, we fulfill this desire when we understand God. Likewise, the virtuous life being the life lived in accordance with reason, it follows that "the greatest good of those who seek virtue is to know God" (IVP36D). This greatest good is one that can be shared by all human beings; it is a good common to all. Thus if we live according to reason and strive to know God, the causes of envy and strife will be removed from the scene and human beings will no longer be "burdensome" to one another. Insofar as we desire that all human beings pursue their advantage, we shall desire that all human beings seek the knowledge of God. Our desire, and theirs, will therefore coincide. Thus Spinoza is led to the principle that "The greatest good of those who seek virtue is common to all, and can be enjoyed by all equally" (IVP36).

Religion, it turns out, coincides with morality. Religion advocates the knowledge of God; morality advocates a life according to reason. Given that a life lived according to reason seeks understanding, and the highest understanding is the knowledge of God, the aim of morality is the same as the aim of religion (IVP37S1).

Acting in Accord with One's Nature: The Life of Reason

The problem of life faced by most human beings is that their lives are controlled by their affects. This produces both internal and external conflict. A person driven by different affects will often desire incompatible things and thus will be torn asunder in the attempt to satisfy all of her conflicting desires. And the prevalence of opposing affects among different individuals leads to conflict and war, either in an effort to impose one's will on others or in an effort to obtain exclusive possession of scarce resources desired by all. Perhaps the most fundamental problem of a life dominated by the affects is that it is a life controlled by the external things we desire. Rather than being guided by our own nature, i.e., our reason, we allow the external world, its attractions and distractions, to manipulate us: "true virtue is nothing but living according to the guidance of reason, and so lack of power consists only in this, that a man allows himself to be guided by things outside him, and to be determined by them to do what the common constitution of external things demands, not what his own nature, considered in itself, demands" (IVP37S1).

One's own nature, considered in itself, is one's rationality – "a man acts entirely from the laws of his own nature when he lives according to the guidance of reason ... " (IVP35C1). Thus the choice we face is between behavior resulting from passions (which themselves have external causes) and behavior resulting from reason (which is an internal cause). Insofar as the rational person behaves according to reason, and reason is her own essential nature, she *acts*, that is, she is the *adequate cause* of her behavior. *And* her behavior is the manifestation of adequate ideas, from which it follows that her affects are active and her behavior results not from passions but from active emotions.

Moreover, as rational agents we must learn to distinguish among affects, seeing that some of them are good, i.e., are to our advantage, and others evil, i.e., are to our disadvantage. Joy, we will recall, "is an affect by which the body's power of acting is increased or aided," whereas sadness is just the opposite. Therefore joy is a good,[8] and sadness an evil. Noting this difference allows Spinoza to evaluate a number of emotions, all of which, we must remember, are functions of joy, sadness, and desire. Take, for example, hope and fear. "There are no affects of hope or fear without sadness. For fear is a sadness ... and there is no hope without fear" (IVP47D). Fear being an expectation of the diminishment of our being, it involves sadness; and hope involves fear because hope is a desire for a possible good in the context of an expectation that an evil will occur if the hope is not realized.

Spinoza appends an important addendum to his comments on hope and fear:

> We may add to this that these affects show a defect of knowledge and a lack of power in the mind. For this reason also confidence and despair, gladness and remorse are signs of a mind lacking in power. For though confidence and gladness are affects of joy, they still presuppose that a sadness has preceded them, namely hope and fear. Therefore, the more we strive to live according to the guidance of reason, the more we strive to depend less on hope, to free ourselves from fear, to conquer fortune as much as we can, and to direct our actions by the certain counsel of reason   (IVP47S).

Why will the counsel of reason free us from fear and hope? Spinoza is very direct in his answer:

> He who rightly knows that all things follow from the necessity of the divine nature, and happen according to the eternal laws and rules of Nature, will surely find nothing worthy of hate, mockery, or disdain, nor anyone whom he will pity. Instead he will strive, as far as human virtue allows, to act well, as they say, and rejoice   (IVP50S).

If whatever happens must happen, then surely hope is irrational, since hope is the desire that one thing (something good) happen when it is also possible that something else (something bad) will happen. Such multiple possibilities are ruled out by the necessity governing all things. Hate and disdain are equally irrational. Hate presupposes that the person who is the object of the hate intentionally did something wrong but could have avoided the wrongdoing. Disdain is directed at a person whose actions or character are thought to be morally deficient, the implication being that the person is to be held responsible for this deficiency because she could have chosen to act differently and to have a different character. Such choices are impossible in a universe ruled by necessity.

The life of reason, clearly, will be very different from the life recommended by many moralists, especially those of a Christian persuasion. It will be a life without hope, without fear, without moral censure, without excessive love, and without humility. Humility is dismissed by Spinoza as "a sadness which arises from the fact that a man considers his own lack of power," hardly a characteristic that lives up to the standard that one should always possess the power of virtue and hence act from the demands of one's own nature. If one does live up to this standard, the result will be a sense of self-esteem, a sense of realizing and being one's own person, of not being manipulated by external causes as they provoke now one affect and then another. Self-esteem, Spinoza tells us, "is a joy born of the fact that man considers himself and his power of acting" (IVP52D). When we achieve a realization of ourselves as rational beings and as having the power to act in accordance with reason, we rise to a form of self-esteem that is really the highest good (IVP52S).[9]

Viewing Things Under a Species of Eternity

To understand all things as flowing necessarily from the nature of God, or to understand them as the necessary consequences of the laws of Nature, is to view them under what Spinoza calls a "species of eternity." This contrasts with our ordinary everyday understanding of things, which views them as contingent (things that may or may not happen) and temporal (happening at a particular point in time and having temporal duration). With contingent, temporal events, we never know with certainty whether they will occur. This leads, of course, to fear that they will (or will not) occur and to hope that they will (or will not). We have already remarked on Spinoza's disparaging attitude toward hope and fear. If, on the contrary, we could understand events as the consequences of the eternal laws of nature, we would be able to know of their existence – past, present, or future – with equal certainty, since we would grasp that they *must* occur. Such knowledge would remove the foundations of fear and hope. Such knowledge would view all events under a species of eternity.

Such knowledge would also remove us from our normal, everyday predicament in which we place greater value on a present event, just because it is present, than on a future one. We do this because we have far more certain knowledge of the present than we do of the (contingent) future. This predicament leads us to value a present good over a future one in spite of the fact that the present good may be less than the future one; and it leads us to value a present good in spite of the fact that it may be the cause of a greater future ill. If, on the contrary, we were to view events as the necessary results of the laws of Nature, and hence under a species of eternity, then "the mind would want the good it conceived as future just as it wants the good it conceives as present" (IVP62S). It is through the use of reason that we grasp things under a species of eternity, and thus reason liberates us from the predicament of ordinary, everyday life. Specifically, "From the guidance of reason we want a greater future good in preference to a lesser present one, and a lesser present evil in preference to a greater future one" (IVP66). We are in a position then to strive for our advantage over the whole of our lives; we escape the uncertainties and temptations of contingency. No longer moved by the passions, which affect only part of the body, we are able to act for the benefit of the whole person.

The Slave and the Free Person

In this way, Spinoza is led to the formulation of a basic distinction – between a slave and a free person. He tells us that if we have understood him so far, then

> we shall easily see what the difference is between a man who is led only by an affect, *or* by opinion, and one who is led by reason. For the former, whether he will or not, does those things he is most ignorant of, whereas the latter complies with no one's wishes but his own, and does only those things he knows to be the most important in life, and therefore desires very greatly. Hence, I call the former a slave, but the latter, a free man   (IVP66S).

The free human being acts from knowledge or reason, not from opinions that result from common sense, imagination, and perceptual experience, and which often are no better than, or even incorporate, ignorance. The free person directs her own life on the basis of her own nature, i.e., her reason; she is self-directed, self-determined by her essential nature as a rational person. She is not the manipulated puppet of outside causes, ever swayed by her blind and often conflicting passions. Spinoza's *Ethics* holds before us the standard and goal of the rational, free human being.

Spinoza gives a few examples of the free person in action. For instance, "a free man will strive, as far as he can, to avoid the favors of the ignorant, so as not to be hated by them"(IVP70D). The ignorant will value the favor they have bestowed "according to their own temperament," which value may be quite different from that placed upon the favor by the free person who receives it. This will lead the ignorant benefactor to be saddened and to hate the beneficiary. Spinoza acknowledges that all of us depend on others, and so we should try to thank our benefactors in a way that they will appreciate. He also notes that the thankfulness to which a person is led by desire "is for the most part a business transaction *or* an entrapment, rather than thankfulness" (IVP71S), and he warns the free person against accepting such gifts: "he shows firmness of mind who does not allow any gifts to corrupt him, to his or to the general ruin" (ibid.).

A free person, according to Spinoza, "always acts honestly, not deceptively"

(IVP72); she keeps her promises and avoids all sorts of treachery. In an anticipation of the moral philosophy of Immanuel Kant, Spinoza justifies these maxims by showing what would happen if they are disregarded. "If a free man, insofar as he is free, did anything by deception, he would do it from the dictate of reason (for so far only do we call him free). And so it would be a virtue to act deceptively ... and hence ... everyone would be better advised to act deceptively to preserve his being. That is (as is known through itself), men would be better advised to agree only in words, and be contrary to one another in fact. But this is absurd ... " (IVP72D). A free person follows the dictates of reason. Reason requires that we will the good of all persons; if, therefore, it advised deception as a means of achieving our own advantage, it would advise deception on the part of all persons. But if everyone deceived everyone else, no one would believe anyone else, and the deceptions would not work and would not, therefore, be to the advantage of anyone.

The free person, Spinoza insists time and again, is the person of strong character. Such a person is able to control her affects, not allowing them to become excessive. The person of strong character resists temptations. Very importantly, "a man strong in character hates no one, is angry with no one, envies no one, is indignant with no one, scorns no one, and is not at all proud" (IVP73S). These traits of the free person follow from the understanding this person has as a result of listening to reason instead of opinion and superstition. Spinoza sums up this wisdom in the following passage:

> a man strong in character considers this most of all, that all things follow from the necessity of the divine nature, and hence, that whatever he thinks is troublesome and evil, and moreover, whatever seems immoral, dreadful, unjust, and dishonorable, arises from the fact that he conceives the things themselves in a way which is disordered, mutilated, and confused. For this reason, he strives most of all to conceive things as they are in themselves, and to remove the obstacles to true knowledge, like hate, anger, envy, mockery, pride, and the rest of the things we have noted in the preceding pages   (IVP73S).

Understanding that all things follow from the divine nature shows us that actions taken against us by others are not wilful, but part of the necessary scheme of things. Realizing this, our attitudes of indignation, blame, and hatred toward the other person are removed. How can a person reasonably be blamed for what he or she could not help doing? When what appears (from the perspective of our passions) to be a disaster strikes us, our recognition that it follows necessarily and inevitably from the divine nature removes our sadness. Free of sadness and the other passions it gives rise to, we are able, in the face of whatever befalls us, to remain calm – indeed, to rejoice. Grasping, as we do, that all things happen necessarily in accordance with the laws of God/Nature, we attain adequate ideas, which replace the inadequate ones according to which avoidable and blameful external causes bring harm to us.

The secret of life, then, is to attain adequate ideas, and this means to obtain the understanding of reason. Reason traces the causes of all things and shows them to be necessary by virtue of according with the laws of God/Nature.

> In life, therefore, it is especially useful to perfect, as far as we can, our intellect, *or* reason. In this one thing consists man's highest happiness, *or* blessedness. Indeed, blessedness is nothing but that satisfaction of mind which stems from the intuitive knowledge of God. But perfecting the intellect is nothing but understanding God, his attributes, and his actions, which follow from the necessity of his nature. So the ultimate end of the man who is led by reason, that is, his highest desire, by which he strives to moderate all the others, is that by which he is led to conceive adequately both himself and all things which can fall under his understanding   (IVAppendixIV).

The contemplative life recommend by Aristotle as the highest form of happiness is Spinoza's ideal as well.

Human Limits

Time and again Spinoza speaks of the need to follow one's own nature instead of allowing oneself to be influenced and shaped by external causes, i.e., allowing oneself to become a slave. He fully realizes, however, that a human being is but a finite mode, a part of the natural order, and hence, to a large degree, inextricably involved in a causal order in which external things do have an impact on her. We cannot avoid being moved about by the events of Nature. And so our ability to act from our own nature alone is limited.

> But human power is very limited and infinitely surpassed by the power of external causes. So we do not have an absolute power to adapt things outside us to our use. Nevertheless, we shall bear calmly those things which happen to us contrary to what the principle of our advantage demands, if we are conscious that we have done our duty, that the power we have could not have extended itself to the point where we could have avoided those things, and that we are a part of the whole of Nature, whose order we follow. If we understand this clearly and distinctly, that part of us which is defined by understanding, that is, the better part of us, will be entirely satisfied with this, and will strive to persevere in that satisfaction . . . Hence, insofar as we understand these things rightly, the striving of the better part of us agrees with the order of the whole of Nature   (IVAppendixXXXII).

Perhaps we can now understand how Spinoza avoids (or tries to avoid) the paradox we alluded to above. This apparent paradox consisted in the fact that while he admonishes us to act from our own nature and avoid manipulation by external causes, his theory of universal determinism entails that all of our behavior is ultimately caused by objects and events that are external to us. But in what sense are they external to us? The internal/external distinction seems to imply that each of us is an independent substance which unfortunately can on occasion be controlled by external causes rather than our own inner being. But there are no finite *substances* in Spinoza's universe. Each of us is but a finite *mode* of the one infinite substance God/Nature. Each of us is what we are because of the nature of this one substance. So in recognizing our place in the eternal and necessary scheme of things, we recognize our essence, our own distinctive being. Causes that we once considered external are only other parts of the one infinite substance, and their actions too are the inevitable results of the laws of God/Nature, i.e., of reason. But reason is also *our* essential nature, not something alien to us. Our essence and the essence of the universe in which we are embedded are one. In understanding these things we remove the cause of sadness; we remove the sense of being coerced or manipulated by external things. We achieve an assurance that our own role in God/Nature is being played out, and played out in accordance with rational laws in an equally rational universe. Hence we come to have a sense of ourselves as active rather than passive, as self-determined, determined by our own essential nature, rather that externally determined. We discover our freedom.

The Intellectual Love of God

It only remains for us to put these conclusions of Spinoza's theory into the language of Part V of the *Ethics*, the part entitled "Of the Power of the Intellect, *or* On Human Freedom." Here Spinoza equates true freedom with the *intellectual love of God*. He also attempts to demonstrate that the mind, in its essential nature, is eternal and does not perish with the body. This demonstration is one of the most obscure aspects of his thought, and we shall not venture into its complexities. But we do need to see clearly what is meant by the intellectual love of God and how, according to Spinoza, it is attainable.

In proposition 14 of Part V he tell us that: "The mind can bring it about that all the body's affections, or images of things, are related to the idea of God" (VP14). To the extent that we understand an affection, or condition, of the body, we understand it as being incorporated in an infinite series of causes. To the extent that we form clear and distinct ideas of this condition, we are able to see that its existence follows from the laws of Nature. These laws are eternal, and express the infinite and eternal essence of God. Thus by coming to understand our body's affections, we see that they are related to the idea of God. Proposition 15 continues the argument: "He who understands himself and his affects clearly and distinctly loves God, and does so the more, the more he understands himself and his affects" (VP15). Spinoza's demonstration of this proposition relies on definitions given earlier in the book. Understanding leads to joy, and when the affect of joy is combined with the idea of an external cause, the result is love. When we understand our affects as being necessitated by God's eternal nature, we see them as having God as their cause. Thus we have joy accompanied by the thought of God as its cause, which means that we love God.

Spinoza describes the love of God as "the highest good which we can want from the dictate of reason ... " (VP20D). He also tells us that it is a love that cannot be destroyed and hence is constant. The essential and eternal nature of God never changes, unlike the character, behavior, and very existence of our everyday loves, who are fickle, the victims of fate, perishable, etc.: "it should be noted that sickness of the mind and misfortunes take their origin especially from too much love toward a thing which is liable to many variations and which we can never fully possess." The love of God is a love "toward a thing immutable and eternal ... which we really fully possess ... and which therefore cannot be tainted by any of the vices which are in ordinary love ... " (VP20S). We fully possess God to the extent that we grasp the divine eternal essence, which is to say, to the extent that we understand the laws of the world which is God's body, and through these laws the things in the world: "The more we understand singular things, the more we understand God" (VP24).

The understanding that leads to the love of God must be of a special kind. The highest form of knowledge "proceeds from an adequate idea of certain attributes of God to an adequate knowledge of the essence of things ... and the more we understand things in this way, the more we understand God ... " (VP25D). For Spinoza, this means that from a grasp of the essential nature of extension (one of God's attributes) we must be able to deduce the properties of particular things in the extended world. This is the type of knowledge that Spinoza thinks is found in modern science. Such knowledge involves grasping the particular things "under a species of eternity."

> We conceive things as actual in two ways: either insofar as we conceive them to exist in relation to a certain time and place, or insofar as we conceive them to be contained in God and to follow from the necessity of the divine nature. But the things we conceive in this second way as true, *or* real, we conceive under a species of eternity, and their ideas involve the eternal and infinite essence of God ... (VP29S).

We grasp them under a species of eternity because we grasp them as instances of eternal laws; we see that they happen necessarily, as the inevitable product of these laws. Insofar as we come to understand our own mind and body, we see them too under a species of eternity, as part of the unfolding of God's essence.

From such knowledge and understanding "there necessarily arises an intellectual love of God. For from this kind of knowledge there arises ... joy, accompanied by the idea of God as its cause, that is ... love of God, not insofar as we imagine him as present ... but insofar as we understand God to be eternal. And this is what I call intellectual love of God" (VP32C). The intellectual love of God constitutes "our salvation, *or* blessedness [happiness], *or* freedom" (VP36S). And Spinoza concludes that the mind that grasps the eternal God is itself eternal.

Grappling with Spinoza

Thus we come to the end of one of the most remarkable books in the history of ethics. Spinoza is often referred to as a philosopher's philosopher whose adherence to a standard of rigor and proof is exemplary. Indeed, in reading through the *Ethics*, one cannot help but think one is in the presence of a mind of the highest order. In spite of this fact, his ethical theory as a whole has not been very influential, probably because most philosophers are unwilling to buy into the rationalistic, pantheistic metaphysical system in which the ethical theory is embedded. The spirit of Spinozism, however, as well as unsystematic items of ethical advice scattered throughout his masterpiece, have had an enormous impact on the lives of individual readers. The author of the present work once knew a man who gave up a highly successful career in advertising as a result of following Spinoza's advice to act always from one's own essential nature and not to let oneself be enslaved by the temptations and traps set by external causes. The goal of a life secure in its understanding of the world, free in its own undertakings, calm in its reactions to the impact of external events, and kind, honest, and loving in its relations to other human beings – this Spinozistic goal has a compelling appeal to many people who think of life in ethical terms.

But what are we to say philosophically about Spinoza's ethics? And how are we to go about it? One well-known commentary proceeds by taking issue with specific features of the Spinozistic system.[10] But one may doubt the value of such an approach – it seems one must take Spinoza "whole" or not at all. For example, one might sympathize with his doctrine of self-interest or with his theory of value that relates values to our emotional reactions to things. But to be fair to Spinoza, one must interpret these aspects of human nature as they become transformed by the achievement of freedom and through the intellectual love of God. Seen from that higher point of view, these aspects of human nature are *transcended*. In other words, Spinoza's is not *just* a philosophy of self-interest. Piecemeal appropriation or criticism seems of little value.

One thing we can say is that Spinoza provides us with an ethical *vision*. It is *a* vision, not necessarily the only one, of how things might look to us in a thoroughly deterministic universe. His theory gives us an ethical perspective that might result from the conviction that all things happen necessarily and as a part of the all-encompassing whole of nature. How should one behave if one happens to believe in a unitary, determined world? What Spinoza shows us is that this view of the world, instead of being one that is thoroughly daunting and overwhelming, can actually, in a Spinozistic fashion, liberate us. It can lead us to see the shallowness and meaninglessness of many of our emotional reactions to things. It can lead us beyond blame and praise, for anything that happens necessarily is inappropriately blamed or praised. If we are moved by Spinoza's vision and come to share it, then, instead of hating the world and the things in it, we can accept them without demurral. Instead of being alienated from the world in which we reside, we can find ourselves at home in it, and we can know the identity between its laws and our own. In a word, Spinoza's vision can bring us *peace.*

But there is a paradox at the heart of this assimilation. It is the same paradox that haunts the thought of the Stoics of old. We are being urged to adopt an outlook on life in light of a comprehensive view of the nature of things. But advice of this sort presupposes that we have the freedom to accept or reject it. And this is just what the vision denies. How, if all things are strictly determined and necessitated, can we take our own lives in hand and direct them in the recommended way? Our essence may be reason, as Spinoza thinks, and reason may dictate a certain way of life. But do we have a choice of being rational or nonrational? Isn't that something that is also determined, and something over which we have no control? If Spinoza is right, then the very notion of deciding to take his advice seems empty.

But is Spinoza really offering advice? He can be, and probably should be, read differently. He can be understood as describing the universe, the human mind, and human action from the standpoint of a deterministic pantheism. In such a universe, *if* we are rational, then we escape the bondage of the passions. *If* we are not, we remain their slave. Reading Spinoza, we may rise, through a process of grasping his thought, to a different level of understanding of ourselves, and thereby achieve a level of freedom hitherto beyond our (less than rational) reach. Seen in this light, the ideas we come to have on reading him are more adequate than our previous thoughts, and being more adequate, they entail more active emotions. As Spinoza sees it, the truth – *as Spinoza sees it* – sets us free. It *entails* our freedom.

8

Butler

Joseph Butler (1692–1752 CE), Anglican Bishop of Bristol and Durham and frequently referred to even today as Bishop Butler, has been described as, "with the exception of Hume, the acutest moral philosopher of the [eighteenth] century."[1] This description serves nicely to indicate the stature of the two philosophers discussed in this and the following chapter. Hume, of course, is one of the greatest philosophers of all time, esteemed not only in ethics but in epistemology, metaphysics, and philosophy of religion as well. Butler himself made notable contributions to the philosophy of religion, but it is in the field of ethics that we hear so much about him today. His ideas are central to many current ethical debates, and he has many defenders as well as detractors.

Butler is known primarily for his attack on psychological egoism and for his defense of a faculty of conscience. Rightly or wrongly interpreting Hobbes to be an egoist, Butler strives to show that it is a confusion of language to say that all human beings are selfish and act only to promote their own well-being. Butler's demonstrations of linguistic confusion are much admired by many recent and contemporary followers of the philosopher Wittgenstein, who is widely known for his claim that the kind of philosophy that tries to prove the falsity of our everyday understanding of things is confused on a linguistic or conceptual level. Butler stoutly defends our everyday view that, although there are many notable exceptions, human beings are both capable of benevolence toward their fellow human beings and actually engage in such benevolent actions. Self-love, although undeniably a motive of many human actions, is actually in Butler's view less likely to exert itself than we ordinarily think; indeed, in his considered opinion, we would actually be better off with more self-love than with less.

Butler is one of the foremost advocates of the faculty or principle of conscience. We have within us, he claims, a reflective power or faculty that judges the moral propriety of actions, motives, and persons, approving of some and disapproving of others. This reflective power possesses what he calls *authority*: its judgments take natural priority over the promptings of particular motives like appetites and passions, as well as over the judgments of self-love and even the feelings of benevolence. Being a devout Christian, Butler believes that God has so structured the human personality as to place conscience within it and give it authority over the other motives. His arguments for conscience, however, do not (always) appeal to theological suppositions, and hence they can be debated, and perhaps accepted, even by those who do not share his religious persuasion. To Butler's mind, it is part of our common experience of ourselves that we have a conscience within us and that this faculty is our foremost guide in moral matters.

Moral Psychology

Butler lived and wrote during the time when moral philosophy was largely conducted from the standpoint of moral psychology. Most moral philosophers of the eighteenth century – including both Butler and Hume – sought to describe the workings of the mind as it engages itself with moral issues.[2] We have already observed Spinoza's interest in the various motives of action, and although his rationalistic approach is very different from the empirical method of most English philosophers, it too reflects the interest in human motivation that prevailed during the century. In the set of *Sermons*[3] in which he set out his moral philosophy, Butler begins in *Sermon I* by mapping out the general structure of the mind in its moral capacity:[4]

> First, There is a natural principle of *benevolence* in man; which is in some degree to *society*, what *self-love* is to the *individual* ...
>
> Secondly ... men have various appetites, passions, and particular affections, quite distinct both from self-love and from benevolence ...
>
> Thirdly, There is a principle of reflection in men, by which they distinguish between, approve and disapprove their own actions. ... This principle in man, by which he approves or disapproves his heart, temper, and actions, is conscience ... (S1/6-8).

Butler views the mind of moral agents as having considerable complexity, and much of his moral philosophy consists of his insistence on acknowledging this complexity and his rebuttal of moral theories that paint a simpler picture (like, for instance, Hobbes's).

Particular Passions

First of all (to change slightly Butler's order of presentation), the mind contains "particular affections," i.e., appetites and passions. These are described as particular because each one has a particular *object*. The object is *what* one has an affection, appetite or passion for. For example, I have an appetite for food, perhaps even a particular item or kind of food; likewise, I experience the passion of love or jealousy toward a particular person; and I want or desire a particular job or salary. We have, that is, many feelings, wants and desires, hopes and ambitions, drives and needs, and the like, all of which have things they aim at or are directed toward (objects) which are definite and concrete (although to varying degrees). When the object of one of the wants or passions is obtained or secured, we shall say that the want or passion has been *satisfied*. Let us call all the motives that have particular objects the set of particular passions or affections.

Butler also describes the particular passions and affections as having *external objects*, as opposed to the *internal* object that he will attribute to self-love – one's own inner state of happiness. Most commentators are agreed, however, that the use of the inner/outer distinction is unfortunate – and, fortunately, unnecessary for Butler's intentions. One could have a particular desire for a very specific state of feeling (a particular sensation, say), and happiness may include certain objective facts (e.g., the health of one's children). In what follows, we shall ignore what Butler has to say about matters internal and external.

Self-love and Benevolence

The particularity of the passions and affections is highlighted when we turn to the second category of mental attributes in Butler's classification scheme. We have, he maintains, a principle of benevolence and a principle of self-love within us.[5] In distinguishing them from the particular affections, he stresses the *generality* of these motives. The principle of self-love is directed toward the overall or long-range well-being of the individual person; the principle of benevolence likewise has as its object the overall or long-range good of other people – in addition to the well-being of other people in general. It is one thing, Butler insists, to want a particular benefit for oneself – a job or salary or promotion or experience. It is another to look to one's well-being in general, to work toward gaining as much benefit overall as possible for oneself. It is the latter, he thinks, that is appropriately called the object of self-love. Self-love is also a *reflective* principle, requiring rational thought and calculation. In this respect it differs once again from particular affections or passions, which may be instinctive and impulsive. Actions, then, that aim at one's overall good and are preceded by reflection on this overall good are actions motivated by self-love. (Butler also refers to them as *interested* actions.) Actions aimed at particular objects, even if these are seen as something good for one, are not actions of self-love but rather actions motivated by particular affections.

Likewise, with regard to benevolence, a person may want a particular loved one or neighbor to meet with success on a particular occasion, but this is distinct from wanting such a person to thrive overall, and it is different from wanting other people in general to meet with success. The motives having a general object are instances of benevolence. (They are also actions that might be called *disinterested*.) When one seeks to promote this general object, the good of others, once again one usually engages in reflection and calculation. Thus, as Butler put it, benevolence is to society what self-love is to the individual. Both are reflective principles and both operate on a higher level of generality than the particular affections and passions.

Unfortunately, Butler is not consistent in his descriptions of benevolence. At times, he appears to equate benevolence with any feeling or action of good will toward another person. Thus he writes, "And if there be in mankind any disposition to friendship; if there be any such thing as compassion, for compassion is momentary love; if there be any such thing as the paternal or filial affections; if there be any affection in human nature, the object and end of which is the good of another; this is itself benevolence, or the love of another" (S1/6). The affections he identifies here are quite particular in nature: I am friendly toward a particular person; I have compassion or momentary love toward a particular person; and my paternal and filial feelings are directed toward specific individuals. If benevolence is a general principle, these affections should not be thought of as benevolence. But if they are instances of benevolence, then Butler uses this term in an ambiguous fashion. It appears that *benevolence* is the name he gives to all affections that prompt us to act in ways beneficial to other people.[6] In insisting on the reality of benevolence, Butler is interested in showing that human beings do, at least on occasion, have the good of another as their object or goal. Certainly it is difficult to deny the reality of friendship, of love of one's parents and siblings, of momentary compassion for the poor or sick. For this reason, Butler thinks, it is difficult to deny the reality of benevolence.

The generality of self-love is more important for Butler than the generality of benevolence. He will often admonish us that we frequently do not take enough interest in our overall good, being swept away by momentary passions (for particular things or people) which actually bring harm to us. In being reflective, the motive of self-love utilizes reason in calculating whether the gain from a particular passion will or will not be outweighed by the losses or pains incurred as a result of this passion. Self-love is best exercised in a "cool hour" when we are not swayed by particular affections and can engage in the reflection and calculation best suited to promoting our overall good. Moreover, self-love can be described as a second-order desire: it is a desire that (some of) our particular passions and appetites be satisfied and that we reap overall enjoyment from such satisfactions. Self-love is the second-order desire for the satisfactions of our first-order appetites and affections to outweigh in the long run the disappointments and pains that result from their frustration.

Conscience

The principle of conscience is the most controversial item in Butler's classification of our mental furniture. Many philosophically-minded persons who are willing to admit particular passions, the principle of self-love, and even the principle of benevolence may want to draw the line with regard to conscience. Butler, however, thinks "it cannot possibly be denied, that there is this principle of reflection or conscience in human nature"(S1/8), and he argues his case by giving us examples of conscience at work. Consider a person befriending another individual who is in distress, and also imagine this same person, in a fit of anger, doing mischief to another individual who had given her no cause for offense. Is there no difference between the two cases? Would the person involved view her two actions as morally equivalent? Clearly not, Butler claims: "to assert that any common man would be affected in the same way toward these different actions, that he would make no distinction between them, but approve or disapprove them equally, is too glaring a falsity to need being confuted" (S1/8). In making such moral distinctions (and we surely make them), the faculty of conscience is at work. We can no more deny the reality of conscience than we can deny the capacity of human beings to make moral distinctions. Conscience *is* moral judgment.[7] While in everyday life we usually restrict the role of conscience to one of informing us of the morality of our own actions, Butler extends this role to encompass judgments on the morality of others as well.

The above three-level classification scheme – containing four categories: particular affections (on the first level), the principle of benevolence and the principle of self-love (on the second level), and conscience (on the third level) – gives us Butler's general view of human nature.[8] He thinks this view is substantiated, not by any philosophical, *a priori* appeal to reason, but by common experience – our experience through sense perception of other people and one's experience of one's own self through introspection. In claiming this, he is solidly within the British empirical tradition. But he is well aware that views such as his are widely disputed, indeed often held up to ridicule, and much of his effort goes into establishing that the distinctions he has drawn are real. Is there truly a principle of benevolence in human beings? Is the principle of self-love distinct from, and higher in authority than, the particular passions and affections? Is there really a faculty of conscience in all human beings, who, after all, so often disagree with one another?

The Reality of Benevolence

Consider first the case of benevolence. Can't the appearance of good will toward others be explained away? Examples leap to mind: the boy scout who helps the elderly lady cross the street may only be trying to impress his scout master and gain points for a merit badge; the hero who risks all to save others may be thinking only of his certain fame or his reward in heaven; the philanthropist who gives to charity may only be generating a tax deduction. What looks like an effort to help others often turns out to have a different motive – a particular passion aimed at some specific good for oneself or the general principle of self-love. May it not be the case that this is always so and that benevolence is merely a sham? Butler himself considers the specific possibility that acts appearing to be benevolent are in reality motivated by nothing more than a covert love of power over others, or by the delight in the feeling of superiority that comes from helping others. In helping others, Butler's cynical foil (Hobbes?) claims, we are really just enjoying our ability to control their fates. We don't really care about them; we only care for ourselves and what we gain from the apparent acts of benevolence.

Butler thinks such arguments are specious and that they are contradicted by plain facts of experience. For example, "Is there not often the appearance of one man's wishing that good to another, which he knows himself unable to procure him; and rejoicing in it, though bestowed by a third person?" (S1/6n). If, for instance, we hear of miners lost in a mining accident, we may wish them well, knowing full well we can do nothing to assist them; and we may rejoice when we learn that rescue teams have saved them. In what sense can such an experience be understood as a delight in the exercise of our own power over others or as delight in our own sense of superiority? Another consideration Butler advances in favor of benevolence is this: if thoughts and acts of good will toward others are nothing in reality but delight in the exercise of our own power, it would not matter how this power is manifested – good will, for all it then matters, might be expressed in acts of cruelty! "Thus cruelty ... would be exactly the same in the mind of man as good-will; that one tends to the happiness, the other to the misery of our fellow creatures, is, it seems, merely an accidental circumstance, which the mind has not the least regard to" (S1/6n). Butler's argument here is a subtle one: equate benevolence with the desire to exercise power; power often is exercised through cruel acts; therefore benevolence is the same thing as cruelty. Such a conclusion, he maintains, amounts to an "absurdity" – thus his argument is what logicians call a *reductio ad absurdum*. If you can show that a theory or claim generates an absurdity – an obvious falsehood – then you have refuted it. It is an absurdity to claim that good will toward others is expressed in acts of cruelty, therefore the theory that generates this conclusion – viz., the theory that benevolence is really nothing more than a desire to exercise power over others – is false. Anyone claiming the principle of benevolence to be "only the love of power, and delight in the exercise of it" (ibid.), is guilty of confusing one thing with another. "Would not every body think here was a mistake of one word for another?" (ibid.), a mistake of not realizing, as Butler is famous for putting it, that everything is what it is and not another thing? Only a person in the grip of a general theory or "hypothesis" of human nature which he is willing to hold to at all costs could be led by it to overlook the obvious differences in human behavior marked by our verbal distinction between benevolence and cruelty, benevolence and delight in one's own superiority, benevolence and the exercise of self-love.[9]

The Distinction Between Self-Love and Particular Passions

Let us turn next to the distinction Butler draws between self-love and the several particular passions. This too, he acknowledges, can be disputed. The egoist who claims that all human beings act always with an end to achieving their own good – let us call this theorist a *psychological egoist*[10] – in effect claims that there is only one motive at work in human beings, namely, self-love. The psychological egoist sees all particular motives as simply so many different and specific ways of seeking one's own advantage, pleasure, or good.[11] If I desire food, in reality, the egoist thinks, I am desiring the good (or pleasure) I will obtain from eating it. If I seek fame, it is really the good or pleasure to be obtained from fame that I seek. Thus for the psychological egoist there is no distinction between the particular passions and affections, on the one hand, and the principle of self-love, on the other.

Once again Butler gives us some commonplace examples to refute the general theory proposed by the egoist:

> One man rushes upon certain ruin for the gratification of a present desire: nobody will call the principle of this action self-love. Suppose another man to go through some laborious work upon promise of a great reward, without any distinct knowledge what the reward will be: this course of action cannot be ascribed to any particular passion. The former of these actions is plainly to be imputed to some particular passion or affection, the latter as plainly to the general affection or principle of self-love (S1/7n).

The first example shows us a person acting upon a particular passion – lashing out, say, in a fit of anger or jealousy toward someone known for his power and ruthlessness. There are cases in which we do things from anger, jealousy, and similar passions that we know full well will bring suffering or ruin upon us – and yet we do them. How can such actions be seen as motivated by self-love? How can actions known to be harmful be seen as promoting our long-range good? Such actions, according to Butler, are the very antithesis of what we mean by actions motivated by self-love.

The second example should be familiar to most students. Working at great sacrifice to oneself for a future academic degree is often what being a student is all about. The degree in itself is not what one seeks, but rather the (indefinite and intangible) rewards that the degree will bring – let us call them "success in life." Success in life, however, is not a specific object; hence it is not the object of a specific passion or affection. It is, rather, the object of the general principle of self-love: one's long-range, overall good. Here, then, we have a case of motivation that is distinct from the operation of the particular passions: motivation by the principle of self-love.

Butler thinks that theorists are prone to miss the distinction between self-love and the particular passions because of some obvious facts about the relationship between the two. In satisfying many of our particular passions, we obtain the *ingredients* of our long-range happiness, namely the enjoyment derived from the satisfaction of these passions. Happiness is the sum of these satisfactions, or the overall balance of satisfactions over frustrations. Hence acting on many of the particular passions and fulfilling them promotes the end of self-interest or self-love. But to see this connection between the two is not to *equate* them. After all, some of the consequences of satisfying particular desires are *not* the ingredients of happiness but rather of misery.

The fact that in satisfying some of our particular desires we obtain the ingredients of happiness (the object of self-love) gives Butler another, very subtle reason for maintaining the distinction between the particular passions and self-love. The reason is this: we *could not* obtain the ingredients of personal well-being, namely pleasures or satisfactions and enjoyments, unless we *really* desired particular objects and obtained *them*, thereby generating the pleasure or the satisfactions and the enjoyment. We get pleasure from an object, he argues, only if we first want the object and then obtain it.

> That all particular appetites and passions are toward *external things themselves*, distinct from the *pleasure arising from them*, is manifested from hence; that there could not be this pleasure, were it not for that prior suitableness between the object and the passion: there could be no enjoyment or delight from one thing more than another, from eating food more than from swallowing a stone, if there were not an affection or appetite to one thing more than another   (S11/6).

More generally,

> ... particular affections tend toward particular external things: these are their objects; having these is their end: in this consists their gratification ...   (S11/8).

By the "prior suitableness between the object and the passion" Butler is referring to the fact that a desire or appetite has an object – one of our desires, for instance, is a desire for *food*. The object of the desire makes it (identifies it as) the particular desire it is and distinguishes it from other desires. Moreover, the satisfaction of a particular desire involves obtaining *its object*. Thus I satisfy my desire for food when I eat *food*, not when, God forbid, I eat a stone. The satisfaction of a desire usually involves pleasure, and thus Butler can claim that pleasure (or enjoyment), the ingredient of happiness, is attained only when *particular desires* are satisfied. The object of self-love, our happiness, requires that there be a separate class of motives and that these separate motives be satisfied. Thus self-love is not the same as the particular passions; rather, it presupposes that they exist as distinct motives.

One might object to this argument in the following way.[12] It may in general be true that only if I want a steak does the fact that I have one for dinner bring about satisfaction. But there could be exceptions to this rule: for example, I might eat a steak without having wanted one and then discover, to my surprise, that it was enjoyable. Thus the pleasure I obtain from eating a steak does not require that I previously wanted one. Butler might reply, however, that even in this case there is, in the background, a desire for some particular kind of experience – say a desire for a hearty meal. I simply was not aware in advance that eating the steak would bring about this experience or satisfy this desire, but the pleasure results only from the fact that this specific desire is satisfied. Or he might posit the prior existence of certain tastes or preferences which are unexpectedly satisfied by the occurrence of an event.

The Confusions of Egoism

Butler has several other arguments against the psychological egoist which we need to consider. These arguments are attempts to diagnose confusions he thinks lead to the egoist's position:

> Every particular affection, even the love of our neighbor, is as really our own affection, as self-love; and the pleasure arising from its gratification is as much my own pleasure, as the pleasure self-love would have, from knowing I myself should be happy some time hence, would be my own pleasure. And if, because every particular affection is a man's own, and the pleasure arising from its gratification his own pleasure, or pleasure to himself, such particular affection must be called self-love; according to this way of speaking, no creature whatever can possibly act but merely from self-love; and every action and every affection whatever is to be resolved up into this one principle. But then this is not the language of mankind ...   (S11/7).

Butler's argument here – against what in the last chapter we called tautological egoism – is very powerful, although not, perhaps, perfectly obvious at first. It must be granted, he points out, that all of a person's desires and wants, affections and passions, are her *own* desires, wants, etc. It is logically impossible for a person to act on a desire not her own: my desire for you to do *x* can't motivate you unless you desire to do what I want done – in which case you still act on your own desire. If the fact that a person always acts from her own desire or motive entails (is a justification for) egoism, then the theory of egoism amounts to no more than the logical truism that a person always acts on her own motives. But then it would be *impossible* for a person not to act out of self-love ("no creature whatever can possibly act but merely from self-love"), since to do so would require her, as is impossible, to act on a motive not her own. But surely egoism is not seen, even by its defenders, as a logical truth – after all, all sorts of empirical evidence and examples are amassed in order to try to prove that it is true, and we would all agree that it is a highly debatable thesis. Logical truths, however, are not debatable, because their denial is inconceivable. If egoism were a logical truth, any efforts to prove it on factual grounds would be irrelevant and the debate concerning its truth wrong-headed, since it is simply *inconceivable* that one person could act on another's motive. It is confused, therefore, to think that the fact that every person acts on her own desires proves that everyone acts from self-love.

In the passage just quoted Butler develops the same line of argument with respect to the fact that the pleasure a person receives from fulfilling some desire is her own pleasure. An egoist may claim that everyone acts from self-love because the satisfaction of any desire brings pleasure to the person who has the desire. Once again a logical truth is adduced in favor of egoism. It is inconceivable that the pleasure I receive from fulfilling some desire of mine is *your* pleasure or that of anyone else. To be sure, you or someone else may receive a pleasure that is qualitatively the same as mine, but having a pleasure that is qualitatively the same as mine is not equivalent to its being *my* pleasure, the pleasure that I feel. Only I can have the pleasure I feel. But if this "fact" – this logical truth – is the ground of egoism, the theory again becomes a logical proposition, not a debatable empirical claim for which evidence can be adduced. It would be *impossible* for a person not to act out of self-love.

If egoism is the claim that every person acts from her own motives, or the claim that the pleasure a person receives from satisfying one of her desires is her own pleasure, then, as we have seen, the statement that all human beings act from self-love means no more than that each person acts from her own motives, etc. But this, Butler affirms, "is not the language of mankind." Such a logical truism is *not* what we mean when we speak of self-love. Well, what *do* we mean? Frequently, we think of a person who always acts from self-love as a *selfish* person. According to Butler, "we often use the word *selfish* so as to exclude in the same manner all regards to the good of others" (S11/11).[13] A selfish person has no interest in the good of others, whereas a person who acts to promote the good of others we normally say is unselfish. But even Mother Teresa – a paradigm case of an unselfish person – acts in such a way that her desire to help others is her own desire, and the pleasure she gets from doing so is her own pleasure. Thus, if we were to accept the egoist's equation of self-love and acting from one's own desires, Mother Teresa would turn out to be selfish! Surely this is a perversion of the way we normally talk about "selfishness." Our normal concept of selfishness is therefore different from the egoist's – the egoist's way of talking is "not the language of mankind."

One of the examples we considered earlier also shows how the egoist distorts our normal way of speaking. Butler's conception of self-love is that of a person acting so as to promote, or attempt to promote, her overall, long-range well-being. If the egoist who claims that we always act so as to promote our self-love means simply by this that an agent always acts on her own desires, then the 90-pound weakling who in anger hits a belligerent 6'6", 220-pound wrestler would be acting from self-love, since she acts from her own desire. But, given our ordinary way of speaking, such a person is manifestly *not* acting in such a way as to promote her overall well-being; she is doing just the opposite, and probably knows she is. Thus she is not acting from self-love in the sense in which we ordinarily do so. The egoist has drastically changed the meaning of the key term in the debate.

But why not change what we mean by "selfish" and "self-love"? Why not say that the selfish person is simply the one who acts from her own motive? Why not equate self-love with the fact that the pleasure derived from fulfilling a desire is the pleasure of the person who has the desire? Aren't the meanings of our words arbitrary? Surely we cannot disallow the egoist her own meanings, different as they may be from our own.

Butler has an answer to this response. If we give the egoist her new meanings, "we should want words to express the difference, between the principle of an action, proceeding from cool consideration that it will be to my own advantage; and an action, suppose of revenge, or of friendship, by which a man runs upon certain ruin, to do evil or good to another" (S11/7). Give the egoist the equation of acting from self-love and acting from one's own desire. Say that yes, in this sense, all human beings act from self-love. We would still need to introduce a distinction, and terms to mark the distinction, between acting from one's own desire in such a way as to promote one's future advantage, and acting from one's own desire in such a way as to risk certain ruin and misery. In other words, we would have to reintroduce the very same distinction we ordinarily draw between the person who acts from self-love and the person who does not. So nothing is gained from the egoist's redefinition of "self-love."

Indeed, if we accept the egoist's new definition of "selfishness," there is no reason to object when she tells us that all human beings are selfish. She just means that all people act from their own desires, and we are perfectly willing to accept that claim – indeed, as we have seen, it is inconceivable that it not be the case. But egoism has now lost its sting. What looked like a highly controversial claim that goes against the common experience of humankind turns out to be a silly truism. If this be selfishness, and egoism, we need not worry about it or disapprove of it. In other words, by changing the meaning of the terms involved in the debate over egoism, the egoist has robbed her thesis of all shock value, and of all interest.

The Reality of Conscience

In Sermon 2, Butler turns his attention to the faculty of conscience and develops his claim that it has natural authority over the other motives at work in human beings. He wants to establish that a person who follows her conscience is one who acts in accord with her nature. In order to demonstrate this, he makes a threefold distinction concerning what we might mean by "nature" and by an act being in accord with or at odds with it. In the first place, nature might be understood to encompass all the motives or principles that human beings act on. One of these motives might be contrary to another, and so in acting on one of them "the same action [might] both follow and contradict [a person's] nature in this sense of the word" (S2/5). To follow nature in the first sense means only that one acts on some human motive. In the second place, human nature might be defined as the strongest motive or principle, the strongest motive being the one that will (usually) prevail over other motives. Thus a person convinced that human beings, though perhaps capable of benevolence, nevertheless always or most often give in to selfishness, would say that human beings are selfish by nature. In this second sense, when a person acts from the strongest motive available, she acts in accord with nature. In the third place, we might mean by nature the principle or principles that *ought* to prevail, whether or not they do and whether or not they have superior strength on any given occasion. If one believes in creation by a divine being, as Butler surely did, one would say that nature is how the creator intended us to act. Human nature, seen in this fashion, is a hierarchy of principles, some having authority over others.

Clearly it is in the third sense that Butler thinks we act in accordance with our nature when we follow conscience. We are then submitting to the faculty within us that ought to prevail. Thus he speaks of "This *prerogative*, this *natural supremacy*, of the faculty which surveys, approves or disapproves the several affections of our mind and actions of our lives, being that by which men *are a law to themselves*, their conformity or obedience to which law of our nature renders their actions, in the highest and most proper sense, natural or unnatural . . ." (S2/9). He also speaks of conscience "magisterially" exerting itself (S2/8) in passing moral judgments and acting on them. Thus conscience is "a faculty in kind and in nature supreme over all others, and which bears its own authority of being so" (S2/8).

The last qualification is important. It shows that Butler does not rely on his theological convictions to justify his belief in conscience. Conscience bears it own authority "on its sleeve," as it were. In being aware of this principle within us, we are immediately struck by its natural supremacy or authority, even when we do not follow it. Conscience speaks to us, we might say, with authority. Its judgments are experienced by us as overriding, as outweighing all other considerations. As C.D. Broad describes the matter: "By saying that conscience has supreme authority Butler means that we regard the pronouncements of conscience, not simply as interesting or uninteresting statements of fact, and not simply as reasons to be balanced against others, but as *conclusive* reasons for or against doing the actions about which it pronounces."[14] As more recent philosophers would put it, conscience is experienced as providing *overriding* reasons for actions, reasons that trump all others. Moreover, it is the recognition of the authority of conscience that leads us to regret and remorse when we do not do as it tells us. Such, Butler thinks, is the common experience of human beings.

When we do not follow conscience, following instead the temptations of some passion or the promptings of self-love, we act in a way that is contrary to our nature. This is true even though the passion, or the principle of self-love, may be stronger than conscience on the occasion of action. "Man may act according to that principle or inclination which, for the present happens to be strongest, and yet act in a way disproportionate to, and violate his real proper nature" (S2/10). The disproportion arises not from the act itself or from its consequences, but from its relationship to the natural hierarchy of principles that constitutes human nature.

A Natural Hierarchy

Butler seeks to justify his theory of a natural hierarchy by considering the relationship between the particular passions and the principle of self-love. "It is manifest," he tells us, "that self-love is in human nature a superior principle to passion" (S2/11). We mark a difference, he notes, between giving in to a present passion when we know full well that in doing so we face immediate ruin or extreme misery, on the one hand, and resisting the passion for the very reason that it will have such disastrous consequences, on the other. We might say that the former action is irrational and the latter rational, or that the former goes against human nature and the latter not. These distinctions cannot be made merely on the basis of strength of motive, since any passion may, unfortunately, have superior strength over a consideration of long-term good. And both the passion and the principle of self-love are equally parts of human nature in the first sense of the term. An animal cannot be blamed for being led into ruin by appetite, because the animal frequently cannot be said to "know any better." But human beings do know better. It is foolish, absurd, to let passion lead us into ruin and misery; it is contrary to what it means to be a rational human being. The nature of human beings is such that we are to be condemned for letting passion get the upper hand; in doing so we are not expressing our true human nature. Thus, Butler concludes, "if we will act conformably to the economy of man's nature, reasonable self-love must govern" (S2/11).

If we can see the necessity of appealing to a notion of supremacy or natural authority to explain the relationship of self-love and the particular passions, we can then more easily acknowledge that conscience has the same kind of authority with respect both to self-love and the passions. Given that we have a conscience, it would be unnatural not to follow its edicts. We are not being fully human when we let the particular passions or self-love overwhelm it.

The distinction he is drawing in Sermon 2 is no more, he reminds us, than the distinction between "*mere power* and *authority*" (S2/14). We easily recognize this distinction in the realm of civil society and government, since in our minds we separate those cases in which a group of people has superior power (a mob, or a dictator and his soldiers) from those cases in which a group has the right or authority to rule, this right being bestowed upon it by the people or (in the minds of the governed) by God. And just as the legitimate constitution of civil society can be violated by power and strength, so the natural constitution of human beings, with its hierarchy of motives, can be violated when passion usurps the rightful rule of conscience. The very idea of conscience, Butler claims, has this notion of authority built into it "insomuch that you cannot form the notion of this faculty, conscience, without taking in judgment, direction, superintendency. This is a constituent part of the idea, that is, of the faculty itself: and to preside and govern, from the very economy and constitution of man, belongs to it" (S2/14). It is a conceptual truth, a more recent philosopher might put it, that conscience has *de jure* authority over the passions and self-love.

Listening to Conscience

Human beings, Butler insists, have "the rule of right within: what is wanting is only that [they] attend to it" (S3/3). In fact, they do not need learned men and clerics, like Butler himself, to tell them what to do – all they require is to listen to conscience: "Yet let any plain honest man, before he engages in any course of action, ask himself, Is this I am going about right, or is it wrong? Is it good, or is it evil? I do not in the least doubt, but that this question would be answered agreeably to truth and virtue, by almost any fair man in almost any circumstance" (S3/4). When conscience speaks, it tells us what is right, what our duty is, what a good person would do. Butler is convinced that conscience commands the same behavior of all human beings, namely justice, honesty, and prudence. Self-love, or one of the particular passions, can momentarily blind us to the edicts of conscience, but a "fair person," one whose vision is not clouded by self-interest or a passion like anger, can full well know what is right or wrong and what is good or evil.

When conscience detects that some acts are right and others wrong, it does so intuitively. "In all common ordinary cases we see intuitively at first view what is our duty, what is the honest part" (S8/14). An intuitive awareness is one that is direct and immediate. While Butler speaks of conscience as reflective, it does not seem for him to involve a process of reasoning or calculation. Hence it is more similar to direct perception than to reason in its discursive moments. The intuitive insights of conscience are, for Butler infallible: they cannot be in error.[15] And they are universal – all human beings perceive the correctness of justice and truthfulness.

What, exactly, does conscience show us when it reveals that some acts are right and others wrong? Butler is fairly clear as to what it does *not* show:

> For there are certain dispositions of mind, and certain actions, which are in themselves approved or disapproved by mankind, abstracted from the consideration of their tendency to the happiness or misery of the world; approved or disapproved by reflection, by that principle within, which is the guide of life, the judge of right and wrong   (S12/31n).

And again:

> The fact then appears to be, that we are constituted so as to condemn falsehood, unprovoked violence, injustice, and to approve of benevolence to some preferably to others, abstracted from all consideration, which conduct is likeliest to produce an overbalance of happiness and misery.[16]

In disapproving of falsehood and injustice in abstraction from their likelihood of producing more misery than happiness, Butler is clearly rejecting a *consequentialist* understanding of right and wrong. A consequentialist is precisely one who locates the rightness of an act in its production of more happiness (or pleasure) than misery (pain). But, then, what *is* it that leads us to condemn "falsehood, unprovoked violence, injustice" and the like? Butler is not very explicit about this matter. In addition to his talk of "the rule of right" he alludes to "moral fitness"[17], and one commentator has likened his view to that of the earlier eighteenth-century moralist, Samuel Clarke, who wrote: "Some things are in their own nature good and reasonable and fit to be done; such as keeping faith, and performing equitable compacts, and the like."[18] Another commentator has deemed Butler a pluralistic *deontologist*, a deontologist being (at a minimum) one who rejects the consequentialist's view that the happiness or unhappiness found in an action's consequences is the determinant of its moral status as right or wrong.[19] A pluralistic deontologist would be one who identifies a multiplicity of duties or rights which cannot be reduced to some common factor. And there is the interpretation of Butler that claims that conscience registers the naturalness or unnaturalness of actions or the principles from which they flow (an action, for example, that proceeds from a particular passion in defiance of self-love would be deemed unnatural).[20] This last view is suggested by Butler's remark that "our perception of vice and ill-desert arises from, and is a result of, a comparison of actions with the nature and capacities of the agent" (D,II,5) and his comment that virtue consists in following nature (S/Pr/13). We shall not attempt to decide the interpretive issues here, but will content ourselves with noting the general agreement that Butler is a deontologist and not a consequentialist. For him, conscience is the rational, reflective ability to ascertain that some acts are right and others wrong without appeal to their consequences.

Why Be Moral?

But why should we do what conscience tells us is right? Why should we be moral? Recall that after telling us that human beings have the rule of right within, Butler goes on to say that "what is wanting is only that [they] should attend to it" (S3/3). But why should they? Sure enough, Butler grants, we may be punished (by the law, other people, or God) if we do what is wrong or if we violate our duties, but it is not the threat of punishment that should prompt us to follow conscience. Conscience is placed in us, not just to tell us what to do, but also to constitute the overriding motive for our doing so.

> But allowing that mankind hath the rule of right within himself, yet it may be asked, "What obligations are we under to attend to and to follow it?" ... The question ... carries its own answer along with it. Your obligation to obey this law, is its being the law of your nature. That your conscience approves of and attests to such a course of action, is itself alone an obligation. Conscience does not only offer itself to show us the way we should walk in, but it likewise carries its own authority with it, that it is our natural guide ... it therefore belongs to our condition of being, it is our duty to walk in that path, and follow this guide, without looking about to see whether we may not possibly forsake them with impunity (S3/5).

Conscience both (a) shows us the "path we should walk," and (b) by virtue of being the superior authority, puts us under an obligation to walk this way.[21] Conscience gives us knowledge of what acts are right and wrong, and the fact that it speaks to us gives rise to our obligations to do what it tells us is right and to forbear those acts it tells us are wrong. It is the source both of moral knowledge and moral obligation.[22]

Commentators often bemoan the fact that, after clearly declaring his non-consequentialist commitments, Butler in many instances will quickly go on to assert that acting from conscience in fact serves self-love. That is to say, he is convinced that doing what is right is the best way to promote one's long-range well-being. In one of the later *Sermons* he writes:

> ... there can no access be had to the understanding, but by convincing men, that the course of life we would persuade them to is not contrary to their interest. It may be allowed, without any prejudice to the cause

of virtue and religion, that our ideas of happiness and misery are of all our ideas the nearest and most important to us ... Let it be allowed, though virtue or moral rectitude does indeed consist in affection to and pursuit of what is right and good as such; yet, that when we sit down in a cool hour, we can neither justify to ourselves this or any other pursuit, till we are convinced that it will be for our happiness, or at least not contrary to it (S11/20).

If we cannot justify the pursuit of rightness and duty unless we convince ourselves, "in a cool hour," that doing so will have as its consequence the promotion of our happiness, then the latter fact appears to be the *reason* for doing our duty, and this is consequentialism pure and simple. Such a claim seems straightforwardly inconsistent with the deontological claim that the perception of rightness or duty and the authority of conscience are the reasons that motivate and justify one in acting morally.

The consensus of scholars seems to be that in the above passage from Sermon 11 Butler is arguing from a premise others accept but he does not. His main goal in this sermon is to prove that the deliverances of self-love and benevolence (which is here identified with virtue) do not conflict with one another. His argument is that even if one thinks that self-love provides the only justification of action, there is still no reason to reject the recommendations of virtue – since they too serve one's own good. Butler can argue this way without actually agreeing that self-love alone justifies action.[23]

Moreover, Terence Penelhum has defended Butler against this inconsistency by pointing out that in the *Sermons* Butler is speaking to his congregation as a pastor and is intent, first and foremost, in getting them to *do* what is right.[24] This goal allows him to admit that human beings are often more swayed by self-love than by conscience (that self-love is frequently the stronger principle) and consequently to urge them to do what they ought because it will promote their own interest – while at the same time he can claim that conscience does not need the defense of self-love. The edicts of conscience are self-justifying, and although human beings are weak, they *can* follow conscience and accept its judgments as overriding. Butler the pastor simply wants them to do what is right, even if not for the best reason.

It also needs to be pointed out that Butler (unlike Kant, as we shall see) does not require of a virtuous or moral act that it be performed solely "for the sake of duty." That is to say, he is willing to allow motivations other than the perception of the authority of conscience to move a person towards doing what is right. The awareness of the authority of conscience may be weak – dulled or worn down by a variety of factors ("laid asleep," as Butler puts it) – in which case the conviction that acting virtuously will increase one's happiness is a perfectly suitable motive to spur one on to moral action. As a deontologist or nonconsequentialist, Butler is committed to the view that what *makes* an act right or wrong has nothing to do with its consequences. But what makes an act right or wrong needs to be distinguished from the motive with which one engages in this act. Thus, while the reasons for judging that an act is right or one's duty have nothing to do with their tendency to promote happiness, we may not be *motivated* to pursue a right action or our duty unless we believe that it will lead to our well-being. In such cases, which may be in the overwhelming majority, appeal must be made to our desire for happiness (to the principle of self-love) in order to explain why we act morally, even though what makes an act moral bears no relation to self-love. The distinction between explaining the reasons an act is right and explaining the motive for pursuing right action may accommodate and render consistent all of what Butler has said.

Be that as it may, we are here confronting several issues that divide moral philosophy throughout the eighteenth century and thereafter. The consequentialist approach, usually in the guise of a form of utilitarianism, is quite popular, while the deontological approach receives a strong defense by Kant. Butler is one of Kant's most important predecessors (and is sometimes referred to as "a poor man's Kant"). One part of this controversy is whether human beings can be motivated by something like reason or conscience, or whether they can be motivated only by a desire for pleasure, happiness or some other form of personal well-being. Another aspect of the controversy relates to the definition of right action; still another to the relationship between this definition and the motive of an act. Butler has not resolved these issues and disputes, but he has certainly introduced us to them.

Butler's Legacy

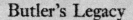

What can we take from this study of Butler? Scholars give him high marks for his criticisms of psychological egoism and hedonism.[25] And he is frequently applauded for his demonstration that self-love and benevolence are not necessarily inconsistent.[26] Butler's observation that the best way to further one's own interest is *not* always to act with the goal of securing this advantage (S11/9) is often credited as the source of the so-called hedonist's fallacy. Furthermore, Butler is the source for many of the objections against consequentialism and utilitarianism that have become standard over the years. He contrasts the certainty that accompanies the pronouncements of conscience with the uncertainty that resides in all of our predictions of the future. Insofar as consequentialism requires us to make these predictions, the fact of irremediable human ignorance tells against the use of the consequentialist standard. Moreover, the certainty we have of the moral propriety of justice, honesty, and the like – as testified to by conscience – allows no exceptions with regard to these basic values. No such certainty of the value of justice, etc. can be obtained through the calculation of consequences, and, indeed, these calculations might throw such values into question in particular circumstances.

Problems

But there are problems with Butler's ethical theory. He asserts, but does not offer philosophical reasons for believing, that following conscience is in the interest of self-love. His own reasons for believing this are theological, relating to the theistic idea that God has designed human nature for its own good. This theological perspective virtually turns God into a utilitarian, and while this view is not logically inconsistent with the nonconsequentialist nature of conscience, it does introduce a tension into Butler's overall philosophy. Moreover, the relationship between Butler's claim that conscience has natural authority and his claim that virtue consists in following nature is unclear and open to conflicting interpretations.

The objection most likely to be raised against Butler relates to the validity of the very idea of conscience. Many philosophers would agree with Elizabeth Anscombe when she writes, "Butler exalts conscience, but appears ignorant that a man's conscience may tell him to do the vilest things."[27] One need not agree with Anscombe's own conception of morality as grounded in divine law rather than human nature in order to harbor considerable skepticism about conscience. A moderately wide experience of the world would suggest to many that the edicts of conscience vary enormously and that they have a suspicious tendency to be consistent with the self-interest of the individuals whose consciences speak. Furthermore, sociological and psychological explanations of conscience abound, most of which have as their goal the debunking of conscience. They interpret it as nothing more than the product of socialization and hence a mechanism of social control, or as the result of the tawdry promptings of infantile desire and the mechanics of repression.[28] In either case, the status of conscience as a source of moral knowledge is seriously called into question.

But Butler is one of those philosophers who insist that we pay attention to our own experience and not be misled by general theories whose credibility is often much less than their authors claim for them. He is convinced that on basic moral issues – concerning justice, honesty, and the like – conscience speaks with one voice to all. And it is by no means obvious that this is not true. To be sure, conscience can be dulled; indeed it can be veritably silenced. But Butler, with his theory of the particular passions and the principle of self-love, has the explanatory apparatus needed to understand why, and when, this happens. Moreover, the regret and remorse we often feel when we violate the dictates of conscience suggest that we hear them clearly enough but simply are not sufficiently motivated (as we know we *ought* to be) to follow them.

Nevertheless, there are serious problems with any theory of conscience. What if the promptings of conscience on the part of two or more individuals disagree? Is there any criterion for settling the dispute? It could not, in the nature of the case, be conscience itself that serves as the criterion. Again, how specific are the dictates of conscience? To side for justice is fine, but the devil is in the details. What particular acts are just? We saw Aquinas struggle with this issue, more acutely so because for him conscience was not (as with Butler) the immediate perception of rightness and wrongness but the activity of deducing specific moral precepts from general ones. And Aquinas was clear that in this matter there is no certainty. Even if we have an immediate perception that justice is right, our moral problems have not been solved – they have just begun.

Butler is perhaps the first philosopher to put conscience at the center of his ethical thinking. In doing so, he taps into widespread agreement that morality and conscience are very closely connected. He gives us ample reason to respect a theory of conscience, but he does not give us a theory sufficiently developed to answer all the questions that arise regarding it. Perhaps the judgment of C.D. Broad best captures the merits and faults of Butler's ethics: "though his system is incomplete, it does seem to contain the prolegomena to any system of ethics that can claim to do justice to the facts of moral experience."[29]

9

Hume

David Hume (1711–76) is one of the most stimulating philosophers of all time, and one of the most notorious. The third of the great British empiricists – John Locke and George Berkeley being the other two – Hume is thought by many to be the most consistent empiricist of the three. Perhaps best known for his unsettling reflections on the self and causality – which force us to reconsider our understanding of self-identity and our ability to predict the future – Hume is also a great moral philosopher.

Hume's contribution to moral philosophy has two parts. First, it consists in a series of reflections on the epistemic source of moral judgments. Second, it is a characterization of the practice of morality, particularly of the kind of reasons that support moral judgments. Hume wants to know, first, how we come to have our moral convictions – from what source we derive them. He is keen to show that, contrary to what moralists throughout the ages have proclaimed, we do not obtain them through the exercise of *reason*. According to him, our moral convictions, for the most part or in essential ways, derive from our *passions* rather than our reason. This is the basic thesis of his moral epistemology. In light of it, it is easy to picture Hume as a moral skeptic, just as he is a skeptic (or appears to be one[1]) with regard to many other areas of knowledge. When he turns to the characterization of morality and the distinctive type of reasons that support moral judgments, he articulates a view that has many subscribers in eighteenth-century and subsequent British philosophy: utilitarianism.[2] According to Hume, it is the *utility* of an action, its ability to promote the public good, the happiness of people in general, that makes it a morally right action and one it is our duty to perform.

Hume's moral epistemology can be characterized as a form of *subjectivism*. Our moral convictions express our passions or sentiments, which, unlike reason, possess no objectivity, i.e., they mark or reflect no mind-independent realities. His doctrine of the nature of morality is a species of *naturalism*.[3] Morality is to be explained solely by reference to the natural qualities of human beings and to natural facts in the world relating to utility. It is to be approached scientifically, by "applying a kind of scientific method to the study of the human mind."[4] Hume rejects any conception of morality that grounds it in a divine order or appeals to faculties (like conscience) that cannot be understood in terms of sense experience and ordinary emotional responses. As we shall see, the subjectivism and the naturalism can sometimes appear to be at odds with one another, and the combination of the two generates tension in Hume's moral philosophy as a whole. We shall have occasion at the end of this chapter to reflect on this tension.

Early in his life, Hume produced a philosophical masterpiece entitled *A Treatise of Human Nature*. Masterpiece or not, this book, in Hume's own words, fell "dead-born from the press; without reaching such distinction as even to excite a Murmur among the Zealots." It received very little notice in his own country (but considerably more in France) and its iconoclastic power went largely unappreciated there. In an effort to generate more interest in his philosophy, Hume later produced two other more popular works, *An Inquiry Concerning Human Understanding* and *An Inquiry Concerning the Principles of Morals*. The latter books, especially the second, are of a more literary nature and sometimes lack the rigor of argumentation found in the earlier *Treatise*. It is also arguable that some of the views on the passions found in the *Treatise* are not fully consistent with those in the second *Inquiry*. We shall not enter deeply into the scholarly disputes concerning the relationship between these two works in moral theory,[5] but shall satisfy ourselves by looking first at the moral epistemology put forth in the *Treatise* and the second *Inquiry* and then at the account of morality given in the *Inquiry*.

The Source of Morality: Reason or Passion?

Early in Part III of Book II of the *Treatise* (entitled "Of the Passions"), Hume remarks on the "suppos'd pre-eminence of reason above passion" (*T*,413)[6] found throughout the history of moral philosophy.[7] He sets himself the task of refuting this perennial point of view: "In order to shew the fallacy of all this philosophy, I shall endeavor to prove *first*, that reason alone can never be a motive to any action of the will; and *secondly*, that it can never oppose passion in the direction of the will" (*T*,413).What he wants to show is that the understanding, the faculty of reason, can never provide considerations that in and of themselves move us to action. That is to say, the understanding alone cannot provide us with reasons that motivate us to act in certain ways. The passions, on the contrary, do have an influence on the will: as a result of having them, we seek or avoid their objects. Thus the fact that an object provokes in a person a desire for it, gives that individual a motive to act in a certain way, namely to seek to obtain this object. Passion motivates, reason does not; hence reason and passion can never produce conflicting motivations.

Hume proceeds to argue for his position by identifying the kinds of consideration that can be brought forward by reason. Here he appeals to some themes of his general epistemology. Reason, in one of its functions, concerns itself with the abstract relations among ideas; in another function it investigates matters of fact about the causes and effects of events. In its first role, reason informs us, for instance, that a round object cannot be square, this because the ideas of roundness and squareness are logically inconsistent or mutually contradictory. Likewise, reason tells us that seven objects added to five yield twelve, the science of arithmetic being the study of abstract relations of quantity. *Demonstrative* reason, of the sort found in logic and mathematics, shows how our ideas connect up with or relate to one another. These relations may hold among our ideas even if these ideas correspond to no actual objects in the world. Thus, even though there are no mermaids in the world, the idea of a mermaid is logically connected to the idea of a creature with a fish-like tail. Demonstrative reason shows us that *if* one idea applies to something in reality, other ideas *must* (or must not) apply as well. For example, if something is a mermaid, it must have a fish-like tail; if Tom is a bachelor, he must not be married; if an object has a square shape, it cannot have a round one. According to Hume, we can know with *certainty* that such relations of ideas hold.

When it comes to knowledge of matters of fact – facts in the actual world – we know these only by experience (the use of the five senses) and by reasoning from experience. Observing two events conjoined in experience, the one always following the other, we reason *inductively* that they will continue to do so in the future. Having observed the sun rise in the east innumerable times, we conclude that it will do so tomorrow as well. Such matter-of-fact reasoning often relates to the causes of events. Thus having observed that bread nourished us in the past, we reason that it will do so now. In the case of matter-of-fact reasoning of this type, certainty is denied us, since our inductive inferences may always be wrong. Having observed thousands of swans and noted that all of them are white, we may erroneously conclude that all swans are white. And one of these days (given some celestial disturbance), the sun may not rise in the east.

Hume thinks it obvious that a knowledge of the relationship between two or more ideas (which, after all, may refer to nothing actual in the world) does not yield a reason for action – although he gives some arguments to this effect which we shall consider later. But it is less obvious that a knowledge of matters of fact, especially of causal connections between events, also fails to yield reasons or motives for action. Doesn't the knowledge that a certain substance will make one sick give one a reason not to eat it? What Hume claims is that knowing that one event causes another – knowing, e.g., that eating a certain kind of food will make one sick – *in-and-of-itself* does not constitute a reason or motive for action (for not eating the food). It is only because we know we shall experience pain if we become sick that we avoid this particular food. The anticipation of pain *does* provide a motive for action. " 'Tis obvious, that when we have the prospect of pain or pleasure from any object, we feel a consequent emotion of aversion or propensity, and are carry'd to avoid or embrace what will give us this uneasiness or satisfaction" (*T*,414). The passions – aversion to pain and attraction to pleasure, hate and love – engage our will. Experience and reasoning from experience only provide information about objects, e.g., their tendency to produce pleasure or pain in us. Such information about an object may lead to an emotional reaction to it (one of aversion or desire), and it is the emotional reaction that gives rise to action. Moreover, experience and reason can guide the passions by pointing us in directions that will allow us to avoid what we dislike and obtain what we desire. "But 'tis evident in this case, that the impulse arises not from reason, but is only directed by it. 'Tis from the prospect of pain or pleasure that the aversion or propensity arises toward any object" (*T*,414). If objects or events do not have an effect on us by way of producing pleasure or pain (or arousing the passions in other ways), then to know that they are cause and effect of one another leaves us indifferent to them – "Where the objects themselves do not affect us, their connexion can never give them any influence" (*T*,414). Thus reason in its capacity for giving us knowledge of causes and effects does not in and of itself provide motives for action. Only the passions – the various desires and aversions – do so.

Likewise, only passions can "prevent volition" (*T*,415) and lead us to refrain from doing something. If I desire a sweet that I know will make me gain weight, my desire not to gain weight can counteract my desire for the object. My knowledge that it will make me gain weight alone cannot do so. Reason, then, cannot oppose passion in the direction of the will. From these considerations Hume concludes that it is improper to speak of a combat between reason and passion – the only combat possible is between one passion and another.

Reason as the Slave of Passion

Hume drives home the above points with one of the most notorious claims in the literature of moral philosophy: "Reason is, and ought only to be the slave of the passions, and can never pretend to any other office than to serve and obey them" (*T*,415). Reason, the understanding, can give us information that will help guide the passions to their fulfillment and help us avoid pain and frustration. But this information does not itself determine what we do or ought to do – only our subjective response to the information has this executive power. Thus reason serves and supports the passions; it has no other function when it comes to human action.

Hume's doctrine can be formulated in terms of the distinction between *means* and *ends*. The knowledge of causes and effects gives us information about the means to achieving certain ends. If I want a high-paying job, I know that education is the most likely means to obtaining one. If I want to be healthy, I know that exercise will lead to this end. Reason is invaluable in giving us information about the best means of achieving our ends, but on the question of ends themselves it is silent. In the *Inquiry*, Hume tells us that ultimate ends – intrinsic values – can never be accounted for by reason, but are derived solely from the sentiments and affections:

> Ask a man *why he uses exercise*; he will answer, *because he desires to keep his health*. If you then inquire *why he desires health*, he will readily reply,

because sickness is painful. If you push your inquiries further and desire a reason *why he hates pain*, it is impossible he can ever give any. This is an ultimate end, and is never referred to any other object   (*I*,111)[8].

Sometimes we desire an object (e.g., money) and pursue it because we know it is a means to other things (e.g., comfort and security). In the final analysis, however, there must be some things we desire on their own account, not because they are means to something else but because of their "immediate accord or agreement with human sentiment and affection" (*I*,111). It is this direct impact on sentiment that gives rise to our ultimate ends. Reason alone can never determine that something is ultimately or intrinsically valuable.

In addition to identifying the means to our ends, there is another way in which reason can serve the passions. The passions, as Hume recognizes, are often accompanied by beliefs about the objects of these passions. If I am angry at a person, I may feel this way because I believe this individual has told a lie about me, and this belief of mine may not in fact be true. I may become furious at a group of people because I think they are in conspiracy against me, but this conspiracy may not exist. Thus the slave, reason, can serve the master, passion, by demonstrating that the beliefs on which certain passions rest are false.

Theory of Motivation

Hume notes that morality naturally has an influence on human actions, which is to say that morality is a *practical* matter, not simply a *theoretical* or speculative one. Morality is concerned with what we are *to do*; it is not just concerned with what the facts are in the world. Moral judgments motivate us to act in certain ways; they have an impact on the will; they constitute reasons for action: "men are often govern'd by their duties, and are deter'd from some actions by the opinions of injustice, and impell'd to others by that of obligation" (*T*,457). We must be able to explain this practical import that moral convictions have. Could we understand this import if moral convictions were the outcome of reason and the understanding? Hume thinks not. Could we understand it if they were the products of passion and sentiment? Yes, Hume tells us.

Hume claims to have shown that reason can operate only to determine the truth or falsity of beliefs associated with our desires. It can comment on the existence or nonexistence of the objects of our passions and on the efficacy or inefficacy of certain means to the fulfillment of our passions. But if we are indifferent to an object, or have no desire for a certain end or goal promoted by an action, then the information provided by reason will have no effect on our actions. Thus reason itself has no direct influence over actions. "Reason is perfectly inert, and can never either prevent or produce any action or affection" (*T*,458). It follows from this that reason cannot be the source of moral convictions, which do move us to act. "Reason is wholly inactive, and can never be the source of so active a principle as conscience, or a sense of morals" (*T*,458). The passions, on the contrary, have a direct effect on action. We seek what we desire or love and avoid what we dislike or hate. Thus only if we take moral convictions to be an expression of the passions, can we understand why morality moves us.

Hume's argument can be summarized as follows: moral convictions are practical, providing an immediate motivation to action; beliefs derived from reason are inert, in themselves having no immediate bearing on action; our passions – our sentiments and desires – have a direct impact on action; therefore, moral convictions cannot be the pronouncements of reason but rather are the results of our sentiments and desires. "Morals excite passions, and produce or prevent actions," Hume tells us, and "Reason of itself is utterly impotent in this particular" (*T*,457).

Hume's argument clearly has some plausibility. A desire or feeling – of anger or love, say – appears to have an immediate relation to action: when angry, we ordinarily strike out or vent our anger in other ways, and we seek to possess what we love. Likewise, jealousy and ambition are expressed in certain typical actions. On the contrary, a belief about some matter of fact does not seem to have any immediate implications for action. If I believe that my house is burning down, nothing follows from this belief alone about what I shall do – I'll do one thing if I want the insurance, another if I want to preserve my abode. So there is great appeal in Hume's view that action and other practical matters are products of sentiment, not rational belief. And if it is true that moral convictions are practical, it seems to follow that these convictions are the product of sentiment and not reason.

It should be pointed out, however, that some recent and contemporary philosophers have rejected Hume's argument. Why accept, they ask, the claim that a belief alone cannot motivate an action? What is there about a desire or passion that better fits it to be a motive of action than a belief. To be sure, belief – the operation of reason – is usually "cool" and passions often "hot and tumultuous." But what does this prove? Critics of this sort suggest that Hume is operating with a mechanical (or "hydraulic") conception of passion whereby a passion is seen to have a push or pull quality directly affecting action.[9] Such a conception, they claim, is purely metaphorical. Moreover, they point out that passions themselves often don't directly lead to action – they do so only under the guidance of belief (a point Hume would accept).[10] But if passions *can* by themselves lead to action, why cannot beliefs by themselves do the same? Considerations of this sort have led some thinkers to seek a purely cognitive, non–Humean theory of motivation.[11]

Passions and Truth

Realizing that his doctrine "may appear somewhat extraordinary" (*T*,415), Hume attempts to defend it by further reflections. Passions, he argues, are themselves neither true nor false; they do not agree or disagree with any facts beyond themselves.

> Reason is the discovery of truth or falshood. Truth or falshood consists in an agreement or disagreement either to the *real* relations of ideas, or to *real* existence and matter of fact. Whatever, therefore, is not susceptible of this agreement or disagreement, is incapable of being true or false, and can never be an object of our reason. Now 'tis evident our passions, volitions, and actions, are not susceptible of any such agreement or disagreement; being original facts and realities, compleat in themselves, and implying no reference to other passions, volitions, and actions. 'Tis impossible, therefore, they can be pronounced either true or false, and be either contrary or conformable to reason   (*T*,458).

If I am angry, my anger can't be said to be either true or false, to correspond or not correspond to any facts; it just exists as an emotional state of my person (complete in itself). If I am in love with someone, this passion does not itself reveal any characteristics of the loved one; it is but a modification of my existence.[12] Nor can my anger or love be logically inconsistent with any other feelings or desires I may have. My being angry at one person, for example, does not entail that I shall or shall not be angry at another person. (Thus a passion implies "no reference to other passions.") It follows that reason or the understanding cannot criticize any passion or set of passions in and of itself, for any cognitive criticism must consist of pointing either to error or to logical inconsistency. From the standpoint of reason, no one passion is preferable to any other. No one passion is "better" than another with regard to truth or logical consistency, since neither of these modes of assessment applies to the passions. From this result the astounding conclusion follows: " 'Tis not contrary to reason to prefer the destruction of the whole world to the scratching of my finger" (*T*,416).[13]

It is necessary to remind ourselves that Hume is denying that reason can find fault with a passion *itself*. As we have noted, reason can come to the assistance of passion by demonstrating that a particular sentiment arises out of a false belief. In such cases, reason corrects, not the sentiment, but the belief responsible for it. Likewise, we may make mistakes about the causes and effects relating to the ends of our desire, and so we may "chuse means insufficient for the design'd end ... " (*T*,416). Once again, reason can correct these beliefs and thereby assist us in attaining the ends of passion. But with these acts of assistance the role of reason comes to an end. "Where a passion is neither founded on false suppositions, nor chuses means insufficient for the end, the understanding can neither justify nor condemn it" (*T*,416). Only when a passion is accompanied by some false judgment can it be said, and even then misleadingly, to be unreasonable.

Most systems of moral philosophy, Hume declares, teach that we have a *knowledge* of good and evil, a knowledge obtained by reason. Hume is the opponent of all such systems. "In order, therefore, to judge of these systems, we need only consider, whether it be possible, from reason alone, to distinguish betwixt moral good and evil, or whether there must concur some other principles to enable us to make that distinction" (*T*,457). He has tried to show that there must be "some other principles" – namely our passions and sentiments – that generate the distinction. And he has still other arguments up his sleeve.

Moral Knowledge?

What kind of knowledge, Hume asks, could be involved in knowing the difference between a right and a wrong action? "If the thought and understanding were alone capable of fixing the boundaries of right and wrong, the character of virtuous and vicious must lie in some relations of objects, or must be a matter of fact, which is discovered by reasoning" (*T*,463). We should recall that the operations of the understanding are two-fold: in addition to the demonstrative knowledge of the relations of ideas (here referred to as relations of objects), there is knowledge of matters of fact in the actual world, a knowledge that Hume maintains is always grounded in sensory experience. Perhaps there is some experiential knowledge of the distinction between right and wrong. But if so, it would be necessary that we *observe* the moral and immoral characteristics of actions.

> Take any action allow'd to be vicious: Wilful murder, for instance. Examine it in all lights, and see if you can find that matter of fact, or real existence, which you call *vice*. In whatever way you take it, you find only certain passions, motives, volitions and thoughts. . . . The vice entirely escapes you, as long as you consider the object. You never can find it, till you turn your reflection into your own breast, and find a sentiment of disapprobation, which arises in you, toward this action, Here is a matter of fact; but 'tis the object of feeling, not of reason. It lies in yourself, not in the object   (*T*,468–9).

Where, Hume asks in the *Inquiry*, are we to locate the crime of ingratitude (*I*,106)? What fact is it? With what sense do we detect it? Can we point to it? Ingratitude consists of ill will or indifference toward a person who has befriended one, and such feelings we may be able to detect. But what about the moral *flaw* in ingratitude? Can we point to *it*? Sense perception affords us a knowledge of myriad qualities and quantities – colors, shapes, smells, tastes, motions – and of facts containing them. But moral qualities and facts are not among these observable items. We cannot observe, with any of the five senses, the *vice* or *crime* involved in an action, or the *virtue* in another. We cannot see (hear, taste, touch, or smell) moral goodness or evil. Thus if we look to sense experience and the knowledge of matters of fact derived from it, we shall not discover the source of moral convictions.[14]

Let us consider, then, the other option, that virtue and vice lie in some "relations of objects" or "relations of ideas," and that knowledge of virtue and vice is the result of the operation of demonstrative reason in detecting these relations. Such is the view of the rationalist philosophers Hume refers to. Do we come to know that an act is right simply by examining our ideas about it and detecting through reasoning that there is a necessary connection between these ideas such as to constitute its rightness? What could these relations be? "Point out distinctly the relations, which constitute morality or obligation, that we may know wherein they consist, and after what manner we must judge of them" (*T*,463). Hume maintains that there are only four relations of ideas the detection of which could yield the kind of demonstrative certainty achievable by reason: resemblance, contrariety, degrees in quality, and proportions in quantity and number. We can detect, with certainty, that two of our ideas resemble one another or are different from one another, just as we can detect that our idea of one quality varies in degree from an idea of another quality or that the idea of one quantity is greater or less than the idea of another quantity. It is relations of one or the other of these kinds that constitute the subject matter of mathematics and other forms of demonstrative reasoning. Do the relations constituting right and wrong fall among them?

Hume argues for a negative answer to this question by claiming that any one of these four kinds of relation could hold, not only with regard to human actions, but to anything whatsoever: ". . . there is no one of these relations but what is applicable, not only to an irrational, but also to an inanimate object; it follows, that even such objects must be susceptible of merit or demerit" (*T*,464). Hume's argument here is a *reductio ad absurdum*: the relations of resemblance, contrariety, degrees in quality, and proportions in quantity and number apply to all things in nature – rational and irrational, animate and inanimate; if moral distinctions were among such relations, then moral distinctions would apply to things irrational and inanimate; but it is absurd to claim that beings who are not rational (animals) and things that are not animate (rocks) are good or evil, right or wrong; therefore moral distinctions cannot consist in one or more of the four kinds of ideas comprehended by deductive, demonstrative reason.

Hume gives a concrete example to drive home this argument against the rationalists. One of the most horrible crimes a person can commit, he claims, is the deliberate causing of the death of one's parent – the crime of parricide. Everyone acknowledges the moral atrocity of this kind of action, but "the question only arises among philosophers, whether the guilt or moral deformity of this action be discover'd by demonstrative reasoning, or be felt by an internal sense, and by means of some sentiment, which the reflecting on such an action naturally occasions" (*T*,466). Hume argues that the latter option will be seen as preferable "if we can shew the same relations in other objects, without the notion of any guilt of iniquity attending them" (*T*,466). Consider then, the act of parricide and the relations involved in it. Aren't these same relations to be found in the case of an oak tree that produces a sapling below it, which sapling "springing up by degrees, at last overtops and destroys the parent tree" (*T*,467)? The sapling destroys its "parent" just as does the child who is guilty of parricide. To be sure, the "will" or "choice" produces the act of parricide, while the laws of biology are responsible for the sapling's action. But, Hume insists, this simply means that the relations constituting the two events have different causes; the relations themselves remain the same.[15] Nothing in the relations themselves – nothing we can detect by the use of reason – serves to distinguish the case of the sapling from that of the child. "Here then the same relations have different causes; but still the relations are the same: And as their discovery is not in both cases attended with a notion of immorality, it follows, that that notion does not arise from such a discovery" (*T*,467). Rational reflection on the relations of ideas does not account for the difference between the *immoral* act of the child who murders her parent and the *amoral* event whereby a sapling brings about the destruction of its parent.

Hume gives a similar argument in the *Inquiry*. What are the relations involved in the grasp of the vice of ingratitude?

> But what are the relations, I ask, of which you here talk? In the case stated [ingratitude] I see, first, good will and good offices in one person; then ill will and ill offices in the other. Between these there is the relation of *contrariety*. Does the crime consist in that relation? But suppose a person bore me ill will or did me ill offices, and I, in return, were indifferent toward him, or did him good offices – here is the same relation of *contrariety*; and yet my conduct is often highly laudable   (*I*,106–7).

Thus the types of relation detectable by demonstrative reasoning hold as much between virtuous actions as vicious ones, and cannot therefore explain the difference between the two.[16]

Hume concludes his critique of the effort to derive moral distinctions from reason with a passage so famous it must be quoted in its lengthy entirety.

> I cannot forbear adding to these reasonings an observation, which may, perhaps, be found of some importance. In every system of morality, which I have hitherto met with, I have always remark'd, that the author proceeds for some time in the ordinary way of reasoning, and establishes the being of a God, or makes observations concerning human affairs; when of a sudden I am surpriz'd to find, that instead of the usual copulations of propositions, *is*, and *is not*, I meet with no proposition that is not connected with an *ought*, or an *ought not*. This change is imperceptible;

but is, however, of the last consequence. For as this *ought*, or *ought not*, expresses some new relation or affirmation, 'tis necessary that it should be observ'd and explain'd; and at the same time that a reason should be given, for what seems altogether inconceivable, how this new relation can be a deduction from others, which are entirely different from it. But as authors commonly do not use this precaution, I shall presume to recommend it to the readers; and am persuaded, that this small attention wou'd subvert all the vulgar systems of morality, and let us see, that the distinction of vice and virtue is not founded merely on the relations of objects, nor is perceiv'd by reason   (*T*,469–70).

"Is" and "Ought"

Here we have the formulation of the notorious "is/ought" problem that has exercised philosophers ever since Hume, and especially those in the twentieth century. Here is perhaps the most famous attack on naturalistic forms of meta-ethical theory ever mounted.[17]

Naturalism is the meta-ethical claim that moral propositions describe facts in the ordinary empirical world and are justified and known by sense experience and science.[18] Hence naturalists are committed to the view that experience or science can discover moral truths by observing facts in nature. In the passage above, Hume calls this widely-held conviction – shared, it would appear, by Aristotle, Spinoza, and Hobbes, among many others – into serious question. Experience of the everyday or scientific variety gives us information about what things exist and what things do not exist. This information is expressed in propositions asserting that something *is* or *is not* – that something is or is not the case, or is or is not of a certain quality, etc. Moral convictions and propositions, on the contrary, often, perhaps always, have to do with what *ought* or *ought not* to be the case: in learning that a certain act is wrong, we learn that we ought not to do it; in being told that something is our duty, we are being informed of what actions we ought to take; even to say that an object is good suggests that it ought to exist; and so on. How, Hume asks, do we derive these moral ought-propositions from is-propositions giving us information about matters of fact? How can ordinary experience or scientific investigation, both of which inform us of what is or is not the case, have any bearing on what *ought* to be the case?

Hume's "observation" about the logical independence of "is" and "ought" constitutes in the mind of many philosophers a devastating critique of much of Western moral theory. The strategy of almost all of the moral philosophers we have studied has been to articulate a theory of human nature and to use this theory to justify moral claims about virtue, the good for human beings, and moral rightness. But theories of human nature, Hume suggests, are descriptive claims about human powers and proclivities and the way human beings actually behave. Such claims are is-propositions. The moral judgments, on the contrary, are normative: they tell us what our characters ought to be like and how we ought to behave. Thus the moral claims are ought-propositions. From the fact that human beings are constituted in a certain way and behave in certain ways, nothing follows about how they *ought* to behave and about the character they *ought* to have. Being what they are, human beings may in fact never do or be what they ought. In sum, one cannot derive moral beliefs or propositions from propositions purporting to describe the way things are.

Hume's is/ought distinction is the source of the distinction many contemporary moral philosophers draw between evaluative (normative) and descriptive (factual) judgments.[19] There is a logical gap, they argue, between making descriptive assertions about how things are and making evaluative ones about how they ought to be. This logical gap is the result of the fact that ought-propositions have a meaning that is distinct from the meaning of is-propositions, and this difference in meaning entails that we cannot *deduce* evaluative propositions from descriptive ones.[20] The gap between "is" and "ought" also casts in doubt our ability to infer inductively any normative propositions from descriptive ones. In a deductive proof, anything said in the conclusion must already be said in the premises, and if normative and descriptive propositions have different forms of meaning, then no normative conclusion is already implicitly contained in descriptive premises. The same problem, but in the reverse direction, occurs in the case of induction. In an inductive argument, we generate a general statement by generalizing from particular statements. If the particular statements are descriptive, we cannot derive from them a normative generalization. Given that deductive and inductive modes of proof seem to exhaust our means of justifying beliefs, Hume's is-ought distinction calls into question our ability to *know* that some acts are right and others wrong, or that certain forms of character are good and others evil. Knowledge requires proof or justification. In light of Hume's distinction, it is questionable whether we can prove or justify our normative convictions on the basis of descriptive truths. Could there be other ways of justifying the normative claims? It is difficult to conceive what they might be. Thus the is-ought distinction can lead to what today we call non-cognitivism, the theory that moral beliefs cannot be justified and hence cannot be the objects of knowledge.[21] The non-cognitivist claims that, contrary to what most of us think, we cannot *know* the difference between right and wrong.

Morality and the Sentiments

The conclusion that Hume himself draws from his arguments is that moral distinctions are not based on the exercise of reason (they are not "discovered" by reason) but rather are the result of our inner sentiments. Reason or the understanding brings certain facts to our attention. We react affectively (on the basis of feeling or sentiment or emotion) to some of these facts. Some of them give rise in us to a sentiment of approbation, others a sentiment of disapprobation. Those acts, persons, or events provoking our approbation we call good or right; those provoking our disapprobation we deem evil or wrong. In Hume's words, "Thus the course of the argument leads us to conclude, that since vice and virtue are not discoverable merely by reason, or the comparison of ideas, it must be by means of some impression or sentiment they occasion, that we are able to mark the difference betwixt them" (*T*,470). Morality, he claims, "is more properly felt than judg'd of ..." (*T*,470).[22]

A virtuous act, according to Hume, occasions an agreeable feeling in us, while an instance of vice provokes an uneasy one: "There is no spectacle so fair and beautiful as a noble and generous action; nor any which gives us more abhorrence than one that is cruel and treacherous" (*T*,470). He also tells us that "to have the sense of virtue, is nothing but to *feel* a satisfaction of a particular kind from the contemplation of a character" (*T*,471). But doesn't this mean that we observe, or reason, that a character is virtuous, and as a result fcel satisfaction or have an agreeable feeling, and would this not imply that we are somehow able to *know* that the character is virtuous, prior to and independent of the feeling? Not so, says Hume. "The very *feeling* constitutes our praise or admiration ... We do not infer a character to be virtuous, because it pleases: But in feeling that it pleases after such a particular manner, we in effect feel that it is virtuous" (*T*,470). As we observe or come to know the *nonmoral* features of individuals, some of these features induce us to feel the sweet, agreeable, satisfying sentiment of approbation – and *these* persons we judge to be virtuous. When we feel a disagreeable sentiment, the sentiment of disapprobation, we call evil whatever occasions this emotional reaction. Hume's subjectivism lies in his claim that virtue amounts to (is "constituted by") the fact that a person's character elicits a sentiment of approbation. The moral nature of the character does not exist independently of this affective response.[23]

Approbation and disapprobation are, respectively, praise and blame, approval and disapproval. In the *Treatise* they are described as faint feelings of love and hatred (*T*,614). Therefore they are instances of "calm passions," unlike the more turbulent forms that love and hatred can assume.

The Philosophical Study of Morality: The Virtues

Given such an analysis of the nature of moral virtue, what form should a philosophical study of it take? Hume's answer is as follows:

> Now since the distinguishing impressions, by which moral good or evil
> is known, are nothing but *particular* pains or pleasures; it follows, that in

all enquiries concerning these moral distinctions, it will be sufficient to shew the principles, which make us feel a satisfaction or uneasiness from the survey of any character, in order to satisfy us why the character is laudable or blameable   (*T*,471).

In asking here for principles, Hume is asking for a general account of what the feelings of moral approbation and disapprobation are – what distinguishes them from other feelings and what gives rise to them. For instance, what *kind* of pleasure do we feel upon contemplating a virtuous act? How does it differ, say, from the pleasure we receive in drinking a glass of fine wine? And on what occasions is the feeling a moral one, as distinct, perhaps, from the feeling of pleasure or satisfaction prompted by the furtherance of our self-interest? We shall now turn our attention to what Hume has to say in *An Inquiry Concerning the Principles of Morals* about these general principles. Having answered questions relating to the source of morality, he proceeds to discuss the issue of the definition of morality and to identify the kinds of factual considerations that lead to moral approbation and disapprobation.

In the *Inquiry* Hume begins by examining the qualities that constitute "personal merit" and by investigating what it is about these qualities that leads us to praise them.

The only object of reasoning is to discover the circumstances ... which are common to these qualities – to observe that particular in which the estimable qualities agree, on the one hand, and the blamable, on the other; and thence to reach the foundation of ethics and find those universal principles from which all censure or approbation is ultimately derived   (*I*,8).

Such an investigation will be founded on "fact and observation" and will proceed to derive general maxims from particular instances.

Among the characteristics commonly thought to be marks of personal merit, we find those that Hume refers to as "the benevolent or softer affections ... The epithets, *sociable, good-natured, humane, merciful, grateful, friendly, generous, beneficent*, or their equivalents, are known in all languages, and universally express the highest merit which human nature is capable of attaining" (*I*,9). Hume notes that these characteristics, or "social virtues," involve "a tender sympathy with others and a generous concern for our kind and species" (*I*,10). Thus an individual who manifests one or more of these characteristics finds favor with us because of "the happiness and satisfaction derived to society from his intercourse and good offices" (*I*,11). We applaud beneficent and humane individuals, and the characteristics themselves, by virtue of the fact that they benefit society. Thus, "may it not thence be concluded that the *utility* resulting from the social virtues forms, at least, a *part* of their merit, and is one source of that approbation and regard so universally paid to them?" (*I*,11) By utility Hume means the power and tendency to bring about benefits, and for him the utility of the social virtues lies in their power and tendency to generate benefit for society at large. It is the effects of benevolence, friendliness, etc. in affecting positively the "true interests of mankind" (*I*,13) that lead us to admire and applaud them. What Hume calls "public utility" (*I*,12) is thus at the basis of much, if not all, of moral approbation. Indeed, the social virtue of benevolence is, in Hume's eyes (and, he thinks, humankind's), the most admirable of all personal qualities: "Upon the whole, then, it seems undeniable that nothing can bestow more merit on any human creature than the sentiment of benevolence in an eminent degree, and that a *part*, at least, of its merit arises from its tendency to promote the interests of our species and bestow happiness on human society" (*I*,14).

Justice

Hume devotes section III of the *Inquiry* to the nature of justice, the idea of property, and the social virtues associated with them. By justice he has principally in mind what today would be called *distributive* justice, the fair partition or distribution of goods among and to individuals or social groups. Such allocation gives rise to the notion of property, to the idea that some goods are *mine* and others *yours*. Hume wants to demonstrate that "public utility is the *sole* origin of Justice" and that "reflections on the beneficial consequences of this virtue are the *sole* foundation of its merit" (*I*,14–15). His argument in favor of this utilitarian conception of justice consists in a series of hypothetical reflections. First of all, he asks what would happen if nature provided us with a "profuse *abundance* of all *external* conveniences." What if there were no scarcity in nature and we had all we could desire to eat and drink – without work? What if the climate were such that we needed no clothes? What if our natural beauty made ornaments of adornment unnecessary? "It seems evident that in such a happy state every other social virtue would flourish and receive tenfold increase; but the cautious, jealous virtue of justice would never once have been dreamed of. For what purpose make a partition of goods where everyone has already more than enough?" (*I*,15) In such a situation, justice would be "totally *useless*." We can see the truth of this, Hume thinks, by observing that, in the world we actually live in, when there is no scarcity of a commodity, such as air, we do not distinguish between the air belonging to one individual and that belonging to another. Consider, in the second place, another hypothetical situation. Imagine that "the mind is so enlarged and so replete with friendship and generosity that every man has the utmost tenderness for every man, and feels no more concern for his own interest than for that of his fellows" (*I*,16). Once again, justice would not be necessary. Its utility would disappear and it would be "suspended."

Instead of such generous assumptions, let us hypothesize that we find ourselves in a situation of extreme scarcity. "Suppose a society to fall into such want of all common necessities that the utmost frugality and industry cannot preserve the greater number from perishing and the whole from extreme misery ... " (*I*,17). Here, too,

Hume maintains, the institutions of justice and property would be of no value – they would not be adequate to rectify the situation so as to restore the minimum necessities to all. What would happen? In Hume's opinion, "it will readily ... be admitted that the strict laws of justice are suspended in such a pressing emergency and give place to the stronger motives of necessity and self-preservation" (*I*,17). When the rules of property no longer have utility, they are abandoned. If "no greater evil can be dreaded from violence and injustice" than from peace and justice, the latter would have nothing to commend them, and they would lose their value for us. In such a situation "the dictates of self-preservation alone" would assume priority and govern our sentiments and judgments.

Justice, then, cannot be said to have value in and of itself, eternally and without regard to the actual situation in which human beings find themselves. The value of justice resides in its utility, and its utility is a function of the concrete circumstances of life in which people exist. In the types of extreme situation described above, justice would no longer have utility. In the actual world, which "is a medium amidst all these extremes," justice and the division of property serve society well. They promote stability and the satisfaction of the minimal needs of most people. Thus in the actual world, justice and property receive our approbation. And the social virtues related to justice – the attitudes and actions towards other people which are required for the implementation of justice, attitudes such as mutual regard and forbearance – these too are admired because of their usefulness. "Where mutual regards and forbearance serve to no manner of purpose, they would never direct the conduct of any reasonable person" (*I*,22).

Why, we might ask, do we not have laws that require absolute equality with respect to the possession of property? It must be granted, Hume thinks, that were such perfect equality achieved, everyone would enjoy "all the necessaries and even most of the comforts of life" (*I*,24), and that all departures from this strict equality "rob the poor of more satisfaction than we add to the rich" (*I*,24). Nevertheless, he argues, perfect equality in the distribution of goods is impractical – it could not be achieved without drastic consequences: "Render possessions ever so equal, men's different degrees of art, care, and industry will immediately break that equality. Or if you check these virtues, you reduce society to the most extreme indigence and, instead of preventing want and beggary in a few, render it unavoidable to the whole community" (*I*,25). In other words, considerations of utility – the production of the greatest social good – speak against laws requiring perfect equality. These considerations must be undertaken in light of the actual realities concerning human nature and the human situation, always with a view to identifying those laws most beneficial to humankind. Basic inequalities among human beings with respect to ability and drive will inevitably lead to a situation in which some people possess more than others, and if laws are passed which negate the consequences of superior "art, care, and industry," everyone will suffer as a result of these laws. Such art, care and industry are necessary for the production of the goods needed to alleviate human misery. Thus we need to encourage and support the qualities of intelligence, ingenuity, and hard work: "Who sees not ... that whatever is produced or improved by a man's art or industry ought forever to be secured to him in order to give encouragement to such *useful* habits and accomplishments? That the property ought also to descend to children and relations, for the same useful purpose" (*I*,25–6). By allowing a person to keep what her special talents produce and to pass on these things to her children, we encourage the development of these talents, whose utilization is beneficial to everyone. Thus the institutions of private property and inheritance are given a classic utilitarian justification.

Hume is contemptuous of those theories that assert there is a *natural* right to property, grounded in some universal human nature. On the contrary "all questions of property are subordinate to the authority of civil laws" (*I*,27) and human beings create civil laws in order to satisfy their needs and interests. Likewise, he rejects the view that there is some innate tendency or "simple original instinct" in human beings that approves of and demands justice. What could such a mysterious instinct be? Indeed, given the intricacies involved in the possession and transferral of property, we would need "ten thousand different instincts" to give us guidance in these matters. The simpler, and therefore preferable, explanation is that we base the myriad distinctions involved in justice and property law on considerations of utility: "The necessity of justice to the support of society is the *sole* foundation of that virtue; and since no moral excellence is more highly esteemed, we may conclude that this circumstance of usefulness has, in general, the strongest energy and most entire command over our sentiments" (*I*,34). We do not need to appeal to mysterious instincts in order to understand the laws and institutions of justice. Calculation of utility is sufficient.

Utility and Rules

Hume adds an appendix to the *Inquiry* entitled "Some Further Considerations With Regard To Justice." The appendix is important, for it shows Hume to be what today we call a *rule utilitarian*. All utilitarians are committed to the view that the consequences of behavior and policy vis-à-vis human happiness or human good are the determining factor with respect to moral rightness. But they divide over the issue of whether one should look to the consequences of single acts or to the consequences of systems of rules and laws, what might be called institutions or practices. Consider the case of a mischievous person inheriting millions of dollars from her parents. In this instance, more harm than good may result from the inheritance, the money being alternately wasted and put to evil ends. Should we judge this particular case of inheritance to be wrong? An act utilitarian would say so. Most rule utilitarians, including Hume, would disagree. In general, they would argue, the institution of inheritance does more good than evil, even though in this particular case this is not so. The possibility of leaving one's wealth to one's children adds incentive to human effort, which effort more often than not produces an increase in human well-being. Thus the practice or institution of inheritance is justified.

Likewise, the laws of possession, which among other things deny possession to someone who acquires goods by mistake, are justified on the grounds of the benefit deriving in general from them. Hume admits that these laws may "deprive, without scruple, a beneficent man of all his possessions if acquired by mistake, . . . in order to bestow them on a selfish miser who has already heaped up immense store of superfluous riches" (*I*,122). In spite of the fact that these laws of possession may have this disastrous consequence in the individual case, in general they produce more good than evil. Still again, Hume claims that the social virtues of justice and fidelity are "highly useful or, indeed, absolutely necessary to the well-being of mankind." But, he acknowledges: "the benefit resulting from them is not the consequence of every individual single act, but arises from the whole scheme or system concurred in by the whole or the greater part of the society" (*I*,121). Indeed, he goes on to say, "the result of the individual acts is here, in many instances, directly opposite to that of the whole system of actions; and the former may be extremely hurtful, while the latter is, to the highest degree, advantageous" (*I*,121). Both with property rights and, to use another of Hume's (now largely outdated) examples, the right of succession, "its benefit arises only from the observance of the general rule" (*I*,121)."It is sufficient if the whole plan or scheme be necessary to the support of civil society and if the balance of good, in the main, do thereby preponderate much above that of evil" (*I*,122). In as much as it is the utility of following the general rule, not the utility of the individual act, that is for Hume the ground of our moral approbation, he is to be placed in the camp of the rule utilitarians.

Related to Hume's focus on the utility of rules is the fact that he usually concentrates on the merit of virtues, i.e., dispositions of character, rather than on the merit of individual acts. "If any *action* be either virtuous or vicious, 'tis only a sign of some quality or character" (*T*, 575). At one point he says that actions are virtuous or vicious only insofar as they are proofs of certain durable principles of the mind. Virtues have a dimension of generality about them – they issue in laudable acts time and again. As such, virtues in general bring benefits – to the individual and society – even though, on particular occasions, they may lead to pain and frustration.

Hume finds utility in almost every corner of our lives. Why do we have governments, which in all cases limit our freedom? "It is evident that, if government were totally useless, it never could have place, and that the *sole* foundation of the duty of *allegiance* is the *advantage* which it procures to society by preserving peace and order among mankind" (*I*,35). What about chastity and the virtue of marital faithfulness? "The long and helpless infancy of man requires the combination of parents for the subsistence of their young; and that combination requires the virtue of chastity or fidelity. . . . Without such a *utility*, it will readily be owned that such a virtue would never have been thought of" (*I*,36). Incest, on the contrary, is morally abominable because of its undesirable consequences. All human interaction requires rules in order to achieve order and promote convenience. Indeed, human beings "cannot even pass each other on the road without rules" (*I*,40). And from the necessity of rules for the maintenance of public order and convenience arises morality: "Common interest and utility beget infallibly a standard of right and wrong among the parties concerned" (*I*,40).

The Approval of Utility: Self-Love or Sympathy?

But why does utility have such an influence over us? Why do we express moral approval of that which promotes the public good? Why do the public virtues have a "natural beauty and amiableness" for us? It must be because the public virtues promote an end which is "agreeable to us" and for which we have some "natural affection." But what is this end? According to Hume, there are two possibilities: self-interest, on the one hand, and the well-being of humankind, on the other. Is it self-love or sympathy for others[24] that makes utility and the public virtues attractive to us? Many moralists have attempted to derive morality from self-love, arguing that we approve of justice and the other public virtues because we see ourselves benefitting from their implementation. Hume disagrees: "the voice of nature and experience seems plainly to oppose the selfish theory" (*I*,44).[25]

Hume gives numerous examples that he thinks the selfish theory, the theory of egoism, has difficulty in accommodating: "We frequently bestow praise on virtuous actions performed in very distant ages and remote countries, where the utmost subtlety of imagination would not discover any appearance of self-interest or find any connection of our present happiness and security with events so widely separated from us" (*I*,44). Moreover, we often admire the bravery and nobility of our enemy (think, for instance, of the widespread American admiration for the Nazi general Rommel), which can hardly be explained in terms of self-interest. If the virtues of ancient heroes or current enemies are admired for their usefulness, it cannot be their usefulness *to us*. "It must therefore be the interest of those who are served by the character or action approved of; and these, we may conclude, however remote, are not totally indifferent to us" (*I*,46). It must be the case that we have some sympathy for the well-being of other people, indeed of mankind, if we are to understand why we express moral approbation of those acts, character traits, and institutions that promote this well-being. Although self-love is admittedly a principle in human nature of "extensive energy," the interests of society also engage our concern, and frequently we can explain our moral approval only by seeing its objects as serving these larger interests. "If usefulness, therefore, be a source of moral sentiment, and if this usefulness be not always considered with a reference to self, it follows that everything which contributes to the happiness of society recommends itself directly to our approbation and good will" (*I*,47).

In fact, Hume claims, "No man is absolutely indifferent to the happiness and misery of others" (*I*,47n1), and he points to the fact that sorrow and mourning affect us with melancholy and that "tears and cries and groans, never fail to infuse compassion and uneasiness" (*I*,48). We sympathize with the stutterer and "suffer for him." We concern ourselves with the fate of people and governments with whom we have little if any connection. Less laudably, Hume points out, our attachment to political parties shows a zealous commitment to concerns extending far beyond personal self-interest. The view that we are indifferent to the fate of others is simply not borne out by the facts of experience. "Would any man who is walking alone tread as willingly on another's gouty toes, whom he has no quarrel with, as on the hard flint and pavement?" (*I*,53) When self-interest is not an issue, we willingly take into account the happiness and misery of others in making decisions of policy and action. So at least *sometimes* we manifest a sympathy for others and a concern for their well-being, feelings far removed from the cold indifference suggested by the egoist. Hume readily acknowledges that we often act from self-interest and that few of us are always free of envy and a desire for revenge, but these motives, he claims, are not always present. Thus, "All mankind so far resemble the good principle that where interest or revenge or envy perverts not our disposition, we are always inclined, from our natural philanthropy, to give the preference to the happiness of society and, consequently, to virtue above its opposite" (*I*,54).

To be sure, our sympathy with others varies with distance, in that we more readily sympathize with family members close to us, and then again with our immediate circle of friends, and with the members of our community, than with human beings at far distance from us in terms of time and space. But the more humane we are, the larger the scope of our concern and the more vigorous our attachment to the needs of others. Such are the lessons of experience, which show that, in addition to any principle of self-love operative in us, there is also a benevolent principle. It is our tendency to find agreeable those actions benefitting others that underwrites and explains why we approve of those actions and practices that bring benefit to others. If we did not approve of the end, we would not approve of the means to it – the social virtues.

Different Forms of Virtue

In addition to the social virtues, there are modes of behavior approved by everyone because they are useful *to their possessor*. Discretion, for instance, is invaluable in the conduct of ordinary life and business. We commend the discrete person, not because her caution and perceptiveness benefit us, but because they benefit her. Likewise, industry and frugality are praised as moral virtues which are useful in attaining success and avoiding disaster. Honesty, fidelity, and truthfulness, in addition to the benefit they bring to society, "are also considered as advantageous to the person himself, and as the source of that trust and confidence which can alone give a man any consideration in life" (*I*,63). And then there is strength of mind, the ability to resist the temptations of the moment so as to secure future pleasure and happiness. Many other virtues benefitting the possessor – *selfish virtues*, Hume calls them – spring to mind: temperance, sobriety, patience, constancy, perseverance, considerateness, order, presence of mind, and so on. Hume remarks of these attributes of character that "the most determined skepticism cannot for a moment refuse the tribute of praise and approbation" to them (*I*,67). Our approval of these virtues – which, again, more often than not bring no benefit to us – cannot be derived from the principle of self-love. On the contrary, "there seems here a necessity for confessing that the happiness and misery of others are not spectacles entirely indifferent to us ... " (*I*,68).

Heretofore Hume has concentrated on the usefulness of certain character traits and dispositions. But some virtues, he grants, are praised because they bring immediate gratification to the person possessing them. They are valuable, not instrumentally, but in and of themselves. Their possession is itself a source of satisfaction or happiness. He places courage in this category, noting that it has "a peculiar lustre which it derives wholly from itself and from that noble elevation inseparable from it" (*I*,77). Likewise tranquillity, the virtue of the sage who "elevates himself above every accident of life and, securely placed in the temple of wisdom, looks down on inferior mortals engaged in pursuit of honors, riches, reputation, and every frivolous enjoyment" (*I*,79). And benevolence, that social virtue *par excellence*, is also a frame of mind immediately agreeable to the person possessing it and to those who behold it: ". . . the very softness and tenderness of the sentiment, its engaging endearments, its fond expressions, its delicate attentions, and all that flow of mutual confidence and regard which enters into a warm attachment of love and friendship – it will be allowed, I say, that these feelings, being delightful in themselves, are necessarily communicated to the spectators and melt them into the same fondness and delicacy" (*I*,80). Because of our "fellow feeling with human happiness," we derive immediate pleasure from an observation of courage, tranquillity, and benevolence in human beings, and thus, in addition to their usefulness, these qualities are "delightful in themselves."

Similarly, there are personal qualities that are praised, not because of their utility or the immediate pleasure they bring to their possessor, but because they are immediately agreeable to other people. Good manners fall into this category. "Among well-bred people a mutual deference is affected; contempt of others disguised; authority concealed; attention given to each in his turn; and an easy stream of conversation maintained, without vehemence, without interruption, without eagerness for victory, and without any airs of superiority" (*I*,84). Apart from the beneficial consequences of such good manners, they bring immediate pleasure to those who behold them. Likewise, *wit* and *ingenuity* communicate "a lively joy and satisfaction" to all who witness them. This immediate enjoyment is "a sure source of approbation and affection" (*I*,84). *Eloquence* and *modesty* are other virtues listed by Hume in this category. And there are also traits of character immediately *disagreeable* to the beholder, e.g., insolence, haughtiness, vanity. Ever the witty and ironic observer of human nature, Hume has this to say of vanity: "It seems to consist chiefly in such an intemperate display of our advantages, honors, and accomplishments, in such an importunate and open demand of praise and admiration as is offensive to others and encroaches too far on *their* secret vanity and ambition" (*I*,87–8). Thus the agreeable or disagreeable nature of some personal qualities is responsible for the approbation or disapprobation voiced in our judgments of people who possess them.

Hume concludes his investigation of the characteristics of personal merit by noting in summary that they consist "in the possession of mental qualities, *useful* or *agreeable* to the *person himself* or to *others*" (*I*,89). He claims to have shown that the virtues constituting personal merit elicit our approbation because of their usefulness or agreeableness. Moreover, the value we place in them arises from the fact that we approve not only what pleases us or is instrumental to our pleasure, but also what pleases others and is beneficial to them. He thinks he has shown that "there is some benevolence, however small, infused in our bosom; some spark of friendship for humankind; some particle of the dove kneaded into our frame, along with the sentiments of the wolf and serpent" (*I*,92).

Morality and the Sentiment of Humanity

In fact, Hume claims, it is only when we are motivated by sentiments favoring our fellow human beings that we enter the realm of morality:

> The notion of morals implies some sentiment common to all mankind, which recommends the same object to general approbation and makes every man, or most men, agree in the same opinion or decision concerning it. It also implies some sentiment so universal and comprehensive as to extend to all mankind, and render the actions and conduct, even of the persons the most remote, an object of applause or censure, according as they agree or disagree with that rule of right which is established (*I*,93).

Here Hume sets forth two conditions for calling a belief or judgment a *moral* one. First, it must be the expression of a sentiment "common to all mankind" – a sentiment shared by all or almost all human beings. Most of the passions are not common in the sense that all human beings feel them with regard to the same objects. Self-love, of course, is directed at the individual's own well-being, and each person's self-love is peculiar to herself and "arising from [her] particular circumstances and situation" (*I*,93). Many other passions – of hate and anger, for instance – are hardly felt by everyone toward the same objects. But the moral sentiment is one we expect all human beings to share with us. When speaking in moral terms, a person must "depart from his private and particular situation and must choose a point of view common to him with others: he must move some universal principle of the human frame and touch a string to which all mankind have an accord and sympathy" (*I*,93). The moral person, then, must be *disinterested* and *impartial*. These conditions are clearly satisfied when one approves an action on the basis of its usefulness to society or the public good. The sentiment of general benevolence, or what Hume calls the affection or *sentiment of humanity* is the moral sentiment *par excellence*. Although weak, it is a feeling found in almost all human beings. It expresses a "common point of view" and "though [the] affection of humanity may not generally be esteemed so strong as vanity or ambition, yet being common to all men, it can alone be the foundations of morals or of any general system of praise and blame" (*I*,93–4). Morality requires the operation of the universal sentiment of humanity.

The second condition imposed on moral sentiments by Hume is that they must "extend to all humanity" in the sense that all human beings must become the subjects of approbation or disapprobation in as much as they serve or oppose utility. Any approval of others that is based on self-love is directed only at those who assist self-interest. Thus the interested sentiment leads a person to judge only a limited number of other people. The case is different when the affection for humanity comes into play – one is thereby concerned with the well-being of *all* human beings and one passes judgment on *anyone* who affects this well-being:

> But if you represent a tyrannical, insolent, or barbarous behavior, in any country or in any age of the world, I soon carry my eye to the pernicious tendency of such conduct and feel the sentiment of repugnance and displeasure toward it. No character can be so remote as to be, in this light, wholly indifferent to me. What is beneficial to society or to the person himself must still be preferred. And every quality or action of every human being must by this means be ranked under some class or denomination expressive of general censure or applause   (*I*,94).

There is a difference, then, between the self-interested passions and the moral one. The moral passion, the sentiment of humanity, encompasses all human beings and societies, whereas the self-interested passions are aimed only at the improvement of oneself. Thus, Hume remarks, we make a distinction in language between morality and self-interest. The language of morality speaks to general usefulness and its opposite, and it presupposes that all human beings share the sentiment of humanity expressed in its judgments. Put otherwise, the principles of morality are "social and universal" (*I*,96).

The Source of Moral Obligation

But why should we obey these universal moral principles? What is the source of the obligation they impose on us? Many philosophers, Hume acknowledges, have maintained that the principles of social usefulness – harsh and demanding as they often are – have a claim on us only because we recognize that we too benefit from practices beneficial to society. In this way, they reduce moral obligation to a form of self-interested or prudential obligation. Hume thinks the reasoning behind such a position is muddled.

First of all, he notes that the tendency to paint morality in a harsh and forbidding light, to conceive of it as something highly demanding and therefore difficult and unpleasant, is far from the truth. We have seen that many moral virtues are immediately agreeable to us, and that, given the sentiment of humanity, the effort to promote general usefulness is also agreeable. Hume reminds us that "the immediate feeling of benevolence and friendship, humanity and kindness is sweet, smooth, tender, and agreeable, independent of all fortune and accidents" (*I*,102). Furthermore, not only is the effort to do our part for humanity and society agreeable, the more we engage in this effort the more we are assured of "the good will and good wishes" of others, which are themselves agreeable. Moral virtue, then, has its "engaging charms," and we "approach her with ease, familiarity, and affection" (*I*,99). He denounces the "monkish virtues" of self-denial, abstinence, and the like, claiming that they are no part of morality and actually are vices. Once we see morality in the right light, "the dismal dress falls off, with which many divines and some philosophers have covered her, and nothing appears but gentleness, humanity, beneficence, affability, nay, even at proper intervals, play, frolic, and gaiety" (*I*,99). The only difficult requirement that morality imposes on us, he claims, is that of "calculation and a steady preference of the greater happiness" (*I*,100).

Why, Hume asks, are we concerned that the pursuit of the moral qualities of justice and beneficence may interfere with the satisfaction of self-love? Only confusions about the nature of the human passions could lead to this concern. The central confusion is the idea that self-love and benevolence are in conflict with one another. In fact, Hume maintains, there is no more of a contradiction between the selfish and social sentiments than between the selfish and ambitious ones, or the selfish and vengeful ones. Here he makes the point Butler established earlier concerning the nature of the passions: "It is requisite that there be an original propensity of some kind, in order to be the basis to self-love, by giving a relish to the objects of its pursuit; and none more fit for this purpose than benevolence or humanity" (*I*,101). In order for a desire to be satisfied, it must attain its object, and it is the attainment of *just this* object that produces pleasure and satisfaction. Thus, the satisfaction of the sentiment of humanity is itself pleasurable, and this is true of all the benevolent passions we have. "Every affection ... when gratified by success, gives a satisfaction proportioned to its force and violence ... " (*I*,101–2). Thus there can be no contradiction between self-love and the sentiment of humanity, the satisfaction of the latter being, on the contrary, one of the means whereby the former is fostered.

But what about the "sensible knave," the person who recognizes that while "honesty is the best policy" may be a good general rule, it is one that has exceptions? The sensible knave observes the rules of justice for the most part, but on those occasions when he can break one of them without detection he does so, pursuing on those occasions his own advantage instead of the public welfare. In response to this objection, Hume urges that we be honest with ourselves concerning our feelings and passions. "But in all ingenuous natures the antipathy to treachery and roguery is too strong to be counterbalanced by any views of profit or pecuniary advantage" (*I*,103).[26] Moreover, the peace of mind we achieve when following moral rules and the awareness of our integrity in doing so are mental states which are themselves very agreeable and cherished by most people. And the knaves, what happens to them? Often they are caught in their own traps, yielding once too often to temptation, and thereby they lose their reputation and the trust of their fellow citizens. The inner mental state of the knave is hardly desirable: the tension, the necessity to be always on guard against detection. And what does the knave get for all his cunning and avarice: "worthless toys and gewgaws" which count for little when compared with the enjoyment of reputation and good character, the joys of society, and the "peaceful reflection on one's own conduct" (*I*,103).

For these reasons, Hume thinks, morality commends itself to us. We need not fear that it endangers our self-interest; on the contrary, it promotes it. But it does so, not because in a cunning and scheming manner we can promote our self-interest by appearing to be moral, but because the social sentiments, pursued for their own gratification, yield a level of satisfaction far outweighing the ever-threatened, ever-insecure pleasures of avarice and selfishness. With the satisfaction of the moral life before our minds, moral obligation should not be seen as a problem.

Thus we come to the end of Hume's moral philosophy. It stands sharply at variance with the moral thinking of many moral thinkers, although the muted subjectivism of Hobbes and Spinoza is not so far removed from it. Its emphasis on the central role of passion, as distinct from reason, makes it a forerunner of more contemporary forms of subjectivism, expressivism, and non-cognitivism. And its description of morality as a practice involving the pursuit of utility makes it a major forerunner of a long series of British utilitarian theories. Inasmuch as moral subjectivism and utilitarianism are central topics of most moral philosophy following Hume, we should see his thought as an important part of the foundation of recent and contemporary moral philosophy.

Critical Observations

We shall end this discussion of Hume's moral philosophy with a few critical observations about it. First, let us consider briefly the tension we noted early on between two components of this philosophy, the epistemological theory of the source of moral convictions and the theory of the reasons supporting these convictions. When Hume speaks of utility and the social virtues – when he is expressing his utilitarianism – it can appear that he is proposing an objectivist theory of morality.

The utility of a practice or institution is an objective matter; it is an observable fact that a particular practice or institution promotes the well-being of an individual or group or humankind as a whole. Any given practice either does or does not have among its consequences such beneficial results. Accordingly, utilitarianism can be seen a form of objectivism which bases moral rights and wrongs on objective facts about human nature and society. But when Hume the moral epistemologist speaks, he claims that morality is based on passion and sentiment, not on the discovery of facts through the use of experience and reason. How can Hume have it both ways?

There is only an appearance of inconsistency here. In his theory of the reasons for moral convictions, Hume is simply investigating the facts, or the beliefs about facts, that give rise to passions or sentiments which are then expressed in moral language. Our passions, he has acknowledged from the first, are often responses to what we believe. Our moral passions, including our sentiment of humanity, are affective responses to beliefs about the well-being of others. If we did not approve of the well-being of others, a belief that a certain practice fosters this end would "leave us cold," i.e., this belief would not translate into a moral conviction that this practice is morally admirable. Thus moral judgments – that a person has behaved virtuously, say, or that a society is a just one – do not (or do not just) describe facts; they express emotional responses to facts or to beliefs about them.

If we accept Hume's factual claim that human beings respond in positive ways to matters of the public good, and if we accept his conceptual claim that morality requires a universal or near-universal sentiment directed at all human beings, it would not be surprising that human beings often agree on moral matters and that their occasional disagreements are over purely factual issues. Noting the moral agreement and the factual disagreements, we might be led to think that morality is an objective, rational affair. But what we have here, in Hume's eyes, is simply widespread agreement in sentiment and occasional disagreement over the facts towards which we express these sentiments. Morality remains, he thinks, a non-objective creation of the passions. The intricacies of this kind of moral theory remained to be worked out by twentieth-century moral philosophers who call themselves emotivists or expressivists.[27] Although currently not a very popular theory among philosophers, emotivism or expressivism nevertheless seems to have enduring appeal and to have established itself as a major option among ethical theories.[28]

Is Hume an Emotivist?

It should not be thought that there is consensus regarding the classification of Hume as an early subjectivist or emotivist. David Norton has argued that Hume is in fact a "moral realist" who believes in the objective existence of moral qualities and who construes the moral sentiments as signs of these external realities and hence as the means by which we *know* of them.[29] The objective moral qualities are the virtues and vices. They are the enduring features of agents that promote or impede utility or the general good. Reason permits us to adduce objective empirical evidence showing that a person does or does not have a character trait that fosters utility, and the sentiment that this knowledge occasions is the sign of the moral worthiness or unworthiness of the trait. Although it is not reason, or reason alone, that detects the objective moral features in the world, the roles of reason and sentiment together suffice to provide us with moral knowledge. Thus, "Hume is a moral realist who believes that virtue and vice have objective status, and a realist for whom both sentiment and reason have significant epistemological roles to play."[30]

Norton's interpretation has been called an exaggeration of some important truths about Hume's ethics,[31] and it is certainly a minority view. Nevertheless it deserves the serious attention of all Hume scholars. Moreover, Norton highlights aspects of the role of reason in morality that are undeniably important for Hume. Reason, as he puts it, may in Hume's eyes be a slave of the passions, but it is not a chattel slave.[32] It can exercise significant control over the passions. For one thing, by showing that a passion is directed at a nonexistent object, or at an ineffective means to an end, it can in effect annihilate this passion. When it comes to the moral passions, reason can call attention to the difference between the operation of the sentiment of humanity and other passions, such as self-interest, that may be mistaken for it. That is to say, reason can detect and correct for our biases, and thereby determine that a certain character trait is truly an instance of moral virtue and that a particular person deserves moral admiration. It can correct for errors of partiality resulting from the fact that we naturally feel a more vivid sense of compassion for those closest to us, biologically and geographically. Reason can ascertain that a sentiment we feel is *not* shared by other spectators, and hence is not the moral sentiment. And, finally, reason provides the necessary information (about utility) on which the sentiment of humanity works, and, when it indicates a lack of utility, it can effectively negate a judgment of moral worth.

Recognizing the extensive role of reason in Hume's ethics allows us to conclude that even if his is a subjectivist theory at heart, such subjectivism is compatible with the claim that judgments of reasonableness are still possible in the moral life. Many contemporary emotivists and non-cognitivists attempt to show the same thing.[33]

The "Is/Ought" Controversy

Finally, there is the matter of Hume's notorious claim that ought-statements cannot be derived from is-statements. This claim exerted enormous influence on moral philosophy during the middle of the twentieth century. The passage in the *Treatise* where it is found (Book III, Part I, Section i, pp. 469–70, and see pages 240–1 above) is in effect the "sacred" text of those theories of non–cognitivism (emotivism, prescriptivism) which deny that moral judgments are true or false statements of fact, and which consequently deny that there can be any moral knowledge. In a related fashion, this passage is often cited in defense of the claim that morality is "autonomous," i.e., that moral judgments and convictions are not derived from, and hence not dependent on, any matters of fact concerning the world, human nature, or God – thus denying that science or theology is the ultimate arbiter of moral matters. But these various appropriations of the "is/ought" passage have not gone unchallenged. There have been scholarly rebuttals attempting to show that Hume did not intend in this passage to deny that moral propositions can be derived from factual ones. And there have been philosophical arguments designed to prove that Hume is simply wrong: that in many cases ought-statements *can* be derived from is-statements. We shall look briefly at both of these contentions.

Alasdair MacIntyre has argued that Hume's intent in the "is/ought" passage was to show only that ought-statements cannot be derived from *some* is-statements.[34] According to MacIntyre, Hume denied that moral judgments follow from theological statements about "eternal fitnesses" or statements about the will of God. There is a "gap" between the two kinds of judgment because the theological statements make no reference to human needs and interests. When the is-statements in question *do* make reference to these matters, then, MacIntyre thinks, Hume is perfectly willing to allow that they may yield moral judgments. This follows because Hume believes morality to be a natural phenomenon relating to human needs and interests, the very things that spark human passion and sentiment. MacIntyre notes the frequency with which Hume cites anthropological and sociological facts about how certain character traits or social rules promote the public interest, for instance in his discussion of justice. MacIntyre then refers to what he calls "bridge notions" – concepts such as *wanting*, *needing*, *pleasure* and the like – which are factual in nature but refer to aspects of human nature that are inextricably tied to our moral experience, including our sense of what we ought to do. MacIntyre argues that these bridge notions allow us to connect the facts to which they refer to moral claims, implying that this is what Hume was actually doing: "we can connect the facts of the situation with what we ought to do only by means of one of those concepts which Hume treats under the heading of the passions" (p. 261). Hume, therefore, should be seen as belonging to the long line of philosophers going back at least to Aristotle who treat morality as a matter of human interest and well-being – such is MacIntyre's verdict.

A similar rejection of the traditional understanding of the "is/ought" passage is given by Geoffrey Hunter.[35] He argues that Hume understood moral judgments themselves to be factual claims, which as such can obviously be derived from other factual claims (or is-propositions). Hunter cites the passage in which Hume says: "So that when you pronounce any action or character to be vicious, you mean nothing, but that from the constitution of your nature you have a feeling or sentiment of blame from the contemplation of it" (*T*, 469). A statement of this type is clearly factual, describing as it does a causal connection between observing an action or character trait and having a certain feeling toward it. Ought-propositions cannot be derived from statements about "relations of reason" or independent external objects, but they can be derived from statements that make reference to human sentiments. After all, Hunter takes Hume to be saying, they *are* such statements.

The re-interpretations of Hume by MacIntyre and Hunter have been vigorously rebutted by Antony Flew and W.D. Hudson.[36] They claim that Hume did not understand moral judgments to be descriptive statements of fact about human sentiments (e.g., "I feel disapproval on those occasions when I witness or hear of someone telling a lie") but rather took them to be *expressions* of sentiments (as, for example, when I express my anger by saying "Damn!" or my pleasure in a musical performance by saying "Bravo!"). If Flew and Hudson are correct about this, then Hume is the direct precursor of twentieth-century emotivism, which makes precisely the same distinction between descriptions and expressions of emotions and aligns moral judgments with expressions of approval and disapproval (Hume's approbation and disapprobation). If this debate over the correct interpretation of Hume teaches us anything, it is the importance of distinguishing between these two kinds of judgment. If moral judgments describe sentiments, then they are true or false and can yield moral knowledge – even if the subject matter of this knowledge is something subjective in nature. The view that accepts this account of them is the *cognitivist* theory of subjectivism. The view that moral judgments *express* such sentiments implies that they are not true or false but at most are sincere or insincere (as "Damn!" can be sincere or insincere). This is the *non-cognitivist* theory of emotivism. According to it, there can be no moral knowledge.

Putting the scholarly debate over the interpretation of Hume's text aside, there remains the philosophical issue of whether an "ought-statement" can be derived from an "is-statement." MacIntyre's view is that this can sometimes occur. He gives us the following example: "If I stick a knife in Smith, they will send me to jail; but I do not want to go to jail; so I ought not to (had better not) stick a knife in him."[37] The question arises as to whether there is a suppressed moral premise that renders the inference a valid deductive argument, a premise of the form "If it is the case that if I do x, the outcome will be y, then if I don't want y to happen, *I ought not to do x*." If there is such a *major premise* presupposed by the inference, then the example does not show an ought-statement being derived solely from an is-statement – rather, it reveals an ought-statement being derived from the combination of an is-statement *and* another ought-statement. The evaluative, moral nature of the conclusion would already be found in the major premise. MacIntyre is of the opinion that the argument should not be construed in this way. He argues that the alleged suppressed premise simply reproduces the original argument (this premise is a conditional statement proceeding from the two factual conditions, "if I do x, the outcome will be y" and "I don't want y to happen," to an evaluative conclusion, "I ought not to do x"). Any problem with the original inference would therefore arise with the suppressed premise. Thus, MacIntyre concludes, adding this premise doesn't help the logic of the situation. Or, conversely, if one accepts the suppressed major premise, one can accept the argument without this premise, in which case the ought-statement follows directly and solely from an is-statement.

Another contemporary philosopher, John Searle, is well known for his alleged derivation of an "ought" from and "is."[38] Consider, Searle suggests, the statement "Jones uttered the words 'I hereby promise to pay you, Smith, five dollars'." From this statement we are able to derive the moral claim "Jones ought to pay Smith five dollars." The initial statement is wholly descriptive and factual in nature. If we add to it definitions or conceptual clarifications of what "promising" means (viz., "to say 'I promise' is to make a promise" and "to promise is to place oneself under an obligation to do what one promises"), then, Searle argues, the ought-statement follows from the is-statement. He claims that none of the intermediate steps – the definitions or clarifications – are moral or evaluative in nature. If this is so, then there are no suppressed moral premises, and an ought-statement is derived solely from non-moral assertions. Searle's critics, of course, are convinced that his argument does involve a suppressed normative premise. And the debate goes on.

However he is interpreted, and whether he is right or wrong, Hume is largely responsible for the shape and direction of much twentieth-century "analytic" ethics. He was not an "analytic philosopher" himself – obviously so, analytic philosophy being a twentieth-century phenomenon – and his failure to make many of the very distinctions found in the works of ethical analysts often renders his writings ambiguous and unclear. But he is at one in spirit with many recent analysts, and he has set the terms for many of the debates in recent and contemporary moral epistemology.

Hume's subjectivism and naturalism contrast sharply with the ethical theory of the philosopher we shall study next, Immanuel Kant. Kant acknowledged Hume as the stimulus for much of his philosophical thinking, and Kant's philosophy is one of the most important critiques of the kind of empiricism Hume represents.

In place of Hume's subjectivism in ethics, Kant will erect a theory of rational objectivism; and in place of his naturalism, Kant will describe the human being in terms that include but also transcend nature. The debate between the two is unavoidable.

10

Kant

"Two things fill the mind with ever new and increasing wonder and awe, the oftener and the more steadily we reflect on them: the starry heavens above me and the moral law within me."[1] Thus does Kant begin the concluding section of his *Critique of Practical Reason*, a book devoted to charting the dimensions of "the moral law within" just as his earlier work, the celebrated *Critique of Pure Reason*, had charted, if not the starry heavens themselves, at least the conditions required for the possibility of our understanding them. As our knowledge of these heavens grows, Kant tells us, we become increasingly aware of our own relative insignificance as creatures of dust on a small speck of a rock within the vastness of the universe. But as our awareness of the moral law within us expands, we recoup our significance and dignity. As Kant puts it:

> The former view of a countless multitude of worlds annihilates, as it were,
> my importance as an *animal creature*, which must give back to the planet
> (a mere speck in the universe) the matter from which it came, the matter
> which is for a little time provided with vital force, we know not how. The
> latter, on the contrary, infinitely raises my worth as that of an *intelligence*
> by my personality, in which the moral law reveals a life independent of
> all animality and even of the whole world of sense   (*CPrR*, 169, 162).

It is as moral beings that we have value – infinite value; it is by virtue of the moral law within us that we transcend our status as mere animal-like creatures doomed to an insignificant life followed by death. It is philosophy, Kant maintains, that gives us insight into the moral law and hence into the source of our value and significance.

Immanuel Kant (1724–1804 CE) was not only one of the major thinkers of the Enlightenment period, he stands today as one of the greatest philosophers of all times. He was a prodigious writer. In addition to the two *Critiques* mentioned above, he wrote a third, the *Critique of Judgment*, which deals with issues in aesthetics. In ethics, there is also the *Groundwork of the Metaphysics of Morals* and the *Metaphysics of*

Morals. Our study of Kant's ethics will focus primarily on the *Groundwork*, a widely studied work which provides an overview of his ethical theory.

The *Groundwork of the Metaphysics of Morals* is a short book but one which is dense and difficult to read.[2] In it Kant stakes out the main contours of a revolutionary moral philosophy at odds with most of the ethical theories we have discussed so far, although echoes of Stoicism and aspects of Christian ethics can be recognized in many of its passages. If, in spite of its radical character, the content of the *Groundwork* appears familiar to the reader, this is possibly because Kant has achieved his aim of representing in his book the fundamental convictions of ordinary morality. His task, he maintains, is to develop a moral philosophy that *grounds* ordinary morality, showing clearly in what it consists and providing a much-needed philosophical defense of it. As we have noted several times already in preceding chapters, many observers agree that Kant does indeed have his finger on the pulse of ordinary morality. Many view him as achieving the most profound and moving expression of it available in the entire history of ethics. It behooves us, then, to study his ethical system with particular care.

The Good Will

"It is impossible to conceive anything at all in the world, or even out of it, which can be taken as good without qualification, except a *good will*"(61, 393). The only thing good without qualification, this first sentence of the *Groundwork* tells us, is a good will. Anything else, Kant warns, be it a talent of mind like intelligence or a quality of temperament like courage, can on occasion be put to ill use and thus be reduced to something vile and evil. A calm and temperate nature, for example, can become no more than the coolness of a scoundrel. Even happiness, Kant thinks, is not unconditionally good, since possessing it might lead a person to excessive boldness or pride. Happiness, which he takes to be well-being and contentment with one's state, cannot gain our unqualified approval unless it is graced by "a pure and good will" – "consequently a good will seems to constitute the indispensable condition of our very worthiness to be happy" (61, 393).

It is important to distinguish Kant's notion of an unconditional good from that of an intrinsic good. An intrinsic good is one that is good in and of itself, and it contrasts with an extrinsic or instrumental good, which is good only by virtue of promoting or leading to some other thing or state of affairs that is good. Kant believes that something might be intrinsically good – happiness or pleasure, for example – without being unconditionally good. As we have just noted, under certain conditions even happiness might fail to be good. Something is unconditionally good only if there are no such conditions that could negate its goodness.

The good will, Kant maintains, *does* have unconditional worth. A will that is good is so no matter what happens, there being no occasions or circumstances in which it can become contemptible. To be sure, a good will may lead one to act in ways that turn out to bring harm and suffering in their wake, but for all that we cannot find fault with the will once we acknowledge that it was good. Likewise, the good will may turn out to be ineffective and succeed in accomplishing little or nothing, but "even then it would still shine like a jewel for its own sake as something which has its full value in itself" (62, 394). This exaltation of the good will leads, of course, to the question what makes a will good. Its unconditional goodness rules out certain answers. The value of such a will clearly does not derive from its good effects, i.e., what it accomplishes in the world, since its effects, through no fault of the will, may not be good. We seldom have complete control over what happens as a result of our actions, and our goodness as human beings and moral agents cannot depend on whether by chance things happen to turn out well. In general, the consequences of acting on a good will cannot be the determinant of its goodness. The goodness of the will must lie, then, in its own nature: "it is good through its willing alone" (62, 394). *How* it wills, the character of its volitions – these are the factors that make it good, and unconditionally so. A will motivated by moral principle is always and necessarily good.

As Kant sees it, our moral status must be altogether within our control; it must be an expression of our status as free human beings. Whether or not we are good depends solely on us, and the one thing we have complete control over, as the ancient Stoics had insisted, is our own will. Thus our moral character is determined by our attitudes of mind, our effort of will – for the rest, who knows what will happen!

Kant believes that as we observe nature we find that no organ is without its distinctive purpose. In his view, nature has so ordered things that every organ or faculty has a function which it is ideally suited to perform.[3] What, then, he asks, is the function of the rational will? Contrary to Aristotle, Kant flatly denies that the purpose of such a will is to attain happiness for its human possessors. Surprisingly – for someone who is often considered a rationalist – Kant maintains that happiness is best achieved through a life of instinct, and that reason, far from promoting happiness, is often an obstacle to it. Reason can induce doubt and uncertainty; it can lead to an estrangement from the emotional life; it can be arid and unnourishing; it can promote chatter and argument, but little contentment. Better to live the life of a simple peasant, Kant seems to think, if happiness is one's goal.

If the attainment of happiness or the guiding of desire (what Kant calls inclination) is not the function of reason, then what is? It cannot be denied, Kant thinks, that reason is a "practical power," that it exists in us for the purpose of influencing the will. By denying it the role of guiding the will so as to achieve the things we want (the objects of inclination), we are forced to grant, Kant argues, that "its true function must be to produce a *will* which is *good*, not as a *means* to some further end, but *in itself*" (64, 396). Reason is given to us for the purpose of helping us attain the highest good of all: the good will.

Duty

Kant maintains that the establishment of a good will through the guidance of reason not only fails to serve inclination (desire) but also may "often involve interference with the purposes of inclination" (64, 396). In Kant's eyes, the moral life is often at odds with the temptations and pressures of inclination. Doing our *duty*, following the demands of reason and doing as we *ought*, doing what is *right*, these acts are often made difficult by the fact that we are driven in the opposite direction by what we desire, by what pleases us, by the demands of our sensuous nature. Contrary to a long line of thinkers who portray the moral life as consisting in efforts to support or perfect desire, Kant views it as a struggle to free ourselves from the influence of desire.[4] More than any other moral philosopher before him, Kant places the stern voice of duty at the heart of the moral life.

The opposition and conflict between inclination and duty does not always occur; there are occasions on which we find it pleasant to do our duty, just as there are people in whom the promptings of inclination and the demands of duty often neatly coincide. We have a duty, for instance, to help our neighbor, and some people, having big hearts and a generous nature, are temperamentally inclined to do just this. Kant warns us, however, that we should not be fooled by an occasional coincidence of inclination and duty into thinking that warm feelings for others bestow moral worth on our actions. Nor is it enough to act *in accordance with duty*, from whatever motive, in order for our behavior to have moral worth. Helping our neighbor is required by duty, but helping our neighbor has no moral worth if done out of an inclination to help others. *Moral worth* is achieved only if we act *from duty*, that is to say, only if we act out of an appreciation of the fact that the act is our duty. The realization that an act is our duty must be our motive for doing it, even if on some occasions inclination prompts us in the same direction. Inclination itself bestows no moral value on our behavior. What Kant alludes to as the *First Proposition* characterizing the concept of a good will is that, in order to have moral worth, an action must be done *from duty* (66,398).

Why, we might ask, is this so?[5] Why could not a motive of sympathy, say, bestow moral worth on an action. Two reasons suggest themselves. First, one might have sympathy toward a person or persons who do not deserve it, and, equally, one might not have it toward individuals who do deserve it. The immediate inclination of sympathy, then, is unreliable in that it might lead one to actions that are not morally right. In general it would be only a fortunate fact if this inclination did incline one to do what was right. Second, the motive of sympathy "lacks moral content" (66, 398), which is to say that the person who acts from it is not interested in doing what is right; such a person is interested only in satisfying the inclination of sympathy. But surely anyone who has no interest in the morality of what she does fails to act in ways that have *moral* worth. Thus, Kant argues, only the motive of duty bestows moral worth on an action.

If moral worth derives solely from the motive of acting from duty, the fact that we sometimes, indeed often, desire to do what it is also our duty to do causes an epistemological problem for us. How, in such cases, can we know that the action was engaged in as a result of an appreciation that it was one's duty? How can we know that an action has moral worth when duty and inclination point one in the same direction – e.g., when warm feelings of sympathy toward others and the duty of beneficence lead to the same action? It is difficult if not impossible to rule out the possibility that such an action is really motivated by inclination rather than by an appreciation of duty. In addition to "immediate inclinations" like sympathy, there is also the possibility of motivation by self-interest. The "dear self" or "self-love," as Kant puts it, often appears on the scene, and our motivation for doing our duty may in fact be our desire to further our own interests.[6] These possibilities lead Kant to suggest that the clearest examples of moral worth are found on those occasions when a person is not inclined to do her duty but does so nevertheless – the only possible motive in these cases being the sense of duty. A person may not like other people but nevertheless still go out of her way to help them, thereby providing us with a clear example of beneficent action having moral worth. A person may have lost all interest in life but nevertheless sustain her life – once again out of a sense of duty. In such cases, moral worth is evident.

Kant is sometimes read as recommending that in order to be moral we must do away with all inclinations when we act as morality demands.[7] This is not the point he is making. He is stressing the claim that one motive only – an appreciation of duty – makes one's behavior moral or gives it moral worth. Inclinations do not do so. When other motives (altruistic or self-interested) are also present, we simply cannot say with any certainty that the moral motive is the effective one. Nevertheless, it remains possible, for example, that a good-hearted person might help others out of a sense of duty, all the while wanting to do so but not allowing the supporting inclination to constitute the decisive motivation. Likewise, a shopkeeper might be honest out of an appreciation of duty, even while realizing that honesty serves her own interests.

Acting on Principle

What, more precisely, is the nature of the motivation that occurs when we act from a sense or appreciation of duty? The motive cannot be the fact that our action will achieve some specific goal or purpose, for such a fact would only show that the act served our desires. Whenever the *object* of our will (the thing in the world or state of affairs we want to obtain or realize) leads us to act, it is inclination that is at work, namely the desire to obtain this object. We don't act morally, for instance, if we help others because such a purpose or goal would be an object of desire, and the action that flowed from this desire would have no moral worth. Duty and inclination, we must remember, are often opposed and always distinct.

But if the motive of a morally worthy action cannot derive from the object of the action, then from what? Kant's answer is that moral worth depends "on the *principle of volition* in accordance with which, irrespective of all objects of the faculty of desire, the action has been performed" (68, 400). This is Kant's *Second Proposition* elucidating the concept of a good will. It is not the purpose or goal – the object of the action – but rather the principle or "maxim" guiding the will that bestows moral worth on the action and thereby on the agent. We act out of a sense of duty when we act *on principle*,[8] when we do what we do because we are enjoined to do so by a principle. A principle motivating our will is what Kant calls a "maxim."

Here Kant puts his finger on an idea that resonates in the minds of many readers. The moral life, he is saying, is the life of principle, and the moral person is the principled individual. Rather than act on the basis of the desires of the moment, the person of principle appeals to a general rule or rationally articulated reason in order to ascertain what to do. The principled individual is motivated by considerations of how in general one should act. But not just *any* principle will do, since one could follow the principle of self-interest and not thereby live a moral life. A moral person is one who is motivated by the principle of the moral law. The person of moral principle is the "man for all seasons" – it is this person who shows forth to the world the jewel that is the good will. The notion of the moral law must now be explained. It will take several steps to do so.

A complication arises with regard to acting on principle. In doing so, I might be motivated by the object of the principle itself, by *what* it enjoins me to do. I might follow the principle "Never tell a lie" *because I want to avoid lying*. But in such a case it is once again inclination, not duty, that motivates me: the desire not to lie is the decisive factor. Hence, in order for my principled act to flow from an appreciation of duty, it cannot be motivated by the object or *content* of the principle. Rather, it must be motivated by the *form* of the principle.

Reverence for the Law

What does Kant mean by the form of a principle? In the first place, a principle *enjoins* or *commands* an action of a certain kind. A principle is not a mere statement of what will happen or has happened or is now happening. It is an imperative telling us *to do* or *not to do* something. Examples of non-moral imperatives are "Shut the door," "Report at noon," "Don't walk on the grass." A moral imperative, in Kant's eyes, has the form of a *law*, e.g., "Always tell the truth." Thus when we act from duty, we must be acting because a law demands it; we are then acting out of respect for law, or, as Kant expresses it, out of reverence for law. And so he writes, *"Duty is the necessity to act out of reverence for the law"* (68, 400). This is Kant's *Third Proposition* articulating the concept of a good will. It is reverence for law *qua* law – "bare law", as Kant puts it – that must be the decisive motive. Acting from duty consists in and derives its moral worth from acting on a principle because it *is* a principle, because it is a law. "Therefore nothing but the *idea of the law* in itself, *which admittedly is present only in a rational being* – so far as it, and not an expected result, is the ground determining the will – can constitute that pre-eminent good which we call moral, a good which is always present in the person acting on this idea and should not be awaited merely from the result" (69, 401).

The notion of the law being present only to a rational being allows us to summarize the course of Kant's argument so far. The role of reason is not to promote happiness or the ends of inclination. The primary role of reason is not even to formulate principles which guide us in attaining certain objects of inclination. The function of reason is to provide a distinctive form of motivation, namely motivation to act because a law requires it. Reason gives us the idea of law, the idea of principles telling us what we must always do, and thus reason makes it possible for the will to achieve goodness.

But why should the idea of law be attributed to, and flow from, reason and reason alone? The answer lies in two formal properties of principles that have the form of laws: their universality and their necessity. A principle tells one what to do – *always* (or always on the occasion of certain circumstances). Some principles have an even higher level of universality: they tell *everyone* (or everyone of a certain description) how (always) to act. Universality, for Kant and many philosophers since the time of Plato, is a mark of reason. Hence only reason can command us to act on universal principles and laws. As we shall see, it is this feature of universality which leads Kant to his first formulation of the fundamental principal of morality, what he will call the "categorical imperative."

Another mark of reason is necessity, the property of being absolutely required. Nature and experience, Kant argues, reveal no necessities to us – at most they show us that some things always happen in certain ways, not that they *must* do so. It is reason, and reason alone, that reveals necessity, as in the case of the geometrical necessity that a straight line bisecting one parallel line at a ninety-degree angle bisect the other at a ninety-degree angle as well. Reason at work in geometry and in logic is able to lay down what must happen or what must be the case. Likewise, the necessity attaching in morality to law – the absolute requirement that we behave in certain ways – must be a product of reason.

If duty is the requirement to act out of respect for the law, what is this law we must obey? As Kant puts it: "But what kind of law can this be, the thought of which, even without regard to the results expected from it, has to determine the will if this is to be called good absolutely and without qualification?" (69–70, 402). We are not to follow a principle or law because of its content or what might result from following it, so the only reason we can have for following it is that it has *the formal characteristics of law*, namely universality and necessity. So, whatever maxim I act on, I must be assured that it has, or can have, the form of universality and necessity. I must know that it is or can be a principle that *all* rational creatures have a duty to obey (*must* obey), and I must obey it because of this formal property. If I obey it for this reason, then, as Kant expresses it, "bare conformity to universal law as such (without having as its base any law prescribing particular actions) is what serves the will as its principle, and must so serve it if duty is not to be everywhere an empty delusion and a chimerical concept" (70, 402). It is not because a principle prescribes some particular action (say helping others) that I should be motivated to obey it; I should be motivated to obey it simply because of its being a universal and necessary law.

The Categorical Imperative

Reason expresses this requirement of duty in the following way: "I ought never to act except in such a way *that I can also will that my maxim should become a universal law*" (70, 402). Formulated in strictly universal terms (addressed to "everyone") and as a command, the requirement of duty reads "Act only on that maxim through which you can at the same time will that it should become a universal law" (88, 421). This requirement Kant calls the *categorical imperative*. As we shall see, there are various formulations of the categorical imperative. The present one is what commentators refer to as the *Formula of Universal Law*. Here we have the first formulation of the *moral law*, or the first elucidation of its nature.

Kant gives an example of how this moral law – this requirement of duty – can guide and constrain one's actions. On some occasion I might be tempted to make a promise (to return some money, say) with no intention of keeping it, simply because I am hard pressed at the moment. The maxim of my act might be something like this: "I will make a false promise if doing so will get me out of difficulty." The question is, can I universalize this maxim and will (decide) to act on the resulting universal principle? Only if my answer is affirmative would my willing have moral worth. Can I, then, will that everyone follow the maxim that enjoins false promises on those occasions when doing so would get them out of difficulty? Kant maintains (for reasons we shall consider presently) that one cannot universalize this maxim, and therefore he concludes that willing to act on the maxim of deceitful promises has no moral worth, and, indeed, that acting on this maxim is wrong and prohibited. This willing and this action have no moral worth because the will cannot be construed as motivated by the fact that its maxim possesses universality (and thus is the expression of a law).

The maxim of false promises, Kant urges, cannot be taken to possess universality – a person cannot will that making false promises as a means of extricating herself from difficulty be a universal law. Why not? Kant's argument at this point is subject to various interpretations[9] and in the end does not succeed in convincing all of his readers. Nevertheless, it is a strong argument, especially if we keep in mind what it is meant to accomplish. The goal of the argument is to show that, if I attempt to universalize the maxim of false promises, I involve myself in an *inconsistency*. This inconsistency will result from the fact that, if everyone were to act on the maxim of lying promises, no one would believe what anyone promises.

There are two ways to bring out the inconsistency involved in attempting to universalize the maxim of a lying promise. First, the inconsistency can be said to lie between my willing the maxim "I may make a promise and not keep it when it is advantageous for me not to do so" *and* my willing the universal maxim "Everyone may make promises and not keep them when it is to their advantage not to do so." The obvious consequence of everyone making false promises would be that no one would trust anyone else. Thus one could interpret the inconsistency involved in willing the universal maxim of false promises to be practical in nature: what I want to obtain by acting on my non-universalized maxim is thwarted by the consequences of everyone acting on the universal maxim. I would not be able to accomplish what I want by making a lying promise if everyone were to make them.

Second, the inconsistency involved in universalizing the maxim of making lying promises can be seen as logical in nature. It is possible to make a promise that others will believe only if there is a general practice of making promises and (for the most part) keeping them. In willing or intending to make a lying promise in a world in which everyone else makes lying promises, I am intending to do so in a world in which the practice of promise-making and promise-keeping will have disappeared. But it is logically inconsistent to talk of making promises in a world in which there are no promises.

The logical inconsistency comes out in another way as well. If my maxim were universalized, the person to whom I promise to repay the loan will not believe that I shall keep my promise. Thus, in making a false promise on the universalized maxim of false promises, I expect my potential benefactor both to believe that I shall pay him back (otherwise I wouldn't make the promise to him) and not to believe that I shall pay him back (because he wouldn't do so if the maxim were universalized). My two expectations clash – they are inconsistent, indeed contradictory. Acting on the maxim of lying promises – making a false promise – presupposes that I believe others will trust me; acting on the universal maxim implies that I believe no one will do so. Here the inconsistency is a logical one between my two beliefs. As a rational person, I cannot will what is contradictory. Thus in making a false promise I cannot universalize the maxim of my action.

In failing the test of universal law (or of universalizability, as one might call it), it follows that the maxim of false promises cannot be a maxim I obey because of its lawfulness (its universality). Thus in acting on this maxim I cannot do my duty and act from duty. Any action actually based on such a maxim, then, has no moral worth, and a will cannot be a good will if it is determined by this maxim. The maxim enjoining false promises "cannot fit as a principle into a possible enactment of universal law" (71, 403). Although I can will to make a false promise or to lie, "I can by no means will a universal law of lying" (71, 403).

Another Formulation

Later in the *Groundwork* Kant provides an alternative expression of the law of duty that commands us to act only on maxims we could will to become universal laws. In willing that a maxim become a universal law, we are in effect willing that it govern the behavior of human beings and thus become a universal law *of nature*, nature being the realm of things and persons governed by law. Thus we have the following rendition of the Formula of Universal Law: "Act as if the maxim of your action were to become through your will a UNIVERSAL LAW OF NATURE" (89, 421). This alternative expression allows Kant to clarify the application of the categorical imperative to concrete cases. In asking ourselves whether we can universalize the maxim of our action, we are in effect asking whether there could be a world, a system of nature, which embodied and was governed by this universal law. Is a world in which this law held sway a *possible* world, one which could exist?

Returning to the case of making false promises, could we will that the world incorporate the law of making false promises as a means of extracting oneself from difficulty? Kant maintains that such a system of nature would be internally inconsistent. As we have seen, universalizing the maxim of false promises would in effect destroy the practice of promising. "For the universality of a law that every one believing himself to be in need may make any promise he pleases with the intention not to keep it would make promising, and the very purpose of promising, itself impossible, since no one would believe he was being promised anything, but would laugh at utterances of this kind as empty shams" (90, 422). There could be no world in which everyone made promises in accordance with the principle of false promises – *promises* would not exist in this world. The very idea of such a world harbors a logical contradiction: it is a world in which everyone makes lying promises *and* a world in which there are no promises.

Kant gives another example of how a universalized maxim would create an internally incoherent world or system of nature. Consider the maxim "From self-love I make it my principle to shorten my life if its continuance threatens more evil than it promises pleasure." By self-love Kant means the motive of acting to benefit oneself, to enhance one's satisfactions, to improve oneself. Thus his question is whether there could be a system of nature in which this motive leads to and justifies suicide. And his answer is no:

> The only further question to ask is whether this principle of self-love can become a universal law of nature. It is then seen at once that a system of nature by whose law the very same feeling whose function is to stimulate the furtherance of life should actually destroy life would contradict itself and consequently could not subsist as a system of nature   (89, 422).

The function of self-love being "to stimulate the furtherance of life," it would be impossible for this motive to justify one in taking one's life or shortening it – the very opposite of furthering life. In identifying the purpose of self-love as being that of "furthering life," Kant is appealing to his teleological conception of nature in which all organs, faculties, and natural tendencies have a purpose. If one accepts this general conception *and* Kant's view of the function of self-love, then to conjecture a world in which self-love leads to a shortening of life would indeed be to involve oneself in an inconsistency – a teleological one. And given that an inconsistent system of nature cannot exist, it would follow that the maxim enjoining the shortening of life out of self-love cannot be a law of nature. Most philosophers today do not accept a teleological conception of nature (and human nature), and therefore they find Kant's argument with respect to this example quite weak.

Kant claims that there are other cases in which, while it is possible to conceive of a certain system of nature existing, we nevertheless cannot *will* that a system of this sort come into being. Such a world would be inconsistent with something else that, as rational creatures, we necessarily will. Consider the case of a world in which all people neglect their natural talents. Such a world is possible; it may even actually exist – Kant gives the example of the South Sea Islanders. But he denies it is possible for a person to will that the maxim of neglecting one's talents become a law of nature: "For as a rational being he necessarily wills that all his powers should be developed, since they serve him, and are given to him, for all sorts of possible ends" (90, 423).

Many find Kant's argument here highly suspect, but, again, it can be interpreted in ways that give it some degree of force (at least from Kant's standpoint). First of all, the argument may point to another teleological inconsistency. If talents exist for the purpose of assisting an agent in obtaining her ends, not to use them for this purpose would be to defy their natural reason for being (*telos*). No rational agent, Kant may be saying, would do this. Second, a rational agent is one who, in willing an end, necessarily wills the means necessary to achieving it.[10] In willing "all sorts of possible ends," a rational agent will therefore will to use the talents which serve her as means to attaining these ends. Insofar as talents are means to her possible ends, a rational agent necessarily wills the utilization of these talents. Not to do so would mean she is not fully rational. Thus a realm of nature in which talents are ignored would be inconsistent with something else a rational person necessarily wills.

One might rephrase Kant's point about talents in the following way (which may or may not be Kantian in its spirit). A *talent* by definition seems to be a characteristic that *benefits* a person, one that can be used to the advantage of that person in many different ways. To acknowledge that one has a talent, then, is to acknowledge that one would be wise to use it. Thus one would be less than rational if one deliberately willed to ignore (all of) one's talents. In doing so one would be deciding not to pursue the advantages and benefits that could be obtained by the use of these talents. Deliberately to avoid benefits to oneself can only be deemed irrational. Hence a rational person cannot *will* to ignore her talents and thus cannot will a world in which the maxim to ignore talents is a law of nature.

A situation similar to the neglect of talents would arise, Kant argues, if we were to attempt to universalize the maxim not to help others who are in need. While there could be a system of nature, a world, in which all human beings are indifferent to the needs of others, it would be impossible, Kant thinks, for a rational human being to will such a world: "For a will which decided in this way would be at variance with itself, since many a situation might arise in which the man needed love and sympathy from others, and in which, by such a law of nature sprung from his own will, he would rob himself of all hope of the help he wants for himself" (91, 423). Would it be possible to will into being a world in which no one sympathized with others and helped them in time of need? Logically, such a world could exist – its description is not self-contradictory. But for a person to will such a world would be to will deliberately that she herself be denied such sympathy and help when she needed them. Given the obvious fact that all of us at some time or another need assistance from others (the fact that none of us is self-sufficient), it would be irrational for any individual to will into existence a world in which this help would not be forthcoming. Thus Kant claims that a rational person would not will into being a world of reciprocal indifference, because such a world would be inconsistent with something else this person necessarily wills, namely that on some occasions others help her. It follows that the maxim which would be the law of such a world cannot pass the test of universalizability.

Perfect and Imperfect Duties

Kant notes a difference between the duties prescribed by reason in the first two examples and those prescribed in the second two. Our duty to preserve our lives (and not commit suicide) and our duty to keep our promises (not to make lying promises) are what he calls "perfect or strict duties"; those to develop our talents and to help others "imperfect duties." The former, perfect duties bind us always: we are, for instance, *never* to make a lying promise, just as we are never to tell a lie. The latter, imperfect duties allow a certain amount of leeway in how we fulfill them – in how we develop our talents (and how much so), or in the matter of whom we help (insofar as we cannot help everyone in need) and how much we do to help them. We cannot make exceptions in the case of perfect duties, since willing to do so would be to will an inconsistent system of nature, one that *cannot* exist. Exceptions are possible in the case of imperfect duties, since no self-contradiction is involved in willing a system of nature in which these exceptions are allowed.

The requirement of universalizability serves as a criterion for determining if an agent manifests a good will. It also is a criterion for determining what acts are morally obligatory and what acts are morally permissible (and impermissible). It does both of these things by identifying those maxims that are, and those that are not, universalizable. If one acts on a maxim that is universalizable (and acts on it because it is so), then one's will manifests a respect for law as such and qualifies as a good will. And if the maxim of one's act is universalizable, then the act enjoined by this maxim is morally permissible. In the case of maxims that *cannot* be universalized, the acts they enjoin are morally *impermissible* and it is our obligation not to engage in them. For example, because one cannot universalize the maxim of making lying promises, it is impermissible to make such promises, i.e., it is one's obligation (to others) not to do so. Because one cannot universalize the maxim permitting suicide, it is one's duty (to oneself) not to commit suicide. When it comes to the imperfect duties, the situation is a bit more complicated. We cannot will to universalize the maxim of ignoring the plight of others, so it is our duty not to do so; but insofar as this duty is imperfect, our obligation is to help others on appropriate occasions, not always. Likewise, it is morally impermissible to ignore all of our talents, but our obligation is only to develop some of them.

In arriving at the command that we always act in ways such that we can will the maxims of our actions to be universal laws (of nature), Kant sees himself as having arrived at the fundamental principle of morality. It is also, he thinks, the first principle of "ordinary human reason" in its practical dimension. The categorical imperative is the analog in the practical area of the principle of non-contradiction in the theoretical area.[11] In bringing this principle to light, he tells us, "we merely make reason attend, as Socrates did, to its own principle" (72, 404). This first principle of practical reason provides us, Kant believes, with a test of both duty and the goodness of the will. It is our moral compass, the one we actually use in everyday life – the one we vaguely have in mind when we ask "what would happen if everyone did that?" In Kant's eyes, this common-sense question probes the logical consistency, or rationality, of everyone willing to do a certain act. It does not inquire into the "utility" – the value or disvalue – of the consequences of so willing.

The categorical imperative commands us with necessity and universality, Kant maintains, and in doing so it turns aside the often insistent, turbulent demands of inclination. Because we are creatures who can be influenced not only by reason but by inclination as well, the demands of reason are received by us as commands. If we were perfectly rational creatures – as we surely are not – what is objectively required by reason would be the natural manner in which we always will and act – it would be what we do as a matter of course (in Kant's terminology, it would be "subjectively necessary"). But being creatures of inclination, what is rationally valid ("objectively necessary") only contingently guides our will (that is, it may or may not do so on any given occasion), and this contingent determination of the will is experienced as *necessitation*, as what we *ought* to do. Such *oughts* or commands are expressed as imperatives, and hence duty speaks to us in the form of imperatives.

Hypothetical and Categorical Imperatives

Imperatives, Kant tells us, come in two forms: they command either hypothetically or categorically. If reason ascertains that a certain act is required (necessitated) in order for a person to achieve a goal set by desire, reason will issue a hypothetical imperative commanding that person to engage in this action. The imperative would say in effect: if you want x, you ought to do y. Thus "Hypothetical imperatives declare a possible action to be practically necessary as a means to the attainment of something else that one wills (or that one may will)" (82, 414). A categorical imperative, on the contrary, commands an action because of the value of that action itself – because of its objective necessity or rational validity: "A categorical imperative would be one which represented an action as objectively necessary in itself apart from its relation to a further end" (82, 414). "One ought never to tell a lie" is an example of a categorical imperative, while "if you want to get out of this jam, you had better lie about your role in what happened" is an example of a hypothetical one. Actions commanded as means to goods other than the actions themselves are the subjects of hypothetical imperatives; actions commanded as good in themselves are the subjects of categorical imperatives.

It is clear that there is a close connection between hypothetical imperatives and inclination. If a person desires a certain object, reason will issue a hypothetical imperative directing her to pursue the means to attaining it. Desires or inclinations notoriously vary from one person to another, and hence a hypothetical imperative directed at one person would not apply to another individual who does not have the desire that grounds or justifies the imperative. And the person who has the desire may escape the necessity of obeying the imperative simply by renouncing the desire.

Hypothetical imperatives deriving from variable and avoidable desires are categorized by Kant as *problematic* practical principles – they are rules of skill. But at least one desire, the desire for happiness, appears to be universal, and hence imperatives that command certain actions as means to the achievement of happiness are not problematic; they are, rather, *assertoric*. In the name of prudence, reason commands all of us to do the things necessary for the attainment of happiness, and, given our ever-present desire for happiness, we have no way of escaping these commands. Still and all, these assertoric commands remain hypothetical: "an action is commanded, not absolutely, but only as a means to a further purpose" (83, 416). Moreover, insofar as it is difficult, indeed near-impossible, to define the content of happiness, which content may vary from one person to another, assertoric hypothetical commands are at best *counsels*, not strict rules.

But when reason sets forth the laws of duty, it does so by issuing categorical imperatives, the commands in question having nothing to do with aiding and abetting desire. The imperative of morality, as distinct from hypothetical imperatives, is *unconditioned*, not being based on any desire, and *absolute*, not being variable because it is not dependent on any variable or contingent desire. It does not amount to a rule of skill (like the problematic imperative) or a counsel of prudence (like the assertoric imperative). It is a *law* which is unconditionally, objectively, and universally valid and necessary. Moreover, "It is concerned, not with the matter of the action and its presumed results, but with its form and with the principle from which it follows ... " (84, 416). It is this imperative of morality, this *categorical imperative*, that reason issues to us in its on-going battle with inclination. Thus we can describe the principle identified above – "One ought never to act except in such a way that one can also will that one's maxim should become a universal law" – as a categorical imperative. As Kant reformulates this principle a bit later, in clearly imperatival form, it reads "Act only on that maxim through which you can at the same time will that it should become a universal law" (88, 421). Insofar as an action has moral worth only if it is done from duty, in a sense there is only one categorical imperative, the one that demands of us that we act on maxims or principles we can universalize and that we act on them *because* they can be universalized, i.e., that we act from respect for the law. Thus Kant often refers to the Formula of Universal Law as *the* categorical imperative.

Are we justified in following the stern taskmaster, reason, who commands us in this categorical fashion? The claims of inclination are as relentless as those of reason and often will push us in directions opposite to those of duty. Why should we follow reason and not inclination? After defining and distinguishing hypothetical and categorical imperatives, Kant raises the question of how we *come by* or *come to have* these imperatives. What form of reasoning leads us to them, and, at the same time, *justifies* them. Most importantly, how can a law that commands us in a universal manner and with necessity be justified? How can it come to have a "grip" on the will. In Kant's terminology, what *grounds* the categorical imperative?

The Ground of the Categorical Imperative

There is little mystery about the ground of hypothetical imperatives and the process of reasoning by which we come to accept them. They command someone to take an action required as the means to obtaining a certain object of inclination of that person, for instance, "if you want to succeed at university, study hard." Such an imperative is derived by a process of reasoning something like the following: first, I desire (will) the end (succeeding at university); second, I recognize the rationality of willing the means to any end that I desire [according to Kant "If I fully will the effect, I also will the action required for it" is a proposition that is necessarily true by definition (analytic) and will be accepted by every rational person (85, 417)]; third, I recognize that studying hard is a necessary means to succeeding at university; fourth, and last,

I will the means (studying hard). In this fashion reason arrives at the hypothetical imperative to study hard. The ground of such an imperative is the contingent and subjective end of succeeding at university.

If this is how we derive and simultaneously justify hypothetical imperatives, it is clear that we cannot use exactly the same model to justify the categorical imperative. The latter is not, as we have seen, a command to engage in an action instrumental to attaining an end of inclination. It commands us absolutely, not hypothetically and relatively. Thus the ground of the categorical imperative cannot be a contingent and subjective end of inclination. How, then, is such a categorical command to be derived and justified?

The derivation of the categorical imperative, although different in crucial ways from that of hypothetical imperatives, nevertheless has the same general form. What if there were something, Kant asks, that is absolutely and necessarily valuable, not simply because, as with happiness, all human beings happen to desire it, but because reason deems it to be an end-in-itself, objectively valuable regardless of whether or not it is recognized by all human beings as such? This objective end could serve as the ground of the categorical imperative. If there were an end of absolute worth, then any action that is a means necessary to attaining it would be required of all human beings – and again, not because they *happen* to desire this end but because it is valuable absolutely in itself. Thus the categorical imperative could be seen as commanding us to do what is necessary to achieve this end-in-itself. In this way, the absolute value of the end and the necessity of the actions required to achieve it would justify the categorical imperative.

Persons as Ends-in-Themselves

At this point Kant postulates that there *is* an end-in-itself having absolute value: "Now I say that man, and in general every rational being, *exists* as an end in himself, *not merely as a means* for arbitrary use by this or that will: he must in all his actions, whether they are directed to himself or to other rational beings, always be viewed *at the same time as an end*" (95, 428). Kant does not attempt to prove the truth of this postulate; in the end he doubts that it can be proved. But he notes that every rational individual conceives of her own existence this way – as an end-in-itself and not just as a means. Thus "Rational nature exists as an end-in-itself" serves as a basic principle or assumption of all rational and moral thinking. We presuppose and appeal to it, Kant believes, when we draw the distinction between a *person* and a *thing*. Each of us is a person, not just a thing to be used, a means to someone else's pleasure or well-being, and our personhood consists in our status as a rational agent of worth. All persons *qua* rational agents have unconditioned value in themselves as ends – such is the pronouncement of reason and morality.

How does the postulate of the rational person as an end-in-herself help Kant with his problem of demonstrating the ground and the derivation of the categorical imperative? His argument here is not explicit or highly developed, but we can take him to suggest something like the following train of thought. If all rational beings are ends-in-themselves, we treat them as such only if we refuse to make any arbitrary distinctions among them, distinctions that would demote some of them to the status of mere things to be used by others. We must, that is to say, act consistently toward all rational beings. Hence whatever we conceive to be right for ourselves, we must also conceive to be right for other rational creatures – *all* of them. And whatever commands to action we give to others, we must give to ourselves as well; whatever duties we assign to them, we must also impose on ourselves. Hence we arrive at the principle of universalizability: "Act only on that maxim through which you can at the same time will that it should become a universal law." This principle, the categorical imperative, enjoins precisely the kind of consistent action required in order to treat all rational beings as ends-in-themselves. To show this, is to demonstrate how as rational beings we can come to accept the categorical imperative.

Kant's postulate of rational nature as an end-in-itself not only allows him to demonstrate the derivation of the categorical imperative, it also leads him to another formulation of this supreme principle of morality. If we accept the postulate of rational nature as an end in itself, a practical imperative follows from it: "*Act in such a way that you always treat humanity, whether in your own person or in the person of any other, never simply as a means, but always at the same time as an end*" (96, 429). This principle, Kant maintains, is simply an alternative expression of the categorical imperative, i.e., of the fundamental principle of morality. It is what commentators call the Formula of Humanity.

In this formulation of the categorical imperative, Kant hits upon a principle that many philosophers today would agree is indeed the most fundamental principle of morality. We are never to treat human beings merely as things; we must always recognize that they are persons and hence have absolute worth in themselves. As we can see if we apply this principle to two of the four concrete examples already considered, it yields intuitively plausible accounts of why we morally should not act in certain ways. To make a false promise to another is surely to *use* that person for one's own ends only and to fail to acknowledge her as an end-in-herself. To refuse to help and support others is to fail to see them as having value in and of themselves, since were we to acknowledge their value, their well-being would be our end as well. Once again Kant notes a difference between our strict or perfect duties and our imperfect ones. In the case of false promises or lies, in so acting I always do wrong to the other person, something I ought never to do. Hence my duties not to make false promises or lie to others are strict. With regard to my imperfect duty to help others, Kant remarks that it is imposed on us not only as a way of acknowledging that others are worthy ends in themselves but also as a way of *advancing* their ends. Fully to appreciate that others are ends in themselves involves – at least on some suitable occasions – making their ends, their goals, our own. My duties to assist them in attaining these personal goals are more flexible than my obligations not to wrong them. My honoring these duties brings merit upon me, even though I am not absolutely required to honor these duties in any specific way. They are "meritorious" duties.

It should be noted that the categorical imperative to treat human beings as ends-in-themselves does not require that we abstain from treating others as means to our own ends. It prohibits us from treating them *merely* as such. Life in society is based on instrumental interactions among people, and we could not survive unless other people served our interests and we theirs. The point is that morally they cannot be reduced to mere servants or slaves. While we appropriately ask and at times demand that they do things for us, we must all the while keep in mind that they too are rational agents, with wills of their own and personalities absolutely valuable in themselves. The moral law resides within them too, and gives them worth beyond their "animal" status.

The Formula of Autonomy

There is still a third formulation of the categorical imperative. It commands us "to act always on the maxim of such a will in us as can at the same time look upon itself as making universal law" (100, 432). This expression of the categorical imperative is called the Formula of Autonomy. Kant believes this formulation follows from the two prior ones, a derivation which proceeds something as follows. Kant tells us that "the will of a rational being must always be regarded as *making universal law*, because otherwise he could not be conceived *as an end in himself*" (102, 434). As we have noted, if we are ends-in-themselves having absolute value as rational creatures, it is morally impermissible for us to be treated as things, and thereby manipulated, used, or exploited by others for their own ends. This implies that in point of fact we do not just move about, act, as the result of external forces – we are not just *things*. We also initiate our own actions; we decide what our ends will be and we set about intentionally and deliberately to attain them. Such a description of ourselves implies that, at least on some occasions, we act freely or *autonomously*. On occasions when our actions are not the product of our freedom, when, for instance, they are the result of forces outside us, they are, to use Kant's term, *heteronomously* produced. Insofar as we are rational beings, and rational beings are those from whom universal laws are derived, we are autonomous beings in our capacity to will according to the principle of universalizability. Thus we come to have the idea "of the will of every rational being as a will which makes universal law" (98, 431). This idea in turn is the foundation for the imperative that we always act in such a way as to see ourselves not only as the subject of law but also as the supreme lawgiver who *makes the law*.

Another line of argument leading to the Formula of Autonomy – the one Kant explicitly uses – proceeds by asking what reason we would have to obey the moral law if we were *merely* the *subjects* of this law. In such circumstances, reason could only indicate to us that it is in our *interest* to obey the law. Such an appeal to interest, however, is an appeal to inclination, and any action resulting from this appeal would be heteronomously produced insofar as it arises out of something outside our rational nature. If our motive for obeying the law is to be respect for it rather than some calculation serving inclination – as it must be if we are to act morally – we must be more than the subjects of this law; we must also be the originators of it, its *legislators*. We can respect the law only if it is self-imposed. Only in this way can the law be *unconditioned*, that is to say, not based on some interest or inclination. Our autonomy requires that the moral law be self-legislated.

Once again Kant seems to have hit upon an idea that is central to the moral thinking of most people, which is to say central to the concept of morality even today. His idea is that as rational agents we are also free agents, and that we must be permitted to act as free agents. To convert us into things to be used and exploited is to deny us this status of autonomy, and doing so is fundamentally wrong from the moral point of view. Hence our duty is to interact with other persons in such a way as to acknowledge and honor their autonomy, and our duty to ourselves is to preserve our own. To do otherwise, either to others or ourselves, would be to convert autonomous persons into mere things. It would be to offend against our *dignity*, since, for Kant, our dignity is the moral characteristic or status we have by virtue of being autonomous rational beings: "*Autonomy* is therefore the ground of the dignity of human nature and of every rational creature" (103, 436).

There is another important idea incorporated into Kant's view that we are creatures who make the law and give it to ourselves. We do not need *to be told* what is right and wrong; we can determine such matters for ourselves.[12] Hence we do not need the minister or priest, the politician or general, or even Plato's philosopher-king as a source of moral authority. On moral matters, we ourselves are the ultimate authority. Each of us has within herself the capacity to distinguish right from wrong, this capacity residing in our reason and our ability to ascertain if maxims of action pass the tests of the various formulations of the categorical imperative. We must *freely* obey the moral law, and this means it must have its source in our own reason. As Kant puts it in his essay "What is Enlightenment?": "Have the courage to use your own intelligence! is therefore the motto of the enlightenment."[13] Kant grants that it is not easy to accept one's freedom and assume the obligation to use one's own intelligence:

> Through laziness and cowardice a large part of mankind, even after nature has freed them from alien guidance, gladly remain immature. It is because of laziness and cowardice that it is so easy for others to usurp the role of guardians. It is so comfortable to be a minor! If I have a book which provides meaning for me, a pastor who has conscience for me, a doctor who will judge my diet for me and so on, then I do not need to exert myself. I do not have any need to think; if I can pay, others will take over

this tedious job for me. The guardians who have kindly undertaken the supervision will see to it that by far the largest part of mankind, including the entire "beautiful sex," should consider the step into maturity, not only as difficult but as very dangerous.[14]

Morality requires, we might say, that we become mature, that we give up childhood and assume control over ourselves. To obey a principle because someone else tells us to do so is not to be a moral person; one's will would be influenced heteronomously if one did one's duty because of a requirement that came from outside oneself. Even to obey God – out of fear or whatever other inclination – would be to fall into heteronomy. Servility of any kind, in Kant's eyes, is inconsistent with morality. The moral person does her duty because she commands it of herself.

The Kingdom of Ends

Morality, in sum, requires that we view one another as rational and autonomous ends-in-themselves. And this perspective gives rise to a concluding Kantian notion of the greatest sublimity and profundity: the idea of rational beings as members of a *kingdom of ends*. A "kingdom" Kant defines as "a systematic union of different rational beings under common laws" (100, 433). As he then reminds us, all rational beings are governed by the law that requires them to treat one another as ends and not merely means. Thus "arises a systematic union of rational beings under common objective laws – that is, a kingdom" (101, 433). All rational beings must be conceived as *members* of a kingdom of ends. They also must be conceived as *head* of the kingdom of ends, as sovereign, for as autonomous creatures they give themselves the law. They are both lawmakers and obedient citizens; they are subject to the very laws they have created. It follows that "a rational being must always regard himself as making laws in a kingdom of ends which is possible through freedom of the will – whether it be as member or as head." (101, 434)

"In the kingdom of ends," Kant tells us, "everything has either a price or a dignity" (102, 434). And he goes on to add, "If it has a price, something else can be put in its place as an *equivalent*; if it is exalted above all price and so admits of no equivalent, then it has a dignity" (102, 434). Rational human beings are unique and irreplaceable, each one having an incommensurable value as an end-in-herself. Only through living the moral life can we participate with dignity in the kingdom of ends. "Therefore morality, and humanity so far as it is capable of morality, is the only thing that has dignity" (102, 435). In this fashion the idea of a kingdom of ends summarizes and integrates the various components included in the notion of morality.

The idea of a kingdom of ends also can be seen as the philosophical backbone of the idea of democracy. A democratic government is precisely one in which the citizens are both lawmakers and free subjects. Democracy alone, its advocates contend, provides the political conditions under which each of its citizens has dignity and not merely a price. Kant lived during the time of the Enlightenment, witnessing both the American and the French revolutions. This was a time when the idea of democracy, so long dormant since the days of ancient Athens, was burgeoning and becoming an overwhelming force in human history. Kant can be regarded as one of the modern fathers of democracy, one who provided its philosophical foundation and justification. The idea of democracy, after all, is and always has been a *moral* one.

Autonomy and Heteronomy

It is important to note at this point that Kant puts a special "spin" on the notions of autonomy and heteronomy. We act heteronomously not only when we are caused to act – coerced, manipulated, controlled – by external affairs or by other agents; we also act heteronomously and without autonomy when we choose to be motivated by *our own inclinations*. These inclinations are external to our rational self, and if our will is motivated by them, the rational self is not bringing about its own actions. We act autonomously only when reason guides the will, imposing its own law on it. Thus we act autonomously only when we act, not from inclination, but from a sense of duty, i.e., when we act morally.

In the *Groundwork*, Kant's disaffection from the life of feelings and emotions, desires, and drives – in short, from the life of the inclinations – is severe and absolute. He pictures the moral life as engaged in a constant struggle with the inclinations – what we *want* to do is seldom what we *ought* to do. Even when we want to do our duty, our actions, as we have seen, have no moral worth unless it is duty itself and not inclination that motivates them. While Kant never denies we are creatures of desire and feeling – far from it! – our real or true self is always equated by him with our rational and moral self. And his emphasis on autonomy is always an insistence on the freedom of this rational, moral self.

Kant is fully aware that this insistence raises many questions of the utmost difficulty. Can human beings in fact guide themselves by reason? Can they obey the dictates of the moral law in the face of intense competition and opposition from the forces of inclination? Can a human being act from free will? Free will and free action are presuppositions of the moral life as Kant pictures it. "Ought," he tells us, implies "can" – what I ought to do I must have the ability, the freedom, to do. It makes no sense to tell a person she ought to do something unless she is free to do it. But Kant is very sensitive to the possibility that human will and action are *never* free. He is painfully aware of the attractions of the thesis, held by many philosophers, that the inclinations are the causes of all actions, and that these inclinations are themselves caused or necessitated by things over which human beings have no control, viz., physiological conditions or external events. The thesis of universal causation or determinism asserts as much. Such a thesis was part of the Newtonian mechanics widely accepted in Kant's time, and Kant himself was a believer in Newton's scientific picture of the world. How, then, he asked himself, can we be moral? If morality requires autonomy, how is morality possible? How is the categorical imperative possible? Having spent most of the *Groundwork* charting the basic principles and presuppositions of morality, Kant is left in the last chapter asking himself whether he has described a chimera, an illusion. Perhaps we are unable to be guided by reason in such a fashion as to obey universal laws, to treat one another as ends, and to act autonomously. Perhaps the kingdom of ends is an idle dream, one incapable of being realized.

The Problem of Freedom

We have not yet plumbed the depths of Kant's problem. He himself had asserted in his earlier *Critique of Pure Reason* that all human experience, and all human knowledge, requires the notion of causal determinism. In attempting to explain the world we experience, science *must* invoke the category of causality and use it to interpret nature as governed by necessary causal laws. If the mind did not interpret experience in the terms of this concept, experience would dissolve into so many subjective and independent impressions of sense, as the earlier philosopher David Hume had in fact asserted. Hume clearly perceived that such a view leads directly to utter skepticism about knowledge. The world of objects and the possibility of knowledge of these objects requires, Kant maintained, the thesis of universal determinism. There can be no denying, he thought, that we have such knowledge – science gives it to us. How, then, is morality possible?

But although Kant's metaphysical and epistemological thought in the *Critique of Pure Reason* makes him acutely aware of the problem of human freedom, this thought also provides him with an answer to the difficulty. In this book he had argued that knowledge (science) is possible only if the objects of experience (and hence of knowledge) conform to the general categories of the human mind. Thus these objects are in effect *appearances* – they are the ways things appear to us, interpreted in terms of the categories of our minds. This is the fundamental theme of Kant's so-called *critical* philosophy. In what he described as a Copernican Revolution in philosophy, he asserts that for knowledge to be possible, objects must conform to the mind rather than the mind conform to the objects. But in addition to regarding objects as appearances that result from the mind imposing its categories and its order on experience, we must also, Kant had maintained, think of the world as consisting of the uninterpreted objects themselves, the world of what he called things-in-themselves. These things-in-themselves are the objects as they are apart from the mind. We don't know and can't know what these things–in–themselves are like, because all knowledge can only be of the appearances. The categories of the mind do not apply to them, since the categories merely structure the world of experience. But we nevertheless can know, Kant thinks, that things–in–themselves exist – at least the rational mind is driven to postulate their existence: "For otherwise we should arrive at the absurd conclusion, that there is phenomenal appearance without something that appears."[15] This world of things–in–themselves, which he speaks of as the *noumenal* world or the *intelligible* world in contrast with the world of appearances or the *phenomenal* or *sensible* world, transcends the causal determinism of nature.

We human subjects, Kant maintains, are part of the natural world of appearances, and our physical and psychological lives are governed by causal laws no less than everything else in nature. But we must see ourselves as having a noumenal, intelligible side as well as a phenomenal, sensible one, and the causal laws of nature cannot apply to this self-in-itself. Precisely herein lies the possibility of morality. The moral self is the noumenal self, the self as it is in-itself, the self that transcends the determinism of nature. The moral self, then, can be free, untouched by the laws of science. It can provide its own laws – the laws of reason – thereby becoming autonomous and an end-in-itself of absolute value. Thus was Kant able to assert the reality of human freedom and affirm the reality of morality. As he asserted in the Preface to the second edition of the *Critique of Pure Reason*, he had placed a limit on knowledge (we only know what happens in the world of appearances) in order to make way for morality. ("I had therefore to remove *knowledge* in order to make way for *belief*."[16])

The Two Standpoints

It is with his critical philosophy of knowledge and reality in mind that Kant reflects on the possibility of morality in the last chapter of the *Groundwork*. There he points out that there are two standpoints we can take toward ourselves: "We can enquire whether we do not take one standpoint when by means of freedom we conceive ourselves as causes acting *a priori*, and another standpoint when we contemplate ourselves with reference to our actions as effects which we see before our eyes" (118, 450). When we look upon our actions as the effects of inclinations, we are looking at them as appearances, as part of nature and regulated by nature's laws. When we see these actions as free, as motivated by our own reason and its principles, we see them as the actions of the self as thing-in-itself. Only in the latter case are our actions the product of our will – our free will. "As a rational being, and consequently as belonging to the intelligible world, man can never conceive the causality of his own will except under the idea of freedom; for to be independent of determination by causes in the sensible world (and this is what reason must always attribute to itself) is to be free" (120, 452).

Kant believes that neither the standpoint of nature nor the standpoint of freedom is avoidable. For purposes of explanation and understanding, we must take up the standpoint of nature – in which natural determinism rules. For purposes of action, we must take up the standpoint of freedom, since in acting we see and must see ourselves as rational agents who prescribe unto themselves the laws of morality. We must, then, view the human being both as part of nature and as free. We can never explain our freedom, since all explanation occurs in the world of appearances, such explanation being a matter of identifying the causes of whatever we wish to explain. In this sense, our human freedom, and the morality that flows from it, is incomprehensible. How there could be a moral imperative requiring us – in total indifference to inclination – to behave in certain ways is beyond our ability to comprehend. It is on this note that Kant ends the *Groundwork*: "And thus, while we do not comprehend the practical unconditioned necessity of the moral imperative, we do comprehend its *incomprehensibility*. This is all that can fairly be asked of a philosophy which presses forward in its principles to the very limit of human reason" (131, 463).

It is very difficult for the contemporary mind to accept Kant's stark dichotomy between the phenomenal world and the noumenal one, and very difficult to accept his claim that as moral agents we transcend nature. But it is also virtually impossible, as Kant himself pointed out, for us to avoid the idea that we are free agents. It is difficult, if we are honest with ourselves, to accept the claim that our wills are always under the control of inclination and the sway of natural causality. Reflection seems to reveal to us that we are capable of *deciding what we want to do*; that we are capable of *acting from reasons* we give to ourselves; that we are capable of saying "no" to the inclinations and natural drives that would cause us to act in immoral ways.[17] As moral agents, we are free – this, Kant thinks, is the message of ordinary reason reflecting on human experience. His critical philosophy has simply shown us how we might conceive of this freedom and this morality.

Even if we agree with Kant about the deliverances of ordinary reason and about the unavoidability of the standpoint from which we appear free, there are still major problems with his own way of thinking about these matters. Most importantly, we must ask how the noumenal will or self could insert itself into the natural world in which we act? How could it interfere with the chain of causality operative in this world so as to lead the agent to follow duty rather than desire? How could it do battle with inclination? Such intrusion into the natural world would entirely upset the causal laws that are supposed to hold with necessity therein. In fairness to Kant, we must remember that the phenomenal and noumenal worlds are simply two ways of looking at the same objects – the phenomenal self is thus the noumenal self from a different point of view. The phenomenal self is not a different entity from the noumenal self. But the problem remains. Are these two points of view consistent? How can one hold both of them at the same time? These are questions that deeply disturbed Kant, and they continue to disturb us today. But to say that these matters are just incomprehensible is hardly a satisfying note on which to rest the argument.

Kant bequeaths to us two extremely important things. He gives us a conception of morality which, as we have said before, strikes many thoughtful persons as an accurate picture of what we ourselves in our inchoate fashion take morality to be; he gives us one of the more probing and profound elaborations of what the moral life requires. But he also leaves us with a problem, the problem of freedom. How is freedom possible in a world governed by natural laws? Is it possible even to conceive of how we can act freely in such a world? Our intuitions about the reality of freedom are strong, but we must ask whether they are philosophically weighty enough to establish that not all things are naturally caused. Or is there some other way to conceive of freedom, a way which is not incompatible with the truth of natural determinism? Is it possible, for instance, to develop a notion of *acting from reasons* that cannot be reduced to a form of *being caused to act*? Much of moral philosophy after Kant is an attempt to answer these supremely difficult questions.

Traditional Criticisms of Kant

At this point we need to consider some of the criticisms that traditionally, and frequently, have been brought against Kant. The first of these relates to the *formal* nature of his fundamental principle of morality, the requirement that we act in such a way that we can will the maxim of our action to become universal law. How, it is asked, can we derive from this first principle any requirement for specific actions? Kant himself insists that in acting morally we cannot focus on the content of a principle but rather must act because of the formal features of the principle, its imperatival, law-like nature and its universality. But how can the appeal to lawfulness and universality alone lead us to the idea of any specific actions being our duty? We shall soon see how a criticism of this sort is developed and elaborated by the great philosopher who followed Kant – Hegel.[18]

However popular, this criticism probably can be turned aside. The Formula of Universal Law (the principle of universalizability), the first (or first two) formulations of the categorical imperative, is intended by Kant as a test to be imposed on specific maxims that an agent might consider as reasons for acting, e.g., the maxim that condones making false promises in times of difficulty. Content is provided by these maxims. We know that we are not to make *false promises* because the maxim of doing so cannot pass the test of the principle of universal law. We know that we ought to help others in need because the maxim of ignoring the needs of others cannot be willed universally. In accepting the duty to help others, our reason is not found in the content of the maxim requiring us to do so but rather in the formal features of this maxim (or in the formal features of the contradictory maxim, e.g., the one which would relieve us from the obligation to help others). What specifically we are to do is indicated by the content of the maxim that passes (or fails to pass) the test of the categorical imperative.

A further answer to the criticism that Kant's first principle lacks content comes from the fact that the other formulations of the categorical imperative (the requirement that we treat human beings as ends and the requirement that we act autonomously) certainly do seem to have content. Insofar as Kant maintains that the various formulations are equivalent, it follows that if we accept the principle of universal law we are also committed to accepting the other principles equivalent to it. The notions of ends-in-themselves and freedom, although abstract, are clearly not devoid of content.

Instead of arguing that the Formula of Universal Law is empty, some critics have urged that it is too generous and would certify maxims that are highly immoral. John Stuart Mill, in the nineteenth century, writes: "But when [Kant] begins to deduce from this precept any of the actual duties of morality, he fails, almost grotesquely, to show that there would be any contradiction, any logical (not to say physical) impossibility in the adoption by all rational beings of the most outrageously immoral rules of conduct."[19] Take, for instance, the case of the sado–masochist.[20] Cannot such a person consistently will that everyone inflict pain on others if it pleases them to do so? The sado–masochist is perfectly happy to have others inflict pain on *her*. If the categorical imperative will not exclude the principle of the sado–masochist, it does not seem to be an adequate test of morally right and wrong actions. Or take the maxim that, in order to get some sleep, I will kill children who tend to cry at night more than average.[21] And again the maxim that mothers shall kill any of their children weighing less than six pounds.[22] Would worlds in which these maxims are universalized be impossible to conceive? It is altogether too unfortunate that we can indeed conceive of such worlds. But if the categorical imperative will not prohibit the killing of low weight or crying babies (surely examples of Mill's "outrageously immoral rules of conduct"), it loses any warrant to count as the supreme principle of morality.

Before one concedes to this form of objection, one must take each case as it arises and study carefully whether the Formula of Universal Law generates the moral absurdity claimed. In particular, one must investigate the various ways in which one can interpret the contradiction arising out of the application of the Formula of Universal Law: as a logical contradiction, teleological contradiction, and practical contradiction. It is always possible that if one of these tests will not exclude an immoral maxim, another will. Moreover, one must also consider individual cases in light of the other formulations of the categorical imperative. Kant himself, in his later *Metaphysics of Morals*, uses primarily the Formula of Humanity to test maxims. The cases of violence considered above would appear to be condemned by application of this formula.

Ought We Never to Tell a Lie?

Another objection often leveled at Kant pertains to his moral absolutism, his belief that acts that are in violation of our perfect duties are *always* wrong. We are *never*, he claims, to lie or make a false promise, because we cannot universalize the maxim that would permit us to do so. Kant gives the example – which has become notorious – of refusing to lie to a person who is threatening to kill a friend of ours who is hiding from him in our house.[23] Surely we are permitted to lie to this person about the whereabouts of our friend! Not so, says Kant – and almost everyone disagrees. In defense of his position, Kant points out it is possible that, while telling the would-be attacker the truth, our friend might escape from the house and avoid the threat. He also notes that while we are telling him the truth neighbors might arrive and help prevent an attack. Furthermore, he could have claimed in his defense that we can never be sure the would-be assailant would in fact harm our friend, or he might have pointed out that we could use other strategies than lying to dissuade or turn aside the attacker. But responses of these kinds fail to convince. Surely, we complain against Kant, we cannot be required by duty to tell the truth in such an instance!

Kant digs in his heels and appeals to his principle of universal law. Truthfulness, he tells us "is a duty that must be regarded as the basis of all duties founded on contract, and the laws of such duties would be rendered uncertain and useless if even the slightest exception to them were admitted."[24] Here we have the principle of universalizability at work. If, in willing to lie, I were to universalize the maxim of my action, "I bring it about that statements (declarations) in general find no credence, and hence also that all rights based on contracts become void and lose their force ... "[25] Truthfulness, he claims, must be an unconditional duty, and this entails for him that there are no exceptions to the rule of truthfulness or to any other principle of perfect duty. A moral principle "does not admit of any exceptions, inasmuch as to admit of such would be self-contradictory."[26] Exceptions to moral principles, he tells us, "would destroy the universality on account of which alone they bear the name of principles."[27]

Must Kant be driven by his own moral philosophy to such extreme conclusions? Is it not possible to maintain that some exceptions might be built into principles which could be universalized without thereby willing a system of nature which was internally inconsistent? What would happen if one tried to universalize the maxim "Tell the truth except when someone almost certainly will be severely harmed by one's doing so." If this maxim were to become a law of nature, would it generate an inconsistent system of nature? Truth-telling would continue to be the norm – that is, in such a world most people would, on most occasions, continue to tell the truth. Truth-telling would be the norm to such an extent that contracts could still be entered into in anticipation of the parties to them being trustworthy. It is, in short, not clearly the case that the maxim of truth-telling with an identifiable exception of this kind cannot pass the test of universalizability for a perfect duty.[28] Kant's own test, therefore, may not lead to the rigid absolutism which he himself endorsed.

Is Respect for Duty the Only Morally Worthy Motive?

We shall now consider some criticisms aimed at Kant's claim that only an action motivated by respect for duty has moral worth. It has seemed to many critics that such a view of moral worth or goodness is entirely too narrow, that, in fact, it fails to capture the ordinary conception of morality that Kant was intent on representing. What of actions done out of love or friendship? Do these have no moral worth? What about *caring* for others? Isn't it morally preferable to help others because one cares about them than to help them out of an abstract sense of duty? Many feminist thinkers have thought so, and as a consequence they reject the Kantian perspective.[29]

In presenting Kant's views on moral worth, we suggested that Kant does not oppose feelings and concerns other than the sense of duty but simply requires that the motive that leads to action be the motive of duty and not any other (supporting) feelings that may be present. But how could we possibly tell, someone might respond, that the other factors present – immediate inclinations or considerations of self-interest – do not play a role in motivating the action? Isn't the notion of supporting but nonmotivating feelings an empty one, in that we could never determine that an inclination fell into this category? If we are inclined to answer this question affirmatively, we might conclude that Kant needs to require that the sense of duty *alone* be present if an act is to have moral worth. And this dour requirement is just too severe to be acceptable. Surely moral worth or goodness does not require such a barren emotional life!

Barbara Herman has argued that the proper response to these critics of Kant requires a better understanding of the notion of a motive in Kant's thought.[30] Motives involve maxims and the activity of practical reason, and they must be distinguished from incentives: feelings, emotions and the like (inclinations) which may be part of experience but are not raised to the level of maxims. According to Herman, Kant requires (for good reasons[31]) that a person act from the motive of respect for duty and only from this motive when doing what accords with duty, but this restriction in no way precludes the additional presence of *incentives* (feelings of love, care, friendship, and the like) in the moral agent. Moreover, when application of the categorical imperative generates the conclusion that an act is morally *permissible*, this judgment in effect authorizes the agent to act on an inclination (or a motive reflecting the inclination). I may want, for example, to save some money. Applying the test of the categorical imperative to this motive of my action, I may determine that it is morally permissible to do so. If, then, I act from the desire to save money *and* the recognition that it is morally permissible to do so, my act, though it has no *moral* worth, nevertheless is morally acceptable from Kant's point of view. My acts have moral worth only when they are morally obligatory and I perform them out of a recognition that they are so. And only in these cases must the sense of duty be *the* (one and only) motive of my action. In those numerous cases in which I act out of a recognition of the moral permissibility of what I do, my motivation may include my wanting to do this thing (or the resulting motive). Thus the Kantian conception of the moral life is not as severe and detached from the life of emotion and feeling as it has sometimes been made out to be.

Critics who are concerned about Kant's (apparently) exclusive focus on the motive of respect for duty frequently take issue with what they see as related aspects of his description of the moral agent.[32] The Kantian agent, they claim, is a rule-follower and someone who is concerned only with universal and impartial moral principles and the motive of duty to follow such principles. Such a view of the moral agent ignores the particulars of the person, those concrete qualities that make her the person she is and give meaning to her existence. It ignores as well those personal pursuits and projects which are central to her life. If morality requires that we put aside these immensely personal aspects of our lives, is morality itself worthwhile? Moreover, it has been said that the Kantian perspective underestimates the moral importance of personal relationships and commitments. In asking that we deal impartially with others, it ignores the fact that some of these others have special claims on us which should not be equated with, or replaced by, the general demands that all human beings have on us. Finally, there is the objection that Kant underestimates the moral importance of happiness in the moral life. The imperatives that tell us how to attain happiness are not, for Kant, categorical in nature, and thus they do not serve as moral commandments. Surely happiness has *some* importance in the moral world!

The Role of Happiness

We shall conclude this chapter by briefly considering this final objection about happiness. Here, fortunately, Kant would agree with his critics, at least to some extent.[33] What Kant denies is that happiness can function as a moral principle. Our act has no moral worth if we engage in it in an attempt to attain happiness for ourselves – or for others if we do so as a result of a desire that they be happy. But this does not mean that happiness has no role to play in his moral theory. He writes in the *Critique of Practical Reason*: "But this distinction of the principle of happiness from that of morality is not for this reason an opposition between them, and pure practical reason does not require that we should renounce the claims to happiness; it requires only that we take no account of them whenever duty is in question" (*CPrR*, 97, 93). Moreover, happiness is something we necessarily pursue – *as rational beings*: "To be happy is necessarily the desire of every rational but finite being" (*CPrR*, 24, 25). Kant, therefore, is no ascetic who urges us to abandon the pursuit of happiness. Happiness for him amounts to the satisfaction of our inclinations, and so the inclinations have a role to play in the life of the rational agent. Kant's task is to define precisely what this role is.

Second, Kant grants that "in a sense" we can have a *duty* to pursue our own happiness. "It can even be a duty in certain respects to provide for one's happiness, in part because (since it includes skill, health, and riches) it contains means to the fulfillment of one's duty and in part because the lack of it (e.g., poverty) contains temptations to transgress against duty" (*CPrR*, 97, 93). He goes on to contrast this duty with a "direct duty," and so we may call the duty to pursue one's happiness an indirect duty.

Happiness, he points out in the *Metaphysics of Morals*, is a means to "the morality of the subject."[34] Skill, health, and riches aid us in attaining moral virtue, i.e., in acting out of a respect for the law. Moreover, the avoidance of frustration, pain, and disenchantment are often necessary if we are to have the frame of mind that permits us to act out of a respect for duty. A happy person, therefore, is more capable of acting as the moral law requires and acting out of an appreciation for the moral law. As a means to the moral life, then, happiness is something we ought to pursue. But we are to pursue it only as a means, not as an end.

For a variety of reasons, the promotion of our own happiness cannot be our direct duty. Our direct duty is to act on principles that satisfy the demands of the categorical imperative. These principles cannot be grounded in contingent ends or inclination, and we have seen that happiness is the object of a universal but contingent human inclination. Moreover, Kant argues that duty always involves constraint, and insofar as happiness is something we all desire, we would not be constrained if the moral law were to command us to seek our own happiness. Thus, "when one's own happiness is made the determining ground of the will, the result is the direct opposite of the principle of morality" (*CPrR*, 36, 35).

In the *Critique of Practical Reason* Kant gives us a theory of the *summum bonum*, the highest or most perfect good. The highest good consists of two parts: morality or virtue is the first, *happiness* the second. Virtue is the required condition for anything being good or desirable, but this does not prove that virtue is the "entire and perfect good" – rather, "for this, happiness is also required" (*CPrR*, 116, 110). Accordingly, Kant describes the highest good as happiness in proportion to worth, or happiness in accord with virtue. The most perfect, complete state of affairs that could exist in the world of finite beings would be one in which human beings are happy to the degree that they deserve to be. Conversely, a world in which one was worthy of happiness but did not attain it would not be a rational world. As Kant puts it in the *Lectures on Ethics*, "the highest created good is the most perfect world, that is, a world in which all rational beings are happy and are worthy of happiness" (*LE*, 6).[35]

Is it a person's duty to pursue the highest good? Do we have an obligation to pursue the goal of a world in which all rational human beings are happy and worthy of happiness? Kant clearly thinks we do have such an obligation: "It is *a priori* (morally) necessary to bring forth the highest good through the freedom of the will" (*CPrR*, 119, 113); "reason commands us to contribute everything possible to its realization" (*CPR*, 125–6, 119); and "the moral law commands us to make the highest possible good in a world the final object of all our conduct" (*CPrR*, 136, 129).[36] Insofar as happiness is part of the highest good, we have an obligation to pursue happiness.

But this obligation does not extend to our own happiness, for, as we have seen, our own happiness cannot be the object of a duty. It is the happiness of others we are impelled by reason to advance. As for ourselves, we should seek our perfection, that is to say, our moral perfection, the goodness of our will. Part of this moral perfection will be the pursuit of the happiness of others *because it is our duty*.

In the *Lectures on Ethics*, Kant writes of a "promise of happiness ... The moral law contains within it a natural promise of happiness: it tells me that if I conduct myself so as to be worthy of happiness I may hope for it; here are the springs of morality and morality thus has a necessary relation to happiness" (77–8). The moral law, then, allows one to hope for happiness. But will this promise of happiness, will this hope for it, be fulfilled? Can the condition of happiness, one's moral virtue, be achieved, and can the happiness proportional to this virtue be attained? Kant's answer is two-fold. First, he denies that we can achieve perfect virtue in this life, and he denies that happiness proportional to this virtue can be obtained by human effort alone. In this world, Kant admits, virtue is unlikely to be rewarded. Second, however, he argues that from the rationality of the demand to secure the highest good, it follows that this demand must be met. Therefore he is led to set forth two *postulates*, propositions that cannot be proved but must be presupposed by our moral experience. Each postulate is "an inseparable corollary of an *a priori* unconditionally valid practical law," i.e., of the moral law.

The Postulates of Immortality and God

The first postulate asserts the reality of personal immortality:

> The achievement of the highest good in the world is the necessary object of a will determinable by the moral law. In such a will, however, the complete fitness of intentions to the moral law is the supreme condition of the highest good. This fitness, therefore, must be just as possible as its object ... But complete fitness of the will to the moral law is holiness, which is a perfection of which no rational being in the world of sense is at any time capable. But since it is required as practical necessity, it can be found only in an endless progress to that complete fitness ... This infinite progress is possible, however, only under the presupposition of

an infinitely enduring existence and personality of the same rational being; this is called the immortality of the soul. Thus the highest good is practically possible only on the supposition of the immortality of the soul ... (*CPrR*, 128–9, 122).

The moral law, then, holding out the promise of happiness to the virtuous, presupposes the condition under which a rational agent can attain the worthiness required for happiness. This condition is the personal immortality of the soul. The "moral destiny of our nature" (*CPrR*, 129, 122) requires endless progress to higher stages of moral perfection, "even beyond this life" (*CPrR*, 130, 123).

The second postulate is that of the existence of God as the guarantor that the virtuous will attain happiness:

> The same law must also lead us to affirm the possibility of the second element of the highest good, i.e., happiness proportional to that morality ... This it can do on the supposition of the existence of a cause adequate to this effect, i.e., it must postulate the existence of God as necessarily belonging to the possibility of the highest good (*CPrR*, 130–1, 124).

The human will cannot "by its own strength" ensure that nature will allot the happiness deserved by the virtuous. But the moral law regards the connection between virtue and happiness as necessary. Therefore only the cause of the whole of nature, itself rational and moral, "contains the ground of the exact coincidence of happiness with morality" (*CPrR*, 131, 125). This moral cause of the whole of nature is God.

Here we have Kant's famous (notorious) moral argument for the existence of God. Thought to be a strong argument by some, and exceedingly weak by others, it clearly presupposes the validity of our moral experience. But this validity, Kant firmly believed, is clear to the rational agent – and inescapable. We can no more deny the claim of morality on us than we can deny the reality of our freedom in moments of choice. What is important for our present purposes is to realize that this concluding commitment of pure practical reason – to the existence of God – is founded on the need to ensure happiness for moral agents. Hence happiness plays a vital role in the Kantian ethical theory. Within this theory it is not the basis of the moral law; it is certainly not the supreme principle of this law. Happiness is grounded in and legitimized *by* the moral law.

Kant and Deontology

We conclude this lengthy discussion of Kant's ethics by raising the question of its relationship to the idea of *deontology*. Kant's theory is usually considered the epitome of deontology, the veritable paradigm that explains what this term means. The notion of deontology derives from the Greek word for duty (*deon*), and Kant clearly elevates the concept of duty to one of the central, if not the most important, moral categories. The philosopher who writes "Duty! Thou sublime and mighty name ... " (*CPrR*, 90, 86) is not in the same ethical boat as those thinkers who emphasize self-interest, pleasure, and the life of prudence. Moreover, the deontological character of Kant's ethics is apparent in his rejection of the idea that duty is determined by calculating the value inherent in the consequences of actions. And finally, Kant can be said to subscribe to a deontological form of ethics by virtue of the fact that for him some actions are wrong in themselves and absolutely so. The wrongness of an action is not derived from variable values (the contingent ends of inclination). Consequently an act that is wrong on one occasion cannot become right or permissible on another just because on that latter occasion it happens to promote these values. If deontology is committed to the belief that some acts are absolutely wrong no matter what the circumstances, Kant subscribes to this type of moral theory. And if deontology encompasses the view that some acts are morally impermissible even though they would lead to morally admirable ends, then Kant is a deontologist.[37]

But if we adopt the standard distinction between deontological and teleological theories first proposed by J.H. Muirhead,[38] matters are not so clear. Muirhead distinguished between an ethics of ends (teleology) and one of duties and rules (deontology). Ends have to do with goodness and value, rules with obligation and rightness. Using this classification scheme, where are we to place Kant? A few observations will show that his ethics is too complex to fit exclusively within the deontological side of Muirhead's distinction. That is to say, if a deontologist is thought of as someone who rejects the importance of *ends* in the moral life, or does not assign a basic role to the idea of goodness, Kant is not so clearly a deontologist.

As we have just seen, happiness is for Kant part of the end of pure practical reason, the highest good (*summum bonum*) being its "entire object" or end. Happiness as a moral end is not ignored, it is simply *qualified* or conditioned: it must be deserved. And at the beginning of the *Groundwork*, the idea of value and *goodness* is at center stage. The *good will* is the only thing having unconditional value. The good will, Kant stresses, "always holds the highest place in estimating the total worth of our actions and constitutes the condition of all the rest" (64, 397). Here we have a value concept elevated to the highest level. The ensuing discussion of duty in the *Groundwork* is "intended to elucidate the concept of a will estimable in itself and good apart from any further end" (64, 397). But this does not make the idea of duty more fundamental. On the contrary, Kant tells us that the concept of duty "includes that of a good will, exposed, however, to certain subjective limitations and obstacles" (65, 397). This implies that we can only understand the idea of duty in light of the idea of the good will in conditions in which it is not "holy" but rather struggles with the forces of inclination.

The absolute value of the rational will is stressed by Kant in his second formulation of the categorical imperative – the Formula of Humanity. Indeed, it is only in light of the postulated value of persons as ends-in-themselves that we can grasp the ground of the categorical imperative and its command that we universalize the maxim on which we act. And the third formulation commands us to regard ourselves as making laws in a kingdom of ends. The "ends" that function in these two formulations of the categorical imperative are not ends or values contingent on inclination. They are absolute and objective ends, but surely ends for all that.

What these reflections show is not that it is wrong to classify Kant as a deontologist but that his theory is too rich to yield to simple classification. Perhaps its greatness lies in the fact that it transcends traditional dichotomies. It certainly offers us a breadth of vision that is unrivaled in the history of Western ethics, except, perhaps, by that of Aristotle and (the next philosopher we are to study) Hegel.

11

Hegel

For some, G.W.F. Hegel (1770–1831) is a philosopher whose importance ranks alongside that of Aristotle and Kant. For others, he is a mere obscurantist whose impossibly dense prose has done little more than inspire the fanaticism of fascists and totalitarians. Many of his defenders see his philosophy of absolute idealism as nothing less than the apotheosis of Western metaphysics, the highest expression of the fundamental principles of metaphysical thought found throughout the preceding centuries. There is no question but that Hegel himself saw his philosophy this way. And there is no question but that the course of Western philosophy changed dramatically after Hegel, many of the later forms of philosophizing constituting a repudiation of the grand metaphysical approach supremely exemplified in his thought. While Hegel has remained influential in Continental philosophy, his influence on British and American thought during the latter three-quarters of the twentieth century has, until recently, been at a very low ebb. But he is gradually being recognized even in the Anglo-American world as a force to be contended with, especially in the area of ethics.

Hegel and Kant

Understanding the general thrust of Hegel's ethical theory requires seeing it in relationship to the moral philosophy of Kant. Understanding the detail of his theory requires viewing it in terms of the comprehensive metaphysics of absolute idealism in which it is embedded – if only, fortunately for us, in a general sort of way.

As we have observed, the principles of morality for Kant emerge from the self's reflection on itself as rational and autonomous. These principles affirm the intrinsic value of the self as an autonomous and rational being, and they direct the self to act in a manner consistent with its rational nature. When the will determines itself by rational principles alone, it acts as an autonomous agent. Such an agent is not influenced by any merely contingent motives such as desires and inclinations; she is guided only by her essential nature *qua* rational. The good will is the will that determines itself as a source of agency transcending the realm of the passions.

Hegel's first criticism of Kant's theory is that the categorical imperative is purely formal and gives us no concrete advice concerning how we should act.[1] The categorical imperative requires only that the motive of our action be one that all rational agents could consistently act on. In Hegel's view, this purely formal requirement does not rule out acting on principles that are intrinsically evil. Thus the formal guidelines do not exclude immoral content.

Hegel's second objection concerns the fact that the moral will for Kant is completely divorced from the sensuous nature of the human being. Kant's philosophy creates an absolute dichotomy between the physical person and the rational one, and the moral will is expressly told to pay no attention to the promptings of the physical self. Hegel rejects this dichotomy. A person must be grasped in her totality, as both physical and rational. In Hegel's eyes, to picture the rational person as being distinct from the physical world is a failure of reason. Any freedom this independent, transcendent self might have would be abstract and empty in as much as it is not the freedom of the whole person.

Absolute Idealism

Hegel's absolute idealism in general can be understood in terms of his dissatisfaction with the Kantian dichotomy between the sphere of nature and the sphere of reason or mind. The theory of absolute or objective idealism is an attempt to show the unity of nature and reason, a unity described forcefully in Hegel's claim that the real is rational and the rational real. According to this theory, the world as a whole is in a process of development, a progressive unfolding in which it becomes more and more rational and more and more aware of itself as essentially rational in nature. At some (early) stages in the development of reality (or the development of what we should call absolute mind), the conscious, rational subject sees itself as distinct and different from the objects in nature – in Hegel's language, the subject is "alienated" from its objects. It perceives itself to be subjective consciousness as opposed to objective reality. But this subject/object distinction is gradually broken down as the mind continually finds evidence of its nature – rationality – in nature. As knowledge of nature advances, the alienation of reason from the physical domain diminishes. Reason comes to see that the real is rational, and the rational real, and hence that the dichotomy between mind and its objects is overcome.

Hegel's doctrine of absolute idealism encompasses not only the domain of physical nature but also the social and cultural realm. Here too something like a progression from alienation to unity takes place. The individual person can see herself as facing a social world which is as different and alien as physical nature can seem to be to the knowing subject. And yet this social world is, in the end, a human product, the result of the reason and will of human beings. It has, in other words, reason and will present in it. The struggle of the individual will or person to find herself at home in the social world is once again an attempt to overcome alienation. Part of the struggle here results from of the fact that each person is an individual – and hence distinct from other human beings – while at the same time each person is human in her essential universal nature and therefore is a social being. It is not difficult to lose one's individuality, or one's sense of it, by immersion into the social world and through conformity with its norms, aspirations, and activities. The problem faced by the individual self, then, is to find a way of escaping the alienation from the social sphere without in doing so abandoning its individuality.

Hegel expresses this dilemma in terms of the concept of freedom. How can we as human selves truly achieve freedom? In one sense we are free when we can simply do what we want, when there are no external barriers preventing us from obtaining what we, as individuals, aspire to do. But this notion of freedom operates within a point of view that sees the individual as set up in opposition to what happens in the natural and social realms. Hence it operates within the point of view of the alienated individual. "Doing what one wants to do" is an inadequate – "abstract" in Hegel's vocabulary – kind of freedom because it is not understood in terms of the individual's essential nature as a social creature. It presupposes an abstract concept of individuality in which the individual is divorced from the rich social context in which she lives and acts. Thus the need to discover a richer concept of freedom, one in which the opposition between individual and society is transcended.

Just as our practical activities – whereby we shape nature into artifacts of our own design – are ways of overcoming the alienation of human spirit from physical nature, so our moral and ethical practices are means whereby we overcome the alienation between the individual and society. Given that the goal of overcoming such alienation is the achievement of true freedom, our moral and ethical activities manifest our attempt to achieve full human freedom.

Finally, in an effort to describe the vantage point from which Hegel develops his moral and ethical philosophy, we must take note of his dialectical method. Dialectic is the process of tracing the development of ideas, not chronologically in time, but logically, in terms of the inherent linkages of meaning between these ideas. It seeks to understand how one idea can give rise – because of its form and content, and its inadequacies – to other ideas, and these in turn to still others. All ideas considered singly are inadequate – or, again, "abstract." Because of their incompleteness and partiality, they come into conflict with other ideas, whose own inadequacy leads to conflict with still other notions. As we follow this progression through one conflict after another, we witness the development of ever more adequate, less abstract ideas. These products of the dialectical advance are equally more rational – and thus more real.

Ethical Life and the Overcoming of Alienation

It is in *The Philosophy of Right*[2] that we find the main expression of Hegel's moral and ethical theory. Here we encounter him tracing the dialectical advance of the normative ideas that shape our thinking about our practical lives. We see, for instance, how the notion of wrongness develops out of prior ideas, specifically out of the notions of private property and contract. The notion of wrongness in turn leads to the idea of morality, which, for Hegel, is still an abstract and inadequate concept. The rational practical life does not come to a conclusion in the moral life but rather in something beyond it. For Hegel, what is beyond morality is the ethical life. The ethical life is what overcomes the separation between the individual and society; it is also the life in which true human freedom is finally made manifest. Thus the dialectical advance from the notion of individual, isolated selfhood, to the concepts of private property, contract, and wrongness, and on to the moral life and then the ethical life, is just another instance of the overcoming of alienation and the unification of self and object. It is an advanced stage in the full development of absolute mind or spirit.

As we proceed at this point to follow the presentation of Hegel's moral and ethical theories as they are found in *The Philosophy of Right*, quotations from the philosopher himself will be provided judiciously. Hegel is simply too difficult to understand for extensive direct quotation to be a sensible approach. The difficulty largely lies in the fact that he brings to his writings a highly technical and obscure vocabulary, one that can be understood only in light of his conception of absolute mind. In the limited space we have, it would be impossible to explain these technical terms. Moreover, for the most part Hegel's basic normative philosophy can be understood without using these convoluted metaphysical underpinnings – that, at least, will be the operating assumption in what follows.

Creating a Self

The task of the practical, normative life is one of creating or determining a self. At first we find ourselves in the world as merely natural creatures: our "immediate" impression of ourselves is one of our bodies and their physical environments. Such a creature does not yet have a personality and does not see herself as a distinct person. The transition to the personal self begins when we become aware of ourselves as conscious creatures, as something more than and indeed distinct from our physical bodies in physical space. Personality requires self-consciousness, and self-consciousness involves an awareness of the self *as consciousness*. In discovering ourselves as selves *aware of* our bodies and their environments, we encounter consciousness itself. We also encounter *will*, since we become aware that we conscious subjects can make changes in the physical domain. Thus the self we become conscious of is the self of consciousness and will. When we define ourselves as consciousness and will, we begin to view ourselves as distinct from the natural world: we are *not* those physical external objects we are aware of and manipulate. Self-consciousness reveals the self "at a distance" from the physical domain, indeed even from the body. We are separate from all such objects, even from our natural desires and drives. So personality first emerges as the personal "I am I" who is conscious of things and, at least to some degree, master of things, but as an entity without any further concrete identity than consciousness, will, and self-consciousness. As Hegel puts it: "Personality begins not with the subject's mere general consciousness of himself as an ego concretely determined in some way or another, but rather with his consciousness of himself as a completely abstract ego in which every concrete restriction and value is negated and without validity" (35).[3] Personality at this stage is pure self-consciousness, "the self-conscious but otherwise contentless and simple relation of itself to itself in its individuality" (ibid.). In other words, I am I.

In being aware of myself as something other than the physical objects in the world and other than my own body, I achieve, Hegel claims, a sense of my freedom. It is a purely abstract freedom, however, the freedom of being something more than a physical body shaped by external and internal factors. As abstract, it is inadequate, but it nevertheless provides us with a one-sided insight into our essential nature. What is needed is to give substance to this freedom, to make it concrete and individualized.

The personality of the self-conscious, self-identical person is the ground and justification of the abstract concept of *right*. "Personality essentially involves the capacity for rights ... " (36). It gives rise to the imperative "Be a person and respect others as persons," which Hegel calls the imperative of right (36). Insofar as the personality we are currently considering consists only in the self's relation to itself in self-consciousness, its rights are not particularized with respect to needs and interests. The command of right goes no further than to say "Do not infringe personality and what personality entails" (38). We are here in the realm of abstract right. But even the imperative of right – the abstract right of personality – rules out slavery as a permissible practice. Slaves are denied personality.

The conception of self or personhood we have arrived at consists in identification with what in fact is the universal essence of self, what all selves have in common: self-consciousness and its right to be. The personality is not yet individuated by having distinguishing properties setting it off from other selves. So far, it is individuated only by being set against the objective world – it is limited to pure subjectivity. But this abstract, alienated subjectivity is not enough; personality demands more: "Personality is that which struggles to lift itself above this restriction and to give itself reality, or in other words to claim that external world as its own" (39). The process of creating a self must go beyond this initial abstract stage. It can do this in several ways. First, it may identify itself with the desires it has as a natural, immediate thing. It determines itself as the self with these desires, interests, needs. Second, in acting on these desires, it determines itself even further: it is the agent who does *this* and *that*, the one who shapes the world in specific ways and thereby lends specificity to its own self.

In doing these things that give determination to the self, it is always possible for the self to overlook the fact that it is the self as *consciousness* and *will* that is at work in determining its personality through choice and action. We can fall into the trap of identifying ourselves with the desires, the choices, and the actions we undertake as if these were somehow natural, given, predetermined. In doing so we lose the self as will and consciousness and become objectified, thereby losing our freedom. Just as the will and consciousness without specific desires and choices is abstract and incompletely determined (being pure subjectivity), the self as a set of desires and actions considered apart from the self as will and consciousness is also abstract and incompletely, inadequately determined (being pure objectivity). True selfhood requires both "moments" or aspects of the self – both objectivity and subjectivity. It also requires an understanding that each moment depends on the other. When we have reached this level of reflection, we have obtained a personality that is no longer merely subjective or merely objective. In this accomplishment, an individual rises to the level of a free personality. She grasps herself as a particular, concrete person, but she also grasps that she is not *just* the concrete aspects of her person: she is also the self-identical consciousness and will that chooses in its freedom to be this particular, concrete individual.

Private Property

In tracing the effort of the abstract personality-as-self-consciousness to give itself concrete substance and to claim the external world as its own, Hegel focuses on the notion of private property. As the personality engages with the world, it grasps, takes possession of, and uses objects in it, claiming them as its own. In this way there arises the notion of private property. My sense of personal freedom is manifested in my possession of things. The abstractness and indeterminacy of this freedom is overcome through the possession of concrete things in the world: I am the free possessor of this property, this house, this car, and so on. And in retaining these things, and in having continuing privileged access to them, I maintain my personal freedom. One of the things I possess is my body, so that I am no longer merely the passive recipient of it. Indeed, the more my possessions, the greater the extent and degree of my freedom. Private property thus becomes the way in which individual freedom is manifested and made concrete.

The possession of property is the exercise of the *right* of self-consciousness: "A person has as his substantive end the right of putting his will into any and every thing and thereby making it his, because it has no such end in itself and derives its destiny and soul from his will" (44). That which can be possessed, an object in external nature, is "the external pure and simple, a thing, something not free, not personal, without rights" (42). Thus the right to private property is "the absolute right of appropriation which man has over all 'things' " (44).

Property, in order to continue to be truly one's own, must be used. The stamp of one's own needs and interests must be placed on it. But the best proof of my ownership of something is that I can sell it to someone else or give it away. I can "alienate myself" from it, but I can do this only because the thing is initially *mine*. The ability to separate myself from my property also demonstrates that I am not *identical* with these external, objective possessions. Hence this ability to sell property confirms itself as the ability of a conscious, wilful person who is free from the immersion in the external world of property.

It is also in the realm of property that we become aware of another person or other people as free, self-relating individuals. As noted, one of the ways in which we can alienate ourselves from our private property is to give it to someone else; another way is to exchange it for something another person owns. Such interactions Hegel refers to as contracts. Reason, Hegel tells us, "makes it just as necessary for men to enter into contractual relationships – gift, exchange, trade, etc. – as to possess property" (71). Exchanging items of property by means of a contract, however, gives rise to the notion of "a common will": "The sphere of contract is made up of this mediation whereby I hold property not merely by means of a thing and my subjective will, but by means of another person's will as well and so hold it in virtue of my participation in a common will" (71). This common will, or "unity of different wills," takes us into the social dimension where other people are encountered as having rights and obligations. Hegel insists, however, that the notion of contract does not encompass the area of marriage or the relationship between the individual and the state; it is restricted to the exchange of private *property*, whereas marriage and citizenship belong to a "sphere of a quite different and higher nature" (75).

Right and Wrong

Private property and the sphere of contracts also constitute the locus for the emergence of normative notions of right and wrong. Taking possession of an object and contracting with another person regarding its possession are, we are told, "grounds of title" (84). But different individuals may attempt to possess the same object, and disagreements can break out over the matter of proper title. "Each person may look upon the thing as his property on the strength of the particular ground on which he bases his title. It is in this way that one man's right may clash with another's" (84). Civil suits arise as means of resolving these disputes, and these suits usually end with a declaration that the thing or things in question are the property of one of the litigants and not of the other. The one party is found to be in the right, the other in the wrong. The wrongness here, however, is *non-malicious*, the outcome of a sincere disagreement over who has the right of possession over particular things. This civil infraction stands in sharp contrast with fraud, which occurs when one party to a contract offers to exchange an item that is not presented in its true light or with its true value, but, as it were, in disguise. The individual committing fraud pretends to abide by the principle of rightness governing exchanges, but in fact merely puts up a show of doing so. Finally, in addition to non-malicious wrongness and fraud, there is the instance of crime, where someone knowingly abrogates the principle of rightness by stealing from another, appropriating something that another person has a right to and that the thief does not even pretend to have a right to.

Hegel discusses crime under the heading "Coercion and Crime," implying that the two go hand in hand. When someone steals something from me, my will, which has become embodied in my property, comes under coercion. Likewise, if I am "constrained to sacrifice something or to do some action as a condition of retaining one or other of [my] possessions or embodiments" (90), we have an instance of coercion. Such coercion or force "is an expression of a will which annuls the expression or determinate existence of a will" (92), and for this reason, Hegel tells us, it is wrong. To overturn this wrong, coercion must be used against coercion, and this leads to the notion of punishment.

Hegel's theory of punishment is straightforwardly and vigorously retributive in nature. Punishment is a means of annulling a crime. A crime is a negation of right, and punishment is a negation of the negation, which is to say, an affirmation of the original right. Punishment is *not* to be seen as a means of reforming the criminal or of deterring future crime. Consequentialist theories of punishment that attempt to justify it on the basis of its reformative or deterrent character treat the punishment as an evil and therefore as something that has to be justified by being shown to lead to desirable consequences. But punishment is not an evil but rather a restoration of right, the righting of wrong. Crime is to be annulled, "not because it is the producing of an evil, but because it is the infringement of the right as right ... " (99). Any discussion of the reformative or deterrent effects of punishment must be based on the acknowledgment that "punishment is inherently and actually just" (99). Indeed, Hegel claims, the criminal as a rational agent desires her own punishment because, being rational, she sees this as the rational way of restoring right, of establishing justice. By being punished, the criminal "is honored as a rational being" (100).

To be sure, in punishing its criminals, a society exercises considerable force or coercion itself. But it has a right to do so: "Abstract right is a right to coerce, because the wrong which transgresses it is an exercise of force against the existence of my freedom in an external thing" (94). Indeed, abstract right may be defined as "a right in the name of which coercion may be used" (94). Hegel carefully distinguishes the right to punish from revenge. Revenge is the act of a particular, "subjective" will – it is something an individual or group of such individuals takes upon itself to perform in order to gratify particular desires. Such actions constitute a *further* violation of the principle of right. But when instituted by the state on the basis of the principle of right and as a means of righting wrongs, punishment is not revenge. It is a demand for or requirement of justice.

In arriving at the stage where we can see punishment as demanded and justified, we have come to a stage where we must distinguish the particular will (based solely upon its subjective, contingent desires) from a higher form of will: "Fundamentally, [punishment] implies the demand for a will which, though particular and subjective, yet wills the universal as such" (103). The demand for punishment is what *all* rational wills require, and require in *all* cases of crime – hence it expresses the will for the universal. Here we encounter the notion of the *moral will* and morality. It is the moral will which "wills the universal as such." With the demands that wrongs be righted and wrongdoers punished, we leave behind us the solitary individual will and its private property – and even the principle of abstract rightness embodied in contract – and we rise to a level where universal principles of conduct emerge. This is morality.

Morality

It is in the arena of morality that a person becomes a *subject*. Prior to the level of morality, an individual may achieve a sense of independence and personality, but this personality is identified only in terms of individual desires and abstract right – the right that flows from ownership of property. Possession of property and contracts themselves rest on individual, i.e., subjective and contingent, preferences. There is no universal law of conduct to which the individual may appeal and with which she may identify at this earlier stage. Insofar as any universal law is a law of reason, and inasmuch as reason constitutes the essential nature of human beings, at the stage prior to morality the individual has not been able to identify fully with her essence. At that earlier stage, universal principles are only implicit in the person. These principles become explicit at the level of morality, so that the person comes to actualize her essence to a greater degree. Mere abstract subjectivity at the level of abstract right changes into concrete, actualized subjectivity as the individual identifies with the universal laws of reason, i.e., the laws of morality. In attaining such subjectivity, the person becomes a *subject*.

Morality appears on the scene as something *required* of the self – in Hegel's terms, as an "ought-to-be, or demand" (108). The universal laws of morality indicate how human beings ought to act and ought to be, not how they actually behave at any moment. Hence in recognizing moral demands – which reveal the self as "lacking" or faulty – the self has not yet achieved identity with universal law, and to this extent the moral subject still remains abstract and incomplete, not yet fully real. The incompleteness of self in light of the demands imposed by moral law gives rise to the notion of an *aim* or purpose. The self seeks to become the embodiment of moral law.

It recognizes its own rationality in this moral law, but at this stage the law appears as an "ought." In its aim or purpose, the self attempts to become, to be, what it ought – it attempts to convert "ought" into "is," to become the actual, objective embodiment of what ought to be.

The moral law, the law of reason, is not just *my* reason and *my* essence; it is the rational essence of all human beings. "The achievement of my aim, therefore, implies this identity of my will with the will of others, it has a positive bearing on the will of others" (112). In the moral sphere, we thus lose our detached individuality. We perceive in the moral law the law common to all, and in seeking to follow it, to achieve our aim and to make actual what is at first merely demanded of us, we seek to become one with the human essence – universal subjectivity, our social being. The fulfillment of our aim thus has three aspects to it: it involves becoming and being something in actuality, that is to say, giving external form and substance to our subjectivity; it involves realizing our human potential or essence; and it involves leaving behind the isolated, individual selfhood of earlier stages and identifying with universal selfhood (112).

How do we externalize our subjectivity and render it objective? Hegel's answer is straightforward: "The externalization of the subjective or moral will is action" (113). To achieve one's aim, one must *act*. This action, however, must be one's own – one for which the agent herself is responsible, one that, as Hegel puts it, is "imputable" to the subject. Furthermore, it must be an attempt to fulfill an "ought" – moral laws require positive forms of action, whereas the earlier laws of abstract right and contract merely prohibited certain actions. And finally, the actions engaged in in order to realize the agent's aim will be ones that relate to other people. Morality has to do with responsible, positive actions as they bear upon the relationship of oneself to others.

Moral action, according to Hegel, has a special content. This content is *welfare*, not simply my welfare but the welfare of others as well. To the extent that welfare is universalized in this way, it becomes identical with the *good*. The good is "the absolute end of the will" (114). Thus the moral law puts us under the demand to realize the good – universal welfare.

Much of the remainder of Hegel's discussion of morality consists of detailed accounts of how to determine when an action is imputable to a particular person (when that person is responsible for it), how welfare is to be determined, and how the pursuit of the good gives rise to the notion of conscience. We shall give only brief consideration to each of these topics.

Responsibility

An action, Hegel tells us, "*presupposes* an external object with a complex environment. The deed sets up an alteration in this state of affairs confronting the will, and my will has responsibility in general for its deed in so far as the abstract predicate 'mine' belongs to the state of affairs so altered" (115). But what aspects of the altered situation are mine? To answer this question, we must first consider what aspects of the context of action the agent is aware of. This situation "may contain something other than what the will's idea of it contains" (117). According to Hegel, the agent is only responsible for the effects of those aspects of the situation that she was conscious of. For instance, if I serve a guest a cup of tea that, totally unknown to me, has arsenic in it, I am not responsible for the death of my guest. Insofar as I am unaware of the aspect of the situation that leads to the death, the deed – my bringing about the death of my guest – is not one that can be imputed to me.

Second, we must acknowledge the fact that every action can have a multitude of consequences, some of which an agent may foresee and others she may not. These consequences often will result from the intrusion of other causal factors. For instance, if someone saved a young Austrian from death and this Austrian, because of early childhood traumas or the like, went on to attempt the extermination of an entire race during the 1930s and 40s, the person who saved him as a youth is not responsible for the later consequences of her action. The purposive consequence of her action – what she anticipated (viz., keeping the Austrian alive) – becomes "the prey of external forces" that "drive it into alien and distant consequences" (118). The modern mind, unlike – Hegel affirms – the ancient Greek mind, does not attribute or accept responsibility for "the whole compass of the deed" but only for those aspects of it that fall within the agent's knowledge. In determining responsibility, what Hegel calls the "right of knowledge" limits a person's responsibility to those aspects of a situation of action and the consequences of the action known to the agent.

There is also a "right of intention", which requires that "the universal quality of the action shall not be implicit but shall be known by the agent and so shall have lain from the start in his subjective will" (120). By "universal quality" Hegel simply means the characteristics or features of an action (including the known consequences of it). By the right of intention Hegel is claiming that an agent is only responsible for those known aspects of an action that she willed or intended to produce. This "content of the intention" constitutes the *end* of an action, and it is because of this end that an action has "subjective worth or interest" to an agent (122).

What in fact are the ends of action? At this stage they are the goals of the self in "its natural subjective embodiment, i.e., in needs, inclinations, passions, opinions, fancies, etc." (123). Here the "natural will" makes its appearance and its ends are "natural and given" (ibid.), the objects of its desires, needs, etc. The attainment of these ends is welfare or happiness. Hegel objects vigorously to the claim that the satisfactions an individual receives upon realizing her ends are themselves the true ends of all action. This view is, in his words, "an empty dogmatism of the abstract Understanding," the latter being a form of thinking that occupies a low position in Hegel's epistemic hierarchy. Indeed, this claim is "pernicious if it passes into the assertion that because subjective satisfaction is present, as it always is when any task is brought to completion, it is what the agent intended in essence to secure and that the objective end was in his eyes only a means to it" (124). In this argument we find clear echoes of Butler and Hume. Hegel, however, uses the argument for his own purposes, which is to declare that the value of an action lies in its *objective* end, what it accomplishes in the external world of fact; its value does *not* lie in the subjective satisfactions an agent derives from achieving her ends. Furthermore: "What the subject is, is the series of his actions. If these are a series of worthless productions, then the subjectivity of his willing is just as worthless" (124). This is a remarkable statement from a philosopher who is sometimes characterized as a dreamy idealist for whom thought and intention are everything and the world of concrete reality an illusion. Judge the person, he is saying, by what she *does*, by the value or lack of value inherent in her actions. The view that personal satisfaction is the sole end of action leads us to "belittle and disparage all great deeds and great men" (124) – after all, the theory would have it, they were only seeking their private satisfaction. Hegel would have us look at the objective ends of their actions – what they *accomplish* – for there is where the value lies.

Welfare and Conscience

The moral will, we should recall, has welfare as its content, but because this will is also universal will, it is the welfare of all – all individual agents – at which it aims. Promoting the welfare of all is "the right." But what is the content of this welfare? Does it consist of the ends that people actually have – what they actually want? Actual ends do not have the normativity of "the right," and so we cannot define the general welfare in terms of these actual, particular ends: "an intention to secure my welfare or that of others ... cannot justify an action which is wrong" (126). Being a person of good heart – seeking the welfare of others – does not guarantee that what we do is right or rational. To do what is right, we must seek, not simply welfare, but the *good*. "Welfare without right is not a good. Similarly, right without welfare is not the good ... (130). The good must subsume both right and welfare. The moral will, therefore, must "make the good its aim and realize it completely" (131). But how are we to determine what is good?

Here we begin to encounter the problems that Hegel has with the philosophy of Kant. Kant believed that reason alone could determine what is right and good. Hegel grants that a subject has a right to listen to reason ("the right of giving recognition only to what my insight sees as rational is the highest right of the subject" [132]), but he maintains that reason at the stage at which we have arrived – the stage of morality – is merely "formal." He contrasts this formal reason with objective reason, suggesting, among other things, that the former speaks only to the form of willing required and not to its content. This, of course, was Kant's view. The moral will for Kant acts on principles having a certain form – universalizability. Hegel thinks of this form as one of rational consistency. Kant believed this formal requirement could distinguish actions that are moral from those that are not, but Hegel, as we noted early on, disagrees. At this point in his argument, however, Hegel is content to point out that formal reason can be correct or incorrect in its judgments. Thus the "right of insight" taken alone would justify a person in acting on the basis of beliefs about the good which turn out to be mistaken. According to this "right," we should listen to our conscience and do what it tells us, even if, as a matter of fact, it misinforms us of what is objectively right or good.

But there is also a "right of objectivity": our obligation, our duty, is to do what *is* right and good (what is objectively right and good), not merely what appears to be so. But how, again, can I know *what* my duty is? We can say that it is to do what is right and to strive after welfare (134), but these are mere abstractions, having no content and specificity. Duty, therefore, is "abstract universality, and for its determinate character it has identity without content ... " (135). This implies, Hegel asserts – having Kant clearly in his line of vision – that the science of morals is reduced "to the preaching of duty for duty's sake" (135). Kant is to be congratulated for giving "prominence to the pure unconditioned self-determination of the will as the root of duty" (ibid.), i.e., for affirming the autonomy of the rational will. But because Kant defines duty as the absence of contradiction, "no transition is possible to the specification of particular duties nor, if some such particular content for acting comes under consideration, is there any criterion in that principle for deciding whether it is or is not a duty" (ibid.). Formal reason, which can judge only of the rational form of a maxim – whether it is logically consistent or not – cannot, in Hegel's eyes, tell us whether any particular maxim is moral or immoral. "Tell a lie when doing so will rescue you from difficulty" or "break promises when doing so is to your advantage" are not self-contradictory maxims, and therefore, Hegel thinks, Kant has no way to repudiate them as immoral.[4]

The right of insight leads us to follow our conscience, but the right of objectivity demands that we do what is right and good. Conscience, at the level of the moral will, has no way of determining what is right and good. Its instrument, abstract reason, distinguishes only what is consistent from what is inconsistent, and this, as we have just seen, is insufficient to give content to the pronouncements of conscience. Ideal conscience, true conscience, as Hegel calls it, "is the disposition to will what is absolutely good" and such conscience is "the expression of the absolute title of subjective self-consciousness to know in itself and from within itself what is right and obligatory" (136). The problem we face, however, is that of knowing whether an individual's actual conscience is this ideal, true conscience. "Conscience [an individual's actual conscience] is therefore subject to the judgment of its truth or falsity, and when it appeals only to itself for a decision, it is directly at variance with what it wishes to be, namely a rule for a mode of conduct which is rational, absolutely valid, and universal" (137). Conscience at the level of moral thinking – formal conscience – is unable to provide us with any assurance that its deliverances have any objectivity.

In this predicament, conscience runs the risk of mistaking the predilections and biases, the impulses and desires, of the individual agent for absolutely valid, absolutely universal principles. For this reason, "it has become potentially evil" (139). Morality arises out of conscience, but so does evil. Evil is not just a matter of acting from natural inclinations but rather a matter of a self-conscious, reflective agent taking these inclinations and deliberately willing them as the embodiment of right and good. The role of conscience in the moral life at the same time opens up the possibility of evil.

Hegel's assessment of the moral life definitely has its negative aspects. At this stage self-consciousness is aware of the notion of universal laws and is aware that these laws are the manifestation of reason, the inner nature of self-consciousness. But moral consciousness or the moral will is unable to give any concrete content to these laws and the duties they entail. Moreover, because it understands the will as self-determining, as deriving from its own nature the moral laws it is to follow, moral consciousness appeals to the inner voice of conscience. But it has no way to distinguish false from true conscience, and this opens up possibilities of evil and hypocrisy. So the moral point of view is hardly ideal. At best, it is one stage, one moment, in the effort of consciousness to achieve an adequate sense of self, a concrete, free identity. Clearly there are other stages beyond it.

But all is not negative in Hegel's treatment of morality. We have left behind the merely natural self, with its accidental and incidental features, and we have left behind the stage of contract, where rights are merely negative and reflect at most the arbitrary desires of the participants. The moral self perceives a higher level of existence, one in which its actions are founded on general principles and principles that are rationally valid. Moreover, it glimpses that these principles are not imposed from without, by external nature or authority, but come from within, from within the human being's own nature. And finally, it achieves, albeit only abstractly, a sense of the social nature of existence. The human being is not an isolated individual who confronts other people as alien, as *other*. On the contrary, the moral sphere is one in which universal human nature, and universal welfare, are dominant considerations. So morality marks a definite advance in the effort of the self to become what it implicitly is. And the problems of morality are precisely those needed to inspire the self to take the next step, to move to the higher level of the ethical life.

Ethical Life

Hegel has high praise for the ethical life – what he famously calls *Sittlichkeit*.[5] It is the realization of true freedom; it is the "good become alive" (142) through self-conscious action; and it is the end that drives self-consciousness forward. Unlike the moral order, the ethical order has "a stable content independently necessary and subsistent in exaltation above subjective opinion and caprice" (144). This content is to be found in the "absolutely valid laws and institutions" (144) of our social existence

– in the family, civil society, and what Hegel calls the state. "Ethical powers" (145) regulate the lives of the individuals who participate in these social realms.

The ethical order has both the objectivity that self-consciousness has been seeking and the subjectivity that is the essence of the self:

> This ethical substance and its laws and powers are on the one hand an object over against the subject, and from his point of view they *are* – "are" in the highest sense of self-subsistent being ... On the other hand, they are not something alien to the subject. On the contrary, his spirit bears witness to them as to its own essence, the essence in which he has a feeling of his selfhood, and in which he lives as in his own element ... (146–7).

In other words, the subject finds in the ethical order a set of laws – and hence rights, duties, and responsibilities – which are objective and which at the same time reflect the real nature of the subject. In following these laws, the subject is following mandates that it gives itself, rules that flow from its own inner being as a rational creature. Thus the subject is free, not because she does what she contingently and capriciously wants to do, but because she follows the laws of her own real essence. "As substantive in character," Hegel tells us, "these laws and institutions are duties binding on the will of the individual" (148). These duties will appear restrictive only from the standpoint of abstract freedom, the standpoint of unformed or indeterminate subjectivity or arbitrary morality. In fact, just the opposite is really the case:

> The truth is, however, that in duty the individual finds his liberation; first, liberation from dependence on mere natural impulse and from the depression which as a particular subject he cannot escape in his moral reflections on what ought to be and what might be; secondly, liberation from the indeterminate subjectivity which, never reaching reality or the objective determinacy of action, remains self-enclosed and devoid of actuality. In duty the individual acquires his substantive freedom (149).

The problem we faced in morality, the difficulty of being able to determine on the basis of abstract or formal reason what our duties are, disappears at the ethical level: "In an *ethical* community, it is easy to say what a man must do, what are the duties he has to fulfill in order to be virtuous: he has simply to follow the well-known and explicit rules of his own situation. Rectitude is the general character which may be demanded of him by law or custom" (150). Participating in an ethical community means assuming certain social roles – for instance, those of husband, father, wife, mother, son, daughter, citizen – and thereby taking on the duties and responsibilities inherent in these roles. As the later British idealist philosopher F.H. Bradley was to put it, a person assumes "his station and its duties."[6] These obligations are not abstract and indeterminate but are, on the contrary, exceedingly concrete and specific. No longer does a person have to depend on subjective conscience or abstract reasoning to know what she ought to do.

We can put too much emphasis on the notion of duties in the ethical sphere. The concept of duty can make the ethical sphere appear more constraining than it really is. Only the person who does not fully participate in his community will sense constraint.

> But when individuals are simply identified with the actual order, ethical life (*das Sittliche*) appears as their general mode of conduct, i.e., as custom (*Sitte*), while the habitual practice of ethical living appears as a second nature which, put in the place of the initial, purely natural will, is the soul of custom permeating it through and through, the significance and the actuality of its existence   (151).

The requirements of our station and our duties are experienced by us as "second nature." In our own minds, they identify us as who we *are*. Individual wilfulness and private conscience vanish and are replaced by "the universal" which "is disclosed in its specific determinations as rationality actualized" (152). A sense of dignity and a sense of stability arise from participation in this universal. And a sense of deep and genuine freedom also arises: "The right of individuals to be subjectively destined to freedom is fulfilled when they belong to an actual ethical order, because their conviction of their freedom finds its truth in such an objective order, and it is in an ethical order that they are actually in possession of their own essence or their own inner universality" (153). Here we have not just negative freedom, freedom from interference by others, but positive freedom, freedom to be who we essentially are. We enjoy this freedom as particular individuals, for it is particular individuals who make up the ethical order. And we enjoy our rights no less than we recognize our duties. When there is an identity of "the universal will" (the ethical order) with the particular will (the individual person), "right and duty coalesce" – "by being in the ethical order a man has rights in so far as he has duties, and duties in so far as he has rights" (155). Ethical life, far from being coercive, is in fact liberating.

There are three moments or stages in the development of ethical life. The first – the natural or immediate phase – is the family; the second is civil society – "an association of members as self-subsistent individuals ... brought about by their needs, by the legal system ... and by an external organization for attaining their particular and common interests"; the third is the state, in which the individuals and their needs and interests are unified (157). We shall look briefly at each of these stages.

The Family

One enters ethical life through the family. The family is an embodiment of *mind* and is characterized by love, "which is mind's feeling of its own unity." In the family, we enter into a social organization in which there is both multiplicity and unity. "Hence in a family, one's frame of mind is to have self-consciousness of one's individuality within this unity as the absolute essence of oneself, with the result that one is not in it as an independent person but as a member" (158). One essentially is a member of a particular family, and one's individuality is expressed through the family and one's role in it.

Marriage itself takes "the natural sexual union" and changes it into "a union on the level of mind, into self-conscious love" (161). Hegel acknowledges that a marriage may subjectively arise from the natural inclinations of the two parties, but the objective source of marriage – even in the case of arranged marriages – is "the free consent of the persons, especially in their consent to make themselves one person, to renounce their natural and individual personality to this unity of the one with the other" (162). It is our ethical duty, Hegel affirms, to enter the married state (162), for in doing so we enter the ethical level of life and transcend accidental passions (which are of interest only to the individual). Marriage may allow for the satisfaction of physical passion, but its primary aim is to attain a "spiritual bond of union" and to rise above "the contingency of passion and the transience of particular caprice" (163). Marriage contains "the sensuous moment, the one proper to physical life," but the ethical bond at the heart of marriage can "subsist exclusively in reciprocal love and support" (164). The physical moment is subordinated to the ethical character of the marriage relation and to the recognition, by the partners, that marriage is an ethical bond.

Monogamy is an ethical requirement imposed by marriage. In entering the marriage state, individual personality is surrendered to the marital tie, whose "truth and inwardness ... proceeds only from the mutual, whole-hearted surrender of this personality" (167). "Marriage, and especially monogamy," Hegel tells us, "is one of the absolute principles on which the ethical life of a community depends" (ibid.). But marriage should not be seen as compulsory, from either the point of view of entering it or staying in it. Once the dispositions and actions of the spouses become "hostile and contrary" and estrangement is total, an objective third party – a civil authority – capable of seeing beyond any passing whims and moods on the part of the two parties, may grant a divorce (176).

The inward tie linking husband and wife is given external embodiment in the family's property and capital. The children of the marriage are also the externalization of this internal unity. "It is only in the children that the unity itself exists externally, objectively, and explicitly as a unity, because the parents love the children as their love, as the embodiment of their own substance" (173). The children have the right to maintenance and education by their parents, and the parents in turn have a right to the service of their offspring. The punishment inevitably involved in the rearing of children has a moral aim: "to deter them from exercising a freedom still in the toils of nature and to lift the universal into their consciousness and will" (ibid.).

Children, Hegel warns, "are not things and cannot be the property either of their parents or others" (175). Indeed, in the children there lies the future dissolution of the family, for when these children come of age "they become recognized as persons in the eyes of the law and as capable of holding free property of their own and founding families of their own" (177). When in this way one family gives rise to several families, "each of which conducts itself as in principle a self-subsistent concrete person and therefore as externally related to its neighbors" (181), we pass from the family into the realm of civil society.

Civil Society

Hegel's conception of civil society is that of a social and economic organization or system of "complete interdependence, wherein the livelihood, happiness, and legal status of one man is interwoven with the livelihood, happiness, and rights of all" (183). The actualization and security of each person's well-being depend on her working within this system, her desires and needs being held in check by the universal laws governing all of its members. Such members of civil society – "burghers," Hegel calls them – exist as private persons and pursue their own personal interests. Indeed, the laws of the society are a means to the fulfillment of personal interests. At the same time, the laws are such as to link up the well-being of the various citizens and to ensure that in working for one's own interest one is at the same time serving the interests of others. This rational system of laws thus enables the satisfaction of all of the interests in society. The "end of reason," as Hegel sees it, it to create an external environment which embodies reason: "by this means alone does mind become at home with itself within this pure externality" (187). When the individual's desires and needs are channeled through this rational system, the individual person is actually liberated – from the "pure subjectivity of demeanor," from "the immediacy of desire," and from "the empty subjectivity of feeling and the caprice of inclination" (ibid.). One achieves fulfillment as a rational person and one attains liberation by being a member of civil society, while at the same time one's individual, subjective needs are met through the mediation of the rational system that serves the entire group. "When men are thus dependent on one another and reciprocally related to one another in their work and the satisfaction of their needs, subjective self-seeking turns into a contribution to the satisfaction of the needs of everyone else" (199).

The system of supply and demand operating in civil society involves a process that conceives of needs and work in the abstract and develops a division of labor to serve these needs and to allocate to individuals the roles and functions needed to do so. It also creates class divisions – in particular, the agricultural class, the business class, and the class of civil servants – and the social distinctions that go with them. The individual person who becomes a member of one or the other of these classes thus becomes "something definite, i.e., something specifically particularized" (207). This class status or social position – one's station – provides concrete identity along with concrete duties and rights.

All members of civil society, however, regardless of their social position, equally count as persons in the eyes of the judicial system: "A man counts as a man in virtue of his manhood alone, not because he is a Jew, Catholic, Protestant, German, Italian, etc." (209) In civil society, "the right becomes positive law," law backed up by the sanctions administered by the judicial system. For the first time, Hegel tells us, universal rights acquire "true determinacy" (211), so that the abstractions and controversies of the moral sphere are left behind. The concrete content of positive law relates to matters of contract (which are no longer personal and arbitrary, as they were in the sphere of abstract right), to the complexity of social, agricultural, and business ties, to family matters, and to the administration of justice.

> By taking the form of law, right steps into a determinate mode of being. It is then something on its own account, and in contrast with particular willing and opining of the right, it is self-subsistent and has to vindicate itself as something universal. This is achieved by recognizing it and making it actual in a particular case without the subjective feeling of private interest; and this is the business of a public authority – the court of justice" (219).

The court of justice resolves issues and disagreements by appeal to the principles of universal law, and the police are called upon to deal with cases in which private interest and desire violate this law. Criminal or penal justice now becomes a matter of annulling crime and restoring the rule of law.

Civil society[7] is for Hegel yet another step forward in the effort of the mind to find its home in the external world. The laws that govern civil society are the product of the rational mind. In general the social world has been rationalized – through the division of labor, the market place, and the social classes, all of which bear the imprint of an abstracting and organizing reason. In civil society, the individual confronts a world made by the mind, and she finds a place in it. Insofar as she commits himself to this world, and acts on the basis of its rational principles, she follows its dictates. But if she sees her own reason as embodied in it, her actions are then guided by the principles of her own nature. Thus she achieves still another level of freedom.

Nevertheless, civil society is not the ultimate incarnation of mind and reason in objective reality. From the standpoint of civil society, we are still dealing with the subjective individual. To be sure, in following the laws and participating in the activities of the society, the individual is securing and maintaining the interests of others as well as her own. But self-interest remains her objective – life in civil society is simply a means to this end. It is basically an *economic* arrangement. We need to take another step forward whereby the individual's interests and very identity come to be equated with and derived from society as a whole. We need to move from the level of civil society to the level of the state, from the economic level to the *political* one.

The State

Hegel's descriptions of the state are often laden with his metaphysical terminology, thus: "The state is the actuality of the ethical Idea" (257) and "an absolute unmoved end in itself" (258). It is, in more accessible terms, the realization in concrete ways of the rational essence of human nature. Here the whole, the state, and the part, the individual, become one, the individual finding her identity as a patriotic member of the state and the state finding concrete actuality through the lives and activities of its members.

The state, Hegel tells us, "exists immediately in custom, mediately in individual self-consciousness, knowledge and activity" (257). Far from denouncing custom, as so many philosophers have, Hegel sees in it a very concrete set of social divisions, demands and goals that have a specificity far surpassing what is ascertained by moral thinking or found in civil society. Participating in the customs of our society, we secure an individual identity for ourselves while we also encounter the actualized values of the society. We no longer confront the mere moral "ought-to-be," for what ought to be is now what *is*. Mere custom, however, remains "immediate" and unaware of what it is; but through the self-conscious commitment of its individuals to it, and through their knowledge of its demands and their self-conscious activities in accord with its rules and expectations, custom is raised to the level of mind aware of itself as such.

Lest it be thought that Hegel is advocating acquiescence to conventions that, as we all know, may be cruel, superstitious, and dogmatic, it needs to be remembered that the advance from civil society to custom and the state is an advance in rationality as well. We might say that Hegel holds before us the ideal of rational customs, or of reason become customary. Rationality must always prove itself, Hegel thinks, and therefore any custom must demonstrate its rational credentials. But this is to be done from *within* the state, through the development of the constitution and the administration of justice. There is no objectively rational point of view apart from the concrete detail of everyday life within the social organism; we must always remember the plight of moral rationality, which can only appeal to rational form and is devoid of rational content. Content is provided by custom and custom made self-conscious in the constitution and life of the state. Rationality – universal validity – is the end, the fulfilling goal of constitutional law. "So far as the authority of any existing state has anything to do with reasons, these reasons are culled from the forms of the law authoritative within it" (258).

The relationship between the individual and the state is different from the individual's relationship to civil society. In the latter case, she can choose to join and thereby benefit from its practices, or she can choose not to. In the case of the state, the state "has supreme right against the individual, whose supreme duty is to be a member of the state" (258). The individual's involvement in civil society is contingent, her involvement in the state, necessary.

> If the state is confused with civil society, and if its specific end is laid down as the security and protection of property and personal freedom, then the interests of the individuals as such becomes the ultimate end of their association, and it follows that membership of the state is something optional. But the state's relation to the individual is quite different from this. Since the state is mind objectified, it is only as one of its members that the individual himself has objectivity, genuine individuality, and an ethical life. Unification pure and simple is the true content and aim of the individual, and the individual's destiny is the living of a universal life   (258).

One's individuality is attained through one's membership in the state and through the roles one assumes in it. In this way, one becomes an objective, substantial human being and more than a mere natural creature or a mere shadow of subjective consciousness.

Just as we tend to think of custom as essentially unthinking and irrational, we may also think of the state as something oppressive, an obstacle to human freedom. Hegel would correct us on both counts. For him, "the state is the actuality of concrete freedom" (260), which he defines in the following fashion:

> But concrete freedom consists in this, that personal individuality and its particular interests not only achieve their complete development and gain explicit recognition for their right (as they do in the sphere of the family and civil society) but, for one thing, they also pass over of their own accord into the interests of the universal, and, for another thing, they know and will the universal; they even recognize it as their own substantive mind; they take it as their end and aim and are active in its pursuit   (260).

The laws and customary practices of the state represent "the universal," what reason demands as far as how life should be lived and society organized. In becoming a member of the state, in obeying its laws and participating in its practices, one finds one's individuality in the universal. Hence in assuming one's station and doing one's duties, one is fulfilling oneself as an individual. And if one recognizes that the laws of reason inherent in the state are the laws of one's own reason – now become objective and concrete – one pursues the aims and ends of the state as one's own. The *isolated* individual may feel in a condition of subjection within the state, but the concrete individual, the member of a state, finds in the performance of her duties her liberation. Her attitude toward the state is one of *patriotism* and *trust*: "the consciousness that my interest, both substantive and particular, is contained and preserved in another's (i.e., in the state's) interest and end, i.e., in the other's relation to me as an individual" (268). When the other – society, the state – "is immediately not an other in my eyes, and in being conscious of this fact, I am free" (ibid.). The state is "mind on earth" (270)[8] and the free human being is the patriot.

The state also expresses a conception of the good, the good for all, and the subjects of the state identify with this conception. This collective end grounds and harmonizes the individual goods of its members.[9] Hence in participating in the state its members are fulfilling, in a concrete fashion, an aim which earlier, in the moral sphere, was merely abstract and unobtainable. The good reaches its fullest manifestation within this highest form of political organization.

Thus we come to the end of the effort of the self to attain both objectivity and freedom. The realization of this goal is found in the ethical life lived within the state. The moments of abstract right and morality do not disappear; nor do the family and civil society. All of these earlier (i.e., rationally more primitive) moments are subsumed within the ethical life. The family remains all important in the state, and the state contains a civil organization for the satisfaction of human need. But these elements are now given new meaning and new goals, for they no longer serve the interests of isolated human beings. On the contrary, they become embedded in the life of patriotic citizens for whom the state provides identity and freedom and goodness.

Assessing Hegel

Hegel's philosophy both attracts and repels us today. Some see it as the intellectual foundation of fascism, and indeed historically it was used for this purpose. We must ask ourselves, however, whether Hegel's insistence on freedom and rationality are consistent with the fascist exploitation of his thinking. Far more positively, some moral philosophers – loosely labeled "communitarians" – see in Hegel's emphasis on custom and the concrete detail of social life a much needed corrective to the rarified abstractions of much contemporary moral philosophy.[10] They claim, much in the spirit of Hegel, that it is in our everyday roles – as spouse, parent, employee, employer, judge, policeman, politician, citizen – that we find the true substance of our duties and responsibilities. These moral obligations cannot be deduced from some general principle, be it Kant's categorical imperative or the principle of utilitarianism. Rational moral thought, they insist, must be employed within the given structures and motivations of our social existence. In communitarianism, the spirit of Hegel is alive and well.

We shall end our study of Hegel by posing one question: is Hegel correct in thinking that only the social dimension of our existence is capable of providing concrete ethical duties and rights? Kant's categorical imperative is clearly an attempt to ground these duties in a principle of pure practical reason. We have seen that Hegel thinks this effort fails, but we have also noted that his arguments to this effect are not completely persuasive. In the next chapter, we shall consider an attempt by philosophers of a very different persuasion from that of Kant to identify a fundamental principle of morality – the principle of utility – which also abstracts from the traditions and conventions of society and indeed puts these social rules to the test. Hegel rejected the utilitarianism with which he was familiar on the Kantian grounds that it erodes the autonomy of reason. But before we can accept the "ethical life" with its stress on norms grounded in the concrete detail of social relationships and goals, we must give the major representatives of utilitarianism a chance to argue their case. Both the Kantian ethics and the ethics of utilitarianism maintain that we are able to devise a criterion of moral value that transcends our social and historical embeddedness and allows us to speak and judge as purely rational creatures. Hegel sees reason as "immanent" in our social practices; he denies that there is any transcendent position from which we can sit in judgment on our personal, economic, and political lives. The difference between the Hegelian position and that shared (uncomfortably) by Kant and the utilitarians, is one of the major divides in philosophical theory.

Hegel is often pictured as an arch-conservative who believes we must do obeisance to whatever traditional convictions govern our society. This is a totally distorted view of him. He criticized the leading conservative views of his day,[11] and he constantly stresses the standards of rationality and freedom. Any given political organization must justify itself by demonstrating the rationality of its laws and government and by showing how its ends are compatible with the subjective ends of its citizens. The state Hegel commends is an idealization, not an existing political organization (although he greatly admired the ancient Greek political community). The idealization called "the state" is the social arena within which concrete freedom and the dictates of reason become objective, without, in doing so, losing the element of subjectivity. It is that achievement of human reason wherein the opposition between subjectivity and objectivity is overcome. The state is an *ethical* institution.[12] Hegel's communitarianism is no defense of any despotic, totalitarian regime or a paean to unthinking traditionalism.

Unfortunately, in much of recent analytic, Anglo-American philosophy and ethics, Hegel is ignored more than anything else. This is unfortunate. For one thing, one must be impressed with the scope of Hegel's ethics. Here is a theory that encompasses the theory of contracts, the erotic urge and marital love, the division of labor, bureaucracy, the theory of punishment, the quest for identity and for concrete, unalienated freedom, and many other aspects of human life not often captured by philosophical reflection. Hegel teaches us that nothing falls beyond the reach of philosophy. Moreover, if "seeing connections" is the aim of philosophical explanation, Hegel provides us with many illuminating insights. In the end, his greatest achievement, perhaps, is that he gives us both a sense of the magnificent achievements of the philosophers who have preceded us – the belief that most philosophers in our history have had something valuable to say, even if not the final word – and, at the same time, a conviction that there is still important philosophical work to be done, higher levels of reflection to be reached.

12

Bentham and Mill

Utilitarianism, the doctrine of the greatest happiness of the greatest number, is the quintessential British moral philosophy. Although Hume was an earlier proponent of utilitarianism, Jeremy Bentham (1748–1832) can with some justification be called its father. He gave the doctrine its most explicit formulation and one of its most vigorous defenses.[1] John Stuart Mill (1806–73), a younger follower of Bentham, produced a more refined version of utilitarianism, making it a doctrine more attractive to many, but, in the minds of his critics, one less consistent. Bentham's *Introduction to the Principles of Morals and Legislation* and Mill's *Utilitarianism* are the classic sources for all discussions of the moral theory of utilitarianism.

Pleasure and Pain

Jeremy Bentham is one of the great, vociferous English reformers. As Mill said in his famous essay on him, "Bentham has been in this age and country the great questioner of things established."[2] He deliberately set himself the task of making English society more rational by ridding it of time-honored practices and institutions which had nothing more than the weight of tradition to recommend them. Institutions based on class privilege, in Bentham's eyes, produced more human misery than happiness, and the practices of government, especially in the area of crime and punishment, were the result of nothing more substantial than superstition and guesswork. If we set aside tradition and superstition and follow the dictates of reason, Bentham argued, we can achieve a society that promotes, as it should, the happiness of its citizens. Following reason meant for him following the principles of his doctrine of utilitarianism. Thus, calling Bentham the "great subversive," Mill crowns him "the father of British innovation both in doctrines and in institutions."[3]

Bentham is a reductive empiricist. He teaches that we must base our understanding of things on the deliverances of the senses, avoiding all metaphysical and religious claims that go beyond the bounds of sense experience. Thus human beings are to be understood in terms of our actual experience of them rather than in terms of philosophical speculations about the powers of reason, conscience, ultimate purposes, and the like. What our senses tell us is this:

> Nature has placed mankind under the governance of two sovereign masters, *pain* and *pleasure*. It is for them alone to point out what we ought to do, as well as to determine what we shall do. On the one hand, the standard of right and wrong, on the other the chain of causes and effects, are fastened to their throne. They govern us in all we do, in all we say, in all we think: every effort we can make to throw off our subjection, will serve but to demonstrate and confirm it. In words a man may pretend to abjure their empire: but in reality he will remain subject to it all the while   (I,1).[4]

In making this bold statement, Bentham is articulating both a psychological theory and an ethical one, and in the process he is attempting to render moral theory a rational science ("Morals," he tells us at one point, "is the medicine of the soul"). According to the psychological theory, pleasure and pain determine how in fact we always act: we are subjugated to them in the sense that anticipation of pleasure or pain are the motives of all our actions. Reflection on the role of pleasure and pain in human behavior will lead us as well to see how we *ought* to act: realistically, only pleasure and the avoidance of pain can be our ends. Proposing a standard of conduct based on the end of pleasure will be consistent with the facts of human nature, and this means that human beings will have a motivation to follow the standard. The science of human behavior that explains its subject matter in terms of pleasure and pain is at the same time in a position to demonstrate how laws and policies can be generated that will prompt human beings to behave as they ought, i.e., so as to promote pleasure and avoid pain. Thus the scientific moralist is able to prescribe beneficial medicine.

The Principle of Utility

The standard that Bentham puts forth he calls the *principle of utility*. This principle alone will harmonize with the fact that pleasure and pain govern our lives:

> The *principle of utility* recognises this subjection, and assumes it for the foundation of that system, the object of which is to rear the fabric of felicity by the hands of reason and of law. Systems which attempt to

question it, deal in sounds instead of sense, in caprice instead of reason, in darkness instead of light   (I,1).

The no-nonsense approach dictated by the principle of utility will replace tradition, speculation, and superstition in the creation of legislation aimed at improving the felicity of those governed by its laws. It will focus inquiry on the consequences of legislation and all other human actions. In its uncompromising consequentialism, it will reject any assertions about duties or rights that are not based on empirically justified claims about the beneficial or harmful consequences of behavior, i.e., the pleasure or pain it produces.

The promotion of happiness is at the heart of the principle of utility:

> By the principle of utility is meant that principle which approves or disapproves of every action whatsoever, according to the tendency which it appears to have to augment or diminish the happiness of the party whose interest is in question: or, what is the same thing in other words, to promote or to oppose that happiness   (I,2).

Bentham makes it clear that the principle is to govern not only the acts of private individuals but those of governments as well. Thus governments and individuals are charged with the duty of promoting the happiness, interest, or advantage of those who are affected by their actions. Happiness, interest, and advantage come to the same thing in Bentham's eyes – they all reduce to pleasure: "A thing is said to promote the interest, or to be *for* the interest, of an individual, when it tends to add to the sum total of his pleasures: or, what comes to the same thing, to diminish the sum total of his pains" (I,5). Thus Bentham is a *hedonistic* utilitarian. The principle of utility enjoins us to produce through our behavior the maximum amount of pleasure, and the minimum amount of pain, that we can.

Bentham believes that for the most part human beings act so as to promote their own interest, that is to say, so as to attain the maximum amount of pleasure and the least amount of pain for themselves. He does not deny the reality of sympathy for others, or disinterested behavior, but he thinks it rare and an exception to be expected only from "heroes." (He frequently saw himself as one of these heroes.) Legislators, he argued, should assume that their fellow citizens will act out of self-interest, and they should design laws accordingly. Bentham is, therefore, a qualified psychological egoist. But he is not an ethical egoist. He believes, on the contrary, that we should act to produce the general happiness – the greatest happiness of the greatest number. He sees the task of the legislator, or the manager of an organization, as one of devising means for attaining the general happiness which at the same time will serve the personal interests of individual citizens, or the members of the organization. In one of his pamphlets he speaks of the *Duty and Interest* junction principle: "No means to be omitted that can contribute to strengthen the junction between *interest* and *duty* ... i.e., to make it each man's *interest* to observe on every occasion that conduct which it is his *duty* to observe."[5] Knowing the laws that govern the actual self-interested behavior of human beings, we are in a position to organize behavior so as to achieve the disinterested end of the general happiness. Bentham has sometimes been accused of deriving "ought" from "is" and thereby violating Hume's strictures in this regard. Bentham professed, however, to believe in Hume's distinction, and if we separate the normative end of general happiness from the factual end of personal happiness we can see how he can have regarded himself as faithful to Hume.

As a good reductive empiricist, Bentham makes it clear that when we talk of serving the interests of the community, we are really talking only of promoting the interests (therefore the pleasure and absence of pain) of the individual members of the community. There is no more to a community than the individuals who compose it. The community itself is a "fiction"; only the individual members are real. Any talk of community can be "cashed out" in terms of statements about individuals. Thus the interest of the community is simply the sum of the interests of its members.

For Bentham, the principle of utility is the fundamental moral maxim. Applying it yields a knowledge of what actions are right and a knowledge of what we ought to do. The action that promotes the greatest happiness of those affected by it will be the right action to engage in, the one we ought to do, the action it is our duty to perform (I,10). "When thus interpreted, the words *ought*, and *right* and *wrong*, and others of that stamp, have a meaning: when otherwise, they have none" (ibid.). Bentham is contemptuous of all talk of natural rights and natural law, precisely because such notions have no relationship to the observable realities of pleasure and pain. Talk of such rights is just so much "nonsense."[6] The principle of utility yields a notion of right action that has a concrete, observable and verifiable sense.

A Proof of the Principle?

An important question arises as to whether it is possible to prove the principle of utility. Bentham admits that in a strict sense it is not, this because utility is the ultimate principle of morality and legislation and hence the principle to which appeal is made in deciding all other questions in these areas ("that which is used to prove every thing else, cannot itself be proved" (I,11). But in an indirect sense, proof is possible. In the first place, human beings often use this principle: "Not that there is or ever has been that human creature breathing, however stupid or perverse, who has not on many, perhaps on most occasions of his life, deferred to it. By the natural constitution of the human frame, on most occasions of their lives, men in general embrace this principle, without thinking of it ... " (I,12). Appealing as we so often do to the principle of utility, we are simply inconsistent when, in philosophical moments, we question or deny it. In fact, many of the arguments against the principle, Bentham claims, involve an unwitting appeal to this very principle. " 'The principle of utility (I have heard it said) is a dangerous principle: it is dangerous on certain occasions to consult it.' This is as much as to say, what?, that it is not consonant to utility, to consult utility; in short, that it is *not* consulting it, to consult it." (I,13,n). The inconsistency is obvious – if, as Bentham assumes, danger is equated with a potential for pain. And if danger is other than this, what is it? Thus if those who disclaim utility do in fact assume it themselves, albeit under a different guise, the principle commending it can be seen as morally inescapable.

According to Bentham, many opponents of the principle of utility who view it as leading to evil do so only because they take note of improper applications of the principle. It is true that many individuals under the influence of passion pursue immediate pleasures without a proper awareness of the considerable pains that are consequent on doing so. Likewise, in acting to benefit herself, a person may do things that bring unimaginable harm to others. Such actions, however, do not impugn the principle of utility, for they involve incomplete and inadequate consideration of the consequences of acting in these ways. "If a man calculate badly, it is not arithmetic which is at fault, it is himself" (II,Objs.). What is useful for the moment, Bentham reminds us, may be hurtful for the ages – but it takes the principle of utility to show this. For utility to be judged fairly, then, it must be presented in a fair light.

Other Objections

Other objections to the principle of utility result from what Bentham refers to as "the perversity of language" (ibid.).

> *Virtue* has been represented as opposed to utility. Virtue, it has been said, consists in the sacrifice of our interests to our duties. In order to express these ideas clearly; it is necessary to observe, that there are interests of different orders, and that different interests are in certain circumstances incompatible. Virtue is the sacrifice of a smaller to a greater interest – of a momentary to a permanent interest – of a doubtful to a certain interest. Every idea of virtue, which is not derived from this notion, is as obscure as the motive to it is precarious   (ibid.).

Properly understood, then, virtue is perfectly compatible with the principle of utility; indeed, it is but an application of it. And if virtue is not tied to utility and the realities of pleasure and pain, it becomes intolerably obscure, indeed mere nonsense. Still another objection to the principle of utility is that many obligations will be undermined when it turns out that breaking them has utility. Consequently, asking individuals to calculate utility will erode the moral fabric. Bentham's answer to this objection is complex. First, he declares that each individual *ought* to calculate the utility of her actions. "Every one will constitute himself judge of his own utility; this is and this ought to be, otherwise man would not be a reasonable being. He who is not a judge of what is suitable for himself, is less than an infant, is a fool" (ibid.). Moreover, some of our obligations, although they have disutility in the particular instance, have great utility in general, and it is this general utility that justifies us in upholding them. Take the case of keeping one's commitments or promises:

> Men are not always held by the particular utility of a certain engagement; but in the case in which the engagement becomes burdensome to one of the parties, they are still held by the general utility of engagements – by the confidence that each enlightened man wishes to have placed in his word, that he may be considered as trustworthy, and enjoy the advantages attached to probity and esteem   (ibid.).

Keeping a particular promise (engagement) may bring about more pain than pleasure to the parties affected. This fact, however, will not excuse the person from the obligation to keep the promise, precisely because a larger consideration of utility – a consideration, say, of the consequences her breaking the promise will have on the general practice of promise-keeping – will recommend in favor of keeping the particular promise. She also needs to consider the consequences of breaking the promise on her own reputation and thus on her future advantage. An account of all the consequences – direct and indirect – is required in order to ascertain what one's obligations are. When this is understood, we can see that the principle of utility will support most of our obligations, indeed all of them that a *reasonable* person can acknowledge.

But, some might complain, aren't our promises binding on us simply because we have made them? No, Bentham replies, his reason being that some engagements are void or unlawful, and so the mere fact of making the engagement cannot impose an obligation. On the contrary, "It is the utility of the contract that gives it force" (ibid.). Obligations and virtues, then, are not threatened by the principle of utility. When derived from this principle, these obligations and virtues are in fact rendered reasonable.

Failure to appeal to the principle of utility leaves our duties and obligations hanging unsupported. Without recourse to this principle, any attempt to justify one of our obligations goes fruitlessly in a circle:

> I ought to keep my promise. Why? because my conscience prescribes it. How do you know that your conscience prescribes it? Because I have an internal feeling of it. Why ought you to obey your conscience? Because God is the author of my nature; and to obey my conscience is to obey God. Why ought you to obey God? Because it is my first duty. How do you know this? Because my conscience tells me so – etc. Such is the eternal round from which there is no exit   (ibid.).

The principle of utility has the substantial advantage of tying our duties and obligations to a secure foundation. When we have calculated the overall utility of an act, no further questions can arise about whether the act ought or ought not be done.

Furthermore, if we were to abandon the principle of utility, how would we conduct our reasoning concerning right and wrong, especially in politics? Are we to judge without any principles whatsoever, or do we appeal to some other, non–utilitarian principle? Bentham suggests that those who pretend to have a different principle in point of fact simply use words that express nothing more than the speaker's "own unfounded sentiments" (I,14). Is a person's own "approbation or disapprobation, annexed to the ideas of an act, without any regard to its consequences" (ibid.) a sufficient justification for moral judgment? To think that it is so would be to breed either despotism (in the event a person's own sentiments are thought by her to be the standard for the human race) or anarchy (in the event each person's unfounded sentiments are allowed to be the standard for that person herself). And, finally, if there is thought to be a fundamental moral principle different from that of utility, what motivation would anyone have to follow it? What would the principle be good for? If we are governed (motivated) solely by the expectation of pleasure or pain, any principle that does not make reference to these feelings would fail to exercise any influence over human beings. As far as action is concerned, such a principle would be worthless.

These, then, are some of the considerations Bentham brings forth to provide an "indirect proof" of the ultimate principle of morality. They amount to pointing out that, correctly understood, the principle of utility is consistent with most of our everyday moral convictions and indeed underwrites them. The indirect proof appeals to the need for an objective base for morality, so that moral judgments generated by applying the fundamental moral principle to particular cases have the weight of fact and do more than express mere opinion and sentiment. Applying the greatest happiness principles yields judgments about the effects of actions and legislation on the pleasure and pain of those affected, and these are facts everyone must accept. And the indirect proof points to the necessity of arriving at a fundamental principle that has motivational efficacy. Bentham is convinced the principle of utility alone has this characteristic.

But could there not be other principles that satisfy the same criteria? Bentham identifies two principles which he believes are the most widely adopted alternatives to the principle of utility. The first is the principle of asceticism, the second the principle of sympathy and antipathy. He has in mind the ancient Cynics and Stoics as advocates of the principle of asceticism, although he groups the members of these philosophical schools together with religious advocates. In his opinion, both had as their "enemy" the "partizan of the principle of utility, whom they joined in branding with the odious name of Epicurean" (II,7). The principle of sympathy and antipathy is a less descriptive term, involving as it does a considerable amount of negative philosophical interpretation on Bentham's part. Once we see what Bentham has in mind, we shall be able to conclude that he takes the advocates of the principle of sympathy and antipathy to include most philosophical moralists who subscribe to deontological principles inconsistent with the principle of utility.

The Principle of Asceticism

Bentham defines the principle of asceticism as follows:

> By the principle of asceticism I mean that principle, which, like the
> principle of utility, approves or disapproves of any action, according to
> the tendency which it appears to have to augment or diminish the
> happiness of the party whose interest is in question; but in an inverse
> manner: approving of actions in as far as they tend to diminish his
> happiness; disapproving of them in as far as they tend to augment
> it   (II,3).

Philosophical defenders of this principle, according to Bentham, are motivated by
hope, the hope that by avoiding the pleasures of life they will attain "honour and
reputation at the hand of men" (II,5). Religious defenders are motivated more by fear,
"the fear of future punishment at the hands of a splenetic and revengeful Deity"
(ibid.). Men and women of education, Bentham avers, are usually those who subscribe
philosophically to the principle ("as more suited to the elevation of their sentiments")
while the vulgar are those more frequently motivated by fear. Bentham aims his attack
primarily at the philosophical defenders of asceticism.

First, he notes, they usually go no further than saying that pain is a matter of
indifference; they do not actually say that it is good. Moreover, they seem to reject
only some forms of pleasure, the gross "organical" kind, and even accept the more
"refined" pleasures, which, of course, they call by another name: "the honorable, the
glorious, the reputable, the becoming ... " (II,6). In making the last point Bentham
is arguing that the philosophical advocates of asceticism in fact operate with
something like the principle of utility, albeit under another name. His next criticism
aims at an alleged inconsistency in their outlook. If pleasure is so abominable, why
restrict oneself, as the advocates of asceticism do, to avoiding it oneself? Why not do
all one can to make other people as miserable as possible? "It should seem, that if
a certain quantity of misery were a thing so desirable, it would not matter much
whether it were brought by each man upon himself, or by one man upon another"
(II,8). The religionists, he remarks, are more consistent in this regard ("witness the
holy wars, and the persecutions for religion" (ibid.)). They are perfectly willing to
make other people miserable, although they too offer special justifications for their
actions ("the just punishments of heretics and infidels") and are unwilling to endorse
in general a policy of causing misery to other human beings. But why should an
advocate of asceticism not pass laws to ensure the misery of all citizens, say by
"stocking the body politic with the breed of highwaymen, housebreakers, or
incendiaries" (ibid.)? Such actions would be entirely consistent with their principle

of asceticism, if they really believed in it. But of course they don't really believe in it, and the principle of asceticism cannot be consistently applied: "Let but one tenth part of the inhabitants of this earth pursue it consistently, and in a day's time they will have turned it into a hell" (II,10). In fact, Bentham suggests, the original advocates of asceticism seem to have adopted the principle because they correctly saw that some pleasures can lead to greater pains (II,9). They should have seen that this fact – and it certainly is a fact – proves not that pleasure is bad and pain good, but that one must look to the overall consequences of an act in order to judge it. That some pleasures lead to pains, in other words, is entirely consistent with the principle of utility, and only to a confused mind suggests the alternative principle of asceticism.

The Principle of Sympathy and Antipathy

Next there is the principle of sympathy and antipathy, which Bentham defines as follows:

> By the principle of sympathy and antipathy, I mean that principle which approves or disapproves of certain actions, not on account of their tending to augment the happiness, nor yet on account of their tending to diminish the happiness of the party whose interest is in question, but merely because a man finds himself disposed to approve or disapprove of them: holding up that approbation or disapprobation as a sufficient reason for itself, and disclaiming the necessity of looking out for any extrinsic ground   (II,11).

This is a strange "principle," and Bentham acknowledges that it is really the denial of all principles. According to it, right and wrong are not determined by external considerations that might warrant the internal sentiments; right and wrong are determined, rather, merely by the sentiments – "whatever you find in yourself a propensity to condemn, is wrong for that very reason" (II,13). Advocating the principle of sympathy and antipathy, then, is really advocating extreme subjectivism, the view that feeling something right or wrong makes it so. Bentham characterizes such a subjectivism by pushing it to extreme lengths: "if you hate much, punish much: if you hate little, punish little: punish as you hate" (II,13). In other words, degrees of right and wrong are reduced to degrees of feeling.

Who has ever adopted such a "principle"? According to Bentham, many thinkers have, including many British moral philosophers of his own, or a slightly earlier, time. He mentions, in a lengthy footnote, Lord Shaftesbury, Hutcheson, Hume, Beattie, Richard Price, and Samuel Clark; and Butler also seems in his line of sight. Some of these thinkers have postulated a moral sense (Shaftesbury, Hutcheson), others a rationalistic knowledge of moral principles (Price), and still others a notion of fittingness or accord with nature (Clarke). But in Bentham's view, such theories are a facade, a cover-up for a reliance on one's own sentiments as a guide to right and wrong. For instance, one person advocates a grasp of moral truth through a moral sense, and "then he goes to work at his ease, and says, such a thing is right, and such a thing is wrong – -why? 'because my moral sense tells me it is'" (II,14n). Clearly, Bentham thinks, this appeal to a moral sense is disingenuous. As for the advocate of reason or understanding, this person is quite prepared to say that "if other men's understandings differ in any point from his, so much the worse for them: it is a sure sign they are either defective or corrupt" (ibid.). And the philosopher who claims that certain practices are conformable to the Fitness of Things is perfectly prepared to tell you, "at his leisure, what practices are conformable and what repugnant, just as he happens to like a practice or dislike it" (ibid.). In other words, the high-blown rhetoric merely disguises an unabashed appeal to what the thinker himself likes or dislikes, approves or disapproves of, has sympathy with or antipathy for. The chief mischief of all these moral "theories," Bentham remarks, is "their serving as a cloke, and pretence, and aliment, to despotism" (ibid.). They simply disguise the acts of the despot who would impose her own feelings on other people. Many is the moralist, Bentham alleges, who engages in this sort of *ipse-dixitism* – who says, in effect, "I say so, therefore it is so."[7] Bentham warns that much harm can be done by such a theorist: "If such a man happens to possess the advantages of style, his book may do a considerable deal of mischief before the nothingness of it is understood" (ibid.). In the area of his special concern, crime and punishment, Bentham notes that the principle of sympathy and antipathy (or the alleged "insights" or "principles" that disguise it) is often invoked to justify punishment far more severe than justified. And the principle is ready at hand to demand punishment of the most trivial incident: "Any difference in taste: any difference in opinion: upon one subject as well as another" (II,16). Beware the moralist, Bentham proclaims, who is ready to condemn and punish because the actions of others do not match her principles – that is, her feelings and opinions.[8]

Bentham singles out for special attention the strategy of those who appeal to the will of God as the basis of moral judgment. This appeal, he thinks, is just another instance of the principle of sympathy and antipathy, or the principle of asceticism, at work. He notes that before the revealed will of God can be applied to practical matters and matters of private conduct, it must be *interpreted*. Taking the precepts of revelation literally, he argues, would be disastrous: "taken in a literal sense, they would overturn the world, annihilate self-defence, industry, commerce, reciprocal attachments" (II,Objs.). But if we do interpret the will of God, such interpretations require some *other* standards or principles of right and wrong in order to be applied.

> The will then which is meant on this occasion, is that which may be called the *presumptive* will: that is to say, that which is presumed to be his will on account of the conformity of its dictates to some other principle ... We may be perfectly sure, indeed, that whatever is right is conformable to the will of God: but so far is that from answering the purpose of showing

us what is right, that it is necessary to know first whether a thing is right, in order to know from thence whether it be conformable to the will of God   (II,18).

We may assume that God knows, and tells us, what is good and right, but to find out *what* he tells us, we must examine matters on our own and find out what *is* good and right. Knowing that, we shall only then know what God tells us to do. The appeal to God is of no assistance in this matter.

Having provided reasons for accepting the principle of utility, and now having disposed of competing principles, Bentham is confident that utility will be accepted as the fundamental principle of morality. Contrary to its competitors, it is honest and workable, and it provides a guide to morality that steers between despotism and anarchy. It does not entangle us in theological disputes or wrap us in metaphysical fantasies. And so he rests his case. We may be less confident than he about the uniqueness of the principle of utility in attaining these ends, but the tests for moral theories Bentham proposes are sensible – and might well be extended to the other theories we discuss in this book.

Utility and Motives

In concluding his discussion of the principle of sympathy and antipathy, Bentham warns us against confusing a *motive* of action with its *ground* or a *reason* for its being the right one to perform. A motive is what moves us to act; the ground of rightness is what justifies the action. Admittedly, when we act on certain motives we often do things that have desirable consequences (according to the principle of utility), and this frequently leads us to commend the motive itself. But a motive that sometimes yields good consequences may at other times yield undesirable ones, and so the motive itself is insufficient to justify any action.

> The only right ground of action, that can possibly subsist, is, after all, the consideration of utility ... Other principles in abundance, that is, other motives, may be the reasons why such and such an act *has* been done: that is, the reasons or causes of its being done: but it is this alone that can be the reason why it might or ought to have been done   (II,19).

The notion of a reason, Bentham is saying in effect, is ambiguous. The reason for an action may be the cause of it, its motive, or it may be the objective consideration that justifies it. In his view, we need always to look for objective considerations. And to his mind, the possession of utility is the only objective reason that renders an action justified.

The Hedonic Calculus

Just how objective Bentham thought the matter of utility to be can be seen from a look at chapter 5 of the *Principles*, a chapter entitled "Value of a Lot of Pleasure and Pain, How to be Measured." Utility is something *measurable*, thus quantitative, scientific, and objective. Here we have the fundamentals of Bentham's *quantitative* hedonism. The aspect of pleasure primarily of concern to him is the *amount* of it, since quantity is something measurable. In examining the consequences of our possible actions, we can determine the quantity of pain and pleasure produced by them and thereby determine which of the options open to us would bring about the greatest balance of pleasure over pain, or the smallest possible amount of pain. It is in chapter 5 that Bentham develops what has come to be called the *hedonic calculus*. This calculus is a quasi-mathematical system for measuring the amount of pleasure and pain brought about by an action, and thus it is a system for determining the utilities that should guide our decisions to do one thing rather than another.

The key to the hedonic calculus is the recognition that pleasure and pain have different dimensions or aspects, each of which is measurable. For instance, they may vary from one another in their duration: one of them may simply last longer than another. They also may vary in intensity: some pleasures are mild, others intense; some pains dull or low level, others excruciating. Less obviously, pleasures and pains can be considered under the aspect of their certainty or uncertainty. Some actions will lead to pain with absolute certainty (try yanking out a tooth without anesthesia); other actions are more problematic in this regard (exercise, for example). Similarly, some actions will undoubtedly lead to pleasure (a connoisseur of fine wines consuming a bottle of 1983 Chateau Palmer) while others may or may not do so (watching your favorite, but inconsistent, sports team play a game). Furthermore, there is the fact that pleasures and pains may vary with regard to the time when they can be expected to occur: some actions lead to immediate pleasures, others to long-delayed ones. Pain follows immediately upon some actions; in other cases (e.g., the next-day hangover) it takes a while before the pain occurs. Bentham refers to this aspect of pleasure and pain as their propinquity (nearness at hand) or remoteness. Thus the first four dimensions of pleasure/pain to be measured by the hedonic calculus are:

1. intensity
2. duration
3. certainty or uncertainty, and
4. propinquity or remoteness.

In applying the calculus, we are to measure each of the pleasures and pains consequent upon each of the several actions open to us.[9] We do this by assigning a number registering the intensity, a number representing the duration, and numbers expressing the certainty/uncertainty and the propinquity/remoteness of each pleasure and pain. Positive numbers signify the amount of pleasure, negative numbers the amount of pain. The numbers representing the intensity and duration of a particular pleasure (or pain) can be multiplied together to obtain the "magnitude" of this pleasure (pain).[10] Insofar as the value of a pleasure is decreased by its uncertainty and remoteness and increased by its certainty and nearness, we can use fractions representing the degree of uncertainty and the distance to reduce the magnitude accordingly. Calculations of this sort will yield a value for each pleasure, and, *mutatis mutandis*, for each pain.

There are still other dimensions of pleasure/pain. Some pleasures have the tendency to produce in their turn, or to be followed by, yet other pleasures, and some pains have the tendency to generate still other pains. The mild pleasures involved in studying or doing homework are likely to be followed by other pleasures that result from getting a good grade in class. The pain of a hangover is likely to lead to other pains – as when one takes an exam with the hangover and gets a bad grade as a result. Thus a pleasure or pain has what Bentham calls its *fecundity* – "the chance it has of being followed by sensations of the same kind" (IV,2). Presumably we can measure this "chance" and assign a number to it. Likewise, we can look at a pleasure or pain and determine the likelihood of its *not* being followed by the opposite sensation. There is a great likelihood that some pleasures will not lead to subsequent pains (the joys of studying, for instance), while other pleasures are highly likely to lead to pains (the pleasures of a drunken spree, for example). Hence we must determine the *purity* of each pleasure and each pain consequent upon an action. It is clear that we should assign a high value to pleasures that are pure, but a low value to pains that are pure; and similarly, a low mark to pleasures that are impure, and a high (or higher) mark to pains that are impure. Thus, in addition to measuring the pleasures and pains consequent upon an action in the four dimensions discussed above, we must also do so in two additional dimensions:

5. fecundity, and
6. purity.

Every action open to a person must therefore be assessed in these six dimensions.

Insofar as fecundity and purity pertain to other pleasures and pains that are produced by an action, it is really unnecessary to consider these dimensions when measuring a single pleasure or pain. The calculation of the totality of pleasures and pains consequent upon an action will pick up the information garnered under (5) and (6).[11]

The resultant numbers assigned to each of the pleasures produced by an action can be added together to give one a sum representing the total amount of pleasure produced by this action. A similar number representing the total amount of pain this action produces can then be subtracted from the pleasure number, and the result will represent the overall balance of pleasure or pain produced by this action. The same procedure can then be applied to each of the possible actions open to a person.

Happiness of the Greatest Number

According to Bentham, the above calculations should first be performed by a person with regard to the pleasures or pains that can be expected for herself. To put it in Bentham's own words: "Sum up all the values of all the pleasures on the one side, and those of the pains on the other. The balance, if it be on the side of pleasure, will give the *good* tendency of the act upon the whole, with respect to the interests of that *individual* person; if on the side of pain, the *bad* tendency of it upon the whole" (IV,5). But the calculation should also be undertaken with respect to the pleasure and pain that *other* people will experience as a result of each possible act. Thus, Bentham tells us, we must add a seventh dimension of pleasure and pain to our considerations:

7. extent.

The overall balance of pleasure or pain for each act will be a function of the amount of pleasure and pain experienced by everyone as a result of the act.

> *Sum up* the numbers expressive of the degrees of *good* tendency, which the act has, with respect to each individual, in regard to whom the tendency of it is *good* on the whole: do this again with respect to each individual, in regard to whom the tendency of it is *bad* upon the whole. Take the *balance*, which, if on the side of pleasure, will give the general *good tendency* of the act, with respect to the total number or community of individuals concerned; if on the side of pain, the general *evil tendency*, with respect to the same community (IV,5).

When all these calculations are concluded, we can ascertain which of the actions open to us will be the right action, the one that ought to be performed: it will be the action measured as having the highest overall balance of pleasure over pain, or the least amount of pain, involved in its consequences – for all persons affected. The final calculation will demonstrate the impact of the right action on the general happiness.

Bentham recognizes that the decision procedure he has suggested is a very complex one which would take a considerable amount of time and involve consideration of numerous consequences. And he admits that because of this complexity it is not to be expected that the process will occur prior to every moral judgment or legislative act. Nevertheless, it should always be "kept in view" (IV,6), and it remains the ideal decision procedure to which one should appeal when necessary. The hedonic calculus, that is, is the ideal of reason. Moreover, Bentham assures us, "in all of this there is nothing but what the practice of mankind, wheresoever they have a clear view of their own interest, is perfectly conformable to" (IV,8). In other words, we already use the principle of utility and the hedonic calculus when we are rational about pursuing our own good or the good of the community.

In his day and ever since, Bentham's proposals have served as a rallying cry for social reformers and philosophers who see the rational life as the calculated pursuit of happiness, happiness for a single person or for the community of persons. Impractical and difficult as it may be, the use of the hedonic calculus represents for these individuals the ideal of rationality. There are, however, a number of problems with Bentham's proposals that must be overcome before one can have much confidence in his decision procedure. We shall conclude our discussion of Bentham by giving a brief indication of some of these difficulties.

Problems of Quantitative Hedonism

The use of the hedonic calculus presupposes that each of the seven dimensions of pleasure is measurable. And this is certainly true of most of them. Duration can obviously be measured in seconds and minutes. But what about intensity? Although we can speak of one pleasure being more intense than another, there is no obvious scale for determining the degrees of intensity. We can, perhaps, rely on a rough estimate of the felt intensity of our own feelings of pleasure, but how are we to assess the feelings of others? And can we say that a moderately intense pleasure for me has the same numerical value as a moderately intense pleasure for someone else? Surely we can have little confidence in the objectivity of such comparisons. And even when we have a clear scale of measurement – such as for duration – there is a question of how the points on the scale are to be understood in relation to one another. Is a pleasure that lasts twenty minutes twice as valuable as one lasting only ten minutes? Is an intense pain that lasts ten minutes simply twice as bad as one lasting only five – or might we not reach a threshold at which point the longer pain becomes unbearable, "not even on the same scale" as the shorter pain? If we hesitate over answers to such questions, we can have less than full confidence in Bentham's calculations. Finally, how are we to compare the values of the different aspects or dimensions of pleasure and pain? Are the degrees of intensity to have the same relative weight as the degrees of duration? Does an intensity of "two degrees" have the same value as a duration of two minutes (or two seconds, or two hours?)? Many problems of commensurability and incommensurability arise in this context.[12]

Bentham himself is aware of the difficulties involved in measuring sensations of pleasure and pain, and at times in his writings he appeals to *money* as a means of quantifying them. He notes that money is one of the best *means* to attaining pleasure:

with money we can purchase pleasure. The amount of money one is willing to pay for a pleasure may be thought of as giving the measure of the value of the pleasure for that person. And if a person equally prefers a pleasure and an amount of money, then the two have the same value for this individual. Likewise, if someone is willing to pay the same amount for two pleasures, then these two sensations can be said to have the same value for her. Money, too, has an objectivity that sensations of pleasure do not seem to have. It is a "common measure" of value in terms of which interpersonal financial interactions take place and by means of which interpersonal comparisons of utility can be made.

Unfortunately, money does not have quite the interpersonal objectivity it seems to have. Does a dollar have the same worth to a pauper and a millionaire? Hardly. Moreover, numerical differences in the amount of money do not neatly equate with differences in value even for a single person. A billionaire probably does not get twice the pleasure from his second billion as he received from his first. And then there are some values on which we cannot put a price – our honor and integrity, say, or the value of a child or spouse. Finally, not all pleasures can be purchased with money, and not all pains avoided with it. Bentham is fully aware of, and openly acknowledges, all of these problems with the use of money as a measure of utility.

Another problem with Bentham's utilitarianism arises with the very notion of pleasure and pain.[13] What are they? It is easiest to think of them as sensations, and Bentham often speaks of them as such. Indeed, the procedures of the hedonic calculus sketched above seem to presuppose that pleasures and pains are sensations. But Bentham himself is noted for the multiple distinctions he draws among the kinds of pleasure (V). There are pleasures of sense, pleasures of skill, pleasures of a good name, pleasures of piety, pleasures of amity, and still others. Few of these other than the pleasures of sense can be characterized as sensations – one doesn't feel a sensation when one experiences the pleasure of a good name. Likewise, the pains of the flesh bear little resemblance to the pains of an ill name. Even among the pleasures of sense, there is, according to Bentham himself, great variation: the pleasures of taste, of smell, of the ear, of the eye, of health. Is there some common quality among these pleasures, a quality that varies quantitatively such that one could add together the pleasures of taste and of health? It is most doubtful that there is. If one were to assume that all pleasures are really the same kind of thing, it would absurdly follow, as one commentator put it, that "sympathy, sex, or religion would all be various ways one could choose of achieving exactly the same thing."[14] The application of the principle of utility and the use of the hedonic calculus assume that all pleasures and pains have common qualities susceptible of measurement by an identical metric. If this assumption fails, what are the prospects for determining utility?

John Stuart Mill

Let us now turn our attention to the utilitarian theory of Bentham's follower, John Stuart Mill. Mill's best known work in ethics, and perhaps the best known of all his many works, is a small tract entitled *Utilitarianism*.[15] It was first published in installments in a magazine and then brought forth as a book in 1863. In this work, he proposes to establish the criterion of right and wrong and to identify the foundation of morality. The latter he takes to be equivalent to the *summum bonum* or greatest good. The principles of morality, the rules of right and wrong, will be derived from this end; they will consist in instructions in how best to obtain it. In Mill's view, specific rules of right and wrong – "it is wrong to tell a lie," "keeping a promise is the right thing to do" – can be seen as applications of a general principle or ultimate standard.[16] This principle is the "greatest happiness principle." Actions will be right or wrong insofar as they promote, or fail to promote, the greatest happiness of the individuals affected by them. It is this happiness which is the *summum bonum*. And happiness, as Bentham had argued, is to be construed as pleasure and the absence of pain.

Much of Mill's little book consists of attempts to answer criticisms of utilitarianism that were directed against Bentham's views.[17] In responding to these criticisms, Mill in fact goes far beyond Bentham and develops a highly distinctive form of the theory. The most important changes are two: a qualitative hedonism that stresses differences in the qualities of pleasures, and a view of human happiness that incorporates virtue as an end in itself. We shall consider these doctrines, and Mill's responses to other criticisms, in the order in which Mill presents them.

The Greatest Happiness Principle

Mill's definition of utilitarianism is very close to Bentham's conception of the principle of utility:

> The creed which accepts as the foundation of morals Utility or the Greatest Happiness Principle, holds that actions are right in the proportion as they tend to promote happiness, wrong as they tend to promote the reverse of happiness. By happiness is intended pleasure, and the absence of pain; by unhappiness, pain, and the privation of pleasure (210).[18]

The theory of utilitarianism accepts the "theory of life" to the effect that "pleasure, and freedom from pain, are the only things desirable as ends; and that all desirable things ... are desirable either for the pleasure inherent in themselves or as means to the promotion of pleasures and the prevention of pain" (210). Mill goes on to say that the *scope* of pleasure and pain – "what things [the Greatest Happiness Principle] includes in the ideas of pleasure and pain" – remains open, suggesting that not all pleasures are encompassed by the concept of happiness, or not to the same degree. This admission leaves somewhat unclear whether for Mill pleasure or happiness is the basic term in defining the *summum bonum*.[19]

A Doctrine Worthy of Swine?

The first objection considered by Mill is that in projecting pleasure as the ultimate end of life utilitarianism puts forward a mean and unworthy goal as the ultimate good for human beings: "To suppose that life has ... no higher end than pleasure – no better and nobler object of desire and pursuit – they designate as utterly mean and grovelling; as a doctrine worthy only of swine ... " (210). Pleasure is something pursued by swine; human beings surely are capable of a higher, more refined good. The objection presumes, Mill counters, that human beings are capable "of no pleasures except those of which swine are capable" (210). On the contrary, he claims, "Human beings have faculties more elevated than the animal appetites and, when once made conscious of them, do not regard anything as happiness which does not include their gratification" (210–11). The life of beasts is indeed inferior when compared to the forms of happiness (and hence pleasure) human beings are capable of. What are these higher forms of pleasure and happiness? They include, and Mill thinks the ancient Epicureans already recognized this fact, "the pleasure of the intellect, of the feelings and imagination, and of the moral sentiments ... " (211). All of these pleasures are distinguished from "mere sensation" (211).

The ancient Epicureans, although they recognized the higher pleasures, saw their superiority to consist simply in the fact that these pleasures have "greater permanency, safety, uncostliness, etc." (211), i.e., are quantitatively greater over the long run than the sensuous pleasures of the moment. In other words, these thinkers (just like Bentham, although Mill does not refer to him) operate with a quantitative form of hedonism. For them, pleasures vary in quantity only, and the basis for preferring the human pleasures to the swinish ones is that, when everything is considered, the former surpass the latter in quantity. Mill proposes, on the contrary, that the human pleasures can be distinguished from their beastly counterparts not only in quantity, but in quality as well. "It is quite compatible with the principle of utility to recognize the fact, that some *kinds* of pleasure are more desirable and more valuable than others" (211). Human beings are capable of these more desirable and valuable pleasures. In stressing them, Mill sees himself as moving beyond Bentham's overly narrow conception of human nature. Moral philosophy should not just be interested in demonstrating how public utility and individual interest can coincide (as Bentham thought) but also in promoting a richness of experience and excellence of character. Mill is as interested (or more so) in the qualities of the "inner life" as he is in legislative arrangements for attaining social goals.

Higher and Lower Pleasures

It has often been argued against Mill that he is inconsistent in first proposing that pleasure alone is desired and then distinguishing between higher and lower pleasures.[20] To make this distinction, the argument goes, there must be some characteristic the presence of which makes a pleasure higher or lower in quality, and this characteristic cannot itself be pleasure. In desiring the higher pleasures, we therefore desire something other than pleasure, namely their distinguishing characteristic. As one writer has put it, "If [a pleasure] is better because nobler, then we have introduced nobility as an independent value."[21]

This argument against Mill can be challenged. Why should not the distinguishing features of the higher pleasures be modifications of pleasure? To take an analogy, colors can be distinguished in terms of their hue and intensity, but these characteristics are not something other than color – they are simply determinate forms of it. Likewise, the distinctions between higher and lower pleasures might be thought of as determinate forms of pleasure. Surely there are qualitative differences between the pleasures of reading Shakespeare and the pleasures of getting drunk!

But, the argument against Mill might continue, these qualitative differences would simply mark different kinds of pleasure but not differences in value, not differences with respect to higher and lower pleasures. How are we to make the latter distinctions? The notion of "higher and lower" implies that pleasures vary in degree, and degree is a matter of *quantity*. Thus it would appear that Mill will have to revert to quantitative hedonism in order to speak of evaluative distinctions among pleasures. Furthermore, if quality isn't converted into quantity, how can Mill compare, as he wishes to do, the value of a small amount of a high quality pleasure with a large amount of a low quality pleasure? If quality and quantity are distinct characteristics or kinds of characteristic, they are incommensurable, i.e., they can't be compared with one another.[22] The argument concludes that either quality and quantity amount to the same thing (in which case Mill is really a quantitative hedonist after all), or Mill cannot speak of degrees of quality and cannot compare quality and quantity (as he does).

Mill was convinced that the quality and quantity of pleasures are distinct characteristics but nevertheless can be compared, just as he believed that different qualities of pleasure can be compared. Distinctions among qualities of pleasure are not a matter of degree – a pleasure of one quality is not "more" or "less" pleasant than a pleasure of another quality but rather superior or inferior to one of another quality. Likewise, a pleasure combining a certain quantity and quality may be superior or inferior to another pleasure with a different combination of quantity and quality. Just as a large amount of ordinary "jug" wine is inferior to a small amount of high quality vintage wine, a large amount of a pleasure of inferior quality has less value than a small amount of pleasure of superior quality.[23]

The Test of Superiority

But what makes one pleasure qualitatively superior to another, and what makes the combined quality and quantity of one pleasure superior to the combined quality and quantity of another? Mill addresses this question by asking how we *know* what pleasures are superior. His answer is this: "Of two pleasures, if there be one to which all or almost all who have experience of both give a decided preference, irrespective of any feeling of moral obligation to prefer it, that is the more desirable pleasure" (211). The preference of competent judges – those who have experience of both kinds of pleasure and attend only to the intrinsic features of the pleasures – is the criterion to be used in distinguishing pleasures in terms of their relative quality. The choice or preference of qualified judges will also serve as "the rule for measuring [quality] against quantity." This rule will determine when quality rules out over quantity, and, presumably, when quantity (perhaps in a great amount) rules out over quality.

Unfortunately, Mill's argument here leaves it unclear whether the choice of qualified judges *constitutes* superiority – so that by definition the pleasure they choose is superior – or whether it is merely a contingent fact that qualified judges will always prefer the superior or higher pleasure.[24] If it is only a contingent fact, then we still need to know in what the superiority of some pleasures consists.

Mill believes that competent judges will prefer the qualitatively superior pleasure even when it is accompanied by considerable "discontent." Thus pain or unhappiness comes into the picture as well. Presumably if the quantity of pain is great, we might reach a point where the value of the quality of the pleasure, no matter how exalted, would be overridden by considerations of the quantity of the pain. If a person had to choose between, on the one hand, a clear mind capable of abstract (pleasant) thought together with extreme pain, and, on the other, relief from the pain but at the expense of the capacity for such thought, which would be preferable? All such questions for Mill are to be placed before competent judges. The preference of qualified judges gives us a general test for the value of hedonic experience.[25]

The Higher Faculties

The higher-quality pleasures are associated, Mill informs us, with the exercise of the higher human faculties. It is the employment of these faculties, and the enjoyment of the pleasures attendant on this employment, which human beings desire above all else. In fact, they would not substitute a human life involving the use of these higher faculties for a lower beastly life even if the latter were filled with (beastly) pleasures. The swine may be more content than the human being who uses her mind, imagination, and moral faculties, but happiness and contentment are not the same thing. There will be some discontent in the lives of most human beings, whereas many animals live lives of what appears to be perfect contentment. Moreover, many human beings often fail to exercise their higher faculties, being satisfied with the lower pleasures of the senses. But the degree of quantitative pleasure is not the mark of human happiness: "It is better to be a human being dissatisfied than a pig satisfied; better to be Socrates dissatisfied than a fool satisfied. And if the fool, or the pig, is of a different opinion, it is because they only know their own side of the question. The other party to the comparison knows both sides" (212). The quality of pleasure involved in the life of a Socrates is so superior to that of a fool, and even more so to that of a pig, that the addition of considerable dissatisfaction to this life leaves it still superior in pleasure.[26]

Mill acknowledges that the "capacity for the nobler feelings is in most natures a very tender plant" (213). This capacity can be crippled by temptation or infirmity of character, and it may be dulled by age or the lack of sustenance, that is, lack of reinforcement, encouragement, or opportunity. In spite of these liabilities, Mill concludes that "it may be questioned whether anyone who has remained equally susceptible to both classes of pleasure, ever knowingly and calmly preferred the lower ... " (213). Again, the verdict of competent judges, those who have experience of both the lower and higher pleasures, is the final court of appeal, and Mill is convinced that this verdict will support the cause of the higher pleasures.

In Mill's eyes, it is the exercise of the higher faculties and the enjoyment reaped from such exercise that best serve to define human happiness. Also included among the components of happiness are a sense of freedom and power, a sense of security, and a harmony among the various elements of the personality.[27] It is this complex end that is expressed in the standard against which we measure human actions, those actions fostering it being right and those thwarting it wrong.

Does Utilitarianism Ask Too Much?

But are human beings capable of happiness? It would be pointless to put this state forward as the goal of human existence if it were unattainable, and numerous pessimistic philosophers have claimed that it is beyond human reach. Mill considers this claim to be an exaggeration of the facts. To be sure, a life of continuous pleasures – a life of constant rapture – is impossible, but this is not what the utilitarians, or the Epicureans before them, are proposing. Their goal is a far more realistic one: a life of frequent and varied pleasures, and momentary raptures, with a "few and transitory pains" mixed in. A balanced mixture of tranquillity and excitement is the type of life desired by most. Such an existence, Mill affirms, is open to most people, and the real obstacles to its being attained by all are "the present wretched education, and wretched social arrangements" (215). Another reason many people fail to attain it is that they care for nobody but themselves. Such an inordinate concern for one's own happiness is the surest way to fail in attaining it. On the contrary, wide and varied interests greatly enhance the prospects for happiness. "A cultivated mind ... finds sources of inexhaustible interest in all that surrounds it; in the objects of nature, the achievements of art, the imaginations of poetry, the incidents of history, the ways of mankind, past and present, and their prospects in the future" (216). Add to these some "genuine private affections, and a sincere interest in the public good" (216), and everyone born in a civilized society should be capable of attaining a life filled with satisfactions. Mill, the liberal believer in progress, has no hesitation in affirming that "most of the great positive evils of the world are in themselves removable ... " (216) and that most vicissitudes of fortune and other disappointments in one's worldly circumstances are "principally the effect either of gross imprudence, of ill-regulated desires, or of bad or imperfect social institutions" (217). All of these obstacles to human happiness can be eradicated.

Mill admits that there are individuals who deliberately do without human happiness – and are often honored for it. Such abnegation of personal happiness is commendable, he admits, but *only* if it is undertaken with a view to increasing the happiness of others. Moreover, an ability to do without happiness – the Stoic capacity for apathy – may be paradoxically the best way to attain pleasure. Freed from an obsession with happiness and anxiety over the many threats to it, a person can then "cultivate in tranquillity the sources of satisfaction accessible to him, without concerning himself about the uncertainty of their duration, any more than about their inevitable end" (218). Mill the utilitarian thus brings the ancient Stoics into the utilitarian camp!

Impartiality

Lest his version of the doctrine sound too egoistical, Mill reaffirms that "the happiness which forms the utilitarian standard of what is right in conduct is not the agent's own happiness, but that of all concerned" (218). Utilitarianism requires an impartial, disinterested, benevolent spectator, a person who will give no preference to her own happiness over that of others and who will pursue the goal of happiness even if she herself does not stand to gain by the effort. This, Mill takes it, was the lesson of Jesus of Nazareth. The Golden Rule ("do unto others as you would have them do unto you") and the admonition to love one's neighbor as oneself are thus perfectly consistent with utilitarianism. Education and society should inculcate in all citizens a desire for the common good and a sense of the harmony between individual happiness and the happiness of all.

But isn't this asking too much? Are human beings capable of acting (always or often) for the common good or promoting out of a sense of duty the greatest happiness of the greatest number? In answering this question, Mill, following Bentham, makes a basic distinction between the standard of duty or right action and our motives for engaging in action. "It is the business of ethics to tell us what are our duties, or by what test we may know them; but no system of ethics requires that the sole motive of all we do shall be a feeling of duty" (219). Motive, according to the utilitarians, has nothing to do with the morality of an action.

> He who saves a fellow creature from drowning does what is morally right, whether his motive be duty, or the hope of being paid for his trouble; he who betrays the friend that trusts him, is guilty of a crime, even if his object be to serve another friend to whom he is under greater obligations   (219).

Serving society at large is seldom a motive that operates in us, Mill grants. More often than not we act to benefit particular persons, and he thinks that this is perfectly appropriate, given that private utility is the most we usually have an opportunity to affect. We are called upon by the principle of utility to perform the action that will result in the greatest overall gain of pleasure over pain; we are not called upon to act out of a love for humanity or an affection for the good of others. Individuals who do act from such motives are highly esteemed, and appropriately so in light of the fact that acting on such motives often brings benefit to society. But it is the benefit, not the motive, that makes it the right thing to do.

Does such a doctrine render utilitarians cold and indifferent to all characteristics of human beings other than the utility of their actions? Not so, says Mill. Utilitarians are aware of, and admire, many other personal characteristics. A good and virtuous character is certainly commendable. None of these human qualities, however, should be praised if it has pernicious consequences for the public welfare. Hence a consideration of utility is called for with regard to human dispositions as well as human actions.

Secondary Principles

But is there time to calculate utility? Won't the moment for action be lost if, prior to acting, we initiate a consideration of the consequences of our action? Is utilitarianism practicable? Mill has a ready response to this line of criticism:

> The answer to the objection is, that there has been ample time, namely, the whole past duration of the human species. During all that time mankind have been learning by experience the tendencies of actions; on which experience all the prudence, as well as the morality of life, is dependent (224).

Human experience leads to the formation of generalizations about the tendencies of certain *kinds* of actions to be beneficial to the public good or harmful to it. We have learned over centuries of experience, e.g., that truthfulness has great utility, and deceit considerable disutility. Moral rules have been formed to mark these tendencies of actions. Mill refers to rules like "telling the truth is the right thing to do" and "breaking contracts is wrong" as secondary or subordinate principles or intermediate generalizations. They are secondary or subordinate to the principle of utility, and they arise when we generalize from experience about the tendency of certain kinds of action to achieve the goal articulated by the principle of utility. Mill warns us that the secondary principles have exceptions and thus tell us only what is generally the case. Nevertheless, given that they are based on longstanding experience of many people and ages, we can use them with confidence, so that there is no need to calculate the utility involved in every single action we undertake. The secondary rules are ready at hand to give us guidance in deciding what we ought to do.

Secondary principles may give rise to a conflict of obligations. One of the secondary principles may require, say, that we tell the truth, while another requires that we protect other people from harm. There may be occasions in the knotty affairs of human beings when telling the truth would involve bringing harm to another person. What are we to do in such a case? Instead of giving free scope to personal desires and partialities, which are subjective and capricious, we are to appeal to the principle of utility, the ultimate principle of morality. "If utility is the ultimate source of moral obligation, utility may be invoked to decide among [the subordinate principles] when their demands are incompatible" (226).

The Sanction of Morality

In the second section of *Utilitarianism*, Mill raises a question about the *sanction* of morality when morality is understood as a utilitarian would have it. What are the motives for obeying the principle of utility and its secondary principles? Why do we feel obligated to obey them? What is the source of their binding force on us? In particular, why do we feel bound to promote the general happiness, even on those occasions when doing so is inconsistent with promoting our own, private happiness? There are, Mill answers, both external and internal sanctions for being a good utilitarian. The external sanctions include the fear of punishment – from God or human beings – when one does not pursue the general good, and the hope of reward or favor when one does pursue it. A society allied to the principle of utility can bring to bear on its citizens powerful incentives for obedience to this principle. Added to these external sanctions are the natural sympathies we have for other human beings; we often are devoted in a disinterested way to their well-being.

Moreover, alongside the above external sanctions is the internal sanction of duty, inner feelings that stand in the way of our doing things that harm others or involve the violation of one of the secondary moral principles. These inner feelings reveal themselves in the form of remorse when in fact we do violate our moral duties. This inner sanction is a subjective one, and it is often enhanced and expanded by education and social acculturation. Nevertheless, it has a natural basis in the social sentiments of human beings:

> This firm foundation is that of the social feelings of mankind; the desire to be in unity with our fellow creatures, which is already a powerful principle in human nature, and happily one of those which tend to become stronger, even with express inculcation, from the influences of advancing civilization   (231).

We grow up with a sense of the oneness of all human beings, a sense that all of us are in the same boat, that we must all work together, and that we must take the interests of everyone into account. These feelings can be strengthened by education to the point that many individuals feel *as a matter of course* that one should give consideration to the good of others. "The deeply rooted conception which every individual even now has of himself as a social being, tends to make him feel it one of his natural wants that there should be harmony between his feelings and aims and those of his fellow creatures" (233). This "feeling of unity" is the ultimate sanction behind the principle of utility, the reason we are motivated to obey it and the reason we feel remorse when we fail to do so.

Proof of the Principle of Utility

The third section of *Utilitarianism* is one of the most controversial parts of the book. In it Mill confronts the question of what kind of proof can be given of the principle of utility. Bentham, it will be recalled, also struggled with this question, and he argued that although no direct proof of the principle of utility is possible insofar as it is the ultimate moral principle, considerable support can be mustered in its favor. Mill likewise maintains that although "questions of ultimate ends do not admit of proof" (234), considerations can be given to sway the mind in favor of the claim that happiness is the end of all action. His "proof" of this proposition has two parts. First, he argues that "questions about ends are ... questions about what things are desirable" (234), and he goes on to maintain that happiness is desirable. Second, he argues that nothing other than happiness is desirable as an end.

What justification does the utilitarian have for claiming that happiness is desirable. Here is Mill's argument:

> The only proof capable of being given that an object is visible, is that people actually see it. The only proof that a sound is audible, is that people hear it: and so of the other sources of our experience. In like manner, I apprehend, the sole evidence it is possible to produce that anything is desirable, is that people do actually desire it. If the end which the utilitarian doctrine proposes to itself were not, in theory and in practice, acknowledged to be an end, nothing could ever convince any person that it was so. No reason can be given why the general happiness is desirable, except that each person, so far as he believes it to be attainable, desires his own happiness. This, however, being a fact, we have not only all the proof which the case admits of, but all which it is possible to require, that happiness is a good: that each person's happiness is a good to that person, and the general happiness, therefore, a good to the aggregate of all persons   (234).

Mill's "proof" is notorious, in that many commentators believe that it commits several obvious fallacies. First of all, the argument that *being desired* is to *being desirable* as *being heard* is to *being audible* is questionable. As the British philosopher G.E. Moore[28] pointed out in the early part of the twentieth century, to say that something is audible is to say it *can* be heard, and surely the best proof of this is that in fact it is heard. But to say that something is desirable is not to say that it *can be desired* but rather that it *ought to be desired*. The fact that people do in reality desire a particular object may show that it can be desired, but it does not show that it ought to be. Hence the fact that people desire happiness does not prove, as Mill claims, that happiness is desirable.

Mill's argument may be strengthened a bit, perhaps, by noting his statement that if something were not already acknowledged as an (ultimate) end, no reasons could ever be given to convince anyone that it was such an end. We can prove that some things are desirable by showing that they lead to other things we admit as desirable, i.e., that they are means to these ends. But the *ultimate* end must be considered desirable in itself, for its own sake, and thus no demonstration of its value which refers us to its instrumentality is possible. What kind of reasons, then, can be given in defense of its value? Mill's answer is that none can be. Unless the end is already seen as desirable, it cannot be proved to be so. Furthermore, if someone does desire an ultimate end, this person at any rate considers it desirable. Thus desiring happiness as an ultimate end is the only way in which a person can come to deem happiness desirable. Given the fact that all human beings in fact desire happiness, it follows that all human beings view happiness as desirable and good in itself. Surely this is all that Mill wants to prove. After all, he rules out a direct proof that happiness is an ultimate end.

But another problem with Mill's "proof" resides in his inference from the fact that individuals desire their own happiness to the conclusion that the general happiness is desirable. He reasons that if a person's happiness, being desired by her, is a good for that person, the general happiness is the good for the aggregate of all persons. Doesn't this argument commit the fallacy of composition, the error of reasoning that consists in concluding that something is true of the whole because is true of the parts? Each part of an elephant is small, but it would certainly be fallacious to conclude that the elephant as a whole is small. Moreover, what exactly does it mean to say that the general happiness is a good to the aggregate of all persons? Does it imply that each person in the aggregate desires the general happiness? If it does, the claim seems false: surely not everyone desires the well-being of others, much less of all others. Does the aggregate of all persons *itself* desire the general happiness? This would require that the aggregate be a sort of person, someone who can desire something, and such a supposition is highly implausible.

It is difficult to defend Mill here, but one could appeal to things he said in his discussion of the sanction of morality in order to explain why he thinks his proof persuasive. If it is true, as Mill believes, that all of us harbor fellow feelings for other human beings, that we have a sense of unity with them and see it as a matter of course that we attend to their interests, then it can be argued that each of us, or at least most of us, desire the general happiness (in addition to our own). And if we desire this happiness, it is an end for us, desirable for its own sake. Hence Mill's proof that the general happiness is an ultimate end could be grounded in his belief that all human beings already take it to be so – their desiring it being the only way in which they can come to believe that it is desirable. Another line of defense might be the following. If pleasures (and forms of happiness) vary in quality, the individuals capable of the highest happiness may in fact desire the general good, the happiness of others. They may view the happiness of others as part of their own happiness; in desiring their own happiness, they therefore desire that of others. And if, having the experience of the higher happiness, they select the inclusive form of happiness over the more selfish form, this demonstrates the superiority – the greater desirability – of a happiness that incorporates the well-being of others.[29]

The Case for Virtue

But is happiness the only thing we desire? A proof of the principle of utility requires that we demonstrate that happiness is the only end in itself. It is here that Mill argues that virtue, the disposition to do what is right, is not only a means to happiness but also a real part of happiness. In this fashion he is able to respond to those who, following Kant, place virtue or a dutiful will at the top of the list of goods. If virtue is a part of happiness, one can admit that virtue is an ultimate end and still retain the thesis that happiness is the only thing that is good in and of itself.

Utilitarians, Mill asserts, "not only place virtue at the very head of the things that are good as means to the ultimate end, but they also recognize as a psychological fact the possibility of its being, to the individual, a good in itself, without looking to any end beyond ... " (235). In defense of this position, Mill points out that individual pleasures, for example those derived from listening to music or from health, are not to be thought of as means to something beyond them, an entity called happiness. Each of these pleasures is desired, and desirable, in itself; it is not a means to, but a component of, happiness. Likewise, it is possible that virtue too is a component of happiness, and therefore desirable in itself.

Mill admits that virtue for a utilitarian is not initially – "not naturally and originally" (235) – a part of the end of happiness; rather, it is capable of becoming a part of it. Initially, utilitarians desire virtue as a means to producing happiness – it is a state of mind or a disposition of character that tends to the performance of actions having utility. But it can be observed that unless a person loves or desires virtue as an end in itself, this person will not be in the state of mind or have the character most conducive to the general happiness. Moreover, because the love of virtue is highly instrumental to the general happiness, an association can be effected between the value of the general happiness and the value of virtue. In this way, virtue itself becomes pleasurable and a veritable component of happiness. Virtue, like music and health, comes to be *included in* happiness: "They are some of the elements of which the desire of happiness is made up. Happiness is not an abstract idea but a concrete whole; and these are some of its parts" (236). The state of mind called virtue is so pleasurable and desirable that it is not just a means to happiness but a part of it, especially in the case of the person who enjoys the exercise of the higher faculties of mind.[30]

Mill believes that he has proved all he needs to prove: happiness is an end in itself and the only end in itself.

It results from the preceding considerations, that there is in reality nothing desired except happiness. Whatever is desired otherwise than as a means to some end beyond itself, and ultimately to happiness, is desired as itself a part of happiness, and is not desired for itself until it has become so (237).

Throughout his "proof" Mill has appealed to psychological facts that he thinks will be apparent through our observations of others and an inner awareness of ourselves. His argument, therefore, is entirely consistent with the empiricism he so ardently espouses elsewhere.

Is This Hedonism?

How are we to assess Mill's contribution to the theory of utilitarianism? Has he answered in a satisfactory manner most of the objections to the theory? Having examined some of the criticisms of his view in the course of our discussion of it, we shall confine ourselves at this juncture to two issues that have recently generated considerable critical commentary. The first relates to one of the observations made earlier. It may be questioned whether Mill's qualitative hedonism is really a form of hedonism at all. Pleasure clearly can vary in quantity – it makes sense to use most of the measures involved in Bentham's hedonic calculus to quantify pleasure (even if we question whether this decision procedure really works to generate an overall hedonic value). But can pleasures really be assessed as higher or lower than one another? Unquestionably the pleasures derived from listening to classical music are different from the pleasures of drinking a fine wine, and both are different from, say, sexual pleasures, but what could it mean to say that one of them is superior in quality to the others? Some of the "higher pleasures" Mill refers to, for instance the ones Socrates allegedly enjoys, probably should not be described as pleasures at all.[31] They are certainly not sensations.

It is open to Mill to claim that superiority simply means that qualified observers – those who have experience of the options and who judge the issue impartially (not being swayed by prior moral convictions) – will prefer one of the pleasures to the others. The good, then, would equate with the preferences of qualified observers. Instead of this being hedonistic utilitarianism, it may be more appropriate to refer to it as preference utilitarianism. And given the difficulties with a straightforwardly hedonistic utilitarianism like Bentham's, the substitution of qualified preference for pleasure may be a step in the right direction for utilitarian thinkers. They wish to stress the objectivity and rationality of utilitarian ethics, but it is difficult to see how there can be a science of the quality of pleasure. Preferences probably can be quantified so as to take into account the number of preferences for each option, the intensity of these preferences, and the like. Thus a science of the good, as envisioned by Bentham and Mill, may make more progress when preferences are taken as basic than when pleasure is the fundamental term of value. Thus the very weakness of Mill's theory – that it fails as a theory of hedonism – may at the same time be its strength as a theory of utilitarianism.

Act- and Rule-Utilitarianism

The second aspect of Mill's thought that has generated considerable attention in the recent literature concerns the question of whether Mill is an act-utilitarian or a rule-utilitarian. These are not terms that Mill himself uses, but they are central to current discussions of utilitarianism, and some scholars have thought it important to identify which camp Mill falls into. Act-utilitarianism is the moral theory that individual acts should be assessed to determine the overall balance of pleasure or pain (happiness or unhappiness) they produce. The right act is then defined as the one among the possible acts open to someone that possesses the greatest utility. Rule-utilitarianism maintains, to the contrary, that what should be assessed for utility is not the individual act but rather a rule or practice that requires a certain kind of act. One must determine whether a rule or practice is justified, and one does this by examining the consequences of following it. If the practice or general adherence to the rule leads to greater pleasure/happiness than would the absence of the practice, or if it leads to more happiness than would general adherence to a different rule, then this practice is morally justified. For a rule-utilitarian, an individual act is right if it falls under a rule or practice that has been morally justified as having maximum utility.[32]

Advocates of rule-utilitarianism defend their theory and criticize act-utilitarianism on a number of grounds. First, they point to the great difficulty of measuring the consequences of individual acts, and they urge that practices, such as the rules making up the practice of punishment, can more adequately be assessed for utility. It is easier to determine the consequences of everyone behaving a certain way (following a certain rule) than it is to ascertain the consequences of an individual behaving in this way. Second, they argue that an act-utilitarian could conceivably justify breaking a promise or telling a lie on a particular occasion by showing that on this occasion the lie or broken promise had greater utility than its opposite. This possibility offends the moral intuitions of many rule-utilitarians. It would undo the binding quality possessed by our obligations not to break promises or tell lies. If the act-utilitarian were right, it would be appropriate, indeed required, prior to every decision to calculate whether telling a lie or breaking a promise had greater utility. For the rule-utilitarian, this is morally unacceptable. Even worse, the rule-utilitarian points out that in principle an act-utilitarian could justify an act of murder, or torture, or injustice, simply by showing that it had greater utility on a particular occasion. Such a consequence is morally outrageous. Rule-utilitarianism does not have these consequences. If the notion of right action is defined as adherence to a rule that has maximum utility, then a lie, breaking as it does the justified rule prohibiting lies, is always wrong; murder, in breaking the justified moral rule against murder, is always wrong; and so on.

Act-utilitarians are not without a response to their critics. They urge that rule-utilitarians are "hung up on rules" – that they would require one to tell the truth or fulfill a promise even if it were obvious that the consequences of doing so were disastrous. This attitude they find intolerable. They can accept the notion of rules if rules are simply generalizations about the tendencies of kinds of acts to promote the public good. Such rules serve as rules of thumb, as guidelines, and they undoubtedly are of assistance in the decision-making process, when it is often difficult to calculate the utility of individual acts open to one at the moment. But these rules or guidelines must be acknowledged to have exceptions, and if a case is encountered in which the violation of a rule would clearly best serve the public interest, it would be *irrational* not to break the rule on that occasion.

Is Mill an act- or rule-utilitarian? The traditional or standard interpretation has been that he is an act-utilitarian,[33] but in 1953 J.O. Urmson urged in an influential essay that he is in fact a rule-utilitarian.[34] And there is a more recent view that he is really neither, at least as these are defined above.[35] The literature on this issue is voluminous, and there is no point in our getting entangled in the many details of the argument. It will suffice to look briefly at those passages in *Utilitarianism* and some of Mill's other works which have led to the rule-utilitarian interpretation, and to note how these passages can equally be interpreted as expressing act-utilitarianism.

Secondary Principles Again

We have seen that Mill frequently speaks of "secondary principles." These are fairly specific rules about what kinds of acts are right and wrong, and they can be seen as derived from the primary principle of utility by showing that following them leads to the greatest good for the greatest number. In one of his essays, Mill suggests that calculation of utility can usually occur only with regard to these secondary principles or "ends": "We think utility, or happiness, much too complex and indefinite an end to be sought except through the medium of various secondary ends" and "Those who adopt utility as a standard can seldom apply it truly except through the secondary principles."[36] This does not say that the principle of utility can only be applied to the secondary principles, but it comes close to doing so. An act-utilitarian, however, can read these passages as saying merely that we will have an easier time of it, and perhaps make fewer mistakes about consequences, if we rely on secondary principles and test them for utility. Mill does frequently comment that the best way to determine the utility of an action is to ask what would happen if everyone acted this way, but this too is susceptible of an act-utilitarian interpretation: it can be seen as recommending an indirect way of ascertaining the consequences of a particular action.

In *Utilitarianism*, Mill introduces the "greatest happiness principle" by saying that it holds actions to be right "in the proportion to which they tend to promote happiness, wrong as they tend to promote the reverse of happiness" (210). Although traditionally taken as the expression of act-utilitarianism, this passage has been given a different reading by J.O. Urmson.[37] Urmson points out that individual actions don't *tend* to promote happiness or unhappiness; they either do or they do not. On the contrary, classes of actions, for instance the class of actions mandated by a rule, may be said to tend to have certain effects, which means that more often than not acts of this type promote happiness (or the opposite). Thus, Urmson concludes, Mill was expressing rule-utilitarianism in the very passage in which he defines the idea of a right action.

This argument, impressive to many, can nevertheless be challenged. Fred Berger points out that there is a sense in which an individual act *can* be said to tend to promote happiness, and that, moreover, this was the sense in which Bentham, Mill, and many others of the day used the term "tend."[38] Any action will have many consequences, some of them being pleasant, some painful. If on the whole or on balance the consequences of the individual action contain more pleasure than pain, then the action can be said to tend to produce pleasure; if the reverse, it tends to produce pain. Such a reading is completely compatible with act-utilitarianism, and indeed seems to require it.

In defending his rule-utilitarian interpretation of Mill, Urmson also points to the passage in which Mill says "There is no case of moral obligation in which some secondary principle is not involved" (226). This passage seems to take moral obligation as the obligation to follow a secondary principle, not the obligation to engage in a particular act because it has utility. This line of thought is developed in later passages of *Utilitarianism* is which Mill is talking of injustice: "For the truth is, that the idea of penal sanction, which is the essence of law, enters not only into the conception of injustice, but into that of any kind of wrong," and "we call any conduct wrong ... according as we think that the person ought, or ought not, to be punished for it" (246). Philosophers generally agree that punishment, in contrast to mere vindictive behavior, occurs only when a rule or law has been broken. If this is so, then if to say that an act is wrong is to say the agent should be punished for it, this wrong must be the violation of a rule, even if the punishment for breaking it is only informal moral condemnation. Accordingly, Mill seems to be defining wrong in such way as to lead to rule-utilitarianism. As David Lyons has put it, "*To show an act wrong, therefore, is to show that a coercive rule against it would be justified.* The justification of a coercive social rule establishes a moral obligation, breach of which is wrong."[39]

This is probably the strongest argument in favor of the rule-utilitarian interpretation of Mill. But it implies that not every action that fails to maximize utility is wrong. This seems inconsistent with Mill's initial definition of right actions, which speaks generally of actions and not a subset of them. But it is possible to interpret the initial definition as part of a general theory of value (the "theory of life"), with morality being but a part of "life," the part in which rules and punishment are appropriate.[40] Seen in this way, the theory of the *summum bonum* would apply to all parts of life – morality as well as prudence and aesthetics – but morality would be distinctive in requiring rules and measuring them, and not individual actions, against the final end of happiness. However that may be, we must leave the matter at this point, confident that the interpretative debates will continue.

Justice

The last section of *Utilitarianism* deals with the foremost objection to a utilitarian theory of morality, the objection that the principle of utility cannot explain justice. This is an objection that has been leveled against all utilitarians – Hume and Bentham were certainly aware of it – and justice is still considered by many to be the Achilles heel of the appeal to utility. Before examining what Mill has to say about justice, we shall look at this criticism in a bit more detail.

Basically, the objection is that whereas the appeal to utility is a consequentialist, forward-looking enterprise, considerations of justice are frequently backward-looking and appeal to factors other than, and often inconsistent with, utility. The requirements of justice are, in this respect, like many of our other obligations. If I make a promise to you, I have an obligation to keep it, and you have a right to expect me to fulfill it, because of what I *did*, viz., make the promise. It would be morally inappropriate for me to calculate the utility of my keeping the promise before I decide to keep it. Sometimes the utility of keeping a promise might be outweighed by the utility of not keeping it. Nevertheless, the balance of utility in favor of not keeping it almost never relieves one of the obligation to do so. (Hard questions arise when the consequences would be extreme and disastrous for the welfare of those affected.) Likewise, the keeping of contracts is not something that should be open to utilitarian calculation – a valid contract is binding, come what may.

The objection to utilitarian consequentialism from the standpoint of justice can be expresssed in terms of the distribution of benefits and punishments. Prizes in a competition should go to those who win or merit them, not to those who would happen be made happiest by receiving them. Insofar as applying the utilitarian standard amounts to measuring the amount of pleasure or happiness that is produced by the actions available to us, it is easily conceivable that the maximum happiness would result from an action that totally ignored the matter of merit. Or the matter of fairness. Treating people fairly does not necessarily correlate with treating them in the way best suited to maximizing overall utility. A store owner might "cheat" on wages, and thereby maximize profits and overall utility, but it would not be fair to the workers to do so. Likewise, the freeloader who does not do her part in a cooperative enterprise should not receive her share of the rewards – she does not deserve it. But the lack of desert seems to have little to do with an overall calculation of utility. An innocent person might be punished and society thereby benefit, but punishment of the innocent is wrong – a great injustice! The innocent do not *deserve* punishment. A petty thief might be severely punished and a greater utility thereby attained – but at the expense of fair treatment.

Utilitarian thinkers have always thought they could answer these justice-based objections.[41] Rule-utilitarians are often motivated by precisely the belief that their form of utilitarianism is in a better position to do so than act-utilitarianism. We shall now turn to what Mill has to say about justice. No attempt will be made, however, to assess whether or not he succeeds in his defense of a utilitarian conception of justice. Such a judgment will be left up to the reader.

Mill begins by acknowledging that "one of the strongest obstacles to the reception of the doctrine that Utility or Happiness is the criterion of right and wrong, has been drawn from the idea of Justice" (240). Justice, he notes, seems to many to be an "inherent quality in things," something "absolute" and therefore different from the relative and changing usefulness of actions and institutions. Our feelings about justice are exceedingly strong and demanding, more imperative than the feelings attaching to simple expediency. There is a binding force about justice that seems to fit uneasily under the notion of general utility.

The Idea of Justice

To show, in spite of these appearances, that justice is an instance of utility, Mill proposes, first, to articulate clearly what is involved in the idea of justice, and, second, to describe the way in which the intense feelings surrounding justice are generated. He thinks that a clearer understanding of what justice is will allow us to see why thoughts of justice are accompanied by feelings of this sort.

He begins his first task by surveying "the various modes of action, and arrangements of human affairs, which are classed, by universal or widely spread opinion, as Just or as Unjust" (241). Most of the cases he considers are instances of *unjust* actions, that is, instances of injustice. The first of these consists of acts that deprive a person "of his personal liberty, his property, or any other thing which belongs to him by law" (241). Justice is served, in this sense, when a person is allowed to possess what he has a *legal right* to. In some cases, however, the civil laws are themselves unjust. When this happens, it is because these laws themselves infringe upon a person's rights. The latter cannot be legal rights, for these are bestowed only by the civil laws. When the laws are unjust, it must be because they infringe upon a person's *moral rights*. This leads to a second kind of injustice, which "consists in taking or withholding from any person that to which he has a *moral right*" (242). Justice is served when the moral rights of people are protected and honored.

A third notion of justice consists in giving people what they *deserve*. This leads, of course, to the question what it is that a person deserves, the general answer to which is that someone deserves "good if he does right, evil if he does wrong" (242). Still a fourth idea of justice (or rather injustice) involves *breaking faith*, not fulfilling one's commitments in an engagement, promise, contract, or the like. Justice in this area is not absolute in that sometimes moral considerations can be given, in particular instances, to justify breaking faith – when, for example, a greater good can be attained by doing so.

There are still two other ideas that are closely connected to justice: impartiality, and the treatment of people as equals. As for the first, it turns out in fact that partiality rather than impartiality is often considered the more appropriate moral response. We should be partial to the weak, the sick, the handicapped, and the like; often we should give them special treatment. Partiality is appropriate in these cases because there are moral considerations justifying the special consideration. But we should be impartial in giving all people their rights. It will frequently be the case that being impartial means considering only certain features of a situation in making a decision, for instance, the desert or merit of people (rather than personal favoritism) in making employment decisions. "Impartiality, in short, as an obligation of justice, may be said to mean, being exclusively influenced by the considerations which it is supposed ought to influence the particular case in hand, and resisting the solicitation of any motives which prompt to conduct different from what those considerations would dictate" (243).

As for equality, Mill remarks that although justice relates to equality, we seldom think all people should be treated absolutely as equals, there being distinctions among them that need to be taken into account if justice is to be served. All people, for example, should be treated equally in being allowed to vote – except children, convicted felons, and those who have not registered to vote! The exceptions, in Mill's eyes, are granted on the basis of general utility.

Justice and Rights

In trying to find the common thread among these various notions of justice, Mill notes that etymologically this idea is almost always connected to the notion of conformity to law, although, among thinkers like the ancient Greeks and Romans, the connection is to laws that *ought* to exist, i.e., moral laws. Legal or moral *restraint* is central to the idea of justice, especially when it is associated with a notion of blame and punishment for breaking the laws. But conformity to moral laws is simply the idea of moral obligation in general. What serves to distinguish the obligations of justice from other moral obligations, e.g., obligations that we have to other people (such as charity and beneficence)? In answering this question, Mill uses the philosophical distinction between duties of perfect obligation and duties of imperfect obligation. The latter duties, which include charity and beneficence, leave it up to the individual person on what occasions, or with regard to what individuals, she is to perform these duties. We have a duty to be charitable, but not to any particular person or charitable organization. Duties of perfect obligation are different: "duties of perfect obligation are those duties in virtue of which a correlative *right* resides in some person or persons" (247). We have a duty of perfect obligation to keep our engagements, because the person with whom we made the engagement has a right to expect that we keep the faith. Likewise, we have a duty of perfect obligation not to hurt another person, because that person has a right to security. Injustice involves a violation of a duty of perfect obligation, which means that when injustice occurs, a wrong has been done and a person has been harmed, specifically by having one of her rights infringed upon.

> It seems to me that this feature in the case – a right in some person, correlative to the moral obligation – constitutes the specific difference between justice, and generosity or beneficence. Justice implies something which it is not only right to do, and wrong not to do, but which some individual person can claim from us as his moral right   (247).

The idea of justice, then, incorporates the notion of protecting the moral rights of people, indeed having a duty to do so that is imposed by the rights people possess. The right is a moral claim that people make on one another; the duty is the obligation to grant or fulfill these claims. Justice exists when rights are upheld and duties performed.

In his analysis of justice, Mill places great stress on this notion of a right and the violation of a right.

> When we call anything a person's right, we mean that he has a valid claim on society to protect him in the possession of it, either by the force of law or by that of education and opinion. If he has what we consider a sufficient claim, on whatever account, to have something guaranteed to him by society, we say that he has a right to it   (250).

The right connected with justice is the right not to be hurt in one or more ways – by having a contract or promise broken, by being dispossessed of personal property, and so on. More generally, it is a right not to be hurt by having one's security threatened or violated. In voicing a right not to be hurt, we are making a claim on society to use its resources to guarantee us this benefit. Society accomplishes this by law or public opinion, in either case threatening to punish anyone who violates our right. If we do not think society ought to take measures to ensure that we have certain benefits, this means we do not think a person has a right to them. For instance, to use Mill's example, we think a person has a right to equal opportunity – a right to what she can earn in fair professional competition – but we do not think a person has a right to earn a certain amount of money a year – which is to say that society should take steps to ensure the former but not the latter.

The Sentiment of Justice

Having defined to his satisfaction the idea of justice, Mill next initiates an inquiry into the feelings (of severity and absoluteness) associated with justice and asks whether they can be explained as arising from considerations of utility. Do we feel so strongly about justice because we see it as promoting general utility? His answer is that "the sentiment itself does not arise from anything which would commonly, or correctly, be termed an idea of expediency; but that though the sentiment does not, whatever is moral in it does" (248). There is, in other words, a nonmoral sentiment at the basis of our feelings about justice, but when this sentiment becomes moralized, it is because of considerations of utility. Let us try to see what Mill means by this.

The original sentiment behind our feelings about justice, he claims, is one of retaliation or vengeance. When we or our loved ones are harmed, we wish to retaliate. This is a very natural feeling, one shared with the lower animals. It is connected with the natural impulse to self-defense also shared by most sentient creatures. Human beings, however, are capable of sympathizing with a broader range of individuals than the lower animals are – they can sympathize with all human beings and indeed all sentient creatures. Moreover, their intelligence allows them to detect a community of interest between themselves and the human society of which they are a part. Any conduct threatening society will then call forth the instinct of self-defense and a desire to retaliate, to punish the ones who bring harm to society and thwart its (and their) interests.

> The sentiment of justice, in that one of its elements ... consists of the desire to punish, is thus, I conceive, the natural feeling of retaliation or vengeance, rendered by intellect and sympathy applicable to those injuries, that is, to those hurts, which wound us through, or in common with, society at large. This sentiment, in itself, has nothing moral in it; what is moral is the exclusive subordination of it to the social sympathies, so as to wait on and obey their call   (248–9).

When our desire for retaliation or punishment is based on our sympathy with the social whole, it is a moral sentiment – the sentiment of justice. It is aimed at promoting the general good. In this way considerations of utility enter into the conception of justice and underlie the strong feelings supportive of it. As Mill puts it:

> the sentiment of justice appears to me to be, the animal desire to repel or retaliate a hurt or damage to oneself, or to those with whom one sympathizes, widened so as to include all persons, by the human capacity of enlarged sympathy, and the human conception of intelligent self-interest. From the latter elements, the feeling derives its morality; from the former, its peculiar impressiveness, and energy of self-assertion (250).

According to Mill, considerations of utility enter into justice in two ways. First, the idea of justice involves, intellectually, the promotion of the rights of people, and the only justification for claiming rights is the utility of doing so. "To have a right, then, is, I conceive, to have something which society ought to defend me in the possession of. If the objector goes on to ask why it ought, I can give him no other reason than general utility" (250). Second, justice serves a particular kind of interest or utility, namely security, which is "to every one's feelings the most vital of all interests" (250). The feelings involved are so strong that the moral obligation to maintain the security of society becomes absolute. "The feelings concerned are so powerful, and we count so positively on finding a responsive feeling in others (all being alike interested) that *ought* and *should* grow into *must*, and recognized indispensability becomes a moral necessity, analogous to physical, and often not inferior to it in binding force" (251). Thus the demands of justice seem to be more absolute than demands to promote happiness. In reality, though, in promoting security they protect the very conditions for attaining happiness – everyone's happiness. Justice therefore possesses the most basic utility of all. Given our animal feelings about security, we are led to say, not just that we ought to promote justice, but that we must.

Mill concludes his discussion of justice by arguing that his utilitarian conception of it can be used to decide the inevitable disagreements that occur over justice when other conceptions of it are initially used. For instance, some claim that it is unjust to punish a person as a means of deterrence – as an example to others – and that punishment is justified only when it is applied for the criminal's own good – to lead her to repentance and rehabilitation. Others on the contrary see punishment that is not aimed at deterrence to be nothing more than the infliction of pain and evil on the wrongdoer. And then there are those who think that no one should be punished – that punishment in general is unjust – because all human actions are shaped and determined by social factors beyond our control. What can decide the debate between these opposing points of view regarding the justice of punishment? Only considerations of utility, Mill claims. Likewise, debates frequently occur over what method of taxation is most just. Some argue for a graduated tax, others for a flat tax, and still others for no tax at all, and each party seems to have good reasons for its position. How are we to decide the issue? Only the principle of utility can give us, Mill thinks, an objective answer not subject to the whims and interests of the individual disputants. Rather than being inconsistent with the matter of justice, then, the theory of utilitarianism is the best way to decide this matter.

Liberty

We shall conclude our discussion of Mill by looking briefly at his essay "On Liberty," a publication perhaps equal in reputation to *Utilitarianism*. In this essay he applies his utilitarianism to the question of the relationship between the state and the individual, inquiring into the areas in which civil authorities have the right to legislate against forms of behavior.[42] He defines his subject as "the nature and limits of the power which can legitimately be exercised by society over the individual" (218).[43] Mill's position on this issue expresses the stance of the classic liberal. According to this view, the individual should be allowed liberty over a broad range of activities, the only limit to this liberty being those actions that harm the interests of others. In the process of arguing for his position, Mill delivers a paean to individuality, applauding individualistic "experiments in living" and condemning the mediocrity and deadening conformity to public opinion found in most societies. He warns against the "tyranny of the majority" that can suppress individuality in the interests of the accepted modes of behavior in a society.

Mill sets out one principle from which the remainder of his argument derives:

> The object of this Essay is to assert one very simple principle, as entitled to govern absolutely the dealings of society with the individual in the way of compulsion and control, whether the means be physical force in the form of legal penalties, or the moral coercion of public opinion. That principle is, that the sole end for which mankind are warranted, individually or collectively, in interfering with the liberty of action of any of their number, is self-protection. That the only purpose for which power can be rightfully exercised over any member of a civilised community, against his will, is to prevent harm to others. His own good, either physical or moral, is not a sufficient warrant. He cannot rightfully be compelled to do or forbear because it will be better for him to do so, because it will make him happier, because, in the opinions of others, to do so would be wise, or even right. To justify that, the conduct from which it is desired to deter him must be calculated to produce evil to some one else. The only part of the conduct of any one, for which he is amenable to society, is that which concerns others. In the part which merely governs himself, his independence is, of right, absolute. Over himself, over his own body and mind, the individual is sovereign   (223–4).

Mill makes it clear that he is defending liberty in the above sense only for "human beings in the maturity of their faculties" (224), not for children or even for people who could not be "improved by free and equal discussion" (ibid.).

There is a sphere of action, Mill claims, in which society should have no direct interest, namely "that portion of a person's life and conduct which affects only himself, or if it also affects others, only through their free, voluntary, and undeceived consent and participation" (225). This sphere includes thought and expression, taste and ambition, and associations with other individuals. Thus there should be, in Mill's view, freedom of thought, opinion, and discussion; freedom of what we might call "life style"; and freedom of association. Only when we pass beyond this private sphere into a distinct public realm in which our actions have a harmful effect on others should there be any curtailment of liberty.

Freedom of Thought

Turning first to freedom of thought, Mill begins by making a bold declaration that "If all mankind minus one were of one opinion, and only one person were of the contrary opinion, mankind would be no more justified in silencing that one person, than he if he had the power, would be justified in silencing mankind" (229). His argument is clearly a utilitarian one, pointing to the desirable consequences that follow from allowing freedom of thought and discussion and the harmful ones that are the products of censorship and control.

> ... the peculiar evil of silencing the expression of an opinion is, that it is robbing the human race; posterity as well as the existing generation; those who dissent from the opinion, still more those who hold it. If the opinion is right, they are deprived of the opportunity of exchanging error for truth: if wrong, they lose, what is almost as great a benefit, the clearer perception and livelier impression of truth, produced by its collision with error (229).

In the first place, to suppress an opinion because society thinks it wrong is to assume that society knows, with absolute certainty, what the truth is. This is an assumption of infallibility – the impossibility of being in error. Such an assumption should quickly be dismissed; it flies in the face of the fact that, given any socially approved belief, "other ages, countries, sects, churches, classes, and parties have thought, and even now think, the exact reverse" (230). This is not to deny that there is any such thing as truth – although some of Mill's critics claimed that his doctrine implies such skepticism – but rather to note that the best, perhaps only, way to avoid error is through public discussion and debate. When society claims, then, to have the truth, in the interest of which it proposes to suppress conflicting opinions, it cannot justify this claim without entering into a debate with the holders of the other view. "Complete liberty of contradicting and disproving our opinion is the very condition which justifies us in assuming its truth for purposes of action; and on no other terms can a being with human faculties have any rational assurance of being right" (231). In the first instance, then, liberty of thought and discussion is justified as a means of ascertaining the truth, since without them there is no justification for claiming to know the truth. Given the fallible nature of the human mind, freedom of discussion is essential: "in an imperfect state of the human mind the interests of truth require a diversity of opinions" (257).

It may be the case, however, that what society believes and propounds is in fact true. Even in this case, Mill argues, freedom of belief and discussion is justified. Beliefs long and widely held, even when true, can come to be dead dogmas, the reasons for their truth being long lost to those who subscribe to them. To refuse to enter into a debate over these beliefs is precisely to avoid the occasions on which the reasons for them are expressed. Thus to be required to put forth *arguments* for beliefs has great benefit, for it rescues these beliefs from the domain of habit, superstition, and prejudice, making of them once again "living truths." Those people who do not enter into debate over their cherished beliefs "do not, in any proper sense of the word, know the doctrine which they themselves profess" (245). Indeed, it can be said that, without debate, society loses not only the reasons for its beliefs but also the very meaning of them: "Instead of a vivid conception and a living belief there remains only a few phrases retained by rote; of, if any part, the shell and husk only of the meaning is retained, the finer essence being lost" (247). We gain immeasurably from freedom of discussion even if, as it turns out, we possessed the truth all along.

Mill considers an interesting objection to his position which urges that the usefulness of some beliefs is so great that society is justified in enforcing them and prohibiting any conflicting opinions. The Church, for example, might claim that some parts of its creed are essential for salvation; a modern state might claim that a conviction of its "manifest destiny" is required in order for civilization to advance; a nation might proclaim that support for its war efforts is essential for success on the battlefield. Mill reminds those who propose usefulness as a justification for enforced belief that "the usefulness of an opinion is itself matter of opinion: as disputable, as open to discussion, and requiring discussion as much as the opinion itself" (233).

The Proper Limits to Human Conduct

Having justified freedom of thought, opinion, and discussion, Mill turns to the question of what limits, if any, should be placed on the human actions that may stem from opinions freely held. And here he is willing to draw a line and separate off a class of actions which society or government is morally permitted to suppress. There are also actions which it is permissible for society to require of individuals. Mill defines these two classes of actions in the following way:

> This conduct consists, first, in not injuring the interests of one another; or rather certain interests, which, either by express legal provision, or by tacit understanding, ought to be considered as rights; and secondly, in each person's bearing his share (to be fixed on some equitable principle) of the labours and sacrifices incurred for defending society or its members from injury and molestation   (276).

The remainder of "On Liberty" concentrates on the first class of actions – the actions legitimately suppressed because they involve harm to others or a violation of the rights of others.

An alternative way of expressing Mill's position is to see it as marking out the areas over which society has jurisdiction. He is particularly concerned to argue that society does *not* have jurisdiction over matters of personal good. In other words, society cannot require that a person do certain things as a means of improving that person's own quality of life. Society should not have a paternalistic relation to its citizens. Individuals should be left alone to pursue their interests, this because they know best what these interests are and are most highly motivated to pursue them. Moreover, individuals must take their own risks and bear responsibility for the consequences of their actions, indeed, responsibility for their own characters. It is only when these actions impinge in a negative way on others that society is warranted in intervening. As Mill puts it, "As soon as any part of a person's conduct affects prejudicially the interests of others, society has jurisdiction over it, and the question whether the general welfare will or will not be promoted by interfering with it, becomes open to discussion" (276). Actions that bring harm to others by damaging their rightful interests may be legislated against.

Mill is aware of what is still today the major objection to his position on liberty: the response that there is no clear line between actions damaging only to the agent herself and actions inflicting harm on others. As he expresses the objection:

> How (it may be asked) can any part of the conduct of a member of society be a matter of indifference to the other members? No person is an entirely isolated being; it is impossible for a person to do anything seriously or permanently hurtful to himself, without mischief at least to his near connections, and often far beyond them   (280).

Here we have the "no person is an island" objection. The drunkard not only thwarts her own chances of a full and productive life, she also harms the members of her family by providing inadequate support. And she constitutes a bad example for all who encounter her. In a case like this, the distinction between self-regarding actions (those having an impact on the agent) and other-regarding actions (those having an impact on others) breaks down. Should not society be authorized, then, in legislating against drunkenness? And likewise against all conditions that cause damage to the agent?

Mill answers this objection by distinguishing between prohibiting and punishing the behavior that inflicts harm on others and prohibiting and punishing the cause of that behavior. If the drunkard violates one of her duties to her family, she can rightfully be punished for doing so. Society has the right to set up laws against dereliction of duty to one's family. But the drunkard should not be punished for her drunkenness, the cause of her dereliction. Likewise, "No person ought to be punished simply for being drunk; but a soldier or a policeman should be punished for being drunk on duty" (282). It is because of the harm (actual or potential) to others that a behavior like drunkenness should be prohibited; to the extent that it harms only the agent herself, it is not a proper subject of prohibition and punishment.

Thus Mill sums up his views on liberty in two maxims:

> The maxims are, first, that the individual is not accountable to society for his actions, in so far as these concern the interests of no person but himself. Advice, instruction, persuasion, and avoidance by other people if thought necessary by them for their own good, are the only measures by which society can justifiably express its dislike or disapprobation of his conduct. Secondly, that for such actions as are prejudicial to the interests of others, the individual is accountable, and may be subjected either to social or to legal punishment, if society is of opinion that the one or the other is requisite for its protection   (292).

Mill's utilitarianism, then, defines a very large area of individual liberty while at the same time taking steps to protect the interests or happiness of society at large.

13

Nietzsche

"We are unknown to ourselves, we men of knowledge – and with good reason. We have never sought ourselves – how could it happen that we should ever *find* ourselves?"[1] So begins Nietzsche's *On the Genealogy of Morals*, one of the most important and one of the most skeptical treatises on morality in the history of Western thought. Nietzsche is certainly not the first to question morality. Many of the Sophists, it will be recalled, thought it was *foolish* to follow moral precepts. Nietzsche goes further: he thinks it is *sick* to do so. Morality for him is a sickness, all the more so because we do not recognize it as such. "We are not 'men of knowledge' with respect to ourselves" (*G*,P,1).

We are in this unfortunate condition, Nietzsche thinks, because we (ordinary folk and ordinary moralists) have never questioned *the value of morality*. We take the importance of morality – indeed in the eyes of most people its *supreme* importance – for granted. Indeed, we do not see that *our* morality is but one of many different moralities! On the contrary, we take our own version to define morality itself, and then we devote ourselves to finding its *rational foundation* (*BGE*,186).[2] But this commitment to "morality" is no better than a *faith*. Instead of seeking a rational justification of it, we would do better, Nietzsche thinks, to engage in descriptions of "moralities" and to develop a typology of morals (ibid.). This effort might open our eyes to the real nature of our own moral convictions. We have never before posed the question, for instance, of "where our good and evil *originated*" (*G*,P,2), but to do so will be revealing – and shocking. Nietzsche would have us raise the following questions: "under what conditions did man devise these value judgments good and evil? *and what value do they themselves possess?*" (ibid.). Such questions call for a genealogy of morals, a study of its history and the social and psychological conditions under which it developed.

In our study of Nietzsche, we shall follow the argument of his main work in moral theory, his *On the Genealogy of Morals*, amplified by claims and observations culled from his earlier book *Beyond Good and Evil*. Some might question the assertion that there is an *argument* to be found in Nietzsche, argumentation not being the type of writing he prefers. His style is always more oracular, aphoristic, and rhetorical –

certainly more impassioned – than the usual "arguments" of philosophers. Nevertheless there is a clearly discernible thesis in Nietzsche, and many observations are made in defense of it. Rather than attempt a collage, an overall picture of Nietzsche's thinking, it is arguably better to trace how he himself develops his thoughts. Thus we shall use the structure of *On the Genealogy of Morals* to organize our presentation of Nietzsche's moral theory.

The Origin of Morality

What is this morality that Nietzsche challenges, this morality whose origins and whose value he questions? It is, first and foremost, the "value of the 'unegoistic,' the instincts of pity, self-abnegation, self-sacrifice"(*G*,P,5). Morality opposes selfishness and stands for disinterested, benevolent, and altruistic action, helping and caring for others, loving one's neighbor as oneself. The attitudinal stance of morality is one that Nietzsche most closely associates with the philosophy of Schopenhauer. He quotes Schopenhauer as claiming that the principle "Hurt no one; rather help all as much as you can" is the basic premise of morality, the moral principle on which all moral philosophers are agreed (*BGE*,186). Nietzsche remarks that philosophers, including Schopenhauer, have notably failed to provide a rational foundation for this basic principle. But that is not the worst of it. The principle, Nietzsche thinks, stands in opposition to the very nature of life, which nature Nietzsche describes in his famous phrase as "will to power." "Whoever has once felt deeply how insipidly false and sentimental this principle is in a world whose essence is will to power" (ibid.), will stop seeking for a justification of it and attempt, rather, to *overturn* it. If we pursue a history of morality, we shall see the origins of this moral attitude, this "turning against life" (*G*,P,5), in a much earlier development. And in understanding it genealogically, we shall be able to call it into question. More than that, we can begin to see new possibilities and put forth a new demand, a demand for an overcoming of morality (*BGE*,32). "Let us articulate this *new demand*: we need a *critique* of moral values, *the value of these values themselves must be called in question* – and for that there is needed a knowledge of the conditions and circumstances in which they grew, under which they evolved and changed ... a knowledge of a kind that has never yet existed or even been desired" (*G*,P,6). And so we set out on a genealogy of morals.

Certain English philosophers, Nietzsche grants, have tried to trace and pin down the psychological origin of our ideas of good and evil (Nietzsche has in mind such thinkers as Hutcheson and Hume). But in reality they have no historical sense and they get it all wrong.

> "Originally," so they decree, "one approved unegoistic actions and called them good from the point of view of those to whom they were done, that

is to say, those to whom they were *useful*; later one *forgot* how this approval originated and, simply because unegoistic actions were always *habitually* praised as good, one also felt them to be good – as if they were something good in themselves"   (*G*,I,2).

Nietzsche thinks these English thinkers, with their constant prattling about "utility," have identified the wrong perspective as the source of moral notions. As he sees it,

> the judgment "good" did *not* originate with those to whom "goodness" was shown! Rather it was "the good" themselves, that is to say, the noble, powerful, high-stationed and high-minded, who felt and established themselves and their actions as good, that is, of the first rank, in contra-distinction to all the low, low-minded, common and plebeian   (*G*,I,2).

For the English, "good" reflects the perspective of those who are acted on by others – it reflects (in Nietzsche's words) the viewpoint of someone who is passive, afraid of others, reactive to others. But the real origin of "good" is otherwise, Nietzsche claims. It derives from those who thought themselves good and who acted on others, who ruled and dominated others, and saw their own actions as good. According to the members of this higher ruling order, the people who are acted upon, those who are "below" them, are *bad* or contemptible. It is thus that the antithesis of good and bad arose in early history.

> It follows from this that the word "good" was definitely *not* linked from the first and by necessity to "unegoistic" actions, as the superstition of these [English] genealogists of morality would have it. Rather it was only when aristocratic value judgments *declined* that the whole antithesis "egoistic" "unegoistic" obtruded itself more and more on the human conscience – it is, to speak in my own language, the *herd instinct* that through this antithesis at last gets its word in ...   (ibid.).

It is the herd instinct that is responsible for the emergence of the equation of morality with the unegoistic, the disinterested, the impartial form of behavior. At the heart of this herd instinct is fear, and therefore "fear ... is the mother of morals" (*BGE*,201). Whereas the aristocrats, the nobles, taught the value of independence and insisted on commanding others, the members of the herd insisted on the value of obedience. (Nietzsche notes how obedience is essential to the conception of morality defended by Kant, who simply codified (in perhaps its most elegant form) the morality of the masses (*BGE*,188).)

In this fashion Nietzsche detects a conceptual transformation during which the initial, aristocratic meaning of the word "good" changed into a plebeian, herd conception of goodness. The aristocratic conception involved the idea of a superior soul, an idea grounded in the social and political superiority of the aristocrats. When, in the historical circumstances that arose, political sovereignty was attained by the church and its "priests," this priestly aristocracy initiated the transformation from the earlier conception of goodness to what Nietzsche clearly sees as the more ignoble conception accepted by the herd, the masses. Most importantly, the priestly caste was responsible for changing the notion of badness – initially denoting the plebeian, base, and worthless soul – into the notion of *evil*, which came to designate anything that threatened the lives and security of the masses. "Everything that elevates an individual above the herd and intimidates the neighbor is henceforth called *evil*" (*BGE*,201). Instead of the contrast between good and bad, we came to have the opposition of good and evil. In the society dominated by priests, with the threat of evil ever present, life became *dangerous* – arrogance became dangerous, and also "revenge, acuteness, profligacy, love, lust to rule, virtue, disease" (*G*,I,6). Whatever threatened the security of the masses became evil. As the possibility of evil confronted human beings, life became, for lack of anything better, "interesting" and deep. All was not "up-front," honest, on the surface – evil lay deep in the heart of human beings and became a constant subject of curiosity and suspicion.

Thus, according to Nietzsche, does the priestly mode of valuation branch off from the knightly-aristocratic mode and then develop into its opposite (*G*,I,7). Whereas the aristocratic soul valued war, strength, powerful physicality, adventure, "vigorous, free, joyful activity" (ibid.), the priestly society opposes war and all things (like strength and freedom) that threaten the herd. The priestly people engage in "nothing less than a radical revaluation of their enemies' values" (ibid.); for instance, Christianity, with its God on the cross, stood all valuations on their head (*BGE*,62). Nietzsche singles out the Jews as one such priestly people, and he has this to say about them:

> It was the Jews who, with awe-inspiring consistency, dared to invert the aristocratic value-equation (good=noble=powerful=beautiful=happy= beloved of God) and to hang on to this inversion with their teeth, the teeth of the most abysmal hatred (the hatred of impotence), saying "the wretched alone are the good; the poor, impotent, lowly alone are the good; the suffering, deprived, sick, ugly alone are pious, alone are blessed by God, blessedness is for them alone – and you, the powerful and noble, are on the contrary the evil, the cruel, the lustful, the insatiable, the godless to all eternity; and you shall be in all eternity the unblessed, accursed, and damned!" ... One knows *who* inherited this Jewish revaluation (*G*,I,7).

Much has been written on the question whether Nietzsche was an anti-Semite, and sympathetic scholars have noted the numerous places in which he condemns anti-Semitism in very harsh terms. His reference to the Jews in the above context is surely an historical, genealogical one. And if his words express wrath and indignation, these emotions are equally leveled at those who inherited the Jewish revaluation: the Christians. The Jews perhaps began, but the Christians supported and extended, the "slave revolt in morality: that revolt that has a history of two thousand years behind it and which we no longer see because it – has been victorious" (*G*,I,7).

Master and Slave Morality

In *Beyond Good and Evil*, Nietzsche introduces his famous distinction between master morality and slave morality, which is simply another way of referring to the morality of the aristocrats and nobles and the contrasting morality of the herd: "The moral discrimination of values has originated either among a ruling group whose consciousness of its difference from the ruled group was accompanied by delight – or among the ruled, the slaves and dependents of every degree" (*BGE*,260). He acknowledges that both of these two moralities are usually found in most higher cultures, sometimes interpenetrating one another, often misunderstanding one another. The two moralities can be found together even in a single soul. That "mixed" cultures have blended them together proves nothing, however, beyond the confusion found in these cultures. In essence the two moralities are totally distinct and totally at odds with one another.

The slave morality that has victoriously replaced the master morality is viewed by Nietzsche as an expression of hatred and revenge against the aristocrats and masters who previously lorded it over the masses, both politically and morally. In fact, the gospel of love taught by Jesus of Nazareth is not, Nietzsche claims, the denial of the thirst for revenge; it is, on the contrary, the triumphant crown of that revenge and hatred. "This Jesus of Nazareth, the incarnate gospel of love, this 'Redeemer' who brought blessedness and victory to the poor, the sick, and the sinners – was he not this seduction in its most uncanny and irresistible form, a seduction and bypath to precisely those *Jewish* values and new ideals?" (*G*,I,8). How better to subdue a morally and politically superior force – how better to take revenge on them – than to spread among them an emasculating gospel of love.

Resentment

A central feature of Nietzsche's genealogy of morals is its psychological explanation of how the slave morality overcame the master morality and inverted its basic values. The key term in this explanation is *resentment* (Nietzsche uses the more resonant French term *ressentiment*). "The slave revolt in morality begins when *ressentiment* becomes creative and gives birth to values: the *ressentiment* of natures that are denied the true reaction, that of deeds, and compensate themselves with an imaginary revenge" (*G*,I,10). Members of the herd are unable to *act*, to express themselves as their basic instincts demand. All they can do is *react* and protect themselves against the threats posed by the masters. Thus they come to resent the masters and all they stand for. In calling these strong ones evil, they take revenge on them, although it is only an imaginary revenge, one that exists merely in their minds. Unlike the masters, who create values by affirming themselves, the slaves create values by negating everything *other than* themselves, everything that the masters stand for.

> While every noble morality develops from a triumphant affirmation of itself, slave morality from the outset says No to what is "outside," what is "different," what is "not itself"; and *this* is its creative act. This inversion of the value-positing eye – this *need* to direct one's view outward instead of back to oneself – is of the essence of *ressentiment*: in order to exist, slave morality always first needs a hostile external world; it needs, physiologically speaking, external stimuli in order to act at all – its action is fundamentally reaction   (*G*,I,10).

In creating values by affirming itself, the noble nature needs no external other – it creates value through its own actions. "Egoism belongs to the nature of a noble soul" (*BGE*,265). The "other" is viewed by the master as something other than *itself*, hence something low, common and bad in comparison with its own character. The nobles are, in their own eyes, "the truthful," "the free," "the happy," "the fortunate," and the members of the masses are the opposite of these. "Slaves," on the contrary, define themselves as "not free," "not happy," "unfortunate," – all the things the masters are *not*.

> The "well-born" *felt* themselves to be the "happy"; they did not have to establish their happiness artificially by examining their enemies, or to persuade themselves, *deceive* themselves, that they were happy (as all men of *ressentiment* are in the habit of doing); and they likewise knew, as rounded men replete with energy and therefore *necessarily* active, that happiness should not be sundered from action – being active was with them necessarily a part of happiness ... – all very much the opposite of "happiness" at the level of the impotent, the oppressed, and those in whom poisonous and inimical feelings are festering, with whom it appears as essentially narcotic, drug, rest, peace, "sabbath," slackening of tension and relaxing of limbs, in short *passively*   (*G*,I,10).

The values of the slaves are derivative and negative, defined by contrast with the values and nature of the masters. These slave values focus not on action but rather on the virtues of not being harmed, being left in peace, getting through life with the least difficulty. When the slaves tell themselves they are happy, they are lying to themselves.

Because of a need to be constantly on guard against the powerful master, the person of *ressentiment* may become very clever, indeed cleverer than the master. Such a person cannot be honest or straightforward – he has to be too much *on guard*. "His soul *squints*; his spirit loves hiding places, secret paths and back doors, everything covert entices him as *his* world, *his* security, *his* refreshment; he understands how to keep silent, how not to forget, how to wait, how to be provisionally self-deprecating and humble" (*G*,I,10). The one and only creation – "out of the cauldron of unsatisfied hatred" (*G*,I,11) – of this clever, ever-alert creature of resentment is the creation of "the enemy": "he has conceived 'the evil enemy,' 'the Evil One,' and this in fact is his basic concept, from which he then evolves, as an afterthought and pendant, a 'good one' – himself!" (ibid.). He himself, merely an *afterthought*, is nothing other than ... "other than the enemy."

Nietzsche stresses the fact that the opposition of good and evil – emerging out of resentment – is quite different from the opposition of good and bad found in the morality of the masters. To be sure, both "bad" and "evil" are opposite of good: "but it is *not* the same concept 'good'" (*G*,I,11). In fact, the person who, for the masters, is good – the superior person, the powerful person, the ruler – is precisely the *evil* person in the eyes of the morality of *ressentiment*. Between the two moralities we have not only a revaluation of values, but a complete inversion of them.

But the morality of *ressentiment* has won – Nietzsche acknowledges this again and again. The victory is so complete that all the "instincts and reactions of *ressentiment*" have become what he calls the instruments of culture. Value-wise, however – at least from the standpoint of the higher noble values – this victory amounts to a regression. The "hopelessly mediocre and insipid man" who has won, and who indeed feels himself to be the goal and zenith of history, is in fact "a disgrace to man and rather an accusation and counterargument against 'culture' in general" (*G*,I,11). Things are always getting "better" – which is to say that human beings are becoming "more good-natured, more prudent, more comfortable, more mediocre, more indifferent, more Chinese, more Christian – there is no doubt that man is getting 'better' all the time" (*G*,I,12). In the face of such "improvement," is there any wonder that, as human beings are feared less, they are loved less as well? Is there any wonder that we have lost our reverence for human nature, abandoned our hopes for humankind, or given up the will to be human? The upshot of all the advance of culture and civilization is in reality an antipathy toward the human, or perhaps more accurately, a complete loss of values: nihilism. "The sight of man now makes us weary – what is nihilism today if it is not *that*? – We are weary *of man*" (ibid.).

Is Nietzsche himself a nihilist? He has often been called one, largely on the grounds that he denies that there are any transcendent, universal standards or values to which human beings must submit. Values are human creations: the masters overtly will theirs into existence, as a manifestation of their will to power, and the slaves too will their values, although their ethic is a sickly, dishonest, hypocritical expression of will to power. In the end, as we shall see, Nietzsche calls for a new creation of values – a revaluation and inversion of the slave ethic – and in doing so he is, in his eyes, repudiating nihilism. In place of the weariness with human beings, instead of the nausea caused by the sight of the sickly modern variety of human beings, he will seek to reinstate the dignified human being, precisely as creator of values.

Conscience

In the second part of *Genealogy of Morals* Nietzsche traces the development of conscience and the emergence of guilt as important facets of herd or slave morality. The first step in this process was the emergence of the notion of responsibility. The responsible person is, in Nietzsche's words, the one who has the "right to make promises" (*G*,II,2). Such a person can be trusted to deliver on her promises, from which it follows that this individual must be calculable (predictable), that her behavior must be uniform and regular. The "morality of mores" – the long history in which custom ruled and shaped the lives of everyone – has created such a person. In following the mores of one's society, in being thoroughly acculturated into it, one becomes the kind of person whose promises can be trusted – "with the aid of the morality of mores and the social straightjacket, man was actually *made* calculable" (ibid.). The responsible human being is not the *natural* person; she is a *fabricated* person.

In one of history's great ironies, the calculable, regular, steady person, the person created by the morality of mores, actually ends up transcending these very mores. For this person becomes the *sovereign individual*, the one who "has his own independent, protracted will and the *right to make promises*" – in a word, the *autonomous* human being. Here we have the "emancipated individual," the "master of a *free* will" who is no longer beholden to the mores or customs from which he emerged. Society creates the regular individual who can be counted on to behave in regular ways; then this person, by making promises, by making *herself* accountable, sees herself as freed from the rules and regulations, the customs and practices, of this society. The "free man" arises: "The proud awareness of the extraordinary privilege of *responsibility*, the consciousness of this rare freedom, this power over oneself and over fate, has in his case penetrated the profoundest depths and become instinct, the dominating instinct" (*G*,II,2). The instinctive sense of oneself as a free and responsible person who answers only to himself – such is the nature of someone who acts from *conscience*.

But the autonomous person of conscience is a "late fruit," Nietzsche affirms, something that had to be created over a long span of time. The process by means of which this occurred is strikingly described by Nietzsche as one of creating a *memory*. How do we come to remember what we promised, and how do we come to remember that we ought to keep our promise? How do we come to remember the "five or six 'I will nots'" one must obey in order to gain the advantages of society? Forgetfulness, he claims, is our natural state. By obliterating the "noise and struggle" of everyday life, it preserves "psychic order" and gives rise to robust mental health. Remembering something thus goes against the grain, and what one remembers must be "burned" into the mind. Pain being "the most powerful aid to mnemonics," such a memory, Nietzsche thinks, is the product of much self- and other-inflicted pain and suffering, much self- and other-inflicted punishment (otherwise known as moral education!). The morality of mores has produced the "man of reason" and the autonomous individual – but "how dearly they have been bought! how much blood and cruelty lie at the bottom of all 'good things'!" (*G*,II,3).

Bad Conscience

Nietzsche's primary target, however, is not so much the notion of conscience as that of *bad conscience*, the consciousness of guilt. He locates the origin of the notion of *guilt* in the concept of a *debt*. The contractual relationship between creditor and debtor gives rise by analogy to the idea that if one person does injury to another, the injured one is owed a debt, a debt that can be repaid by injury in turn to the offender. The pain inflicted on the culprit through punishment is the repayment of this debt (*G*,II,4). The aggrieved creditor's pleasure at the sight of the pain inflicted on the culprit is just compensation for the injury initially done to the creditor (*G*,II,5). "To see others suffer does one good, to make others suffer even more: this is a hard saying but an ancient, mighty, human, all-too-human principle ... " (*G*,II,6).

If punishment viewed in this way is regarded as cruelty, so be it. In earlier days, Nietzsche claims, human beings were not ashamed of being cruel, and in those days "life on earth was more cheerful than it is now that pessimists exist" (*G*,II,6), pessimists who see the reality of pain and suffering as an argument *against* existence. Modern human beings have a "queasy stomach" for reality, this being the result of "the morbid softening and moralization through which the animal 'man' finally learns to be ashamed of all his instincts" (*G*,II,7). We moderns have forgotten that "disinterested malice" was long regarded as a normal quality of human beings. In earlier times, "men were unwilling to refrain from *making* suffer and saw in it an enchantment of the first order, a genuine seduction *to* life" (ibid.).

In a manner not far removed from that of Hegel, Nietzsche locates the origin of morality in the world of contracts and debts: "It was in *this* sphere then, the sphere of legal obligations, that the moral conceptual world of 'guilt,' 'conscience,' 'duty,' 'sacredness of duty' had its origin ... " (*G*,II,6). The personal relationship between buyer and seller, creditor and debtor, is at the heart of morality and indeed all forms of social organization. "The community, too, stands to its members in that same vital relation, that of the creditor to his debtors" (*G*,II,9). The lawbreaker is one who has failed to pay for the advantages of society by obeying its laws; it is only *just*, then, for society to exact payment by punishing the criminal and enjoying the spectacle.

The *mercy* a society may show a lawbreaker is simply an expression of the fact that the society is so strong it does not have to worry unduly about the criminal's transgression. The demand for justice is the response of a creditor who has not received her due. The institution of laws takes the administration of justice out of the hands of those who would act on the basis of grudges, rancor, and resentment and turns it into something impersonal. The rule of law represents a struggle against the reactive feelings of resentment and revenge. In fact, Nietzsche claims, " 'Just' and 'unjust' exist ... only after the institution of the law" (*G*,II,11). No injury or assault is essentially unjust in itself, since "life operates *essentially* ... through injury, assault, exploitation, destruction and simply cannot be thought of at all without this character" (*G*,II,11). Hence justice and punishment are forms of *impersonal* violence involving the collection of the debt that social deviants owe to their society. But in the end, a legal order is simply a means "in the struggle between power-complexes" (*G*,II,11). It is not an attempt to end all struggle, since that would be hostile to the very nature of life.

Guilt

The punishment demanded by justice, however, is not enough to explain the notion of *guilt*. "Punishment," Nietzsche tells us, "makes men hard and cold; it concentrates; it sharpens the feeling of alienation; it strengthens the power of resistance" (*G*,II,14). The criminal sees society committing, in the name of justice, the very same acts she herself stands accused of: deception, bribery, robbery, violence, torture, murder. It is not from such feelings and insights that a person will come to see herself as guilty and will develop a bad conscience. The explanation of the bad or guilty conscience is otherwise.

> I regard the bad conscience as the serious illness that man was bound to contract under the stress of the most fundamental change he ever experienced – that change which occurred when he found himself finally enclosed within the walls of society and of peace ... suddenly, all their instincts were disvalued and "suspended" ... [I]n this new world they no longer possessed their former guides, their regulating, unconscious and infallible drives: they were reduced to thinking, inferring, reckoning, co-ordinating cause and effect, these unfortunate creatures; they were reduced to their "consciousness," their weakest and most fallible organ! ... [A]nd at the same time the old instincts had not suddenly ceased to make their usual demands! Only it was hardly or rarely possible to humor them: as a rule they had to seek new and, as it were, subterranean gratifications (*G*,II,16).

The guilty conscience has its origins in the fact of society itself and the brutal restraints it imposes on one's natural instincts and urges. It is the social, or socialized, creature who feels herself guilty. Let us see how this happens.

Nietzsche argues that "all instincts that do not discharge themselves outwardly *turn inward* – this is what I call the *internalization* of man: thus it was that man first developed what was later called his 'soul'" (ibid.). (This anticipation of one of the basic tenets of Freudian psychoanalysis is uncanny.) When society is successful in protecting itself against the instincts of the "wild, free, prowling man," these very instincts turn inward against civilized human beings themselves. When these human beings cannot, because of social constraints, vent their hostility and cruelty against others, *they vent them against themselves*. Being sundered from her animal past, the human being turns like an animal against herself and declares war "against the old instincts upon which his strength, joy, and terribleness had rested hitherto" (ibid.). Such a person comes to feel guilty for still having these instincts and for still feeling the need to give expression to them. It is in this fashion that the modern person comes to have a guilty conscience.

We can see, then, that the civilization of human beings, the creation of a state, was a "fearful tyranny," an act of violence against the animal drives of the human creature. All talk of the state arising out of a contract is for Nietzsche just so much sentimentalism. The state was created by "blond beasts of prey," by which Nietzsche does *not* mean members of the Aryan race (he mentions numerous races in this regard) but rather the *lionlike* nature of natural conquerors. These conquerors, free and brutal themselves, suppressed the instinct for freedom in the citizens of their communities, and in doing this they generated the greatest control mechanism of them all: the guilty conscience. "This *instinct for freedom* forcibly made latent ... this instinct for freedom pushed back and repressed, incarcerated within and finally able to discharge and vent itself only on itself: that, and that alone, is what the bad conscience is in its beginnings" (*G*,II,17).

The instinct for freedom is what Nietzsche calls "the will to power" (*G*,II,18). "A living thing seeks above all to *discharge* its strength ... " (*BGE*,13). Turned inward, against the "ancient animal self," the will to power creates a soul "at odds with itself that makes itself suffer out of joy in making suffer" (ibid.). This tortured soul, taking delight in being cruel to itself, is the source of all those values that come to define herd morality: selflessness, self-denial, self-sacrifice – in a word, the unegoistic (ibid.): "Only the bad conscience, only the will to self-maltreatment provided the conditions for the *value* of the unegoistic – " (ibid.). Out of the illness of bad conscience arises the "beauty" of the moral ideals.

It is but a short step from moral bad conscience to a cosmic conception of guilt: the guilty conscience becomes guilty before *God*. God becomes the antithesis of the animal instincts which the human beings hate in themselves; indeed, these very animal instincts become a form of guilt before God. And the Devil? This is but the idea of the evil instincts abroad in the world. These instincts can taint the world, so that worldly existence itself becomes evil. Interpreting itself religiously, the bad conscience lays upon itself a degree of guilt that can never be atoned for, and the punishment it receives for its evil, sinful nature never is quite equal to the degree of its guilt. " ... his *will* to erect an ideal – that of the 'holy God' – and in the face of it to feel the palpable certainty of his own absolute unworthiness" (*G*,II,22) – here is the will to power in its ultimate, perverted expression. And here, Nietzsche shouts, is "sickness, beyond a doubt, the most terrible sickness that has ever raged in man" (ibid.).

Nietzsche ends the second part of the *Genealogy* with a plaintive question: could the bad conscience ever direct itself against the *unnatural inclinations* in the way it now levels its hatred and invective against the natural ones? "The attainment of this goal," he writes, "would require a *different* kind of spirit from that likely to appear in the present age" (*G*,II,24). It would take a person "of the future" to accomplish this grand goal. Such a person would be the "Antichrist and antinihilist," one who "would redeem us not only from the hitherto reigning ideal but also from that which was bound to grow out of it, the great nausea, the will to nothingness, nihilism ... " (ibid.). Representing "great health," this person would be "victor over God and nothingness," and although only the future can bring such a person "*he must come one day*" (ibid.).

Ascetic Ideals

The Third Essay in the *Genealogy of Morals* is an investigation of what Nietzsche calls "ascetic ideals." These ideals – so important to the moral life – include disinterestedness, self-denial, simplicity, apathy toward the things of the world, antipathy toward sensuality, spirituality, and (expressly highlighted by Nietzsche) poverty, humility, and chastity (*G*,III,8). Why are these virtues and attitudes important to the person leading the moral life? Nietzsche's answer is: the moralist "wants *to gain release from a torture*" (*G*,III,6). We need to see what this torture is, and what release from it involves.

Often enough, the ascetic "virtues" function simply as means to the attainment of certain goals. This explains a *philosopher's* attachment to these virtues: they provide her the independence and serenity she needs in order *to think* and live the life of the mind. The philosopher's pose *par excellence* is that of a person withdrawn and hostile to life, suspicious of the senses, freed from sensuality (*G*,III,10). Consider the typical metaphysical theory, which emphasizes the reality of the permanent and unchanging and downgrades the reality of the world of the senses. When it inspires metaphysical philosophy, the ascetic ideal leads to a renunciation of the ego, a denial of one's own reality, and even a rejection of reason. Or consider Kant's definition of beauty: that which gives us pleasure without interest. "Without *interest*?" Nietzsche screams, and compares this typical, ascetic philosophical attitude with that of the novelist Stendhal, who described beauty as a promise of happiness (*G*,III,6). Many fruitful, inventive spirits (philosophers, artists, and, indeed, athletes), Nietzsche thinks, seek out ascetic ideals simply as means for the attainment of their spiritual or creative activities. Such efforts are, in the end, merely laughable.

The Ascetic Priest

But the case of the *ascetic priest* is more dangerous and serious than the above, for in the mouth of this creature, who "appears in almost every age" (*G*,III,11), the ascetic ideals have a more sinister function. In advocating the ascetic life, the ascetic priest is contrasting and opposing to actual life (with its natural impulses, its worldliness, its transitory nature) a different form of existence altogether; this priest is recommending an ideal form that *denies* life. In this ascetic life, *ressentiment* and bad conscience rule without equal, overpowering life itself and turning life against itself (*G*,III,11). In this mode of existence, pleasure is "felt and *sought* in ill-constitutedness, decay, pain, mischance, ugliness, voluntary deprivation, self-mortification, self-flagellation, self-sacrifice" (ibid.). The ascetic priest urges us, not just to escape life momentarily – to think, to create, to train for a match – but to *hate* life.

But, Nietzsche asks, is not such a life that denies life a self-contradiction, an absurdity? Surely the interpretation of life offered by the ascetic priest must involve some misunderstanding of the facts, since the ascetic ideal cannot be taken seriously on its own terms. What is the truth that the ascetic ideal veils?

> Let us replace [the self-contradiction the ascetic appears to represent] with a brief formulation of the facts of the matter: *the ascetic ideal springs from the protective instinct of a degenerating life* which tries by all means to sustain itself and to fight for its existence; it indicates a partial physiological obstruction and exhaustion against which the deepest instincts of life, which have remained intact, continually struggle with new expedients and devices. The ascetic ideal is such an expedient; the case is therefore the opposite of what those who reverence this ideal believe: life wrestles in it and through it with death and *against* death; the ascetic ideal is an artifice for the *preservation* of life   (*G*,III,13).

In this fashion, Nietzsche thinks, the prevalence of the ascetic ideal testifies to the sickliness of the tamed human being of recent history. In holding before the herd the image of a different kind of life – the ascetic life – the ascetic priest denies actual life in the interest of saving human beings from the torture that *ressentiment* has created in the human soul, saving the human species from the disgust it feels toward itself. The ascetic ideal is an antidote to the great unhappiness produced by the *bad conscience*. By denying life, the ascetic priest paradoxically is among "the greatest *conserving* and yes-creating forces of life" (ibid.).

But this effort at conservation is hypocritical and self-contradictory. It is, after all, an effort to conserve the weak, to conserve those who, in being weak, have turned their instincts against themselves and who suffer nausea at the sight of themselves. The dominance of the ascetic ideal is only "the will of the weak to represent *some* form of superiority – where can it not be discovered, this will to power of the weakest!" (*G*,III,14). Those who preach, and those who accept, the ascetic ideal are all creatures of *ressentiment* who wish to take revenge on the fortunate and happy, the strong and superior. And their greatest success is attained when they poison the minds and consciences of the fortunate ones to the extent that these fortunate ones themselves abdicate their good fortune (as disgraceful) and embrace the misery of the weak. When the "happy, well-constituted, powerful in soul and body" begin to doubt their right to happiness, the greatest calamity has occurred. The world is inverted, feeling is emasculated, the higher is degraded to the status of an instrument of the lower. We must therefore be on guard against the ascetic priest and the ascetic ideal. They represent the two worst contagions to which human beings can be subjected: "the *great nausea at man*" and "*great pity for man*" (*G*,III,14).

Now we can understand the role of the ascetic priest. "*Dominion over the suffering is his kingdom*" (*G*,III,15). Here we have a case of the sick leading the sick. To maintain their dominion, the ascetic priests of this world must first maintain the sickness of those over whom they exercise leadership and control. They must keep open the wound, and infect it even more. And they must protect their flock against its enemies, the healthy and happy ones. But their most important function, Nietzsche tells us, is to alter the direction of *ressentiment*. When creatures feel miserable because they cannot express their desires, when they feel cramped, empty, impotent, they are inclined to lash out at some external cause of this miserable condition. They need to find someone or something else guilty in order to deaden their own pain. *Ressentiment* naturally reacts outwardly against its enemies. But the ascetic priests change the direction of this reaction – thus their message to their flock: " 'Quite so, my sheep! someone must be to blame for it: but you yourself are this someone, you alone are to blame for it – *you alone are to blame for yourself!*' " (*G*,III,15). The ascetic priests maintain their dominion by increasing the suffering of their flock. To their aid come the concepts of guilt, sin, depravity, damnation. And, as in the witch trials of yesteryear when the accused themselves came to believe that they were witches, the sinful and the wretched come to interpret themselves as sinful and wretched. But this is, Nietzsche instructs us, an *interpretation*, not a *fact*.

Ascetic priests, especially in their activities within Christianity but also within the other great world religions, treat not the cause of the suffering – after all, they wish it to continue – but only the pain. And for this purpose they have many narcotics to dispense. One way of alleviating the pain is to "reduce the feeling of life in general to its lowest point. If possible, will and desire are abolished altogether" (*G*,III,17). Thus the priests inculcate "selflessness" and "sanctification" in their flock. These states can in turn produce such "spiritual disturbances" as redemption, a mystical union with God, the hypnotic sense of nothingness, i.e., "deep sleep." Another way to numb the pain generated by inward-directed *ressentiment* is through "mechanical activity" (*G*,III,18) – what some call the blessedness of work: "absolute regularity, punctilious and unthinking obedience... fully occupied time, a certain permission, indeed training for 'impersonality,' for self-forgetfulness" (ibid.). The cultivation of "petty pleasures" helps us get through life. Still another means of combatting depression is that of devoting oneself to the task of giving pleasure to others – the "love of the neighbor," the "happiness of 'slight superiority,' involved in all doing good, being useful, helping and rewarding ... " (ibid.). When the herd is formed, and the sick and depressed huddle together in "community" to ward off the suffering of inward-directed *ressentiment*, "a new interest grows for the individual, too, and often lifts him above the most personal element in his discontent, his aversion to *himself*" (ibid.). The weak congregate together – "all the sick and sickly instinctively strive after a herd organization as a means of shaking off their dull displeasure and feeling of weakness ... " (ibid.). And ascetic priests are always on hand to assist in the effort.

The above are what Nietzsche calls *innocent* means of combatting depression; there are also *guilty* ones that involve an *orgy of feeling* (*G*,III,19–20). The immersion of the soul in "terrors, ice, flames, and raptures," the enthusiasm of idealism, the letting loose of the "pack of savage hounds in man" – thousands of examples of such guilty techniques can be found in history. Exploiting a sense of guilt is itself one of the ascetic priests' chief tricks in this regard. What "heart-rending, ecstatic music" has been produced by the self-punishment brought on by a sense of guilt – "everywhere the scourge, the hair shirt, the starving body, contrition" (*G*,III,20). Instead of protesting against pain, the victim of inner-directed *ressentiment* now *thirsts for* pain. The sick become sicker. In short, "the ascetic priest has ruined psychical health wherever he has come to power ... " (*G*,III,22).

Who Will Stand Up For Life?

Where, Nietzsche asks toward the end of the *Genealogy*, is the *opposing* ideal, the one that can counter the ascetic ideal and overcome the sickness caused by it? Not in science, with its ideal of obedience to the truth (in Nietzsche's eyes just another way of stifling the will to power). Moreover, science does not generate values; it only finds them outside itself. And the picture of human nature painted by science reduces even more the importance of human life; instead of faith in the dignity and uniqueness of the human being, science gives us a picture of the human being as an *animal*, an "arbitrary, beggarly, and dispensable form of existence." The free-thinkers of the world, the "pale atheists, anti-Christians, immoralists, nihilists," (*G*,III,24) these skeptical Nay-sayers of the modern world are also too devoted to the truth, too much in the grip of the will to truth, to achieve the freedom to create values. Perhaps the opposing ideal can be found in art – often a subversive activity and one where the will to deception, and the creative will to power, may still be found. But only in uncorrupted art, and the artist is easily corrupted.

Where today can we find opposition to the "*impoverishment of life*"(*G*,III,25)? In a sense there is, Nietzsche concludes, no answer to this question. The best we can do is laugh at the ascetic ideal and subject it to ridicule. " ... the ascetic ideal has at present only *one* kind of real enemy capable of *harming* it: the comedians of this ideal – for they arouse mistrust of it" (*G*,III,27). (The comedians – those who mock and laugh at ascetic ideals – see something "higher" as a human possibility.) Only when we can pass beyond the stage of viewing nature as a product of the goodness and providence of God, only when we no longer see history as the unfolding of a moral world order, of a plan imposed by divine reason; only when we can reject the notion that everything is preordained and beyond our control – only then will we no longer subject ourselves to given ideals but rather aspire to create them ourselves. Only when, like the masters of old, we project values outward from ourselves; only when, unlike the slaves and members of the herd of the past thousands of years, we no longer have values imposed on us from the outside – only then will human life be restored. Only when we can get over the feeling that the human being *lacks* something, only when we no longer seek a meaning for human existence outside of itself, only when we no longer hate human life and seek to escape it, only then can the will to be human be restored. Only then can we say "Yea" to life and oppose the "Nay-sayers" who represent the ascetic ideal.

Nietzsche certainly holds out hope for the "new philosophers," the "coming philosophers." They will be spirits strong and original enough "to revalue and invert 'eternal values' " (*BGE*,203). Unlike the moral philosophers of the past and present, they will no longer be content to gather data about morality and attempt to systematize it or press it into formulas (like Kant and Hegel) (*BGE*,211). On the contrary, their task will be to *create values*. "Their 'knowing' is *creating*, their creating is a legislation, their will to truth is – *will to power*"(ibid.). In creating values they are at last embracing the will to power, not fearing it or being ashamed by it – and not hypocritically expressing it even while they denounce it in favor of higher ideals. These philosophers, these strong souls, are "world-affirming" (*BGE*,56) – they affirm life *as it is*, that is to say, as will to power. They acknowledge that "Life is *essentially* appropriation, injury, overpowering of what is alien and weaker, suppression, hardness, imposition of one's own forms, incorporation and at least, at its mildest, exploitation ... life simply *is* will to power" (*BGE*,259). Instead of attempting to escape from life, instead of being afraid of it, they choose ... to live it. Their goal: "To translate man back into nature" (*BGE*, 230).

This new philosopher is the person of the future who, in *Thus Spake Zarathustra*, Nietzsche celebrated as the Overman – the "man beyond man." Her most remarkable achievement will be to embrace, not just life, but *the eternal recurrence of all things*. This is how Nietzsche expresses this fantastical doctrine in *Beyond Good and Evil*:

> the ideal of the most high-spirited, alive, and world-affirming human
> being who has not only come to terms and learned to get along with

whatever was and is, but who wants to have *what was and is* repeated into all eternity, shouting insatiably *da capo* [from the beginning] – not only to himself but to the whole play and spectacle, and not only to a spectacle but at bottom to him who needs precisely this spectacle – and who makes it necessary because again and again he needs himself – and makes himself necessary – – What? And this wouldn't be – *circulus vitiosus deus* [a vicious circle made god]? (*BGE*,56)

Who is capable, we can still hear Nietzsche asking, of imagining such a being? Who is able to will that *this life*, the actual one we have, be repeated infinitely. Such a person would indeed *love* life!

Shocking, But Is It True?

Nietzsche's genealogy of morals can be shocking, eye-opening, and inspiring. But is there any truth to it? Philosophers who have rejected Nietzsche's account have usually not found fault with the genealogy *per se*. The question they most often pose is, so what? Even if our moral doctrines evolved in the manner described by Nietzsche, this has no tendency to show that these doctrines are false or irrational. It would be to commit the genetic fallacy to argue that a proposition is false simply because it was derived in a questionable manner. The origin of a belief has little if anything to do with its truth. So, the argument goes, the Nietzsche who rejects morality because of its genealogy can be dismissed as irrelevant.

But what Nietzsche wants is not so much to show us that morality is false – what interest, after all, does he have in *truth* – as to show us that morality stinks. His goal is to get us to see the hypocrisy and small-mindedness inherent in morality and to provoke us to turn away from it with contempt. He thinks that an honest and courageous mind which looks at the history and the psychology of the subject will reject morality on the basis of higher values – which is to say little more than on the basis of *honest* values. Nietzsche wants us to know ourselves for what we are, to be courageous enough to accept what we are, and, finally, to be thrilled by being human. If we accomplish this, we *surpass* humankind, and morality!

One must grant Nietzsche that small-mindedness, meanness, and hypocrisy often characterize "high-minded" moralists. But if one looks at the picture of morality drawn by an Aristotle, or Kant, or Mill, does it reveal a sickly and contemptible creature as the moral ideal? Is morality in the hands of these great thinkers nothing more than a form of revenge and an expression of *ressentiment*? The reader must decide for herself. The author of this work thinks not.

Epilogue

Into the Twentieth Century

The study of moral philosophy from the time of Socrates and the Sophists in the fifth century BCE to the time of Nietzsche at the end of the nineteenth century CE prepares us well for the doctrines and controversies in twentieth-century moral philosophy. Most if not all of the positions held by recent and contemporary thinkers have their parallels in earlier theories, and indeed many of these twentieth-century theories involve attempts to update and improve upon their predecessors. We shall end our study with a brief look at what the new century (soon to be over) has to offer. Doing this will make abundantly clear the relevance of a study of the history of ethics.

Our focus will be almost exclusively on the development of ethics in the Anglo-American world of the twentieth century. At the turn of the century neo-Hegelian approaches dominated this scene. F.H. Bradley's *Ethical Studies*, first published in 1876 but revised for a second edition in 1927, is probably the most important idealist work of this period.[1] In it, Bradley promotes the ethical end of self-realization.[2] Soon, however, there began a realist backlash against idealism, led in large part by G.E. Moore, whose *Principia Ethica* is a classic which is still read and appreciated today.[3]

Intuitionism

Moore articulates an intuitionist account of ethics according to which we have a capacity for direct, perception-like insight into the presence of the property of goodness as it inheres in states of affairs. The property of goodness he describes as being simple, unanalyzable, and non-natural. In saying that goodness is non-natural, Moore is claiming that it is not reducible to any properties that are scientifically observable, such as pleasure. He attempts to prove that this moral feature is non-natural by showing that all theories that attempt to equate it with a natural feature of the world commit a fallacy, the Naturalistic Fallacy. They confuse one thing, goodness, with something else, e.g., pleasure. He goes on to define the notion of right action in terms of an action's ability to maximize non-natural goodness. Thus Moore proposes a form of what is called ideal utilitarianism.

Intuitionism soon caught on – but without Moore's commitment to utilitarianism – and a number of intuitionists developed deontological theories according to which notions of right and duty cannot be derived from ideas of the good. W.D. Ross was an extremely influential deontological intuitionist, as was H. A. Prichard.[4] Ross claims that we can be intuitively (directly and immediately) aware that certain rules of obligation are binding on us, and Prichard launches a vigorous attack on the idea that duty and right action can be a function of self-interest or the ends of desire. Although there are many differences of detail among them, the intuitionists and Bishop Butler walk similar paths. In many ways Ross's and Prichard's notion of intuition sounds like Butler's conscience. And by denying that "ought" can be defined as what is instrumental to the good, all of them reject utilitarianism and declare their deontological commitments.

Consequentialism

Perhaps the central debate in twentieth-century ethics has been over the merits of consequentialist ethics. Consequentialism is the ethical theory which determines the rightness of actions by reference to the value or disvalue found in their consequences. Many philosophers admire the consequentialist utilitarianism of Bentham and Mill for its conception of instrumental rationality and for the fact that it deals with those issues that are squarely on the agenda of most governments today, issues concerning the problems of welfare and attempts to improve the quality of life for their citizens. The scientific cast of utilitarianism is also appealing in an age in which the prestige of science has reached mythic proportions. But consequentialism has had numerous critics. It has been said to reduce the concept of the human person to that of a consumer of pleasure, and to picture moral decision-making as nothing more than calculation and maximization of pleasure. It has been charged with disregarding the concrete relationships people find themselves in and ignoring matters of personal integrity and deeply important personal projects. Furthermore, as we briefly saw in our discussion of Mill's thought, this form of ethics has been accused of justifying, at least in principle, morally outrageous actions such as torture and the punishment of the innocent – both of which could conceivably maximize utility in certain circumstances. Consequentialists have denied these charges, and they have worked hard to show that, properly understood, their theory is consistent with our normal moral intuitions or convictions – with what might be called "ordinary morality." But the critics of consequentialism have not been satisfied. We are left with a choice between the belief that consequentialist utilitarianism provides us with the ideal rational approach to ethical decision-making, and the belief that it runs roughshod over everyday morality.[5]

In chapter 12 we had a brief preview of one way in which some consequentialists have attempted to respond to the claim that their theory threatens morality. Concerned that evaluating the consequences of individual actions (as proposed by act-utilitarianism) could indeed in some circumstances justify things like punishment of the innocent and torture, these philosophers have developed theories of rule-utilitarianism to replace act-utilitarianism. According to rule-utilitarianism, rules, not consequences, fix what we are to do in individual cases, and the absoluteness and inflexibility of these rules can preserve the values of ordinary morality. But the rules themselves must be given a consequentialist justification if we are to have any assurance that they are rational and serve the interest of human well-being.[6]

Deontology

Many advocates of ordinary morality see the ethical philosophies of Immanuel Kant and Joseph Butler as best capturing its spirit, and to some extent its letter.[7] A focus on respect for persons, or alternatively on respect for their rights, serves as the moral linchpin of many of their theories, most of which can be characterized as deontological in outlook.[8] The duties and obligations we have toward others constitute in the minds of these theorists the unshakable foundation of morality, a foundation that should not be subjected to the uncertainties and contingencies involved in calculations of utility. The requirements of justice must always be honored if we are to maintain the dignity and integrity of persons. And the Kantian value of autonomy is central to this idea of personhood. Respect for others is required of us at all times; disrespect is wrong in and of itself. Most contemporary deontologists are committed to the belief that, as Charles Fried puts it, "There are some things which a moral man will not do, no matter what ... "[9]

Contractarianism

An alternative to all of the above theories is a form of contractarianism that descends from Hobbes. The rules that dictate our duties and obligations as well as our rights are understood by this theory to be the consequences of a sort of bargain we have struck with one another. We have, as the title of one contractarian work expresses it, "Morals by Agreement."[10] We can understand the rules we agree to as strategies we would adopt in situations of some uncertainty in which we can expect others to act in their self-interest but in a rational manner. This way of thinking about moral rules does not require that there be any actual, historical moment at which we entered into a contract with one another. Thought experiments in which we demonstrate what behavior would be acceptable to rational beings is all that is required.

One of the most esteemed and influential theories of this type was developed by John Rawls.[11] Rawls attempts to explain the origination of our moral principles by seeing them as the results of a hypothetical bargaining process occurring in what he calls the "original position." In this purely hypothetical position, we have only limited knowledge of what people take to be basic goods. With this limited knowledge, what principles would we choose to guide us in the affairs of life? We do not have knowledge of our own abilities or preferences (we are behind a "veil of ignorance"), and so we cannot agree to a set of rules that would unfairly favor us. In such a position, we must calculate what rules we would be willing to live under no matter what our talents, incapacities, tastes and preferences turn out to be. In making up our minds, we will assume that everyone acts from self-interest – we simply don't know in any detail what our own interests or those of others are. Under such circumstances, Rawls argues, we would only accept rules that would not be inconsistent with our self-interest come what may in our actual situation in life, and we would propose rules we believe others can accept in a similar way out of their self-interest. The principles we would all accept, and agree among ourselves to accept, would be rules of fairness or fair treatment – the rules of justice. Insofar as we would agree to these principles under these circumstances, they should become the basis of the rules that will guide our moral and political lives. In Rawls' theory we hear clear echoes of Hobbes, but also of Kant. For the question posed in the original position may be thought of as asking what kind of life and society we would be willing to accept in order to protect human dignity and the basic value of freedom, regardless of the contingent circumstances we face in actual life.

Virtue Ethics

In addition to consequentialism, deontology, and contractarianism, a fairly new participant in the debate over moral theory is virtue ethics.[12] Here we have the obvious influence of Aristotle, and to some extent that of all the ancient Greek philosophers. The virtue ethicists are dismayed by the emphasis on rules in much recent ethical debate – rules of right action, rules of justice, rules of utility. These thinkers believe the essential focus of the moral life should be on what kind of person one is, not on what rules one should obey. For them *character* is the essential concept. Hence they recommend the development of what the ancient thinkers called virtues – dispositions of character that best express human nature and help us achieve those values embodying the ideals of our humanity. The moral individual is not the rule-follower but rather the individual whose character is that of a good person and good citizen. Such a person is sensitive to the detail of our moral lives and is disposed by character to behave appropriately in particular circumstances. One prominent virtue ethicist, indeed one of the philosophers largely responsible for the emergence of this type of ethical theory, is Alasdair MacIntyre.[13] MacIntyre views the virtues as dispositions of character that permit the attainment of values inherent in and arising out of the many practices constituting our lives: family practices, business practices, religious practices, the practices of local and national government, and the like. The virtuous person is the good father or mother or child, the good merchant or lawyer, the good educator, the good politician, and so on. In focusing on the concrete relations we already have with other people and groups and identifying the concrete values that arise out of participation in the activities of these groups, MacIntyre also reflects a point of view that goes back to Hegel and his emphasis on the concrete ethical life.

Meta-Ethics

So far we have looked at a variety of normative theories that have populated the recent scene in ethics. These theories propose ways in which we ought to act, or define the kinds of lives we ought to live. But much of twentieth-century ethics has been meta-ethical in nature, seeing its task as the conceptual one of analyzing the *meaning* of moral terms and judgments and characterizing the logical relations (or lack thereof) in moral arguments. Such an approach (usually) disavows any attempt to arrive at answers to normative questions about how we ought to behave or live our lives (indeed, in some instances it denies the very possibility of a *philosophical* attempt to arrive at such answers). Meta-ethical analyses are supposed to be value-neutral.

The meta-ethical approach began as early as the first decade of the century, when G.E. Moore inquired into the meaning of the word "good."[14] But it developed a full head of steam only when the logical positivists of the thirties and forties were in the ascendancy.[15] These thinkers were enamored of the view that only natural science gives us knowledge of the world, and that only those propositions or assertions that are empirically verifiable (i.e., the propositions of science) are meaningful. Most of the positivists deny that moral utterances are empirical, scientific claims, and therefore they are led to the conclusion that these utterances are meaningless, at least cognitively meaningless (without cognitive content). Consequently, they argue, moral utterances do not convey any kind of knowledge. In this fashion the positivists develop what is called non-cognitivism, the view that there is no such thing as moral knowledge. They usually characterize moral judgments as expressing feelings or attitudes, or as expressing commands that prescribe how one is to behave. Neither expressions of feeling nor commands have a "truth value" (they are neither true or false) and thus they cannot be true statements that are descriptive of facts in the world.

Emotivism and Prescriptivism

Emotivism is the non-cognitivist meta-ethical theory committed to the view that moral judgments have emotive meaning.[16] These judgments are said to express the speaker's own attitudes and, through a complicated psychological process, to provoke similar attitudes in those who hear or read the judgments. One of the consequences of this emotivist analysis is that there can be no such thing as validity in moral argumentation. At most we can be successful, through persuasive means, in getting other people to share our attitudes.

The non-cognitivist theory of prescriptivism interprets moral judgments as implying something like imperatives, and it argues that as a consequence of this prescriptive status moral judgments cannot be derived solely from factual descriptions.[17] Descriptions alone do not entail imperatives. Most prescriptivists allow for a form of valid moral argumentation, but such arguments presuppose ultimate moral principles that themselves cannot be demonstrated to be true. Hence there is the possibility of rationally irreconcilable disagreements among those who accept different ultimate moral principles.

Relativism

Clearly the non-cognitivism of the emotivists and prescriptivists smacks of Hume. As we have seen, Hume has been interpreted as himself offering an emotivist analysis of moral judgments. But if the spirit of Hume is still with us in a variety of ways, so is that of the ancient Sophists, especially those who accepted something like Protagorean relativism. Relativism is the view that there are no universal moral truths.[18] Cultural relativists claim that different cultures and societies have in fact adopted different moral codes, and ethical relativists maintain that none of these codes can be shown to be valid for anyone other than those people who subscribe to them. Likewise, ethical relativists claim that none of the many different moral codes can be invalidated. Thus for this moral theory it turns out that a set of moral propositions is true for those who believe them, but false for those who do not. Moral propositions are *relatively* true, relative, that is, to their advocates. Some very sophisticated forms of relativism have been developed in recent years which suggest ways in which moral judgments can have a truth value (and hence are not just emotive or prescriptive utterances) but a truth value relative to a particular group.[19]

Relativism reminds us of Nietzsche as well as the Sophists. Nietzsche's perspectivism leads to this kind of view, and his abhorrence of ordinary morality – as deceitful and sick – sits well with the view that moral judgments have no universal validity or warrant. In point of fact, Nietzsche has had little impact on British-American analytic ethics during our century, but he has exercised enormous influence over so-called "Continental" philosophy, e.g., existentialism and forms of power-philosophy identified with the recent French philosopher Michel Foucault. These continental theories at least appear to espouse forms of relativism.

"Good Reasons" and the Moral Point of View

From what we have observed, it is clear that a major strand of twentieth-century moral philosophy has been subjectivist in its orientation. Advocates of this perspective deny that moral judgments have objectivity – i.e., they deny that these judgments register facts that must be accepted by any rational person. But objectivism is by no means dead. During the middle part of the century many analytic philosophers moved away from subjectivism and non-cognitivism by describing the distinctive form of reasoning found in moral arguments. By focusing on the "logic" of moral argumentation, they shifted the focus of attention from the question whether moral judgments are true or false to the question of what constitutes a "good reason" for a moral conviction. Similarly, by describing what they called "the moral point of view," many meta-ethical philosophers identified the distinctive kinds of considerations appropriate to moral questions.[20] Both the "good reasons" and "moral point of view" approaches led meta-ethics away from the skepticism about moral rationality found earlier in emotivism.

This shift from subjectivism to objectivism can, perhaps ironically, be seen as developing a particular theme in Hume's moral philosophy. Hume, it will be recalled, stipulated some conditions that must be fulfilled if a feeling or sentiment is properly to be called moral. It must be the "sentiment of humanity," a sentiment directed at all of humanity and one that sets requirements on everyone. It must be, that is to say, the sentiment of an impartial and disinterested observer, and it must issue in universalized moral requirements. Similar demands were placed by Mill on the "competent judges" who select the higher pleasures. This type of approach has led in the twentieth century to what has been called the "ideal observer theory."[21] According to this point of view, moral judgments are the expressions of belief or attitude of well-informed and impartial persons, and these judgments can be criticized if they are thought to lack one or more of these qualifications. Hence they are subject to rational correction.

The foremost of the prescriptivists, R.M. Hare, proposed a very influential theory of moral reasoning. Hare's theory relies heavily on the Kantian notion of universalizability.[22] In judging morally, he maintains, we must be willing to affirm universal imperatives that prescribe the same form of behavior for everyone in the same situation. Other philosophers who have attempted to identify the distinctive form of moral reasoning have claimed that such reasoning by definition takes the well-being of others into account.[23] The spirit of utilitarianism is evident here.

Naturalism

Some philosophers, unwilling to accept the view that moral judgments do not express factual propositions but nevertheless believing that they are simply the product of our feelings and affective/conative states, claim that moral judgments *describe* the emotional conditions and feelings of the speaker or a community of agents. This kind of view has not been widely adopted in recent times (except, perhaps, among beginning philosophy students). But it is one form of a more prevalent philosophy of *naturalism*, whose basic tenet is that moral judgments are statements about what happens in the natural world (statements about feelings are after all descriptions of natural facts, even if subjective ones). A number of American philosophers of the early part of the century concentrated on how values arise out of interests and desires.[24] This form of naturalism lost much of its appeal as a result of the charge, inspired by Moore, that it commits the naturalistic fallacy and, more generally, as a consequence of the non-cognitivist turn in meta-ethics. Another form of naturalism, one that has become increasingly popular in recent years, interprets moral claims as making statements about evolutionary advantage or disadvantage, i.e., human survival and threats to it.[25]

While a moral theory like utilitarianism can be formulated within a subjectivist, emotivist framework,[26] it can equally be adopted by a naturalist (who believes moral judgments are but a species of scientific ones), by an ideal observer theorist (who believes a fully informed, impartial observer would favor the greatest happiness of the greatest number), by a "good reasons" approach, and by others committed in one way or another to objectivism. Thus a great many ethical theorists adopt moral epistemologies purporting to show how moral knowledge, or at least rationally responsible moral conviction, is possible. They may differ in the way they characterize the epistemological status of moral judgments, but they agree in rejecting skepticism. Rational choice theorists, many of whom subscribe to a contractarian moral theory, believe that valid arguments can determine what principles we should follow. Kantianism is by no means dead in this regard: an appeal to what would happen if everyone behaved in a certain manner is one way of expressing the notion of rational choice. And some contemporary philosophers go so far as to claim that we can give a deductive proof of the basic moral principles. In the work of Alan Gewirth, for example, even the spirit of Spinoza, dressed up to be sure in very different attire, is still with us.[27]

The Possibility of Moral Knowledge

Some of the most influential of current moral philosophers call themselves moral realists.[28] They believe in the reality of moral facts and the reality of our knowledge of these facts. An intuitionist branch of realism asserts that, somewhat as Aristotle suggested, we have a perception-like capacity to perceive the presence of moral facts – to see that some acts are wrong and others required of us. Other realists picture moral knowledge more along the model of scientific hypothesizing. They interpret moral judgments as hypotheses about the unobservable moral properties of things, and they claim that these judgments can be evaluated, like any other scientific theories, on the basis of their ability to explain our moral experience.

Recent Topics

In addition to these many theories, there are numerous topics in recent and contemporary moral philosophy that take us back into the history of the subject. We shall consider just two of these. First, there is the question whether reasons for action must make reference to desires or whether on the contrary they need only record objective facts about the circumstances or consequences of action.[29] This debate should remind us of the views of Hume and Kant, the first accepting the "desire"-requirement, the second affirming the possibility of the will being moved by purely rational considerations. In a way, the current controversy is simply asking: who was right, Hume or Kant?

Another issue hotly debated for a period of time concerns the definition of morality.[30] Is morality a distinctive practice to be identified on the basis of the *form* of moral judgments or on the basis of the *content* of these judgments? Those opting for a formal definition often put forth Kantian-sounding requirements to the effect that moral judgments must be universalizable and overriding (taking precedence over all others) in nature. Theorists opting for a material definition in terms of content often urge – in a fashion reminiscent of Hume, Bentham, and Mill – that moral judgments must make reference to the well-being of others and to the effects of our actions on others.

This, then, sketched in the broadest possible strokes, is twentieth-century moral philosophy. The picture demonstrates that, if only in loose and general ways, history repeats itself. As one of Faulkner's characters in *Requiem for a Nun* observed, "the past is not dead; it's not even past."

Recommended Readings

(*advanced)

Socrates

Benson, Hugh H., ed., *Essays on the Philosophy of Socrates* (Oxford: Oxford University Press, 1992).

Brickhouse, T., and Smith, N., *Socrates on Trial* (Princeton: Princeton University Press, 1989).

*Irwin, T., *Plato's Moral Theory: The Early and Middle Dialogues* (Oxford: Oxford University Press, 1977).

Prior, William J., *Virtue and Knowledge: An Introduction to Ancient Greek Ethics* (London and New York: Routledge, 1991).

Santas, G., "The Socratic Paradoxes," *Philosophical Review*, 73 (1964), 147–64.

Santas, G., *Socrates* (London: Routledge and Kegan Paul, 1979).

Sesonske, A., and Fleming, N., eds, *Plato's Meno: Text and Criticism* (Belmont,CA: Wadsworth, 1965).

*Vlastos, G., *Platonic Studies*, 2nd edn (Princeton: Princeton University Press, 1981).

Vlastos, G., ed., *The Philosophy of Socrates: A Collection of Critical Essays* (Garden City, NY: Doubleday, 1971).

The Sophists

Guthrie, W.K.C., *The Sophists* (Cambridge: Cambridge University Press, 1971).

Prior, William J., *Virtue and Knowledge* (see above).

Plato

Annas, Julia *An Introduction to Plato's Republic* (Oxford: Clarendon Press, 1981).

*Irwin, T., *Plato's Ethics* (Oxford: Oxford University Press. 1995).

Kraut, R., ed., *The Cambridge Companion to Plato* (Cambridge: Cambridge University Press, 1992).

Popper, K., *The Open Society and Its Enemies*, vol. 1 (*The Spell of Plato*), 5th edn (New York: Harper and Row, 1966).

Prior, William J., *Virtue and Knowledge* (see above).

Reeve, C.D.C., *Philosopher-Kings: The Argument of Plato's Republic* (Princeton: Princeton University Press, 1988).

Sachs, D., "A Fallacy in Plato's *Republic*," *Philosophical Review*, 72 (1963), 141–58.

White, N., *A Companion to Plato's Republic* (Indianapolis: Hackett Publishing Co., 1979).

Aristotle

Cooper, John M., *Reason and Human Good in Aristotle* (Cambridge: Harvard University Press, 1975; Indianapolis: Hackett Publishing Co., 1986).

Hardie, W.F.R., *Aristotle's Ethical Theory*, 2nd edn (Oxford: Clarendon Press, 1980).

Hutchinson, D.S., "Ethics," in Jonathan Barnes, ed., *The Cambridge Companion to Aristotle* (Cambridge: Cambridge University Press, 1995).

Meyer, Susan S., *Aristotle on Moral Responsibility* (Oxford: Blackwell, 1993).

*Reeve, C.D.C., *Practices of Reason* (Oxford: Clarendon Press, 1992).

Rorty, A., ed., *Essays on Aristotle's Ethics* (Berkeley: University of California Press, 1980).

Urmson, J.O., *Aristotle's Ethics* (Oxford: Blackwell, 1988).

White, Stephen A., *Sovereign Virtue: Aristotle on the Relation Between Happiness and Prosperity* (Stanford: Stanford University Press, 1992).

Hellenistic Ethics

Annas, Julia, *The Morality of Happiness* (Oxford: Oxford University Press, 1993).

Long, A.A., *Hellenistic Philosophy* (London: Duckworth, 1974).

Nussbaum, Martha C., *The Therapy of Desire* (Princeton: Princeton University Press, 1994).

Sandbach, F.H., *The Stoics* (London: Chatto and Windus, 1975).

Medieval Ethics

Armstrong, R.A., *Primary and Secondary Precepts in Thomistic Natural Law Teachings* (The Hague: Nijhoff, 1966).

Copleston, F., *A History of Western Philosophy*, vol. 2 (London: Burns, Oates and Washbourne Ltd., 1950).

Copleston, F., *Thomas Aquinas* (New York: Barnes and Noble, 1955).

Copleston, F., *A History of Medieval Philosophy* (New York: Harper and Row, 1972).

Davies, Brian, *The Thought of Thomas Aquinas* (Oxford: Clarendon Press, 1992).

Gilson, E., *History of Christian Philosophy in the Middle Ages* (New York: Random House, 1955).

Kirwan, Christopher, *Augustine* (London: Routledge, 1989).

Maurer, A.A., *Medieval Philosophy* (New York: Random House, 1962).

McInerny, Ralph, *Ethica Thomistica* (Washington, DC: Catholic University of America Press, 1982).

McInerny, Ralph, *A History of Western Philosophy* (Notre Dame and London: University of Notre Dame Press, 1970).

O'Connor, D.J., *Aquinas and Natural Law* (London and New York: Macmillan and St Martin's Press, 1968).

Wetzel, James, *Augustine and the Limits of Virtue* (Cambridge: Cambridge University Press, 1992).

Hobbes

Baumrin, B., ed., *Hobbes's Leviathan: Interpretation and Criticism* (Belmont, CA: Wadsworth, 1996).

Boonin-Vail, David, *Thomas Hobbes and the Science of Moral Virtue* (Cambridge: Cambridge University Press, 1994).

Gauthier, David, *The Logic of Leviathan* (Oxford: Oxford University Press, 1969).

Kavka, Gregory S., *Hobbesian Moral and Political Theory* (Princeton: Princeton University Pres, 1986).

Spinoza

*Bennett, Jonathan, *A Study of Spinoza's Ethics* (Cambridge: Cambridge University Press, 1984).

Broad, C.D., "Spinoza," in *Five Types of Ethical Theory* (London: Routledge and Kegan Paul, 1930).

Curley, E. *Behind the Geometrical Method: A Reading of Spinoza's Ethics* (Princeton: Princeton University Press, 1988).

Hampshire, Stuart, *Spinoza* (London: Faber and Faber, 1956).

James, Susan, "Spinoza the Stoic," in Tom Sorell, ed., *The Rise of Modern Philosophy* (Oxford: Clarendon Press, 1993).

Lloyd, Genevieve, *Part of Nature: Self-Knowledge in Spinoza's Ethics* (Ithaca: Cornell University Press, 1994).

Wolfson, Harry A., *The Philosophy of Spinoza*, 2 vols, (New York: Schocken Books, 1969).

Butler

Broad, C.D., "Butler," in *Five Types of Ethical Theory* (London: Routledge and Kegan Paul, 1930),

Cunliffe, C., ed., *Joseph Butler's Moral and Religious Thought*, (Oxford: Clarendon Press, 1992).

McNaughton, David, "British Moralists of the Eighteenth Century: Shaftesbury, Butler, and Price," in Stuart Brown, ed., *British Philosophy and the Age of Enlightenment*, Routledge History of Philosophy, vol. V (London and New York: Routledge: 1996).

Penelhum, Terence, *Butler* (London: Routledge and Kegan Paul, 1985).

Hume

Chappell, V.C., ed., *Hume* (Notre Dame and London: University of Notre Dame Press, 1968).

Hudson, W.D., ed., *The Is/Ought Question* (London and New York: Macmillan and St Martin's Press, 1969).

Norton, David, *David Hume* (Princeton: Princeton University Press, 1982).

Penelhum, Terence, *David Hume* (West Lafayette, IN: Purdue University Press, 1992).

Smith, Norman Kemp, *The Philosophy of David Hume* (London: Macmillan, 1941).

Kant

Aune, Bruce, *Kant's Theory of Morals* (Princeton: Princeton University Press, 1979).

Guyer, Paul, ed., *The Cambridge Companion to Kant* (Cambridge: Cambridge University Press, 1992).

*Herman, Barbara, *The Practice of Moral Judgment* (Cambridge: Harvard University Press, 1993).

*Hill, Thomas E., Jr, *Dignity and Practical Reason in Kant's Moral Theory* (Ithaca: Cornell University Press, 1992).

Korsgaard, Christine M., "Kant's Formula of Universal Law," *Pacific Philosophical Quarterly*, 66 (1985), 24–47.

O'Neill, Onora (Nell), *Acting on Principle* (New York: Columbia University Press, 1975).

Paton, H.J., *The Categorical Imperative: A Study in Kant's Moral Philosophy* (Philadelphia: University of Pennsylvania Press, 1947).

Paton, H.J., *The Moral Law* (New York: Barnes and Noble, 1950).

*Sullivan, Roger J., *Immanuel Kant's Moral Theory* (Cambridge: Cambridge University Press, 1989).

Sullivan, Roger J., *An Introduction to Kant's Ethics* (Cambridge: Cambridge University Press, 1994).

Wike, Victoria S., *Kant on Happiness in Ethics* (Albany: State University of New York Press, 1994).

Wolff, Robert Paul, *The Autonomy of Reason: A Commentary on Kant's Groundwork of the Metaphysics of Morals* (New York: Harper and Row, 1973).

Wolff, Robert Paul, ed., *Kant: A Collection of Critical Essays* (New York: Doubleday Anchor Books, 1967).

Hegel

Beiser, Frederick C., ed., *The Cambridge Companion to Hegel* (Cambridge: Cambridge University Press, 1993).

Taylor, Charles, *Hegel* (Cambridge: Cambridge University Press, 1975).

*Wood, Allen W., *Hegel's Ethical Thought* (Cambridge: Cambridge University Press, 1990).

Bentham

Harrison, Ross, *Bentham* (London: Routledge and Kegan Paul, 1983).

Parekh, B., ed., *Jeremy Bentham* (London: Frank Cass, 1974).

Mill

Berger, Fred. R., *Happiness, Justice, and Freedom: The Moral and Political Philosophy of John Stuart Mill* (Berkeley: University of California Press, 1984).

Donner, Wendy, *The Liberal Self* (Ithaca, NY and London: Cornell University Press, 1991).

Ryan, Alan, *J.S. Mill* (London: Routledge and Kegan Paul, 1974).

Schneewind, J.B., ed., *Mill: A Collection of Critical Essays* (Notre Dame and London: University of Notre Dame Press, 1969).

Smith, J., and Sosa, E., eds, *Mill's Utilitarianism: Text and Criticism* (Belmont, CA: Wadsworth, 1969).

Twentieth-Century Ethics

Arrington, Robert L., *Rationalism, Realism, and Relativism: Perspectives in Contemporary Moral Epistemology* (Ithaca: Cornell University Press, 1989).

Hudson, W.D. *Modern Moral Philosophy* (Garden City, NY: Doubleday and Co., 1970).

Kerner, George C., *The Revolution in Ethical Theory* (New York and Oxford: Oxford University Press, 1966).

Singer, Peter, ed., *A Companion to Ethics* (Oxford: Blackwell, 1991).

Warnock, Mary, *Ethics Since 1900* (Oxford: Oxford University Press, 1960).

Notes

Chapter 1 Socrates and the Sophists

1 Plato, *Five Dialogues*, trans. G.M.A. Grube (Indianapolis and Cambridge: Hackett Publishing Co., 1981).
2 Ibid.
3 The actual accusation against Socrates was one of being *"to parapan atheos"* – going against the gods, namely the gods of the city. In other words, the Athenians accused him of going against their civic religion. While the charge is not what is meant by "atheism" today, it does suggest an alternative notion of atheism.
4 Ibid.
5 Ibid.
6 Plato, *Laches and Charmides*, trans. Rosamond K. Sprague (Indianapolis and Cambridge: Hackett Publishing Co., 1992)
7 Gregory Vlastos, "The Unity of the Virtues in the *Protagoras*," in his *Platonic Studies* (Princeton: Princeton University Press, 1973, 1981), pp. 221–69.
8 Quoted by Vlastos, *Platonic Studies*, p. 232.
9 Plato, *Protagoras*, revised edn, trans. C.C.W. Taylor (Oxford: Oxford University Press, 1991).
10 G. Santas, "The Socratic Paradoxes," *Philosophical Review*, 73 (1964), 147–64; reprinted in A. Sesonske and N. Fleming, eds, *Plato's Meno: Text and Criticism*, (Belmont, CA: 1965).
11 Plato, *Cratylus* 386a, in *The Collected Dialogues of Plato*, ed. E. Hamilton and H. Cairns, trans. B. Jowett (Princeton: Princeton University Press, 1961).
12 Plato, *Theaetetus*, trans. M.J. Levett, revised M. Burnyeat (Indianapolis and Cambridge: Hackett Publishing Co., 1992).
13 Plato, *Republic*, trans. G.M.A. Grube, revised C.D.C. Reeve (Indianapolis and Cambridge: Hackett Publishing Co., 1992).
14 Quoted by W.K.C. Guthrie, *The Sophists* (Cambridge: Cambridge University Press, 1971), p. 101.

Chapter 2 Plato

1 Plato, *Republic*, trans. G.M.A. Grube, 2nd edn, revised C.D.C. Reeve (Indianapolis and Cambridge: Hackett Publishing Co., 1992).
2 Some commentators see the argument of the dialogue as addressed, not directly to Thrasymachus, but to the position developed in Book II by Glaucon and Adeimantus (see below). I interpret it as a response to both.
3 It is sometimes argued that Plato does not adequately defend his claim that it is beneficial for the guardians to give up pure contemplation of the forms and turn their attention to political leadership.
4 See Richard Kraut, "The Defence of Justice in Plato's *Republic*," in *The Cambridge Companion to Plato*, ed. R. Kraut (Cambridge: Cambridge University Press, 1992), p. 325. Plato points to the consequences of these unchecked desires in his discussion of the tyrannical person (*Republic*, 571ff).
5 See David Sachs, "A Fallacy in Plato's *Republic*," in *Philosophical Review* 72 (1963), pp. 141–58.
6 I am grateful to an unidentified reader of the manuscript for expressing the issue in these terms.
7 See S. Freud, *Civilization and its Discontents*, ed. and trans. James Strachey (New York: W.W. Norton, 1962).
8 See J.-P. Sartre, *Existentialism*, trans. B. Frechtman (New York: Philosophical Library, 1947).

Chapter 3 Aristotle

1 Aristotle, *Nicomachean Ethics*, trans. Terence Irwin (Indianapolis and Cambridge: Hackett Publishing Co., 1985).
2 See Stephen A. White, *Sovereign Virtue: Aristotle on the Relation Between Happiness and Prosperity* (Stanford: Stanford University Press, 1992), chapter 1.i.
3 See John M. Cooper, *Reason and Human Good in Aristotle*, chapter 2 (Cambridge: Harvard University Press, 1975; and Indianapolis: Hackett Publishing Company, 1986).
4 Stephen A. White, *Sovereign Virtue*, p. 20.
5 Cooper, *Reason and Human Good in Aristotle*, p. 93.
6 Another scholarly debate is over whether the ultimate end must be one determinate thing/ activity or can be a composite of determinate things/activities. Some scholars have argued that happiness consists exclusively of one thing, intellectual activity, whereas a more traditional interpretation sees happiness as an inclusive notion and hence consisting of a number of component ends. See W.F.R. Hardie, *Aristotle's Ethical Theory*, 2nd edn (Oxford: Clarendon Press, 1980), chapter 2; Richard Kraut, *Aristotle on Human Good* (Princeton: Princeton University Press, 1989); J.L. Akrill, "Aristotle on Happiness," *Proceedings of the British Academy*, 60 (1974); and Stephen White, *Sovereign Virtue*. This debate is a fundamental one, and we shall encounter it again when we examine the last book of the *Nicomachean Ethics*.
7 See D.S. Hutchinson, "Ethics," in *The Cambridge Companion to Aristotle*, ed. Jonathan Barnes (Cambridge: Cambridge University Press, 1995), p. 200.

8 D.S. Hutchinson, "Ethics," p. 201.
9 For a salutary demonstration of how a philosopher's concepts mirror those of her culture, see Stephen White's portrayal of the attitudes toward happiness among the people and poets of ancient Greece (*Sovereign Virtue*, chapters 2.i and 2.ii). White is able to show what aspects of the common view Aristotle finds acceptable and what aspects he rejects. While rejecting the popular emphasis on fortune/luck and material prosperity, Aristotle is nevertheless able to find a place for them is his account of happiness.
10 J.O. Urmson, *Aristotle's Ethics* (Oxford: Blackwell, 1988), p. 12.
11 But, as we shall see, even for Kant happiness plays a very important role in the moral life. The *summum bonum*, the objective end of life, Kant maintains, is the happiness of human beings proportioned to their worthiness in deserving it. What Kant denies is that the motive of one's action should be that of attaining happiness for oneself.
12 Aristotle thinks that the components of true happiness are pleasant in themselves (*NE* 1099a10–15).
13 It is in this context that the translation of "*eudaimonia*" by "success" has much to recommend it. A successful person is one who excels over a long period of time, indeed, perhaps, over the period of a lifetime. And success in life is to some degree dependent on external factors, and events that may happen after one's lifetime. See D.S. Hutchinson, "Ethics," p. 204.
14 A person's apparent success in life could be shattered by post-mortem disgrace.
15 See the last chapter of this book for a brief discussion of contemporary virtue ethics and for references to the literature.
16 To be sure, for Aristotle the virtuous person must do the right thing. But the Aristotelian notion of right action is *derived* from that of a virtuous person; it is *what the virtuous person must do*. It is not, as in later deontological, Kantian ethics, prior to and independent of the concept of virtue and the ends of desire.
17 D.S. Hutchinson, "Ethics," p. 219.
18 But *not* in the Protagorean sense in which there can be no such thing as a false moral judgment.
19 See J.O. Urmson, *Aristotle's Ethics* (Oxford: Blackwell, 1988), pp. 28–9.
20 That a person acts voluntarily is one of the conditions for ascribing moral responsibility to her for this act. It can be questioned whether Aristotle is engaged in developing a theory of moral responsibility or is only discussing conditions under which praise and blame are effective in shaping future human behavior. For a discussion of the issues, and a defense of the view that he is giving us a theory of moral responsibility, see Susan S. Meyer, *Aristotle on Moral Responsibility* (Oxford: Blackwell, 1993).
21 Aristotle's discussion of practical reason in the *Nicomachean Ethics* is complex and often obscure, thus lending itself to a variety of interpretations. A particularly good and clear discussion of the issues involved is found in W.F.R. Hardie's *Aristotle's Ethical Theory*, revised edn (Oxford: Clarendon Press, 1980), chapter 11. One might also consult the very detailed discussion in C.D.C. Reeve, *Practices of Reason* (Oxford: Clarendon Press, 1992), part II.
22 Aristotle himself does not use this term, but it is firmly associated with him. His discussion of what we call practical syllogisms occurs not only in the *Nicomachean Ethics*, book VI, but also in *De Anima* III and *De Motu Animalium* 701.
23 Commentators disagree over the way in which one is to characterize a practical syllogism. An alternative to the description just given is the following: the major premise states that a certain kind of action is a means to a certain end; the minor premise identifies a particular

act as an instance of this kind; and the conclusion is the particular act itself. See Hardie, *Aristotle's Ethical Theory*, pp. 229–32. The example discussed below is patterned after this second model.

24 See C.D.C. Reeve, *Practices of Reason*, p. 42.

25 Here we encounter once again the disagreement of scholars over whether Aristotle intended to equate the ultimate end of happiness exclusively with the life of study or contemplation, or whether he intended it to contain as well the activities achieved through practical reason. See note 6 above.

26 Alasdair MacIntyre, *After Virtue* (Notre Dame: University of Notre Dame Press, 1981), p. 139.

27 Ibid.

28 See Robert Nozick, *The Nature of Rationality* (Princeton: Princeton University Press, 1993).

Chapter 4 Hellenistic Ethics: Epicurus and the Stoics

1 See A.A. Long, *Hellenistic Philosophy* (London: Duckworth, 1974), p. 3; and F.H. Sandbach, *The Stoics* (London: Chatto and Windus, 1975), p. 23.

2 As reported by Diogenes Laertius, *Lives of Eminent Philosophers*, trans. R.D. Hicks, Loeb Classical Library (Cambridge: Harvard University Press, 1966), pp. 203–5.

3 See his *Either/Or*, vol. 1 (New York: Anchor Books, 1959).

4 All references to the *Letter to Menoeceus* are from the translation found in *Greek and Roman Philosophy After Aristotle*, ed. Jason L. Saunders (New York: The Free Press, 1966); references to this work in the text will subsequently be indicated by the letter *M*.

5 Diogenes Laertius, *Lives of Eminent Philosophers*, vol. 2, p. 66.

6 Epicurus, *Principal Doctrines*, in Saunders, *Greek and Roman Philosophy After Aristotle*; subsequent references to this work will be indicated in the text by *PD*.

7 A.A. Long, *Hellenistic Philosophy*, p. 42.

8 Cicero, *De finibus bonorum et malorum* ii 17; quoted by A.A. Long, ibid., p. 63.

9 W. Windelband, *A History of Philosophy*, vol. 1. (New York: Harper Torchbooks, 1958), p. 176.

10 See A.A. Long, *Hellenistic Philosophy*, p. 107.

11 Marcus Aurelius, *Meditations*, trans. M. Staniforth (Baltimore: Penguin Books, 1964), book IV, section 40.

12 These stories come from Diogenes Laertius, *Lives of Eminent Philosophers*, vol. 2.

13 Ibid., p. 195.

14 From the collection of Stoic writings by J. von Arnim, *Stoicorum veterum fragmenta* (Leipzig, 1905–24, 4 vols). Quotations from this work are indicated by the volume number and the fragment number – the above quotation, for instance, being *SVF*, I, 181. The quoted fragments are also contained in the translations found in Saunders, *Greek and Roman Philosophy After Aristotle*; the above quotation is found on p. 111.

15 Diogenes Laertius, *Lives of Eminent Philosophers*, vol. 2, pp. 195–7.

16 Ibid., p. 197.

17 Ibid.

18 A.A. Long, *Hellenistic Philosophy*, p. 108.

19 *SVF*, III, 72; p. 115.

20 Ibid., III, 151; p. 120.

21 Ibid., III, 166; p. 120.
22 Ibid., I, 191; p. 118.
23 Ibid., III, 117; p. 118.
24 Diogenes Laertius, *Lives of Eminent Philosophers*, vol. 2, p. 211.
25 *SVF*, I, 230; p. 129.
26 Ibid., III, 497; p. 129.
27 Ibid., III, 282; p. 124.
28 Ibid., III, 443; p. 128.
29 Diogenes Laertius, *Lives of Eminent Philosophers*, vol. 2, p. 217.
30 Ibid., p. 219.
31 See F.H. Sandbach, *The Stoics.*, pp. 59–60.
32 Diogenes Laertius, *Lives of Eminent Philosophers*, vol. 2, p. 229.
33 *SVF*, III, 340; p. 126.
34 W. Windelband, *A History of Philosophy*, vol. 1, p. 176.
35 *SVF*, III, 333; p. 125.
36 Diogenes Laertius, *Lives of Eminent Philosophers*, vol. 2, p. 233.
37 *SVF*, III, 323; p. 124.
38 Epictetus, *Manual*, section 1, in Saunders, *Greek and Roman Philosophy After Aristotle*; subsequent references to the section numbers of this work will be given in the text.
39 New York: New Directions Books, 1941, pp. 76–9

Chapter 5 Ethics During the Medieval Period

1 *Romans.* 13.13, *New English Bible.*
2 St Augustine, *The Writings Against the Manichaeans and Against the Donatists*, trans. R. Stothert, in *A Select Library of the Nicene and Post-Nicene Fathers of the Christian Church*, vol. 4, ed. Philip Schaff (Grand Rapids, Michigan: Wm. B. Eerdmans Publishing Co., 1979), p. 42.
3 Ibid.
4 Ibid.
5 Etienne Gilson, *History of Christian Philosophy in the Middle Ages* (New York: Random House, 1955), p. 72.
6 *The Writings Against the Manichaeans and Against the Donatists*, ed. Schaff, p. 42.
7 Ibid., pp. 44–5.
8 *De Moribus Ecclesiae Catholicae*, I, 25, 46.
9 See *The Writings Against the Manichaeans and Against the Donatists*, ed. Schaff, p. 46.
10 See James Wetzel, *Augustine and the Limits of Virtue* (Cambridge: Cambridge University Press, 1992), p. 41.
11 St Augustine, *City of God* in *Basic Writings of Saint Augustine*, vol. 2, ed. Whitney J. Oates (New York: Random House, 1948), book XIX, chapter 12, p. 485.
12 Ibid., p. 487.
13 Ibid., book XIX, chapter 13, p. 488.
14 Ibid.
15 Augustine's attitude toward war is somewhat ambiguous. While war and violence can never be "just" acts in a pure and ideal sense, true justice, he thought, is not of this world. In our fallen state, we are sometimes required to do what is less than ideal.
16 *City of God*, ed. Oates, book XIX, chapter 131i, p. 488.

17 Ralph M. McInerny, *A History of Western Philosophy*, vol. 2 (Notre Dame and London: University of Notre Dame Press, 1970), p. 46.

18 *City of God*, book XIV, chapter 28, p. 274.

19 *De Spiritu et Littera*, 19, 34.

20 *Enarrationes in Psalmos*, xv, 22.

21 *City of God*, ed. Oates, book XV, chapter 22, pp. 306–7.

22 *De Trinitate*, xi, 6, 10.

23 *City of God*, ed. Oates, book XIV, chapter 7, p. 247.

24 Ibid., book XII, chapter 7, p. 185.

25 Ibid., book XII, chapter 8, p. 186.

26 Ibid.

27 Ibid.

28 See, for instance, Alvin Plantinga, *God, Freedom and Evil* (London: George Allen and Unwin, 1974), pp. 29ff.

29 See E. Gilson, *Abelard and Heloise*, trans. L.K. Shook (1951); and D.W. Robertson, Jr, *Abelard and Heloise* (New York: The Dial Press, 1972).

30 *Peter Abelard's Ethics*, trans. D.E. Luscombe (Oxford: The Clarendon Press, 1971), p. 3. The page numbers of all subsequent references to this volume are given in the main text.

31 For a highly regarded contemporary version of this theory, see Harry Frankfurt, "Freedom of the Will and the Concept of a Person," *Journal of Philosophy*, 68, pp. 5–20.

32 *Peter Abelard's Ethics*, trans. D.E. Luscombe; see the editor's note 5, p. 25.

33 See A.A. Maurer, *Medieval Philosophy* (New York: Random House, 1962), p. 70.

34 Aquinas, *Summa Theologiae* Ia.12.5; numbered references to this work are to part, question, and article.

35 F. Copleston, *A History of Medieval Philosophy* (New York: Harper and Row, 1972), p. 180.

36 *Summa Theologiae* 1a2ae.1.5.

37 Ibid. 1a2ae.3.1.

38 See Armand A. Maurer, *Medieval Philosophy* (New York: Random House, 1962), p. 187.

39 The notion of "irascible appetites" is discussed by A.A. Maurer in *Medieval Philosophy*, p.186.

40 *Summa Theologiae* 1a2ae.90.4.

41 Ibid. 1a2ae.91.1 and 91.3.

42 Ibid. 1a2ae.91.2.

43 See A. Donagan, "The Scholastic Theory of Moral Law in the Modern World," in *Aquinas: A Collection of Critical Essays*, ed. A. Kenny (New York: Anchor Books, Doubleday and Co., 1969).

44 See R.A. Armstrong, *Primary and Secondary Precepts in Thomistic Natural Law Teachings* (The Hague: Nijhoff, 1966), p. 39.

45 Ibid., p. 38.

46 Aquinas is not always helpful in identifying what these general precepts are, and commentators disagree over precisely what precepts reflect the *inclinationes naturales*.

47 Armstrong, *Primary and Secondary Precepts in Thomistic Natural Law Teaching*, p. 48.

48 *Summa Theologiae* 1a2ae.94.2.

49 Ibid.

50 Aquinas makes it clear that setting aside a secondary precept requires a special dispensation from God.

51 See R. McInerny, *Ethica Thomistica* (Washington, DC: Catholic University of America

Press, 1982), p. 40.

52 Ibid., p. 46.
53 See Brian Davies, *The Thought of Thomas Aquinas* (Oxford: Clarendon Press, 1992), pp. 221–5.
54 For a good discussion of this concept, see ibid., pp. 233ff.
55 Ibid., pp. 235ff.
56 *Summa Theologiae* 1a2ae.58.1.
57 Davies, *The Thought of Thomas Aquinas*, p. 246.
58 See D.J. O'Connor, *Aquinas and Natural Law* (London and New York: Macmillan and St Martin's Press, 1968), p. 75.
59 See Ludwig Wittgenstein, *Philosophical Investigations* (London: Macmillan, 1953).
60 "Paris Reports," book I, distinction 2, question 1; quoted by F. Copleston, *A History of Medieval Philosophy*, p. 253 from the Vives Edition of the "Opera Omnia," XXII, p. 512 (1891–5).
61 I have benefitted in this discussion of Scotus from the accounts found in F. Copleston, *A History of Western Philosophy*, vol. 2 (London: Burns Oates and Washbourne, Ltd., 1950) pp. 545–51; F. Copleston, *A History of Medieval Philosophy* (New York: Harper and Row, 1972) pp. 225–9; A. Maurer, *Medieval Philosophy* (New York: Random House, 1962), pp. 240–1; and Allan B. Wolter, "General Remarks," in his translation of Scotus's ethical writings, *Duns Scotus on the Will and Morality* (Washington, DC: The Catholic University of America Press, 1986).
62 Maurer, *Medieval Philosophy*, p. 286.
63 Ibid.
64 Ockham, *Reportata*, book II, Qu. 5, H; cited by Copleston, *A History of Medieval Philosophy*, p. 253.
65 Ibid., p. 287.
66 Ockham, *Reportata*, book IV, Qu.9, E-F; cited by Copleston, *A History of Medieval Philosophy*, p. 252.
67 Copleston, *A History of Medieval Philosophy*, p. 253.
68 See Copleston, *A History of Medieval Philosophy*, pp. 229, 254.

Chapter 6 Hobbes

1 As we shall see at the end of this chapter, there are a number of very different interpretations of Hobbes's moral theory, including one that claims he has no moral theory. Rather than consider the interpretive disagreements as we proceed, we shall follow a single interpretive line throughout most of the chapter and only later take note of the disagreements.
2 All references in the text to *L* are to Hobbes's masterpiece, *Leviathan*, ed. Edwin Curley (Indianapolis and Cambridge: Hackett Publishing Co., 1994); citations are given to chapter and section.
3 One recent interpretation of Hobbes as a virtue ethicist puts an entirely different light on the matter; see David Boonin-Vail, *Thomas Hobbes and the Science of Moral Virtue* (Cambridge: Cambridge University Press, 1994).
4 I borrow the terminology of moderates and dominators from Gregory S. Kavka. See his *Hobbesian Moral and Political Theory* (Princeton: Princeton University Press, 1986), p. 97.
5 Thomas Hobbes, *De Cive*, English version, ed. Howard Warrender (Oxford: Oxford

University Press, 1983); citation is to chapter and section.

6 See Bernard Gert, "Hobbes and Psychological Egoism," in *Hobbes's Leviathan: Interpretation and Criticism*, ed. Bernard Baumrin (Belmont, CA: Wadsworth, 1996), pp. 107–26; and "Hobbes, Mechanism, and Egoism," *Philosophical Quarterly*, 15 (October, 1965), 341–9. Also see F.S. McNeilly, "Egoism in Hobbes," *Philosophical Quarterly* 16 (July, 1966), 193–206.

7 *Human Nature*, chapter 9, section 10.

8 I take this term from Kavka, *Hobbesian Moral and Political Theory*, pp. 35ff, who credits Gert for it in his "Introduction to Thomas Hobbes," *Man and Citizen* (Garden City, NY: Doubleday, 1972), p. 7.

9 See Kavka, *Hobbesian Moral and Political Theory*, pp. 35ff.

10 Ibid., pp. 64ff.

11 One recent commentator, Gregory Kavka, has interpreted Hobbes as defending a theory of rule-egoism, a sophisticated version of the doctrine. Rule-egoism requires that we follow rules that foster our self-interest, not that each of our actions be the one that best serves our self-interest. See Kavka's *Hobbesian Moral and Political Theory*.

12 See David Gauthier, *The Logic of Leviathan* (Oxford: Oxford University Press, 1969), p. 91.

13 I am indebted in what follows to David Boonin-Vail's excellent discussion of the issues in his *Thomas Hobbes and the Science of Moral Virtue*, chapter 3.

14 It must be granted that Hobbes is inconsistent in this regard. In the Preface of *De Cive* he writes that "there are no authentical doctrines concerning right and wrong, good and evil, besides the constituted laws in each realm and government." Insofar as the authority of each government extends only over those who consent to it, the constituted laws of any realm and government have no validity for all human beings.

15 See the work of Howard Warrender.

16 See Kavka, *Hobbesian Moral and Political Theory*, pp. 107–8.

17 See Will Kymlicka, "The Social Contract Tradition," in Peter Singer, ed., *A Companion to Ethics* (Oxford: Blackwell, 1991), p. 187.

Chapter 7 Spinoza

1 All references to the *Ethics* are to the translation by Edwin Curley contained in *A Spinoza Reader*, ed. E. Curley (Princeton: Princeton University Press, 1994).

2 He does, however, assert the immortality of thought or mind, although not in an individuated form.

3 God is these things plus an infinite number of other attributes of which we have no knowledge.

4 In citing passages in the *Ethics*, the first, Roman numeral refers to the Part of the book; the following capital letter refers to a preface (Pr), an axiom (A), a definition (D), or a proposition (P); the next Arabic numeral refers to the number of the axiom, definition, or proposition; and the concluding capital letter refers to a Scholium (S), Corollary (C) or Demonstration (D) following a proposition.

5 Stuart Hampshire, *Spinoza* (London: Faber and Faber, 1956), p. 94 and passim.

6 This notion will become very important later on.

7 Harry A. Wolfson, *The Philosophy of Spinoza*, vol. 2 (New York: Schocken Books, 1969), p. 195.

8 Although not always. If a joy is based on a confused idea of the self, as we noted above, it is a passion that inhibits the person's *conatus*.

9 It should be recalled that forms of self-esteem based on confused ideas of the self are *not* commended by Spinoza as a good.

10 C.D. Broad, *Five Types of Ethical Theory* (London: Routledge and Kegan Paul, 1930), chapter 2.

Chapter 8 Butler

1 Leslie Stephen, *History of English Thought in the Eighteenth Century*, vol. 2 (New York: Harcourt, Brace, and World, 1962), p. 39.

2 Two of the other most important English philosophers of this period were Shaftesbury and Hutcheson, who are often labelled "moral sense" philosophers. This label is sometimes applied to Butler as well, but, as we shall see, there are important differences between Butler's views and those of these two contemporaries.

3 The official title of the sermons is *Fifteen Sermons Delivered at the Rolls Chapel*.

4 References to passages from the *Sermons* will indicate the sermon number (e.g., S1) followed by an indication of the number of the paragraph in the sermon. All references are to the J.H. Bernard edition of *The Works of Joseph Butler*, vol. 1 (London: 1900). Most of the passages are reprinted in *Moral Philosophy from Montaigne to Kant*, vol. 2, ed. J.B. Schneewind (Cambridge: Cambridge University Press).

5 Some scholars debate this classification scheme and put benevolence among the particular passions. Some reasons for this debate will be mentioned below. See David McNaughton, "Butler on Benevolence," in Christopher Cunliffe, ed., *Joseph Butler's Moral and Religious Thought* (Oxford: Clarendon Press, 1992). McNaughton provides a useful list of philosophers who have taken Butler to classify benevolence as a general principle (p. 270).

6 See Terence Penelhum, *Butler* (London: Routledge and Kegan Paul, 1985), p. 32.

7 It is sometimes debated whether for Butler conscience is a matter of feeling or one of knowledge. In the philosophical context of his day, many thinkers were stressing the importance of feeling and sentiment. Butler does not explicitly take a stand on this issue, and on the occasions when he alludes to it, he is deliberately vague and evasive, e.g., when he asserts its existence "whether considered as a sentiment of the understanding, or as a perception of the heart; or, which seems the truth, as including both" (*Dissertation or Virtue*/1). But in referring to conscience as *reflective*, he seems to show that for him it is a rational activity and a matter of knowledge, even though it may have feeling tone attached to it. As we proceed, further reasons for interpreting him this way will unfold.

8 As noted above, this classification scheme is debatable. R.G. Frey has argued that there are three competing interpretations: the standard one (adopted here), the one which denies that benevolence is a general principle and places it among the particular passions, and the one (adopted by Frey) that claims there are only two levels, the first containing the particular passions and benevolence, the second containing self-love and conscience. See R.G. Frey, "Butler on Self-Love and Benevolence," in Cunliffe, ed., *Joseph Butler's Moral and Religious Thought*.

9 As Leslie Stephen puts it with a rhetorical flourish, "Butler shows conclusively the inadequacy of the analysis of all heroism and philanthropy into a love of our own trumpery individuality," *History of English Thought in the Eighteenth Century*, p. 46.

10 See chapter 6 above, p. 175ff.

11 A psychological egoist who thinks that one's own good is always conceived to be one's own pleasure or balance of pleasure over pain is a psychological hedonist.

12 A similar argument is found in David McNaughton, "British Moralists of the Eighteenth Century: Shaftesbury, Butler and Price," in *British Philosophy and the Age of Enlightenment*, Routledge History of Philosophy, vol. 5, ed. Stuart Brown (London and New York: Routledge, 1996), p. 216. Penelhum also objects to the argument on similar grounds, *Butler*, pp. 52–3.

13 A less drastic conception of selfishness would be a disposition of character in which desires for the good of others are too weak and desires for the good of ourselves too strong – see McNaughton, "British Moralists of the Eighteenth Century: Shaftesbury, Butler and Price," p. 217.

14 C.D. Broad, *Five Types of Ethical Theory* (London: Routledge and Kegan Paul, 1930), p. 78.

15 Penelhum has argued that Butler's theory does not require that the pronouncements of conscience be infallible; all it requires is that they be overriding. See Penelhum, *Butler*, pp. 76–7.

16 Joseph Butler, *Dissertation on Virtue/8*, in the Bernard edition of *The Works of Joseph Butler*, vol. 2, (D); included in Schneewind, *Moral Philosophy from Montaigne to Kant*.

17 In his *Analogy of Religion*, part II, chapter 8, paragraph 11.

18 From *A Discourse of Natural Religion*; cited by Stephen Darwall, "Conscience as Self-Authorizing," in Cunliffe, ed. *Joseph Butler's Moral and Religious Thought*, p. 214.

19 McNaughton, "British Moralists of the Eighteenth Century: Shaftesbury, Butler and Price," p. 213. Penelhum (*Butler*, p. 79) refers to Butler as a dogmatic deontologist.

20 See Nicholas Sturgeon, "Nature and Conscience in Butler's Ethics," *Philosophical Review*, 85 (1976), 316–56.

21 One of the most lively debates in recent Butler scholarship has arisen from Nicholas Sturgeon's claim that the authority of conscience is superfluous. Sturgeon argues that the only reason conscience can offer for doing an act is that this act, or the principle that motivates it, is natural, and the only reason for not doing something is that it, or the principle from which it flows, is unnatural. Thus conscience, as he sees it, merely registers the facts that actions and their principles are natural or unnatural. Its authority does not enter the picture. See Nicholas Sturgeon, "Nature and Conscience in Butler's Ethics." This argument has been vigorously rebutted and the standard interpretation (presented here) defended by Terence Penelhum, in *Butler*, by Stephen Darwall, in "Conscience as Self-Authorizing," and by Darwall in his recent *The British Moralists and the Internal 'Ought': 1640–1740* (Cambridge: Cambridge University Press, 1995), pp. 244–83.

22 There remains the question of how conscience can generate obligation. Must this explanation be a theological one, in terms of the order or hierarchy that God intended in creating human beings? For this view, see Brian Hebblethwaite, "Butler on Conscience and Virtue" in Christopher Cunliffe, ed. *Joseph Butler's Moral and Religious Thought* (Oxford: The Clarendon Press, 1992), pp. 197–208. Or does the authority of conscience derive from something like the fact that without it we could make no sense of a rational agent acting autonomously from reasons ("being a law unto herself")? For the latter view, see the works of Stephen Darwall cited above.

23 See Penelhum, *Butler*, pp. 73–4.

24 Ibid. pp. 4, 20, 25, 74. Penelhum writes, "To get more moral practice, Butler is happy to pay the price of theoretical overdetermination" (p. 25).

25 Although sometimes with reservations about particular aspects of his arguments – see, for

example, T. Penelhum, *Butler*, pp. 45–7.

26 Satisfying the desire to help others, or satisfying the desire for the good of others, thereby increases one's own satisfaction or pleasure, and hence serves self-love. McNaughton, for instance, has deemed Butler's argument here "masterly" ("British Moralists of the Eighteenth Century: Shaftesbury, Butler and Price," p. 216).

27 G.E.M. Anscombe, "Modern Moral Philosophy," reprinted in *Collected Papers*, vol. III (Oxford: Oxford University Press, 1981), p. 27; quoted by Hebblethwaite, "Butler on Conscience and Virtue".

28 See Hebblethwaite, "Butler on Conscience and Virtue," for a good discussion of these issues.

29 C.D. Broad, *Five Types of Ethical Theory*, p. 83.

Chapter 9 Hume

1 Scholars disagree over the extent to which Hume actually is a skeptic. See Norman Kemp Smith, *The Philosophy of David Hume* (London: Macmillan, 1941).

2 Leslie Stephen traces the "primary impulse" behind utilitarianism to the seventeenth-century philosopher John Locke (see Stephen's *History of English Thought in the Eighteenth Century*, p. 68). But Hume is clearly the leading forerunner of the classic expressions of utilitarianism found in Bentham and Mill in the nineteenth century.

3 We shall see later, however, that when naturalism is interpreted in a different way (as a meta-ethical theory), Hume is a severe critic of naturalism.

4 J. Kemp, *Ethical Naturalism: Hobbes and Hume* (London: Macmillan, 1970), p. 29.

5 There will be an occasion to comment briefly on one possible difference – see notes 24 and 25 below.

6 All references to Hume's *A Treatise of Human Nature* are indicated by *T* and page number. All references are to the L. A. Selby-Bigge edition, 2nd edn revised by P.H. Nidditch (Oxford: Oxford University Press, 1978).

7 He was particularly concerned to refute the views of philosophers he called "rationalists," two of whom were Samuel Clark (1675–1729) and William Wollaston (1659–1724).

8 All references to Hume's *An Inquiry Concerning the Principles of Morals* are given by *I* and page number. All references are to the Library of Liberal Arts edition, ed. Charles W. Hendel (Indianapolis and New York: Bobbs-Merrill Co., 1957).

9 See John McDowell, "Non-Cognitivism and Rule-Following," in *Wittgenstein: To Follow A Rule*, ed. S. Holtzman and C. Leich (London: Routledge and Kegan Paul, 1981), pp. 154–5.

10 I am angry at a person *because* I think she has lied to me; I approve of the Democratic party *because* I believe it will bring a better life to the poor.

11 See Jonathan Dancy, *Moral Reasons* (Oxford: Blackwell, 1993). Dancy points out that at times Hume himself speaks of beliefs as giving rise to actions, as when he describes their "force and influence" which "renders them the governing principles of all our actions" (*T*, 629). But Dancy, a major advocate of a cognitive theory of motivation, simply shrugs off this passage as one of many inconsistencies in Hume's text.

12 Terence Penelhum has characterized Hume's argument as being based on the notion that passions are impressions, not ideas, and that only ideas (which are *copies*) can be true or false – true if they copy correctly, false otherwise. See his *David Hume* (West Lafayette, Indiana: Purdue University Press, 1992), p. 143.

13 The reasoning that leads to this shocking conclusion has been described by Penelhum as "one of Hume's worst arguments, and unfortunately one of his most important," ibid., p. 143. Penelhum's rebuttal consists in pointing out that the notion of rational assessment includes more than judgments of truth or falsity. A passion like gratitude or anger can be unreasonable, not because it is based on a false judgment, but because it is disproportionate to the benefit or harm a person thinks she has received. Hume would probably respond by asking how we ascertain proportionality. Is it a relation of ideas? An observable matter of fact?

14 Contemporary moral realists urge that Hume has gone wrong here by missing the *resultant* nature of moral properties. Vice is not a property on the same level with the properties we observe, but it results from those properties. As Jonathan Dancy has put it, in a specific situation "the vice consists in those properties and the way they relate to one another" (*Moral Reasons*, p. 75). Thus one should not expect to observe vice in addition to, and separate from, the observable properties in the case of the resultant properties.

15 Hume's argument here seems artificial. Surely the causal relation itself makes a difference, and the total set of relations in the parricide case is therefore different from the total set in the sapling case.

16 But surely the *direction* of the relation – going from good offices to ill will in the one case and from ill will to good offices in the other – makes a difference to the moral character of the relational situation?

17 A *meta-ethical* theory is one that analyses the meanings of moral terms and judgments as well as the logical structures of moral arguments. Such a theory is to be distinguished from the kind (or aspect) of ethics in which normative claims are made, that is to say, in which it is *asserted* or claimed that some kinds of thing are good or some types of action wrong.

18 Thus "naturalism" in this sense is different from that in which, on p. 231 above, we said that Hume himself is a naturalist. To remind ourselves, Hume's naturalism consists in his rejection of any supernatural origin of morality and his insistence that morality pertains only to the empirical characteristics of human nature. The meta-ethical naturalism he rejects is a thesis about the semantic character of moral judgments and the relationship between these judgments and their reasons. Hume himself did not speak in these terms – indeed meta–ethics as a self-conscious and deliberate enterprise is a twentieth-century phenomenon. But he can be seen as a precursor of a meta–ethics that rejects naturalism.

19 See Charles Stevenson, *Ethics and Language* (New Haven: Yale University Press, 1944), and R.M. Hare, *The Language of Morals* (Oxford: Oxford University Press, 1952). Stevenson's classic book contains an *emotivist* appropriation of Hume's distinction, and Hare's equally classic work represents a *prescriptivist* use of it.

20 For the emotivist, ought-propositions have emotive meaning: they express attitudes; for the prescriptivist, ought-propositions have evaluative meaning: they entail something like imperatives that prescribe actions. The non–moral emotive expression "Damn!" does not follow logically from any set of descriptions; the non–moral command "Shut the door!" is an imperative that equally fails to follow logically from any set of descriptions. For the emotivist and prescriptivist, moral judgments similarly fail to follow logically from descriptions.

21 The theories of emotivism and prescriptivism, cited in notes 19 and 20 above, are classic theories of non–cognitivism.

22 In Section ii of Part I of Book III of the *Treatise*, Hume speaks of moral distinctions being "derived from a moral sense," and this fact has sometimes led to his being classified as a moral sense theorist in the tradition of Shaftesbury, Hutcheson and other British

thinkers. This classification can be confusing. Although most moral sense philosophers thought of the moral sense as a matter of sentiment rather than reason, it seems they also understood it to be a source of knowledge and hence a faculty capable of detecting moral properties and facts. Hume rejects any such faculty and any such knowledge – moral convictions express feelings, not insight. His "moral sense," if we wish to call it that, is a certain kind of non-cognitive sentiment. We shall see later precisely what this moral sentiment amounts to. Later we shall also see how this non-cognitivist reading of Hume can be challenged.

23 Moral characteristics, then, are similar to *secondary qualities* such as color and taste. Secondary qualities are constituted by the subjective responses of perceivers caused by the objective primary properties of external objects. According to the theory of secondary qualities, an object is red if it causes a perceiver to have the subjective experience of red; the object itself has only the primary, measurable, qualities of extension, motion and the like. Hume rejects, in the field of metaphysics, the primary quality/secondary quality distinction, which he attributes to "modern philosophy" (*T*,225ff), but he himself notes that his theory of *value* can be understood in its terms.

24 In the *Treatise*, Hume uses the term "sympathy" in a technical sense to indicate a mechanism of association whereby we are able to recreate in ourselves the feelings and passions of others. In the later *Inquiry*, this technical notion is apparently abandoned and is replaced by ordinary, original sentiments of benevolence and compassion, and what Hume comes to call "the sentiment of humanity" (see below). When I refer to "sympathy" in what follows, I do not intend Hume's earlier technical notion.

25 Hume seems to have changed his opinion on this matter since the time of the *Treatise*, for in this book he wrote, "In general it may be affirmed that there is no passion in human minds as the love of mankind, merely as such, independent of personal qualities, of services, or of relation to oneself" (p. 481). Moreover, in this earlier work benevolence is of quite limited scope. The *Treatise*'s doctrine of sympathy (see note 24) was designed to explain how we can favor people to whom our limited passion of benevolence does not extend. After admitting that there is no one whose happiness or misery does not affect us, Hume goes on to write, "But this proceeds merely from sympathy, and is no proof of such an universal affection to mankind ... " See Penelhum, *David Hume*, pp. 153–6.

26 With respect to this claim, many may think Hume naive. Or have "the times" changed enough since Hume's day to explain our current opinion of the strength of the profit motive?

27 See A.J. Ayer, *Language, Truth, and Logic* (New York: Dover Books, 1946), chapter 6; Charles Stevenson, *Ethics and Language* (New Haven: Yale University Press, 1944); J.L. Mackie, *Ethics: Inventing Right and Wrong* (Harmondsworth: Penguin Books, 1977); Simon Blackburn, *Spreading the Word* (Oxford: Oxford University Press, 1984).

28 See the recent book by Allan Gibbard, *Wise Choices, Apt Feelings* (Cambridge: Harvard University Press, 1990).

29 See his *David Hume* (Princeton: Princeton University Press, 1982), chapter 3.

30 Ibid., p. 109.

31 By Terence Penelhum, *David Hume*, p. 149.

32 Ibid., p. 126.

33 See in particular the works of Stevenson and Hare cited above.

34 A.C. MacIntyre, "Hume on 'Is' and 'Ought'," *Philosophical Review*, 68 (1959); reprinted in V.C. Chappell, *Hume* (Notre Dame and London: University of Notre Dame Press, 1968), pp. 240–64; all references are to the reprint.

35 Geoffrey Hunter, "Hume on *Is* and *Ought*," *Philosophy*, XXXVII (1962), pp. 148–52.
36 See Antony Flew, "On the Interpretation of Hume," *Philosophy*, XXXVIII (1963); reprinted in Chappell, ed., *Hume*, pp. 278–86; and W.D. Hudson, "Hume on *Is* and *Ought*," *The Philosophical Quarterly*, XIV (1964); reprinted in Chappell, pp. 295–307. Also see Hunter's response to Flew and Flew's parting shot in Chappell, pp. 287–94.
37 "Hume on 'Is' and 'Ought'," p. 256.
38 See John Searle, "How to Derive 'Ought' from 'Is'," *Philosophical Review* (1964), 43–58; a useful collection of essays dealing with Searle's argument is W.D. Hudson, ed., *The Is/ Ought Question* (London and New York: Macmillan and St Martin's Press, 1969).

Chapter 10 Kant

1 Immanuel Kant, *Critique of Practical Reason*, 3rd edn, trans. Lewis White Beck (New York: The Library of Liberal Arts, Macmillan, 1993), p. 169; p. 161 of the Prussian Academy edition of Kant's works, volume 5. Subsequent references to this book (*CPrR*) will be cited in the text by first giving the page number of the Beck translation and then the number of the page in the Prussian Academy edition.
2 All references to the *Groundwork* are given in the body of the text to page numbers of the translation found in H.J. Paton, *The Moral Law*, trans. H.J. Paton (New York: Barnes and Noble, 1950), followed by the page number of the Prussian Academy edition.
3 This teleological conception of nature, unacceptable to most contemporary thinkers, is developed in greater detail in Kant's *Critique of Judgment*.
4 The *Groundwork* stresses the struggle between morality and desire more than some of Kant's later works such as the *Metaphysics of Morals*.
5 An excellent discussion of this issue can be found in Barbara Herman, *The Practice of Moral Judgment* (Cambridge: Harvard University Press, 1993), chapter 1, esp. pp. 1–6. In what follows I am indebted to what she has to say in this chapter.
6 Such cases of self-interest are easier to distinguish from motivation by duty, Kant suggests, than those in which there is an immediate inclination that coincides with duty.
7 There is some justification for this way of reading him. At one point Kant gives the example of a person whose mind is clouded over with sorrow to the extent that all sympathy for others is extinguished. In this context he writes, "suppose that, when no longer moved by any inclination, he tears himself out of this deadly insensibility and does the action [helps others] for the sake of duty alone; *then for the first time his action has its genuine moral worth*" (66, 398). The last clause certainly suggests that only when the motive of duty operates alone is moral worth attained. In spite of this passage, the interpretation offered here seems more consistent with the text as a whole. For a discussion of this passage, and similar ones in the *Groundwork*, see Barbara Herman, *The Practice of Moral Judgment*, pp. 18–22.
8 But not just *any* principle, as we shall see.
9 For an excellent discussion of these interpretations, see Christine M. Korsgaard, "Kant's Formula of Universal Law," in *Pacific Philosophical Quarterly*, 66 (1985), 24–47. Also see Barbara Herman, *The Practice of Moral Judgment*, chapter 7; and Onora (Nell) O'Neill, *Acting on Principle* (New York: Columbia University Press, 1975), chapter 5.
10 See below, p. 275.
11 See Roger Sullivan, *An Introduction to Kant's Ethics* (Cambridge: Cambridge University Press, 1994), pp. 48ff.

12 See J. B. Schneewind, "Autonomy, obligation, and virtue: An overview of Kant's moral philosophy," in Paul Guyer, ed., *The Cambridge Companion to Kant* (Cambridge: Cambridge University Press, 1992), p. 309.

13 I. Kant, "What is Enlightenment?" in *The Philosophy of Kant*, ed. and trans. Carl J. Friedrich (New York: The Modern Library: 1949), p. 132.

14 Ibid., pp. 132–3.

15 I. Kant, "Preface to the Second Edition," *Critique of Pure Reason*, trans. M. Müller, in *Kant Selections*, ed. T.M. Greene (New York: Scribner's, 1929), pp. 19–20.

16 Ibid., p. 22.

17 Here we hear echoes of the Stoics and Abelard.

18 See below, pp. 296, 306–7.

19 John Stuart Mill, *Utilitarianism*, in *Collected Works of John Stuart Mill*, vol. 10, ed. J.M. Robinson (Toronto and London: University of Toronto Press and Routledge and Kegan Paul, 1969), p. 207.

20 See the discussion of this example by Bruce Aune in his *Kant's Theory of Morals* (Princeton: Princeton University Press, 1979), pp. 50–1.

21 Christine Korsgaard, "Kant's Formula of Universal Law."

22 Paul Dietrichson, "Kant's Criteria of Universalizability," in *Kant: Foundations of the Metaphysics of Morals: Text and Critical Essays*, ed. Robert Paul Wolff (Indianapolis: Bobbs Merrill, 1969), p. 188; cited by Korsgaard, "Kant's Formula of Universal Law."

23 See I. Kant, "On a Supposed Right to Lie Because of Philanthropic Concerns," trans. James W. Ellington, in Ellington's translation of Kant's *Grounding for the Metaphysics of Morals*, 3rd edn, (Indianapolis and Cambridge: Hackett Publishing Co., 1993).

24 Ibid., p. 65.

25 Ibid., p. 64.

26 Ibid., p. 67.

27 Ibid.

28 It is possible, however, to imagine a defender of Kant arguing that in a world in which everyone tells the truth except when a certain condition prevails, no one would believe anyone when this condition holds, and this fact would undermine the general climate of trust.

29 See Carol Gilligan, *In a Different Voice: Psychological Theory and Women's Development* (Cambridge: Harvard University Press, 1982); and Nell Noddings, *Caring: A Feminist Approach to Ethics and Moral Education* (Berkeley: University of California Press, 1984).

30 See Barbara Herman, *The Practice of Moral Judgment*, chapter 1. The remainder of this paragraph consists of an attempt to express her argument. For another discussion of the issues involved here, see Onora (Nell) O'Neill, *Acting on Principle*, pp. 117–24.

31 See above, pp. 264–5.

32 See, in this context, the work of Bernard Williams: *Moral Luck* (Cambridge: Cambridge University Press, 1981), especially the first essay, "Persons, Character and Morality"; *Problems of the Self* (Cambridge: Cambridge University Press, 1976); and *Ethics and the Limits of Philosophy* (Cambridge: Harvard University Press, 1985). Also see Lawrence A. Blum, *Friendship, Altruism, and Morality* (London: Routledge and Kegan Paul, 1980).

33 In this discussion of happiness, I am indebted to Victoria S. Wike, *Kant on Happiness in Ethics* (Albany: State University of New York Press, 1994).

34 I. Kant, *The Metaphysics of Morals*, ed. M. Gregor (Cambridge: Cambridge University Press, 1996, p. 388.

35 I. Kant, *Lectures on Ethics*, trans. L. Infield (London: Methuen and Co., 1930).

36 Some commentators think, however, that he should not have committed himself to this obligation inasmuch as it would involve something other than the form of one's principle (the moral law) as the determining ground of the will, and hence would throw the will into a state of heteronomy.

37 Herman points to some other ways in which Kant's ethics is clearly deontological, *The Practice of Moral Judgment*, p. 210, note 5.

38 J.H. Muirhead, *Rule and End in Morals* (Oxford: Oxford University Press, 1932); cited by Barbara Herman, *The Practice of Moral Judgment*, p. 208. Herman argues that the standard understanding of Kant as a deontologist is, at best, unhelpful. See especially chapter 10. My discussion of the issue has been influenced by her argument.

Chapter 11 Hegel

1 See the discussion of this issue on pp. 285–6.

2 *Hegel's Philosophy of Right*, trans. T.M. Knox (Oxford: The Clarendon Press, 1942).

3 All references are to the numbered sections of the Knox translation.

4 For a Kantian response to this type of criticism, see pp. 287–8 above.

5 The English translation of this term is "customary morality." Because of this conventional meaning, it is important to remember that Hegel uses the term to refer to "ethical life" as distinct from morality.

6 F.H. Bradley, "My Station and its Duties," in his *Ethical Studies*, 2nd edn (Oxford: The Clarendon Press, 1935).

7 Some forms of liberalism, but not all, would consider Hegel's civil society as the equivalent of modern liberal society. Highly individualistic forms of liberalism would be unlikely to do so.

8 Sometimes this passage is translated so as to equate the state with "God standing in the world." See Kenneth Westphal for a discussion of how the state (as God) is seen by Hegel as fulfilling the functions Kant assigned to God, viz., assuring that virtuous agents receive happiness: "The basic context and structure of Hegel's *Philosophy of Right*," in Frederick C. Beiser, ed., *The Cambridge Companion to Hegel* (Cambridge: Cambridge University Press, 1993), p. 240.

9 See Allen W. Wood, "Hegel's Ethics," in Frederick C. Beiser, ed., *The Cambridge Companion to Hegel*, p. 231.

10 See Michael Sandel, *Liberalism and the Limits of Justice* (Cambridge: Cambridge University Press, 1982); and Michael Sandel, ed., *Liberalism and its Critics* (New York: New York University Press, 1984).

11 See Kenneth Westphal, "The basic context and structure of Hegel's *Philosophy of Right*" in Frederick C. Beiser, ed., *The Cambridge Companion to Hegel* (Cambridge: Cambridge University Press, 1993), pp. 234–69.

12 Allen W. Wood, "Hegel's Ethics," p. 230.

Chapter 12 Bentham and Mill

1 The doctrine, however, was by no means original with him, as Bentham himself acknowledged. The earlier French philosopher Helvétius (1715–71) spoke of "public

utility" as "the principle on which all human virtues are founded," and the phrase "the greatest happiness of the greatest number" comes from the Italian criminologist Beccaria (1738–94) – see Ross Harrison, *Bentham* (London: Routledge and Kegan Paul, 1983), pp. 107, 114–16.

2 J.S. Mill, "Bentham," in *Collected Works of John Stuart Mill*, vol. 10, ed. J.M. Robson (Toronto and London: University of Toronto Press and Routledge and Kegan Paul, 1969), p. 78; also contained in *Jeremy Bentham*, ed. B. Parekh (London: Frank Cass, 1974), p. 2.

3 Ibid., p. 79; p. 3.

4 Unless otherwise indicated, all references to Bentham's work are to his *An Introduction to the Principles of Morals and Legislation* in *The Works of Jeremy Bentham*, vol. 1, ed. John Bowring (New York: Russell and Russell, 1962); citations are to chapter and section.

5 Cited by Harrison, *Bentham*, p. 118.

6 "Nonsense upon stilts," he says of "imprescriptible" (inalienable) rights.

7 See Harrison, *Bentham*, p. 174.

8 Undoubtedly many of the moral philosophers criticized in this fashion by Bentham would view his refutations as crude caricatures and *ad hominem* arguments.

9 An excellent discussion of this procedure is found in Wendy Donner, *The Liberal Self* (Ithaca, New York and London: Cornell University Press, 1991), pp. 23–6.

10 See J. Bowring, ed., *The Works of Jeremy Bentham*, vol. 4, p. 540.

11 See Harrison, *Bentham*, p. 156.

12 For an excellent discussion of the issues surrounding incommensurability, see James Griffin, *Well-Being* (Oxford: Oxford University Press, 1986), pp. 75–92.

13 See H.L.A. Hart, "Bentham," in *Jeremy Bentham*, ed. B. Parekh, p. 78; the essay first appeared in the *Proceedings of the British Academy*, 48 (1962).

14 R. Harrison, *Bentham*, p. 149.

15 We shall have occasion later in this chapter to examine one of the other well-known works of Mill, his essay *On Liberty*, but it should be noted that some of Mill's other writings, especially the *Subjugation of Women* and Book 6 of the *Logic*, are also important for understanding his moral philosophy.

16 This reference to rules of right and wrong raises the question of whether Mill is an "act-utilitarian" or a "rule-utilitarian." For definitions of these terms and a discussion of the issue, see below, pp. 347–50.

17 And much of the commentary on it consists in attempts, as Alan Ryan puts it, "to expose the feebleness of Mill's arguments and to expose other commentator's misunderstandings of those arguments"; *J.S. Mill* (London: Routledge and Kegan Paul, 1974), p. 96.

18 All references to Mill's *Utilitarianism* are to the version contained in volume 10 of the *Collected Works of John Stuart Mill*, ed. J.M. Robson (Toronto and London: University of Toronto Press and Routledge and Kegan Paul, 1969). Citations are given in the text by page number.

19 Fred Berger argues that only insofar as a pleasure is a constituent of a person's happiness does it have value, thus suggesting that for Mill "happiness" is the more basic term. At one point Berger writes, "the ultimate criterion of the value of all actions ... is what is requisite for the happiness of man *as a creature of elevated faculties*." See Berger's *Happiness, Justice, and Freedom: The Moral and Political Philosophy of John Stuart Mill* (Berkeley: University of California Press, 1984), chapter 2; the quotation comes from p. 43. I have frequently relied on this excellent study of Mill.

20 An excellent discussion of this issue, and an able defense of Mill's position, is found in Wendy Donner, *The Liberal Self*, chapter 2.

21 A. Ryan, *J.S. Mill*, p 111.

22 Arguments of this sort can be found in F.H. Bradley, *Ethical Studies* (London, 1962), pp. 118–19.

23 Wendy Donner draws an interesting parallel between the evaluation of the sensory qualities of wine and the evaluation of the qualities of pleasures. See her *The Liberal Self*, chapter 4.

24 See below, p. 346.

25 Interesting questions arise about the qualifications of competent judges. Wendy Donner makes some important observations about the kind of intellectual, affective, and moral development Mill thought competent judges must undergo. See her *The Liberal Self*, chapters 5 and 6.

26 Critics have argued that 'a Socrates' choice of the refined pleasures of the mind over the pleasures of the pig is unconvincing: "The philosopher who is a half-hearted sensualist cannot estimate the attractions of a debauched existence, any more than the sensualist flicking through the pages of Hume can estimate the pleasures of philosophy" (A. Ryan, *J.S. Mill*, p. 111).

27 See Berger, *Happiness, Justice, and Freedom*, pp. 39–44.

28 See G.E. Moore, *Principia Ethica*, revised edn (Cambridge: Cambridge University Press, 1993), pp. 118–19.

29 See Berger, *Happiness, Justice, and Freedom*, p. 61: "Persons capable of the highest happiness *do* desire the general happiness; it *is* desirable in the eyes of those whose judgment is determinative of intrinsic value."

30 Mill has been criticized here for taking virtue to be desired, not for itself, but because it enhances happiness. The genuinely virtuous person, the argument goes, does not look upon virtue this way. See Berger's response to this charge, *Happiness, Justice, and Freedom*, pp. 35–6.

31 As Alan Ryan notes, "To say that Socrates prefers his way of life, even if he is constantly dissatisfied, is to say that he thinks it better, not that he thinks it more pleasant" (*J.S. Mill*, p. 111).

32 See David Lyons, *Forms and Limits of Utilitarianism* (Oxford: Clarendon Press, 1965) for a discussion of various kinds of utilitarianism. Also see John Rawls, "Two Concepts of Rules," *Philosophical Review*, 64 (1955), 3–32.

33 G.E. Moore, whose views on the matter were very influential during the early part of the twentieth century, interpreted Mill as an act-utilitarian in his *Principia Ethica*.

34 J.O. Urmson, "The Interpretation of the Moral Philosophy of J.S. Mill," *Philosophical Quarterly*, 3 (1953), 33–9. See the response to this essay by J.D. Mabbott, "Interpretations of Mill's *Utilitarianism*," *Philosophical Quarterly*, 6 (1956), 115–20.

35 See Fred Berger, *Happiness, Justice, and Freedom*, chapter 3. Berger's discussion of the issue is one of the best available. And his "rule-strategy" interpretation of Mill is an exciting and highly plausible alternative to the rule- and act-utilitarian categories.

36 "Bentham," in Parekh, ed., *Jeremy Bentham*, p. 33.

37 See note 34.

38 Berger, *Happiness, Justice, and Freedom*, pp. 68–9.

39 David Lyons, "Mill's Theory of Morality," *Nous*, 10 (1976), 109; cited by Berger, *Happiness, Justice, and Freedom*, p. 108.

40 See D.G. Brown, "What is Mill's Principle of Utility?" *Canadian Journal of Philosophy*, 3 (1973), 1–12.; and Berger, *Happiness, Justice, and Freedom*, pp. 105–6.

41 A good collection of essays in which these issues are discussed is *Consequentialism and its*

Critics, ed. S. Scheffler (Oxford: Oxford University Press, 1988).

42 For an interpretation that sees Mill's views on liberty as part of his theory of justice, see Fred Berger, *Happiness, Justice, and Freedom*, chapters 4 and 5.

43 All references to "On Liberty" are to the version included in *Collected Works of John Stuart Mill*, vol. 18, ed. J.M. Robson (Toronto and London: University of Toronto Press and Routledge and Kegan Paul, 1977). Citation is by page number.

Chapter 13 Nietzsche

1 Friedrich Nietzsche, *On the Genealogy of Morals*, trans. Walter Kaufmann and R.J. Hollingdale (New York: Vintage Books, 1989). All references to the *Genealogy* are given in the text to the Preface (P), First Essay (I), Second Essay (II), or Third Essay (III) and to the section therein.

2 Friedrich Nietzsche, *Beyond Good and Evil*, in *Basic Writings of Nietzsche*, trans. W. Kaufmann (New York: Modern Library, 1968); reference is to section number.

Epilogue: Into the Twentieth Century

1 See F.H. Bradley, *Ethical Studies*, 2nd edn (Oxford: Clarendon Press, 1927).

2 See Mary Warnock, *Ethics Since 1900* (Oxford: Oxford University Press, 1960), chapter 1.

3 G.E. Moore, *Principia Ethica* (Cambridge: Cambridge Press, 1903; revised edn 1993).

4 See W.D. Ross, *The Right and the Good* (Oxford: Oxford University Press, 1930) and *The Foundations of Ethics* (Oxford: Oxford University Press, 1939). H.A. Prichard is best known for his essay "Does Moral Philosophy Rest on a Mistake?" *Mind*, 21 (1912).

5 For an excellent discussion of the pros and cons of utilitarianism, see J.J.C. Smart and Bernard Williams, *Utilitarianism: For and Against* (Cambridge: Cambridge University Press, 1973). A useful anthology is Michael D. Baynes, ed., *Contemporary Utilitarianism* (Garden City: Doubleday Anchor Books, 1968), and a fairly comprehensive collection of essays on a more advanced level is P. Pettit, ed., *Consequentialism* (Aldershot, England and Brookfield, Vermont: Dartmouth, 1993). One might also consult David Lyons, *Forms and Limits of Utilitarianism* (Oxford: Oxford University Press, 1965); S. Scheffler, ed., *Consequentialism and its Critics* (Oxford: Oxford University Press, 1988); S. Scheffler, *The Rejection of Consequentialism*, revised edn (Oxford: Oxford University Press, 1994); and S. Kagan, *The Limits of Morality* (Oxford: University of Oxford Press, 1989).

6 See the references in note 5 above. Three important essays (contained in the Baynes anthology) are John Rawls, "Two Concepts of Rules," *Philosophical Review*, 64 (1955), 3–32; J.J.C. Smart, "Extreme and Restricted Utilitarianism," *Philosophical Quarterly*, 6 (1956) 344–54; and Richard B. Brandt, "Toward a Credible Form of Utilitarianism," in H.-N. Casteñeda and G. Nakhnikian, eds, *Morality and the Language of Conduct* (Detroit: Wayne State University Press, 1963).

7 For approaches to ethical issues directly reflecting the influence of Kant, see Onora O'Neill, *Acting on Principle: An Essay on Kantian Ethics* (New York: Columbia University Press, 1975); Onora O'Neill, *Constructions of Reason* (Cambridge: Cambridge University Press, 1989); and Barbara Herman, *The Practice of Moral Judgment* (Cambridge: Harvard

University Press, 1993).

8 See A. Donagan, *A Theory of Morality* (Chicago: Chicago University Press, 1977); Alan Gewirth, *Reason and Morality* (Chicago: University of Chicago Press, 1978); and C. Fried, *Right and Wrong* (Cambridge: Harvard University Press, 1978). Also see Nancy Davis, "Contemporary Deontology," in Peter Singer, ed., *A Companion to Ethics* (Oxford: Blackwell, 1991), pp. 205–18.

9 Fried, *Right and Wrong*, p. 7; cited by Nancy Davis, "Contemporary Deontology," p. 205.

10 See David Gauthier, *Morals by Agreement* (Oxford: Oxford University Press, 1986); also see Gauthier's "Morality and Advantage," *Philosophical Review*, 76 (1967), and his "Why Contractarianism?" in P. Valentine, ed., *Contractarianism and Rational Choice* (New York: Cambridge University Press, 1991).

11 See John Rawls, *A Theory of Justice* (Cambridge: Harvard University Press, 1971); also see Rawls' essay, "Justice as Fairness," *Philosophical Review*, 67 (1958).

12 See A. MacIntyre, *After Ethics* (Notre Dame: University of Notre Dame Press, 1981); Michael Slote, *Goods and Virtues* (Oxford: University of Oxford Press, 1983); Michael Slote, *From Morality to Virtue* (Oxford: Oxford University Press, 1992); Philippa Foot, "Virtues and Vices," in her *Virtues and Vices and Other Essays in Moral Philosophy* (Berkeley: University of California Press, 1979); and Lawrence Blum, *Friendship, Altruism and Morality* (London: Routledge and Kegan Paul, 1980).

13 In *After Ethics*.

14 In *Principia Ethica*.

15 See A. J. Ayer, *Language, Truth, and Logic* (New York: Dover, 1946), chapter 6.

16 The most sophisticated theory of emotivism is that of Charles Stevenson in his *Ethics and Language* (New Haven: Yale University Press, 1944). Also see J.O. Urmson, *The Emotive Theory of Ethics* (London: Hutchinson University Library, 1968; and New York: Oxford University Press, 1968).

17 The classic source for prescriptivism is R.M. Hare's *The Language of Morals* (Oxford: The Clarendon Press, 1952). Also see his *Freedom and Reason* (Oxford: Oxford University Press, 1963).

18 See M. Krausz and J.W. Meiland, eds, *Relativism: Cognitive and Moral* (Notre Dame: University of Notre Dame Press, 1982).

19 See Gilbert Harman *The Nature of Morality* (Oxford: Oxford University Press, 1977); and David Wong, *Moral Relativity* (Berkeley: University of California Press, 1984).

20 See S. Toulmin, *An Examination of the Place of Reason in Ethics* (Cambridge: Cambridge University Press, 1950); and Kurt Baier, *The Moral Point of View* (Ithaca, NY: Cornell University Press, 1958).

21 See Roderick Firth, "Ethical Absolutism and the Ideal Observer," *Philosophy and Phenomenological Research*, 12 (1952).

22 See *The Language of Morals* and *Freedom and Reason*.

23 See the works mentioned above by S. Toulmin and K. Baier.

24 See, for instance, Ralph Barton Perry, *General Theory of Value* (Cambridge: Harvard University Press, 1926). The writings of John Dewey also express this point of view.

25 See E. Sober, ed., *Conceptual Issues in Evolutionary Biology*, 2nd edn (Cambridge: MIT Press, 1993).

26 See J.L. Mackie, *Inventing Right and Wrong* (Harmondsworth: Penguin Books, 1977).

27 See Alan Gewirth, *Reason and Morality* (Chicago: Chicago University Press, 1978).

28 See G. Sayre-McCord, ed., *Essays on Moral Realism* (Ithaca: Cornell University Press, 1988).

29 See Bernard Williams, "Internal and External Reasons," in Ross Harrison, ed., *Rational Action* (Cambridge: Cambridge University Press, 1980); reprinted in Bernard Williams, *Moral Luck* (Cambridge: Cambridge University Press, 1981); also see Jonathan Dancy, *Moral Reasons* (Oxford: Blackwell, 1993).

30 See G. Wallace and A.D.M. Walker, *The Definition of Morality* (London: Methuen and Co., 1970).

Index